TEACHING METHODS
FOR TODAY'S SCHOOLS

TEACHING METHODS FOR TODAY'S SCHOOLS

Collaboration
and
Inclusion

J. Scott Hewit
Rollins College

Kathleen S. Whittier
Plattsburgh State University College

Allyn and Bacon
Boston • London • Toronto • Sydney • Tokyo • Singapore

Series Editor: Frances Helland
Marketing Manager: Kathy Hunter
Senior Vice-President and Publisher, Education: Nancy Forsyth
Editorial Assistant: Kris Lamarre
Production Coordinator: Susan Brown
Editorial-Production Service: Matrix Productions
Photo Researcher: Susan Duane
Cover Administrator: Suzanne Harbison
Composition Buyer: Linda Cox
Manufacturing Buyer: Suzanne Lareau

Copyright © 1997 by Allyn & Bacon
A Viacom Company
160 Gould St.
Needham Heights, Mass. 02194
Internet: abacon.com
America Online: keyword: College Online

Library of Congress Cataloging-in-Publication Data

Hewit, John Scott.
   Teaching methods for today's schools : collaboration and inclusion
/ by John Scott Hewit and Kathleen S. Whittier.
     p. cm.
   Includes bibliographical references and index.
   ISBN 0-205-15413-1
   1. Teaching teams—United States. 2. Mainstreaming in education—
United States. 3. Teaching—United States. 4. Learning.
5. Curriculum planning—United States. 6. Educational change—
United States. I. Whittier, Kathleen S. II. Title.
LB1029.T4H48 1996
371.3'95—dc20   96-41529
                                                CIP

Printed in the United States of America
10 9 8 7 6 5 4 3 2 1   01 00 99 98 97 96

*This book is dedicated with love
to our families
Sally, Dusty, Jesse
Ken and Kenny
No more lost weekends*

CONTENTS

PREFACE

This project began several years ago. We were teaching in separate programs at a state university, and over lunch, arrived at two interesting realizations. First, we learned that students in Elementary Education were taking a junior practicum course very similar to the junior practicum course students were taking in Special Education. Second, we acknowledged that special educators and classroom teachers in area schools were beginning to communicate routinely to improve the educational services offered to pupils with special needs in the classroom setting. The result of these realizations was that the teacher education program at our university was not preparing preservice teachers to collaborate or to work together to improve programs for all students, with or without disabilities.

Our first attempt to resolve this problem was to join with two other colleagues, John Madison and Byrne deGrandpré, and design a team taught course in mainstreaming for Elementary, Secondary and Special Education majors. The only problem was that the course was an elective, and as such, was not going to be taken by all students in those areas. We then went about developing a junior practicum course for students in Elementary and Special Education to take together as an alternative to their separate respective junior practicum courses. As we planned the details of the new course, called Collaborative Curriculum and Instruction, we searched for a text suitable for the course, and had to settle for an anthology of readings from a wide range of sources. It was clear that someone needed to write a book on collaborative teaching methods for inclusive classrooms and schools, and *Teaching Methods for Today's Schools: Collaboration and Inclusion* was begun.

While working on this project, we have spoken with hundreds of educators in all sorts of schools, and found that they are often being told that they will be in an inclusive program. We do not support inclusion when educators are forced to participate, where educators do not have time to adequately prepare, or where inadequate support exists. We also do not support inclusion when there is little or no attention given to the development of collaborative professional relationships.

Where there is inadequate choice, preparation, or support, inclusion is inherently flawed.

Where educators embrace the concept of inclusion, there is still the need for preparation and support. Educators who want to work toward inclusion must understand that their roles will change, and that they must be able to develop collaborative skills if the process of inclusion is to succeed. Our goal in writing this text is to help preservice teachers learn to collaborate as they plan, implement and evaluate curriculum in inclusive settings. Therefore, we hope that this text will be useful in:

- elementary and secondary education curriculum and instruction courses
- special education curriculum and instruction courses
- collaborative curriculum and instruction courses for special education and elementary and secondary education students

The first four chapters provide readers with a transition from foundations coursework to methodology coursework by looking closely at schools, curriculum, learning and teaching in today's world. Basic understanding of these four components of the educational process is prerequisite to beginning to actually work together on curriculum and instruction.

Chapter 5 is totally devoted to professional collaboration. Why is it so important? When is it needed? Who is involved? How is it actually achieved? Collaboration is distinguished from consultation, peer coaching, and other related terms, and potential barriers are explored.

Chapters 6, 7, and 8 present the tools of the profession, including the development of goals and objectives, lesson and unit planning, and instructional management. Chapters 9 through 12 detail four major approaches to instruction, the expository, discovery, discussion, and inquiry strategies, plus a separate section on cooperative learning. Each chapter includes planning suggestions, adaptations for students, and assessment techniques.

Chapter 13 takes a look into the future of schools of the 21st century, and examines the students, teachers, schools, and communities of tomorrow. It serves as a challenge to all educators as we work to provide the very best for the next generation of learners.

Several special features make *Teaching Methods for Today's Schools: Collaboration and Inclusion* more accessible to the reader. The first twelve chapters begin with key terms, objectives, and Profiles of learners, teachers, and schools which serve to illustrate the key aspects of each chapter. Scattered throughout each chapter are opportunities for readers to stop and reflect upon the material, a feature called Reflect for a Moment. In addition, the four chapters on instructional strategies include practice activities and detailed examples of lessons using each strategy. Finally, the instructor's manual includes key terms, chapter objectives, test items, detailed chapter outlines, suggested activities, and suggested readings.

This has been a labor of love, and we want to thank several friends, colleagues, and coworkers for their time and support. Our dear friends John Madison and

David Bedworth were there whenever we needed encouragement, advice, and technical assistance. John gave us in house editing suggestions, and David enthusiastically coached us through the process of contract negotiations. We owe them both a great deal. Kimberly Byrnes and Karen Rankin, graduate students, worked diligently with us to create a comprehensive instructor's manual. The people at Allyn & Bacon who helped us through the maze of publishing a textbook included two editors, Virginia Lanigan and Frances Helland, and two outstanding editorial assistants, Nihad Farooq and Kris LaMarre. In addition, we would like to thank Susan Brown, production coordinator, Kathy Hunter, marketing manager, and Lizzy Rausen, advertising projects coordinator for their support and guidance at important stages of the writing. We would also like to thank Merrill Peterson and Matrix Productions, the independent editorial-production service, and Gail Farrar of Publishers' Design and Production Services, Inc. for their prompt and supportive role in the final production stages.

We would also like to express our gratitude to those reviewers who willingly offered their suggestions as the book took shape; their comments and questions were extremely helpful during the revision process: Greg Bryant, Towson State University; Amy P. Dietrich, The University of Memphis; Joanne Gurry, University of Massachusetts, Boston; Nancy Lourie, San Jose State University; Michael Meloth, University of Colorado; Billie Jean Thomas, Northern Illinois University; and Sarah Weidler, Buffalo State College.

Last, but certainly not least, we would like to thank the many students, teachers, and administrators who encouraged us in our work and provided great stories of collaboration and inclusion. You taught us more than you will ever know.

PART I

INTRODUCTION

This textbook presents a new approach to curriculum and instruction that encompasses ongoing changes in the structure of public schools. An increasing diversity of children and families in our society, major concerns about students' knowledge and ability in academic areas, and the state of the national economy all demand that we reexamine the basic manner in which we go about educating young people. The future of our existence clearly depends to a large degree on our ability to develop more effective means for bringing up generations of learners who can lead us into the twenty-first century

In recent years, efforts at restructuring the educational system have included such features as the mainstreaming of students with mild or moderate handicapping conditions, school-based management, developmentally appropriate practices, competency-based instruction, whole-language and thematic instruction, cooperative and collaborative learning and teaching, and alternatives to standardized assessment, to name but a few. Amid all these movements is a student population that is changing rapidly. More and more students are coming to school with identifiable handicapping conditions that interfere with their learning, and more and more of these students are being placed into elementary classrooms with twenty to thirty other students for part or all of their formal education.

Teacher candidates at most colleges and universities are completing either an elementary education program or a special education program, and both groups are ill equipped to enter the schools, where the range of student abilities is far greater then ever before. However, under closer examination the similarities between the two programs far outnumber the differences, and students from both programs benefit greatly from shared course work and field experience. The elementary education major gains knowledge and experience in identification, referral, and instruction of students with special needs, and the special education major gains knowledge and experience in curriculum, group management, and group instructional strategies.

It has become very clear that the traditional notion of a teacher working with the same twenty-five students in one classroom all day, every day, with no other adults present, is no longer the case. Instead, the teacher of today—and that of the twenty-first century—will be a member of many teams, needing to organize materials and time carefully, communicate effectively with a wide variety of personalities, and work productively with others to deliver the best educational program possible to each student. Therefore, this text places considerable emphasis on professional collaboration, or the joint planning and delivery of educational services. This collaboration is not *reactive*, in which teachers meet when a problem arises. Rather, it is *proactive* collaboration, undertaken before students begin the school year, that plans curriculum and instruction in advance to minimize difficulties each student might have during the year. Realistically, this teamwork is more likely to succeed whenever problems do arise because of the communication network that has already been established.

Behind the reform that is the basis for this text lies a paradigm shift that requires educators, administrators, politicians, parents, and others to move away from the cyclical pattern of reform. Educational change in the new paradigm has moved from focusing on external factors and adult roles to placing the student at the center of the learning environment. The impetus that created a need for change is the understanding that the student "is the producer of the educational outcome: learning" (Lipsky & Gartner, 1992, p. 5). The process of learning production must be reconceptualized when we envision the learner turning from the role of passive recipient to that of active player in the learning environment.

INCLUSION

Making students the focus of the educational system requires movement away from the concepts of mainstreaming and integration toward full inclusion. Clear differences exist among these three concepts, although they are often inappropriately viewed as interchangeable. The following definitions clarify the differences.

> *Mainstreaming* occurs when the primary placement of a child with disabilities is in a self-contained special education class and she or he is given opportunities to attend appropriate classes with nondisabled children.
>
> *Integration* occurs when the primary placement of a child with disabilities is in a self-contained special education class in a school where there are also children without disabilities.
>
> *Inclusion* occurs when the only placement of a child with disabilities is in an age-appropriate, heterogeneously grouped classroom in the learner's neighborhood school.

Clearly, mainstreaming and integration imply that one environment is superior to another, that one group of persons is more socially desirable than another, and that therefore certain placements should be sought out. Both concepts imply that students must earn the right to be placed where they were before being "labeled" and removed for their own good. "The concept of inclusion is being adopted because it more accurately and clearly communicates what is needed—all children need to be *included* in the educational and social life of their neighborhood schools and classrooms, not merely placed in the mainstream" (Stainback, Stainback, & Jackson, 1992, p. 3). The focus of inclusion is on the development of a supportive and nurturing school community, one that benefits all learners, not just a selected category of students. In inclusive schools every learner's "gifts and talents, including those of students traditionally defined as having profound disabilities or chronically disruptive behaviors, are recognized, encouraged, and utilized to the fullest extent possible" (Stainback, Stainback, & Jackson, 1992, p. 5).

COLLABORATION

Inclusive schools provide all students with the opportunity to become effective workers in the development of their own learning. This paradigm shift does not discount the impact of external factors on the educational environment, nor does it ignore the role of adults; parents and communities are sought out as members of a child-centered educational system. The roles of school adults will be changed dramatically by this shift. General and special educators will need to focus on collaboration (see Chapter 5) to ensure that every learner has an educational program that is geared to challenge his or her unique needs. School adults will need to transcend their traditionally narrow categorical responsibilities, develop cross-disciplinary collaborative teams, increase and vary their interactions with students, and become more involved with adults outside the school. Graden and Bauer (1992) point out that an essential component of inclusive schools is the development of a schoolwide "collaborative ethic," an acceptance of the nature and importance of collaboration. According to such an ethic, "all of the resources and efforts of school personnel can be spent on assessing instructional needs, adapting instruction, and providing support to students" (Stainback, Stainback, & Jackson, 1992, p. 7).

1

SCHOOLS TODAY

Key Terms

Automated system
Case management approach
Choice
Collaboration
Cooperation
Distance technology
Educational law
Empower

Expanded resources
Inclusive schools
In loco parentis
Public Law 94-142
Public Law 101-476
Representative teams

Objectives

After completing this chapter, the reader will be able to:

1. Identify the major historical, economic, and political influences on education in the twentieth century.
2. Describe how modern technology influences children's lives.
3. Discuss the influence of the U.S. Constitution and its amendments on education.
4. Discuss the major educational litigation.
5. Contrast Public Law 94-142 with Public Law 101-476.
6. Describe how legislation related to education is influenced by economics.
7. Compare the varying impacts education has had on the economic structure of the United States.
8. Discuss the formal control and informal influences of political factors on education.
9. Describe the hierarchy of formal educational control.
10. Discuss the three cycles of educational reform in the United States.
11. Compare and contrast paradigm shifts that have resulted in educational restructuring.

PROFILES OF HIGH SCHOOL GRADUATES

Heather Stewart

It was early June, and 225 seniors at Summerville High School were preparing for the big day. Heather Stewart was looking forward to celebrating with her friends. Most of them knew where they were going to be in the fall. Heather was excited about going to Redford State because two of her good friends were going there, too. The thought of living in a college dorm was exciting to her. It was also a pretty good school, she thought. She could drive home on weekends, since the campus was only three hours from Summerville.

In the meantime, Heather was going through a typical senior slump. She was a good student, although she struggled at times with algebra. In fact, she would probably be lucky to get a C in this class for the year. Mr. Bowen, her English teacher, had noticed that Heather still made some pretty fundamental writing errors. Bemoaning the lack of basic writing skills among graduating seniors had become a ritual of spring among Summerville's teachers. But Heather was a polite young adult, and they figured that she would do fairly well in college even though her SAT scores were not terrific. In fact, there seemed to be quite a few low SAT scores among the Summerville students.

Heather was still trying to get a good job for the summer. She knew she could always just stay at the video store where she'd worked for the past year, but she wanted to make more than five dollars an hour. Besides, she wanted to quit August 1 and take off with her friends for a week. They'd already talked about going to Florida, and her mom had even worked it out so that Heather could have the car.

But for now, it was time to gear up for graduation. Amanda Haley was definitely having a party, and so was Curt Morrow. Heather was psyched for the big event.

Michael Johnson

Michael was hungry. Those school lunches weren't enough to keep him going all afternoon. He told Joey, his friend, that he was hungry. Joey told him to go get something to eat. Yeah, right. Without any money? He could go home. Not much going on here on the street anyway.

Michael's birthday was coming up, three days after graduation. One more year and he was legal. Sneaking beer around was getting to be a drag. He just wanted money so he could get some nice clothes, but his mother had told him not to expect much. She was back to just one job, and it barely paid the rent.

Michael had looked around the Jefferson Heights shopping district for a job. Anything. He even offered to sweep the sidewalk in front of the Pro-Mart, but they said they already had someone who did that type of work. His home economics teacher had tried to help him get a job with the school for the summer, but they weren't hiring anyone new. It looked like another summer hanging out on Oak Street, jawing with Joey and Luis, watching the women.

Graduation, big deal. It was good for some heavy partying. Michael had to wonder just how he actually qualified for graduation. He still couldn't read his science book or his reading skills workbook. He figured they just wanted him out of there. The only teacher he felt comfortable around was Ms. Walsh, his special studies teacher. He had to admit she had put up with more of his venting than just about anyone.

How could they say he was ready to graduate? He was only passing three of his six classes, and all three were below general track. Even Ms. Walsh couldn't perform miracles. But still they said he was graduating. Joey sure wasn't, and Luis was only eighteen, so he could keep going. A lot of other kids hadn't even stayed in school. Some of them were getting into some serious trouble now, too.

So Michael would graduate. Then what? He had thought of joining the army but didn't think he could pass their written entry tests. He just wanted a job and some money.

INFLUENCES

What has brought students like Heather and Michael to this point in their lives? How has Heather managed to succeed at gaining acceptance into higher education and the workforce while Michael has failed? Why is Heather graduating at age eighteen, excited and enthused about her future, while Michael, at almost twenty-one, simply wonders how he qualifies to graduate?

Although there are no simple answers to these questions, influences in society do affect students as they move through school. These influences, which can be seen as historical, economic, or political in nature, are explored to a limited extent in this text. A number of influences, however, clearly cross all historical, economic, and political lines and therefore require closer examination if there is to be improvement in the quality of formal education: for example, the influence of the family and modern technology on the educational success of students will dramatically increase during the next century. This chapter examines these factors in detail.

A quick glance at the structure of the current school system suggests a strong historical influence. Numerous educational practices (grading systems, departmentalization, grade levels, subject areas, and school calendars, to name but a few) are rooted in social concepts of days gone by. Despite challenges from progressive thinkers and practitioners (Dewey, Montessori, Piaget, Illich, Kozol), the resistance to significant structural change has been strong enough to retain many school practices that came into existence before the twentieth century. The concepts of professional **collaboration** and **inclusive schools,** which were not part of these past practices, likewise encounter resistance when educators attempt to introduce them.

Other influences on our schools have an economic basis. For example, school consolidation, class size, and the design and construction of school buildings are all determined by economic considerations. As the United States moves from being the world's biggest lender to the world's biggest debtor, economic restrictions leave many school districts with the task of meeting higher educational goals with shrinking budgets. Communities across the country are struggling with tax increases and have had to cut services—and in some cases close their schools—to avoid paying higher school taxes. For many communities, the suggestion that educators need additional professional time to plan collaboratively and to study inclusion is economically unappealing. At the same time, it is interesting to note that the economy is significantly affected by the state of education. Clearly, many of the economic problems in the United States are the result of problems in education.

Reflect for a Moment

Can you recall some changes that took place in your home school district as the result of economic factors? How were the changes received? What effect did the changes have on the students themselves?

Politics have always exerted considerable influence on schools. Concern over American schools reached new heights in the 1950s, when low academic standards, incompetent teachers, and a watered-down curriculum all came under attack. The launching of the Russian satellite Sputnik in 1957 resulted in unprecedented pressure on the federal government to allocate more funding for the improvement of education. During the 1960s, Presidents Kennedy and Johnson signed massive legislation into effect, establishing such programs as Head Start, Title I remedial instruction, and bus transportation for children. Minority populations were the focus of major legislative activity during the 1960s and 1970s as the government sought to provide equal opportunity for all children. One of the most significant laws enacted was Public Law 94-142, the Education for All Handicapped Children Act, which was passed in 1975.

During the 1980s, the political process moved into a reform phase, prompting some observers to recall the critics of the 1950s (James & Tyack, 1983). However, the many published reports during this decade led to *America 2000: An Educational Strategy*, announced in 1990 by President George Bush and signed into law by President Clinton in 1994 as the Goals 2000: Educate America Act. (Morrison, 1997). Among the major aims of this legislation are school readiness, nonviolent drug-free schools, lifelong literacy and learning, successful high school completion, professional development for educators, overall student achievement and service to community, math and science excellence, and parent involvement. Reform was clearly being carried over, at least on paper, into the 1990s.

State government has traditionally funneled more funds into public education than any other single body. Each spring, local communities across the nation anxiously await the outcome of state budget meetings to see how much they will receive for school operations. State curriculum guides are common in most states, as are state-level standardized tests. Teachers and administrators are certified at the state level, and school buildings are inspected by state health and safety officials. Local districts in many states choose their textbooks from among a state-approved collection. Without a doubt, the influence of state government on schools is significant.

Local governance, in the form of school boards in most cases, exerts considerable influence on school operations. Parent advisory boards, community task forces, and, more recently, business leaders all contribute to the overall quality of educational services at the local level. It is at this grassroots level that successful efforts at structured collaboration and inclusive education have emerged.

Family Influences

Heather Stewart and Michael Johnson are not real people, but in many respects they mirror students in modern American society. The family still serves as the primary source of experience and learning for children outside school. What is no longer the same is the nature of the family in modern society.

In what ways has the family changed in recent years, and how have the changes influenced children in school? Record numbers of children are living in single-parent households, and most of them are experiencing a declining standard of living (Jellinek & Klavan, 1988; Dodson, 1987). Families headed by females are increasing at ten times the rate of two-parent families (Carlile, 1991). The traditional family with two parents, one working outside the home, made up about 60 percent of America's family population during the 1960s. Today they number around 7 percent (Elkind, 1986). As single parents (remember Michael's mother) struggle financially, their children find that they have less time with either parent and are forced to deal with new and often difficult emotions. The number of families experiencing divorce is not decreasing. Although not all single-parent families are the result of a divorce, studies have found that children of divorce are late to school, miss school altogether, and skip school more often than children from intact families (NAESP & Charles F. Kettering Foundation, 1980).

Although large numbers of women involuntarily join the workforce as a result of the financial changes accompanying a divorce, it is also clear that many more women are choosing to pursue employment than in generations past. In 1950, 31 percent of women in the United States were employed, but in 1990 the figure had risen to 70 percent (Shane, 1989). When every parent in the household works all day outside the home, it simply becomes more difficult to find time for fundamental parenting responsibilities like reading to children, preparing well-balanced meals and sitting down with children over dinner, or helping them with their homework. It must be understood, however, that although many parents have entered the workforce so that they can provide basic food, clothing, and shelter for their children, other parents have gone to work in order to acquire modern conveniences like a second car, air conditioning, or a new set of furniture, and still others have gone to work for reasons relating to personal fulfillment. Whatever the motivation for working, the change in the family brought on by women entering the workforce has been significant.

Reflect for a Moment

It might be interesting to go around the class and discuss the family routines people had when they were in elementary school. How many of your classmates experienced the traditional two-parent, one-career family structure just described?

The effect of this family change on school success is seen perhaps most easily in the expanded role of the schools. Several responsibilities formerly held by families (child care, meals, and the teaching of basic values and behaviors) have been transferred to the schools. When schools successfully accept this new role, more resources and time are required. In most cases, however, the transition has been less than thoroughly anticipated. Many educators lack the counseling skills to meet the emotional needs of an increasingly diverse school-age population. Programs designed to bring parents and schools closer together in meeting children's basic needs have not been widely implemented.

In short, schools were not adequately prepared to meet the needs of children from families in which all parents were employed outside the home. As children attempt to learn to read, solve word problems, or write poetry in school, many are distracted by hunger, family concerns, or uncertainty over who will be home. Their ability to concentrate and their receptivity to instruction is often compromised.

A third change in the structure of the family has been the number of families living in poverty. In the vast majority of the fifty states, the numbers are increasingly alarming. More children are hungry, more are suffering from preventable diseases, more are homeless, more are abused, more are entering the foster care system, more are in state custody, more are having children themselves, more are failing in school and dropping out. School districts throughout the nation report that more than half of their students qualify for free lunches. It is important to remember that restructuring education will not solve basic economic and social problems. But the reality in classrooms today includes many children who have difficulty attending to learning activities because they are hungry, tired, physically ill, or psychologically distressed. There is no political influence at work here. Millions of children are unable to develop their minds and bodies in school because they suffer the ill effects of poverty.

One type of family bears reckoning with: teenage mothers and their children. These families are largely poor and less educated, and their future is bleak (Stevens-Long & Cobb, 1983). The United States has a higher rate of teenage pregnancy, teenage childbirth, and teenage abortion than any other industrialized nation in the world (Wattleton, 1989). A teenager with poor grades is more likely to become pregnant than a teenager who is experiencing success in school. More than a million American teenagers become pregnant in a year, and in many of these cases the father does not remain actively supportive of the mother.

The majority of teenage mothers have children with greater health and developmental risks. Their children are more likely to experience low birthweight and/or be gestationally premature, with more disabilities later in life. Children of teenage mothers are more likely to experience emotional disturbance in early childhood and be held back more often in school (Anastasiow, 1983). As a group, children of teenage mothers are educationally at risk and ultimately are more likely to become teenage mothers themselves.

Reflect for a Moment

Chances are that you or a classmate know someone who became a mother in her teens. What was that person's experience in school like as a teen mother?

Yet another family influence on schools today is the increasingly diverse cultural background of the school-age population. It is projected that by the year 2000 about 46 percent of the school age population, but only 5 percent of the teachers, will be of color (Pallas, Natriello, & McDill, 1989; American Council on Education and the Education Commissioner of the States, 1988). Immigration, higher during the 1980s than during any decade since the turn of the century, was expected to increase during the 1990s (Huelskamp, 1993). Over 150 different languages are now spoken in schools across the country, with some single districts having close to that number within their own boundaries.

Among these diverse groups, nearly half of all African-American children and around 40 percent of all Hispanic children live in poverty (Snyder, 1988). This pattern of poverty applies to families with both parents present, placement of children in special education programs, and high school graduation rates. In some urban high schools, the dropout rate for Hispanic and African-American children runs from 70 to 80 percent (Hochschild, 1985). It appears abundantly clear that schools have yet to find ways to successfully educate children of color and that the percentage of children of color in the school-age population is continuing to increase.

Numerous other changes in the composition of American families have implications for schools and educators. Families in modern society have changed dramatically. Many children are part of blended families, gay families, or single-parent-by-choice families. Single-parent families continue to increase in number. Women continue to enter the workforce. Poor families are on the rise. Finally, families of color, particularly African-American and Hispanic families, make up a greater proportion of our population than ever before.

Because families are changing so radically, schools are finding it increasingly difficult to meet the needs of children. It is almost impossible for a classroom teacher to effectively plan and teach a class of such diverse learners without collaborating with colleagues, parents, and community agencies. School officials are increasingly calling on social service agencies, health officials, specialists in related fields, and various other community resource personnel in an effort to provide the nonacademic structure that is a prerequisite to academic success. It is often the effective coordination of these services that is the key to a child's future in school, and in life. If inclusive schools are to succeed, then these collaborative efforts must be carefully planned and utilized.

Reflect for a Moment

What types of extended services does your home school district offer to changing families? How are these services coordinated? Are they in great demand? Do you think they should be the school's responsibility?

Technology

Technology is defined by Morrison (1993) as "the application of scientific, material, and human resources to the solution of human needs" (p. 411). How is modern technology influencing people's lives? It would not be an overstatement to say that society is in the midst of a technology explosion. Technology has contributed significantly to the emerging image of the global village. Interdependence among societies throughout the world has been facilitated by recent advances in technology, which affects where people work and when they work, how they get places, what they buy, and just about every aspect of life in which communication is beneficial. Technology also offers tremendous opportunities for educators who wish to collaborate efficiently and for inclusive classroom programs. It has, in consequence, a multidimensional effect on both teaching and learning.

At the core of any discussion of the influence of technology on schools today is the challenge of communication, together with its role in learning. Nineteenth-century schools primarily used lectures, tests, grades, chalkboards, books, and paper and pencil to communicate knowledge and demonstrate learning. During the first half of the twentieth century, technological developments included the telephone, camera, radio, television and motion pictures, but few if any of these tools were truly used for instructional purposes until the second half of the century. Today, although the variety of printed materials continues to increase with the proliferation of curriculum guides, teachers' manuals, journals, newsletters, booklets, brochures, worksheets, and the infamous ditto, the use of audiovisual materials and electronic technology has grown enormously. The use of microcomputers in education is perhaps the single most visible sign of this change in the school setting. In just one year, the number of schools with microcomputers increased from 13,986 to 30,493, or over 200 percent (National Center for Educational Statistics, 1984). In a relatively short period of time, the influence of the tiny microchip has been profound. Currently, the use of computers in classrooms is being carefully examined so that their value can be more widely recognized.

Although schools have moved slowly to take advantage of twentieth-century technology, the communities they serve have moved more quickly. The vast majority of homes and businesses have telephones, many with expanded capacities for messages, conferences, and multiple lines. Parents with teenage children can attest to the value of the telephone in their homes and to how it can become the technology of choice for their children for long periods of time. The telephone has become an invaluable tool for businesses, community organizations, government workers, and virtually anyone who values rapid, accurate communication. Live conversations take place around the world, around the clock, thanks to fiber-optic cables and satellite communications. Schools could benefit greatly if conference lines were installed, permitting groups of learners to communicate with resource people and the community or around the world. Even school based telephone networks could facilitate communication from room to room among faculty, staff and administration. Many other possibilities exist as well.

With the emergence of the radio in the 1920s and television in the 1940s, people found that they could hear and see live events from around the world simply by turning a knob on a box. With better access to radio, learners could follow fast breaking events, such as elections and local events. They could participate in talk shows focusing on topics of educational importance. Many families today have two or more television sets situated around the house so that they can watch it during meals, while cleaning, or in the relative seclusion of their bedrooms. In recent years, researchers have found that in many homes the television is turned on and left on for hours and hours every day and that many children spend more time watching television than they spend sleeping or even attending school. As the amount of time spent watching television increases, the amount of time left for reading and writing decreases, and concerns have been expressed about the literacy of adults and children (Kozol, 1985; NAEP, 1985).

Although television has often been seen as a less than positive influence on education and school learning, many other forms of technology have served to facilitate learning, particularly among students with disabilities. A number of different electronic communication devices have made it possible for students to take in information and express their understanding in ways previously unimagined.

Children with cerebral palsy use speech synthesizers, and children with severe hearing impairments have access to auditory trainers (microphones worn by teachers and receivers worn by students) and tactile aids which help the student "feel the sounds". Laser technology provides severely physically handicapped children with a means to respond to questions by tracking their eye movement. After centuries of having their personalities and thinking abilities stifled, thousands of people are finally able to interact with others and gain a newfound respect and identity in their schools and communities. These and other technological breakthroughs in the schools are the result of scientific advances, followed by professional collaboration among educators. Technology clearly can make a significant contribution to the building of an inclusive learning community.

Mecklenburger (1990) suggests that the role of technology in modern America be examined and used to support education. He finds that even though businesses everywhere have been restructured by modern technology, most schools are still operating with outdated information and equipment. Consider, for example, that with the help of modern technology knowledge will probably increase fourfold in the next ten years (Shane, 1990). Consider that "five year olds today experience more information in one year than their grandparents did in a lifetime" (Gayle, 1990, p. 12). Then consider the impact of such changes on our beliefs and ways of learning and communicating. Schools, businesses, and governments will have to restructure themselves to manage the massive flood of new knowledge and information capable of being stored and retrieved with current technology. Today people need to develop a more expanded view of technology, a view that takes into account everything from the chalkboard and eraser to electronic mail and interactive video. Educators must be able to adopt this overview if students are to realize the full benefits of modern technology.

Reflect for a Moment

Check your technology IQ: Do you have your own computer? Do you use a computer every day? Do you communicate with others via electronic mail? Do you know how you would use computers and other current technology in your classroom?

Educating citizens to be technologically literate is a community's responsibility and has become a central mission in current school-restructuring efforts. How well prepared are Heather and Michael, the two students profiled at the beginning of the chapter? There is less and less demand for workers who have not yet mastered the basic skills of mathematics and communication (Kelly, 1990). Businesses are looking for people who are alert to change in marketing, production, and management, for people who think and learn quickly. Our modern society needs workers who can operate computers, lasers, and robots (Ornstein, 1989). They also must possess the skills of team decision making, **cooperation,** and collaboration (Dettmer, Thurston, & Dyck, 1993). Many learners who, because of a disability, have historically been denied access to general education, are finding modern technology a means to achieve their academic and vocational goals in inclusive school settings.

Dealing with these rapid changes effectively will only be possible if the educational community is willing to let go of the worn-out strategy of simply modifying past practices. A very compatible relationship exists between current practices and classrooms enhanced by technology (Newman, 1992). At the same time, fundamental changes will occur, changes that some people naturally resist. But unless a school is utilizing technology across the curriculum in various ways, students will be less prepared for the future.

The potential role of teachers in technologically supported classrooms is unique. Instead of lecturing, testing, and grading, teachers collaboratively create plans for group projects, consult with students individually and in groups, and organize learning expeditions outside the classroom. Many teachers have already capitalized on opportunities with technology and have made fundamental changes in their roles. Elementary science teachers help students learn how to use technology to solve problems. From a satellite teleconference with a class of ten-year-olds in Germany to a recycling music video students have choreographed, directed, performed, and filmed themselves, technology offers unlimited possibilities.

Providing students with access to unlimited information is empowering them to take responsibility for their learning, giving them choices for research, and motivating them to search for solutions to real problems. Caution, however, must be taken. Equal access is absolutely essential if technology is to be used successfully for the benefit of all citizens (Grunwald, 1990). Otherwise a two-tiered system of learners will emerge, those who are computer literate and those who are not. Workers who are not computer literate will be as unprepared for tomorrow's world as those who cannot read are for today's (Wishnietsky, 1991).

EDUCATIONAL CHANGES

Educational Law

Before any discussion of the law as it relates to public education can take place, the origins of **educational law** must be understood. Although a great deal of law relates specifically to education, most legal governance comes from another area. Education as it operates in the United States is a function of state government and as such is affected by an infinite number of laws designed to regulate government functions. Perhaps the strongest set of laws are those set forth in the U.S. Constitution. All laws or statutes passed by Congress, state constitutions, state legislation, ordinance of local government units, and rules and regulations of boards of education are subject to the provisions outlined in the Constitution. Interestingly, although the Constitution covers a wide range of powers, duties, and limitations relevant to education, it does not specifically refer to education. As a result, education becomes a state function under the Tenth Amendment, which provides that powers not delegated by the Constitution to the federal government are passed on to the states. It is important to recognize, therefore, that education is not a constitutional right but, rather, a privilege granted to people through state government. We should not conclude, however, that the federal Constitution does not affect public education. The number of educationally related cases taken to the Supreme Court has increased rapidly over the past twenty-five to thirty years. Generally these educational cases focus on violations of Article I, section 10, and the First, Fifth, and Fourteenth Amendments. As stated earlier, laws or statues may be passed by a variety of government bodies. The actual interpretation of laws, however, is achieved through rules, regulations, and litigation.

Support in the United States for free public schools began as early as the 1820s. In their access to free and appropriate public education, some groups were treated differently from others. By the 1850s a number of states had enacted compulsory attendance laws, with the exception of children with disabilities. Unfortunately, this situation continued through the first three-quarters of the twentieth century.

In 1964, the number of students in public education programs topped 40 million. Of that number, only 2.1 million were students with disabilities (National Center for Educational Statistics, 1990). The notion of mainstreaming children with disabilities in general education classrooms paralleled the movement away from racial segregation and helped people to realize that arbitrarily segregating children in any way was and is adverse to their development. Preliminary efforts were made by Congress in 1965 (Elementary and Secondary Education Act PL 89-10), 1966 (Amendment to Title 1 of the Elementary and Secondary Education Act PL 89-313), and 1969 (creation of the Bureau of Education of Handicapped PL 89-750) to provide for students with disabilities through the enactment of grant programs that were primarily incentive programs with few specific guidelines and no real enforcement capabilities.

As stated previously, there is no federal constitutional right to education. However, when a state undertakes to provide education, the Fourteenth Amendment comes into play. When it provides education, the state must do so on equal terms and must not deny any state-granted right without due process.

Student civil rights were at the forefront in the decades of 1960 and 1970. Supreme Court decisions reflected favorably on the rights of students to due process and expanded on freedom of assembly, speech, and dress. Mandated procedural and substantive guarantees were established in all schools to protect students' rights, and equity and equal opportunity became buzzwords for public education systems.

Since 1945 there has been in this nation an ongoing struggle between the ideals of "excellence" and "equity" in the public schools. Excellence proponents want more academically demanding schools with ever-increasing standards. Equity proponents seek public schools that offer programs appropriate for *all* students (e.g. disabled, Hispanic, African-American, Native American, at-risk, and homeless).

Before 1954, many African-American children were being funneled into special classes and schools. The Supreme Court addressed these problems in the case

Brown v. the Board of Education of Topeka, which stated that separate (segregated) but equal is not equal. Subsequently, the Civil Rights Act of 1964 (PL 88-352) authorized the U.S. Commissioner of Education to give support to both state and local school districts to assist in their efforts to racially desegregate public schools in the United States, an effort that has little lasting effect when examining the current equity and racial balance of inner-city school systems (Kozol, 1967; 1992). The *Brown v. Board of Education of Topeka* decision gained new meaning with the enactment of Public Law 94-142, the Education of All Handicapped Children Act (1975). By 1972, more than thirty separately filed cases appeared throughout the United States, using the principles set forth in the Brown decision as the basis for their legal theory with regard to segregation of disabled students (see *Pennsylvania Association for Retarded Children (PARC) v. Pennsylvania, 1971; Mills v. Board of Education, 1972*).

As the courts of the 1980s and 1990s became more conservative, so did the outlook on the individual rights of students. Schools have resumed once more the edict of *in loco parentis,* a legal term meaning "in place of the parent". The class action suits that had done so much in the previous twenty years became burdensome, their utility gone. With the influx of drugs and weapons, many schools had become places of danger; violence was no longer something that took place on inner-city streets. Every seven minutes, a child is arrested for a drug offense. Every thirty-six minutes, a child is killed or injured by a gun. Every day, 135,000 children bring their guns to school. The local, district, and Supreme courts, reacting to these changes, gave back to school administrators the authority to control student publications and speech and to provide for search and seizure. This is not to say that school administrators were granted unlimited authority; however, the more conservative courts of the 1980s and 1990s have become far more sympathetic to the plight of authority.

In the past thirty-five years, consequently, litigation has become intricately involved in the development of policies and procedures for public education. Among the most influential concerns are freedom of speech, search and seizure, drug testing, discipline of students with disabilities, expulsion, and suspension (see Rossow & Hiniger, 1991, for a brief analysis of major legal issues).

The Supreme Court decision in *Tinker v. Des Moines Independent School District* in 1969 firmly established students' right to free speech in regard to social, political, and economic issues. Three students who had been suspended for wearing black armbands to protest the Vietnam War were reinstated. The Tinker court ruling stated that students' freedom of speech could not be restricted by school officials simply because they have a different point of view. According to the Supreme Court, students do not shed their constitutional rights to freedom of speech or expression at the school door. Decisions in the late 1980s have served to clarify parts of the Tinker ruling. *Bethel School District No. 403 v. Fraser* made it clear, on the other hand, that respect for civility of public speech was a necessary function of school officials and allowed appropriateness to be defined by the school administration, not the courts.

Other forms of expression, such as student dress and hairstyles, have never been ruled on by the Supreme Court as First Amendment issues. However, state supreme courts and federal appellate courts have rendered a variety of opinions on the topic, some conferring constitutional protection for students and others for school districts. Although hairstyle has become something of a moot point, the increase in gang activities and wearing of gang "colors" may create a surge of new litigation.

Many difficulties have risen from the lack of clarification in the application of the Fourth Amendment to the educational setting. The Fourth Amendment forbids unreasonable search and seizure and provides that warrants describing the place or thing to be searched, and the persons or things to be seized, can only be issued on probable cause. This amendment only becomes germane in the educational setting, when criminal prosecution develops based on evidence obtained on school premises with the involvement of school authorities. The Supreme Court ruled that a balance must be maintained between students' privacy rights and the administration's interest in maintaining a safe and orderly learning environment (*New Jersey v. TLO*, 1985). Using reasonableness as the guidepost, local-level judicial interpretations and procedures that were appropriate yesterday may be wrong today. As a result, the legal stage is set for revisiting this issue. With metal detectors and drug-sniffing dogs becoming more important to schools than art and music rooms, search and seizure is an ever-present problem.

Reflect for a Moment

Think for a minute about a court decision that affected your education. Decisions are made in all areas of education quite regularly. Was it prayer in schools? Athletic requirements? Censorship?

Public Laws 94-142 and 101-476

In the last one hundred years, Congress has passed only a handful of statutes governing education, with none perhaps as powerful an agent for change as **Public Law 94-142** (Education for All Handicapped Children Act). The enactment of PL 94-142 in 1975 and its amendment in 1990 by PL 101-476 (Individuals with Disabilities Education Act, or IDEA) have granted students with disabilities and their families many powerful rights. A number of provisions were made under this federal law, including procedural safeguards for parents and students, individual education programs (IEP), and education in the least restrictive environment (LRE); active parent participation was a critical element in each of the major provisions cited. PL 94-142 marked the beginning of free and appropriate public education services to *all* school-age children and youth, regardless of disability.

By altering all references to handicapped children to children with disabilities, however, PL 101-476 amended PL 94-142, changed the title of the act, and reinforced the importance of considering the child first. Additionally, two new categories were added (autism and traumatic brain injury); requirements for transition services for students sixteen years of age or older were tightened; and collaboration among all special education teachers, general education teachers, and related services personnel was strongly emphasized.

Economic Factors

From the 1940s to the 1980s, economic prosperity gave rise to the expansion and modernization of American education. Following World War II, educators had time to examine current practices; calls for increased attention to math, science, and foreign languages began in the late 1950s. The postwar economy provided major funding support for curricular changes in these areas in the form of the National Defense Education Act (NDEA) in 1958. Textbooks were upgraded, teacher education was supported, and new teaching materials were developed (Armstrong, Henson, & Savage, 1983).

As the nation's postwar economy continued to expand, so did the size and composition of the school-age population. During the 1960s and 1970s, social issues such as racial segregation, the plight of the disabled, and poverty all resulted in massive increases in spending for education. Desegregating the nation's schools required extensive busing of students, and the cost of this commitment was enormous. Presidents Kennedy and Johnson, both champions of human rights and equal educational opportunity, supported efforts to establish school lunch programs, remedial instruction, and Head Start, a preschool program for children from low-income families. The Head Start program constituted a free educational experience for children never before considered part of the system of public education, and as such required huge investments of federal funds. Funding has fallen far short of the demand, however, with only about one-third of eligible children currently being served.

Programs for children with disabilities became required by law in 1975 with the passage of Public Law 94-142. Large amounts of tax revenue were promised to meet the mandate of a free, appropriate education for all children with disabilities. In spite of these significant increases in spending, many critics remained as the decade of the 1980s arrived, and considerable financial support was extended so that educators could reexamine the country's educational system. Results of these studies (*A Nation at Risk*, 1983; *The Holmes Report*, 1986, and others) indicated that costly changes were necessary to save the nation's schools. Because of this ongoing concern over the quality of schooling, funding for schools continued to increase during the 1980s.

Public education is supported by a combination of federal, state, and local tax dollars, with states contributing the largest amount of the three. Locally, most schools are funded by property taxes, paid by property owners at the local level. Many taxpayers, however, are not willing to pay higher taxes to support increased funding for schools (Elam, Rose, & Gallup, 1991). More and more people are presently demanding quality education but refusing to pay the price for supporting that quality. The reasons go beyond dissatisfaction with schools that have been well funded over the past twenty-five years. For the first time since the Great

Depression, schools across the United States are feeling the effects of a weakened national economy.

Reflect for a Moment

Recall a financial situation in your home district. Was it a need that went unfulfilled because of a shortage of funds? Was it a school budget that was approved or defeated? Was your school district well funded? How do you know whether it was or was not?

Management Factors

Gray (1993) suggests that this economic tragedy can be traced to American high schools, where students gravitate to either the "in" crowd or the "out" crowd. These students carry these attitudes into the adult work force, where American businesses and industries are characterized by one group who makes the decisions and another group who does the work. This structuring of the workforce, which originated with the scientific management theory of Frederick Winslow Taylor, contrasts with more contemporary, collaborative theories such as participatory management, or total quality management (TQM).

Seen in this light, the situation challenges schools to change their current practices of student recognition as a prerequisite for improving the quality of the work experience and rejuvenating the national economy. Rather than having the economy influence the schools, school restructuring can dramatically influence the economy. Educators must communicate to highly talented students the importance of teamwork in building a stronger economy. One of the most immediate and perhaps lasting ways for educators to do this is to establish a collaborative climate among themselves, and to demonstrate collaborative behavior naturally and routinely around students. They must also convey to those more educationally challenged that they are acquiring skills that are essential to overall team success and that their ideas are actively sought. Educators working as a collaborative team helping all students truly believe that they are critical players on the larger schoolwide team will take the first step in changing the structure of the working nation.

Reflect for a Moment

To what extent did you feel like a part of the team or part of a successful effort while you were in high school? Middle school? Elementary school?

O'Looney (1993) offers a slightly different version of the relationship between school structure and economic production, suggesting that schools are currently organized for mass production, in the same way that Henry Ford approached automobile manufacturing. This model—characterized by high-volume, low-skilled, but specialized workers; a separation of production workers from management; and linear production—was convenient for most of this century. Schools reflect a similar approach, with most students in basic classes and only a few in advanced classes. Many students are moved on as long as they attend classes, tolerate rote tasks, and are not disruptive. Collaborative planning and teaching are not features of these schools.

Foreign competition, complete with new technologies, has challenged this outdated approach to both the workforce and the system of schooling in the United States. Models of production quite different from Fordism guide the management of firms in other countries. These models rely on multiskilled workers who can contribute to what is called *flexible production.* These workers are literate and skilled at team problem solving and decision making.

Using management design principles created by Michael Hammer, O'Looney suggests that American schools could benefit from reexamining existing school practices in ways such as the following seven strategies: forming representative teams, using a case management approach, empowering teachers, providing distance technology, adding expanded resources, providing more choices, and automating administrative tasks. Strategy 1 would develop **representative teams** to rethink existing procedures, teams who are willing, in collaboration, to create new ways to conduct necessary school business. Instead of the processing approach, in which a student is channeled through all the required phases of school, strategy 2 would shift to a **case management approach,** in which a teacher, with the benefit of modern technology and collaborative support, could more fully educate a child by teaching and facilitating learning over an extended period of time and could conduct all the related educational business (grading, reporting, assessing, financing) related to that child. Strategy 3 would **empower** teachers who have all this data on a child to make more decisions about the child's education, particularly those relating to problem situations, resources, and related services. Strategy 4 would use **distance technology** to reach students across a much greater geographical area. Strategy 5 would utilize **expanded resources** for interdisciplinary learning, bringing parents and other professionals into the information system for a child in a meaningful way. Strategy 6 would consider giving parents, teachers, and students **choice** about whom they worked with in the school. Strategy 7, finally, would plan an **automated system** for more of the tedious paperwork, such as attendance and correspondence. All of these strategies would require additional funding, but O'Looney emphasizes that a commitment to significant redesigning is a prerequisite to the much-needed capital investment. Inclusive schools have employed these strategies effectively and found that through a collaborative effort, all learners can succeed.

Creating quality education by integrating it into the plan instead of fixing the problems of the end result is the basis of another management theory by W. Edward Deming (Holt, 1993). Deming's first emphasis is on the understanding of a clear and stimulating sense of purpose. He opposes traditional assembly-line management and insists that workers be educated in statistics so that they can test their own methods of work instead of just carrying out orders from managers. Applied to current education, this theory of management requires a change in who makes decisions. Instead of national or state systems of curriculum and assessment, teachers should assume the role of primary decision makers and actively pursue site-based management. Management at this level is necessarily particular to each school, rather than generic across schools, and is consistent with the smaller, neighborhood school concept that is integral to inclusive schools (Stainback, Stainback, & Jackson, 1992).

The school, for Deming, includes the student as consumer and the parent as sponsor, with both involved in all basic school-related decisions. Assessment would be informal because it would be particularized at each school. Curriculum would be based on students' own cultures and backgrounds and would truly link educational theory and practice. All these features are conducive to the building of inclusive schools and can be achieved more readily through professional collaboration. Overall, Deming's management model represents a dramatic change from the rational managerial model that has been used by so many American corporations and school systems, and as such will surely meet with resistance.

One common theme in each of the models described is collective decision making (Schmoker & Wilson, 1993), a concept that is very much like collaboration. Wherever this practice is observed, either in industry or in the schools, workers (teachers) are motivated and enjoy their work and consumers (students) are satisfied with their product. In these models, workers (teachers) feel that their efforts are valued and see improvement in their work, at least in part because of the presence of constant feedback. Significantly, in schools where these practices are in place, the cost of education does not increase. With such potential for economic change in the schools, the future certainly is bright.

Political Factors

Political influences on educational policy and reform date back to the beginning of public education in the United States and take two forms: formal control and informal influences. The power delegated to individuals or groups through statutes or laws and regulations is *formal control* and functions in a hierarchical fashion (see Figure 1.1).

Along with these formal controls come *informal influences*, exerted by individuals or groups on those who formally possess power to control the educational system. Although these groups or individuals have no legal authority, they are just as powerful a force in educational reform and change as those with delegated powers. The delivery of their agenda is well organized, and their lobbying efforts are extremely structured. Examples of informal influence groups are teachers' unions, parent groups (PARCs), businesses, civil liberties unions, and other lobbying groups. Unfortunately, often change is not initiated in the politics of education because it is appropriate but as a result of loud and active informal influences. Informal influence groups are frequently driven by a single issue and fail to take into consideration the impact their suggestions will have on all children or the totality of the educational system.

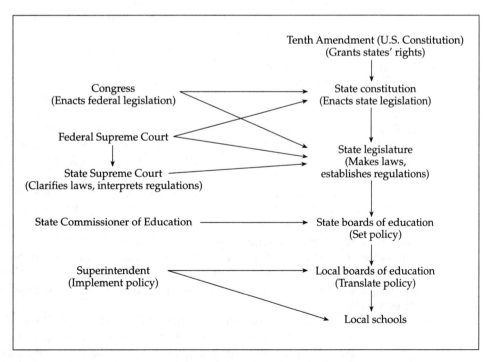

FIGURE 1.1   Hierarchy of formal educational control

Reflect for a Moment

Can you think of a situation (not necessarily related to your school experience) where a relatively small group of energized, vocal people made themselves heard and brought about a change in policy of some nature?

The Tenth Amendment (see the earlier discussion of educational law) does not eliminate Congressional control over education but rather creates a system of indirect influence. Although Congress is not prohibited from enacting legislation that affects public schools, its power is diminished unless significant funding is involved. The larger the funding package, the greater the federal control over education becomes. Before the beginning of the twentieth century, the role of Congress was limited to providing land grants for schools (the Ordinance of 1785 and the Northwest Ordinance of 1787) that were used primarily for the maintenance of public schools within specific townships.

The twentieth century has seen increased congressional influence over the educational system in a variety of areas. The emergence of legislation such as the Smith-Hughes Act (1917), which allocated millions of dollars for vocational education; the National School Lunch Act (1946), which provided funds for free milk and low-cost lunches for children from economically deprived families; and the National Defense Education Act (PL 85-684, 1958), which granted funds to improve education in mathematics, science, and foreign language, changed the role of federal involvement in education. These acts were seen by many as Congress's first real attempt at setting educational policy.

During the 1960s and 1970s, Congress expanded its role as policy maker through a significant increase in federal legislation directed primarily at ensuring equal educational opportunities (Economic Opportunities Act, PL 88-452; Elementary and Secondary Education Act, PL 89-10; Education for All Handicapped Children Act, PL 94-142). Through this legislation the federal government was able to exert power over the states via regulations attached to the receipt of funding. Dye (1985) believes that this expansion of the federal role through legislation and funding limited state control so severely that it destroyed the meaning of the Tenth Amendment.

More indirect than the influence of Congress is the effect that U.S. presidents have had on public education. Although some presidents have exerted more influence than others, their input is frequently limited to establishing legislative agendas and setting the tone of the Supreme Court (Reed & Bergemann, 1995). The issue of decentralization of education has changed depending on presidential leadership, ranging from Thomas Jefferson's belief in almost total control by the people to John F. Kennedy's and Lyndon B. Johnson's desire for federal direction.

Article 3 of the U.S. Constitution states: "The judicial power of the United States shall be vested in one Supreme Court, and in such inferior courts as the Congress may from time to time ordain and establish." The Supreme Court has the power to interpret the Constitution and as such is able to exert a significant amount of indirect influence on public education—indirect, that is, only in the sense that the Supreme Court acts to resolve problems and does not solicit cases. The Supreme Court's involvement in education increased dramatically between 1954 and 1970, when some 2,000 cases were heard as compared to approximately 200 cases before 1954 (Reed & Bergemann, 1995). So significant was the Supreme Court's influence on education during the 1960s and 1970s that it was often referred to as the "black-robed school board."

Not unlike the President, state governors play an indirect role in public education. Governors set legislative agendas and in all states except North Carolina have the power to veto legislation. State governors began to increase their role in the educational system during the late 1980s by forming the Educational Commission of the States. In conjunction with the National Governors' Association and the Council of Chief State School Officers, the Educational Commission developed several task forces to examine leadership and management, school facilities, parent involvement and choice, technology, readiness, teaching, and college quality. These task forces established six major goals for education that heavily influenced the formulation of The Bush administration's *America 2000*. Although the National Governors' Association developed an agenda for reaching these goals, they can only be realized if passed into law by state legislatures and then interpreted and implemented by state boards of education.

With the authority to create and design school districts, control teacher certification, prescribe curriculum, mandate attendance laws, regulate aspects of school administration as well as raise revenue and distribute funds, state legislatures have direct formal control over their educational systems. Additionally, state legislatures may establish agencies to implement laws and carry out school administrative functions. With the exception of Wisconsin, state legislatures have invested these formal controls in state boards of education and either a superintendent of public instruction or a commissioner of education. Although the function of both officials tends to be regulatory in nature, they have a great deal of informal influence on legislation and policy.

Local school districts or educational agencies directly administer local public schools. This task is generally accomplished through the work of both the local school board and superintendent. School board members, often between five and nine in number, are elected, generally serve staggered terms, and frequently serve without pay. Although individual school board members may exert a great deal of political pressure on the group, the board must act as a single body to translate policy. It is at this level that many decisions supporting professional collaboration and inclusive education need to be made.

Local superintendents act as liaisons to the community. They are responsible for the educational and business administration of all schools within the district or educational agency. Among their duties are budget preparation and implementation, curriculum selection, professional development of teachers and staff, and implementation of school boards' goals and policies.

Governmental and political factors exert a powerful influence over the educational system. Concerns about centralization of governmental power have state legislatures reexamining their role in the development of educational systems. Educational reform is becoming more than a plank in an election year platform, visible only if good for gathering voter support.

International Factors

The United States has possibly one of the most culturally, ethnically, and racially diverse populations of any nation in the world. Reflecting their international mixture of origins, very few U.S. schools have populations that are culturally homogeneous. English is the second language for many learners in the United States. It is imperative, therefore, that for children and youth to function in a diverse and complex world they develop knowledge, skills, and attitudes that promote global awareness. Federally funded educational improvement projects have found it necessary to look internationally for resolutions to curriculum concerns in the United States. The University of Chicago School Mathematics project, for example, has translated forty mathematics texts (from Japan, the former Soviet Union, and Hungary) and held three international conferences since 1983 to assist in the development of an appropriate mathematics curriculum (Usiskin, 1993).

The increase of technology in the areas of communication and travel has also helped to shrink the distance between countries. Economies of most nations are no longer self-supporting and must rely on world trade to grow. The stock exchanges in Tokyo and Paris are as important to the United States as those in New York and Chicago. Children who come from monolingual homes are at a disadvantage in today's world. Bilingual backgrounds (once considered as a problem in public school environment) provide for students a leg up in the international job market.

The practice of comparing educational standards from one state to another has, consequently, given way to international comparisons. It is not uncommon to see reports in the daily newspaper regarding the substandard educational system, lower test scores, and overall lack of higher-level thinking skills exhibited by students in the United States when compared to those in other nations. Statements such as "The United States has the weakest elementary school mathematics curriculum in the world" (Usiskin, 1993, p. 14), from the director of the University of Chicago School Mathematics Project, are issued every day on all the classic curriculum areas (math, science, social studies, and reading).

It is not enough simply to compare students and bemoan their inadequacies. The slogan "Think globally, act locally" needs to be the theme of education in the United States. Educators must act to institute programs that prepare all children to be world citizens.

Reflect for a Moment

What activities or projects did you participate in during your school years that reflected the idea of "Think globally, act locally"?

Reform and Restructuring

Within the United States, reform in public education has a long history—from the Olde Deluder Satan Act (1647) to the Goals 2000: Eductate America Act (1994). Education reforms have been proposed by politicians, state and local school boards, associations, governmental agencies and commissions, university boards of regents, and individuals. "Too frequently, however, the suggested reforms have been contradictory in nature, poorly implemented, and eventually abandoned" (Orlich, 1989, p. 513).

In 1983, the National Commission on Excellence in Education presented its findings regarding the need for educational reform in a report entitled *A Nation at Risk*. The United States was perceived to be at risk in large part because too few people understood the complexity of problems facing our country's children and youth, problems that did not necessarily focus on education but were having an enormous impact on the learning environment. What held true in 1983 still holds true: "Today—tens of thousands of studies and reports, pilot projects, and conferences later—we're at risk because we've not made the national commitment necessary to rescue our children and our schools" (Geiger, 1993, p. 15).

There is little doubt that historians will look back at the 1980s as the decade of education, not because problems were solved, but because for the first time the totality of the educational dilemma we as a nation face has achieved national significance (Doyle, 1991). Whatever its ultimate worth may be, Goals 2000 is the first serious reform initiative to address the issue of increasing the federal role in education and if so, who should benefit from this expanded involvement.

This is not to say that bits and pieces of the educational dilemma have not broken away and risen to the top, gaining national significance. But the totality of problems that schools face has never before been examined with such interest or intensity. Since World War II, the national reaction to these individual problems has been legislation. The Servicemen's Readjustment Act (known as the G.I. Bill), the Individuals with Disabilities Act (1990), and Chapter 1 are but a few examples of ways the federal government has intervened to seal the smaller cracks of the educational dam. The waters of disenchantment, however, continue to rise toward the top.

School reform efforts have historically targeted very specific student populations (Native Americans, Hispanic Americans, African Americans, students with low socioeconomic status (SES), students with disabilities). Reform efforts, although they may differ by degree, have for these minority groups followed a rather predictable pattern and focus primarily on external factors or the roles of adults within the educational system. Access and funding, curriculum change and program effectiveness, and improved student outcomes and program accountability have been the three major cycles of school reform.

Equal Access and Funding

The first cycle of educational reform examines the dilemma of equal access and funding for all children and youth to the public education system in the United States. The fallacy that these benefits were granted through *Brown v. the Board of*

Education of Topeka and the Civil Rights Act has long plagued the educational system. There is no doubt that in the United States every child has the opportunity to attend public school and that compulsory education is the norm. However, *opportunity* to attend school is very different than *access* to an education. In other words, being there does not mean you will be provided the chance to learn. One of the major factors that results in what Kozol (1992) has termed as "savage inequalities" in the development and delivery of sound education to all children is the ridiculous manner in which public schools are funded. Funding alone does not guarantee a quality educational experience. Funding, however, is a major issue when monies are so scarce that students must sit in buildings that are crumbling. Property-poor areas such as inner-city or large rural districts cannot make up the difference between what the state sets as per-pupil cost and the reality of expenditures. This inequity results in overcrowded classrooms, substandard equipment, buildings in disrepair, and a less than enthusiastic staff.

Although initiated as early as 1971, it was not until the beginning of the 1980s that students, parents, and administrators from poor inner-city and rural districts began to strike out against state school finance systems through litigation. During the last twenty-five years, ten State Supreme Courts struck down as unconstitutional state school finance systems that they believed resulted in stark disparities among rich and poor districts in per-pupil expenditures for education. The ten states that have had their finance systems determined to be unconstitutional are, in chronological order of rulings, California (1971), New Jersey (1973 and 1991), Connecticut (1977), Washington (1978), Wyoming (1980), West Virginia (1982), Arkansas (1983), and Kentucky, Montana, and Texas (all in 1989). Additionally, at least fourteen more states have pending court cases challenging the constitutionality of state funding systems for education.

More revolutionary than the flood of litigation that began over two decades ago, this current battle, which is focused on funding, has been fueled by courts less tolerant of inequities among districts not just in spending but in educational opportunities as well. Unfortunately, although courts have been explicit about how the funding systems are inequitable, they have failed to provide strong recommendations for rectifying the problem. That is not to say that states are not taking seriously the court rulings. Oregon's 1993–1995 kindergarten through twelfth grade budget is a 66.4 percent increase over their 1991–1993 school budget, an unusually high increase. Other states, such as Delaware, North Carolina, New Hampshire, and Ohio, are more conservative, proposing increases ranging from 3 to 7 percent (Legislative Update, 1993, p. 15).

Curriculum Change and Program Effectiveness

The second cycle in school reform consists of curriculum change and program effectiveness. In the period from 1860 to 1990, at least a half dozen reform movements were undertaken to effect curriculum change and improvement in elementary and secondary schools. Of these, three related to what the curriculum should be and three identified the bases of curriculum planning. These historic U.S. curriculum movements or reforms looked to (1) establishing, organizing, and re-organizing schools; (2) opening, augmenting, and broadening the curriculum; (3) reducing, concentrating, and tightening curriculum; (4) focusing on children and youth as learners and the ways they learn; (5) focusing on the problems and requirements of diverse cultures and the society as a whole; and (6) focusing on subject matter and students' learning success (Doll, 1992, p. 9).

One of the greatest problems facing the curriculum reform movement is what is most important to include from the vast quantities of subject matter and information available. (Chapter 2 addresses curriculum in greater detail.) There is a great debate over whether curriculums should be composed of classic subject areas (mathematics, language arts, and science) or should respond to sociopolitical pressures (HIV/AIDS prevention and combative drug abuse programs). According to Doll (1992), although a great need exists to restructure curriculum delivery in the classic subject areas, societal pressures are forcing additional topics (religion, unwanted pregnancies, HIV/AIDS, drugs/alcohol addiction, grief education, global awareness) into the schools. This growing curriculum is out of balance with the basic structure of the learning environment as time that was once devoted to the study of the fine and performing arts has been gradually decreased to make way for these newly evolved areas of learning. Recognition of the necessity to become globally aware, the dramatic increase in youth violence that creates the need for grief education (formally death education), and a growing demand for programs geared towards economics and personal finance are all areas of special interest and pose additional demands on a curriculum that is already overflowing.

Reflect for a Moment

Take a few minutes to carefully address the big question, "What should all students learn?" Start with broad generalizable statements. (This may take a while.)

Perhaps at the core of these reform movements is the belief that the most challenging diversity faced by our schools is not cultural, but rather curriculum or academic diversity. Quality or the search for educational excellence has been the foundation for the belief in a need for a common national curriculum. One such common curriculum was developed by Hirsch in 1986 through an organization called the Core Knowledge Foundation. Hirsch (1993) states "to achieve excellence and fairness in education, an elementary school needs to teach a body of shared knowledge, grade by grade" (p. 23). The Core Knowledge Sequence for Grades 1–6 recommends content that will "provide a solid, coherent foundation of shared knowledge for students in elementary grades" (Hirsch, 1993, p. 25). Urban blight is evident in the South Bronx neighborhood surrounding the Mohegan School: crack houses, prostitution, uncollected trash, and abandoned cars are common features. All the students at Mohegan qualify for free lunch and most are either Hispanic or African American. Since adopting the Core Knowledge Curriculum, students at this school have moved from an educational environment focused primarily on remediation to one that is enriched and integrated.

Outcomes

The third cycle of educational reform attempts to strengthen the rigor of public education in the United States through the accountability of educators and improvement of student outcomes. Interestingly enough, experts seem to have reached the conclusion that both of these reforms can be accomplished through increased assessment. The concept of using measures such as the National Teachers' Examination as a tool for developing more universal teacher certification in this country, however, has never come to fruition. Measurement of student outcomes, on the other hand, brought cries from legislators for mandated national standardized assessments. "Underlying the proposal for national testing are the assumptions that uniform tests will improve the education system as a whole, that instruction will necessarily improve as a result, and that teachers and students will benefit" (Lieberman, 1991, p. 219). Proponents believe that these mandated tests will measure only the most important educational outcomes, ones that school systems should be held accountable for, standards by which success and failure can be measured. They also believe that mandated national testing is a means of motivating and directing educators and learners.

It is difficult to understand how the creation of more test anxiety in an already overassessed group will serve to motivate. Until the late 1980s, debates on "high-stakes standardized testing" (Shepard, 1991) were largely rhetorical because there was little research in the area. However, since 1987 a body of research has evolved that adds substance to the debate on the effects of mandated standardized testing. Cannell (1987) and Linn, Graue, and Sanders (1990) found that political pressure and media attention on tests results in an atmosphere of manipulation, causing scores to become inflated and creating a false impression of student achievement. Additionally, mandated standardized "high-stakes" testing was found by Smith (1989) to narrow the curriculum. As a result of externalized tests, general education teachers gave up reading "real books", writing, and long-term, in-depth learning projects for word recognition, language usage, punctuation, and arithmetic operations. In districts where testing is emphasized, teachers actively help students prepare for these tests throughout the school year (Shepard, 1991).

Reflect for a Moment

Do you remember preparing for standardized tests? Throughout your schooling, what do you recall about teachers "teaching to the test" or having students practice for the tests?

The type of drill-and-practice instruction that these mandated standardized tests reinforce is based on outmoded learning theory (Resnick & Resnick, 1992). Contemporary research on cognition has rejected assumptions about decomposability and decontextualization as a means of developing higher-order thinking skills. Educators who teach to mandated standardized tests by providing daily skills instruction through drill-and-practice that closely resembles the test format are not simply using noneffective methodology but have instructional practices that produce detrimental effects. Research in cognitive psychology demonstrates the error in learning theory that suggests that basic skills learned through rote memorization can be reassembled into more complex understandings. On the contrary: For learners to develop those higher-order skills, they must be constantly challenged to think and actively construct mental models or schemata.

Conversely, although reform in this cycle targets all children and youth, the fear of being accountable and the need to demonstrate high test scores seems to result in the rejection of those students who need the educational system the most. Shepard (1991) reports that there appears to be

> a direct correspondence between the extent of pressures regarding accountability and the number of children who are denied entry to kindergarten programs, who are assigned to two-year kindergarten programs, who are referred to special education, who are made to repeat a grade, or who drop out of school. (p. 234)

Hatch and Freeman (1988) found that both professional knowledge and the status of educators were reduced by the dictates of externally mandated standardized testing. Educators experienced stress and role conflict as a result of allowing their instructional decisions to be dictated by testing rather than learning theory or best practice. Often the most intellectually able educators with the strongest professional code of ethics do not remain in the teaching profession, and many of those who choose to remain are forced to shield themselves from this moral dilemma by caring less about their teaching and their students.

The argument against standardized testing should not be taken as a stance against teacher and student accountability. Accountability must be a major concern for educators in the twenty-first century. However, to believe that learning will be enhanced through the use of nationally mandated standardized examinations is short sighted. Alternative assessment techniques such as portfolios, knowledge demonstrations, and other types of authentic assessment are currently being adopted in several states. No additional time is required for truly authentic assessment because the day-to-day student work is the evidence of learning.

Multicultural Education

Multicultural education, another spoke in the wheel of the education and school reform movement, is directed at assuring that students from all social classes and racial, intellectual, cultural, and gender groups will have equal opportunity to learn. In addition to advocating equal access, multicultural education has striven to prompt the infusion of varying cultures into all curriculum areas. Perhaps one of the critical features that sets this reform movement apart from the others is its clear recognition that the ultimate goals will never be reached but nonetheless should always be sought.

> Educational equality, like liberty and justice, are ideals toward which human beings work but never fully attain. Racism, sexism, and discrimination against people with disabilities will exist to some extent no matter how hard we work to eliminate these problems. When prejudice and discrimination are reduced toward one group, they are usually directed toward another group or they take new forms. Because the goals of multicultural education can never be fully attained, we should work continually to increase educational equality for all students. (Banks, 1993, p. 4)

SUMMARY

Schools today have a two-way relationship with modern society. On one hand, schools have exerted a constant influence on society in the form of graduates, young people who possess a wide range of knowledge, skills, and attitudes that allow them to participate with varying degrees of success in society. Many observers have determined that schools must change in order to prepare future generations for the world of the twenty-first century because graduates today lack the critical knowledge, skills, and attitudes needed for success. Educational programs that segregate learners from one another fail to provide valuable opportunities for cooperative effort. On the other hand, society continues to exert an equally powerful influence on schools. Many of the influences on schools can be traced to historic precedent in the form of economic theories or a series of governmental/ political structures.

More recently, the influences of changes in the family and technology on the educational system have been recognized for their importance. Family structure in the United States has altered dramatically. The high incidence of divorce has created generations of students whose emotional and social well-being are clearly at risk and whose success in school is routinely placed in jeopardy. The percentage of mothers who have entered the workforce has increased dramatically. Schools have become community centers, providing child care, breakfast, routine medical services, and moral support to children everywhere. More families with children are living in poverty than ever before in the nation's history, leaving schools to create and coordinate support networks for children and families who are homeless, hungry, violent, or psychologically harmed. Yet another family influence is the ever-increasing number of teenagers having children. Many of these children are born at risk and many of their mothers are school dropouts unprepared for either parenthood or the workforce. Finally, the cultural diversity of families in modern society is greater than ever, with a dramatic mismatch emerging between the cultural backgrounds of teachers and students in many urban areas. The challenges facing schools as a result of these and other changes in families will require educators to reorganize the process of schooling in order to meet the demands of the future.

2

CURRICULUM TODAY

Key Terms

Affective domain
Analysis
Application
Basic fundamental movements
Characterization by value
Cognitive domain
Comprehension
Constructivism
Curriculum
  Planned
  Unplanned
    hidden
    informal
  Student centered
    activity centered
    child centered
    humanistic
    relevant
  Subject centered
    back to basics
    competency based
    essentialist
    integrated
    subject area
    subject structure

Essentialism
Evaluation
Expressive, interpretive
  movements
Knowledge
Organization
Perceptual abilities
Perennialism
Physical abilities
Progressivism
Psychomotor domain
Receiving
Reconstructionism
Reflex movements
Responding
Skilled movements
Subject structure
Synthesis
Valuing

Objectives

After completing this chapter, the reader will be able to:

1. Describe curriculum.
2. Identify significant characteristics of five major curriculum philosophies.
3. Explain historical influences on contemporary curriculum.
4. Develop strategies for addressing curriculum for the next century.
5. Compare and contrast subject-centered and child-centered curriculum.
6. Identify which curriculum types are compatible with collaborative teaching and inclusive schools.
7. Discuss psychological forces which may influence curriculum development.
8. Discuss social forces which may influence curriculum development.
9. Identify contemporary curriculum trends.
10. Distinguish the basic features of the three domains of learning.

PROFILES OF CURRICULUM

Rigorville Central School

No one thought it could be done, no one perhaps except Sandra Fothergill, superintendent of the Rigorville Central School district. After years of reading about declining test scores, light homework loads, and disciplinary problems, she led a major transformation of the district's philosophy. It was time to demand more of students and stop pampering them. The result of a year of meetings with school boards and building administrators was the most academically focused curriculum people in Rigorville had ever known.

Teachers from kindergarten through twelfth grade would deliver a no-frills academic program that stressed intellectual exercise and focused on an agreed-on core of knowledge. Students would have no choice of courses; reading, writing and arithmetic would be the main menu items. No more self-awareness, decision making, or sex education in the curriculum. The teaching materials would consist of textbooks, pencil and paper tasks and, on occasion, films. There was little need for learning centers, field trips, or group projects. Students would have to learn to sit and listen, and take notes. Recitation was the preferred method of instruction, and students either succeeded or failed and dropped out. Groups would be used, but only as tracks of students according to ability. Students with low scores on the standardized tests administered each spring would be pulled out of general classrooms and taught separately. Teachers would be rewarded with merit pay based on their students' test scores.

After two years of this regime, the scores of the Rigorville students on standardized tests had improved over 10 percent! Citizens applauded the superintendent's initiative. But there was a group of concerned citizens, some of them teachers in the district, who were disturbed by the direction the community was taking.

Lake Change Community Schools

Like Rigorville, the townspeople of Lake Change were painfully aware of the problems in their schools. Students were increasingly disruptive, preferred driver's education over Shakespeare, and came to school unprepared more often than not. So many of them just didn't seem to be motivated to do anything.

Over morning coffee at Al's Diner, the superintendent of schools, Jesse Adams, expressed his concern to Jeannette Staples, executive director of the Chamber of Commerce. The two decided to invite the community to a town meeting to discuss what might be done to change the situation. Child care was provided free of charge, and refreshments were served. Almost one hundred people came, and Adams and Staples received support to go ahead and organize a school/community steering committee to research and recommend strategies for improving conditions in the schools.

After almost a full year of public hearings, the teachers' union and the school board agreed on a set of strategies designed to bring new life to the teaching/learning environment. The purpose of the curriculum was redefined, with the main focus placed on teaching all students how to learn instead of teaching all students a set body of information. Students, not the curriculum, would become the focus of schooling. Curriculum would be thoroughly reexamined, with a likely shift toward a more community-conscious, problem-oriented, project-centered course of study. Teachers would have release time each week to plan collaboratively with support personnel, a strategy designed to enhance the learning environment in the general classroom for all learners regardless of age, ability, interest, or past school performance.

WHAT IS CURRICULUM?

Given such different learning needs and experiences, it is important to have a clear understanding of just what curriculum means. The curricula experienced by each of the two districts just mentioned reflects the values of the society they live in and their own individual strengths and needs. But is curriculum simply subject area content? Or is it the broader set of experiences that students acquire during the entire time they are in school? MacKenzie (1964) sees curriculum as "the learner's engagements with various aspects of the environment which have been planned under the direction of the school" (p. 402).

The extent to which schools actually plan all of a student's experiences has long been a matter of debate, so other interpretations of curriculum have been broader. Hass and Parkay (1993) have attempted to synthesize several approaches, offering a definition of curriculum as:

> all of the experiences that individual learners have in a program of education whose purpose is to achieve broad goals and related specific objectives, which is planned in terms of a framework of theory and research or past and present professional practice. (p. 3)

They identify four fundamental blocs of knowledge that must be seriously considered in designing a curriculum: social influences, child development, learning theory, and the nature of knowledge and knowing (Hass & Parkay, 1993). For the sake of clarification, **curriculum**, from this point on, will refer to all of the learning that children do in school.

Curriculum Philosophies

So that we may approach the issue of curriculum with a clear perspective, it is critical to think through several philosophies that relate to the purpose and content of what should be learned in school. A brief survey of perennialism, essentialism, progressivism, reconstructionism, and contructivism can offer some insight into how curriculum has evolved through the past and may develop in the future.

Perennialism

Perennialism is based on the belief that the purpose of education is to develop intellectual strength and discipline the mind. This view of education can be traced back to the traditions of Plato, Aristotle, and St. Thomas Aquinas (Oliva, 1992). The goals of a perennialist education are pursuit of truth and preservation of the intellectual traditions of Western culture. The truth, found through a detailed study of the great books of the Western world, is viewed as eternal and unchanging. Every student is expected to understand the intellectual tradition in which she or he lives and be able to read, understand, and talk about this tradition in an intelligent manner.

Over half a century ago, Hutchins (1938) addressed what he saw as a population of illiterate university students, observing that they were being required to read fewer and fewer books as part of their studies. Regarding the increased student interest in such extracurricular events as football, school newspaper, and drama club, he saw students who viewed the general curriculum as useless and void of great writers and artists. Hutchins argued that the fundamental questions of humankind were the same in 1938 as in ancient Greek and Roman civilizations and, as perhaps the leading perennialist of his time, advocated a rigorous and demanding curriculum that included grammar, logic, rhetoric, and the "great books."

Hutchins favored examinations as a way to demonstrate student learning and urged that they be taken only when students were ready. He disdained such frills as vocational training and meeting the immediate needs of students, and rejected such nonabsolutes as emotions, feelings, and motor development as unrelated to strengthening of the mind.

Although a few schools adhere to Hutchins' principles, perennialism has not enjoyed widespread acceptance in America's schools. If the five philosophies of curriculum were arranged from most liberal to most conservative, perennialism would be the most conservative.

Essentialism

Perhaps almost as conservative as perennialism is **essentialism**, the most commonly found philosophy in practice in American schools. The roots of essentialism can be traced to the creation of the Boston Latin School in 1635. With the exception of a brief period of progressivism during the 1940s and 1950s, essentialism has remained the dominant educational philosophy in America.

At the heart of essentialism is the transmission of a society's heritage, both its culture and goals. Most of those goals are intellectual, requiring mental discipline from the learner. Essentialists believe that the mature must instruct the immature in a wide range of situations, imposing discipline as a means to helping learners develop self-discipline. The curriculum is set, and learners adapt to it. One of the most respected essentialist scholars of the early twentieth century was Bagley (1941), who asserted that the essentials included recording, computing, measuring, a broad and balanced knowledge of the world, a sense of one's history, investigation, invention, creative arts, health, natural science, fine arts, and industrial arts. All these areas of learning were seen as fundamental to a formal education.

The influence of essentialism has been both significant and enduring. In contemporary American education, the **back to basics** curriculum movement has been fueled by essentialists, who support an academically rigorous, traditional course of study. The Rigorville transformation at the beginning of the chapter is a reflection of this reemergence of essentialism. Since the 1950s, the essentialist approach to curriculum has been most evident in junior and senior high schools in the United States, with the teacher-centered classroom, subject-centered curriculum with its Carnegie Units, ability grouping, formal examinations, and traditional systems of assessment (paper and pencil tasks, tests, quizzes) and grade evaluation. Educators using an essentialist approach in the classroom present a rule and follow up with a series of practice opportunities so that learners will learn the rule well enough to use it in new and different situations. Behaviorists have found this approach compatible to their thinking about learning (see Chapter 3).

Bagley (1941) drew clear distinctions between the essentialist perspective and that of the progressivists, to be discussed shortly. Progressivists, in his view, emphasize student interest as the driving force behind effort. Essentialists, while not denying their value, assert that such interests, at least those of the enduring, higher-level type, often emerge from efforts at tasks not initially appealing to the learner. Progressivists, in Bagley's opinion, see teacher-initiated learning as an undesirable reality of some educational experiences, whereas essentialists see this type of learning as part of responsible adult care and support of younger, more dependent learners. Bagley also asserted that what the progressivists see as innovative child-centered curriculum is really a return to a less civilized, less culturally literate plan for learning. He claimed that the progressivists, in their zeal to focus on learning that relates to the present, dismiss the past as dead, a view to be cautioned against. Finally, Bagley regarded the Progressivists, with their movement away from a subject-centered curriculum, as hindering even the most competent learners from a course of study that would in fact prove rigorous and, in the long run, rewarding.

Progressivism

Just as essentialism espouses a subject-centered, pencil and paper–driven curriculum, **progressivism** counters with a **child-centered, activity-centered curriculum** based on a strong democratic ideal. More than a transmission of heritage, curriculum to the progressivists should promote the interests of the learner and the larger society. The citizens of Lake Change, with their focus on the learner and the community, were clearly interested in a more progressivist curriculum. The natural sciences are viewed as the ideal vehicle for the emergence of a "method of intelligence" that the learner can apply to a wide range of situations. John Dewey, perhaps the most well known progressivist, (1902) referred to this "method of the mind" as a process of assimilation in which the student actively captures meaningful new learning. The child in a progressive school actively experiences learning rather than passively absorbing content. Learners in the progressive tradition are encouraged to be creative, motivated, and democratic in their thinking.

William Heard Kilpatrick (1941) advocated progressivist principles when he described the source of a student's learning as

> a situation of his own, such that he himself feels inwardly called upon to face it; his own interests are inherently at stake. And his response thereto is also his own; it comes out of his own mind and heart, out of his own very self. He may, to be sure, have had help from teacher or book, but the response when it comes is his. (p. 231)

This mode of learning is quite contrary to examination and recitation in a school- or teacher-directed curriculum, which Kilpatrick sees as meaningless and boring. "It does little for mind or heart, and possibly even less for character, for it hardly gets into life" (Kilpatrick, 1941, p. 231).

Kilpatrick makes a strong case for progressivism, describing six significant features. First, he views the success of the child as a member of the larger society, characterized by lifelong learning and a positive attitude and disposition, as the center of the educational endeavor. Second, as stated, the source of learning lies within the child; it is not set down by the teacher or school. Third, the school has a responsibility to engage the student in socially useful work through participation in real-life events and activities. Fourth, according to Kilpatrick, is the emphasis placed on helping young learners think for themselves, adapt to changing conditions around them, and use their learning productively. The teacher's role in a progressivist school is to not dictate learning to students, but to help develop and guide them toward a desirable life. This type of curriculum clearly cannot be planned, published, and imposed on masses of students all at once. Therefore, the fifth feature is that the curriculum is jointly constructed by students and teachers together, with teachers as guides and students as active doers. The sixth feature reflects back on the impact of such a curriculum on learners. Kilpatrick sees students actively learning, using textbooks as but one of many tools of learning, and building meaningful relationships with others along with a strong sense of self-discipline as members of a positive, productive learning community.

One of the most well-known progressive techniques is the scientific method, where learners identify a problem, hypothesize, gather information, analyze the information, and come to logical conclusions. This process was seen as the means to approach a myriad of problems posed by life and pursued in progressive schools. Furthermore, while essentialists aligned their curriculum philosophy with the learning theories of the behaviorists, progressivists found their philosophy compatible with aspects of experimental psychology, Gestalt psychology, and perceptual psychology (Oliva, 1992). The experimental psychologists' emphasis on active involvement, the Gestalt psychologists' focus on the "big picture," and the perceptual psychologists' examination of self-concept all found a place in the approach to curriculum taken by the progressivists.

During the 1930s and 1940s, progressivism received a boost from the Eight-Year Study, which followed groups of learners from experimental schools and conventional schools through their college years and found that the conventional course of study was not a necessary prerequisite for success in college (Aikin, 1942). However, the progressivist era soon fell into decline. Among the contributing factors were concern over students' failure to learn basic skills, the extremes that some progressive schools went to in pursuing their ideals, alarm over the American education system in general brought on by the launching of the Russian satellite Sputnik, and the attraction of the familiar, clearly structured subject matter of the essentialist philosophy.

Reconstructionism

Early **reconstructionism**, led by Counts (1932), branched away from the progressivists during the Great Depression of the 1930s when they saw progressive education failing to address societial ills. Unemployment, hunger, shelter and ethnic problems were among the challenges early reconstructionists took on as they moved to an almost militant level of activism. Brameld (1935) exhorted teachers to "influence their students, subtly if necessary, frankly if possible, toward acceptance of . . . the collectivist ideal" (p. 55).

Those who adhere to a reconstructionist perspective on curriculum see schools as the means to change or reconstruct society. The school is responsible for teaching students to analyze and question social practices that result in whole groups of people living with poverty, war, racism, or some other significant societal ill. Hence the reconstructionist curriculum is centered around studies of the major problems of a particular society, and students are taught to be empowered and have an influence on their community.

Because of its almost socialist orientation, reconstructionism did not grow in favor during the middle of the twentieth century. Beginning in the early 1970s, however, a new radical academic left of critical theorists emerged, among them Paulo Freire, Joel Spring, and Henry Giroux. The new academic left adapted the reconstructionist philosophy and advocated for empowerment of the student; they criticized schools as totally ineffective change agents that also acted as a highly repressive influence on young minds. The attack came with a paucity of alternative proposals as reconstructionists distanced themselves from the public schools (Tanner & Tanner, 1995).

Although democracy is seen as the goal of education among reconstructionists, many of the attacks from this group of critical theorists have been too radical for the American public to accept. As a result most reconstructionist influences have been limited to alternative schools outside the mainstream of public education. In spite of the reconstructionists' extreme position, and particularly that of the new radical academic movement, however, it should be remembered that Americans continue to look to education as a way to improve society.

Constructivism

As researchers increasingly learn about what takes place during the learning process, they have recognized the active role that students can and should take in acquiring new knowledge and understanding (Flavell, 1992; Forman, Minick, & Stone; Poplin, 1988). McNeil (1995) describes a curriculum of **constructivism** as not a prior body of knowledge to be transmitted but rather the knowledge and meanings students construct as they form goals and act upon materials and other aspects of the classroom environment, exploring with others a matrix of ideas. (p. 1)

Fosnot (1989) defined constructivism according to four principles: The first principle is that **knowledge** is made up of prior constructions. These prior constructions are the result of the learner's past experiences connecting known and unknown information through a process of self-regulation. The second principle is that assimilation and accommodation play a major role in a learner's construction of new knowledge. *Assimilation* takes place when the learner uses existing framework to process new information. *Accommodation* takes place when the learner finds it necessary to modify and adapt existing framework to process new information. A young child assimilates when she or he uses an existing framework to count pennies. The same young child finds it necessary to accommodate when she or he is given a nickel and some pennies because counting by ones does not work.

The third principle is that "learning is an organic process of invention, rather than a mechanical process of accumulation" (p. 20). Inherent in this principle are the learner as constructer of knowledge and the teacher as enlightened mediator. The fourth principle is that learning that has meaning takes place when cognitive conflict is examined and resolved because this process allows the most complete understanding of new or only partially resolved information. A child who asks about Santa Claus in the mall has experienced *cognitive conflict* (Santa should be in his workshop supervising the elves) and is actively seeking a more complete (and accurate) understanding of the concept of Santa Claus.

The purpose of schooling, according to constructivism, is the lifelong use of knowledge in a wide range of circumstances and with a wide range of other people (Reid, Kurkjian, & Carruthers, 1994). Learners, the central focus for curriculum development in the constructivist tradition, actively construct new knowledge through interactions with their physical and social environment. Teachers therefore must develop curriculum continuously in the classroom. They come to expect different strategies to reach a common understanding and have different understandings arising from a common activity (McNeil, 1995).

Reid, Kurkjian, and Carruthers (1994) describe constructivism as an epistemology, or way of knowing, and offer several implications for curriculum. The constructivist curriculum, they say, is process based, student centered, holistic, and higher order. Students are driven to construct new learning by connecting existing and prior knowledge with new material. This is the learner's strategy for resolving confusion or filling a perceptual gap in their understanding. For example, a young reader who encounters an unfamiliar word uses either existing knowledge of phonics or the surrounding words, or both, to figure out what the unfamiliar word might be. Errors are seen as opportunities to reach a better grasp of the new learning. The teacher's main responsibility is to provide activities that learners will use to construct some type of meaning through self-regulation.

Another implied tenet of the constructivist curriculum is the changing nature of educational and instructional goals brought on by the dynamic change in learners over time. Reid, Kurkjian, and Carruthers (1994) acknowledge that problem solving is a learning activity often employed by the constructivist educator: "When content to be learned is addressed holistically and is at an appropriate level of complexity, students invent ways to (a) organize their knowledge and procedures (i.e., skills and strategies) and (b) to compensate for weaknesses" (p. 269).

The constructivist curriculum is consequently idea and problem centered. Learners take time to describe how they see themselves as learners, what learning is, and what they think different students actually learn. The influence of constructivism on public schools has been limited to date, due in part to the magnitude of change necessary in educators' thinking that implementing this curriculum would entail.

Reflect for a Moment

Look back over the five philosophies and find the one you feel most comfortable with. Why did you choose that philosophy? Is it different from the prevailing philosophy of the school(s) you attended as a child?

A Brief History

Historically, the nature of curriculum has tended to be consistent with the child's status in society. When children had little value, perennialist curriculum prepared them for social stratification and hard work. When they were valued, curriculum became more child oriented and progressive.

Early Puritan schools were mostly for boys only, and curriculum was reading, religion, writing, Latin and Greek, and some arithmetic. During the westward movement, vocational subjects were offered. After the Revolutionary War, new townships established their own schools, and free public schools followed. By the 1860s, females were admitted to schools, but instructed separately. Children read from *McGuffey's Readers*, the first sequenced reading program, and secondary students enjoyed a more diverse curricular offering than ever before.

Urbanization and immigration during the period from 1870 to 1920 meant that schools had to Americanize throngs of children. New ways of thinking about curriculum, including John Dewey and the progressive movement, also emerged. European influences included Johann Herbart (literature, history, morality, and mastery learning), Maria Montessori (the prepared environment in preschool and primary school), and Friedrich Froebel (the kindergarten) (Morrison, 1997). Because of these influences, American schools became more student centered and integrated. Language arts and social studies were each created from a blend of several formerly separate subjects. This integration was especially apparent with the emergence of the junior high school.

After World War I, all students were eligible for high school. James Conant is largely credited with the development of the comprehensive high school and its multitrack programs of study. Unfortunately, during the 1930s and 1940s, it became apparent that a family's financial resources played a major role in determining who qualified for the college track.

Since the 1950s, curriculum changes have reflected a need to meet the needs of an increasingly diverse population. Schools have been criticized for becoming anti-intellectual, and for failing to prepare students for modern society. The fundamental questions of what students should learn and how they can best learn have continued to challenge educational leaders. During and after the Vietnam War, curriculum was slanted toward more relevant learning, a focus which still exists as evidenced by such curriculum offerings as drug education, sex education, multicultural education, and environmental education.

Since the early 1980s, a series of reports, beginning with *A Nation At Risk*, have kept experts busy trying to meet society's expectations. Basic skills have been reemphasized, and expectations have been raised in most communities. In 1994, President Bill Clinton signed the Goals 2000: Educate America Act of 1993 into law. The goals of this legislation are (1) all children will begin school ready to learn; (2) the graduation rate will rise to 90%; (3) American students will demonstrate basic competencies in grades 4, 8, and 12; (4) they will be first in the world in mathematics and science achievement; (5) all American adults will be literate and be able to compete in a global economy; (6) all schools will be drug and violence free, and offer an environment conducive to learning; (7) teachers will continuously pursue professional development schedules; and (8) school/home partnerships will increase parental involvement and support all phases of children's development.

Reflect for a Moment

How has school curriculum changed since you were in elementary school? Given the evolution of school curriculum, what changes would you predict over the next fifty years?

Curriculum for the Future

Several schools of thought exist on what the future focus of curriculum should be (Doll, 1992). Under what conditions should schools be responsible for attracting students and their families in an open market of school choice? To what extent should schools be responsible for preparing students to be productive economically, thus serving the nation's economic interests? What would be the effect of simply increasing standards and demanding more of students and teachers by means of national tests and standardized curricula? Who should be the main decision makers, providing leadership for the restructuring of schools? How important is equity in curriculum change—ensuring a more balanced educational experience and access for all learners regardless of their different characteristics? These are among the important questions to be addressed as schools attempt to meet the challenges of the twenty-first century world.

Several other themes, closely tied to curriculum, exist in discussions about the curriculum of the future: (1) The explosion of knowledge over the last fifty years, as detailed in Chapter 1: Students must learn how to access that knowledge and use it with confidence, using modern technology. (2) The continued deterioration of the environment has captured the concern of citizens around the globe. Students must learn how to become "earth friendly" and commit to an environmentally sound lifestyle. They must also recognize and be prepared to contribute to a stronger interdependent "global village." (3) The population in North America is becoming more and more diverse, heightening the importance of learning about and valuing differences among people and resulting in the emergence of inclusive educational settings (Ford, Davern, & Schnorr, 1992). (4) The changing nature of the family and rate of teenage pregnancy demands that students be more aware of the responsibilities of family life and the health risks involved in sexual activity and drug use (Ford, Davern, & Schnorr, 1992).

The Alpha Team (1991) at Oakland University in Rochester, Michigan has designed a curriculum for the twenty-first century which focuses on change and adaptability, global interdependence and cultural diversity, quality of life, technology, and self-actualization.

This curriculum empowers all students, motivating them toward lifelong learning. It also reflects the need for students to realize the interrelatedness of all aspects of living and learning, and to value the uniqueness of each individual. Woven throughout these basic curriculum components is the constant attention given to the student's sense of self-worth and ability to self-evaluate.

Reflect for a Moment

Think about the classrooms you have visited recently. What must change about those classrooms to better prepare the students for the future?

Curriculum Types

Planned

If, according to the definition used earlier in this chapter, curriculum includes all of the learning that children do in school, a clear division of curriculum exists between what is planned and recognized on one hand and what is unplanned and often not considered on the other. **Planned curriculum** is usually organized into subject areas with some sequential hierarchy. Textbook publishers, state departments of education, and school districts all detail the formal curriculum for educators, who are then expected to deliver it to students. Although a planned curriculum attempts to adapt to the wide range of students in a given school or age group, there are definite limits to such attempts, and at some point in planning curriculum educators must be prepared to consider the needs of the students actually attending that school or class.

Unplanned

Informal **unplanned curriculum** can be viewed in two ways: as informal curriculum and as hidden curriculum. **Informal curriculum** consists of those nonacademic aspects of school that students and teachers learn in order to function effectively in the school environment. School rules and policies contribute substantially to the informal curriculum in the form of clearly articulated procedures for conduct in the hallway, the cafeteria, the classroom, and other areas. The feeling tone in a given classroom, built from teacher-student relationships and expectations, also contributes to the informal curriculum. Other aspects of the informal curriculum would include home-school-community relations, extracurricular activities, fashion trends, certain slang expressions, and of course, affectionate relationships between students. The informal curriculum exerts a significant influence on the formal, planned curriculum.

Hidden

Hidden curriculum, on the other hand, is seen by several scholars as a divisive influence, a collection of subtle school practices that serve to reinforce inequality (Morrison, 1993; Apple, 1982). This curriculum includes but is not limited to the types of classes and learning activities students are offered, the ways in which teachers interact with students, the expectations that teachers and other school personnel have for different students, and the related degrees of self-worth that different students possess. Researchers have, for example, carefully examined the way that teachers treat males and females, and concluded that females consistently are given less attention and lower expectations than boys (Maccoby & Jacklin, 1974; Matyas & Kahle, 1986). Any time a teacher calls on a student to answer a question that is clearly beyond his or her reach and then turns to another student whose arm is waving wildly in the air, a hidden curriculum is also being taught and learned: that one student does not know anything, that another knows quite a lot, and that both are learning how to fulfill their roles at the bottom and top of the class's and, to a certain degree, society's caste system. Other students who sit silently and witness this event are learning that they have no power to help each other combat this unequal treatment.

Still another far-reaching aspect of the hidden curriculum is the way that women, minorities and laborers are largely ignored and that the general proliferation of untruths related to political, economic and social life are depicted in the study of history (Aronwitz & Giroux, 1985; Anyon, 1980). The prevalent use of such curriculum materials has, over a period of many years, served to maintain dominant enfranchised population groups at the expense of minority groups (Ernst, 1993).

The critical issue of hidden curriculum in all its forms is how many teachers fail to fully consider its existence and impact on children (Morrison, 1993). Educators must be sensitive to these elements of the hidden curriculum if they are to be effective leaders in inclusive settings.

Reflect for a Moment

Think back to your high school days. What examples of the hidden curriculum were present in your school? What do you think were the effects on student learning?

Although curriculum content can be described as formal, informal, or hidden, the way that content is organized is not as clearly delineated. One of the most manageable approaches to understanding the various organizations of curriculum is to first view them as either subject centered or student centered.

Subject-Centered Curriculum

Subject-centered curriculum organizations are the more common and convenient of the two types and can be readily discerned in existing school subject area organizations and departments from the early grades right on through the university level. Educators who support a perennialist or essentialist philosophy defend this organizational scheme as more logical and therefore easier to plan, teach and learn; more expertly taught by professionals trained in specific subject fields; and more fully supported by texts and other teaching materials. There are several subtypes of subject-centered content organizations (see Table 2.1).

Subject area curriculum dates back to ancient Greece and Rome, and remains today as the most dominant organizational approach, particularly beyond the elementary grades. It includes basic content (3Rs, English, history, science), special areas (art, music, band, industrial arts), and electives (advanced calculus, creative writing, photography). **Essentialist curriculum**, closely aligned with an essentialist philosophy, is far more conservative, and includes only the three Rs, English, science, history, and foreign languages. Its focus is on rigorous intellectual training and, in modern-day schools, an abundance of workbook and drill activities. The **back to basics curriculum** is much like the essentialist organization but places even greater emphasis within each subject area on reading, writing, and mathematics. These two types also have different purposes. Whereas the essentialist organization is aimed at intellectual strength, the back to basics approach is primarily a reaction to relaxed academic standards and declining standardized test scores

TABLE 2.1   Content and Curriculum Organization

Content Organization	Philosophy of Curricula	View of Curricula
Subject Centered		
Subject area	realism	traditional
Essentialist	perennialism	traditional
Back to basics	perennialism	traditional
Competency based	realism	traditional
Subject structure	pragmatism	progressive
Integrated	reconstructionism	progressive
Student Centered		
Child centered	pragmatism	progressive
Activity centered	reconstructionism	progressive
Relevant	pragmatism	progressive
Humanistic	existentialism	progressive

among students over the past thirty years; it represents primarily an effort to establish minimum levels of academic proficiency for all students.

Competency-based curriculum, which has emerged over the last twenty years, is based on B. F. Skinner's philosophy that measurable behavior can be used to determine competency in curriculum learning and that student outcomes, not teacher input, are the focus of curriculum structure. This organizational scheme relies heavily on the way a particular subject area is broken down into smaller, more identifiable knowledge, skills, and concepts and on student performance on a series of criterion-referenced tests to determine whether or not competencies have been attained. Many students with individual educational plans (IEPS) are instructed using a competency-based curriculum, whether they are in a segregated setting or an inclusive setting. **Subject structure curriculum** came into being during the 1950s and 1960s largely as a result of concern over inadequate science and mathematics curricula in the United States. In an effort to improve student learning in these and other areas, this approach disposed of rote memorization and drill and sought out rules, concepts, and principles that characterized each subject area. The intent was to promote research and inquiry as learning strategies and reject the notion of knowledge as permanent. This content organization maintained curriculum in its traditional subject fields.

Integrated curriculum, on the other hand, unifies several subject areas around a particular topic or theme. For example, if the theme is outer space, then mathematics, literature, history, writing, economics, and even art and music can and should be integrated into the study. The integrated curriculum is subject centered because it is preplanned, teacher directed, and logically organized and presented. This type of curriculum has often been implemented with thematic units of instruction and has also been used in inclusive settings because of (1) the natural overlap of traditional subject areas is more sensible to all students, (2) its flexibility in offering a variety of learning activities to a wide range of students, and (3) the opportunities it provides for collaboration among educators.

Student-Centered Curriculum

If, however, students help decide on the themes and learning activities—in accordance with the progressivist, reconstructionist, or constructivist philosophies—the integrated curriculum can be regarded as a form of student-centered curriculum. Whereas subject-centered approaches to organizing curriculum focus primarily on cognitive learning, **student-centered curriculum** emphasizes student interests and needs, offering a more affective version of content organization than other approaches. Curriculum development in inclusive settings usually features more affective learning than in a noninclusive setting, and therefore student-centered approaches are more often utilized in inclusive settings (Stainback, Stainback, & Moravec, 1992). Those who defend these curriculum schemes cite the child's need for creativity and freedom from adult-imposed curriculum and learning experiences. John Dewey, one of the strongest supporters of student-centered curriculum, was convinced that students' intrinsic motivation was much more likely to emerge when their interests and needs were considered. He was not, however, an advocate of a totally student-directed curriculum and was very critical of those overly permissive educators who provided little or no cognitive content to students.

Several content organizations can be identified as largely student-centered. **Child-centered curriculum** is originally the work of a series of progressive early childhood educators (Rousseau, Pestalozzi, Froebel, Montessori) who used songs, manipulative materials, play, and kindness in their curriculum organizations. Children's development was seen as unfolding, and activities were loosely organized so as not to impose on or interfere with the naturally occurring development of each child. These programs were characterized by a high degree of freedom for the children, and modern-day versions still emphasize many of the same basic beliefs. In child-centered curriculum, conformity is devalued and uniqueness is prized. A variant of student-centered curriculum is **activity-centered curriculum**, a product of private schools during the early part of the twentieth century. Beginning with the efforts of William Heard Kilpatrick, a student of John Dewey's, this scheme centered on lifelike, purposeful activities, and grew to include group games, dramatizations, field trips, interest centers, and projects. Accompanying these activities was a further emphasis on socialization and stronger school-community relations. More recently, activity-centered content organization has grown to embrace career education and internships in an effort to better prepare students for citizenship, the working world, and the social demands that come with being an adult. Such a curriculum is being utilized in many inclusive settings because of its emphasis on building social relationships and relating learning to the world beyond the school doors.

During the 1960s and 1970s, when the United States was caught up in the Vietnam War, many educators realized that their curriculum was out of step with reality. As a consequence, **relevant curriculum**, an approach to content that reflects social change and student interests, became a prominent force in curriculum planning during this era. Student demands, in fact, played a major role in creating these changes, including the addition of more independent projects; revisions of existing courses and development of new courses in such pressing areas as environmental protection, drug abuse and urban blight; more overall freedom of choice in course selection; and a continuing expansion of school walls to embrace work-study programs, community service projects, and credit for life experiences (Apple, 1982; Penna, Giroux, & Pinar, 1981).

One final type of student-centered curriculum is **humanistic curriculum**, an organizational approach that rose in opposition to a perceived emphasis on excessive cognitive learning during the 1950s and 1960s. Well-known psychologists Arthur Jersild, Arthur Combs, and Donald Snygg all contributed to a movement that focused on the relationships between good teaching, knowledge of self and students, and students' own self-concepts (Jersild, 1952, 1955; Combs & Snygg,

1959). Obviously, then, the humanistic organization of curriculum stresses more affective learning than other schemes, and its goal is Maslow's self-actualized individual (1962). According to its proponents, students learning the humanistic curriculum will form more meaningful relationships, be more independent and self-directed, and accept themselves and others more readily.

Reflect for a Moment

In what category or type would you place the curriculum in the schools you have most recently visited? Do preschools, elementary schools, and secondary schools differ in the type of curriculum they employ?

CURRICULUM DEVELOPMENT

Curriculum development is essentially a process that begins with a series of decisions about what learners should acquire in the form of knowledge, skills, and attitudes. Wiles and Bondi (1993) identify four essential tasks of curriculum development: analyzing the purpose of schooling, designing the program, implementing the activities, and evaluating the entire process. To analyze the purpose of schooling, there must be a clear and acceptable set of beliefs concerning instruction, followed by the formulation of agreed-on outcomes of education (goals) and more specific observable learning behaviors (objectives). The next step, program design, must be based on an accurate assessment of learners' needs and is followed by a process of planning out instructional activities and delivering them to the learners. Finally, the outcomes of instruction need to be measured to determine the success of the curriculum development process.

As straightforward as this four-step model may appear, it becomes almost unmanageable in reality. During the twentieth century, curriculum has been developed to cope with specific social, psychological, or cultural demands rather than being designed from a global or holistic point of view. Hilda Taba, a highly respected curriculum expert, finds that "decisions leading to change in curriculum organization have been made largely by pressure, by hunches, or in terms of expediency instead of being based on clear cut theoretical considerations or tested knowledge" (1962, p. 9). In the midst of such reactionary approaches, there emerged by the 1950s a consensus that the educational process was basically the interaction of three factors: (1) learner, (2) society, and (3) subject matter. Soon the learning process itself became a widely accepted fourth factor in the educational endeavor, and together these four components comprise what experts today consider when they develop curriculum.

At this point Tyler's model of curriculum development, a four-step process described earlier, is useful in specifying curriculum (Tyler, 1949). Taba took the process a bit further by identifying not four but seven steps:

1. Diagnosis of needs
2. Formulation of objectives
3. Selection of content
4. Organization of content
5. Selection of learning experiences
6. Organization of learning experiences
7. Determination of what to evaluate and the means of doing it. (Taba, 1962, p. 12)

A series of important considerations for each of the steps was also included. Taba's work has had a significant influence on curriculum development and allows for continuous review of curriculum content. Curriculum planners, however, must consider other factors as well before taking even the first step.

Psychological Forces

Two major considerations in curriculum development are the process of learning and the nature of the learner. Learning processes or theories, particularly behaviorism and developmentalism, will be addressed in Chapter 3, but amid years of discussion and debate over the merits of various theories, there are certain principles, which most psychologists can subscribe (Hilgard 1956; Watson 1960; Piaget, 1965; Gagne, 1977; Weiner, 1980)

Several of these generally accepted principles center around the student: Students will differ in important ways no matter how they are grouped, and there will always be "loners." A student's personal history can be either a help or a hindrance to learning, depending on the teacher involved. Students who experience success are better prepared to cope with failure and are more likely to succeed when the tasks and materials are meaningful. Although the tasks themselves should not be too easy or too difficult, students without specific motivation will learn only as much as they think is needed; therefore it is wise to challenge students because under challenging conditions, students are more inclined to try and solve problems. Students will have more success when they routinely set realistic goals for themselves and are involved in selecting and planning activities. In fact, although active participation is well documented as a key to learning, conceptual learning is strengthened when it is presented in several different situations and then applied by students to other situations. This transfer of learning will take place more readily if the learner discovers the transfer and application for himself or herself. Finally, students will learn more efficiently when they work with peers and ask questions.

Other basic principles of learning are focused on content and how it is presented: No one subject in school is significantly better at building mental strength than the others. Information that fits the learner's existing attitudes will be more easily remembered than information that does not fit the learner's existing attitudes. Retention is enhanced with repetitive practice when this practice is spaced out over a long time. Finally, positive and constructive feedback is valuable to all learners.

Even when teachers understand and apply these learning principles, they will still have to come to terms with certain other realities imbedded in an honest appraisal of the learning process. For example, some students simply cannot read, write, and calculate at a socially acceptable level, no matter what approaches to learning and instruction are attempted. The next step, then, is to accept the responsibility for providing educative and productive learning experiences for these students so they can participate constructively in their schools and communities. The challenge that this and other realities pose to those who design curriculum is clear.

Another example is found in motivation. Doll (1992) suggests that goal setting is central to helping students become motivated and that students who regularly practice setting realistic goals for themselves are more motivated to learn. Where this student-directed goal setting exists, curricula are appropriate for all learners.

A final important principle of learning that relates to curriculum development is related to conceptual development. Basically, students will learn any fact or skill much more successfully in context than in isolation. That is, any new information must somehow be seen by the learner as a part of a larger, more continuous whole, whether it is using basic multiplication facts in determining costs of grocery items or remembering the dates of the Civil War to get a deeper perspective on the economy of the antebellum southern United States.

Reflect for a Moment

Look back over the various psychological principles of learning. Which were the most evident in your experience as a student? Which do you think were less critical to your success as a learner?

Because the nature of the learner is all too often ignored in the curriculum planning process, the result is typically a pervasive sense of academic dread, frustration, and failure for many learners. Student-centered curriculum and subject-centered curriculum have already been described briefly, and it is unlikely that either type will totally dominate curriculum development. Regardless, it is hard to deny that there is an enormous amount of data on any individual learner that should be known and considered in collaboratively developing curriculum (see Table 2.2).

Furthermore, it is far more productive to identify and plan for specific individual learner characteristics than it is to label learners based on a single characteristic. Instead of planning for the learning disabled, the culturally different, or the gifted student, educators must plan for the individual learner based on everything that the learner brings to the classroom. This type of planning is enhanced when educators collaborate.

Besides examining data on individual learners, it is critical for educators who are involved in curriculum development to keep a current list of developmental

TABLE 2.2   Important Learner Data

vision	hearing
motor skills	handedness
verbal expressive language	nonverbal expressive language
listening vocabulary	reading vocabulary
stress responses	social skills
emotional functioning	fears
talents	likes and dislikes
academic achievement	personality type
interests	favorites
memories	nutritional needs
learning modalities/styles	best friends
family customs	family characteristics

characteristics close at hand so that they are never inclined to drift away from a curriculum appropriate for the developmental profiles of the students they are planning for at that particular time. In fact, it is quite appropriate to plan curriculum needs directly from these developmental characteristics.

In the process of planning a curriculum, educators should be aware of several changes in the overall population of students. Certainly the diversity within any group of learners has expanded during the past twenty years as a result of rapid increases in enrollment of African-American and Hispanic children and children from single parent and blended families. Compared to students from a few generations ago, today's students are bigger and healthier, enter puberty earlier, and are exposed to far more information via television and the rest of the technological explosion than any preceding generation. Adult authority has, in many cases, become capricious, and many younger children are being left at home alone; children appear more and more confused about what is and is not acceptable in people's relationships with each other. The implications for those involved in curriculum development are not as simple in this case. It is clear, however, that all families can help make school curriculum more meaningful for learners, and that one of the very clear needs among today's learners is a need for consistent, challenging expectations, both academically and socially.

Social Forces

Several social forces are at work during the process of curriculum development. Probably the most powerful is the national and state economy, because schools are challenged constantly to meet the workforce demands of a changing world. The world of the twenty-first century will be a technologically advanced world, and the workplace will require more education than ever before. Modern careers require skills that are more technologically complex, and also more interactive. Successful workers in the modern world must possess both an understanding of electronic technology and the ability to work cooperatively with others to solve problems of a highly intricate nature. The curriculum must change to meet these needs.

Another social force that impacts curriculum development is the women's movement. As women gained a new level of confidence in themselves during the 1960s and 1970s, they entered the workforce in large numbers though their salaries were often unequal to those of their male counterparts. In spite of the fact that most professions have attracted more women into their ranks, careers are by and large still gender oriented. The curriculum has clearly not met the needs of the female population as they attempt to enter traditionally male professions. As a result, a significant human resource remains underutilized in our society.

Minorities represent yet another significant social influence on curriculum development and, like women, are sadly underrepresented in the process of updating school curriculum. When reliable sources indicate that a greater percentage of white students (77.7%) complete high school than blacks (66.7%) (National Center for Education Statistics, 1990), it becomes abundantly clear that the curriculum is not meeting the needs of a large minority population. Banks (1991) argues that the curriculum remains ethnocentric, and that as long as the history of minorities is taught within an English and European framework, students from minority groups will not excel at the levels of their white age mates.

A social influence internal to curriculum development is tradition. Many educators who are trying to plan changes in the curriculum confront actual laws as well as time-honored practices and psychological resistance (Doll, 1992). Part of the development process, then, is the way in which tradition is viewed and utilized. It should be remembered, however, that questions should be raised about the success of traditional practices in many areas of the curriculum.

Reflect for a Moment

What changes have taken place in your home school district that constituted a threat to traditional schooling practices? What was the public response to these changes?

As society changes, so do the boundaries of acceptable behavior, and no one questions the influence of student and family behavior on the curriculum of the schools. As stated earlier, curriculum is formal, informal, and hidden. Informal curriculum is most affected by the behavior of people in schools, and it is a curriculum that is deteriorating in many cases. Standards of acceptable behavior for adults (educators, parents, and adults in general) and students have declined, and the result has been a code of ethics too confusing for most young people to understand, let alone internalize. Many families have become fragmented, in some cases forcing children to try and construct their own set of values. Many students demonstrate a lack of self-discipline that has in turn had a less than desirable effect on their behavior at school. Although the formal curriculum may have to change to meet these students' needs more adequately, it is the informal curriculum, including that of the family and the surrounding community, that will have to be strengthened if violence and disciplinary problems in the schools are to be reduced.

Other social factors, including the financial burden schools have placed on taxpayers and changes in the student population, have already been discussed in Chapter 1. Taken as a collection, these social influences have made it more challenging than ever for educators to develop curriculum appropriate for all students. The responsibility cannot, however, simply be laid at the feet of teachers and administrators. Clearly there is a much larger sphere of influence, encompassing the family, the community, the media, the national economy, and the changing international scene, that brings an unprecedented variety of learners to the schoolhouse door each day—and consequently an unprecedented demand for curriculum development as well.

Reflect for a Moment

How much diversity exists in your home school district? Who benefits most from the existing school curriculum? What efforts have been made to make the curriculum more responsive to all learners?

Curriculum Trends

Before leaving the discussion of influences on curriculum development, it is valuable to examine several current trends and how they can contribute to the curriculum of the twenty-first century (O'Neil, 1990). Amid, and to a large degree in lieu of, the influences already suggested, these trends hold promise in moving toward what curriculum can be.

Enough is Enough

The result in part of an attitude of "Add to, but don't take away," the present curriculum is overstuffed—high on coverage but low on depth. The fundamental question remains: What is essential to learn?

Let's Review . . . All Fall

A second trend concerns the amount of review time many teachers feel obligated to lead. The more time spent reviewing past material, the less time spent learning new material. Educators are now seriously examining the curriculum they plan for the fall to see if there is excessive review.

Make Them Think!

Another trend is the persistent call for active learning. For years, there has been a universal discussion about students who are involved in their learning. Such students, tomorrow's leaders, are able to reflect critically on their learning experiences, both formal and informal. All students can benefit from a concerted effort by educators to increase the amount of active learning in their classrooms.

Integration, not Segregation

Integrated curriculum has commanded the attention of educators for generations, but perhaps never as openly as today. School leaders are openly, and in concert with state departments, moving to integrate their subject matter, and encourage students to see the natural links among the traditional subject areas. Educators can use social studies as a readymade meeting place for both the humanities and the natural and physical sciences. Mathematics, technology, and science are now being integrated nationwide.

Access for All

Finally, the traditional practice known as tracking, in which students are grouped by some vague interpretation of ability, is being rejected in schools at every age level in favor of a solid core for all students, followed by enrichment and remediation where necessary for individual students. This shift in curriculum planning is particularly consistent with inclusive schooling. In far too many schools, students branded as "low ability" are subjected to endless drill and review, while "advanced" students find themselves in active, fascinating activities. All students must have an updated, integrated, engaging, and challenging curriculum. This trend suggests the need for including all learners in the general education program.

Curriculum Content

Every generation of educators must answer the question "What should be learned?" To organize a response, however, it is crucial to have a framework in which to place content deemed important enough for students. Traditionally, schools have used subject areas and grade levels as categories for this content, but with more and more integrated curricula and multiage classrooms being developed, there remains a need for additional structures into which content may be placed.

Doll (1992) offers the categories of substance and process, which can be used when planning instruction. *Substance* is the subject matter itself, and *process* is how the subject matter is used. Using history as an example, he describes substance as the historical data and process as the recording of that data for making subsequent decisions. Another, perhaps more comprehensive organizational structure is found in the three domains of learning: cognitive, affective, and psychomotor. Because these three taxonomies, or classification systems, provide an organized scheme for curriculum content, an introduction to each domain follows, with brief examples of the different levels within each domain. Each taxonomy begins with the lowest level and builds to the most complex level of learning. It is important to keep in mind that, while the examples that follow draw primarily from one domain, most learning involves all three domains. For example, a learner who is composing a business letter, while primarily applying cognitive behavior, is also valuing the task (affective domain) and utilizing fine motor skills (psychomotor domain). The three domains are revisited in Chapter 6, as a critical aspect of the planning process.

Cognitive Domain

Although the three domains overlap frequently, by far the most well known and heavily emphasized is the **cognitive domain**, which deals with "the recall or recognition of knowledge and the development of intellectual abilities and skills" (Bloom et al., 1956, p. 7). Therefore, subject matter most often falls into the cognitive domain and can be organized into six categories that reflect simple to more complex forms of thinking (Bloom et al., 1956). The cognitive domain offers the educator a structure not only for organizing curriculum and planning lessons, but for preparing questions for a given lesson and for planning assessment procedures as well.

Knowledge, the simplest form of thinking, requires rote memory and recall of facts, definitions, rules, sequences, and the like. When students memorize multiplication facts or the fifty states, they are operating on the knowledge level of the cognitive domain. Unfortunately, because of the unjustified emphasis many teachers place on knowledge-level learning, many students see school as one large memorization task. The next level of the cognitive domain is **comprehension**, which requires students to translate, interpret, restate, or give examples to demonstrate their understanding. Students who are summarizing a story they have heard, or describing lab safety procedures, are thinking at the comprehension level. At the **application** level, students typically use their knowledge in actually working out problems or adapting to a new situation. Students are working on the application level when they write a business letter or when they use an algebraic formula to solve a problem with a building project.

The fourth level, **analysis**, is evidenced by the learner's ability to break down new information into meaningful parts in order to gain a clearer understanding of both the parts and the whole. Students find cause and effect relationships, distinguish properties of objects or concepts, and specify strengths and weaknesses in written work at the analysis level. When they dissect a frog in biology or survey the student body on environmental awareness, students are using analytic thinking behaviors. At the **synthesis** level, students produce or create stories, structures, and the like, showing their ability to combine elements and even theories. Solutions and new ideas are evidence of thinking at this level. Therefore, when students are expected to compose a musical piece or hypothesize about how a settlement will grow over a long period of time, they are thinking at the synthesis level. Finally, there is the **evaluation** level, the most complex of all the levels of the cognitive domain. Students judge information, compare arguments, and evaluate theories, providing criteria for their judgments and comparisons in the process. When students draw conclusions based on sound logic after listening to a debate, they are using the evaluation level of the cognitive domain. When a student, based on factual information, recommends a particular change in the way the student elections are conducted, she or he is thinking on the evaluation level.

In developing curriculum, the cognitive domain should be used to provide opportunities for students to think at all levels, regardless of the subject area or the grade level. It is particularly important, in an era of information deluge, to place a greater emphasis on the levels that require using knowledge so that students become more capable of selecting the knowledge they need for a given task.

Reflect for a Moment

Can you think back to high school, or earlier, and describe a project or activity you worked on that clearly emphasized Bloom's higher levels of thinking?

Affective

The **affective domain** is primarily concerned with educational outcomes such as interests, appreciations, values, attitudes, responses, and convictions. These areas of learning have traditionally been less of a focus for instruction in the classroom than cognitive outcomes, in part because of the hesitation to impose values and attitudes on any group of learners who usually represent a variety of belief systems, class values, and cultural customs. But in recent years many educators, including the Educational Policies Commission of the National Education Association (1951) and Sizer (1984), have maintained that certain values can and should be taught, and that such values must be determined by those planning curriculum. Contemporary curriculum in many districts includes such topics as drugs and alcohol, sexuality, leadership, community service, and values clarification.

A hierarchy of affective outcomes has been developed so that if certain values are endorsed, teachers can actively plan learning to achieve positive affective outcomes. Krathwohl, Bloom, and Masia (1964) described five categories, beginning with **receiving**, which is the student's willingness to attend to a stimulus through one of the senses. Students who are listening to a concerto or noticing the changes in the seasons are operating on the receiving level of the affective domain. The second level is **responding**, where the student willingly answers to a stimulus, showing some form of active participation and leading to a desire to seek out particular activities. When a student argues a point during a discussion or contributes to a small group brainstorming activity, she or he is demonstrating the responding level. **Valuing**, the third level, suggests that the student attaches a certain worth to an object, person, or other phenomenon. It may mean just accepting a value or it may mean a more comprehensive commitment to a level of personal responsibility. Therefore, when a student stands up for a classmate during a disagreement or keeps his or her desk organized and neat, valuing is taking place.

The fourth level, **organization**, anticipates that learners will construct a system of values as a result of considering several different beliefs and resolving the differences. This level includes both the acquisition of a value by a learner and the development of a value system. Value systems are emerging when a student decides to do homework before going outside to play, or when another student steers clear of parties where drugs might be present. The final, highest category of the affective domain is **characterization by value or value complex**. At this level, the individual's value system has remained the driving force for his or her behaviors and choices for a long period of time, long enough to constitute a lifestyle (Krathwohl et al., 1964). A student's behavior becomes predictable because of the strength of her or his value system. A student who has worked with senior citizens long enough to become the leader of a group of student volunteers is one example of characterization. Another example is the fourth grade student who has shown such a love for reading that he volunteers to read to the younger kindergarten students every Thursday during his recess period.

Regardless of whether or not one feels that values should be taught at school, there has been a resurgence of interest in the affective domain in part because of its acknowledged influence on cognitive and psychomotor learning. To ignore affective learning is to risk placing all learning at a disadvantage, and educators in today's schools are finding affective curriculum goals and objectives more and more crucial to the success of the diverse school age population.

Psychomotor

While the cognitive domain deals primarily with thinking behaviors and the affective domain focuses on attitudes and beliefs, the area of motor learning is organized under the **psychomotor domain**. Table 3.3 in Chapter 3 provides five levels designed by Simpson (1972) and six clarifying actions adapted by Harrow (1972). These levels and actions, while not as thoroughly hierarchical as those in the other two domains, still show a sequence that is useful in long-term curriculum planning.

The first level consists of **reflex movements**, those actions that are largely involuntary but still occur in response to particular stimuli. Most if not all of the reflex movements are present at birth. **Basic fundamental movements**, the second group of actions, include crawling, walking, any dynamic movement in one place, running, jumping, and a variety of manipulations such as drawing and kneading. Therefore, when a student is climbing a tree, he or she is utilizing basic fundamental movements.

The third group of actions, **perceptual abilities**, are really a combination of cognitive and motor abilities. Included in this group are body awareness, directionality, body image, awareness of one's body in space, sensory discrimination, and hand-eye coordination. Whenever a student is correctly following verbal instructions, walking on a balance beam, or playing Simon Says, perceptual abilities are being used. Next are **physical abilities**, which are highly motoric in nature and serve as the foundations of advanced movement skills. They include strength, endurance, flexibility and agility and are exemplified by long distance running, basic ballet, weight lifting, and other skilled physical abilities.

Skilled movements at the next level are those specific to sports and sports equipment, dance, and other organized forms of recreation. They differ from physical abilities in requiring a more complex series of movements. Part of these movements are body mechanics related to such activities as diving, gymnastics, painting, sculpture, or playing the piano. Finally, there are **expressive and interpretive movements**, collectively referred to as *nondiscursive communication* because their primary purpose is to communicate through movement. Expressive movements are gestures, postures, and facial expressions, whereas interpretive movements come from aesthetic motion and creative movements. Included at this level are such movements as pantomime and opera.

All three domains should be used to identify the levels of learning students are operating on and then to plan curriculum activities appropriate for particular students. A middle school student may be a highly skilled gymnast but struggle with reading for understanding. His psychomotor activities would therefore be higher in complexity than his cognitive activities when reading. Finally, while the domains provide guidance for planning in terms of levels of learning, educators must carefully take into account the nature of the learner and the value of the material being considered.

Reflect for a Moment

Think of an example of learning in the cognitive domain in this course. Can you identify the level of learning? Can you think of an example of learning in the affective domain from this course? The psychomotor domain?

SUMMARY

Curriculum, or the content students learn in school, is largely a reflection of what the predominant culture determines to be important at any given time. Although several philosophies of curriculum exist, American education has been largely dominated by the essentialist tradition, which places traditional subject matter at the center of the curriculum plan. With the exception of a brief flurry of progressivism in the 1940s and 1950s, the essentialist philosophy has prevailed. Perennialism, reconstructionism, and constructivism have had lesser influence on public education, but their presence has been felt in the form of alternative schools.

As curriculum planners look ahead, they must consider that only part of the curriculum is actually planned. To fully grasp the entire curricular influence, educators must also acknowledge and capitalize on the presence of unplanned and hidden curricula. They must also understand a variety of curriculum organizations, most classified as either subject centered or student centered.

Curriculum development essentially consists of four steps: determining the purpose of the curriculum, designing the curriculum, implementing the curriculum, and evaluating the curriculum. In reality, however, the process is heavily dependent on the learner, the learning process, the subject matter, and the nature of society at a given time. Characteristics of individual learners, and of groups of learners, must be very carefully considered during the curriculum development process. There are also a number of principles of learning, related to the learning process, that educators need to take into account when planning curriculum. Social factors that impact heavily on curriculum include the economy, the changing role of women in society, the growing population of minority students and families in school communities, the general conduct of students and families, the role of tradition, and the tax burden being placed on citizens in communities across the country.

One popular method of organizing subject matter is to organize it into three domains: cognitive, affective, and psychomotor. Each of these domains can be broken down into a hierarchy of learning, from simple to complex, and used to examine or assess the content of any curriculum.

3

LEARNING TODAY

Key Terms

Acquisition
Adaptation
Analytic learner
Articulation
Attitude
Attention and disposition
Attribution theory
Behaviorism
Characterization
Cognitive development
Commonsense learner
Disposition
Domain-specific knowledge
Dynamic learner
Entry
Essential cognitive processes
Generalization
Imaginative learner

Information processing
Learning styles
Learning theory
Maintenance
Manipulation
Mediational strategies
Memory
Metacognition
Motivation
Multiple intelligences
Naturalization
Precision
Proficiency
Readiness
Reversion
Social-cognitive theory
Social context theory
Sociohistorical

Objectives

After completing this chapter, the reader will be able to:

1. Describe the four functions of theories.
2. Compare and contrast the four learning theories presented.
3. Identify the stages of learning.
4. Discuss the various learner characteristics.

5. Describe how learner characteristics effect knowledge acquisition.
6. Discuss the importance of mediational and metacognitive strategies.
7. Describe the importance of thinking skills.
8. Identify Gardner's seven intelligences.
9. Discuss why it is important to understand how the three domains (psychomotor, cognitive, affective) effect readiness.
10. Compare and contrast different learning styles.
11. Distinguish between testing and assessment.
12. Explain the importance of alternative assessment techniques.

PROFILES OF LEARNERS

H.K.

She lost her sight and hearing as a result of "brain fever" before her second birthday. Since her hearing loss occurred before she had developed enough language to retain its sound in her memory, she failed to develop speech until much later. Until the age of seven she was virtually shut off from the rest of the world. Her means of interacting with and understanding her environment were incomprehensible to those around her. However, this seemingly untouchable, unteachable child named Helen Keller graduated with honors at the age of twenty-four from Radcliffe.

Jacob

Jacob dislikes cooperative learning activities, preferring to work on his own. He is frequently in trouble with the teacher because he has difficulty conforming to school rules. The principal has sent him home three times this semester to change his clothes because he felt they were too distracting to others. Jacob is often absent because it is his duty to stay home and take care of his sick mother. His homework is rarely completed as he is responsible for making dinner and getting his younger siblings in bed. Jacob is African American.

T. E.

Three of his siblings died before he was born. At birth he had a large head and most of the family felt he was abnormal. He started school at age six but left after three months because he was diagnosed as being mentally handicapped ("addled"). His mother homeschooled him and he also had individual tutors. However, in spite of experiencing early problems in school, being declared ineducable by his teachers, and having a severe hearing loss (not detected until age twelve), Thomas Edison contributed more perhaps to conveniences of humankind than any other person.

Maria

Maria enjoys working in cooperative learning groups when everyone is responsible for the group's achievements. She dislikes going anywhere alone, so she rarely volunteers to run errands for her teacher. If her teacher asks her to come after school, Maria always brings a friend. Maria is embarrassed by praise and is sometimes taunted by peers for her superior grades in math. Maria is Hispanic American.

B. J.

He was a letterman in football, basketball, and track while in school, having a need to win, to be successful at something. Academically, however, he was a slow reader and felt unsuccessful and dumb. To compensate for his poor reading ability, he would memorize facts. It wasn't until he was in high school that Bruce Jenner was told for the first time that he was dyslexic.

Hero

Hero spends hours on his homework at night, methodically checking and rechecking his answers. At age nine he already speaks three languages fluently. His father and mother hope he follows in either of their footsteps and becomes a successful cardiologist or attorney. They've already been discussing choices for college. Hero especially enjoys both science and math, actively participating in the school science fair since first grade. Hero is Asian American.

M. M.

Born outside Chicago in 1965 with perfect hearing, she developed a severe case of roseola, a virus which left her totally deaf in one ear and 80 percent deaf in the other ear. Although she learned to read lips and mastered sign language as a young child, incessant teasing at school contributed to violent temper tantrums. She performed on stage at age eight, but quit in high school to pursue a college degree in criminal justice. During her last college semester, she won a minor role in *Children of a Lesser God.* At age 21, Marlee Matlin became the youngest winner of an Oscar for best actress for her stunning role in that very same show, *Children of a Lesser God.*

H. C. A.

Born into poverty, his father died when he was eight years old. His schooling was intermittent, much of it occurring in the city school for poor boys. He disliked academics, preferring instead to daydream, sing (soprano), and play with dolls—and he continued to play with dolls until he was sixteen. He was seen by adults as an unhappy, isolated, feminized boy who cried easily and was afraid of the dark. At fourteen, he left school to pursue his dream of being famous. He did become famous, perhaps the most famous author Denmark has ever known—Hans Christian Andersen.

A. E.

His motor development was normal, but he did not speak at all until he was three years old. To use language was torturous for him, and until seven he had to practice saying each sentence to himself before he used it aloud. His behavior was impulsive and violent. He threw a chair at his tutor when he was five. Much of his rage was directed at his sister, and he often made attempts to physically harm her. In school, where rote learning and memorization were stressed, he had difficulty, especially in arithmetic and foreign languages. He thought in pictures, not words and used visual imagery to solve complex problems. At age fifteen, Albert Einstein transferred to a school where the curriculum encouraged thinking based on visual imagery; the rest is history (Lerner & Egan, 1989).

The first conclusion we can draw from these profiles is that students with a wide range of abilities can succeed in school and in life. Perhaps more important, however, we need to realize that what students learn in school depends to a great extent on their individual needs. Bruce Jenner never learned to read well, but he learned to run, jump, and throw extremely well. Helen Keller never learned to drive a car, but she learned to write well enough to publish seven books, all translated into fifty languages. In both cases, the individuals learned what they needed to learn to survive—and even thrive—in society.

HOW STUDENTS LEARN

Learning begins the day an infant is born (some cultures believe that it begins even *in utero*). The first time a baby has a sensory perception, holds its rattle, or says "Momma" or "Daddy," she or he has completed a learning negotiation. These negotiations and skills are different for each and every individual, not only because of each individual's uniqueness, but also due to cultural uniqueness.

Educators are becoming increasingly aware of the importance of understanding cultural diversity among students when developing curriculum and planning daily lessons. However, it should be noted that although culturally based similarities and differences do exist, all learners are unique and complex individuals. To develop teaching methods based on culturally based generalities may be presumptuous and, in many cases, simply inappropriate. The most valid approach to planning curriculum for a diverse group of learners is to understand and acknowledge each learner as an individual who is also a member of the school learning community.

In attempting to provide all learners with an effective learning environment, educators must first view children as *active learners*. As active learners, students define the educational environment through their own activities (Reid, 1988). By defining the learner in this way, educators recognize that each learner, though unique, brings to each learning experience four basic characteristics: knowledge of the world, capacity, strategies, and metacognition (Reid, 1988).

These characteristics, although common to all humans, are uniquely expressed by each child. Learners are able to make sense of new learning events largely as a result of their previous knowledge of the world. An inadequate knowledge base (prerequisite skills) may cause the learner to become frustrated. To build any structure, even an intellectual one, it is necessary to begin with a strong foundation.

The ability or capacity to learn is a unique feature of every child; it can be both increased or decreased, and the learner's functional capacity increases as he or she develops. The truly effective educator assesses each learner's capacity and stretches every child to his or her maximum limit.

Strategies are those deliberate activities (both mental and physical) used by learners to acquire knowledge. Some learners have highly developed, well-organized strategies; others may have complex, ineffective ones. It is the educator's responsibility to assist learners in the refinement and expansion of strategies.

Metacognition, the characteristic involved in learners' understanding and regulating of their own learning, is a complex and vital process in learning and will be discussed in greater depth in later chapters. To build on these basic learner characteristics using the most effective teaching strategies, an educator must understand how learning occurs. Learning theory is a broad subject that will be explored briefly here.

Learning Theories

"Man's power to change, that is, to learn, is perhaps the most impressive thing about him" (Thorndike, 1931, p. 3) The almost unlimited capacity for learning is an important characteristic that sets humankind apart from all other species. A variety of sources provide information about the history of learning, including philosophy, folklore, empirical research, and learning theory (Gredler, 1992). A **learning theory** is an organized set of principles that provides a conceptual framework from which to build practice. Learning theories are helpful because they provide educators with principles that are testable.

Suppes (1974) identifies four general functions of theories. First, because they are composed of testable principles, theories provide a framework for conducting research. Second, they provide an organized frame of reference for specific items of information. Third, theories unmask both the complexities and subtleties of simple events. Fourth, they provide us with a means of reorganizing prior experiences into testable principles. Learning theories also have an additional unique function: they address the underlying psychological dynamics of events. Thus, learning theories provide educators with a mechanism for understanding, in both informal and formal settings, the implications of events related to learning (Gredler, 1992).

Learning, cognitive, and social development are multifaceted events. Therefore, no single theory addresses all the complexities present in various settings in which learning can occur (Gredler, 1992). To fully understand how individual children learn, it is vitally important for educators to have an overview of the wide range of the major learning theories and theorists.

Learning theory is a maze of authors and ideals that has been conceptualized in a variety of ways. Wiles and Bondi (1993) identify three major approaches to learning: (1) behavioral, (2) drive theory based, and (3) environmental. Hass and Parkay (1993) recognize four families of learning theory that stress (1) stimulus-response association, (2) "field" theory (Gestalt, cognitive, and perceptual), (3) Freudian thought, and (4) social learning. Gredler (1992) groups the theories into three theoretical categories: (1) learning process, (2) cognitive development, and (3) social context. How educators chose to classify or group the various theories is of relatively little importance (for purposes of this text, a modification of Gredler's classification system will be used; see Table 3.1). What is of importance is the fundamental understanding of how students learn these theories. We will briefly summarize them here in historical sequence.

By the 1920s, American psychologists had focused a great deal of their research attention on the study of how children, adolescents, and adults learn. From that time until the late 1950s, behaviorism became the dominant movement in this study of learning.

Behaviorism

"A baby shakes a rattle, a child runs with a pinwheel , a scientist operates a cyclotron—and all are reinforced by the results" (Skinner, 1968, p. 153). The theories of both B. F. Skinner and Robert Gagné come under the category **behaviorism,** a

TABLE 3.1   Learning Theories

Focus	Theorist	Basis for Theory
Behaviorism	B. F. Skinner	Operant conditioning
	Robert Gagné	Conditions of learning
Information	David Ausubel	Advance organizers
Processing	Various others	Cognitive psychology, memory
Cognitive	Jean Piaget	Cognitive development
Development	Lev Vygotsky	Sociohistorical psychological development
Social Context	Albert Bandura	Social-cognitive
	Bernard Weiner	Attribution

theory that addresses the events and conditions necessary to produce a desired learning outcome. Skinner's principles of *operant conditioning* are a continuation of the behaviorist approach established by John Watson in the 1920s. According to Skinner, learning is a behavior. As a student learns, his or her response rate increases. As the student unlearns, the rate decreases. Therefore, learning can be viewed as a change in the probability that a desired response will occur. Skinner established a three-component sequence (discriminative stimulus–response–reinforcing stimulus) by which learning is increased.

Gagné believes that "human skills, appreciations, and reasonings in all their great variety, as well as human hopes, aspirations, attitudes, and values, are generally recognized to depend for their development largely on the events called learning" (1985, p. 1). From his research in educational settings, Gagné established five distinct domains of learning: verbal information, intellectual skills, cognitive strategies, motor skills, and attitudes (Gredler, 1992). Each of these domains for Gagné represent different types of performance that are learned in different ways.

Information Processing

Dissatisfaction with behaviorism during the 1970s resulted in a new approach to the study of thinking: information processing. **Information processing,** simply stated, is the manner in which people gather information from the environment and form useful patterns that allow them to understand and predict events in their experience (Eggen & Kauchak, 1988). Goals of this theory center on learners' acquisition of knowledge through an analysis of information from their environment. Information processing focuses on learners' active investigations as the foundation for intellectual growth.

Information processing theory is founded on fundamental assumptions about the ways in which information is represented and stored in memory as well as on research on problem solving. This theory views the process of learning as occurring in three distinct stages: (1) attending to stimuli, (2) encoding stimuli, and (3) storing (long-term memory) and retrieving knowledge. Encoded messages are stored internally in one of three structural levels, which function as semantic networks linking the verbal elements of learning together. The three structural levels in information processing are: (1) sensory or intake register, (2) working memory, and (3) long-term memory (Romberg & Carpenter, 1986). Romberg and Carpenter believe "all operations on information occur in the working memory. In other words, this is where conscious thinking occurs" (1986, p. 853).

Reflect for a Moment

When you look up a phone number and then dial it, you are using working memory. What other examples of working memory can you describe from your everyday life?

Difficulty arises when we attempt to define information processing as a single theory because there are significant differences in the various information processing approaches. One such approach is based on Ausubel's (1963) advance organizer model. This model presents abstract generalizations of information to be learned in advance of the actual information.

Cognitive Development

Cognitive development approaches to the learning process differ from the behaviorist and information processing models just described. Theorists such as Piaget and Vygotsky believe in the necessity first to identify the capabilities that represent the various levels of human thought and then to describe the events and conditions needed to reach those levels (Gredler, 1992). However, Piaget and Vygotsky describe thinking in different ways. Piaget focuses on the manner in which learners manipulate and interact with objects in their environment as a means for constructing a more complex level of cognitive development. "To present an adequate notion of learning one must first explain how the individual manages to construct and invent, not merely how he repeats and copies" (Piaget, 1970, p. 703). Additionally, Piaget views knowledge as "an ever-changing process" rather than "as a product or a thing" (Gredler, 1992, p. 216). Thinking begins with infants and their actual physical reaching, grasping, and pulling of objects, progressing to the young adult, who is able to manipulate ideas cognitively.

Vygotsky, in contrast, viewed cognitive development as culturally based. Using a **sociohistorical** framework, Vygotsky established three types of experiences that form human behavior: inherited, social, and repeated (passive and/or active adaptation). Additionally, he emphasized the development of complex mental functions such as categorical perception, logical memory, conceptual thinking, and self-regulated attention that make use of both given stimuli and created stimuli.

Social Context

Social context theories of learning place the social environment of the individual at the center of the learning process. Albert Bandura's social-cognitive theory and Weiner's attribution theory focus on the relationship among the student's social environment, beliefs about self and the world, and learning. Bandura's **social-cognitive theory** is based on three assumptions that examine the learning process in naturalistic settings, the relationship of the learner to her/his environment, and the meaning of what is learned. Of critical importance to the learning process is the use of internal standards that help govern the student's ability to self-regulate and self-reflect before imitating a previously modeled behavior. Students "monitor their ideas, act on them or predict occurrences from them, judge the adequacy of their thoughts from the results, and change them accordingly" (Bandura, 1986, p. 21).

To account for the acquisition of both prosocial and antisocial behavior, Bandura suggests a single paradigm that encompasses modeled behaviors, effects of those behaviors on the model, and the cognitive processes (attention, retention, motor reproduction, and motivation) that the student chooses to implement. Thus, learning in this model is seen as a three-way interaction (reciprocal determinism) that occurs among the environment, learner's internal events, and the learner's behavior. The three work in a reciprocal fashion, with no single factor being more important than the other. The learner's behavior occurs as a result of his or her internal events. The environment then acts on the behavior, which in turn alters the internal state, creating a change in behavior.

Bernard Weiner's **attribution theory** links attribution research, motivation, and emotions to form an explanation of the learning process. "A central assumption of attribution theory . . . is that the search for understanding is a basic 'spring of action'" (Weiner, 1979, p. 3). All learning behavior is motivated by the search for understanding. The three major components of Weiner's theory involve the explanation of success or failure and the impact that it has on subsequent behaviors. The explanations given vary along the dimensions of stability, controllability, and locus of causality; they generally focus on ability, effort, task difficulty, luck, illness, mood and other persons (Gredler, 1992). Differing future expectations and emotional reactions are generated by each of the dimensions.

This summary of twentieth-century theories on learning helps us see that learning theories are not the only important factors that should be investigated in deciding what and how to teach each child. Theory must always be viewed in relationship to a variety of more individual factors that may affect the learning process of a student. Among the most important of these factors are learning stages, learner characteristics, and learning styles.

Learning Stages

The learning process consists of a sequence of learning stages that all persons go through regardless of their individual differences (Katims, 1990). The design and implementation of effective teaching strategies demand a thorough understanding of the seven stages of learning: entry, acquisition, reversion, proficiency, maintenance, generalization, and adaptation (see Table 3.2).

Far too often, educators fail to recognize the diversity of learning stages in their classrooms and either leave children dumbfounded or bored because of inappropriate materials or presentation (teaching strategies related to learning stages are discussed in Chapter 6). Each student has an individual level of preexisting

TABLE 3.2   Stages of Learning

Stage	Rate of Progress	Goals
Entry	none	
Acquisition	0–80%	accuracy (90–100%)
Reversion	erratic	accuracy (0–100%)
Proficiency	high rate, accurate	fluency (desired rate)
Maintenance	high rate, accurate	retention
Generalization	transfer to new setting or responses	
Adaptation	capitalize on knowledge	extension

Adapted from: Smith, D. D., *Teaching the learning disabled.* Copyright © 1989 by Allyn and Bacon. Adapted by permission.

knowledge that helps him or her make sense of the learning experience. Because learning stages are fluid, a child may be at the entry level for a math lesson and the generalization level for science. Moreover, learners progress through each stage at different rates depending on a variety of factors. When educators recognize each student's existing stage of learning, they can provide instruction that enables the child to progress from one level to the next (Katims, 1990).

Children who are at the **entry** stage come into the learning experience with little or no prior learning on the topic. They possess the prerequisite skills needed to benefit from the learning event, but the task at hand is completely new to them. Acquisition, the initial development of a skill or block of knowledge, is defined by Haring, Liberty, and White (1980) as "the period of learning when if performance falters, changes designed to provide information to the learner about how to perform the desired response have a higher probability than other strategies of promoting pupil progress" (p. 171–172). Students at the **acquisition** stage of learning come to the learning experience with a rate of progress that ranges from 0 (no ability)–25 percent (initial) to 65–80 percent (advanced). The learning event is not unfamiliar, but at this level students are still developing the block of knowledge, combining new skills with those possessed already to develop an accuracy level in their performance they feel comfortable with.

During the stage described as **reversion,** a student demonstrates great fluctuation in the performance of the new activity, often falling back on more comfortable past practices as a result of being uncertain of his or her new learning. Being able to perform the skill or task both accurately and quickly without thinking is the learning feature at the **proficiency** stage. Students know how to do the task or understand the material but now must focus on performing it proficiently. Some learners may have difficulty at this stage because they have problems appraising the accuracy of their performance. Here the educator must provide students with constant feedback as well as a means for creating their own feedback.

Students who have retention (memory) difficulties may experience frustration at the next stage, **maintenance.** During this stage learning is focused on maintaining high levels of performance without corresponding direct instruction. Learners must retain the acquired skill over long periods of time with no practice or delivery of reinforcement connected to the skill given by the teacher.

At the **generalization** stage, students perform the skills they have learned but at varying times and in different situations. Generalization has occurred when a child learns to divide and can go to the store and calculate the cost of one item when it sells at three for 99 cents. For some students, this too is a difficult stage and the carryover develops only if it is specifically taught. Ellis, Lenz, and Sabornie (1987) have described four levels of generalization: *antecedent generalization*, the altering of negative learner attitudes that may affect generalization behaviors; *concurrent generalization*, the learning of a skill so well that generalization will occur; *subsequent generalization*, the learner's application of the new skill to a variety of situations or settings; and *independent generalization*, the mediation of generalization through student self-instruction.

In the final stage, **adaptation,** the learner alters the skill without benefit of new instruction to fit into a new area of application. Mercer and Mercer (1989) refer to this as the *problem-solving* stage: The student who has mastered an understanding of parts of speech such as adjectives, for example, adapts that knowledge to create elaborate descriptions of the characters in his stories. Again, some students must be taught problem-solving skills deliberately through direct instruction.

Reflect for a Moment

Think of something you would learn, if you started today, at the entry stage. Then think of a different area where you are learning something at the acquisition stage. Try to think of learning experiences you are presently engaged in at the different stages just described.

Learner Characteristics

Each student brings to the classroom a set of unique learner characteristics that must be considered in developing an instructional model. Unlike factors such as gender, race, and socioeconomic status, learner characteristics are those attributes that are unique from one individual to the next. Among these characteristics are attentional variables, mediational strategies, memory, motivation, thinking skills, multiple intelligences, and readiness.

Attention

A complex phenomenon, **attention** may be the fundamental characteristic linked to all learning. Zeaman and House (1963) identified a two-stage model of learning with attention first and learning second. Alabiso (1972) helps to clarify the term by separating it into three distinct components: attention span, focus, and selective attention. *Attention span*, the length of time a learner spends on a task, is situational in nature. Lack of attention span has often been erroneously connected with distractibility; teachers may have said of Hans Christian Andersen that he had no attention span when in fact he was distractible. A student with no attention span is unable to attend to anything, whereas a distractible student actually has a problem with the other two components of attention—focus and selective attention. *Focus* is the inhibition of distracting or incidental stimuli, and *selective attention* is the ability to discriminate important stimulus characteristics. Distractibility, then, is the inability of a student to focus and select the proper stimuli, thereby attending to everything and consequently comprehending little.

Wittrock (1986) suggests that attention be viewed as composed of two distinct components, short-term or *phasic* attention and long-term or *tonic* attention. Short-term or phasic attention is largely involuntary and often referred to as either an arousal or orienting response. Tonic or long-term attention is largely voluntary and as such is frequently cited as a problem for children with learning disabilities, behavior disorders, and mental retardation (Zeaman & House, 1963). In determining the attentional demands of any instructional task, an educator needs to examine four areas of ability students must draw on: maintaining the level of arousal needed to attend, scanning the field of possible stimuli to select those that are relevant, shifting attention rapidly to accommodate changes in relevant stimuli, and maintaining attention over time (Mercer & Snell, 1977).

Mediational Strategies

When their mental processes are activated, students often find learning tasks easier. These processes can collectively be described as **mediational strategies** because in mediating between stimuli and responses they assist in problem solving, retention, or recall. Mediational strategies such as verbal rehearsal and repetition, labeling, classification, association, and imagery are commonly employed by mature learners (Polloway, Patton, Payne, & Payne, 1989). A critical fact about mediational strategies is the inability of some students to develop and implement them. Researchers have identified two subtypes to help educators form a base for understanding this problem: mediation deficiency and production deficiency (Flavell, Beach, & Chinsky, 1966). Learners who cannot use mediational strategies effectively even when assistance is provided demonstrate a *mediation deficiency.* Conversely, learners with *production deficiency* can use mediators provided to them by others but are unable to develop mediational strategies on their own. Implications for teaching are very different for each of these deficiencies, with the former being a much more difficult problem to remediate.

Memory

A third learner characteristic of great importance when designing instruction is **memory.** Memory is an integral component of the learning process. However, it is important that educators understand that memory should not be seen as a learning goal apart from the content to be recalled. "Memory is not the goal of instruction but rather a vehicle to facilitate learning" (Polloway et al., 1989, p. 32).

A variety of definitions of memory have emerged in the research literature. Hulse, Egeth, and Deece (1980) describe the memory process as having three distinct components: the ability to (1) classify information, (2) mentally store information for future use, and (3) retrieve, or recognize and recall stored information.

Reid and Hresko (1981), on the other hand, view memory as an individual learner's capacity to interact with incoming information as a means of making sense out of her or his environment. Basically, memory is the ability to store and retrieve information on demand. The learner's ability to store and retrieve information on demand goes beyond simple rote recall to include both short- and long-term memory stores. There are many types of memory discussed in the research literature, but perhaps the most crucial to learning are short-term, long-term, rote, and sequential. A learner with good *short-term memory* is able to hold and retrieve information for short periods of time (seconds or minutes). Retention and retrieval of information over longer periods of time such as hours or days indicates good *long-term memory.* Students who are able to remember something they do not understand, such as a statistical formula, have excellent *rote memory.* The ability to retrieve information in a specific order (counting, reciting letters of the alphabet or the Gettysburg address) indicates good *sequential memory* but not necessarily an understanding of the material.

Memory deficits are not easy to remediate. Memory performance, according to Schonebaum and Zinobar (1977) is

> influenced by the manner in which items are learned and maintained in memory, the rate of loss from memory (or forgetting), and the manner in which items that have been learned and retained are located and retrieved from memory. Accurate short term recall reflects the combined efficiency of all these processes. [(p. 262) cited in Polloway et al., 1989, p. 31]

Motivation

A great deal of literature (Adelman & Taylor, 1983; Deshler, Schumaker, & Lenz, 1984; Wittrock, 1986) emphasizes the relationship between the learner characteristic of **motivation** and problems with learning and performance. Wittrock (1986) views motivation as "one of the most frequently studied and useful thought processes involved in learning" (p. 304).

> If a student is motivated to learn something, s/he often can do much more than anyone would have predicted was possible. Conversely, if a student is not particularly interested in learning something, resultant learning may not even be close to capability. (Adelman & Taylor, 1983, p. 384)

Motivation is the process of initiating, sustaining, and directing activity and can be intrinsic or extrinsic in nature. *Motivators* are the specific influences that cause a learner to become involved in one experience over another (attending to a lecture versus napping during class). When motivators come from within, such as the tendency to daydream, they are seen as *intrinsic.* When they are directed by the environment, such as teacher attention, motivators are said to be *extrinsic.* The educator's key to motivating learners is bringing the sources of intrinsic and extrinsic motivation together in ways that actively engage students in the learning negotiation (Borich, 1992). Linking intrinsic and extrinsic motivation to educational activities is thus a critical variable in engaging the student in the learning process. Perhaps the most important sources of motivation are the learner's interests, needs, and aspirations (intrinsic and extrinsic). The effective educator understands these important personal characteristics and expands the learning environment to encompass all three.

Reflect for a Moment

Think of something you have, at some time in the past, put your mind to achieving. Hopefully it is something that you did succeed in achieving. What motivated you? What other motivators have you had in the past?

Motivation is also a function of one's thoughts (Ames & Ames, 1984). Recent research in this area has focused on learners' perception of the causes of their academic successes and failures and has shown that students' conception of the relationship among ability, effort, and achievement evolves from an undifferentiated state to a more analytical one (Wittrock, 1986). Many six-year-olds are unable to separate ability, effort, and achievement, believing that hard work (effort) is equal to intelligence (ability) and success (achievement) (Nicholls, 1978). Generally, seven- and eight-year-olds are able to differentiate the three concepts and relate effort to achievement. However, they are still unable to understand the connection between ability and achievement. Although children from ages nine to eleven have linked ability to achievement, they still equate effort with intelligence and success. Learners begin to realize at about age eleven that effort and ability are basically nonrelated entities, each influencing achievement in an independent fashion.

Learners also develop their understanding of locus of control in a progressive manner. It is important to distinguish the two points of origin for locus of control. Children who believe that the events they experience (both successfully and unsuccessfully) are under their own control have an internal locus of control. Children who believe that the events they successfully experience are under the control of forces outside themselves have an external locus of control. Piaget and Inhelder (1975) point out that young children exhibit a very strong internal locus of control, often times overestimating their ability to manipulate events, including such phenomenon as the weather. Unfortunately, what often occurs is the systematic erosion of a child's internal locus of control as a result of educational experiences that consistently ignore the unique learning strengths and needs of each individual child. Researchers (Andrews & Debus, 1978; Wang & Stiles, 1976) have demonstrated that children who believe that their hard work (effort) influences their achievement are more likely to learn than those who believe that learning is dependent on teachers. Furthermore, LeMehieu (1981) advocates teaching techniques that use encouragement to help cultivate ideas and stresses the avoidance of techniques that promote conformity and self-discouragement. Moses (1985) also stresses the importance of the link between critical and creative thinking on one hand and motivation on the other, maintaining that when educators promote thinking skills, students are encouraged to pursue their own self-interest, thus increasing their motivation to learn.

Attribution theory examines what a student attributes his or her learning success or failure to. Learners consistently tend to attribute their successes and failures to one of the following: effort, ability (both internal factors), nature of the task , and luck (both external factors). Morrison (1993) points out that attribution theory has major implications for both curriculum and the classroom environment because "once children get into a pattern of failure, it is difficult to get them out of it" (p. 71). *Learned helplessness* occurs when students attribute their success to external factors but are unable to attribute their failures to the same thing.

Additionally, Ames and Ames (1984) feel that motivation is directly linked with a learner's desire to protect his or her self-concept. A learner deemed an overachiever may be less able than other students but as a direct result of increased effort will seem to have higher ability. Conversely, this same student may put forth little or no effort if she or he perceives that the end result will be failure because to do so would make him or her appear less able (Ritter, 1988). Therefore, in an attempt to protect self-esteem and self-worth, the learner displays corresponding low-effort behavior or motivation (Ritter, 1988).

Glasser (1986) further supports the importance of the motivation–self-esteem connection, contending that if educators want to motivate learners to work harder, they must provide learners with a clear understanding of the end benefit. "Students who are not motivated are among those who fail to recognize that acquisition of knowledge and skills in school can result in something meaningful for them" (Ritter, 1988, p. 3). Figure 3.1 presents Stipek's (1988) comprehensive list of behaviors associated with high motivation. Educators should take these behaviors into account when they are adjusting both the curriculum and their teaching strategies to meet the unique needs of all the learners in their class.

Thinking Skills

Since 1970, perhaps the most influential orientation in educational and psychological research has been the inactive learner perspective. Although often focused on the lack of involvement of children with disabilities in the educational process, it is an approach that can and has been broadened to encompass *all* students who appear to lack motivation. As a result of this research, methods for teaching and refining children's thinking skills, especially in the area of metacognitive strategies, have been developed. Use of these skills and strategies assists students to become more actively involved with the learning environment.

Nickerson (1988) and Pressley, Woloshyn, Lysynchuk, Martin, Wood, and Wiloughby (1990) have identified four common dimensions of thinking: essential cognitive processes (Presseisen, 1986), domain-specific knowledge, metacognition, and attitudes and dispositions. **Essential cognitive processes,** the first and perhaps most nuclear dimension, are those tools a learner uses in thinking. While the learner is engaged in thinking, he or she often applies these essential processes to **domain-specific knowledge,** the second dimension of thinking. Third, the learner

Does the student pay attention to the teacher?

Does she volunteer answers in class?

Does he begin work on tasks immediately?

Does he maintain attention until tasks are completed?

Does she persist in trying to solve problems herself rather than giving up as soon as a problem appears too difficult to solve?

Does he work autonomously when he can?

Does she ask for assistance when it is really needed?

Does he turn assignments in on time?

Is her work complete?

When given a choice, does he select challenging courses and tasks even though he might not initially succeed?

Does she accept initial errors or less-than-perfect performance as a natural part of learning a new skill?

Is her performance fairly uniform on different tasks that require similar skills?

Does his test performance reflect as high a level of understanding as his assignments?

Does she engage in learning activities beyond course requirements?

Does he appear happy, proud, enthusiastic, and eager in learning situations?

Does he follow directions?

Does she strive to improve her skill even when she performs well relative to peers?

Does he initiate challenging learning activities on his own?

Does she work hard on tasks when not being graded?

FIGURE 3.1   Behaviors associated with high motivation

Source: Stipek, D. J. (1988). *Motivation to learn: From theory to practice.* Englewood Cliffs, NJ: Prentice-Hall, p. 14. Reprinted by permission of Allyn and Bacon.

must use **metacognition** to determine if he or she is employing the appropriate and efficient process to understand the material presented. To use their thinking skills most effectively, students must exhibit a positive **attitude and disposition** toward using the essential cognitive processes.

Essential Cognitive Processes.   As their name implies, essential cognitive processes are the fundamental tools of thinking, such as observing, finding patterns and generalizing, forming conclusions, evaluating conclusions, and analyzing critically (Kauchak & Eggen, 1993). With these tools, the learner is able to access, convert, and assess information.

The importance of helping learners use and enhance their essential cognitive processes has been addressed in a variety of sources. Bruner (1969) and Carnine (1990) point out that essential cognitive processes assist learners in making sense of the knowledge they are collecting by helping to integrate information coherently.

Kauchak and Eggen (1993) state: "The ability to reason inductively—to generalize—and the ability to reason deductively—to infer, predict, and hypothesize—are described as characteristics of intelligence itself" (p. 291). Additionally, each of these processes is founded on the cultural perspective that information becomes knowledge once it is validated by examining the evidence thoughtfully (Kauchak & Eggen, 1993).

The cultural dimension involved in thinking skills involves how the learning task is viewed and interpreted and which essential cognitive processes are employed. Interestingly, cultural background seems to have profound effects on essential cognitive strategies that are used in the content areas of mathematics and writing. Stigler and Baranes (1988), for example, suggest that students learn to use mathematics based on important concepts that are introduced through their culture. Mathematics as a science cannot be separated from the language, tools, and practices that children bring to the learning experience from the social and cultural environment in which they reside. African American students seem to have difficulty in this content area because Black English Vernacular does not use some of the prepositional constructs necessary for the comprehension of certain quantitative relationships (Banks & McGee-Banks, 1993; Orr, 1987). The Chinese languages appear to facilitate the development of counting skills because they help the learner think about important abstract mathematical concepts by providing a synchronous conceptualization of numbers (Banks & McGee-Banks, 1993; Stigler & Baranes, 1988).

Farr (1986) believes that writing is a mirror of cultural understanding. As a result, the writings of those students whose cultural backgrounds do not imitate the language of convention used in most schools are judged inadequate by teachers. Heath (1983) found that learners from cultural backgrounds other than Anglo-American are made to write using essential cognitive processes and linguistic patterns and conventions that differ from their own. This finding has also been reported (Madison, 1995) as prevalent in the deaf culture, whose language of preference (sign) differs syntactically from Standard English.

The essential cognitive processes must be taught and practiced before children can become proficient in them. Although there are numerous separate thinking skills curricula, these processes are most effectively learned and applied by students when they are taught within the specific content area(s) being studied.

Reflect for a Moment

A good way to understand essential cognitive processes is to cite examples from our own lives. I sit outside on the picnic bench and observe the summer day. I conclude, after watching the storm clouds move in, that it is time to unplug the computer. How about you?

Domain-Specific Knowledge. Thinking is a multidimensional process that is highly dependent on the context in which it occurs—in this case, the content discussed and the expected outcome. It is therefore critical that essential cognitive processes be taught and used with domain-specific knowledge, defined as the knowledge in a specific content area such as mathematics, science, or U.S. history.

Metacognition.   Flavell (1979) distinguished essential cognitive processes, those used to make progress in cognition, from metacognitive strategies, those used to monitor that progress. Metacognition is, therefore, an individual's understanding about how she or he learns, and provides that learner with skills and abilities to direct their essential cognitive processes. "Metacognition has . . . come to connote the management of one's own cognitive resources and the monitoring and evaluation of one's intellectual performance" (Nickerson, 1988, p. 19). Metacognitive skills are extremely important for essential cognitive processing because they play a central role in helping to direct not only learning but feelings of competence (Meichenbaum, 1977). Students employ metacognition when they use some type of strategy to help themselves learn or remember information. Such strategies include outlining, rehearsing, classifying, checking, evaluation, or prediction (these strategies are discussed in depth in later chapters).

Interestingly, culture appears to influence metacognitive style by providing guidelines that help a learner select which strategies she or he will use. "The basic premise is that culture induces different approaches to how individuals use their mind by providing a set of rules that become preferred methods of acquiring knowledge" (Banks & McGee-Banks, 1993, p. 321).

Attitude and Dispositions.   Ennis (1987), Resnick (1987), and Swartz (1987) suggest that learners' attitudes play an important role in the development and use of thinking skills. The power that thinking provides is often overlooked by students. Emphasis can be placed on the power of thinking skills by asking learners to explain how they arrived at an answer or conclusion, by challenging students to find ways to balance the federal budget, or by staging a courtroom trial, complete with a jury. Learning is knowledge and knowledge is power!

Students who fail to use metacognitive strategies generally do so because they have not learned effective ones. "To be valuable, thinking skills must not only be learned but also used" (Kauchak & Eggen, 1993, p. 293). It is assumed that as students develop an understanding of the essential cognitive processes and metacognitive strategies they are learning, a disposition will emerge to use them spontaneously (Kauchak & Eggen, 1993).

Over time, cognitively productive attitudes and dispositions can be developed, but only if students have a chance to experience opportunities to use thinking skills that produce positive results. A behavior (use of thinking skills) that has rewarding outcomes is more likely to reoccur.

Hallahan, Kauffman, and Lloyd (1985) suggest that metacognition should be divided according to specific cognitive processes. They believe the use of categories such as metamemory, metaattention, metalinguistics, and metalistening would enhance research efforts in the field of metacognition. By categorizing, researchers are able to focus on a single cognitive process, and advance learning strategies more readily, one category at a time.

Multiple Intelligence

Not unlike the identification of multiple types of metacognition, researchers (Armstrong, 1994; Gardner, 1983, 1993; McKim, 1980) have recognized that all learners have multiple intelligences. Gardner (1983) challenged the long-held belief in a single intelligence that could be measured and labeled as IQ. Believing that intelligence had been defined too narrowly, Gardner proposed that intelligence has much more to do with one's capacity to solve problems and fashion products in a naturalistic, context-rich environment (Armstrong, 1994). In the scope of human potential there are at least seven basic intelligences: bodily-kinesthetic, interpersonal, intrapersonal, linguistic, logical-mathematical, musical, and spatial.

Bodily-Kinesthetic Intelligence. *Bodily-kinesthetic intelligence* deals with specific physical skills as they relate to using one's entire body to express both ideas and feelings. This type of intelligence includes skills such as balance, coordination, dexterity, flexibility, speed, and strength as well as haptic (predisposed to touch); proprioceptive (intramuscular); and tactile (touch) senses.

Interpersonal Intelligence. *Interpersonal intelligence* is the ability to understand the messages of others, whether these messages are overt or covert. Capabilities in this type of intelligence are commonly thought of as "people skills", being able to respond to the cues that individuals give you in some practical and productive way.

Intrapersonal Intelligence. The ability to adapt one's behavior based on an accurate understanding of one's strengths and weaknesses, motivations, emotions, and needs is the basic component of *intrapersonal intelligence*. A working knowledge of self that enables an individual to use the skills of self-discipline, self-understanding, and self-esteem to function well in any situation is fundamental in this form of intelligence.

Linguistic Intelligence. This ability involves the effective use of words in oral and written communication. *Linguistic intelligence* is the manipulation of the structure (syntax), sound (phonology), meaning (semantics), and practical (pragmatics) uses of language.

Logical-Mathematical Intelligence. This type of intelligence allows a learner to be aware of logical patterns and relationships, if-then statements and cause-effect propositions, functions, and abstractions. Thus, *logical-mathematical intelligence* is the capacity to use numbers effectively and to reason well, employing processes that include categorization, generalization, and hypothesis testing (Armstrong, 1994).

Musical Intelligence. "The capacity to perceive, discriminate, transform, and express musical forms" (Armstrong, 1994, p. 3) is *musical intelligence*. An individual can demonstrate an understanding of music that may be either global/intuitive

("top-down"), analytic/technical ("bottom-up"), or both. Musical intelligence encompasses an awareness of melody, rhythm, pitch and timbre of a musical piece.

Spatial Intelligence. *Spatial intelligence* is the ability to transform accurate visual-spatial perceptions, attending to the elements of color, line, shape, form and space, and understanding the relationship that exists among them. Components include the potential to orient oneself in a spatial array and to visualize and graphically represent both visual and spatial ideas.

Gardner (1983) believes that all children possess each of the seven intelligences we have just examined. Further, children have the capability of developing each intelligence to high levels of proficiency. However, Gardner (1993) suggests that children begin to demonstrate *proclivities* at a very early age. As a result of these proclivities, by the time they begin school, children have established methods of learning that tend to favor certain forms of intelligence over others.

In addressing the instructional issues related to multiple intelligences, educators must keep in mind that these intelligences work together in complex ways. It must also be noted that although a few skills were highlighted in the definitions, there are a variety of ways to be intelligent within each category.

Reflect for a Moment

Think about your own learning proclivities. Which types of intelligence did you favor? For example, was it easier for you to learn the alphabet by singing than by other means? Do you still sing it to yourself when alphabetizing?

Readiness

Readiness is a learner characteristic that often seems only important to the preschool teacher who believes in developmentally appropriate practices. In any assessment of the level of readiness that a student brings to the learning event, perhaps the most common areas examined are the learning domains: cognitive, affective, and psychomotor. The importance of these domains to readiness for learning at the elementary and middle school level has been well documented (Epstein, 1977; 1981; Epstein & Toepfer, 1978; Huston, 1985; Toepfer, 1986). Toepfer (1986) cites the absolute necessity that educators understand students' levels of readiness if they want to make learning challenges appropriate. Unfortunately, students who lack the appropriate cognitive, affective, and psychomotor readiness skills for a certain learning task are often considered deficient and therefore in need of remediation. How can a learner be remediated for something for which she or he is not developmentally ready? Often what results from premature exposure to a learning event are persons who learn from a failure experience to dislike, fear, and avoid that event at all costs.

Ausubel (1959) defines readiness as the "idea that attained capacity limits and influences an individual's ability to profit from current experience or practice . . . the adequacy of existing capacities in relation to the demands of a given learning task" (p. 146). The fact that readiness crucially influences the efficiency of the learning process is seldom debated. Readiness often determines whether a given cognitive, affective, and psychomotor skill is even learnable at any given stage of development.

Psychomotor.   Of the three domains, the psychomotor (see Table 3.3), is probably the least emphasized. This domain has as its primary focus the development of muscular strength and coordination.

However, the psychomotor domain also involves the teaching of skills and endurance as well. Students who lack endurance, strength, and coordination may have difficulty in a variety of academic and nonacademic subjects such as reading, music, art, physical education, social skills, mathematics, language arts, and science. All of these areas need some level of readiness in the psychomotor domain for the manipulation of materials. Accurate interpretation of a learner's psychomotor level allows the educator to make meaningful selections of learning strategies (Jacobsen, Eggen, & Kauchak, 1993).

Cognitive.   Jacobsen, Eggen, and Kauchak (1993) "estimate that anywhere from 80 to 90 percent of the average elementary and secondary student's school time is devoted to the achievement of cognitive goals " (p. 91). With this much of the school day being spent engaged in activities focused on the cognitive domain (see Table 3.4) it is clear why this area is so important. The cognitive domain consists of the rational and analytical thinking process that a student goes through during learning. Therefore, it is critical for educators to be able to recognize learner characteristics so that they may determine what cognitive skills a student is ready to learn.

TABLE 3.3   Psychomotor Domain

Level	Actions	Learner Characteristics
Imitation	reflex movements	nonvoluntary movement
Manipulation	basic-fundamental movements	visual tracking reaching grasping manipulating
Precision	perceptual abilities physical abilities	interpretation of stimuli skilled movement (foundation) endurance flexibility strength agility
Articulation	skilled movement	task proficiency complex movement
Naturalization	nondiscursive communication	communicative movement body language

Sources: Simpson, E. J. (1972). The classification of educational objectives in the psychomotor domain. *The psychomotor domain*, vol. 3, Washington, DC: Gryphon House. Harrow, A. J. (1972). *A taxonomy of the psychomotor domain: A guide for developing behavior objectives*. New York: Longman.

Affective.   Development of attitudes and values are the two major attributes that must be considered in assessing a student's readiness to learn as it relates to the affective domain (see Table 3.5). How a learner feels about ideas, objects, people, or a particular learning event is an important consideration in instructional design. Like other types of behavior, *attitudes* are learned as a result of previous experiences. Berliner (1987) found that positive attitudes toward school are related to achievement and success. When students feel better about themselves and school, they learn more.

Unlike attitudes, *values* are more global in nature, relating to abstract ideas about how individuals ought to lead their lives. Values and attitudes about education and learning are intertwined with cultural and ethnic background.

TABLE 3.4   Cognitive Domain

Level	Learner Characteristics
Knowledge	recalls previously learned material
Comprehension	grasps meaning
Application	used learned material
Analysis	examines parts to understand whole
Synthesis	reorganizes learning to develop new understanding
Evaluation	judges value of material learned

TABLE 3.5   Affective Domain

Level	Learner Characteristics
Receiving	open minded
	neutral attitude
Responding	positive attitude
	interest
	involvement
	commitment (limited)
Valuing	learner-initiated behavior
	commitment (unlimited)
	supports position openly
Organization	justify
	accept
	reject
	adopt more complex point of view
Characterization	developed/exhibit large group of attitudes
	attitudes as part of character

Learning Styles

For educators to serve all students, they must focus not just on what students learn but how they learn. Educators need to understand just how different students really are and how these differences shape learning. All learners are unique and present profound differences in learning styles. It is imperative that educators celebrate those differences and adjust their teaching styles to fit the learner. Albert Einstein's ability to learn and be successful changed dramatically when he was introduced to a learning experience that complemented his learning style. McCarthy and Lieberman (1988) define learning styles as "approaches to learning developed by individuals over time" (p. 40). **Learning styles** indicate the manner in which an individual perceives, interacts with, and responds to the learning environment. **Learning styles**, therefore, are the cognitive, affective, and physiological traits a learner uses to approach learning events (Jacobsen, Eggen, Kauchack, 1993; Keefe, 1982, Schmeck, 1988).

The way in which learning styles differ from student to student has a great deal to do with the reciprocal interaction of the individual child and his or her environment. As children interact with experiences and information, they adapt their styles, emphasizing some orientations more than others. These "adaptations or possibility-processing structures form the personal bases [sic] of learning" (McCarthy & Lieberman, 1988, p. 40). According to Kolb (1984), there are two major differences in the way people learn: how they perceive information and how they process it.

Every individual perceives reality in a somewhat different manner. All we need to do is listen to the various eyewitness accounts of an accident and that fact will become very clear. Some witnesses rely more heavily on their senses (concrete), feeling their way through the event, whereas others contemplate what was seen, thinking (abstract) carefully about their account. Although both types of perception are demonstrably different from each other, they are complementary and equally valuable. Both have strengths and weaknesses, and every person needs each mode of perception to experience any event to its fullest. However, Kolb (1984) points out that for learning to occur, perception must be followed by processing.

How learners process experiences or information is the second major difference in learning. Some persons jump right into the middle of an experience (active processing), while others watch and reflect (reflective processing). As with perception, both styles are valuable, with strengths and weaknesses. Watchers reflect on what is new, filtering it through personal experiences and deliberately creating connections. Doers, on the other hand, act immediately on new information, pausing to reflect only after they have interacted with what the new experience has to offer.

Operating as a continuum, processing ranges from the desire to act to the need to internalize. Persons on either end of the spectrum need to adjust their processing by taking on characteristics of the opposing point of the continuum. Concrete and abstract perception, reflective and active processing, are of equal value to the learner. Students should be given the opportunity to move from one mode to another, leaving the style that is most comfortable for them and taking the chance to grow.

Using the four facets that make up the two dimensions of perceiving and processing, Kolb (1984) delineated four major types of learners: imaginative, analytic, commonsense, and dynamic. Type 1, the **imaginative learner,** perceives concretely and processes reflectively, preferring to learn by watching, sensing, and feeling. These learners tend to ask why. "They seek a connection between their values and how learning relates to those values" (Hilgersom-Volk, 1987, p. 7). Students who learn best by listening and sharing ideas are imaginative thinkers who believe in personal experience. Because imaginative learners have a need to see an event or information from many perspectives, they may have a difficult time making decisions (McCarthy & Lieberman, 1988).

Analytic, or type 2, **learners** perceive abstractly and process reflectively, preferring to learn by watching, asking why, and thinking. Their learning behaviors include devising theories, seeking continuity, thinking sequentially, and being thorough and industrious. Analytical learners enjoy the "traditional" classroom model because they need to know what the expert (teacher) thinks (McCarthy & Lieberman, 1988).

Type 3, or **commonsense learners,** perceive information abstractly and process actively. Pragmatic commonsense learners are able to integrate theory and practice and resent being given the answers because they derive pleasure from the problem-solving process, thinking and doing. "They edit reality, cut right to the heart of things" (McCarthy & Lieberman, 1988, p. 43). Asking the question how, "they are doers who search for practical application of knowledge" (Hilgersom-Volk, 1987, p. 7).

Dynamic type 4 **learners** perceive concretely and process actively, preferring to learn by sensing, feeling, and doing. They learn by trial and error, integrating experience and application. Flexibility is a critical feature of their learning style. Seeking out risks, dynamic learners desire to enrich reality. Often viewed as manipulative and pushy, dynamic learners seek to influence (McCarthy & Lieberman, 1988).

In addition to creating parameters for classification of learning styles, Kolb's model presents a cycle of learning, one in which the learner moves from experience through reflection and conceptualization to experimentation (see Figure 3.2). Based on the new experience or information created from experimentation, the cycle begins anew on a higher learning level, encompassing a wider sphere of information with each completed cycle.

Reflect for a Moment

Study Figure 3.2 and try to identify yourself on the model. Which quadrant describes you best? Find others who share the same quadrant and explore each other's school experiences. You might be surprised!

Kolb employs the research on left and right hemispheres of the brain to provide a further dimension to his learning styles model. Torrence (1982) suggests that the logical, sequential, analytical, temporal processor of information relies heavily on her or his left hemisphere. The learner who depends more on the right hemisphere of his or her brain tends to process information in a nonverbal, concrete, spatial, emotional, and aesthetic manner. Not unlike the schools attended by Albert Einstein, the majority of education today focuses on information that is best processed

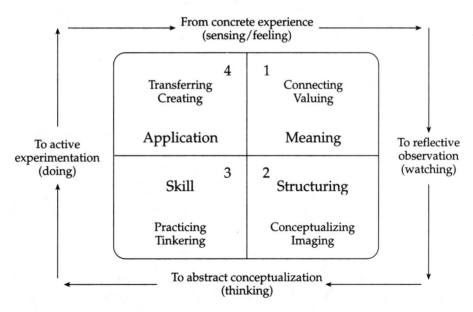

FIGURE 3.2   Four quadrants of learning

Source: McCarthy, B., & Lieberman, M. (1988). Learning styles dialogue. In *Report of the New York State Board of Regents' Panel on Learning Styles*, p. 47.

by the left hemisphere of the brain. This emphasis results in difficulties for those students who think visually and see problems holistically rather than verbally.

In their investigation of learning styles, Witkin, Moore, Goodenough, and Cox (1977) identified yet another dimension on which students differ: field dependence and independence. This dimension is primarily concerned with how much the environment affects the perceptual judgments or interpretations of the learner (Wallace & McLoughlin, 1988) and examines the learner's ability to select relevant from irrelevant information when the background may be complex or confusing. A word problem in math, for example, contains both useful (relevant) and useless (irrelevant) material. In solving the problem, the *field-dependent* learner (concrete) would have difficulty selecting necessary information from the fluff. Conversely, the *field-independent* learner (abstract) would have no difficulty filtering out unnecessary information and developing a solution. Farr and Moon (1988) believe that field dependence/independence is strongly influenced by development. As the learner matures, she or he is less likely to be distracted by irrelevant information and thus able to focus learning on what is important.

Kagan, Pearson, and Welch (1966) focus on *conceptual tempo* as an important aspect of learning style. The rate at which students respond to questions and problems relates to whether they are active or reflective processors. Active processors tend to be more impulsive, rushing into an answer without being fully aware of the question. Active processors tend to have higher error rates when reflection is needed but are much better at speed games that target low-level factual information (Jacobsen, Eggen, & Kauchak, 1993). Blackman and Goldstein (1982) found evidence that students seen as underachievers tended to be more active (impulsive) processors, while reflective learners appear to perform better in school, exhibiting superior attentional behavior.

A variety of factors affect the learning styles a student develops. Gender, race/ethnicity, social class, religion, and exceptionality are among the most well researched. There is strong evidence for the relationship between culture and learning styles (Banks, 1988; More, 1990). Banks (1993) suggests that "membership in a particular group does not determine behavior but makes certain types of behavior more probable" (p. 14). Based on his work with minorities (predominantly African Americans and Mexican Americans), Banks (1988) states that researchers "have found that ethnicity has a powerful effect on behavior related to learning" (p. 461). Many African-American and Mexican-American students have learning styles that are field sensitive and prefer more personalized learning approaches (Ramirez & Castaneda, 1974). Clearly the research does not suggest that all members of an ethnic or racial group have the same learning style, but membership in a group does influence students' behaviors.

Besides membership in an ethnic or racial group, educators must also consider the interaction of socioeconomic class and gender in the formation of learning styles. Banks (1993) states:

> Knowledge of the characteristics of groups to which students belong, about the importance of each of these groups to them, and the extent to

which individuals have been socialized within each group will give the teacher important clues to students' behavior. (p. 15)

Mexican-American students who are middle class and more assimilated demonstrate more field independence than do Mexican-American students who are from a lower socioeconomic class and less assimilated (Banks, 1993). Caucasian students tend to be much less field dependent than African-American students. Female learners, compared to male learners, demonstrated a greater degree of field dependence.

Rhodes (1990) found clear differences in learning styles between Native Americans and Caucasians. In his study Native-American students preferred a more holistic, observational style, whereas Caucasians processed information using a much more linear approach that focused on categorization of information. Navajo and Ute children see their language as an essential element of life (Banks & McGee-Banks, 1993), developing learning styles that incorporate a great deal of auditory processing. Curriculum materials and teaching strategies that best meet the needs of these learners' styles must incorporate oral history, legends, and language structure.

However, a learning styles approach to teaching may alter the instructional procedures more than the curriculum. Synthesizing the research on learning styles of African-American students, Shade (1989) concludes:

> From all indications their knowledge is gained most effectively through kinetic and tactile senses, through keen observation of the human scene, and through verbal description. This difference in perception manifests itself, not only in worldview, but also in modality preference, cue selection, and pictorial perception. (p. 110)

Again, racial or ethnic membership is not the only critical variable in the development of unique learning styles. Finding that girls appear to learn math better when taught through cooperative rather than competitive instructional procedures, Fennema and Peterson (1987) suggest that gender plays an important role in learning styles and therefore must be considered when designing instructional strategies.

Although one of the most widely discussed concepts in education, learning style needs to have continued research into its empirical efficacy. Problems with the research to date stem from wide variations in the definition of learning styles. A clear, consistent definition should be developed and research must be continued.

HOW WE KNOW THAT STUDENTS HAVE LEARNED

Traditionally, educators have judged student learning through a series of summative tests (both formal and informal). For those students who have learned how to manipulate the "evaluation process," good grades and not necessarily real learning are the reward. Banbury (1987) relates a story about a young Cajun boy from a small bayou town in Louisiana who, when "presented with the IQ test question.

'What are the four seasons of the year?' . . . responded enthusiastically, 'That's easy. Shrimping, crabbing, hunting, and fishing'" (p. 177). This story should create an uneasy feeling about the discriminatory nature of evaluation. The young boy gave a logical and accurate answer to a test question for which he will receive no credit because he will have failed to produce the "correct answer."

Overton (1992) states that "teachers must test. Testing is one method of evaluating progress and determining individual student needs" (p. 3). Teachers *do not* need to test. They need to assess in a continuous manner. Assessment (or *ecological assessment*) means looking at the whole child, gathering information in a variety of ways from the learner's total environment. It should be a formative process that is carefully and systematically structured to monitor progress and assist in making appropriate educational decisions. Effective educators are able to adjust their teaching because they monitor learners' progress through the use of continuous ecological assessment.

To be of value, educational assessment must no longer be seen as practical if it is summative in nature. The cycle of teach–test–move on must be altered if educators are to grant every child a high-quality learning experience. Educational assessment needs to be seen by practitioners as formative: preassess–teach–assess–reteach–reassess–and move on only when the information is understood. Is it logical to teach a higher-level skill when a child has grasped only 50 percent (or less) of the prerequisite skill?

Reflect for a Moment

This is a good time to think and talk about ways to determine student learning. Brainstorm a list, on your own or with classmates, of ways to determine or measure student learning.

Assessment Techniques

Each profile at the beginning of this chapter portrays a student who brought to the learning event a different set of experiences and expectations. Their teachers' failure to consider the unique backgrounds of these students and consequent misassessment of their abilities resulted in embarrassment, apathy, anxiety, frustration, hostility, and a variety of other problems that interfered with or prevented them from learning. Educational assessment of all types is influenced by society's beliefs and mores and therefore reflects the dynamic values of the dominant culture (Sax, 1989). Standardized test content is especially closely connected to the prevailing values and needs of the predominant culture. It is imperative, then, for educators to use standardized tests wisely, with a clear understanding of who designed them and for whom they are specifically intended.

Assessment occurs every time an educator grades homework, an essay, or an art project or observes student behavior of any kind. Assessment may be organized under two major headings, formal and informal. Both formal and informal assessment may be categorized by characteristics that relate to amount of time permitted (power and speed), degree and type of language (verbal, performance, nonlan-

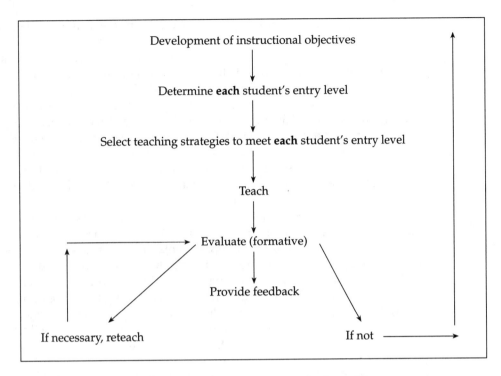

FIGURE 3.3   Relationship between assessment and teaching

Adapted from: Sax, G. (1989). *Principles of educational and pyschological measurement and evaluation (Third Ed.).* Belmont, CA: Wadsworth, p. 13.

guage tests), or whom the test is designed for (a group of students or an individual). However, *formal assessment* involves the systematic collection of data by means of norm-referenced or standardized tests. *Informal assessment* is the collection of data by any other systematic method. Collection of data by means of structured observations or criterion-referenced or teacher-made tests is generally considered informal assessment.

To teach without assessing is a contradiction in terms. "By its very nature teaching requires innumerable value judgments to be made by the teacher ... many that have lasting and significant effects" (Sax, 1989, p. 12). As a result, the educator's judgments must be founded on a careful analysis of relevant information and cannot be based on intuition, arbitrariness, or custom. There must be a strong relationship between teaching and assessment (see Figure 3.3).

Alternatives to Testing

Each child is unique, and so is each curriculum and its delivery. On the other hand, everyone who is being tested or assessed experiences anxiety. Not every child can write an essay under pressure, especially when spelling and grammar are included in the analysis of the response. True or false questions create meaningless stress in children who tend to think abstractly because they analyze every word, reading much more into the questions than necessary. Multiple choice questions are often biased against the child who is distractible, especially when the writer uses foils such as *all of the above, none of the above,* and *a and c but not d or f.*

Educators have a variety of assessment types to choose from, but the key to appropriate and academically profitable use of any assessment procedure is systematic and organized data collection. Additionally, the assessment procedure needs to fit the unique nature of each child. To assess students accurately and to provide for individual differences, educators must always modify tests and data collection procedures. Thus, the selection of appropriate procedures demands planning, preparation, and collaboration among educators.

Banbury (1987) reports that the predominant determinants of a learner's grades and class standing are written tests and daily written assignments. Whenever grades are determined only from assessments of written assignments, students (such as those profiled earlier) are penalized if they experience difficulty with reading, writing, or information processing. This traditional form of assessment accentuates deficits and prohibits children from demonstrating their true understanding of the content. To ameliorate this problem, an educator must implement alternative testing techniques. This will not come easily and requires the dispelling of some long-held beliefs about the need to have all students demonstrate learning in the same manner.

Assessments need to be developed so that they do not "'dumb down' kids" (Harmon, cited in Rothman, 1993, p. 13). The use of a computer or tape recorder may be helpful to students who are experiencing difficulty with writing skills. These devices allow learners to communicate their understanding of the content without the frustration of writing. Oral reports and verbal reviews of the content materials are additional methods that may be helpful for assessing learners with reading difficulties. Demonstrations, experiments, exhibits, projects, and pictorial or photographic essays will provide students with an opportunity to demonstrate mastery of concepts. Debates, panel discussions, role-playing activities, interviews, and class participation can all be analyzed to determine a student's proficiency in content areas.

Educators using written assignments or exams should clearly explain grading standards. If grammar and spelling are to be assessed, a separate grade should be given for content. It should be noted, however, that grading grammar and spelling may cause students to become overly concerned with the mechanics of writing, drawing their energy away from producing high-quality content.

Skill levels are not the only variable an educator must consider in establishing an assessment battery. Geographic location, ethnic background, and socioeconomic level are also variables that need to considered. Presently, Boston College's Center for the Study of Testing, Evaluation, and Educational Policy is working on an assessment designed specifically for urban school districts. This new assessment is being developed to "more accurately tap a range of student abilities than do traditional tests" (Rothman, 1993, p. 13). The three-part assessment examines four subject areas: reading, writing, mathematics, and science. The assessment's three parts deal with questions from the National Assessment of Educational Progress (NAEP), open-ended questions (both long- and short-answer), and performance tasks. In field tests of this new assessment device, students were asked to manipulate geometric shapes, tape-record their retelling of a story, write an essay about a video they had viewed, and determine the effect filling glasses with water has on pitch. Rothman (1993) reported that the learners enjoyed taking the test; one student even remarked, "It shows how smart you are" (p. 1).

Authentic assessments, which use students' work on worthwhile, real-life activities as the means of measuring learning, include many of these alternative techniques. Their use is still in the beginning stages but appears to be a direction that some states are taking to assure that educators have thorough, valid performance indicators and that learners truly profit from their educational experiences.

Reflect for a Moment

Authentic assessment: How is it different from weekly spelling tests and science lab reports? How is it different from tests and papers?

To many, using alternative assessment techniques may sound as if it is a great deal of extra work. However, with planning and organization, they can be implemented without undue difficulty. Mr. Conway, for example, did not believe in tracking, so his sophomore U.S. History class was composed of students with a variety of ability levels. Students were permitted to demonstrate their understanding of the historical period under study in their own individual way. Some students wrote extensive research papers, others built dioramas (to scale), still others did oral reports, and one enterprising student, aspiring to be a teacher himself, constructed a life-sized set of stocks. The stocks became a permanent addition to Mr. Conway's class and a future educator learned a great deal about alternative assessment from a master teacher.

SUMMARY

Students come to school with a complex set of unique characteristics that always influence the content and degree of what they are able to learn. Without a sound understanding of the learning process, educators are unlikely to be able to meet the needs of their students. Four major learning theories can be applied to any learning situation: behaviorism, information processing, cognitive development, and social context.

Learning stages make up another crucial component of the learning process. Educators must keep learning stages in mind as they teach. All students who are presented with new information, regardless of their learning styles, tend to relate to the information through a series of stages: entry, acquisition, reversion, proficiency, maintenance, generalization, and ultimately adaptation.

Furthermore, all students exhibit certain characteristics of thinking, such as attention, mediation, memory, motivation, locus of control, thinking skills, multiple intelligences, and readiness.

Utilizing any of these theorical approaches is more effective when educators carefully consider the differences in learning styles among students. Learning styles are the traits an individual uses to successfully interpret various learning presentations. One approach to organizing individual learning styles categorizes them as dynamic, imaginative, common sense, and analytic learners (Kolb, 1984) and ensures success for all students regardless of their style. Other dimensions of learning styles include field dependence and independence, conceptual tempo, culture, gender, and socioeconomic class.

The assessment of student learning is a complex and often misunderstood process. Contrary to common belief, it is not mandatory to test students to determine what they have learned. Continuous, formative assessment techniques, systematic in their use, are superior to any testing procedures in use today. Educators must be aware of the need for organized, systematic data collection if assessment is to provide accurate information for subsequent curriculum planning and implementation. Alternative forms of assessment and grading that take the data collected fully into account will lead directly to more satisfactory educational outcomes for all learners then traditional assessment does.

4

TEACHING TODAY

Key Terms

Community
Content-centered
Reciprocal process
Reflective behavior
Shared decision making
Teacher expectations

Teaching styles
   Student-centered
   Teacher-centered
Thought
   Interactive
   Preactive
   Postactive
Withitness

Objectives

After completing this chapter, the reader will be able to:

1. List several aspects of teaching that improve student performance and attitude.
2. Apply Eby's (1992) model of reflective behavior.
3. Compare and contrast the three teaching styles.
4. Predict how his or her own beliefs will impact on students and the classroom.
5. Identify ways an educator can contribute to a sense of community.
6. Analyze his or her own teacher preparation program for elements of collaboration, inclusion, and teaching practice.

PROFILES OF TEACHERS

Janice Pelkey

Janice Pelkey was entering her fourteenth year teaching seventh grade remedial reading at Normandy Cove Middle School. The new comprehension series she ordered was in, but Janice was wondering now why she had let Mr. Joyce, her principal, talk her into changing texts. She had been so familiar with the stories in the old series, and now she had a whole new set of stories to read. Well, she figured that as long as she read them along with her students, she would do fine.

Janice arrived at school for the required staff development day and checked to be sure no one had taken the tables and chairs from her tiny room. She saw no need to rearrange the room. The only change was the text. Dreading the hassle of scheduling her students, she wished she could just teach them and not worry about other people's schedules. She worked steadily, making up vocabulary sheets, homework questions, and tests for the first three stories. Just like the previous thirteen years, she would give students the vocabulary sheets to work on in class, then have them take turns reading out loud, and give them the comprehension questions for homework.

The number of students she had been assigned was larger than ever before. The fact that more and more students could not read at grade level was a clear sign to Janice that parents were just becoming more irresponsible, probably letting their children sit around and watch MTV all evening. There would be no real improvement until parents started doing their share.

Othelia Williams

Othelia Williams was excited about the changes in her second grade bilingual program at Broken Arrow Elementary. Now, as she applied the finishing touches to the dramatic play area, she relived the events that had led to this day. She recalled the sense of urgency she had felt trying to use so many commercial texts and worksheets with students whose native language was not even English. They deserved so much more, and Othelia was determined to provide them with the best possible learning experiences. She first acknowledged her own commitment to the students, then sought out others who had information about the students, including parents, neighbors, and past teachers. Next she entered into a regularly scheduled dialogue with each student so she could better plan for individual needs and interests.

Othelia spent hours and hours reconstructing the class to be responsive to the students, always keeping each student's aims and aspirations foremost in her work. There were new roles and responsibilities for all the adults and children involved. After a few weeks, she discovered a noticeable change in the classroom atmosphere. Enthusiasm was evident everywhere, and students attacked their work with new-found motivation. When the school year ended, Othelia was more certain than ever that the developments in her thinking about teaching would continue throughout the summer and manifest themselves in dramatic program innovations for the coming year. The students had helped her to rethink everything she had learned about teaching.

"TYPICAL?"

The profiles in this text are often exaggerated to make a point. Using measures reported in demographic studies, however, Feistritzer (1983) has developed a profile of the "typical" teacher, as follows:

> the "typical" American teacher suggests a woman approaching her 40th birthday. She has taught for 12 years, mostly in her present district. Over those dozen years, she returned to her local college or university often enough to acquire enough credits for a master's degree. She is married and the mother of two children. She is white and not politically active. Her formal political affiliation, if she has one, is with the Democratic party. She teaches in a suburban elementary school staffed largely by women. In all likelihood the school principal is male. She has about 23 pupils in her class. When counting her after-hours responsibilities, she has put in a work week slightly longer than the typical laborer, and brings home a paycheck that is slightly lower. (p. 1)

Reflect for a Moment

What is your reaction to Feistritzer's profile? What about the description surprises you?

All learners today are increasingly needful of special attention. The complexity of social issues and problems impacting directly on children at the end of the twentieth and beginning of the twenty-first century translates into more children in need of extra help, regardless of the presence of a special educational classification. Educators will need to do more than assist children with their schoolwork. They may need to help their students find adequate food, a safe haven from abuse, and motivation to learn. The intent of this chapter, therefore, is not simply to describe the "typical" teacher. Rather, the focus is exclusively on those characteristics that help to define the effective master teacher.

Given the vast diversity of today's schools, a child with a disability may possibly have more needs than other students, but certainly needs no more severe than those of students already present in the noninclusive classroom. The most effective educators in inclusive classrooms are quite simply the most effective teachers. Effective educators teach each individual learner rather than targeting instruction to the average of the class. Highly aware of classroom dynamics, effective educators demonstrate "with-itness" (Kounin, 1977). Effective educators are able to utilize a wide range of materials and techniques, shifting smoothly among them as the need arises. Effective educators have developed continuous reflective practices that allow them to monitor and adapt. Effective educators enjoy, value, and are excited about all students as well as the act of learning. Anyone who watches an effective educator teach can see this excitement and enjoyment at once (Rogers, 1993).

EFFECTIVE TEACHING RESEARCH

Since the early 1970s, school-based research has been used to help educators identify and strengthen a number of traits or behaviors that have collectively become known as effective teaching. This research has been conducted at all grade levels in a wide range of urban, suburban, and rural schools, with students representing various achievement levels, socioeconomic levels, cultural backgrounds, and personalities. The focus of this research has been the effects of various teacher behaviors on students' performance and attitudes. A great deal of literature is available on effective teaching, enough to fill several books; what follows is only a limited discussion. Effective teaching will be explored in more practical ways in Chapters 9 through 12.

Borich (1992) identified a number of teacher behaviors that have consistently been supported by school-based research (Rosenshine, 1971, 1983; Dunkin & Biddle, 1974; Walberg, 1986; Brophy & Good, 1986; Brophy, 1989). The first is *lesson clarity*, or the ability to present curriculum to students in a straightforward, understandable manner. This set of behaviors includes giving directions, organizing a sequence of information, and using language familiar to students. *Instructional variety* is also a critical aspect of effective teaching. This refers to the use of a number of different materials, strategies, feedback techniques and questioning procedures during a given lesson. Teachers who use a variety of visual aids, reading materials, audiovisual technology, and other resources tend to have a significantly positive effect on student performance and attitudes. A third teaching behavior that supports students is *task orientation*, or the extent to which the teacher uses class time for curriculum instruction. Some teachers have developed ways to minimize the time needed for class routines and instructional transitions, giving students more time for learning. These teachers clearly define their instructional goals and maintain high but realistic and positive expectations of all students.

Related to task orientation is the amount of time students actually spend engaged in learning. Although academic time, or the amount of time a teacher spends on curriculum material, is enhanced whenever task orientation is strong, *engaged time* refers to time when the student is actually performing curriculum exercises or activities (Berliner, 1984; Rosenshine, 1983). Even as the teacher may be very focused on using class time for academic instruction, the students may be largely uninvolved (Berliner, 1987). Strategies for increasing engaged time through active participation will be discussed in Part III. Linked with engaged time is the practice of *using student ideas.* Teachers who consistently acknowledge, modify, summarize, or apply student comments experience higher levels of student participation and elicit higher levels of thinking from the learners. Students welcome opportunities to restructure learning by using their own experiences and thoughts, and these occasions serve to motivate them further. Finally, research clearly suggests that students who engage in learning with a minimum of errors have higher achievement and better attitudes toward school (Wyne & Stuck, 1982; Brophy & Evertson, 1976). Therefore, the actual *rate of success* of students during engaged time is also a critical factor in effective teaching.

Reflect for a Moment

Think about something you recently did which you did well. Now think about how it felt as you were working on it successfully. Then think of a task you recently attempted unsuccessfully. How did you feel as you were working on that task?

Borich (1992) describes *structuring* as "teacher comments made for the purpose of organizing what is to come, or summarizing what has gone before" (p. 18). Although in this context structuring might be viewed as highly teacher directed, it can take on a more interactive nature by using questions to help students recall previous learning at the beginning of a lesson or draw conclusions at the end of the lesson. Regardless of the relative amounts of teacher and student talk, the critical component is the carefully placed organizer at both ends of the lesson. A similar organizational structure can certainly be created for the main phase of a lesson, and this strategy will be discussed in greater depth in Chapter 8.

The *questioning* strategies a teacher uses are yet another key factor in effective teaching. Content questions are those used by the teacher to check student understanding of literal content materials, whereas process questions are used to elicit deeper, more complex student thinking required for logical reasoning, problem solving, decision making, and other higher level skills (Borich, 1992). Content questions have a stronger relationship to student achievement than process questions, largely because student achievement is measured by knowledge of content. However, it is vital for teachers to use process questions consistently. Teachers can actually provide a demonstration of the thinking that contributes to solving a particular problem or even responding to a question (Duffy, Roehler, & Herrmann, 1988). A related behavior is *probing*, in which a teacher directs students to clarify, elaborate on, or shift the direction of the initial response to a question. All of these probing requests constitute shifts to higher levels of student thinking. Another questioning strategy aimed at increasing student achievement is *prompting*. When students offer no response or an incorrect response, teachers prompt by offering a clue to help the same student move closer to the desired response. Student achievement is improved most when these shifts occur systematically, in effect empowering students to seek and discover new learning, with the teacher serving as a facilitator rather than a lecturer.

Last, although difficult to glean from research, is the importance of *teacher affect*. Students universally observe the degree of enthusiasm in a teacher's manner and more often than not respond accordingly. The teacher's voice, movement, facial gestures, and eye contact all communicate emotion to students, and the use of enthusiasm in a selective, skillful manner can contribute to the level of engagement and achievement.

Meese (1994) has summarized numerous studies on teaching effectiveness with mildly disabled and at-risk students that focus on the lesson itself, and uses a direct instruction model (see the Hunter model in Chapter 8) to organize lesson components. Before any lesson component comes the critical planning that should take into account prior student learning (see Chapter 6). The first component, *opening the lesson*, should include a combination of teacher behaviors, including gaining students' attention, reviewing previous learning, reminding students of class rules if necessary, and stating the purpose of the lesson and why it is important learning. A second component is *demonstrating the learning* by using organized, sequential explanations; repetition; and examples that focus students' thinking on the intended learning outcome. The next component, *guided practice*, includes questioning for student understanding (in a narrow and brisk manner when needed), using various active participation techniques, and providing quick and specific feedback to both accurate and inaccurate student responses or efforts. Guided practice is followed by *independent practice* on the lesson objective providing an opportunity for students to demonstrate their proficiency with the new learning. Finally, the *closing* of a lesson should actively involve students in a summary or review of the new concept or skill learned and specifically direct them to the next activity.

Meese (1994) also includes *evaluation* in her discussion of teaching effectiveness. This evaluation must occur immediately following a lesson or even, as a formative process, throughout the lesson itself in order to provide information for teachers to use in making immediate, short-term, and long-term adjustments to instruction.

REFLECTIVE BEHAVIOR

The differences between the two teachers Janice Pelkey and Othelia Williams are numerous, but together they represent the basic difference between nonreflective and reflective teachers. John Dewey (1933) provided a comprehensive description when he wrote of reflective thinking as the "active, persistent, and careful consideration of any belief or supposed form of knowledge in light of the grounds that support it" (p. 9). Skillfully elaborating on this definition, Eby (1992) indicates that an active, persistent, and careful thinker is one who acts responsibly, is committed to taking on difficult challenges, and is sincerely concerned about doing the best for herself or himself and the students. In addition, Eby suggests that Dewey's definition points toward an open-minded, inquisitive thinker who does not accept knowledge or practice without questioning it in some manner. Finally, instead of just drawing an instant conclusion and moving on, the reflective thinker carefully examines and weighs evidence before passing judgment in any circumstance. Schon (1987) concurs, noting that "reflection gives rise to on-the-spot experiment. We think up and try out new actions" (p. 28).

Any reflective behavior by teachers is only as valuable as its effect on students. We can observe the moment-to-moment thinking of a reflective teacher in the following example: Othelia Williams is circulating among the students as they use various play stations around the room. She hears Jerry and Rick arguing in the dramatic play area; the bright yellow hard hat is the choice of both students, and they are each trying to tug it away from the other. During a period of time lasting no more than a few seconds, Othelia considers (a) intervening and taking the hat from both students; (b) intervening and conferencing with the two students; (c) simply calling over to them and directing them to take turns using the hat; or (d) observing the students' ability to solve the problem on their own. She chooses (d) because, based on what she knows about their interpersonal skills, she expects Jerry and Rick to resolve the situation. Over the next 15 to 30 seconds, she monitors the boys' problem solving until they have taken care of the situation.

An essential characteristic of **reflective behavior**, therefore, is listening to and acting on one's inner voice, or being able to consider alternative actions during one's teaching, usually as a result of any number of astute observations involving students. A second essential characteristic is maintaining of ethical principles throughout the reflective process (Tom, 1984; Bullough, 1989), which in turn requires reflective teachers to identify and nurture their own individual moral development. Using Kohlberg's stages of moral development (1987), educators can interpret their ethical behavior as preconventional, conventional, or postconventional, with the understanding that, as public school professionals working with young people, most will operate on a conventional level. Perhaps just as important as interpreting one's moral conduct is staying aware of, and consciously applying, a set of these ethical principles to the hundreds of judgments an educator must make everyday.

Using Dewey's work on reflective thinking, Eby, Tann, and Pollard have constructed a useful graphic model of reflective teaching (Eby, 1992; see Figure 4.1). In

REFLECTIVE TEACHING

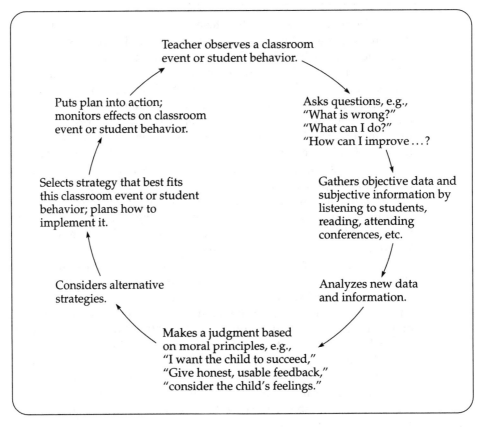

Teacher observes a classroom
event or student behavior.

Puts plan into action;
monitors effects on classroom
event or student behavior.

Asks questions, e.g.,
"What is wrong?"
"What can I do?"
"How can I improve ...?

Selects strategy that best fits
this classroom event or student
behavior; plans how to
implement it.

Gathers objective data and
subjective information by
listening to students,
reading, attending
conferences, etc.

Considers alternative
strategies.

Analyzes new data
and information.

Makes a judgment based
on moral principles, e.g.,
"I want the child to succeed,"
"Give honest, usable feedback,"
"consider the child's feelings."

**REFLECTIVE
PLANNING**

**REFLECTIVE
EVALUATION**

FIGURE 4.1   A Model of Reflective Teaching

Source: Eby, J. W. (1992). *Reflective planning, teaching, and evaluation for elementary school.* New York:
Merrill, p. 14.

the example of the dramatic play center, Othelia Williams proceeded through each
of the steps in this model, resulting in a plan that respected and supported the students' abilities to solve problems. She also decided to ask Jerry and Rick how
they resolved the problem during her next visit to that center. If Othelia had put
a different, less successful plan into action, she would, as a reflective educator,
have analyzed the outcome and approached similar future scenarios in a different
manner.

Reflect for a Moment

Is resolving conflict a curriculum priority? Although it may be actively taught in preschool, is it actively taught in elementary school? Or is it taught incidentally?

In schools where educators are committed to students, reflective behavior is becoming more common among all participants. Administrators are openly supportive, actively encouraging teachers to reflect on their actions. Team teaching, where two or more educators jointly plan and deliver instruction, lends itself to the process of reflective practice. As shared decision making becomes more widespread in schools, more educators and community members will be exposed to and actively participate in reflective practice.

Underlying all of these situations is the prevailing belief that schools do in fact have a significant effect on society. Potential effects of schools where reflective behavior is the norm might include higher academic achievement, more positive attitudes toward learning, more gainful employment after leaving school, and less delinquent behavior (Eby, 1992). Moreover, school effectiveness research has reached a point where academic measures no longer represent the only outcomes needed or desired. A positive school climate, where students, teachers, parents and community members all contribute to a strong sense of pride and commitment in an atmosphere of academic competence, has more far-reaching value to the larger society. To this end, teachers, as the focus of this chapter, are involving themselves more in the leadership and collective decision making of their school communities, often in highly innovative ways.

TEACHING STYLES

Before examining the knowledge and concerns teachers must bring to bear on their teaching, it is wise to carefully reflect on substantive differences among teachers in the field. Contrary to the claims of some observers, teachers are not all the same. They have a full range of personalities, values, aptitudes, communication skills, and personal backgrounds that collectively contribute significantly to what emerges in the classroom as a teaching style (Reed & Bergemann, 1992).

Although all teachers understandably work toward student success in their teaching, the ways they go about pursuing this common goal are often remarkably diverse. Rubin (1985) refers to **teaching style** as

> a composite of the teacher's demeanor and conduct, apparent in the things teachers emphasize, in the procedures they use and in their reactions to opportunity, adversity, failure, success. It is reflected in both good teaching and bad, because each teacher-practitioner goes at his or her work differently. (p. 19)

This style takes time to develop and even tends to change over time. However, it consistently reflects the individual's beliefs about himself or herself and others and self-perceptions as a teacher. In addition, teachers draw strength from knowing that they have facilitated student learning through their own teaching style.

Teaching style needs to be distinguished from teaching method. *Teaching methods* include lectures, discussions, small group activities, cooperative learning, mastery learning, questioning, and other well-known techniques and will be examined in Part III. Most teachers use several of these methods, but each teacher will apply her or his own unique teaching style to a given method. For example, if two teachers are using questioning in their lessons, the first teacher may direct certain questions at particular students, planning so that students with below-average reading skills confirm a literal comprehension while other students are challenged at a more complex level. The second teacher also uses questioning as a method but directs each question at the entire class and waits a few seconds before calling on an individual student to respond. The ways that each of these teachers uses questioning reflects their teaching style.

Two teachers will also teach the same content in different ways because of their teaching styles. If the topic is magnetism, one teacher may allow students to explore a variety of materials using magnets; a second teacher may demonstrate magnetism at the front of the room as students observe. Again, the content and even the expected learning outcome are the same in both classes, but the ways the teachers proceed toward the outcome are quite different, reflecting their individual teaching styles.

How, then, may the variety of teaching styles be organized and understood? One clear scheme is to look at three groups of styles: teacher-centered, student-centered, and content-centered. To adequately grasp the meaning of each group, remember that teaching styles reflect an individual's personality, values, experiences, sense of self and others, and perception of the teacher's role. As such, they are highly personal and unique despite any attempts to categorize them. In addition, most teachers demonstrate characteristics of each of the three groups but may have a dominant set of behaviors belonging to one group.

With this qualification in mind, the **teacher-centered** group of teaching styles is characterized by an instructor who models learning for his or her students in all academic and interpersonal respects. This teacher may demonstrate either open enthusiasm or a decidedly unemotional persona while teaching and relies heavily on his or her own understanding of any new information to be learned by students. These teachers also tend to be the decision makers when it comes to what will be learned, how it will be learned, and what level of performance constitutes success. Recordkeeping is also teacher generated and usually very systematic in nature. Evaluation of student learning always reflects the individual teacher, even within the teacher-centered group, but the highly dramatic, heavily interpretative teacher will usually evaluate student learning more subjectively than the emotionally detached, highly prescriptive teacher who systematizes each task.

Teachers with **content-centered** teaching styles will openly confirm that their first priority is to present the required material in a coherent, systematic manner. They will also be regarded by colleagues and students as experts who are highly knowledgeable in the subject matter they teach and who have generally high expectations of students. Methods tend to be lecture and discussion, although in some cases teachers are quite skilled at such methods. Textbooks are used heavily, and so are assignments taken directly from the texts. Organization of material, again, is carefully attended to, and learners are monitored closely. In some unfortunate situations, teachers who are content centered are determined to "cover" material at any cost and ignore the learner. The result in such cases is a group of students who simply limp along or, even worse, just do not learn, and eventually fail in school.

The third group of teaching styles is the **student-centered** style. The role of the student-centered teacher is as facilitator, not as expert or the central figure in the learning process. This style is easily distinguished from the other two because of the emphasis placed on the learner in just about every conceivable aspect. Curriculum is planned and delivered on the basis of students' readiness, interests, and developmental needs. In fact, much of what takes place in the student-centered classroom is the result of shared decision making involving the teacher and the students. In some classrooms, students are even the primary decision makers. Students find this type of teacher more approachable than other teachers and usually can establish a comfortable relationship. Group discussions, experimentation, creative dramatics, and learning by doing are frequently utilized methods. Students often learn as much from their peers as they do from the teacher or the textbook. Teachers use data on individual learners to plan lessons and also tend to emphasize all three domains of learning rather than just the cognitive domain. They consistently value student input and strive to encourage independent thinking, critical questioning, and risk taking among all learners.

Reflect for a Moment

Review the three styles briefly. Which style strikes you as the best fit for you? Why?

In retrospect, most teachers combine the three styles in their own unique way, but student-centered styles and teacher-centered styles both seem to have successful results. Several studies have found that teachers who direct students are less effective than teachers who allow learners to work independently and discover learning for themselves (Walberg, Schiller, & Haertel, 1979; Macrorie, 1984; Rosenshine & Furst, 1971). On the other hand, some studies have found a positive correlation between teacher-centered styles and academic achievement (Evertson, Anderson, Anderson, & Brophy, 1980; Stallings, Cory, Fairweather, & Needles, 1978). It appears, then, that different teaching styles are effective depending on the students involved and the situational context. However, it does seem that successful teachers are able to flex and adjust their teaching style in response to a range of student and setting specific features.

KNOWLEDGE OF SELF

"Thinking, planning, and decision making of teachers constitute a large part of the psychological context of teaching. Teacher behavior is substantially influenced and even determined by teachers' thought processes" (Clark & Peterson, 1986, p. 255). Therefore, it is vitally important for educators to reflect on their own thought processes in order to gain a strong knowledge of self. Clark and Peterson (1986) offer a heuristic model depicting two domains—(1) educators' thought processes, and (2) educators' actions and their observable effects—as a way for educators to organize and reflect on their teaching (see Figure 4.2).

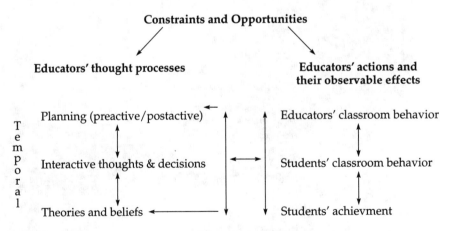

FIGURE 4.2   Educators' Thoughts and Actions

Source: From Clark, C.M., & Peterson, P.L., "Teachers' Thought Processes." Reprinted with permission of Simon & Schuster Macmillan from *Handbook of Research on Teaching*. Third Edn., Merlin C. Wittrock, Editor, pp. 255–296. Copyright © 1986 by the American Educational Research Association.

EDUCATORS' THOUGHT PROCESSES

Clark and Peterson (1986) believe that educators' thought processes encompass three categories (1) preactive and postactive thoughts (planning); (2) interactive thoughts and discussions; and (3) theories and beliefs. There are temporal distinctions in the first two categories that relate directly to when the thought process occurred in relationship to the classroom interaction.

Preactive and Postactive Thoughts (Planning)

The first category, planning, occurs either before or after, while the second takes place during classroom interaction. In addition to the temporal differences between the first two categories there is a qualitative difference. **Interactive thought** processes engaged in with students are qualitatively different from those that occur during either the preactive or postactive planning time.

Because of the cyclical nature of the effective teaching process, difficulties may occur in trying to clearly distinguish between preactive and postactive thought processes. Planning that occurs as a result of an effective educator's reflection process seems to be clearly **postactive thought**. However, an educator who alters teaching strategies for the next day has engaged in **preactive thought**.

Educators' theories and beliefs represent the third category. The vast store of understanding, experiences, and knowledge possessed by educators lays a foundation that affects their preactive, interactive, and postactive thought processes and therefore their teaching decisions. That is not to imply that theories and beliefs are unchangeable. Effective educators refine their theories and beliefs constantly as a result of reflection on their classroom interactions.

Intrapersonal Attitudes

Every person, no matter what his or her profession, has a set of intrapersonal attitudes shaped by a unique set of values, beliefs, and experiences. Regardless of the profession an individual selects, the understanding and refinement of intrapersonal skills enhances that person's ability to work with others. The ability to reflect on personal values, beliefs, and experiences helps the educator to adjust intrapersonal attitudes to best meet the unique needs of all learners.

Idol, Nevi, and Paolucci-Whitcomb (1994) present eleven intrapersonal attitudes that they believe effective educators and collaborators need to reflect and build on. Among these attitudes are facing fear, sharing a sense of humor, behaving with integrity, taking risks, using self-determination, thinking longitudinally, creating new norms, responding proactively, and adapting upward (see Idol, Nevin, & Paolucci-Whitcomb, 1994, p. 33).

Fear is the feeling of anxiety that is created by the actual or perceived presence of danger. Danger in this sense is given a wide interpretation that encompasses more than physical harm. In reality, much of what creates the physiological feeling of fear within human beings has little to do with worry about actual physical harm.

Modest amounts of fear are healthy, and they are often experienced when educators alter their traditional teaching patterns, expand their beliefs, or cast off familiar theoretical perspectives. By examining what creates fearfulness, educators can use this emotion productively. Facing what is frightening and understanding why it brings forth that emotion is an attitude that helps the educator gain perspective.

Humor is an intrapersonal attitude essential for effective teaching and collaboration. "Humor is the ability to perceive, appreciate, or express what is funny, amusing, or ludicrous" (Idol, Nevin, Paolucci-Whitcomb, 1994, p. 34). Laughter is perhaps one of the universal communication media. The ability to reflect on our own actions and appreciate the humor of a situation is essential for personal and professional growth. Humor becomes the ultimate equalizer, enabling the educator to communicate with students and colleagues.

Reflect for a Moment

How easily do you laugh? When was the last time you had a really good laugh?

Effective educators must always reflect on their own level of moral development and consistently pursue a higher level. A student does not learn about integrity from a textbook but rather by model. Educators must be honest and sincere in their actions with others as well as with themselves. Educators need to know themselves, accepting personal accountability (behave with integrity), which in turn maintains self-respect.

Effective educators need to have the self-confidence necessary to be risk takers. They need to be able to try a new teaching technique, to allow students to respond to a problem using media other than paper and pencil tests, to give up the sanctity of "my classroom" for the excitement of a collaborative relationship. Risk takers are able to gain from situations that were less than successful because they see "failure" as a learning experience.

Closely related to taking risks and integrity is using self-determination, which in action is the ability of an educator to select a course of action after examining all the alternatives. Self-determination, the ability to make one's own decisions, does not come without a strong sense of responsibility. The effective educator examines choices to be certain that decisions made do not harm others. Therefore, it is important for the educator who demonstrates self-determination to act with integrity, and understand the risks involved.

Norms are the underlying expectations and practices of the dominant group. Norms can take the form of prevailing beliefs and attitudes or overwhelming biases and are often discriminatory. Norms are also comfortable, because they provide teachers with a standard from which no one should deviate. Effective educators are able to recognize the attitudes and beliefs that shape the norms they hold as important, altering them to create new practices as needed. For example, under prevailing norms educators view the teachers' lounge as a safe haven where they "often speak in derogatory ways about their learners" (Idol et al., 1994, p. 36). However, the educator who is an effective master teacher would "adopt a norm to only speak publicly and positively about a learner's strengths" (p. 36). Working collaboratively to improve the education of all learners is creating a new norm, and so is becoming more reflective and self-aware about one's own teaching.

Theories and Beliefs

A knowledge of one's own thought processes, attitudes, values, and beliefs also enables the educator to be proactive rather than reactive. The reflective educator anticipates change, viewing it as an opportunity rather than an obstacle. The educator who responds proactively sets a tone for his or her learners by providing an environment that deals with challenges in a calm and organized manner. Additionally, by responding proactively the educator is modeling higher-order thinking skills for her or his students. Proactive responses also assist in time management as one must be thinking ahead in order to troubleshoot future problems. The reflective educator has thought through his or her lesson plan and has already designed alternative ways of explaining a concept.

If the future of education is to remain "bright with promise" (Skopp, 1989), reflective educators must constantly adapt upward. This calls for discarding past practices and beliefs about learners as a collective whole and viewing learners as a group of individuals whose needs are unique. Adapting upward also calls for the abolition of past beliefs about learners who are different from the perceived "norm." It calls on the teacher to reflect on the immorality of using the educational system to maintain social control, a covert action that has effectively maintained class and social barriers since the beginning of public education in the United States.

Reflective educators must examine how they translate their beliefs, attitudes, values, and thoughts into actions. Clark and Peterson's (1986) second domain—educators' actions and their observable effects—provides a means for examining how beliefs, attitudes, values, and thoughts are translated into actions. Additionally, this domain examines the reciprocal effects that result from those actions.

EDUCATORS' ACTIONS AND THE OBSERVABLE EFFECTS

Three categories can be identified within the educators' actions and their observable effects domain: (1) educators' classroom behavior; (2) learners' classroom behavior; and (3) learner achievement. This is the domain in which classroom teaching occurs. Researchers (Brophy & Good, 1986; Doyle, 1977; Dunkin & Biddle, 1974) who believe in the process-product model believe that teaching has a unidirectional nature. Typically, the process-product model sees teaching-learning as the educator producing a behavior that affects student behavior, which in turn affects student achievement; the educator behaves, producing some observable action from students. However, the effective educator recognizes the reciprocal nature of these three categories and guards against negative changes in student behavior. She or he understands that each of the categories affects the other, producing changes that in turn create new effects and additional change. It is imperative that educators reflect on the ways in which their behaviors and actions are modified both covertly and overtly by their interactions with students. The teacher who responds in a supportive manner to incorrect answers creates an environment that allows students to feel free to attempt difficult problems, which in turn helps the teacher feel more comfortable about exploring higher cognitive levels with students.

CONSIDERATION OF THE STUDENTS

A strong connection exists between knowledge of self and educators' abilities to understand how their underlying assumptions about students shape their teaching behavior and, subsequently, their students' behavior. Educators must develop a clear awareness of themselves to fully recognize how their actions toward students are altered by their presumptions about and interactions with individual learners.

To teach effectively, educators must understand the type of subliminal messages they are sending to students. The inferences educators make about the future success of students are referred to as **teacher expectations**. A direct result of the educator's personal values, beliefs, and experiences, teacher expectations manifest themselves in a variety of teacher behaviors. Unfortunately, too often educators are not fully aware of the inequity of their behaviors.

Reflect for a Moment

Be honest. What kind of people really irritate you? What do you really dislike in a child? Knowing your own biases toward people in general is important to keeping these biases in check.

Students with low ability may not learn to their potential in part because of teacher behaviors extending over several years. Research by Cooper (1979) and Weinstein (1983) indicates that some educators treat students with high ability differently than students with low ability and that learners clearly perceive those differences in teacher behavior (see Table 4.1). Educators who reflect routinely will benefit from checking their own behavior using these criteria.

Teacher expectations focus not only on the dichotomy of high versus low ability, but also on cultural background, socioeconomic status, gender, presence of a disability, or family name. Brophy and Evertson (1981) found that educators tended to respond to students whom they "rejected" differently than other students. "Rejected" students were monitored more closely, frequently being reminded of their responsibilities with their personal requests being refused more often. Additionally, the "rejected" students met with impatience and were held up as bad examples before the other learners.

All of the data on achievement among learners from nonwhite backgrounds strongly indicates that schools are not successful in meeting the educational needs

TABLE 4.1   Principal Findings of Studies* on the Treatment of High- and Low-Ability Students

Compared to their treatment of high-ability students, teachers tended to:
Seat low-ability students far away from the teacher.
Call on low-ability students less often.
Wait less time for low-ability students to answer questions.
Criticize low-ability students more frequently.
Praise low-ability students less frequently.
Provide low-ability students with less detailed feedback.
Demand less work and effort from low-ability students.
Prompt low-ability students less after incorrect responses.
Teach low-ability students for shorter periods of time.
Spend more of low-ability students' instructional time on interruptions, routines, and
    idleness.
Provide low-ability students with less academically oriented curriculum.
Conduct more unfocused activities with low-ability students.
Present material less clearly and more slowly with low-ability students.
Explain objectives less often to low-ability students.
Maintain less rigorous, more vague standards with low-ability students.
Use texts with low-ability students that have less information and fewer questions.

*Anyon, 1981; Brophy, 1983; Cazden & Mehan, 1989; Collins, 1986; Good, 1970; Hilliard, 1989; Irvine, 1990; Lehr & Harris, 1988; McDermott, 1977; Oakes, 1986; Rist, 1970; Rosenthal, 1973; Villegas & Watts, 1991; Wong-Fillmore, 1990.

of African-American, Hispanic, and Native-American children (Ballantine, 1989). Although several theories have been put forth to explain the low achievement of students from these groups, teacher expectations play a significant role (Kauchak & Eggen, 1993). When teachers treat students in lower-ability groups in certain negative ways (see Table 4.1), they are working with a disproportionate number of children from the three groups mentioned. Leacock (1969) found that educators generally rated African-American students less favorably than they rated Caucasian students. Additionally, educators showed hostility and rejection toward the brightest African-American students, a complete reversal of the usual findings in studies involving Caucasians. As a result, Good and Brophy (1987) caution that educators "need to be aware of differences in students that they may overreact to if not careful" (p. 34).

Aside from the contribution of grouping and tracking to teacher expectations of *culturally diverse students*, there are also fundamental cultural differences between home and school that can impede student learning. Language patterns alone have major implications for academic success. Many students are not expected to participate actively in conversations with adults at home and are therefore very reluctant to speak with adults in school (Villegas, 1991). In other cases, the types of questions adults use at home are so different from those that teachers use at school that certain students are unlikely to participate in discussions at school (Heath, 1983).

If teachers are going to be effective with students from culturally diverse backgrounds, they must actively pursue several strategies (Kauchak & Eggen, 1989). First, they should get to know children's families, read literature from different cultures and get to know teaching colleagues from those cultures. Second, they should openly embrace cultural diversity among students, emphasize the positive aspects of different cultures, and encourage sharing and mutual respect among students. Third, teachers should develop and implement curriculum content and instructional strategies that both accommodate and accurately inform students from a diversity of cultural experiences. Fourth, teachers must present curriculum content from a genuinely multicultural perspective.

Observers have noted that the percentage of U.S. students from non-Caucasian backgrounds has grown to over 20 percent and will continue to grow to 40 percent by the year 2000 (Villegas, 1991). On the other hand, if current trends continue, some 95 percent of the teachers in the United States will be white. The discrepancy between the cultural background of students and teachers has become a driving force behind a strong effort to provide guidelines to help all teachers work effectively with culturally diverse classes of students. Cultural awareness and culturally responsive pedagogy are critical considerations in studying teacher expectations of students from different cultural backgrounds.

Rather than being used as a guide to direct educators, often times the *socioeconomic status* of a student is used as an excuse for failure. However, Brophy and Evertson (1976) suggest that knowledge of a student's socioeconomic status will provide educators with insight into which teaching behavior will be most effective. As Table 4.2 shows, the effective behaviors used for one group are not simply reversed for the other. There are specific critical areas for each group that seem to result in a more positive learning environment.

Although much of the research to date has focused on educators' interactions with high and low ability levels, there is information available that addresses *gender issues* as they relate to teacher expectations. Hyde (1981) and Maccoby and Jacklin (1974) have clearly demonstrated that the pattern of school achievement varies for boys and girls. Gender differences in intellectual functioning are, however, quite small. Additionally, although males and females achieve in somewhat different ways, innate biological differences do not pose a reasonable explanation for the gaps in achievement. The greatest contributing factor to performance differences between the genders appears to be societal, parental, and teacher expectations. Therefore, gender differences as they relate to school achievement seem largely the result of learned behavior.

Educators must guard against developing unwarranted expectations of learners based on gender. A variety of studies (Brophy & Good, 1974; Cooper & Good, 1983; Good & Findley, 1985; Morse & Handley, 1985; Motta & Vane, 1977; Simmons, 1980) have shown that educators tend to perceive students differently based on gender. Motta and Vane (1977) found that educators perceived females as more dependent, creative, and achievement oriented than males. Additionally, males were viewed as more aggressive. Simmons' (1980) research regarding teacher expectations reflects results similar to Motta and Vane. Male students

TABLE 4.2   Important Teaching Behaviors for Low-SES and High-SES Pupils

Findings for Students with Low SES

Teacher affect	Warm and encouraging; let learners know that help is available.
Student responses	Before moving to the next learner or question, elicit response from the student asked.
Overteaching/Overlearning	Present materials in small chunks, at a slow pace, with opportunity for practice and success.
Classroom interaction	Stress factual knowledge; monitor learner progress; minimize interruptions by maintaining smooth transitions from one activity to another; and help learner who needs assistance immediately.
Individualization	Supplement standard curriculum with specialized material to meet the individual needs of learners.

Findings for Students with High SES

Praise and criticism	Correct poor answers immediately when learner fails to perform.
Individualization	Ask questions that require associations, generalizations, and inferences; supplement curriculum with challenging material; and assign homework and/or extended assignments.
Classroom management	Be flexible; let learners initiate teacher-student interaction; and encourage learners to reason out correct answer.
Verbal activities	Actively engage learners in verbal questions and answers.

Source: Borich, G. D. (1992). *Effective teaching methods* (2nd ed.). © 1992, p. 26. Reprinted by permission of Prentice Hall, Upper Saddle River, New Jersey.

were seen as more aggressive, independent, and possessing better physical skills, while females were thought of as more emotional, intuitive, ambitious, and empathetic. Grant (1985) has found evidence to suggest that some educators actually socialize young females to be responsible and dependable but not initiating and assertive.

Reflect for a Moment

Recall a situation in your elementary or middle school experience that relates to gender treatment by educators.

Additionally, educators must be aware of how student gender affects the quality and quantity of their interactional communication. Studies by Brophy and Good (1974) and Cooper and Good (1983) demonstrated that male students had consistently more interactions with educators than did females. Morse and Handley

(1985) found that female initiated verbal interactions decreased rapidly as they matured whereas male interactions increased.

Curriculum areas may also affect educators' treatment of males and females. Bossert (1981) noted that students assigned to mixed-gender projects, took on certain roles within the group. Males tended to manipulate the materials, whereas females were more likely to record results. Educators need to be aware of the different interests that students bring to the learning negotiation and encourage them to try out different roles.

Some evidence also suggests that the educator's own content specialty areas may alter his or her expectations of students based on gender (Morse & Handley, 1985). For example, teachers of secondary science spent more time reinforcing questions and providing feedback (thus prolonging interactions) for males than for females.

Furthermore, educators need to recognize the reciprocal nature of student behavior and its influences on their own behavior. Brophy and colleagues (1981) found that

> boys misbehaved much more often and more disruptively, but were not more likely than girls to be alienated from teachers or to express negative affect toward them. Nor were teachers alienated from them, although they were slightly more likely to express negative affect in interactions with boys than in interactions with girls. All in all, the sex difference data reviewed here reinforce and extend the patterns observed in earlier research: Teachers perceive girls more positively than boys and share more positive patterns of interaction with them, but most, if not all, of these differences are attributable to differences in the behavior of the students themselves and not to significant teacher favoritism of girls or rejection of boys.(p. 118)

Good and Brophy (1987) report that most students with disabilities will do well if they receive acceptance and support from their teachers. Educators' "attitudes and expectations are critical" (Good & Brophy, 1987, p. 412). It is essential for the success of the inclusive classroom that the student with a disability have as much chance of success as the nondisabled. Educators' attitudes must reflect a feeling of acceptance. Children with disabilities must be "bonafide members of the class, not seen as visitors on loan from the special education teacher" (Good & Brophy, 1987, p. 412).

Preexisting notions of what disability means must be cast aside. In part, the educational system itself has done much to perpetuate fallacies about children with disabilities. The concept that children need to be labeled to obtain appropriate educational services is ludicrous because it implies that all other children should be left to twist in the wind. *All* children *need* appropriate educational services. Additionally, the labeling process does as much to take away the unique individuality of a child as it does to "enhance" his or her educational services. Labels serve to package a child into a group whose members, if truth be told, are probably more different than alike. Labels conjure up images and expectations that often have little to do with the individual child.

A critical step in developing positive attitudes and expectations is looking first at the capabilities of children with disabilities—reflecting on what they can do and how they contribute positively to the classroom. Their weaknesses cannot be ignored, but they should never be used to define who these learners are. No human being wants to be known only by his or her flaws.

Anyone who has an older sibling, cousin, or other distant relative with the same last name has experienced the *family name phenomenon*. Many children have been forced to either live up or down to a teacher's expectation of them based on previous encounters with students with the same last name. Many a first grade teacher has been seen running in terror from the teacher's room after hearing comments about his or her class based solely on last names. "You know those Sullivans, they're all troublemakers." "I had his sister, she did nothing the entire year." "Oh no, not another Jones! Do you know all the older children are emotionally disturbed?" Although not a highly researched phenomenon, the reality of the name bias cannot be denied. Educators must reflect on how they form initial opinions about learners. Educators tend to forget that every child is a unique individual and no two children are the products of identical environments; the reciprocal nature of any interaction creates uniqueness and difference, even for identical twins.

KNOWLEDGE OF THE COMMUNITY

Although **community** is a difficult concept to define, educators must have an understanding of what is meant by the word. Only through knowledge of what a community is can educators hope to promote a feeling of it in their classroom and school. Flynn (1989) defines true community as

> a group of individuals who have learned to communicate honestly with one another, whose relationships go deeper than their composures and who have developed some significant commitment to rejoice together, mourn together, to delight in each other, and make others' conditions their own. (p. 4)

Effective educators develop an awareness of the community in which they work. Effective educators seek to develop and nurture a sense of community among their students and colleagues. This cannot be accomplished without a knowledge of and involvement with the larger communities in which a classroom exists—namely, the school and neighborhood. Without a sense of community, the goals of inclusive classrooms and schools will fail.

Being an effective educator means addressing the needs of *high-risk children*. Societal conditions within the community, family, and the school are the sources of risk (Comer, 1987). Therefore, educators must carefully consider what their role

within the community should entail. Comer (1987) states that risk "began its upward spiral after World War II when education became the ticket of admission to
good jobs, and television and rapid transportation fragmented the sense of community that once gave support and direction to families" (p. 13). Additionally, the
1950s saw rapid movement away from the city neighborhood setting and its stoops
and front porches to the suburbs with their expansive lawns and backyard patios
or decks. The sense of community declined along with this movement of family activity from the front porch to the backyard.

Although educators responded to the postwar conditions by "raising creden-
tial standards, and improving course content and teaching methods," little attention was given "to the affective content of education" (Comer, 1987, pp. 13–14). The
quality of relationships between educators and learners, among school personnel,
and between personnel and community, particularly parents, was ignored. Educators joined with social and behavioral scientists to examine the increase in affective
and behavior problems among learners without truly recognizing the supportive
function of community relationships.

In an interview, Ratzki (1988) relates that the sense of community established at
the Köln-Holweide school in Cologne, Germany is the prevailing factor in a greatly
reduced student dropout rate (1 percent compared to a national average of 14 percent) and a college admission rate more then double the national average (60 percent
versus 27 percent). The Köln-Holweide school has a balance of students from high-,
middle-, and low-ability groups representing middle- and low-income levels. The
school has low teacher absenteeism, almost no truancy, and only minor discipline
problems. Educators, administrators, parents, and community members worked together to transform the school environment into one that supports students for their
learning efforts. Cooperative learning, peer tutoring, and collaborative teaching are
just a few of the techniques used to enhance the sense of community.

As can be seen from Flynn's definition and the Köln-Holweide school, a community is not determined by its size but rather by the level of member commitment. Inclusion and collaboration embrace the sense of community. Many of the
characteristics identified by Stainback, Stainback, and Jackson (1992) should be
considered by any educator trying to foster a sense of classroom and school community. Among them are the development of an inclusive philosophy and the creation of an atmosphere of mutual respect, in both cases reflecting a strong belief in
diversity and individuality. Educators must also model commitment before they
can expect their students or colleagues to demonstrate it. A sense of commitment
is similar to laughter in that both must first be encouraged but, once begun, can
quickly become contagious.

Effective educators have developed a teaching philosophy that directs their
classroom behavior. The development and demonstration of an inclusive philosophy by educators is the first step in creating a sense of community. To foster a sense
of community requires a philosophy that affirms that diversity and individuality
are valuable components of any environment.

Mark is a student with extensive behavioral challenges. He has been known to bite, scratch and fight. Mr. Nichols, the sixth grade teacher, has carefully led his whole class through the process of problem solving and open discussion about Mark's behavior and ways in which they can be his friends and support his positive behavior changes. (Sapon-Shevin, 1991, p. 10)

Persons with diverse ability levels, cultural backgrounds, and socioeconomic status must learn together in order to live together. "As society becomes increasingly multicultural," educators "must recognize that learning to celebrate differences is critical for cohesive communities" (Sapon-Shevin, 1991, p. 10). The educator who embraces this inclusive philosophy takes a giant step toward creating Flynn's true community.

Although Flynn does not directly address the concept of mutual respect in his definition, the ideal comes through. The ability to model mutual respect comes from educators' reflections on their own sense of self-respect. To truly give respect, one must have respect for oneself. Therefore, educators must develop rules that reflect the rights of all students in their classroom community. Creating this standard will foster an atmosphere in which individuality is balanced with a sense of group commitment to prevent isolation and fragmentation.

Reflect for a Moment

In high school, did you feel alienated, did you feel part of a small group, or did you feel a part of the entire school community? Why?

KNOWLEDGE OF THE CURRICULUM

Collaboration is facilitated, and inclusive classrooms are more smoothly managed, when educators recognize how much of a common core curriculum exists for all learners. More specifically, collaborative curriculum planning for inclusive classrooms should strive to minimize special education jargon, focus on broader contexts rather than precise behaviors, and work toward a format to use in outlining educational programs for all students, not just those with special needs (Ford, Davern, & Schnorr, 1992).

Certain approaches to curriculum also invite inclusivity and collaboration. Educators who are familiar with thematic and project-based curriculum planning can work together to organize learning for students with a wide range of characteristics. Students involved in whole language curriculum can succeed in an inclusive classroom. When educators collaborate to provide cooperative learning experiences and peer teaching opportunities in inclusive classrooms, students can excel both academically and socially.

To be able to pursue such approaches to school curriculum, educators must have confidence in their knowledge of curriculum content, its connections to broader educational goals, and their ability to plan in different ways that are responsive to diverse student characteristics. This requires a thorough knowledge of, and appreciation for, not only the cognitive curriculum but the affective and psychomotor curriculum as well. Many students, some identified as needing special services and some not, experience frequent frustration and failure in school, not because an academic task is too difficult, but because they do not feel accepted or secure in a particular setting. If more students are going to be successful in academic areas, educators must pay closer attention to these affective needs and plan carefully for affective curriculum outcomes.

Progressive educators are becoming more dissatisfied with the traditional standard curriculum and some of the implications of its continued use. Smith (1986) has identified several problems. First, he sees the futility of a set body of knowledge, stressing instead the importance of teaching students how to learn. Second, a standard set curriculum is totally inappropriate for the unprecedented diversity of students in public schools. Third, when a standard curriculum is predefined, there is a tendency to teach the curriculum instead of the student. Fourth, a set curriculum too often invites an equally rigid and unimaginative delivery system that many students, regardless of backgrounds and abilities, find boring and largely meaningless. Finally, the creation of a set curriculum, usually by state department personnel and textbook writers, leaves powerless those who are at the center of the educational system—namely, the students and teachers.

For these and perhaps other reasons, educators must assume more responsibility for designing and modifying the curriculum, taking a constructivist approach that respects both children's individual strengths and needs as well as time-honored theories of learning and development. To provide appropriate curriculum in inclusive settings, they need to become more flexible with lesson objectives, more able to adapt learning activities to individual differences, and more ready to seek out team approaches and collaborative arrangements to increase the overall effectiveness of the curriculum being delivered (Stainback, Stainback & Moravec, 1992).

What students should learn has been covered extensively in Chapter 2, and curriculum content has been written about extensively in state curriculum guides, publishers' syllabi, and other formal documents. A number of sources have identified a strong relationship between a teacher's knowledge of subject matter and effective teaching (Hall, 1981; Sizer, 1984; Rubin, 1985; Bennett, 1986; Futrell, 1989). Unfortunately, several indicators suggest that many educators do not have a solid background of general knowledge, and suggest the need for more liberal arts preparation for students planning to enter teaching (National Commission on Excellence in Education, 1983; Solorzano, 1983; Holmes Group, 1986).

It is hard to deny that one must know something well in order to teach it to someone else. Content knowledge includes not only facts, dates, and details but the structure and organization of content and key concepts as well (Bellon, Bellon, & Blank, 1992). The middle school social studies teacher who wants to teach students about the Industrial Revolution in nineteenth-century America must not only be well versed in a wide array of historical data but be able to link this data to additional information about that period in history and address possible implications of that data for events that occurred later in time.

Furthermore, the teacher must be able to take all of this information and communicate it to students who each have their own unique, personal way of receiving information. In other words, the teacher must translate the information into a form that has meaning to each and every student. In the case of the middle school teacher and the Industrial Revolution, it is totally unacceptable to expect all students to read, understand, and put into useful context five pages of print summarizing a particular time in history. However, if the teacher provides visual examples, helps students draw links from major achievements of that era to contemporary industry, and even takes students to a museum to see actual machinery, photographs, and other evidence of life during the Industrial Revolution, then students will have a much deeper, lasting experience with the curriculum content.

It is important to understand curriculum as Bruner presented it in his epic book, *The Process of Education* (1960). Bruner's concept of *spiral curriculum* is based on the notion that topics are presented in a relatively simple form in the early years of schooling, taking on more and more complexity as learners progress through the grades. Text publishers and state departments of education exemplify this form of curriculum development quite clearly when they provide scope and sequence charts, in many cases for an entire K–6 or even K–12 curriculum. Unfortunately, some teachers, because of either a basic lack of confidence in their own knowledge of the long-term goals of the curriculum or a perceived lack of planning and teaching time, rely so heavily on commercial texts and workbooks that they lose sight of the importance of purposeful, personalized planning and instruction.

One vital aspect of the teacher's knowledge of curriculum, therefore, is the ability to add to or delete learning activities presented by publishers of commercial materials (Louisell & Deschamps, 1992). Without this skill, the curriculum becomes little more than one worksheet after another, with students and teachers largely ignorant of the long-term purpose and goal of any given lesson or assignment. In addition, all those involved are less likely to be enthusiastic about and motivated by such a mechanical system of schooling, and this lack of excitement has a decidedly negative impact on student achievement and teacher development.

One current concern of some educators is the apparent discrepancy between the school curriculum and programs planned for individual learners with special needs. Many teachers see two types of curriculum in school: regular and functional (Ford, Davern, & Schnorr, 1992). The first type is what most students learn; the second, what students with significant disabilities learn. However, a deeper understanding of both students and the curriculum allows educators to recognize what is simply an increasingly wide range of student needs within a universal set of broad-based educational goals which apply to all learners. These basic educational goals include writing, reading, and mathematics skills, but also citizenship, social skills (cooperation, respect, concern for others), and self-esteem. It is crucial for educators to view curriculum as a logical and coherent vehicle for guiding all learners toward those broad educational goals and to reflect on this relationship on a daily basis as they plan instruction.

In conclusion, educators must possess curriculum knowledge at several levels. At the first level, they should have a thorough understanding of the cognitive, affective, and psychomotor goals and objectives appropriate to the individual students they are teaching, allowing them to adjust and alter materials and activities so that all students can find meaning and interest in the lessons provided. A second level of understanding requires educators to maintain a clear link between daily instruction and the broad educational goals which are intended for all students. Collaboration with other professionals in planning appropriate experiences is essential if all students are to be given equal opportunity and access to the universal goals of public education. A third and final level is the one at which educators critically examine traditional standard curriculum and take a proactive role in reforming what students learn. Curriculum for inclusive schools should be geared less to facts and details and more toward learning how to learn; less to a norm and more toward diverse school-age populations; less to a content-centered perspective and more toward a learner-centered perspective; less toward texts and worksheets and more toward engaging the active learner, and less to control from afar and more to student and teacher design and development.

Reflect for a Moment

Were there opportunities for you to construct your own learning in high school? Independent studies? Projects? Was it geared toward facts or learning how to learn? How was it assessed?

CONSIDERATION OF THE SETTING

Classrooms are complex social settings. An elementary teacher may engage in more than 1,000 interpersonal exchanges with learners in a single school day (Jackson, 1968). Many of these interactions are lost in the shuffle unless the educator has carefully structured his or her classroom environment. (For a more detailed discussion of the classroom environment and instructional management, see Chapter 7.)

Discussions about classroom management generally focus on establishing and maintaining order in the classroom environment (Doyle, 1986). This simple, straightforward statement masks, however, the complexity of classroom management. Conceptions of what constitutes orderliness vary across situations (e.g., snack versus silent reading time), individuals (e.g., "traditionalists" versus "progressives"), and settings (whole group versus small group; learning stations versus seat work). The actions educators take to maintain order vary from planning lessons to distributing materials, interacting with learners, discussing rules, and reacting to behavior (both individual and group) (Doyle, 1986). Additionally, the appropriateness of any action is governed by the circumstances under which it occurs; the who, what, where, how, and why of an activity.

Unfortunately, Good and Brophy (1987) contend, many educators fail to perceive much of what occurs in their own classrooms. This happens for three reasons: "(1) classroom interaction involves fast and complex communication, (2) teachers are not trained to monitor and study their behavior, and (3) teachers rarely receive systematic or useful feedback about their behavior (p. 26)." Collectively, these behaviors focus on the need for educators to develop their reflective skills. Further, the second and third reasons reinforce the importance of peer collaboration. Collaboration provides educators not only a source of systematic feedback about their behavior but helps strengthen observational skills.

In considering setting, educators must examine classroom climate. Borich (1992) defines *classroom climate* as the atmosphere or mood in which interactions between a teacher or collaborative team and students take place. Climate is a product of the way in which an educator uses authority, models warmth and acceptance, encourages collaboration and cooperation, celebrates diversity, and allows for independent actions.

Reflect for a Moment

Have you ever been in a strict classroom climate? A warm climate? How about a collaborative classroom climate? Did the teachers involved plan it that way?

Unfortunately, in many classrooms, climate is allowed to develop randomly. The effective educator, however, is proactive in the development of classroom climate, looking carefully at both the social and physical environments. Although social climate has been the emphasis in this section, the physical setting and the environment for learning are also important. A more in-depth analysis of classroom climate and instructional management is provided in Chapter 7.

TEACHER EDUCATION

With the advent of total inclusion, the once dual system for the education of children with special needs and those of "normal progress" is changing (Whittier & Hewit, 1993). This change in the delivery of educational services must also bring about a restructuring of teacher education programs. If, as human beings, we are in part products of our learning, it should come as no surprise, given traditional teacher preparation programs, that colleges and universities are creating yet another generation of separatists—those educators who as a result of their preparation believe that general and special education should forever remain separate entities. Separatists understand *Brown v. Topeka Board of Education* but fail to realize how this ruling pertains to students with disabilities, tracking, or cultural diversity.

All educators need to acquire the skills and knowledge to work in a collaborative and cooperative partnership, and the unification of teacher education programs would be the first positive step in this direction.

> Given the increasing complexity of the student population, as well as the unprecedented fact that the cultural background of most novice teachers will differ from those of their students in the years to come, such a position should strike no reader as a surprise. (Pugach, 1992, p. 255)

The general and special education faculties in universities and colleges have a responsibility to model collaboration and inclusion. As Pugach (1992) states, "The stakes are extremely high and the best thinking of every professional is warranted in all aspects of the educational enterprise" (p. 255). To modify and evolve the present preparation programs will require the breaking down of traditional territorial issues. Pugach and Lilly (1984) state that "schools, colleges, and departments of education must be in the business of predicting the future in education and adjusting teacher education programs in relation to projected trends in the field. Our teacher education programs must anticipate needs in the future to provide optimum teacher preparation today" (p. 48).

Any education program, be it a nursery school or a university, is recognized for the quality of its graduates. A graduate of a teacher education program should possess a thorough working knowledge of theoretical perspectives; research and ongoing issues in the areas of social, psychological, and technological foundations; and learner diversity (cultural, ethnic, ability level). Additionally, these new educators will possess other knowledge, including how to locate and use human print and electronic resources, community and cultural awareness, subject matter, and pedagogy. Pedagogy must include teaching models, both general and specific as well as planning, collaboration, evaluation, climate, management, and reflection.

Reflect for a Moment

How much are you learning to collaborate in your current program? How much are you learning to practice teaching models? How much are you learning to adapt instruction for various students?

The new teacher preparation programs must prepare educators who have demonstrated the ability to teach in the inclusive classroom, applying the knowledge described here in a variety of settings with a wide and diverse range of students. Of equal importance will be the ability to collaborate with a multitude of professionals and nonprofessionals, both in and out of the classroom, and to be an advocate for children. Last, such a program will need to help the future educator develop ongoing reflective practices both in and out of the classroom, based on a commitment to lifelong learning.

Desired Professional Outcome	Yes	No	To Do

1. I have thought about and written my philosophy of teaching.
2. I have a professional career plan for the next year that includes goals and objectives I will endeavor to meet as a professional.
3. I engage in study and training programs to improve my knowledge and competence related to teaching.
4. I am a teachable person. I am willing to change my ideas, thinking, and practices based on study, new information, and the advice of colleagues and professionals.
5. I have completed or am working on a degree in order to enhance my personal life as a professional.
6. I try to improve myself as a person by engaging in a personal program of self-development.
7. I practice in my own life and model for others good moral habits and ethical behavior. I encourage others to act ethically.
8. I act professionally and encourage others to do the same.
9. I place the best interests of children, parents, and the profession first in decisions about what constitutes quality teaching.
10. I know about and am familiar with my profession's history, terminology, issues, contemporary development, and trends.
11. I consciously and consistently find ways to apply concepts about what is best for students to my teaching.
12. I belong to a professional organization and participate in professional activities such as celebrations, study groups, committees, and conventions.
13. I am an advocate for and on behalf of my profession and the needs and rights of students.
14. I involve parents in my classroom and school. I encourage parents in their roles as supporters of their children's education.
15. I seek the advice of and cooperate with other professional groups in my work with students and parents.

FIGURE 4.3   Fifteen Steps for Becoming a Professional

Source: From *Education and Development of Infants, Toddlers, and Preschoolers* by George S. Morrison. Copyright © 1988 by George S. Morrison. Reprinted by permission of Addison-Wesley Educational Publishers Inc..

SUMMARY

Over the past twenty-five years, classroom-based research on teaching effectiveness has provided educators with a comprehensive set of recommendations for improving student performance and attitude. It is important for all educators to have opportunities to study and apply this information in their individual settings. Aspects of teaching consistently supported in this research include lesson clarity, instructional variety, task orientation, engaged time, using student ideas, rate of success, structuring, questioning, probing, and teacher affect. Aspects of teaching that are specific to the direct instruction model of teaching include attention to opening the lesson, demonstrating new learning, guided practice, independent practice, lesson closure, and evaluation of instruction.

The development of ongoing reflective practices is an essential component of effective teaching. Reflective behavior encompasses more than simply looking back at what was done. Individual differences are what helps to shape teaching style. Teaching styles develop slowly and, in the effective educator, are in constant revision. The educator's teaching style dictates the effectiveness of his or her teaching methods. Overall, teaching styles fall into one of three categories: teacher centered, student centered, and content centered.

Self-knowledge goes beyond simple awareness; it provides the effective educator with a means for change. Effective educators recognize that one's personal values, beliefs, and experiences are an integral part of teaching behavior.

The effective educator is able to envision how his or her actions affect and are altered by the learner. The recognition that any action creates an interactive environment that will result in change to both the learner and the educator is crucial.

Incumbent in knowing oneself is the recognition that one's perceptions and beliefs about a given student impact on that student's ability to learn. Teacher expectation is a powerful force that governs a child's learning environment. Educators' perceptions of what high- versus low-ability students can accomplish color not only the teacher-student interaction but also the student-learning interaction.

Without a sense of community, the concept of inclusive classrooms and schools will fail. The effective educator seeks to understand the community in which she or he works.

The understanding that classrooms are amazingly complex social settings is necessary to the development of a learning environment. Effective educators have carefully orchestrated classroom climates. Collaboration and reflection help the effective educator refine the classroom environment, making it conducive to learning.

5

PROFESSIONAL COLLABORATION

Key Terms

Collaboration
Collaborative consultation
Collaborative skills
Collaborative teaching
Consultation
Diversity
Face-to-face interaction
Full collaboration
Group processing

Inclusive school
Individual accountability
Mentoring
Peer coaching
Positive interdependence
Problem solving
Resource attractor
Team

Objectives

After completing this chapter, the reader will be able to:

1. List the different types of people who contribute to a collaborative team or a collaborative ethic.
2. Explain the five factors essential to team productivity.
3. Model collaborative skills.
4. Discuss why collaboration is essential to effective education.
5. Analyze the changes necessary for collaboration and inclusion to occur in a school community.
6. Compare and contrast the various approaches to teamwork with full collaboration.
7. Describe ways an administrator can promote collaboration in a school.
8. Develop roles for parents and community members in establishing a collaborative, inclusive school community.

PROFILES OF A TEAM

Sadie Standish

When I arrive at 7:45, the school is quiet and the classrooms where doors are open are devoid of life. Some muffled noises are coming from behind closed doors but no real distinguishable voice that tells me I'm not alone. I enter my classroom and close the door, shutting out contact with the outside world.

The feeling of isolation, though sometimes cozy, prevents me from finding answers to unvoiced questions about my teaching. When my students are pulled from my room, I sometimes wonder where they go and what they learn. When they're pulled out, I never know if what they're learning is different from what I'm teaching. How do I provide them with missed information? How do I adapt curriculum to meet the unique needs of all my students? Are my ideas and techniques for adaptation valid? Whom do I turn to when I need resources and materials to make those ideas and techniques real? How do I communicate with the parents of my students? How do I go about assigning grades?

What about socialization of students? How can I arrange instruction to support social acceptance of all students? Why do those who are pulled out always miss the special events I try so hard to schedule into my busy academic calendar?

Mr. Bordeau, my principal, never comes into my room to see how my students are doing. I've never even met the speech therapist who takes Jamie on Thursdays; I have no idea what they do. Mrs. Jacobsen, the resource teacher, just left some papers in my mailbox with a note about accommodating Brian. Right. Let her do the accommodating. After all, he's labeled special ed. Maybe I shouldn't be worrying so much about all of this. They never offer any real help. Besides, I like the privacy of my own room and the comfort of my routine. When I took this job, Mr. Bordeau talked about the excellent "teamwork" at this school. No way! As long as I just do my job, who cares?

Callie Collins

We're meeting before school today to begin planning a unit on outer space. All the teachers in the third/fourth grade group will be there. Karen, the resource teacher, is going to share some of the exciting ideas we talked about after school yesterday. Ever since this group of teachers began collaborating, we've all been more enthusiastic about our work. I never saw myself as creative until I began brainstorming ideas for curriculum innovation with my colleagues. Just having time scheduled every week for talking about our teaching beliefs has helped so much. Sure, my day is a little bit longer, but I can already see the benefits. Many of the questions I had about my teaching have been clarified. It was exciting to find out that I wasn't the only teacher feeling isolated, that other team members had similar questions and concerns.

For the first time, I had a chance to find out that even though Karen and I actually shared the same goals for students, some were falling behind their peers academically because of lack of curriculum clarity. By having the opportunity to discuss curriculum and students' needs, we were able to provide an integrated program in some academic areas.

Mrs. Daley, the principal, worked out a schedule that allowed us to visit each others' classes. I spent some time in Karen's class and saw her materials, her presentation strategies, and her management techniques. Karen and I have planned a schedule so that we can work with groups of students in my classroom during the language arts block.

Our collaborative teaching also seems to have had a positive effect on students. It's almost as if seeing us as a team has made them more willing to work together, too. They really look like they're enjoying each other's company, and all their schoolwork has certainly shown improvement. Students who seldom if ever participated before are leading discussions and being actively sought after for group projects. In fact, Michael's mother stopped me at the bank last week. He had told her that this year he felt special, not because of his disability, but because other students liked and used his ideas for several creative writing assignments.

We've noticed some new, unexpected friendships emerging, too. Pamela, who has cerebral palsy, and Jessica have become inseparable and are cohosting a slumber party this coming weekend at Pamela's house.

I am finding myself in some new surroundings. Teaching is much more than going into your room in the morning, closing the door, and working alone with children till the end of the day. I really don't know how I ever got along without my colleagues.

THE NATURE OF A TEAM

All persons, young and old alike, have a basic need both to belong and to feel that they have the power and freedom to contribute to a group (Brandt, 1988; Glasser, 1986). Later in this chapter, the distinctions among consultation, peer coaching, mentoring, collaborative consultation, collaborative teaching, and full collaboration will be detailed. The elements that distinguish full collaboration from team structure are not as clear, however. The characteristics that define a **team** and the relationship among team members are very similar to those of **collaboration** because the element of collaboration is what distinguishes a team from a group or committee. Friend and Cook (1992) define team as "a relatively small set of interdependent individuals who work and interact directly in a coordinated manner to achieve a common purpose" (p. 32). The development of inclusive schools and communities requires the collaboration of a variety of team members. Teams of adults, teams of students, and teams with both adults and students all exist in inclusive schools. Everyone in an inclusive school must work in various collaborative groups. Friend and Cook (1992) further suggest that effective teams must also have a clear understanding of group goals and that members' personal needs must not be frustrated by the experience. All collaborative members contribute unique qualities, perspectives, understandings, and expertise to the team process.

Reflect for a Moment

Pause to recall an experience you have had in which you were part of a small team working together for a common goal. How did the team succeed?

Johnson and Johnson (1987) define team as "a set of interpersonal relationships structured to achieve established goals. Successful team performance requires interpersonal competencies" (p. 397). They identify five characteristics essential for the productive functioning of a team: positive interdependence, individual accountability, face-to-face interaction, collaborative skills, and group processing.

Positive Interdependence

Positive interdependence is the essence of collaboration—it promotes working together and sharing resources, highlights mutual support and celebrates team success (Friend & Cook, 1992; Johnson & Johnson, 1987; Vandercook & York, 1990). Positive interdependence is also based on a sense of trust, trustworthiness and loyalty. A single member cannot succeed unless the entire team does. Status is coordinate, not superordinate or subordinate; each collaborator is an equal contributor, adding his or her experience to the team (Mittler, Mittler, & McConachie, 1987; Sileo, Rude, & Luckner, 1988; Vandercook & York, 1990; Zins, Curtis, Graden, & Ponti, 1988). Additionally, positive interdependence is closely aligned with cooperative goal structures (see Chapter 6) and the four features of collaborative consultation identified by Nevin and colleagues later in this chapter.

Positive interdependence is a state in which individual group members perceive that mutuality exists. This mutuality occurs because the collaborative team is working for mutual benefits through mutual obligation and investment. Thus, shared identity develops that binds the team together emotionally. In addition, collaborators share the feeling of having a common fate. They have all gained or lost based on the overall collaboration and performance of the team. As a result of developing this sense of common fate, team members have an expectation of joint celebration. Camaraderie, a sense of belonging, and pride in both individual efforts and group outcomes emerge. Therefore, mutual benefits are a key to a well-developed team. All members understand that their productivity benefits not only them as individuals but everyone else as well.

Individual Accountability

When the performance of each team member is assessed, **individual accountability** exists. Evaluating individual contributions reduces the likelihood of duplication of effort by team members and also provides a mechanism by which team members can better channel their support and assistance to one another. Reflection by individual members on their contribution and accountability for collaborative success or failure serves to strengthen the entire team process.

Face-to-Face Interaction

Although team effectiveness may be influenced by positive interdependence, the interaction patterns of members have the most powerful influence on productivity, morale, and efficiency (Johnson & Johnson, 1987). It is suggested that meaningful **face-to-face interaction** occurs in a small collaborative team. Members' perception of their participation and efforts decrease as the size of the group increases.

Collaborative Skills

Collaborative skills are an essential element of effective and successful teamwork and, like technical skills, must be taught and practiced. They include, but are not limited to, listening to different, sometime opposing views, giving up one's own "turf," sharing ideas and responsibilities, solving problems interpersonally, showing respect for colleagues, reconsidering one's own opinion, resolving conflict, managing resistance, and reflecting on current practices. Because many educators and administrators have never been required to work as part of a team, they may lack the necessary collaborative skills. Often educators may believe they are collaborating but, because of a lack of necessary social skills, they are actually engaging in activities that are counterproductive to true collaboration (Graden & Bauer, 1992).

Listening

Educators will find it easier to appreciate the importance of listening by recalling experiences where they were *not* listened to, whether with colleagues, during a social affair, or in the classroom. Listening to others shows concern for them, enhances one's understanding of the situation, and reduces the likelihood of misinterpretation. Ineffective listeners often tend to daydream, prematurely organize a response, overfocus on individual words, or simply become distracted by external stimuli. Educators can improve their listening skills by taking notes or repeating and organizing mentally what they hear.

"Turf"

Many educators have established a clear understanding of their roles in the educational system and may feel threatened by a proposal that clearly changes that role. Both general educators and special educators have become comfortable with having their own classrooms and even their own students. Sadie Standish likes the privacy of her own room and the comfort of her routine. This relative isolation is truly a safeguard, and those who give up their territory must feel confident about the nature of change taking place and safe in their role as a change agent. Callie Collins, in spite of finding herself in new surroundings, now wonders how she ever got along without her colleagues.

Reflect for a Moment

How do you feel when you are comfortably settled in a role (job, routine) and are forced to give up that comfort?

Sharing

Consistent with giving up one's "turf" is the willingness to share responsibility for all students in a given team or school. Instead of viewing a group of students as "my class," the collaborator becomes a member of a schoolwide group of adults who are collectively concerned with every student at the school. This shared responsibility also requires educators to share ideas for working successfully with any student in the school. Third grade teachers offer assistance to kindergarten teachers who are developing a dramatic production. Speech therapists receive learning center ideas from fifth grade teachers. All adults share ideas and responsibilities.

Solving Interpersonal Problems

Just about any professional task or activity involves a problem of one sort or another (Friend & Cook, 1992). If educators are going to collaborate successfully, they must develop interpersonal **problem-solving** skills. Although situations are handled more effectively when they are proactively managed (that is, before the problem has actually occurred), many problems cannot be anticipated and must still be effectively addressed when they emerge.

During the interpersonal problem-solving process there are times when *convergent thinking* is necessary—when the collaborative team must agree. Conversely, there are also moments when it is essential to encourage *divergent* thinking—to bring as many diverse perspectives to the problem as possible. Identifying the problem is the first and perhaps most critical step in the problem-solving process. At this point it is imperative for the group to be of one mind, to converge on a clear identification of the problem being discussed. The problem should represent a discrepancy between the existing and desired situations, be viewed by participants as a problem, and be free of explicit assumptions regarding a possible solution.

Generating possible solutions is the next step in problem solving, and each possible solution should be carefully evaluated in terms of its positive and negative implications. Divergent thinking is necessary during this step, when team members must produce a variety of ideas. Brainstorming is a common method used to generate many different ideas in a relatively brief time span, and it engages the full participation of all group members. At this point, evaluation is suspended so that ideas may develop freely. This is not to say that each solution should not be evaluated in terms of implications. That step follows the act of brainstorming, when all ideas are categorized and critically analyzed by the group for inclusion on a narrower list of solutions.

After the initial list of ideas has been narrowed, the remaining possible solutions should be outlined to see what steps would be involved in implementing each. Then, through criteria such as extent of intrusiveness, feasibility, and individual preference, a solution is selected. This is the second point at which convergent thinking becomes critical. The collaborative group needs to agree on a course of action before they can implement it.

Implementation involves making necessary arrangements, establishing a schedule for implementation as well as criteria for its success. The solution is carried out and its success is evaluated by all participants as success, partial success followed by modification, or no success. This evaluation is followed by an analysis of each step of the problem-solving process and a return to the point where the process broke down. This process, if used diligently, can create truly effective collaborative relationships.

Respect

Collaboration requires educators not only to hold respect for each other, but to demonstrate it consistently through their actions. When colleagues seek ideas from one another, ask for advice, volunteer to work together, make commitments to one another and deliver on those commitments, and communicate constructively, they are demonstrating respect.

Reflect for a Moment

Have you ever worked with someone who showed genuine respect for you and your thinking? How did you know that person had such respect for you?

Reconsider

Whenever broad-based educational goals are examined, the development of a lifelong learner is usually a primary criterion. Lifelong learners are persons who constantly reflect on their experiences and willingly alter their thinking in various ways. Because collaborators are continuously reflecting, discussing their beliefs and actions, and adjusting subsequent beliefs and actions as they take in new knowledge and information, they must be lifelong learners. There is no room in true collaboration for cognitive dissonance, and educators who hold fast to existing beliefs in the face of new and valuable information will participate less successfully on collaborative teams. It is critical that collaborators be able to examine their own judgments, broad based and case specific, and be willing to adjust their views and opinions to meet changing circumstances.

Conflict

Current school reform efforts often entail changes in leadership roles and responsibilities. All change brings with it inevitable conflict between and among educators. Conflict by itself is a natural occurrence and can have positive and negative outcomes. Positive outcomes include high-quality decision making; a strong sense of commitment; sharper thinking; more open, trusting relationships among colleagues; and more effective communication skills (Friend & Cook, 1992).

To resolve conflict successfully between individuals or even within an individual, there are several strategies to consider. The problem-solving process described earlier is one strategy. Communicating effectively, using questions and clarifiers, is another widely recommended practice. Finally, negotiation, which includes direct, clear, professional and responsive communication, is frequently used successfully to resolve conflict. Regardless of the strategy used, it is important to focus on issues, not people; avoid emotional conflict; consider bringing in a third party if necessary; and certainly, if valid reasons exist, not rule out the possibility of dismissing the situation.

Resistance

Resistance, in effect, means avoiding what one doesn't want. Like conflict, resistance is a naturally occurring phenomenon, especially in the face of change. Many professionals with good intentions resist change because of a wish to keep things way they are, a fear of failure, a perceived threat to their teaching behavior, or an honest difference of opinion about the need for change. Professionals who are successful in managing resistance will utilize administrative support, respect the values of colleagues and involve them actively throughout the change, and provide ample evidence that the proposed change has been successful in other schools. Additionally, they will demonstrate clearly how the change will benefit educators, consider highlighting the novelty of the process being proposed, establish an open communications network to help maintain a trusting relationship with colleagues, and plan to proceed slowly and openly with the proposed changes (Friend & Bauwens, 1988).

Professionals are not the only individuals resistant to inclusion and collaboration; parents are as well. Resistance focuses primarily on two areas of concern: the possibility of negative peer interactions and reduction in quality of their child's educational program. The possible benefits are often "overshadowed by parental desires to protect their children from verbal abuse, isolation and ridicule" (Galant & Hanline, 1993, p. 293). Parents of children in inclusive classrooms have, however, reported that their children experienced relatively few difficulties with peers and believe the collaborative setting promotes positive academic and social contact for all children (Green & Stoneman, 1989; McDonnell, 1987; Villa, Thousand, Stainback, & Stainback, 1992).

Practice

Identify the collaborative skill illustrated in each of the following brief scenarios.

A. Whenever the collaborative middle school team meets, Cindy notices that Roberta and Tony are almost constantly taking notes. She realizes that she frequently rephrases their comments in her mind.

B. Although as colleagues they disagree on whether theoretical foundations or teaching methodologies are more important in a teacher education program, Rodney and Mark value each other's opinions and have worked diligently to create a first-rate program.

C. Joanna Jackson and Molly Reed, a third grade teacher, sharply disagree on the best method of reading instruction for Mrs. Jackson's daughter, Danielle. After four long meetings and assistance from Joe Strand, the reading specialist, they have reached a solution and now have a deeper sense of commitment to their plan.

D. The primary grades team meets weekly to discuss their successes and frustrations from the week. They offer each other suggestions, celebrate each other's victories, and take turns sharing brief readings about teaching.

E. Sarah Jones has a great idea for a unit on local customs but is relatively new to the area. Mary Clement knows several of the town's old timers, so they decide to work together on developing resources for the unit.

F. The atmosphere in Katie Berwick's sixth grade classroom was almost dull. She didn't have any management problems to speak of but was not satisfied with the climate. A group of girls were even beginning to complain, saying Katie was favoring the boys over the girls. Mark Boardman, the special educator who worked in the classroom frequently, admitted that he concurred with Katie's assessment. They spent several afternoons making up a list of possible changes, analyzed the list carefully, and selected a strategy they could implement and monitor closely.

G. Jerry Oswald had done just fine for eighteen years in his fourth grade classroom. He didn't see a need to hold all these meetings with the other teachers in his hallway. But after observing the positive outcomes for students that resulted from the collaboration between Sue and Karen, he asked them if he might sit in on their next meeting to learn more about collaboration.

H. Hanna Williams, a high school music teacher, was getting nowhere in her efforts to include students from Mike Schwinn's self-contained special education class in the sophomore chorus. Mike insisted that they would be made fun of and that she would not know how to handle them. Hanna discussed her dilemma with Gloria Washington, the building principal, and together they devised a plan to include both Mike's students and Mike himself in the chorus schedule. Gloria also showed Mike an article about disabled high school students in another urban school who participated successfully in that school's chorus.

I. At the beginning of the school year, Ernie Dean had been upset about sharing his classroom with other teachers. It took a few months, but he was finally starting to feel a little more comfortable having Julie Davenport in his room during second and fourth period history. He even found himself referring to classes as "the students" instead of "my students." Besides, several students were writing much better essays with Julie's help.

Reflecting

Collaboration is not an entirely new concept to many educators. Many have been involved in various forms of team teaching, peer coaching, and collaborating for years. Beyond these existing forms of collaboration, however, educators are obliged to reflect on both their own and others' practices. This can be achieved through regular meetings in which educators share recent practices they have implemented and professional literature that describes current collaboration efforts in other schools. A careful examination of collaboration across many settings will provide professionals with new and exciting possibilities in the delivery of educational services.

Group Processing

Each collaborative team needs to set aside specific time to discuss how well they are achieving their goals and maintaining an effective working relationship. **Group processing,** then, involves an analysis of successful and unsuccessful strategies, and promotes reflection and positive change. Further, such group or team processing facilitates the consistent use and refinement of collaborative skills through constructive feedback. Team processing can also have a decidedly positive effect on team productivity; Johnson and Johnson (1987) found that teams increased their productivity by developing insight into how to interact more effectively and/or generating feedback that reinforced members when they engaged in collaborative behavior.

The success of collaborative teams depends on the foundation of a collaborative culture that by its very nature must be inclusive. Essential for the development of full collaboration is knowing *why* it should happen, *when* it should take place, *who* should be involved, and *how* it can be accomplished.

WHY?

The importance of establishing a collaborative culture has been highlighted by the Carnegie (1986) and Holmes (1986) reports. Collaboration among all areas of the educational community is viewed by both studies as central to a successful school experience for all students in the twenty-first century.

Collaborative work emphasizes teachers' experiences and supports the act of reflecting on practice. According to Fuchs and Moore (1988), "teaching can be an isolated profession. Most teachers plan, teach, and reflect on their teaching by themselves" (p. 412). Students in the junior high where teachers collaborated reported a more varied and interesting classroom environment. The authors also indicated that the benefits of their collaborative planning, teaching, and reflecting far outweighed the challenges and extra time required.

Wiedmeyer and Lehman (1991) identify several problems that existed before the implementation of their collaborative teaching program. Among those problems were a lack of curriculum coordination, resulting in students' difficulty in generalizing skills learned in the resource room; general and special educators' failure to take ownership of each child's learning needs; and loss of important special events time (and socialization) as a result of students' removal from the classroom for educational interventions. Following a year of collaborative teaching, a variety of benefits emerged. Students with disabilities stated, "I feel like I'm not even in L.D. at times. [I have the] sense that I'm like the others, I don't care that anyone knows now. But last year I was trying to make friends and didn't want my learning disability to get in the way" (Wiedmeyer & Lehman, 1991, p. 9).

Although this model was established to enhance the education of students with special needs, positive outcomes exist for other students as well. According to Simpson and Smith-Myles (1990), at least 20 percent of the students who are not labeled experience difficulty in the general education classroom. Will (1986) states that among this 20 percent are children who possess low self-esteem; exhibit social, conduct, and behavior problems; have difficulties understanding or using language; or are deemed to be slow learners. In a full collaboration model, benefits for all students are the goal from the outset.

Reflect for a Moment

At the next class session, look around at your classmates. Can you tell which ones are disabled? Chances are at least one is. Do you think that the current system of identifying students with disabilities is identifying all of the right students?

The notion that schools are communities of educators and learners has become central to the inclusive movement (Stainback, Stainback, & Jackson, 1992). Changes in the composition of the family, the cultural makeup of the school-age population, and the basic decisions concerning what students should learn in school mandate a new and more effective delivery of educational services.

Thousand, Villa, Paolucci-Whitcomb, and Nevin (1992) have detailed several benefits of a new organization of educators that closely resemble full collaboration. First, they suggest that collaboration creates an enhanced and shared expertise that allows schools to more adequately meet increasingly diverse student needs. The teaching teams that result will create environments in which a more elaborate exchange of ideas leads to instructional outcomes that benefit all students, not just those with special needs. As a result of this type of collaborative culture, Skritc (1989) believes that students will be provided with services more appropriate to their unique academic and affective needs and will successfully manage more complex learning.

Central to this shared expertise are: (1) shared "ownership" of problem definitions and solutions, leading to greater goal commitment and more successful implementation; (2) shared knowledge and expertise resulting in the acquisition of new skills; (3) increased cohesiveness and willingness to work together on future projects; and (4) new conceptualizations and novel solutions, in which students themselves engage in higher-level thinking processes, show higher-quality cognitive and moral reasoning, use more metacognitive strategies, and simply generate more solutions than when they work individually.

A second major benefit of the full collaborative model is the inherent paradigm shift among educators that is a prerequisite to the establishment of shared expertise. The collaboration culture recognizes and embraces the need for an entirely new way of thinking about school organization, a shift that is already in evidence in inclusion-oriented schools. Such a shift has been necessitated by the massive societal changes described above.

Third, the school with a collaborative culture is better positioned to prepare students for the demands on their communication and social skills that will be necessary to successfully work in the world of the twenty-first century. An unprecedented emphasis on learning how to learn and sharing this knowledge with others is fundamental to the collaborative culture. The possibilities for student-student and adult-student learning exchanges can serve to empower students to become highly active learners (Thousand et al., 1992).

The fourth aspect of the collaborative culture is the emerging establishment of schools in the midst of this paradigm shift. This shift is not without emotional turmoil and will need to occur gradually, with schools retaining at least temporarily some of the more traditional structures of their current organization. If the new schools are to be truly inclusive, then the community must be included in their planning and ultimately be actively supportive in their creation and operation. The ongoing interaction and communication required to make this shift are extremely complex, increasing the quality of the collaboration that will eventually be the focus of the delivery of educational services to all students.

WHEN?

Collaboration does not happen by itself. There are particular conditions in school, district, and community climate that seem to encourage this relationship among educators. Kent (1987) states that "the creation of these conditions requires effort, not only on the part of teachers, administrators, and school support staff, but also of district and school board officials, professional organizations, parents, and community leaders" (p. 52).

One condition supporting full collaboration is the concept of inclusive schools. Historically, many schools have actively sought to "mainstream" students with disabilities into their general education classrooms, which suggests that these students did not belong there all along. More recently, districts have taken to "integrating" students with disabilities, which implies that schools must be mandated to accept a less desirable element; integration is a quota to be maintained rather than a celebration of uniqueness and diversity. Both mainstreaming and integration have created tension, bias, and a general sense of confusion and antagonism in the school community.

An **inclusive school** is one that emphasizes the school as a community of learners and educators. Too often, attempts to establish a collaborative culture are shortcircuited by administrators who believe that simply placing teachers in a room together during common planning times will lead to collaboration. Lytle and Fecho (1991) suggest that "collaborative cultures take time to develop, rely on trust and mutual understanding, and arise from both the day to day as well as the long term relationships of the participants" (p. 8). The essence of the collaborative culture indicates clearly that it must be developed before the delivery of educational services.

The reality of significant change in educational systems suggests that full collaboration may occur only after several other forms of quasi-collaboration have been attempted. These strategies, some of which are described later in the chapter, may be successful for some groups of children, but over time may prove less beneficial for other groups of children. For example, the collaborative teaching style that Peggy Robinson, Gary Van Heusen, and Joy Adair have developed works splendidly for students with special needs in their two classes, but other students with special needs in the same school are still shuffling back and forth from general to special education classes.

When all teachers begin to accept new and different roles, then full collaboration will emerge (Graden, 1989). Special educators must not be seen just as "experts" who provide technical instruction and remain separate, unwilling to collaborate. Likewise, general educators must not be seen just as "helpful," able to work only with other general educators. A shared language must also be established. Jargon specific to special education, lesson planning, or a certain subject area must be softened to facilitate better understanding among colleagues.

Even when educators accept these new, expanded roles, full collaboration must wait until local school boards and administrators are willing to provide educators with the time needed to learn about collaboration, recognize its value, and then plan and reflect collaboratively on a regular basis. Several districts in Vermont and other states have adopted a school schedule that includes a half day per week devoted exclusively to collaborative planning. Schedules must be drawn that facilitate and support collaboration. It does little good to schedule educators for instructional time together when the students are at lunch or in a special art or physical education class. When commitments are made in terms of roles, time, and scheduling, full collaboration will begin to emerge.

All of these factors collectively suggest that groups of educators with good intentions may try to implement full collaboration prematurely or hold unrealistic expectations for the change. Full collaboration takes time to prepare for, and still more time to successfully implement. Resistance, frustration, and breakdowns in communications and/or momentum must be anticipated, but the benefits are well worth the struggle.

Reflect for a Moment

Have you ever had a really great idea and been so excited to put it into place that it flopped? Looking back, just why did your idea fail?

WHO?

The *why* and *when* of collaboration are important to the process, but they cannot be accomplished without a full understanding of *who* needs to be involved. A variety of people are necessary to promote the collaborative ethic that is critical for the development of an inclusive school environment. Administrators, school board members, educators, students, families, community members, and support personnel are among the groups of actively involved persons needed to ensure that collaboration and inclusion are successful.

Students

Students are traditionally seen as receivers of education even though schools, as they are currently structured, fail to be effective for a large number of learners. A large part of this failure lies in just this assumption that students are passive recipients rather than active producers of learning. Gartner and Lipsky (1990) discuss the need to help students become instructional agents, more effective workers in the production of their own learning and that of their peers. Hamre-Nietupski, McDonald, and Nietupski (1992) highlight the importance of students' roles as instructional agents.

Stephanie, a first grader with multiple disabilities (moderate to severe mental retardation coupled with visual impairments and physical disabilities) has difficulty in the winter putting on her shoes and tying them after removing her boots. To avoid missing the important opening activity, Stephanie removes her boots and brings her shoes to circle. Once in circle, Stephanie asks a peer for assistance in putting on and tying her shoe. Stephanie's peer has been shown how to help with difficult steps and to encourage her to attempt easier steps. Positive interactions have developed between Stephanie and her peers, she is able to participate in opening routine, and her self-care skills have increased (Hamre-Nietupski, McDonald, & Nietupski, 1992).

Strully and Strully (1989) believe that such interaction is necessary because it facilitates the development of friendships and long-lasting supportive relationships. Both parties benefit as a result of positive interactions by expanding their understandings of, and appreciation for, each other's uniqueness.

Schools are social institutions that cannot evolve and grow without taking into consideration societal and cultural influences. Issues such as homelessness, hunger, pollution, aggravating childhood illnesses (asthma, chronic ear infections), inadequate vaccination practices, fundamental changes in the family structure, immigration of people from a variety of cultures, and the shrinking world culture make collaboration and inclusion a necessary component in school reform. Societal and cultural trends will require learners of the future to interact with people from varying family structures, cultures, languages, levels of ability, and other personal characteristics.

This increased heterogeneity will naturally result in increased demands for graduates to value and cooperate with people who have diverse characteristics. The ability of people with diverse backgrounds and characteristics to live harmoniously in an increasingly interdependent world will be influenced by society's decision to pursue inclusion-oriented or separate schooling for various groups. (Giangreco, 1992, p. 243)

Students with or without disabilities (Stainback, Stainback, & Wilkinson, 1992) from varying cultural, ethnic, or racial backgrounds will benefit from peer support and friendship provided by schools that are inclusion oriented. Positive interaction styles are developed when students collaborate, laying the foundation for forming future friendships and providing one another with support. Students learn that to be liked and supported by their peers they must also like and support others.

Through inclusion, learners with diverse backgrounds and ability levels develop the ability to establish areas of compatibility. This does not mean students look for carbon copies of themselves, but rather that they learn how to find out about other individuals and make comparisons with their own interests, values, and experiences. In this way they grow, developing the ability to take another's perspective, to be supportive and sensitive to both similarities and differences. Hinde (1979) points out the necessity for all students to develop a moral and ethical code to guide their behavior toward others. Among the most important components of the learner's code is the need to develop trust, trustworthiness, and loyalty. Not unlike positive interdependence, these qualities serve as the acid test that determines the limits or intensity of a relationship, be it a friendship or professional collaboration.

Another benefit of inclusion and student collaboration is the development of skills that enable learners to deal effectively with conflict. "Conflict resolution requires a student to be able to make known and protect his or her own rights and needs while being sensitive to and respecting the rights and needs of peers" (Stainback, Stainback, & Wilkinson, 1992, p. 9). (A description of how conflict resolution can be fostered was provided in the collaborative skills section of this chapter.)

However, it is important to understand that collaboration between children does not develop through physical integration but must be facilitated, nurtured, and modeled (Guralnick, 1980). Lavoie (1985) states that children will learn more in a 30 second behavior modeling session than in a five-day intensive course. As a result of full collaboration through modeling, facilitation of these skills becomes second nature. Full collaboration provides learners with teachers, administrators, support personnel, community resource persons, and families who are consistently modeling positive interaction, celebration of diversity, moral and ethical codes of trust, trustworthiness and loyalty, and conflict resolution.

Reflect for a Moment

How do you think children learn to make fun of each other? Is it just the result of their age, or is there some other source of learning? Are children born to help each other, or do they learn that behavior?

Families

Families are a necessary component in the development of a collaborative school ethic. Because the idea of full inclusion and collaboration is new for many, offering up exciting possibilities and scary unopened doors, it is imperative that educators empower families to share their ideal of what is possible for their child or children (Buswell & Schaffner, 1990). Parents bring a great deal to this process because they have a much clearer perspective on the totality of the child's life, concerned not just with the present day but how happy and productive their adult child will become.

Empowerment of families provides them the opportunity to share with administrators, educators, and other school personnel three fundamental attitudes that promote and support inclusion of children not only in their own families but in the full range of school life. *Unconditional acceptance* and *commitment* are two of the attitudes directly tied to family inclusion (Biklen, 1985). Children are accepted by their families just as they are and are supported in their efforts to become successful. Educators must extend this attitude or belief to the school community. A third attitude is families' ability to "focus upon the capabilities or strengths of the child rather than the challenges" (Buswell & Schaffner, 1990, p. 222). This has to be the essence of any learning experience and any environment that hopes to promote learning.

Communities

Another essential player in the development of inclusive schools and the collaborative ethic is the community as a whole. Communities can help to provide people with a sense of belonging. Additionally, the community holds an untapped wealth of knowledge, experiences, and resources. As Callie Collins noted, teaching in an inclusive school means much more than going into her classroom and closing the door. It involves having Joe the postman come in to discuss how the community streets are organized and visiting Pam's great-grandmother in the nursing home to hear about the community's history. Field trips to local industries are fundamental if students are to learn how industrial development has impacted on community growth and environment.

Reflect for a Moment

How involved was your community in your classroom? How many members of the community do you recall visiting your classroom? How many field trips did you take to different places in your community?

Educators

Graden and Bauer (1992) point out that to build a successful collaborative ethic and an inclusive school, all educators must be "responsible for all students, rather than being responsible for a category of students (e.g., 'special' and 'regular' educators are responsible only for their particular students)" (p. 86). This must be an essential aim and philosophy for educators who engage in full collaboration. As previously mentioned, teachers must relinquish ownership of a group of students and assume instructional responsibility for all students. This may be the most difficult hurdle for the collaborative process. Educators traditionally have been given complete custody of their class, with visitors often regarded as unwelcomed annoyances. Any college supervisor involved in the placement of practicum students or student teachers can share the frustration of encountering educators who were unwilling to allow preservice teachers into their classrooms. This denial of opportunity does not generally come from educators' lack of confidence but rather an inability or unwillingness to allow an outsider to work with their children. Unfortunately, this problem does not just develop for the preservice teacher but also for support personnel who wish to provide in-class services rather than pulling children out.

Support Personnel

Perhaps nowhere is the need for collaboration more obvious than in the area of support personnel who provide specialized services to children. Individual children display a remarkable variety of specialized needs. If all children in a school district are to have their special needs met, a comprehensive system of related services must be in place. Only when the professionals in supportive roles are treated as essential contributors will full collaboration be possible.

Although most educators think of therapists, counselors and specialists as support personnel, it is important to include all who work with children, including custodians, office staff, and cafeteria workers. Support is inclusive, but it can be counterproductive without collaboration. York, Giangreco, Vandercook, and Mac-Donald (1992) break down support into four types: (1) *resource,* or tangibles (computers, funds, professional journals, peer tutors), (2) *moral,* or interactions that validate the worth of individuals, (3) *technical,* or in-service and peer coaching, and (4) *evaluation,* or help with assessment of other support that will drive decision making.

The inclusive school includes each of these types of support. In fact, all who work with children in an inclusive school will more likely than not demonstrate true support, caring deeply about children and their families, keeping children in focus as the primary players in the educational forum, acknowledging efforts of colleagues, and providing instructional experiences that promote positive interdependence and active learning for all students.

Supportive personnel identified for an individual student's individualized education plan (IEP) are charged with the responsibility of enhancing the student's progress toward specific developmental behaviors. Despite the fact that several student needs require such assistance, Biklen (1987) and Giangreco and Eichinger (1990) urge collaborative educators to provide only the necessary supports. Even in an inclusive school, support services normally reduce the time students can interact socially, disrupt the flow of learning in classrooms, confuse families, and complicate the communications network among educators. Furthermore, regardless of the supportive person's expertise, the effectiveness of support depends equally on that person's ability to collaborate.

Administrators

The educational administrator is the person responsible for articulating the mission of the school district and assuring congruence among the actions of the educators, support personnel, students and the philosophy. In this critical position to shape the organizational structure and values of the school, the administrator may facilitate or obstruct the development of an inclusive environment.

Administrators may, through their placement of children within neighborhood schools, facilitate learner friendships and collaboration. In a study of superintendents' attitudes about the inclusion of students classified as severely and profoundly disabled learners in neighborhood school and general education classrooms, Stainback, Stainback, and Stainback (1988) found that 50.5 percent agreed with inclusion, whereas only 15.5 percent disagreed. By maintaining oversight that children remain in their neighborhood schools, participation in afterschool programs and activities becomes more feasible (Brown, Long, Udarvi-Solner, Davis, Van Deventer, Algren, Johnson, Gruenewald, & Jorgensen, 1989; Hamre-Nietupski, McDonald, & Nietupski, 1992). Additionally, administrators can develop afterschool social opportunities that allow all learners to interact.

Administrators also set the tone for inclusion and collaboration within a school. The principal in Stephanie's school believed strongly in total inclusion and the promotion of positive cooperative social interactions. As a result, the educators in this 350-student elementary school "had a heightened awareness of the social aspects of education and focused on promoting positive relationships among students" (Hamre-Nietupski, McDonald, & Nietupski, 1992, p. 8).

Administrators must recognize that they are driven not only by their own assumptions and beliefs about the goals of inclusive education, but also by their faculties' and students' abilities to achieve these goals (Villa & Thousand, 1990). Administrators who embrace the three fundamental assumptions of total inclusion—

> (1) all children can learn, (2) all children have the right to be educated with their peers in age-appropriate heterogeneous classrooms within their local schools, and (3) it is the responsibility of the school system to meet the diverse educational and psychological needs of all students. (Villa & Thousand, 1990, p. 202)

—need to help their faculties and students understand these assumptions. The provision of multiple and extensive in-service and the development of activities will help expose all members of the school community to theoretical, ethical, and data-based support for inclusion and collaboration.

To further foster support for inclusion and collaboration, the administration needs to encourage school and community members to participate in developing the school's mission. A sense of "ownership" is more likely to emerge in those persons directly involved in the decision-making process and the development of inclusionary constructs.

Reflect for a Moment

Think back to your favorite principal. What are three words you would use to describe her or him?

School Boards

School boards help administrators foster an inclusive school climate by providing both moral and financial support. A school board that truly believes in the concept of inclusion allows administrators to promote the continued education of their staff and freedom to structure the time needed to collaborate. School boards, like administrators, are in a position to shape the inclusive school and develop the needed school-community link. Opening up schools to become once again the focal point of the community structure is a critical feature of total inclusion that the school board can bring about. In fact, the National Association for State Boards of Education has published a report that calls for state boards to create fully inclusive education systems (Viadero, 1992). The report recommends setting uniform standards for the education of all students and calls for teacher licensure that requires candidates to be prepared to teach children with or without disabilities.

HOW?

Team building and networking are essential to the development of a collaborative culture. Developing collaborative teams and networks calls in turn for necessary changes in attitudes, school structure, and utilization of resources. Stainback and Stainback (1990) believe that although most parents, professionals, students, and advocates agree with the movement to educate all students in an inclusive environment on a philosophical and social justice level, there have been major difficulties implementing the collaborative ethic.

In some schools, teachers who are not fully committed to inclusion and its philosophy are asked to teach in inclusive classrooms. In others, teachers are not given adequate training or advance notice, resulting in their understandable resistance or indignation. Some schools create inclusive groups of classrooms within a traditional school structure, and two often conflicting service systems emerge. Often the amount of time needed to collaborate effectively is not provided, and teachers feel inadequately prepared to meet the educational needs of whole groups of students. For true inclusion to take place, three major aspects of the profession must be carefully transformed: professional attitudes must be healthy, the basic school structure needs to be reconstructed, and resources should be redistributed.

Attitudes

Teacher commitment, fundamental to the development of collaborative teamwork, can be hampered before individuals even enter the profession. Traditional teacher education divides and separates college students into majors in which they are taught to focus their study on different groups of school children. General education majors are in some cases actually taught to exclude certain children from their instructional planning; they subsequently devalue groups of children, making full collaboration a very difficult process once they enter the profession. Conversely, special education majors are typically taught to plan only for children with disabilities and become focused primarily on children's limitations. These teachers-to-be also come to view children with disabilities as their sole responsibility and feel threatened when collaboration activities draw them or the children they teach into general classroom programs. Furthermore, because traditional teacher education programs fail to address multicultural issues, beginning teachers from both programs are likely to neglect children from minority groups.

Traditional practices are being altered at some teacher education colleges such as Syracuse University, Keene [NH] State College, and the University of Vermont (Meyer & Biklen, 1992; Whittier & Hewit, 1993) in which programmatic barriers are being dismantled and students are preparing to teach all children. These inclusive teacher education programs emphasize full collaboration activities and provide school-based practicum experiences with collaborative teams of educators. Such changes in teacher education are intended to build a commitment to teaching all students among preservice teachers.

Reflect for a Moment

Examine the teacher education program at your institution. Is there coursework that focuses on professional collaboration, team processing, or inclusive education?

Johnson, Johnson, Holubec, and Roy (1984) delineate four levels of social skills that collaborative team members use at various stages of group development: forming, functioning, formulating, and fermenting. All four levels involve the exploration and redefinition of personal and professional attitudes. Although members of a team will be at varying levels in their collaborative skills, newly established teams should be expected to focus on *forming* skills (see Figure 5.1 for the timeline), which enhance the building of trust and facilitate the sharing of ideas, resources, and feelings.

Functioning skills develop as the team continues to meet. The growth of communication and leadership skills enables the collaborative team to organize and manage activities so that tasks are completed and group integrity is maintained. Throughout this level of development, team members are encouraged to assume individual responsibility for effective team work. Collaborative teams will also want to *formulate* the specific skills necessary to stimulate creative problem solving and decision making. Additionally, they will explore new methods for creating deeper comprehension of unfamiliar information.

Evidence that the collaborative team has successfully managed conflict and controversy by uncovering divergent perspectives and developing new solutions indicates, finally, that *fermenting* has taken place: "The competence and confidence of individual team members in handling conflicts increases as a function of a positive attitude toward and an appreciation for differences of opinion within the team" (Thousand & Villa, 1991, p. 12).

Collaborative relationships cannot be forced on teachers or parents. Many of the collaborative skills discussed earlier in this chapter will take time to foster among certain educators. In order to build committed collaborative teams among parents and in-service professionals, highly interactive workshops and extended educational programs are, of course, important. Just as critical is the allocation of time for parents and educators to engage in formal and informal discussions with others who are knowledgeable about collaboration and inclusion, to spend time with children with disabilities, and basically to become acquainted with a more diverse student population. Both of these strategies are aimed at helping parents and professionals develop positive attitudes toward collaboration and inclusive schooling practices.

January	**Communication of Program Objectives** Information meetings with school board members, administrators, teachers, support personnel. Support and involvement are sought.
February	**Continue Communication (see January)** **Student Identification** All students with special needs are identified, and special needs are documented and reviewed.
March	**Continue Communication*** **Teacher Identification and Inservice** Special educators, general educators, and support personnel who wish to work collaboratively are identified and brought into the process. Inservice for these educators begins.
April	**Curriculum Planning** Team members examine and analyze curriculum outcomes by subject area. Units of instruction are identified, broken down, and sequenced. Strategies for delivery of curriculum with varied activities that meet different student needs are selected. Development of instructional materials. Authentic assessments are developed.
May	**Curriculum Planning** Continuation of above procedures.
June	**Curriculum Implementation** Schedule is established for collaborative meetings. **Curriculum Planning** Continuation of April activities.
August	**Problem Solving** Team members determine process for problem solving.
September	**Curriculum Implementation** The planning is implemented. Team members constantly learn from each other, redefining their roles, sharing talents and expertise, and combining strategies. Assessment of student outcomes is continuous. Parent contact is instituted and maintained.
October	**Program Evaluation** Multidisciplinary meetings are scheduled for teachers, parents, administrators, school board members, support personnel and students to discuss successes and concerns. Modifications are suggested and made when needed.

*Continue Communication through October.

FIGURE 5.1 One Approach to Planning a Collaborative Instructional Model

School Structure

A second challenge to parents and professionals who are planning collaborative networks lies in overcoming the traditional school structure in which educators work in isolation. This physical isolation extends to behavior in the classroom, where educators function as sole authority and use a relatively directive style with students. The transition from such solitary roles, which lead educators to believe that their problems exist in isolation, to collegial, collaborative relationships, in which discussions, negotiations, and mutual understandings are expected, is necessary for collaboration and inclusion to take place. Many other current school structures and roles, such as committees on special education, must be thoroughly reconceptualized. Existing roles on such committees and in schools in general contribute to the current dual system of educational services.

To influence these traditional structures schoolwide, it is important to use a systematic approach, beginning with establishing a school philosophy that places a priority on collaboration. The role of the administration and the school board is essential in creating a philosophy that supports not only collaboration but the placement of all children in the general classroom and the community beyond. If educators and parents are committed to such priorities, their encouragement and support can enable administrators and school boards to adopt an appropriate district philosophy statement.

Stainback and Stainback (1992) suggest the establishment of support networks to complement such a philosophy, including cooperative learning activities, buddy systems, peer tutoring, student assistance teams, and friendships for students along with team teaching, teacher assistance teams, professional peer collaboration, and planning time for educators. Cooperative learning activities, buddy systems, and peer tutoring—all strategies that allow students to interact productively with each other in pursuit of academic goals—will be examined in more detail in the chapters on teaching strategies.

Friendships have been cited in the literature on support networks as a major ingredient in successful integration (Forest, 1987; York & Vandercook, 1988). "In the final analysis, the only true protection and advocacy that any individual has is caring peers, friends, family and community members" (Strully & Strully, p. x, in Stainback & Stainback, 1990). These friendships vary greatly, just as children's friendships naturally do, but they can, to a certain extent, be encouraged and facilitated by educators and parents. The techniques are many, including pairing students without friends with popular students (Forest, 1987), seating these types of students near each other, planning lessons designed to allow classmates to report each other's positive characteristics to the class through drawings or essays, or focusing on health topics that emphasize the support needed by each person that can be provided by classmates (Stainback, Stainback, & Wilkinson, 1992).

Classes can include welcoming committees who extend social invitations to out-of-school events to new students or ongoing peer support committees who work on ways to help all class members gain support and experience success. Student assistance teams, composed of school personnel and students, can help form a circle of friends, people who will stand up for one another. Adults working with children can, on occasion, simply suggest to students that they work together. Amid these strategies, it is always wise to reinforce student actions that are supportive of others, either verbally or through some other mode of communicating appreciation. Students who lack friendship can themselves be helped to develop a positive interactive style, establish common interests with peers, take others' perspectives, provide support themselves, develop their own code of conduct, learn to resolve conflict, and actually practice these friendship skills (Stainback, Stainback, & Wilkinson, 1992).

Educators can also present learning about personal similarities and differences through curriculum material in all subject areas. Such lessons will help all classmates realize that students without friends often have many of the same interests, beliefs, and dreams that they have themselves. Differences among students can and should always be used in constructive situations so that an individual student's uniqueness is seen as a positive contribution to the smooth functioning of the class.

Among the most powerful influences on the development of friendships among classmates is the behavior exhibited by those adults present. When every class member experiences positive interaction with adults in the class, both directly and through observing others, a climate is created that promotes repeated positive interactions among students. This modeling extends to the ways in which the adults interact with each other and other adults in the school community.

It is not always necessary for a student to have lots of friends, and none of the friendships nurtured in classrooms will endure unless they are voluntarily maintained. Collaborative teams, however, are more effectively developed in schools where students openly support each other. School structures that actively support these networks are a key ingredient in building teamwork.

Reflect for a Moment

Do you now or have you ever had a friend with a significant disability? How did you meet? What did you find out about that friend?

Support networks that focus on adult relationships are crucial to team building. Team teaching is defined by Thousand and Villa (1990) as "an organizational and instructional arrangement of two or more members of the school and greater community who distribute among themselves planning, instructional, and evaluation responsibilities for the same students on a regular basis for an extended period of time" (pp. 152–153). The purpose of such a collaborative arrangement is to increase the individualization of instruction and the opportunity for students to learn collaboratively with same-age peers in inclusive schools. When team teaching takes into account the major features of a team (positive interdependence, individual accountability, face-to-face interaction, collaborative skills, and group processing), the instructional benefits are unlimited. They may include more active learning experiences, expanded and enriched curriculum, more peer interaction, increased opportunities for cooperative learning, and more comprehensive social and cognitive challenges. In fact, adult teaching teams closely resemble cooperative learning groups among students.

Strategies among teaching teams vary, but they may include weekly or daily planning meetings, shared classroom space, jointly selected assessment procedures, shared expertise and teaching ideas, individual preparation time and space, complementary areas of professional concentration, coordinated unit planning, and jointly scheduled parent conferences. It is also not uncommon for other adults to contribute to the success of a teaching team, most notably teaching assistants who can come into the classroom and organize student groups and peer tutoring situations.

Resources

Full collaboration enhances the inclusive education system in a variety of ways. The development of a collaborative ethos contributes to making an inclusive school a resource attractor. A **resource attractor** is an attribute (collaboration) that tends to attract other resources because it gives the inclusive school an advantage in competition for these resources (Johnson & Johnson, 1987). The collaborative ethos will draw resources such as federal or state grants for the improvement of education, private funds from business and industry, and volunteers to the inclusive school.

Additionally, collaboration promotes the innovative and effective utilization of resources. Schenkat (1988) reports that billions of dollars and hundreds of thousands of personnel are spent working in educational programs that are segregated or compensatory. With collaboration, all of these funds and personnel can be incorporated into the inclusive educational system. Specialized knowledge from all educational personnel will be shared, class size can be reduced, and supportive networks can be developed.

Educators who previously worked in self-contained classrooms (be they general or special education) can now be freed up to become team teachers. Services that were provided to a few students in segregated settings will be brought into the classroom, increasing the number of students who can benefit from these services and personnel. Additionally, materials previously reserved for selected groups of students will now be available to all students.

An additional and often neglected resource are parents. Parents are an invaluable resource to any educational system and the collaborative ethos calls for increased involvement of all parents in the education of their children. Stafford Middle School, for example, relies heavily on parent volunteers to conduct their annual whale watch trip to Boston. Having parents working with groups of students on such field trips helps to improve educational outcomes. Parents help to model appropriate interactions and build relationships with the school. Parents provide support to the educational system in other ways as well. They elect school board members and speak with administrators. Parents may develop lobby groups directed at soliciting policy change and additional resources. Parents can also provide insight into their children that educators can use to structure the educational environment.

Reflect for a Moment

Have you ever participated in an extensive field trip with a group from school that included parents? Did you get to know certain other students and parents better as a result of this trip?

THE MANY FACES OF COLLABORATION

The two profiles at the beginning of this chapter demonstrate the differences in school climate and colleagiality when a collaborative culture has been established. However, before an understanding of collaboration and a collaborative culture can be established, a clear distinction must be made about what constitutes true collaboration. A variety of terms have been introduced in the research literature and often times are misinterpreted as being synonymous with collaboration. Distinctions must be drawn among such concepts as consultation, collaborative consultation, peer coaching, and mentoring. Additional distinctions need to be made between the function of collaborative teams and other types of educational teams, such as teacher assistance and prereferral intervention.

To begin the distinction process, *Webster's New Twentieth Century Dictionary* (1990) was consulted to provide definitions of consultation, coaching, mentoring, and collaboration. *Consultation* is defined as seeking the advice of another, taking counsel, whereas *collaboration* is working together with and cooperating with others. Coaching is the process of instructing a person in a subject or preparing a person for a specific thing. Mentoring is the formal and comprehensive counseling of another person, typically employing advice and cautions. These definitions are, of course, simplifications of complex processes and must be explored in depth to understand the true differences among them.

Some have suggested that the distinction between consultation and collaboration is one of expert and colleagial consultative relationships, each with clearly different structures and definitions that are mistakenly referred to simply as consultation (Phillips & McCullough, 1990; Johnson & Pugach, 1992). However, the distinction must go one step further and distinguish among consultation, peer coaching, mentoring, collaborative consultation, collaborative teaching, and full collaboration.

Consultation

The expert form of collaboration, **consultation,** pairs a person with a consultee because of the former's special knowledge and ability to listen and provide possible solutions. "Central to this relationship is the special expertise of the consultant, without which there would be no basis for the relationship" (Johnson & Pugach, 1992, p. 217). This consultation process has played a central role in several configurations, including teacher consultation (Knight, Meyers, Paolucci-Whitcomb, Hasazi, & Nevin, 1981), teacher assistance teams (Hayek, 1987), and prereferral assistance teams (Graden, Casey, & Bronstrom, 1985).

Consultation is further seen as a special delivery model (Friend, 1988). Consultation certification patterns have been developed for special education teachers, with school districts arranging staff development opportunities not for all personnel but generally only for special services persons. Information consultation has been developed almost exclusively in school and counseling psychology and special education literatures. "Professionals who support consultation services are sometimes mistakenly assumed to be advocates of the wholesale return of all mildly and moderately handicapped students to general education settings" (Friend, 1988, p. 11). The restrictive nature of the consultation service delivery model eliminates the active participation of many school professionals. General educators are often relegated to the position of passive recipient of information about the learners with whom they are actively involved. It is important to understand, therefore, that consultation in this form is not a viable service delivery model for collaborative and inclusive schools.

Brian has been identified as having a learning disability and has been placed in a regular fifth grade class for all academic instruction. Mrs. Jacobsen, the consulting teacher, is certified in special education and is familiar with Brian's learning needs. She meets every other day with Brian in the fifth grade class and teaches his reading group, which includes two other students also having difficulty with reading. Mrs. Jacobsen tells Sadie Standish, the fifth grade teacher, what to do to adapt other lessons that require Brian to read independently.

Reflect for a Moment

Think of a person whom you consult about something. Now think of a person whom you meet and work together with on a task (it need not be school related).

Peer Coaching

Peer coaching is the process of instructing a colleague in the subject of effective teaching by using observational data from classroom visitations. As such, it is clearly a form of reciprocal consultation that closely resembles the "expert" model. In some peer coaching arrangements, two teachers will provide each other with instructional suggestions. The purpose of peer coaching is ultimately to improve the educational experience of students in the two classes.

With support from the school administration, Ralph Graves and Anna Newman, two experienced teachers at Standish Elementary, have scheduled visits to each other's classes in order to videotape lessons: Ralph will videotape one of Anna's science lessons, and Anna will videotape one of Ralph's math lessons. Because Ralph has a strong background in science education, he can study the videotape and then meet with Anna to discuss his observations and offer strategies for increasing student learning. Anna's background is mathematics education, and she will follow a similar procedure in assisting Ralph with his math lessons.

Mentoring

In an educational setting, **mentoring** usually involves a veteran teacher and either a beginning teacher or a teacher who is experiencing difficulty in some area of teaching. Mentoring, like peer coaching, exemplifies the "expert" model of consultation. It, too, is designed to improve the educational experience of those students in one teacher's class.

Here is an example of mentoring in the collaborative classroom. It's been a challenging and exciting first year of teaching for Maria Martin. Thank goodness, she thinks, for the mentoring program in her district, and the fantastic support of Joanie Klein, her mentor. They have been scheduled for one half day per week of release time and usually meet in the school conference room, or the nearby library, to examine various aspects of Maria's professional life. They may review Maria's lesson plans, discuss Joanie's observations of Maria's teaching, or examine the effectiveness of her classroom management: one day it may be parent conferences, another day the use of the computer in her classroom. They may visit other classrooms together, or attend in-service as a team. Maria's confidence and competence have grown tremendously during the year, and she is really enjoying her teaching more than she had thought possible.

Collaborative Consultation

From a colleagial perspective, special expertise is not essential for **collaborative consultation.** What is important is that the relationship focus on mutual sharing of a body of knowledge, individual ideas, and the subsequent problem-solving process. In spite of the fact that the process is a shared one, it does result in one person, usually the general classroom teacher, carrying out the plan formulated by the group.

Nevin and colleagues have identified four features of collaborative consultation: (1) because all participants, including the student, have important expertise to contribute, the process is multidirectional; (2) participants share an understanding that the responsibility for determining tasks and relationships is carried by all members and is not the domain of a single leader; (3) all participants are committed to frequent face-to-face interactions in order to distribute leadership, reexamine the effectiveness of their group process skills, and hold each other accountable for predetermined tasks; and (4) they agree to adjust the amount of emphasis placed on tasks versus relationships within the group as a result of individual participants' willingness and ability to support group goals (Nevin, Thousand, Paolucci-Whitcomb, & Villa, 1990).

Phil Kerwin was skeptical at first, but the collaborative consultation that has been in place at his school for two years now seems to be having some positive results. The three teams he has been involved in have all been different, but the most recent, focusing on ways to help Melissa get along with her peers in his third grade class, has been particularly successful. Melissa, her mother, Phil, the resource teacher, and the school counselor all met to solve the problem collectively, working just as hard on communicating with each other as they did on the student's problem. Early on, the group had agreed that Phil, Melissa, the other students in Phil's classroom, and Melissa's mother were the people who had to assume primary responsibility for addressing the problem but that ultimately Melissa was responsible for her own conduct. Although this approach seemed foreign at first to Phil, he realized that it was having a noticeably positive effect on Melissa's social skills, not only at committee meetings but in the third grade class, too.

Collaborative Teaching

Collaborative teaching, according to Wiedmeyer and Lehman (1991), is "a cooperative and interactive process between two teachers that allows them to develop creative solutions to mutual problems" (p. 7). The assumption is that each educator brings valuable knowledge to each step of the problem-solving process. Collaborative teaching has emerged as a response to problems in the delivery of instruction to students whose disabilities are compounded when they are separated from other students. It has also been established on the basis of the general educator's need for assistance.

Peggy Robinson and Gary Van Heusen both had strong academic backgrounds in English and social studies, respectively, and through their teaching experience had come to realize that most of their curriculum could be taught in an integrated fashion. They began meeting and planned a teaching schedule for their tenth graders that involved groupings and strategies to include students who had previously left their classes for resource room assistance. This small group of students, most of whom were identified as having learning disabilities, would no longer miss out on any English or social studies instruction. Peggy and Gary knew they would have to continue to schedule a study skills class for these students, so they planned one for the entire class and used their curriculum as the focus for teaching study skills. The data, although denoting only short-term results thus far, were encouraging. The cooperative learning tasks, close monitoring of students' seatwork time, and expanded repertoire of teaching methods and materials they were jointly bringing to their teaching all contributed to some enthusiastic class discussions and activities.

Beyond their own collaborative teaching, Gary and Peggy found that Joy Adair, the resource teacher, was more than happy to collaborate by adjusting her schedule so that she could work with groups of students in their classes during their lessons. Joyce's assistance was greatly appreciated by both Peggy and Gary because they found that all their students, regardless of ability, could now work with each other on the various thematic tasks they had planned during the year.

Full Collaboration

Full collaboration differs from all the above processes in a number of ways. First, it is established to enhance schooling for all students, not just those with special needs (Nevin, Thousand, Paolucci-Whitcomb, & Villa, 1990). Second, it relies not on the roles of the people involved (general educators, special educators, school psychologist, etc.), but on the knowledge and skill each person brings to the process (Graden, 1989). Third, though the school that utilizes collaborative consultation is characterized by numerous ad hoc problem-solving committees, the fully collaborative school establishes problem solving as a responsibility of all community members from the outset, instilling in the process an across-the-board commitment to continuous problem solving.

Ellis (1990) suggests that teacher collaboration allows opportunities for reflection, interaction, and shared learning. Core characteristics for collaboration include carefully managed indirect service delivery for students; a positive, trusting, confidential relationship in which individuals operate as equals; a voluntary colleagial relationship with the right to reject ideas generated; and active involvement and empowerment for all participants (Gutkin & Curtis, 1990; Graden & Bauer, 1992).

In addition, the concept of full collaboration extends to what Phillips and McCullough (1990) call a collaborative school ethic, evidenced by joint responsibility and accountability for all problems, belief in mutual benefits resulting from pooling talents and resources, belief in the time needed to solve problems, and belief in the value of collaboration correlates (morale, alternative solutions, and cohesion). In this manner, the school community with a collaborative ethic is an inclusive school. A school cannot be inclusive without the collaborative ethic; likewise, the collaborative ethic cannot exist without the inclusive school.

Because full collaboration is the essence of the inclusive school community, then, the goal of such collaboration is not only to remediate current concerns related to a student's performance or functioning but, more important, to prevent future problems for that student and all other students: "Inclusive schools tend to build upon the notion that the school is a community of learners and educators. This sense of community is based on the commitment that all educators are responsible for the success of all students" (Graden & Bauer, 1992, p. 86).

Callie Collins is part of a fully collaborative team. It is clear from the focus of her team's energy that all students, not just the students with disabilities, are being considered. The different professionals who make up the team bring knowledge, ideas, and skills, not just titles and areas of expertise, to the team process. Whereas Mr. Bordeau, Sadie Standish's principal, talked about teamwork and appointed committees whenever needed, the teams in Callie's school were established before the school year started and became a fundamental unit of pedagogy in the school ethos. The spirit of enthusiasm that has emerged from the teamwork has extended to the students in several classes and all students appear to feel valued.

Reflect for a Moment

It is very important at this point to distinguish between full collaboration and the other forms of professional teamwork. A quick review of all the teaming strategies will be helpful here. Though all these strategies have value, the inclusive school operates most effectively with full collaboration.

Problem Solving

Problem-solving adequacy must be high in a full collaboration setting. Problems need to be resolved in a manner that eliminates them permanently with the exertion of a minimal amount of energy. Although problem solving is central to all the processes described, it operates differently within the various models. Problem solving in the collaborative skills model has already been described. In the consultation, peer coaching, and mentoring models, a teacher brings a problem to the attention of an expert, coach, or mentor, who provides potential solutions. In the collaborative consultation and collaborative teaching models, problem solving is still the foundation for teaming, but the solution is arrived at by utilizing the expertise of each of the persons involved.

In these two models, teams are created in order to solve problems. In a fully collaborative school culture, teamwork is established before any students enter the picture and before any problems are evident. At the forefront of full collaboration are teaching teams, curriculum design, and instructional methodology and adaptation, rather than a situational concept demanding consultation or teamwork from individuals. What brings a team together is not individual students, but the belief that schools must proceed as a community if they are to succeed. Thus, education for all students within the community becomes the instructional responsibility of every teacher. Fully collaborative schools have procedures in place for sensing problems, implementing solutions, and evaluating their effectiveness. Thus problem solving is just another activity undertaken by the collaborative team rather than their sole reason for existence. The fact that full collaboration is not undertaken simply as a reaction to a problem assists team members in developing innovative methods of troubleshooting.

LEADERSHIP

On a broad level, a leader is someone in a group who "exerts more influence on other members than they exert on him" (Johnson & Johnson, 1987, p. 48). However, studies of leadership have found that this influence may be varied and circumstantial. Although extensive research has identified several types of leadership, three basic approaches can be distinguished: autocratic, laissez-faire, and democratic.

The *autocratic* model of leadership, in which the leader dictates orders and determines policy without input from group members, may be necessary when an urgent decision has to be made. The *laissez-faire* model, in which the group makes decisions independent of the leader, may work best in situations where the group is clearly ready to decide on an action and has the resources needed to implement this action. The *democratic* model, in which the leader encourages interaction, consideration, and cooperation and policies and actions are determined by group discussion, usually works best whenever considerable member commitment to a potential action is crucial.

Given the magnitude of change inherent in the shift to a fully collaborative school, it appears that some form of democratic leadership would be most effective in this situation. Helping group members cooperate with each other in establishing both long-term goals and short-term strategies is a primary responsibility for collaborative educators in leadership positions. Included in this group of leaders may be district administrators, school board members, members of a collaboration task force, and perhaps a support facilitator.

Administrators

Several strategies exist for administrators who wish to promote collaboration in their school structure. A prerequisite to the success of any strategy, however, is the strength of one's beliefs about the importance of collaboration and inclusion. Articulating for oneself, and then among school staff, a clear philosophy about these fundamental practices, though not sufficient by itself, can facilitate the administrator's efforts with the strategies that follow. These educational leaders should keep in mind that no single strategy will suffice and that individual schools and school districts will find success with their own unique combinations of strategies.

In-Service and Professional Development

Workshops, guest speakers, seminars, and college courses can all provide data to educators on current practices that exemplify collaboration and/or inclusion. This information, if accompanied by a theoretical link, can spark interest and generate a higher level of involvement among educators. Articles documenting successful collaboration can be distributed among faculty and become the focus of small or large group discussions. Administrators can also enhance thinking about collaboration and inclusion by facilitating visits to schools in which successful practices are already in place, where educators can meet and discuss these issues with colleagues from the host schools.

Administrators should always construct a comprehensive in-service agenda rather than the all-too-common "one shot" sessions. This may require several years in some cases, but it is critical if educators are to have the opportunity to fully internalize the collaborative/inclusive ethic. Full participation from the administrator is important during the in-service period. In many cases, administrators will also benefit from comprehensive in-service related to their role as curriculum and instruction supervisors and managers in the inclusive school.

Reflect for a Moment

Will you go beyond this chapter in your search for a fuller understanding of collaboration and inclusion? Articles and chapters written by Stainback and Stainback, Thousand and Villa, Johnson and Pugach, Friend and Cook, Wang and Reynolds, Forest, and Gartner and Lipsky will help you in your search.

School/District Philosophy

Another vital area in which administrators can build support is the development and/or reexamination of a school or district philosophy that recognizes and supports collaboration and inclusion. Immediate and substantial involvement of school faculty, staff, and members of the community in this central decision-making process is an effective way to build collaborative "ownership" of the subsequent implementation of collaboration and inclusion practices.

There will, in most cases, be clear differences of opinion about full collaboration and inclusion because of the diversity of individuals being charged with this important task. Such differences can be embraced, and the ensuing risk minimized, if some members of the group already have a thorough understanding of collaborative and inclusive concepts and all have opportunities to become familiar with the theory and data supportive of such a philosophy.

Esprit de Corps

Any time a school is successful, as a community, in taking a new direction, it is partly the result of a sense of excitement shared by everyone, an enthusiasm that energizes the members of a collaborative school community. Administrators can enhance this esprit de corps by committing time and resources to recognizing groups and individuals whose activities are highly collaborative.

Evidence of such an effort from an administrator includes frequent recognition of groups as opposed to individuals, significant time spent with teachers, staff and students rather than with other administrators, knowing what kinds of incentives different people value, and recognizing the contributions that all people can potentially make to the collaborative/inclusive ethos. The school administrator can take a variety of actions to contribute to the esprit de corps in a school or district working toward full collaboration (Villa and Thousand, 1990):

- Sending brief handwritten notes of praise or appreciation
- Bringing school visitors to classrooms and highlighting the collaborative atmosphere with educators and students present
- Creating and supporting opportunities for educators to present their collaborative work to school boards, community groups, and colleagues at meetings of professional organizations
- Making sure that teachers, staff, students, and community members are well represented on all hiring and planning committees
- Inviting teachers to serve in leadership roles as mentors to college students, new teachers, and community volunteers
- Developing and supporting collaboration among educators beyond the school day in the form of courses taught in the district, professional retreats, or summer workshops

OVERCOMING TRADITIONAL BARRIERS

Several obstacles to full collaboration and inclusion are present within the organization of schools. Curriculum is dictated by grade level, not by individual needs. Tracking still abounds. Special education operates as a separate system, with its own policies and programs. Little, if any, time is slotted specifically for educators to plan together.

Strategies for enhancing collaboration and inclusion within the prevailing organizational structure must address the major components of the school system.

First, administrators must lead the way in acknowledging the essential sameness of curriculum for all students. All adults within a community, with the help of educational leadership, can come to realize that curriculum and methods of instruction are largely the same for special education as they are for general education. What is different is the place a given student falls along that continuum of curriculum. Adults can be helped to see this sameness if administrators assist them in examining the content of the curriculum and assign them instructional responsibility for common content, regardless of their former role as special or general educator.

A second major strategy that administrators can work with concerns the roles of various staff personnel. A successful leader will clearly communicate his or her expectations for adult-student and adult-adult interactions and support higher levels of collaboration in those interactions. Certain interactions can lead to increased adult-student ratios in classrooms as well as more frequent collaborative exchanges on behalf of students who might otherwise be segregated.

One model for redefining roles consists of four steps (Villa & Thousand, 1990). The first step is to identify a group of adults willing to change their job functions, a group that includes special and general educators. Next, this group must receive training in collaborative techniques for planning and delivering instruction to heterogeneous groups of learners. During this step administrators must recognize and utilize peer teaching opportunities and understand the importance of continuous professional development beyond the induction stage. The third step, establishing a timeline for implementing the changes, is perhaps the most challenging for the administrator. Gathering information from group members about the efficacy of various components of change and developing a plan of action that ultimately comes from the core group are both activities that require the administrator to be an expert in politics and public relations (Skrtic, 1987). The fourth step in this process requires the administrator to obtain a final commitment from the group about their new job functions. If the process has been highly participative up to this point and group members are given a final opportunity to modify the changes being proposed, it is unlikely that the administrator will have to move to mandate the plan. After the plan is implemented, all those involved will need to engage in ongoing review of its effectiveness and suggest modifications wherever necessary.

A third strategy to help overcome organizational barriers is for administrators to hire new educators who will promote collaboration and inclusion. Such persons can be identified during the hiring process and, once a member of the school community, can enhance the ability of the staff to work together on behalf of a diverse student population.

The fourth strategy focuses on the administrator's ability to bring out the talents of each adult in the community and to encourage them to share their respective areas of expertise. New teachers can be assigned to veterans who can clearly communicate the collaborative ethos of the school, and demonstrate collaborative strategies. Teaching teams can be created, taking into consideration each educator's needs, areas of expertise, personality, and flexibility. The goal is to contribute to the establishment of trusting, professional partnerships that have a positive effect on student success in the classroom. As students move on from year to year, team structures are reexamined for possible reconfiguration; the expanding body of professional services that such teams provide is a significant benefit to all involved. Another way for administrators to fully utilize the talents of educators is to support situation-specific peer visits and observations, in which professionals can become more familiar with each other's roles, or provide instructional assistance to each other.

A final strategy for dealing effectively with organizational barriers is to develop master schedules that fully support collaboration. An important step in constructing such schedules is knowing how educators want to collaborate and how time can be organized to best meet those collaborative needs. Collaborative structures within a school must also be scheduled in concert with schoolwide and districtwide collaborative structures. This scheduling must be highly responsive to professional collaborative needs and will vary from one district or school to the next.

Reflect for a Moment

Do you know of any schools where any of the reforms discussed here are taking place? Alternative grading systems, multiage classrooms, mentoring, collaborative planning time, and other changes are but a few such innovations.

COLLABORATIVE/INCLUSIVE TASK FORCE

If a school community is planning to become highly collaborative and inclusive, it may help to create a task force that will serve as a general advocacy group for collaboration and inclusion efforts (Stainback, Stainback, & Jackson, 1992). This task force will usually include teachers, parents, students, administrators, school board members, and support personnel and will take responsibility for helping other members of the school community understand how to establish and maintain a friendly, compassionate, and inclusive school.

Specifically, the task force can develop a collection of literature and videotapes on collaboration and/or inclusion and make them available to all groups within the community. They may also plan visits to other districts where collaboration and inclusion are being pursued. They may schedule informational workshops or seminars for community members in which invited speakers discuss their experiences with collaboration and inclusion. A colleague who has worked in the classroom for years brings more credibility as a guest speaker than a so-called expert.

One of the most challenging responsibilities of a collaborative/inclusive task force may be the development of a detailed plan for achieving full collaboration and inclusion. Such a plan should address utilization of resources and personnel, in-service education, short- and long-term objectives, and student needs.

Support Facilitators

There may be one person in a school community who is the designated *support facilitator.* Support facilitators are often responsible for organizing support in general classrooms, and they collaborate with teachers and support personnel to enhance full inclusion. During these collaborative meetings, there are no experts, supervisors, or evaluators; each group member contributes to the educational planning.

In practice, support facilitators take on other roles as well. They need to encourage natural support networks in inclusive classrooms by promoting peer interdependence through buddy systems, peer teaching, cooperative learning, and emerging friendships. A second role is as resource persons who will locate needed materials and equipment, communicate instructional needs to other members of the community, utilize personnel strengths for the benefit of all students, and recruit volunteers who can assist in the general classroom. Support facilitators can also be team teachers and offer their own expertise in classrooms through direct instructional experiences with students. In all these capacities, the support facilitator functions as a resource and a leader for all members of the collaborative community.

Reflect for a Moment

A support facilitator does not have to be a special educator. Looking at the role to be filled, what qualifications would you want this person to have?

School Boards

The school board's leadership role has already been described in an earlier section of this chapter. The emergence of fully collaborative inclusive schools in many states and Canadian provinces suggests that many school boards are supportive of collaborative inclusive efforts. This support is crucial in light of the organizational barriers and situational resistance that exist in many communities.

THE ROLE OF THE ADULT/PARENT

"The intergenerational link between adults and youngsters is especially strong as it relates to issues surrounding culture and school success" (Briscoe, 1991, p. 13). Everyone has a role to play in the collaborative educational process of inclusive schools.

"Reaching the family is as important as reaching the child" (Rich, 1987, p. 64). Hansen, Himes, and Meier (1990) found that strong home-school collaboration provides students with support for development and learning. Involvement with the school by a learner's parents enhances his or her chances for success in school (Epstein, 1989) and significantly improves achievement (Henderson, 1987; Kroth & Scholl, 1978; Rich, 1987).

Murphy (1981) demonstrates that learners are not the sole recipients of benefits resulting from parent involvement. Parents also gain, developing improved feelings of self-worth and self-satisfaction and an increased incentive to augment the educational environment in their homes. Home-school collaborations provide parents with an opportunity to learn skills and techniques that enhance interactions with their children. Educators and administrators also benefit from parental collaboration by developing a better understanding of the learners' cultural and familial background. Parents are an invaluable source of information about their children's culture, interests, and needs.

Home-school collaboration provides benefits for the school and community because it promotes improved attitudes and advocacy, not just directed from parents to school but also from school to parents. The Yale Child Study Center (Comer, 1989) found that after school personnel, parents, and community members (from diverse areas of expertise) developed a collaborative ethos, school failure declined. Additionally, parent involvement also creates possibilities for children who have previously been devalued.

Reflect for a Moment

How much were your parents involved in your education? Do you think it would have helped if they were more involved? What keeps adults/parents from taking a greater role in their children's school experience?

Anna Lovich, concerned by the negative attitudes of professionals about her four-year-old daughter Sally, started meeting with other parents unwilling to accept the life sketches drawn for them about their children with disabilities. Anna met the Woronkos, and they brought the Goldsteins, the Goldsteins in turn introduced the Laubachs, and the Laubachs talked with the Perrons . . . . In their search for answers, they encountered several people who had broken the bondage of their labels to become fully participating members of society. Inspired by these models, the group began to question why there was a double standard for children who differed from the "norm."

This small group of parents, determined not to be content with the status quo and wanting an opportunity to voice their convictions and values, founded the Integration Action Group. A Canadian-based group, these families developed the following statement of principles:

- All children can learn and develop.
- All children have the right to live at home in a family.
- All children have the right to share educational experiences with others their own age.
- All children have the right to neighborhood friends and relationships.
- All children have the right to supports and services needed, and these should be available in the neighborhood school, in regular classroom settings.
- All children have the right to an education that will prepare them to live and work in the real world.
- All children have the right to acquire the daily social and coping skills that develop through life in the community.

- All children have the right to be "just one of the kids."
- Successful integration of a child with extra needs benefits not only the child, but also his or her friends and peers, the school system, and society as a whole. (Forest, 1986, p. 6)

Be a child physically or mentally impaired, from a cultural minority, awkward, or poor, the vision that child's parents have is the same one all parents have for any children. Although the Integration Action Group focuses on parents and their roles in the process of developing inclusive schools, it is crucial to understand every adult has an important part to play. Teachers, social workers, administrators, businesspersons, politicians, or interested community members—the greater the diversity of those who become involved in the collaborative ethos, the more accessible and permanent change will be.

Inclusive and collaborative education will allow students to learn with and from each other, their teachers, parents, and community members (Falvey, Coots, & Bishop, 1990). The opportunity for students to interact with adults from the community other than their parents or teachers is essential in an inclusive environment. Adult volunteers in the schools come from a diversity of backgrounds and provide students with valuable models. A child who never experiences an adult volunteering his/her time may never learn what a valuable contribution volunteering can be, contributing not just to those receiving the service but to the person giving of himself or herself. Grandparents who come to read during story time, local artists in residence who share their talents, a Native American story teller who spins tales providing both ethnic and moral richness, all contribute to the learning process. Conversely, all these volunteers also learn from sharing their time and talents with students; students change the adults they come into contact with just as the adult contributes to the changes in students. This sharing does not always have to occur within the confines of the school. A local dairy farm, nature center, post office, bank, or restaurant can become a classroom.

DIVERSITY AND THE COMMUNITY

Learners do not exist in an educational vacuum. Children leave school at the end of the day and return home to their parents or other adult caregivers. A very important resource for the success of inclusive schools and motivation for collaboration may be overlooked if educators fail to recognize family structures as they are defined by the cultural group and/or community. The role of the family and its strength within different cultural communities must be recognized and used to achieve positive educational changes. To ignore the social context (community) in which the learner operates is to eliminate a vital connection required for educational success.

Fundamental to the development of both inclusive schools and communities and the building of a collaborative culture is a celebration of **diversity.** Successful educational experiences for diverse populations will never be an obtainable goal unless educators understand and recognize that each learner has a set of individual needs and that the learning environment must be altered to accommodate these needs (Briscoe, 1991). For the diverse populations of students involved in inclusive schools, understanding the elements of their culture and their influences on the learning process is a necessity. All learners must be allowed to participate fully in the educational process without being made to believe that important cultural norms must be rejected for them to be successful.

Diversity must be viewed as a strength, to be reinforced as a positive characteristic that is desired and valued. The aim, then, is not to be oblivious to diversity, because avoidance creates in children the belief that differences should not be discussed. Neither students nor adult members of a community can develop a sense of belonging if they feel it necessary to ignore diversity among their peers. Diversity becomes a source of weakness when those who are obese, use wheelchairs, celebrate different holidays, come from single-parent families, speak a different dialect or language, or come from different ethnic backgrounds are ignored instead of having their differences explored and talked about in a learning context. Inclusive communities would lack character and teaching power if everyone looked and thought the same way.

"A community is not only a geographic location, but also a network of interactions between people. Schools are viewed as both communal entities and elements of the surrounding community" (Falvey, Coots, & Bishop, 1990, p. 231). Creation of a collaborative community that encompasses diversity is a complex process, and a variety of considerations must be examined. Involvement in the collaborative community must be structured in such a way that enables all participants to share a sense of responsibility in the educational process. Educators, administrators, school board members, and community residents must be able to identify important goals and problems that are commonly shared and need joint problem solving to effect change. Additionally, specific organizational structures and schedules must be developed to ensure that formal collaboration occurs.

Since school staff often live in communities apart from where they teach, it is essential that an awareness of the community in which the school exists be developed. Additionally, school staff must become actively involved in all school-community activities. Staff involvement provides community residents with reassurance that their unique and diverse needs are being taken into consideration for more than just an "8 to 3" daily time span. The educational process takes on greater importance when the members of a community feel that they are valuable contributors to the schools around them.

Reflect for a Moment

When you were in school, did you see any of your teachers in the community? How many? What other roles did these teachers fill in the community?

The development of a community in which members actively participate in everyday activities and care about and assist one another is essential to creating a collaborative community-school relationship. Today it is possible for teenagers to finish high school without ever having been asked to participate responsibly in life activities in or out of the school, without ever having been encouraged to spend time and recognize the wisdom of the elderly, pick up a littered playground, help paint the house of a person who is disabled, or teach a young child how to throw a Frisbee (Boyer, 1983). Learners need to be encouraged to develop solutions to critical community issues such as gang violence, homelessness, pollution, and inadequate child and health care. Dusty, a student at Plattsburgh High School, is one of the twelve original founders of a community-based soup kitchen that provides hot meals to anyone who wishes to drop in. He has collaborated with community members to raise funds and recruit volunteers. Recently, Dusty was given release time from his studies at the high school to meet with classes of middle school students about volunteering. The soup kitchen now has a group of middle school students who help out on a regular basis. This collaboration has not only enhanced Dusty's awareness of community issues but has given Plattsburgh a much-needed and valuable service.

Although this example highlights the involvement of learners and schools within the greater community, the reverse is also needed. Community volunteers are an integral part of any inclusive school. The need to introduce not only parents but volunteers into the school setting has been a major focus of school reform literature (Macchiarola, 1989). To provide high-quality educational opportunities for a diverse population of students, members of the community must become involved in the educational process of all children. Falvey, Coots, and Bishop (1990) point out that "business leaders, community organizations, college students, and other groups, including senior citizens and retired citizens, should be sought after and welcomed into the school" (p. 233). Opportunities exist within communities that, when brought into the schools by volunteers, enhance the available resources.

Within a collaborative relationship between school and community lies the hope that people will begin to view the school as a source of education, entertainment, social life, and community identity (Schmuck & Schmuck, 1990). In essence, the school and not the mall should become the gathering point for the community. Community theatre groups engaging talented students to complete their casts, musical presentations from a community-school orchestra, the artistic talents of young and old alike on display in the hallways—all these events serve to refocus the community eye toward the school. The community and all of its diversity must be embodied and appreciated in the school setting if all children are to learn to function effectively and contribute positively to society (Falvey, Coots, & Bishop, 1990).

SUMMARY

Inherent in the development of inclusive schools and communities is the need to form collaborative teams. Such teams may consist of a variety of people: parents, students, teachers, administrators, citizens, school board members, and support personnel. Collaboration is the key element in the smooth functioning of such a diverse team. Five factors essential to team productivity have been highlighted: positive interdependence, individual accountability, face-to-face interaction, collaborative skills, and group processing.

The need to develop a collaborative culture has been established as a critical component for the education of all children now and into the twenty-first century. Collaboration creates enhanced expertise among school personnel that results in the ability to meet a greater diversity of student needs. The collaborative model facilitates the paradigm shift necessary to establish an educational culture in which shared expertise will be permitted to develop. Collaboration places an unprecedented emphasis on learning how to learn and share knowledge with others that influences both educators and students. Collaboration has also become the impetus for the emergence of fully inclusive schools, where all students learn in general classrooms.

Collaboration has many faces. Quasicollaborative models such as consultation, collaborative consultation, peer coaching, mentoring and collaborative teaching have often been incorrectly used in research literature as if they were synonymous with full collaboration.

These quasicollaborative models differ from full collaboration in three ways. Full collaboration is established to enhance schooling for all students, not just those with disabilities. In full collaboration, the knowledge and skills brought to the process are far more important than the professional titles of people involved. Finally, in fully collaborative schools, teams are brought together before there is any need for problem solving; when a problem comes up, each team member participates actively in finding a solution and takes responsibility for implementing the chosen strategy.

Everyone has a role in the collaborative educational process. The inclusion of all children is not enough to make the system fully functional; parents and community members must also be included.

Diversity must be recognized and celebrated as a strength in the collaborative school community. In such an environment, learners participate in the educational process without being made to feel that their cultural norms must be rejected for them to achieve success.

PART II

TOOLS OF THE PROFESSION

Regardless of the student involved, or the school that student attends, or the age or experience the teacher has, there are a number of tools all teachers can and should use to become more effective collaborators in an inclusive school environment. These tools are the essentials of good teaching no matter what instructional strategy is being practiced.

The first tool is **planning for instruction**, both the short- and long-term variety. It is fairly easy to see (from our personal experience) that "when we fail to plan, we plan to fail." Considering the breadth and depth of the public school system, it becomes absolutely critical to plan at the state, district, school, and classroom levels. Classroom teachers are usually charged with the responsibility for translating educational aims and goals into actual learning objectives. To meet this challenge effectively, teachers must not only know their subject matter well, they must also know their students well.

Educators are increasingly finding it helpful to meet with colleagues to plan instruction collaboratively. Grade-level or age-group teams of professionals pool their resources and collectively provide a far more enriching educational experience for learners in inclusive settings than ever before. As more and more schools move toward inclusive education, the time allotted for collaborative planning will always be less than ideal because of the structure of the school day and year. Therefore, it is imperative for members of instructional teams to schedule time to meet outside school so that they have sufficient time to plan for the short- and long-term needs of learners.

Although the vast majority of instruction taking place in schools is aimed at learning in the cognitive domain, educators have increasingly offered learning opportunities in the affective domain through cooperative learning and in the psychomotor domain through physical learning experiences found in drama, art, and outdoor education. The complementary nature of the three domains should help educators recognize ways to address all three areas in their planning.

Perhaps an even more complex issue facing educators is that of **instructional management**. Although behavior management, a popular topic at teacher in-service days, presents an ongoing challenge to most educators, the focus on behavior should not draw away from the enormous importance of managing the instructional setting overall. Instructional management, the second of three tools for the profession, oversees the physical space and materials, the time allocated for instruction, the instructional plan and its implementation, and student conduct.

Teachers who manage their environments effectively have taken all these factors into account and made conscious decisions about the synergy that exists among them. These educators realize the amount of influence they have in the classroom and utilize it to lead students through a well-organized instructional endeavor on a consistent basis. They may choose to rely on one specific strategy or one instructional routine for managing time and have great success. But they also know when they need to examine some aspect of the teaching/learning dynamic and consider modification or overall change in that interaction.

Successful teachers tend to have successful learners and work constantly to ensure their success. They also work with colleagues in ways that enhance their instructional management, whether it means coteaching a unit on the swamps of south Florida or employing older students during a story-sharing experience. Little if any time is wasted in the classroom, where these educators have organized their efforts carefully. All learners are actively involved all of the time, with appropriate tasks and materials. Transitions are anticipated and often become part of the instructional sequence.

One of the most exciting aspects of inclusive schools is their empowerment of educators. This empowerment can result in, among other effective changes, scheduling that supports collaborative planning and teaching. This planning can also lead to more efficient recordkeeping systems among collaborators and more accurate and meaningful information from all learners. Many collaborative teams have even instituted student self-monitoring strategies and self-evaluation techniques in an effort to help learners themselves become more empowered in their education. Such efforts require a high degree of organization, and at the same time, an equally high degree of flexibility, from all educators involved. There is never any substitute for carefully planned environments in which students can confidently explore new and meaningful learning.

Last is the tool of writing out **unit and lesson plans**. Beyond the broad planning of curriculum lies the daily, weekly, and even yearly planning of actual instructional time, beginning with goals and objectives and collaboratively proceeding through details of integrating the curriculum, gathering appropriate materials, scheduling instruction, and adapting instruction to meet the diverse needs of students. In an inclusive classroom these instructional activities are less likely to be lecture-driven, pencil and paper tasks and more likely to be innovative, interactive, intellectually challenging events.

Students preparing to be educators may find, in their field experiences, that many of the teachers they work with do not write long, detailed lesson plans. To some extent this practice is a reflection of their experience. It is highly unlikely that any creative and innovative lesson or unit will occur without a carefully planned written description of the experience. Students will find that carefully planned lessons and units will lead to more enjoyable and satisfying teaching episodes. The preservice educator who includes a good introduction or anticipatory set, carefully organized presentations of new learning, adequate checks for understanding, sufficient time for guided practice, and of course time for extended practice and reflection will find his or her lesson-planning efforts worthwhile more often than not.

The additional benefit of carefully detailed planning of units and lessons lies in the confidence it brings that allows educators to collaborate more freely and openly. In an inclusive setting, a self-confident educator can be more positive and supportive of all learners.

6

PLANNING FOR INSTRUCTION

Key Terms

Aims
Behavior
Capacity
Competitive goal structure
Conditions for learning
Condition
Cooperative goal structure
Criterion
Doctrine of contingent value
Goal
Individualistic goal structure

Instructional planning
Learning stage
Metacognition
Mode of presentation
Motivation
Objective
Outcome
Self-concept
State anxiety
Temperament
Trait anxiety

Objectives

After completing this chapter, the reader will be able to:

1. Translate educational aims to instructional goals.
2. Convert instructional goals into instructional objectives.
3. Identify several cognitive, affective, and observable factors to consider in planning instruction.
4. Identify four reasons that instructional objectives are important to planning.
5. Write instructional goals in each of the three domains.
6. Write instructional objectives in each of the three domains.

PROFILES OF PLANNERS

John Madison

It is June 25, the first day of summer vacation. John Madison thinks back on the school year and smiles. The planning he did last summer certainly paid off; his students, individually and as a group, made excellent progress in all areas of the curriculum. He will take a few days to reflect on the successes and frustrations of the past year before beginning to plan for the coming year. But he will definitely use a planning procedure very similar to last year's.

One of the most time-consuming aspects of last year's planning, John recalls, was the study of district and state curriculum goals and objectives. Since he is going to teach the same grade again, that stage of the planning process will not be as detailed the second time around. He had worked hard to be sure his units and lessons were consistent with district and state curriculum guidelines because he wanted to concentrate more on instructional methods that would benefit all learners. The district had approved the inclusion of a sex education curriculum during the year and he had helped pilot the program in his fifth grade. In addition, the district had provided in-service workshops on cooperative learning, and he was excited about planning more activities for groups of learners in the coming year. There would inevitably be some other minor changes in the organization of the curriculum over the next nine months, but the overall outline of goals he had prepared in each subject area last summer would make an excellent draft for the coming year.

Another critical feature of John's planning procedure was familiarizing himself with the subject matter content and its organization. He was very strong in the language arts area and often provided assistance to other educators who were working on contemporary assessment techniques that reflected learners' actual learning experiences. He was less confident, however, about science and would need to practice the experiments and activities related to the important science concepts before the school year began. John wasn't sure whether the sequence of curriculum presented in the teacher's manual would be manageable in a district so far north. He had lived and taught in Florida for several years, and was used to conducting science activities outdoors all year long. Maybe Janice Brooks, that third grade teacher who had such a great science program, would help him. Bosworth, the town where he was teaching, was gearing up for its bicentennial celebration in two years, so a few meetings with the county historian were in order. John wanted to prepare a social studies curriculum that would highlight the history of the community and provide students with basic social studies skills and concepts at the same time. He could already envision much of the mathematics curriculum being taught within the context of this community study.

Perhaps the most important aspect of John's planning was having knowledge of the learners themselves. He already knew the students who would be in his class this coming year, and he would have the benefit of reading through their portfolios that were begun in kindergarten. Their writing samples, science experiment laboratory reports, problem-solving activities from mathematics, social studies research projects, and lists of books read and reported on would help him greatly in his planning. In addition, he would have the end-of-the-year reports from the IEP committee for the four students who were receiving special services. He had already spoken with their former teachers and knew of several promising adaptations he could plan on for each student. Three years ago, he had started doing home visits in August so that he could meet with every child's family and had benefitted from the information he had gathered. This year John would contact families in late July to arrange the visits. He hoped to better understand individual students' learning preferences, their interests, their fears, and of course their academic and social strengths and needs. All of this information would inevitably help him in grouping strategies, objective writing, and his assessment and grading procedures.

No planning program would be complete without a careful examination of methods of teaching the curriculum. The cooperative learning workshops were exciting and reinforced many of his existing techniques. Because the state and district had clearly identified the need for all students to work effectively with one another, he felt confident about planning cooperative group activities whenever appropriate. At other times he knew that the learning centers he had developed over the past five years would offer a tremendous opportunity for students to practice their newly acquired skills in an independent setting or to explore the features of a new area of learning. In fact, he decided to design a new center on whales to help students explore in more depth the mammals they would be seeing when they took their spring field trip to Boston. Of course, he would continue to use both direct and indirect methods of instruction because he felt some topics in mathematics and writing were most effectively learned by students through formal presentation. He usually had no trouble identifying students who needed another approach to these topics and typically used a more indirect approach with them, relying more heavily on the knowledge that these students brought to the new learning. Oh, and he mustn't forget the huge success students had with peer teaching this past year. He would be watching carefully from the first week of school to determine what types of student-student learning pairs might be worth pursuing. The success of this technique, for both "teacher" and learner in the pairs, was overwhelming last year, and he was convinced of its value.

Observing students in this way was a perfect example of the final and perhaps most complex aspect of the planning process for John Madison—using information gathered on a daily basis in the classroom. He had found tremendous value in listening to students talk to each other about their out-of-school experiences in the neighborhood, at play, at home, in the mall, with their family, just about anywhere. He had integrated this information into his weekly lesson planning and discovered that it greatly enhanced student learning. He also had begun seeking direct feedback from students about his lessons and used it together with his own written reflections to redirect subsequent plans. The results were very satisfying, and he now appreciated the importance of flexible planning.

Yes, it would be well worth the time this summer to spend a few weeks planning carefully to meet students' educational needs. John Madison felt comfortable knowing that his planning procedures would reap benefits for all the students in his class and for his own professional development.

Ellen Baker

June 25—summer vacation, finally! Now Ellen Baker knew why she decided to go into teaching. She just couldn't wait to get out of this school, and out of this town. Oh, yeah, she had to turn in her plan book. Better get out the textbooks and write some page numbers in the little boxes. It didn't matter, really. It seemed as if no matter what she did, there were always some students who did great and some who failed miserably. Most were somewhere in the middle—not great, but good enough to pass.

Ellen just didn't understand why some of the teachers spent so much time at school during the summer. The teacher's guide had everything in it anybody needed to know. She never thought those state guides made any sense, anyway. By the way, how did they expect her to teach sex education on top of all the other requirements? Cooperative learning? Every time she tried to group her students for round robin reading, they got out of hand. Why bother? They did just fine the old way.

As a result of failing to plan, Ellen Baker has little time to collaborate with colleagues with expertise in content areas other than her own. Just because her undergraduate degree was in art, why did the principal suggest that Suzanne McShane, the sixth grade English teacher, come to her for help with a mural project? If they want an art consultant, they should offer her additional pay. Besides, whenever she needed help with those new science experiments, she'd just look in the manual.

She did have one question, though. She wondered why John Madison was always able to teach his students so much. John's students always seemed ready to begin, while hers were constantly having to go find their books and other materials. Transitions from some activity to another were havoc. Ellen Baker has heard of sponge activities, but since they aren't in her teacher's manuals, they must not really work that well. She tried learning centers (or collections of dittos) once, but found them much too bothersome. Every student had to come to her for directions, and they didn't treat the materials carefully enough. Maybe if there had been written rules and directions for use—but that took too much time.

PROPERTIES OF PLANNING

These two profiles highlight one of the fundamental differences between effective and noneffective teaching—planning. Effective teaching involves more than reading the teacher's manual and filling in a lesson plan book with page numbers. Essential to the learning process is the need for **instructional planning**. In a review of research articles examining the concept of planning, Clark and Peterson (1986) describe eight different types of planning that occur in the course of a school year. Six of these are tied to time spans (weekly, daily, long range, short range, yearly, and term), and the remaining two (unit and lesson) describe content. These types of planning will be addressed in later chapters. At this point it is important to realize that each teacher plans somewhat differently and that it takes years for a dedicated professional to become a comprehensive planner who is integrating both academic and nonacademic data into her or his planning behavior. More urgent to the issue of planning is the knowledge base necessary for successfully carrying out any of the types of planning presented by Clark and Peterson.

There are four forms of knowledge one must possess in order to plan appropriately. These include a knowledge of aims, goals, and objectives; learners; teaching methods (Borich, 1992; Morine-Dershiner & Pfeifer, 1986); and subject matter and its organization. Establishing societal aims is a top priority, but effectively completing the process of developing goals and objectives requires a thorough understanding of learners, available teaching methods, and subject matter content.

Teaching methods will be thoroughly examined in subsequent chapters of this text. This chapter examines societal aims, constructing goals, and developing curriculum objectives. The chapter concludes with a look at what we know about learners and content.

AIMS OF EDUCATION

Overall disenchantment with the quality of public education in the late 1970s and early 1980s fueled the establishment of several national task forces, including the National Commission on Excellence in Education (1983), the Carnegie Forum on Education and the Economy (1986), and the Holmes Group (1986). Reports issued by these groups were designed to assist schools in the development of their curricular aims for the 1990s. Consensus was reached on several matters regarding future educational aims. Perhaps one of the most important and recurring concerns was the belief that our public education system had lost sight of their role in teaching learners to think. Additionally, the requirements of living within a technological society were addressed as were concerns about back to basics issues, higher-order thinking skills, and creativity.

Ten years have passed since these reports were issued, yet little has changed in public education. As we approach the twenty-first century, carefully formulated societal aims must be given more than lip service. Such factors as our shrinking planet, ideological upheaval, and rapidly deteriorating communities must become priorities for future survival. Professionals involved in public education have a moral obligation to act as catalysts in the transformation of these aims into goals and objectives for learners.

Aims give a sense of direction to curriculum and planning. They must be sufficiently broad to appeal to a wide variety of schools across a school district or state. Because they are broad-based generalities, aims are difficult to implement and even more difficult to measure. Therefore, once clear aims are established, they must be transformed into measurable goals and objectives. Before this feat can be accomplished, educators must become intimately acquainted with learners' cognitive, affective, and skill development. Aims cannot be converted into goals and objectives unless educators have a clear picture of their students.

Reflect for a Moment

For a clear example of educational aims, revisit Goals 2000, signed into law by President Clinton in 1994.

CONSTRUCTING GOALS

The narrowing of aims to goals can be achieved with the development of a knowledge base in the areas previously described in this chapter. Not unlike aims, **goals** give curriculum a sense of direction. Goals are, however, both more specific and tangible than aims; they address the needs of the curriculum in the affective, cognitive, and psychomotor domains. Goals convert aims into implementable curriculum while remaining flexible enough to provide a variety of individual interpretations.

Goal Structures

In addition to the three developmental domains, goal structures must also be considered. The goal structure of any task reflects the way the educator organizes the task for student learning (Good & Brophy, 1991). Three major goal structures identified by Johnson and Johnson (1991) are competitive, individualistic, and cooperative.

Competitive goal structures are based on the concept that the learner can only succeed at the expense of others. Degree of success is measured by the extent to which others fail. For example, when an educator establishes a goal of spelling words correctly and uses a common spelling bee activity—known as the "Whatdyaget" syndrome—students fail one by one until only one actually succeeds. In this manner, the educator ensures that one student or small group of students will obtain the goal only if other students fail.

Individualistic goal structures are developed to make the learner's success totally unrelated to any other student. This is an independent, do-it-alone, approach to learning. Using the same spelling goal, when an educator dictates a pretest on Monday to decide which words will be on each student's test on Friday, he or she is organizing the task as an individualistic goal structure.

The focus of **cooperative goal structures** is interdependency. The learner can only succeed if everyone with whom she or he is working succeeds. According to Johnson, Skon, and Johnson (1980), cooperative activities, structured correctly, can produce peer support, encourage learning, and result in higher-level metacognition and response to task. Cooperative goal structures have been as successful as more traditional competitive and individualistic goal structures in promoting achievement and are more successful in fostering mutual concern and positive social relationships among learners, improved self-concept, and liking of school as well as other affective outcomes (Johnson, Maruyama, Johnson, Nelson, & Skon, 1980; Sharan, 1980; Slavin, 1980). Although competitive and individualistic goal structures represent the more traditional approach, cooperative structures are more viable for the inclusive school and the collaborative approach. Educators could develop the spelling goal, for example, into a cooperative structure by having small groups of students create stories using the spelling words. Each group member would be expected to write at least one sentence, and credit would be given only when all words were included and correctly spelled.

Affective Goals

Krathwohl, Bloom, and Masia (1964) developed a taxonomy to help educators classify affective goals. Goals in the affective domain focus on learning that describes changes in interest, attitudes, and values. As learners progress through each level of the affective domain, they develop more self-reliance and commitment and become more involved in the learning process. The taxonomy, which begins with receiving, progresses through responding, valuing, and organization until the learner reaches characterization. Goals within the affective domain primarily involve adaptive behavior, social development, and emotional development. Interestingly, such goals are often difficult to specify because of the unobservable nature of human feelings. The following goals, however, are designed to follow the progression just described:

> Receiving: The student will be aware of body language.
>
> Responding: The student will practice positive body language.
>
> Valuing: The student will display generally appropriate body language.
>
> Organization: The student will select body language specific to his or her own needs.
>
> Characterization: The student will resist inappropriate types of body language.

Cognitive Goals

Goals in the cognitive domain must take into account each of the levels of complexity established by Bloom, Englehart, Hill, Furst, and Krathwohl (1956). Most goals developed in the areas of mathematics, reading, language arts, science, and social studies fall within the cognitive domain. As with other domains, our assumptions about the cognitive domain are based on a belief that the skills developed are hierarchical in nature. Accordingly, cognitive skills are seen as ranging from the lowest or most common level, knowledge, to the highest level, evaluation. The following goals related to mathematics facts illustrate the range of the cognitive domain:

> Knowledge: The student will memorize math facts in addition.
>
> Comprehension: The student will add two-digit numbers.
>
> Application: The student will use math facts in word problems.
>
> Analysis: The student will know when she can use math facts and when she cannot.
>
> Synthesis: The student will create a new set of math facts.
>
> Evaluation: The student will know the value of math facts.

Reflect for a Moment

Look at the six levels of cognitive skills just listed. Which goals look most interesting to you? These are also probably the most interesting goals for many learners as well. What does this fact tell you about planning goals?

Psychomotor Goals

Goals in the psychomotor domain typically require that the learner demonstrate some physical/motor ability. Simpson (1972) developed a method for categorizing these goals in which each level within this domain has distinct characteristics that must be considered in planning educational goals. Development in the psychomotor domain reflects a progression from gross to fine motor skills. The following goals, which reflect the levels of imitation, manipulation, precision, articulation, and naturalization, constitute yet another hierarchy and emphasize increasing levels of dexterity within the area of neuromuscular skill:

Imitation: The students will copy drawings of basic shapes.

Manipulation: The students will depict the four seasons in drawings.

Precision: The students will draw important people in their lives.

Articulation: The students will draw pictures of different animals.

Naturalization: The students will doodle.

OBJECTIVES

A variety of teaching skills are incorporated into the planning process. Educators create instructional plans based on goals. To lend specificity and measurability to goals, however, they must also develop objectives. The relationship between goals and objectives is an intimate one and is shared as well with the aims from which both were originally derived. To formulate objectives, therefore, the educator must reflect on not just the goals but the aims of education.

Objectives that are well defined clarify learning outcomes in terms of measurable or observable student performance. When educators have clearly defined curriculum objectives, better instruction occurs, learning is more efficient, evaluation is better, and students are better able to conduct self-evaluation or self-reflection (Berliner, 1987; Kibler, Barker, & Miles, 1970; Rosenshine & Stevens, 1986). Further, the most successful instructional approaches (expository, discovery, inquiry, and discussion) rely heavily on well-defined curriculum objectives.

Mager (1984) cites four major reasons that make explicit objectives important in the learning process: selection of content or procedures, evaluation of instructional success, provision for students to organize thoughts and activities necessary to accomplish the learning event, and reflection about the curriculum.

There is no sound basis for planning, selecting, or developing instructional materials, content, or methods when explicit objectives do not exist (Mager, 1984). If you know your destination, in other words, you are more likely to get there. John Madison finds it easy to select content, methods, and materials for each lesson because of his carefully written objectives. He finds that his objectives actually help direct these educational decisions. Ellen Baker, on the other hand, relies heavily on teaching guides to direct her instruction, with less than adequate results. She fumbles not only with the content but with the materials as well because she has failed to develop explicit objectives.

The second important reason for stating objectives explicitly deals directly with the assessment of teaching and learning outcomes. Assessment is designed to help educator and learner alike reflect about the nature of their success in achieving the lesson objectives. Ellen Baker, who relies heavily on end-of-unit tests, is often confused about why her students do so poorly—after all, she felt she taught them what they needed to know! John Madison uses his objectives from each lesson to develop test questions. He is sure his students will do well because he reteaches a lesson when they haven't successfully reached these objectives.

The third reason for planning clear objectives is to help learners organize their own efforts toward successfully accomplishing the learning event. Students also need to know where they are going so that they know what to bring on their trip. Students in Ellen Baker's classroom are always out of hand, constantly asking questions to clarify some trivial point in the lesson. Often there are exasperated sighs when the response they give is wrong because "they" failed to interpret Ellen Baker's questions correctly. They also seem to take a great deal of instructional time organizing themselves, constantly returning to their cubbies or desks to get materials needed to complete an activity. In John Madison's class, students know what is expected. John has written the lesson objective on the board so that students know how to organize their questions, materials, and efforts to accomplish the learning tasks. By planning explicit objectives, John Madison provides both his students and himself with a road map for the learning event. This road map gives everyone in the classroom a means for understanding where they are going, thereby providing a better chance of arriving there.

The fourth important advantage of formulating explicit objectives concerns the reflective process that takes place in writing. "The drafting of objectives causes one to think seriously and deeply about what is worth teaching, about what is worth spending time and effort to accomplish" (Mager, 1984, p. 6). Objectives can serve as a means of examining the worth of curriculum and materials already in existence and provide a base from which to make adaptations or deletions.

Objectives are perhaps one of the most important and useful tools in the planning, implementation, and evaluation of instructional events. An explicitly stated objective is one that succeeds in communicating the educator's intent. Regardless of the subject area, domain of learning, or stage of learning, the educator should be able to identify the performance or behavior, the condition, and the criterion of the learning outcome in any objective. An explicit objective, therefore has three characteristics that communicate the intent of the learning event and should clearly answer the following questions:

1. Behavior: What is the learning outcome?
2. Conditions: What tools will be needed to demonstrate the learning outcome?
3. Criterion: At what level must the learning outcome be demonstrated?

The focus of any one objective should be on the expected learning outcome. Because the act of learning occurs within a realm that the educator cannot see—the student's mind—learning can only be measured in terms of observable outcomes. Learning outcomes are the **behavior** that results from the learning process. The following are sample behavior segments of objectives:

Knowledge: Be able to name the major battles of the Civil War.

Comprehension: Be able to summarize the outcomes of the major battles of the Civil War.

Application: Be able to predict outcomes of major Civil War battles.

Analysis: Be able to differentiate between the qualities of battle commanders.

Synthesis: Be able to create a scenario in which the South wins the Civil War.

Evaluation: Be able to compare and contrast the battle strategies of Robert E. Lee and U. S. Grant.

Perhaps the most difficult task in formulating objectives is identifying observable learning **outcomes**. Gronlund (1991) suggests that the objective writing process can end here, that the two components of conditions and criterion are not necessary. Conditions and criterion "result in long cumbersome lists that restrict the freedom of the teacher" (Gronlund, 1991, p. 10).

The second characteristic cited by Mager (1984) is **conditions**, or the tools students need to demonstrate the learning outcome. As stated before, one of the reasons for writing an explicit objective is to provide the students with appropriate means for organizing the learning conditions. Conditions, therefore, do not limit the educator, as Gronlund (1991) believes. Instead, they free up instructional time that would otherwise be spent attempting to organize the learning. Conditions statements often begin with phrases such as "given a," "when provided with," "using a," or "without the aid of." The previously cited examples of behaviors have been coupled with the following conditions to provide clear examples.

> After reading a book at the appropriate reading level, be able to name the major battles of the Civil War.
>
> Following a discussion, be able to summarize the outcomes of major battles of the Civil War.
>
> Given scenarios with events altered, be able to predict outcomes of major Civil War battles.
>
> Given various biographies, be able to differentiate between battle commanders.
>
> Given information sheets, be able to create a scenario in which the South wins the Civil War.
>
> Using information from the Civil War unit, be able to compare and contrast the battle strategies of Robert E. Lee and U. S. Grant.

Criterion consists of the acceptable performance levels of the learning outcome. The criterion for success varies from student to student and should be related carefully to each student's ability level. Because students will live down to our expectations of them, acceptable performance levels should be set high enough to encourage but not frustrate the learning process. Criterion may be related to the speed, accuracy, or quality of learning outcome.

Speed is a common criterion to determine whether a successful learning outcome has been achieved, but it is often misused. In fact, speed is a valuable criterion only in a very narrow realm of learning experiences. If student responses must be automatic, speed may be a critical factor. If behavior or performance focuses on completion time, such as evacuating a building in under 2 minutes, speed is important. But for many students, a time limit automatically creates a losing situation. Learners with processing problems take longer to interpret and understand, and those who are awkward may take longer for a physical response. Therefore, speed should only be used as a measure of success when it is absolutely critical for the activity. Does it matter how quickly the obese student runs a race, or is it more important that she or he ran and finished?

Accuracy may also be a criterion used to determine successful completion of a learning event. Accuracy can be demonstrated in terms of percent of correct responses (90%) or number of times performed (four out of six times). There are two common pitfalls in using accuracy as a criterion. The first is having unattainable percentages, such as 95 percent accuracy when there are twenty-five responses. The second is overuse of 100 percent accuracy. Because very few learning outcomes must have such a high level of accuracy, the level of 100 percent (or twenty out of twenty times) should probably be reserved for only those learning outcomes that involve safety issues such as looking both ways when crossing the street.

Quality of learning outcome is another criterion. Mager (1984) suggests that this criterion may be achieved by defining "the amount of acceptable deviation from perfection or some other standard" (p. 83). (For example, students must write a story containing no more than one misspelled word.) Another aspect of quality is the inclusion of essential features. (For example, students must write an essay that evokes fear.)

The learning objectives cited earlier follow, with criteria added.

Accuracy: After reading a book at the appropriate reading level, be able to name at least four major battles of the Civil War.

Accuracy: Following a discussion, be able to summarize the outcomes of two major battles of the Civil War.

Accuracy: Given scenarios with events altered, be able to predict outcomes of major Civil War battles with 75 percent accuracy (or three out of four battles).

Quality: Given various biographies, be able to differentiate between the qualities of battle commanders, identifying no less than two differences.

Quality: Given information sheets, be able to create a scenario in which the South wins the Civil War that includes effective battle strategies.

Quality: Using information from the Civil War unit, be able to compare and contrast the battle strategies of Robert E. Lee and U. S. Grant, using supportive data from no less than three confrontations.

To prevent frustration during the learning process, the educator must reflect on where students are at any given point in each of the three domains. Additionally, objectives must be carefully planned to further the student's stage of learning.

Cognitive Domain

Within the cognitive domain there are six levels of learning: knowledge, comprehension, application, analysis, synthesis, and evaluation. Students' cognitive development must be carefully considered when determining the level of learning expected. The level of learning influences how long students will take to achieve an objective and the nature of the learning outcome.

The individual levels have been described in Chapter 2. Table 6.1 provides

TABLE 6.1   Learning Outcomes, Time Intervals, and Verbs in the Cognitive Domain

Domain	Learning Outcome	Verbs/Behaviors/ Performance	Time Interval
Knowledge	Knows facts Knows theory Knows terms	recites, defines, recalls, names, identifies, lists, labels, matches, counts, recognizes, repeats	Immediate 1–4 days
Comprehension	Summarizes readings Understands principles Interprets charts Discriminates properties	explains, predicts, converts, distinguishes, describes, gives examples, summarizes, translates, paraphrases, estimates, rewrites	5 days– 2 weeks
Application	Applies knowledge Uses information Builds a model Determines amount needed	computes, demonstrates, constructs, organizes, makes, uses, solves, develops, carries out, changes, produces	2, 3, or 4 weeks
Analysis	Compares and contrasts two items Subdivides a group Analyzes a passage Draws relationships	classifies, outlines, selects, differentiates, illustrates, points out, diagrams, relates, breaks down, separates	4, 5, or 6 weeks
Synthesis	Produces a new item Creates a story Designs a different form	creates, devises, constructs, organizes, compiles, draws, integrates, formulates, prescribes, generates, proposes	6 weeks to 1 semester
Evaluation	Appraises a product Defends an opinion Justifies a decision	judge, validates, compares, critiques, decides, evaluates, selects, determines, concludes, appraises, supports	1 semester to 1 year

examples of general learning outcomes, verbs that can be used to describe student behaviors and performances, and estimated time needed for completion.

During the previous discussion of the behavior and performance segment of the objective, each of the cognitive levels was addressed. The following examples have been developed using information from Table 6.1.

Knowledge: From memory, be able to list the four basic parts of a plant.

Comprehension: Using text drawings, be able to describe major stages of the life cycle of a plant.

Application: Following written instructions, be able to produce a healthy flowering plant.

Analysis: Given a list of ten plants, be able to separate the plants by genus.

Synthesis: With information from independent readings, be able to propose a feasible plan to stop the destruction of tropical plant life.

Evaluation: Given a choice of 5 plants, be able to select the plant best suited for the existing environment and cite no less than four valid reasons for the choice.

Affective Domain

It is extremely important to recognize and plan for each of the levels in the affective domain—receiving, responding, valuing, organization, and characterization. As the learner moves through the levels of this domain, a clearer system of attitudes and values emerges. During this process, the internal sense of self serves as a steadily greater influence than external factors.

As with the cognitive domain, individual levels have been presented in Chapter 2. Table 6.2 includes general learning outcomes and verbs at each level of the affective domain.

The following set of objectives is developed from the information in Table 6.2.

Receiving: In a small group setting, be able to attend to a guest speaker for no less than ten minutes.

Responding: While at the water table, be able to share the toys with others without a prompt.

Valuing: On the playground, be able to persuade another student to join in a game.

TABLE 6.2   Learning Outcomes, and Verbs in the Affective Domain

Domain	Learning Outcome	Verbs/Behaviors/Performance
Receiving	Is aware of material Listens to someone Attends to a presentation	notices, hears, pays attention to, looks at, listens to, holds, replies
Responding	Follows directions Participates in conversation Responds to a question Becomes involved in an activity	discusses, participates, obeys, volunteers, shares, answers, plays, complies, helps, tells, performs
Valuing	Demonstrates a preference Acts consistently Initiates a discussion Expresses an opinion	argues, selects, convinces, debates, persuades, defends, supports, commits
Organization	Makes a decision Presents a position Plans a strategy Accepts responsibility for behavior	justifies, accepts, rejects, decides, theorizes, formulates, organizes, generalizes, realizes, arranges
Characterization	Develops a global view Incorporates beliefs Reflects upon personal attitudes Exhibits respect	avoids, displays, manages, resists, resolves, serves, verifies, uses, maintains, demonstrates, practices

Organization: When asked, be able to accept responsibility for leaving a task unfinished.

Characterization: During a group discussion, be able to resist joining others who ridicule a classmate.

Psychomotor Domain

Table 6.3 illustrates each of the levels in the psychomotor domain by providing learning outcomes and verbs associated with student behavior or performance.

The hierarchical levels have different characteristics that are demonstrated by the verbs used. The following examples represent objectives using behaviors included in Table 6.3.

Imitation: Given a basketball, be able to hold it correctly for a chest pass.

Manipulation: Given a basketball, be able on request to show the correct grip for a chest pass.

Precision: With a partner, be able to execute a correct chest pass.

Articulation: During a half-court game, be able to throw chest passes when appropriate.

Naturalization: In competition, be able to throw chest passes routinely without error.

TABLE 6.3   Learning Outcomes, and Verbs in the Psychomotor Domain

Domain	Learning Outcome	Verbs/Behaviors/Performance
Imitation	Uses visual model Repeats an action Copies a pattern Traces a shape	follows, holds, places, reproduces, kicks, hops, bends, jump
Manipulation	Follows verbal directions Holds the tool correctly Sets up equipment Uses written directions	many of the verbs listed above and constructs, shows, positions, repeats, copies, writes, carries out
Precision	Balances objects Hits the target Writes legibly Measures amount needed	catches, bounces, controls, plays correctly, draws, pours
Articulation	Coordinates arms and legs Moves smoothly Writes quickly (and legibly) Types with all ten fingers	dances, uses calculator, builds, paints, adjusts, changes, improves, adapts, performs, prepares
Naturalization	Writes automatically Draws without effort Climbs without effort Skates naturally	runs, throws, writes, sculpts, doodles, sketches, swims, drives, dresses, plays, carries

Learning Stages

Both domains of learning and stages of learning must be considered in planning instructional objectives. It is important, however, to remember that they are separate, not interrelated entities. A student may be at the most complex level in a domain (evaluation, characterization, or naturalization) and still require instruction at the lowest stage of learning (acquisition).

Learning stages (Smith, 1981) are discussed here as they relate to the writing of instructional objectives. Each of the stages (entry, acquisition, reversion, proficiency, maintenance, generalization, and adaptation) will be discussed briefly and examples of objectives will be provided where appropriate. In applying different stages of learning to instructional objectives, behavior and performance usually stay the same, but the criteria and conditions may need to be modified.

Although the *entry* stage of learning must be considered in planning instructional objectives, educators do not develop objectives for this level. They determine the skills or knowledge needed to begin and the level of the domain at which instruction will take place.

> Entry level: No objective writing at this stage. Student knows what the concept of angle is in geometry, recognizes the numbers 45 and 90.

At the *acquisition* stage, the learner is in the process of acquiring new skills or knowledge. Instructional objectives should focus on assisting learners at the initial acquisition stage to demonstrate knowledge or perform skills accurately. As students move on to the advanced stage of acquisition, the focus of the objective shifts to making the learner become more reflective about completing the task or transferring new knowledge to long-term memory.

> Acquisition: Given a protractor, be able to draw 45 and 90 degree angles.

Reversion, not unlike acquisition, has accuracy of response as its primary instructional aim. During the process of acquiring a new skill, the learner often performs erratically. The student's performance at this stage generally indicates an understanding of how to perform the new skill accurately but the newfound knowledge is not always secure and will occasionally revert to the entry level.

> Reversion: Given examples of two angles, will correctly identify one as a 90-degree and the other as a 45-degree angle.

Speed of performance becomes an integral part of an objective's focus for students at the *proficiency* level. So do continuation of reflective learning, development of learning management, and retrieval of information.

> Proficiency: Given a protractor and a list of five angles, be able to draw them all correctly within 3 minutes.

During the *maintenance* stage, instruction focuses on the continuation of a high level of accurate performance. One component of the objective for this stage is a level of performance that does not necessitate direct instruction.

Maintenance: During a learning center activity, be able to draw each angle requested correctly.

Educational objectives for students at the stage of *generalization* focus on the occurrence of skill performance or the application of knowledge at different times and in a variety of situations. At this level the knowledge or skill itself does not change; the learner expands its usage to encompass new settings and varying conditions.

Generalization: During a woodworking class, be able to draw angles needed for sketch of planned wood sculpture.

Adaptation has as its aim the extension of knowledge or skills to new areas. This level differs from generalization because it involves the altering of knowledge to fit into unique new situations. In writing objectives at this stage, behavior and performance, conditions, and criteria may all need to be modified.

Adaptation: When problems arise in completion of woodworking sculpture, be able to draw new angles needed for accurate representation of sculptured object.

KNOWLEDGE OF STUDENTS

Comprehensive knowledge of the student is critical to the design and implementation of goals, objectives, and instruction (Haring, Lovitt, Eaton, & Hansen, 1978; Idol-Maestas, 1983; Mercer & Mercer, 1989; Smith, 1981). If they are to plan successful school experiences, educators must understand how each student's learning is influenced by his or her cognition, affect, skills, and environment. Goals, objectives, and teaching strategies can then be carefully matched to student characteristics to more fully enhance learning.

All educators should be expected to reflect on their responsibilities long enough to determine which is more important to their planning efforts—teaching the content or teaching the students. Much of current curriculum development can be linked to societal aims and should be relevant to the needs of a world in constant transition. But when it comes down to planning instruction, short or long term, too many educators turn to their text manuals before they consider the characteristics of the learners. Such misguided planning priorities can and do often lead to inappropriate choice of content, methods, and materials, minimal student engagement and success, and, over the long run, a sense among educators and learners alike that what goes on in class is often meaningless and of little use.

Reflect for a Moment

Think about what you did and did not learn in high school. What do you now wish you had learned more about in high school? What could you have spent more time learning about in school?

Learner characteristics and individual differences that have an impact on the planning process form a long list. Therefore, we have divided them into the following sections: cognitive/academic factors, affective attributes, observable skills, and environmental influences.

Cognitive/Academic Factors

The effective planner must take into consideration the unique cognitive and academic factors demonstrated by each student. Educational researchers have linked a number of cognitive and academic factors to student learning. Among these are prior academic achievement, visual and auditory perception (Stanovich, 1986; Richek, List, & Lerner, 1989), intelligence, vocabulary, style of learning (Blakeslee, 1982), use of cognitive strategies (Hallahan, 1980; Pressley & Levin, 1983), memory (Reid, 1988), and metacognition (Flavell, 1979). These, of course, are but a few of the many factors that can and do influence student learning and they will vary from task to task.

Learners' task-relevant prior knowledge is a critical consideration in planning new learning, regardless of whether the order of reasoning is simple to complex, general to detailed, concrete to abstract, or some other logical progression of ideas. Content organization, basic to all types of planning, must take each student's prior knowledge into account. When educators fail to consider such information, students are less likely to attain higher level concepts and are more likely to become inattentive and/or frustrated.

Intelligence is fluid and multidimensional, depending on circumstances and conditions. All learners display varying intelligence. Jesse may be unable to memorize basic addition facts but have no difficulty comparing two characters in a story. Samantha is adept at evaluating a scientific theory but struggles to participate in a class discussion. Tests of general intelligence, though fair predictors of school grades, are inadequate measures of future success in the business world, the chemist's lab, or career life in general. It is imperative, therefore, that educators know each learner's specific strengths and weaknesses and plan instruction accordingly instead of simply using results of general intelligence tests.

Many specific cognitive abilities must be taken into account in planning for student success. Among these are visual perception, auditory discrimination, vocabulary, spatial relations, general reasoning, and vocabulary. Each contributes in varying degrees, depending on the demands of the task. Every learning experience, from rote memorization to detailed analysis of data to evaluation of interpersonal conflict, relies to some degree on these and other specific cognitive abilities.

An understanding of the learner's information processing is fundamental to the planning process. The primary focus of information processing is an explicit and detailed understanding of how a student's cognitive system works in dealing with a task or problem (Reid, 1988). Important features of cognitive information processing include capacity, conditions, and metacognition.

Capacity

Capacity is the amount of information a learner can attend to at one time, encompassing ability to work using both short- and long-term memory. Worden (1983) defines working or short-term memory as the hypothetical buffer in the information processing system in which incoming material is "held momentarily for the purpose of decoding and further processing" (p. 134). Short-term memory is, as the name implies, a space of limited size from which information is rapidly deleted to make room for new input. Who has not experienced the exasperation that comes from looking up a phone number, being interrupted before getting a chance to dial it, and then having to look it up all over again even though less than a minute has elapsed?

Memory, therefore, can be visualized as a set of capacities that enable the student to interact with incoming information in order to make sense of the tasks or learning (Reid, 1988). To maintain this new information, a learner must be able to store information in his or her long-term memory. To enhance students' long-term memory, educators must be aware of the methods in which learners use past experiences to organize new learning. For students who are experiencing difficulty with memory processes, Polloway, Patton, Payne, and Payne (1989) have outlined the following set of strategies:

- Instruction should focus on rehearsal strategies and related mediation tools, such as labeling and verbal associations.
- Students should receive information in manageable units and should be given assistance in grouping or clustering items.
- Information to be learned and retained should be meaningful and relevant.
- Students should be given mnemonics for specific content and should be assisted in using them.
- When they learn memory strategies, students must be given opportunity to practice and apply them.
- Direct instruction should be provided to demonstrate to students how to group information.
- Visual imagery can be used to provide a picture into which verbal information can be placed.
- Paraphrasing information—putting it into one's own words—facilitates storage and recall.
- Incentives should be provided as needed, with a subsequent shift to self-regulation.
- Overlearning, repetition, and constant use and application of learned material and strategies should be ensured. (p. 32)

Reflect for a Moment

Do you remember a teacher who actively taught learning or study strategies to you or your class? If so, share these strategies with the class. If not, did you devise your own?

Conditions

Recent brain behavior research has provided evidence that educators should take into account certain cognitive **conditions for learning** a student operates with in seeking to make sense of new experiences. *Simultaneous processors* of information prefer the right hemisphere and typically benefit from more visual, emotional, hands-on instruction. Students who are *sequential processors*, in contrast, favor the left hemisphere and benefit from more traditional, verbal teaching approaches. All subject matter includes content that can be processed by both hemispheres, so educators must be careful not to rely too heavily on the traditional verbal approach in planning their presentations (Blakeslee, 1982).

Perhaps an even greater challenge to the educator planning instruction is the student who demonstrates cross-dominance. *Cross-dominance*, or a failure to develop laterality, occurs when the two hemispheres of the brain, neither of which have become dominant, come into conflict as the learner attempts to process information. This condition can negatively affect the capacity for learning language (Lerner, 1993). The educator who can closely observe the effects of different types of instructional delivery on different learners will also be able to detect a learner who displays cross-dominance.

Metacognition

Metacognition, the process of knowing about one's own thinking, can include self-questioning, self-monitoring, and mnemonics (memory aids). When Marco completed a mathematics problem, John Madison asked him, "Tell me how you solved this." This example of a metacognitive strategy helps the student verbalize the thinking process he or she employed to solve the problem. Students will use metacognition to help understand content but will benefit even more if educators demonstrate different mental models and allow them to practice the reasoning involved in various models (Duffy, Roehler, & Herrmann, 1988). Some students may use a talk-aloud model; others may use a self-interrogation model for the same task.

Educators who become aware of the different metacognitive strategies students use can more easily plan successful instruction for a diverse group of learners. Likewise, students who know when and why they are using different models will employ metacognition readily and efficiently to different learning tasks. Students use this "inner speech" with increasingly complex tasks, but they can be helped along by educators who demonstrate and practice metacognition.

Affective Attributes

Several affective attributes of learners have been identified in the research on personality and school learning. The most important are student anxiety, self-concept, motivation, and temperament.

Anxiety

Anxiety can make any task difficult. The most capable learner can become paralyzed if fearful, tense, or threatened. A student who becomes panicked before taking a test faces **state anxiety**, or fear related to a specific situation. This type of anxiety varies across different circumstances and can also have positive aspects. JoAnne is preparing a speech and is fearful, but the fear will likely cause her to organize her material more carefully.

Instructional goals and objectives will typically evoke a degree of state anxiety from the student. Grades, report cards and assignments may also contribute to high levels of state anxiety and may cause a student to become mentally paralyzed. This heightened anxiety can result in plagiarizing, skipping classes, studying past exhaustion, and displaying symptoms of illnesses such as a headache or upset stomach.

Reflect for a Moment

How severe is your nervousness over tests? Speaking in front of a group? What other situations make you highly anxious?

Student state anxiety can and should be managed effectively by educators (Weiner, 1972). Full understanding of the exact value of any test or assignment will help students avoid extreme anxiety. In addition, using a variety of requirements to determine a grade will reduce students' tendencies to exaggerate the importance of any single outcome and help lower state anxiety.

Trait anxiety, on the other hand, is a form of anxiety that extends across a range of conditions and over longer periods of time, making it a more stable personality characteristic. High trait anxiety is common among individuals with high levels of motivation; like state anxiety, however, it can become unhealthy and lead to mechanical, uninspired learning behavior in an otherwise highly motivated student. The educator who provides a warm, caring, and encouraging environment can help an anxious student regain his or her desire to do well. Organizing task outcomes so that a range of acceptable responses exists is one strategy educators can use to support this type of student.

Self-Concept

The **self-concept** of a learner is derived from his or her interactions with others throughout life. As a child uses these interactions to create an image of himself or herself, a self-concept emerges.

A long history of theory and research has linked self-concept with school success, and recent reviews continue to indicate consistently positive relationships between the two (Hansford & Hattie, 1982; Kash & Borich, 1978). Beyond the research on this subject, having a positive self-concept is generally regarded as important to success in all phases of life, whether it be school, marriage, career, or any other aspect of human experience.

Clearly the student who experiences success in school is likely to improve his or her self-concept, which in turn will have a positive effect on other life events. Therefore, educators are reminded of the importance of planning so that every student experiences success on a regular basis. This is even more true in the case of low SES students whose home life provides little opportunity for success and as a result exhibit lower self-concepts. Because most students use educators' feedback on a regular basis in rethinking their self-images, personal interactions between educators and students need to be constantly reexamined. Messages sent to students by educators, whether intentional or not, may have a lasting impact on students' self-concepts.

The educator who is aware of his or her own self-concept and how it influences interactions with students will usually be able to communicate in a warm and encouraging manner. Ultimately, these interactions are supported by a belief that each student has inherent value as a unique and talented individual.

Motivation

Motivation, both intrinsic and extrinsic, contributes greatly to student learning (Michaels, 1977), and a teacher will need to monitor through observation what sources of motivation exist for each student. Contracts, games, self-paced learning, grouping, grades, praise, and many other extrinsic motivators can be part of the planning process and add to a more successful learning experience for both learners and educators.

However, the student who is tired, hungry or ill will bring very little intrinsic motivation to the learning setting, thus greatly reducing the effects of any of these extrinsic motivators. Maslow (1954) recognized that an individual's basic physical and emotional needs had to be met before the individual could consider needs for academic achievement and cognitive stimulation. A child who is rested and well fed but feeling threatened by an autocratic or permissive classroom environment will not be fully able to pursue success in academic work. Maslow's work has demonstrated how intrinsic motivation can be accessed and nurtured in all students. The classroom that functions as a community, with a shared sense of commitment and a cooperative esprit de corps, allows students to reflect more fully on their learning experiences and become motivated by the anticipation of new learning. Class meetings, high expectations for students and educators, and an overall sense of community all contribute to the learner's intrinsic motivation.

Reflect for a Moment

How do you feel around 10:30 in the morning on a day when you got up early, ate a decent breakfast, and possibly took time to exercise? How about on a day when you got up late, grabbed some cookies, and arrived 2 minutes late for class?

Caution must be used when planning the learning environment not to confuse lack of motivation with lack of instruction. For the student who does not understand the concept being taught, no amount of motivation can force understanding. If Harry doesn't know what "cow" is, he will never know, even if promised the world, unless he is provided with instruction about cows.

Temperament

Chess and Thomas (1985) define **temperament** as the "manner of thinking, behaving, or reacting characteristic of an individual" (p. 167). The way in which a learner deals with the educational environment is dictated by temperament. Children from birth exhibit individuality in the way in which they respond to their environment and the way others, particularly educators, respond to them and their needs. Nine characteristics have been identified: activity, rhythmicity, approach/withdrawal, adaptability, threshold of responsiveness, intensity of reaction, mood, distractibility, and attention span and persistence. Temperamental characteristics should not be confused with actual behavioral acts, however, because the former are not implicitly positive or negative.

In structuring a learning event, it is extremely important to incorporate activities that will enhance temperament rather than create conflict. Adjustments in response to the range of student activity level are helpful. Some students may need much more physical involvement with material during an activity than others. *Rhythmicity*, as it relates to temperament and learning, involves the timing of certain learning activities to match the student's natural physiological functions. Activities requiring greater amounts of concentration need to be scheduled when the learner is best able to focus his or her thoughts.

The educator must carefully scrutinize the nature of a learner's response to new stimuli needs. Determining how to present new materials and information needs to encompass whether a student responds with willingness and excitement (approach) or negative expressions and behaviors (withdrawal). Although all new learning should be clearly connected to existing knowledge, it becomes an even more critical feature of instruction for those students who have withdrawal as part of their temperamental makeup. Adaptability is the ease or difficulty with which the learner adjusts to new or altered learning situations. Some students flow easily from one activity to another; others need to have transitions clearly delineated before they occur. Changes in the physical environment of the classroom, such as lighting and noise levels, may alter the responsiveness of individual learners. Soft background music may enhance the productivity levels of some and interfere with those of others. In addition to the quality or direction of a student's reactions, the educator must take into account the intensity of such reactions. Intensity of reaction is extremely important in the planning of learning motivators. Children with high intensity levels may need less external motivation than others with lower reactive levels.

The attribute of temperament termed *mood* encompasses the amount of pleasant, happy, friendly behavior exhibited by a student in comparison with unpleasant, unhappy, unfriendly behavior exhibited when instructional situations vary. Reactions to variations in instruction and educators should be noted and dealt with positively before they turn into behavioral problems.

The concept of *distractibility* is not to be used interchangeably with *attention span* or *persistence*. Distractibility involves the ease with which a child's attention is diverted by external stimuli; attention span or persistence applies to the length of time a child pursues a given activity and continues it. In planning instruction, educators must remember to vary not only the content area but the response mode in order to decrease distractibility and increase attention span or persistance. To simply move from reading a science text to reading a history text is not enough. The students must be given variation in the task as well—moving, for example, from a creative writing assignment to a science experiment to a quiet reading time to a historical reenactment.

Observable Characteristics

Planning effective learning experiences requires all educators to be aware of and plan according to the observable physical/motor characteristics of the learners, including vision, hearing, and both gross and fine motor skills. In addition, educators must plan for learners who differ in gender, handedness, strength, endurance, and other factors of physical/motor development. Physiological maturation is an important variable in motor and perceptual-motor skills. Age is directly related to the maturation progress of these skills. A six-year-old should not be seen as lacking stamina or motor ability because he or she can not run for as long as a ten-year-old. Six-year-olds are generally not as large as ten-year-olds and lack the corresponding strength and muscular development. The physiological difference between six- and ten-year-olds is clear, and no educator would expect them to perform at the same level of motor and/or perceptual-motor skill development. An educator planning learning events needs to be aware of the various levels of stamina and other aspects of physical development that exist within a given group of students. The role of each individual student in highly active learning experiences should be carefully thought out so that each child's potential is maximized.

What is not quite as clearly understood are the intragroup differences that occur in development. In Ms. Perky's first grade class, for example, the motor and perceptual-motor abilities vary greatly. Three of her students are able to jump rope with ease, yet four others have great difficulty balancing on one foot.

Reflect for a Moment

Think about your own fifth grade class. Remember how big most of the girls were and how small most of the boys were? Remember how highly coordinated some kids were, and how clumsy others were?

In spite of a wealth of literature on gender issues, it is clear that students have very different experiences and opportunities in classrooms as a function of their gender (Good & Brophy, 1994; AAUW, 1992; Sadker, Sadker, & Klein, 1991). Morse and Handley (1985) studied seventh and eighth grade students for two years in science class and found that student-to-teacher interactions initiated by females dropped from 41 percent to 30 percent over the two-year period. Leinhardt, Seewald, & Engel (1979) studied students in thirty-three second grade classrooms and found that whereas girls had more academic contact and instructional time with teachers in reading, the boys who had more contact with teachers in math. Reading abilities of girls and boys were the same initially, but by the end of the year girls had significantly higher reading achievement.

Gender may still systematically limit the kinds of activities in which the learner engages. Influences such as peer pressure, modeling, or response to perceived attitudes of educators may enhance these activity limitations. Educators' expectations, based on gender, have an effect on student learning and should be carefully examined in planning. Intellectual challenges and opportunities for success must be devoid of gender bias.

Teacher expectations have a consistent influence on student learning outcomes. Palardy (1969) found that when teachers expected boys to have more trouble learning to read than girls, the boys indeed did perform at a lower level. Doyle, Hancock, and Kiefer (1972) found that both male and female students whose IQ scores had been overestimated by teachers had higher reading achievement than those whose IQ scores had been underestimated. Even more disconcerting is the fact that in several studies (Beez, 1968; Schrank, 1968) students expected to do well by their teachers did in fact achieve higher levels of performance than students not expected to do well. Taken together, these studies indicate that educator's expectations of their students can have a direct effect on subsequent student achievement.

Environment

Planning instruction that has intellectual and social relevance for students is of primary importance to ensure that learning will occur. The child's world, including his or her prior school experience, home and family, standard of living, and peer group, can have a decided effect on learning outcomes and will need to be taken into account in the instruction planning process.

Newson and Newson (1976) studied socioeconomic status (SES) and learning and found real differences in learning style between high and low SES families. Generally speaking, low SES families tend to emphasize rote learning rather than self directed. Other researchers have found clear differences among learners from different racial and cultural groups. With few exceptions, students from minority groups score lower than nonminority children on intellectual measures and academic achievement (Roberts, 1971). This may be because minority students have been systematically excluded not only from quality education (Kozol, 1967, 1992) but also from the standardization samples of many of the instruments used to assess their abilities. Educators, then, should use their knowledge of learners' SES and ethnicity to provide more successful classroom experiences for all (Sleeter & Grant, 1986).

One final aspect of the learners' environment that educators should consider during planning is peers. When Goodlad (1984) surveyed thousands of school students, he found that students regarded friends as the most valuable aspect of their schooling. The importance of the peer group to effective instructional planning, therefore, is clear. Educators must utilize their knowledge of student friendships and social groupings in a way that stimulates active, enthusiastic learning and minimizes disruptive classroom activity. Whereas aggressive and outspoken learners present planning challenges, the passive student will require adaptive planning as well. Many strategies exist for supporting school success using many types of peer relations. The reflective planner will consider these strategies carefully.

KNOWLEDGE OF CONTENT

The substance of teaching is content. Content is simply subject matter; it is what one teaches. Content is also transient. Knowledge of subject matter grows and changes rapidly, and what is basic today may be obsolete tomorrow. Content must be reflective of and related to ethnic, racial, and cultural groups. Although clearly defined opportunities for the infusion of ethnic and cultural content exist in social studies and language arts, educators with a thorough understanding of their subject matter are able to integrate multicultural information in mathematics, science, and other content areas. Educators' understanding of their content area is too narrowly defined when they are unable to see how their subject matter is related to cultural and normative issues (Banks & McGee-Banks, 1992).

For an educator to thoroughly understand content, she or he must be a perpetual student of it. Faded yellow lecture notes and standard textbooks cannot be the tools of an educator in the twenty-first century. Old news is just that; content must be continually revisited, analyzed, and updated. Subject matter cannot be separated from the teaching method. It consists not only of facts and concepts but of skills, attitudes, and appreciation. Knowledge of content goes beyond a simple conveying of factual information.

As society changes, the promotion of aptitudes for learning takes precedence over teaching today's facts (Corno & Snow, 1986). More important than the educator's understanding of the "what" of content is their ability to foster the "how." The development of intellectual skills and appreciation of subject matter is far more vital than rote memorization of information. Without development of critical thinking, problem solving, problem finding, and expressive skills, the value of instruction may be reduced to memorization and regurgitation of facts today and only useful in answering game show questions later in life.

Through careful selection of methods and content, the skills and understanding necessary for assimilating new knowledge that can be generalized to new situations will be obtained. Callahan and Clark (1988) discuss the need for understanding the **doctrine of contingent value**. Basically, this doctrine implies that the selection of instructional content must be based on its importance and usefulness to the student. Since all subject fields contain volumes of content, a thorough coverage of the most vital information is more appropriate than a superficial glance at everything.

Content itself is not an end but rather the means to knowledge (Callahan & Clark, 1988).

Reflect for a Moment

Some of your classes have surely been full of unrelated facts, but we hope some of them have been full of highly interwoven learning that you were helped to organize as you critiqued, analyzed, solved, built, and utilized the content.

KNOWLEDGE OF METHODS AND MATERIALS

Areas of equal importance in curriculum and instruction planning are the selection of teaching methods and instructional materials. Both will be discussed briefly here and elaborated on in subsequent chapters. Within the four basic teaching methods (expository, discovery, discussion and inquiry), there are many teaching strategies and techniques to be examined and a variety of other factors that must be considered (Jacobsen, Eggen, & Kauchak, 1993).

Teaching and learning styles, appropriate sequencing and pacing (Freiberg & Driscoll, 1992; Kauchak & Eggen, 1993), mode of presentation, learning stages, the three domains of learning, classroom arrangement, and management procedures are a few of the factors to be considered in developing productive teaching methods. Necessary to the planning process is not only an understanding but a purposeful selection of these skills and factors so that they may be strategically interwoven during the presentation of subject matter. Teaching methods must clearly establish connection, relationship, transition, and sequence so that individual threads of knowledge can be woven into blankets of understanding.

Sequencing and pacing are both facilitated when educators reflect on student success rates and group responses. Commercial materials may assist educators in sequencing content, but educators must examine such materials daily to determine how well they meet specific student needs and what additional activities or materials would further enhance student learning. Reflective educators constantly assess the relationship between a given lesson, the previous lesson, and subsequent lessons.

Pacing takes place within a given lesson, and across lessons over longer instructional periods. Student responses, verbal and written, will significantly influence when an educator moves from one phase of a lesson to the next, or from one section of a unit to the next.

Mode of presentation must be intimately linked with the student's learning style. Learning styles are often thought of in terms of student reception of information (see Chapter 3). There are a variety of presentation modes that an educator may use when presenting materials and information. To discuss those modes more easily, we have grouped them under the type of *input modality* they represent: auditory, visual, tactile, or kinesthetic.

Every mode of presentation both benefits and limits the teaching and learning process. Although all presentations should preferably be done using a multisensory approach—one that involves more than one modality—traditional forms of presentation often focus on only a single mode. An *auditory* mode prevails when all the material or information is presented by the educator orally and students must listen to learn. Lecture, discussion, and/or audio recordings must be perceived through sound for the learner to derive meaning. Generic across subject areas and grade levels, the lecture approach is the primary auditory mode and has its roots in ancient teaching. Lecture has survived because it is both an efficient and familiar device.

Despite negative student reports, (Birkel, 1973) analysis (Hillocks, 1981) and metaanalysis (Henson, 1980; Smith, 1978)) of the research has indicated that the lecture approach is no less effective than others when used with secondary or postsecondary students. However, Evertson, Emmer, and Brophy (1980) and Good and Grouws (1977) found that effective mathematics instruction in grades four through eight involved a multimodal or multisensory approach. Effective mathematics instruction was characterized by twice as much time spent in lecture coupled with visual demonstration and discussion than ineffective mathematics instruction.

Discussion, while still primarily focused on auditory input, has as an added factor verbal interaction between the educator and student. Where lecture is a teacher-directed approach, discussion is teacher facilitated. Discussion enables students to receive auditory input from a variety of sources. Additionally, discussion provides students opportunities to engage in higher-level cognitive thought processes.

A second group of presentation approaches focuses on the student's ability to receive information through the *visual* mode. Demonstrations are visual and provide a variety of stimuli to students by showing rather than telling, although they are most effective when the two devices are linked. Modeling varies from demonstration in two ways. (1) the added component of telling while showing is often not used; this is significant because values and morals are generally learned not by what the student hears an educator say but through observation of everyday actions. (2) Modeling, unlike demonstration, is frequently unplanned, and gives rise to a magnitude of unanticipated learner behaviors.

Tactile input guides the third mode of presentation and has as its focus the sensation of touch. The use of manipulatives, tracing, building or constructing, and fingerpainting are examples of tactile presentation. Tactile approaches are most often combined with visual and auditory presentations; they are rarely used in isolation.

Simulations, role playing, dance, and creative dramatics are approaches that use the *kinesthetic* mode as a focus for learning. Kinesthetic input has as its primary strength the opportunity to allow students to learn by doing, thinking, feeling, and responding physically to a variety of stimulus. It is the integration of physical movement with thought that brings a deeper, more tangible meaning to the learning experience.

In selecting teaching methods, it is also important to recognize that certain teaching strategies may be more appropriate than others, depending upon the student's learning stage (see Chapter 3). For students at the initial stage of acquisition, Smith (1981) recommends the use of physical guidance, shaping, modeling, demonstration, cueing, prompting, errorless learning, and backward and forward chaining. As acquisition advances, teaching methodology includes specific directions, feedback, and error drill (i.e., practicing items missed).

A learner who is at the stage of reversion responds erratically to the new skill being acquired (Idol, 1989). Because the student responds correctly some of the time and reverts back to entry level part of the time, teaching methods that reinforce correct responses and ignore incorrect responses or pinpoint error patterns are appropriate.

Mercer and Mercer (1989) point out that because learners approach skills in an automatic manner at the proficiency level, teaching tactics must vary from those used at either the acquisition or reversion stage. Strategies appropriate at this level involve positive reinforcement as well as an altering of reinforcement schedules. Teaching techniques such as periodic practice, overlearning, intermittent reinforcement schedules, social reinforcement, and intrinsic reinforcement or self-management are important for learners at the maintenance stage. Fundamental teaching methods at this stage focus on maintaining high levels of learning.

Stokes and Baer (1977) provide specific teaching suggestions that help the student generalize learning such as direct instruction, varying the setting and educator, gradual altering of instructional stimuli and reinforcers, and teaching in the natural environment. Conversely, research by Deshler, Schumaker, and Lenz (1984) and Ellis, Lenz, and Sabornie (1987) demonstrates that specific strategies should be employed throughout preceding instructional stages to promote generalization. Specifically, Ellis, Lenz, and Sabornie identify four generalization levels (antecedent, concurrent, subsequent and independent) that should be considered throughout the learning process.

Strike (1975) and Idol-Maestas (1983) suggest that discovery learning may be the most appropriate method for the adaptation stage. Previously learned skills are used in newly discovered ways without direct instruction.

Reflect for a Moment

Think for a minute about a teacher you have seen in action with a group of young learners. What "tricks of the trade" do you remember seeing? What did that teacher do that simply worked?

Selecting Materials

Besides possessing the knowledge of various teaching methods and techniques, educators must select and use appropriate materials. Decisions about using textbooks, audiovisual aids, student slates, response cards, experience charts, manipulatives, and other instructional materials change for every teaching situation, depending on anticipated learning outcomes, student needs, and the situational context.

Reflective teachers are always equipped with a wish list of materials, knowing that the need to obtain different materials arises whenever new units or topics of instruction emerge. They are familiar with a number of catalogues and routinely mark items in them so they may quickly and efficiently place orders whenever possible.

Reflect for a Moment

Quickly brainstorm a list of classroom materials. Give yourself 1 minute to list as many as possible. Compare your list with those of others in your class.

Examining potential instructional materials with a brief but effective procedure is also important to the successful selection process. Whenever possible, securing materials for a trial period is encouraged so that educators can actually field-test the items with students. Sometimes a checklist or rating scale can be developed for use with a certain type of materials, such as math manipulatives or primary texts.

As with teaching methods, educators must take into account the many characteristics of learners and the nature of the content to be taught when choosing which materials to use. Aside from general factors such as target age, cost, durability, and skill appropriateness, materials should be judged in terms of a number of instructional and managerial criteria (Gall, 1981; Mercer & Mercer, 1989). The sequence of skills should be easy to follow and logical. The organization of content should accommodate a range of student interests and abilities and be flexible enough to allow the use of a variety of outside materials and activities. Directions for educators and students should be clear and should apply to all stages of a given lesson, from warmup to assessment and remediation (when needed). Although much of the content may focus on cognitive learning, the content should show a clear commitment to affective and psychomotor learning along with ample opportunities for students to progress through all levels of each domain. Additionally, materials should provide for a variety of stimulus-response modality combinations (e.g., visual stimulus–motor response) to meet the range of preferred styles among students.

Management issues to be considered in selecting materials include a need for recordkeeping strategies, use of space, time needed for materials setup, student interest level, and extent of teacher assistance required. The considerations, while designed for educators who are considering the purchase of materials, are equally important in selecting materials during instruction planning.

For the reflective planner, selection of materials continues during and after instruction. Educators clearly must plan for students' preferred mode(s) of learning (see Table 6.4). Observing students as they work and asking them to assess the value of various materials will provide valuable input for the future use of instructional materials. In many circumstances, modifications in the materials themselves or in the way they are used will enhance student success and subsequent interest in learning.

It would be foolish to consider instructional materials without making use of the natural learning environment outside the classroom. Educators who fail to take

TABLE 6.4   Presentation Modes and Possible Materials/Activities

Auditory	Visual	Tactile	Kinesthetic
tapes	videotapes	sand	simulations
lectures	chalkboards	water	role playing
	books	clay	writing
	maps	fingerpainting	creative dramatics
	slides	art activities	rhythm activities
	overheads	displays	
	charts	flannel boards	
	pictures	magnet boards	
	posters	sand paper	

advantage of community resources are robbing students of living examples of practically every conceptual understanding ever taught in school. Field trips, resource people, local resource materials, community groups and area businesses, industries, and agencies must be carefully selected, but all these resources can bring students significantly closer to vital knowledge and experience too often limited to the printed word. One educator, frustrated with a social studies text, planned a year-long series of walking field trips to local sites where students became involved firsthand with all aspects of their community. Students recorded information from each trip and created a series of fully illustrated community story books. Using the community as a resource in this case allowed students not only to understand basic concepts more easily, but also to appreciate the interdependent nature of their own hometown.

Two other groups of materials to select from are teacher-made materials and free or inexpensive materials. As long as an educator is willing to make his or her own materials, the result is usually more closely matched with student needs than materials provided by a commercial manufacturer. Often only a letter or phone request is required to obtain free or inexpensive materials. Careful examination of such materials is, however, necessary, to avoid involving students with biased, useless, or irrelevant materials.

Finally, educators who wish to plan for a wide range of students will want materials that

- Pretest to help determine where to begin.
- Review previously learned objectives.
- Allow students to achieve objectives in multiple ways.
- Are adaptable to individual, small group, and large group settings.
- Allow students to proceed at their own rate and skip certain objectives already mastered.
- Have reinforcement activities. (Smith, 1983)

SUMMARY

An essential aspect of the learning process and a necessary element of effective teaching is instructional planning. The ability to convert aims to goals and then to objectives is a key feature of the organized educator.

Goals provide aims with a means for implementing curriculum. Goals are written to include either the cognitive, psychomotor, or affective domains. Additionally, goals maybe structured to be competitive, individualistic, or cooperative. After goals have been established, the collaborative team must develop objectives so that they can measure learning outcomes. Instructional objectives are drawn directly from goals to ensure their specificity and measurability.

There are four major reasons to plan instructional objectives. The first is to enable the educator to select content and procedures—what to teach and how to teach it. The second concerns the evaluation of the learning event—did the students learn and were the teaching methods, materials and content appropriate? The third deals directly with assisting students to organize for the learning event. The fourth is that objective writing enables the educator to reflect on the curriculum, eliminating what is obsolete and adding new information whenever necessary.

Educators must take into account the three domains of learning when writing objectives as well as goals. Objectives should be arranged in a hierarchy to be sure they match a student's learning stage.

Therefore it is clearly necessary for educators to have a thorough understanding of learners during the instructional planning process. Each student brings to the learning event unique characteristics and environmental influences. The learner's cognitive and academic levels, affective attributes, and observable skills must be carefully analyzed.

A variety of affective attributes contribute to the unique learning process of each student. All affective attributes focus on the emotional factors that may impact on the learner in either a positive or negative manner.

Content is the substance of teaching. It is vital that an educator develop a clear and ever-growing understanding of their content. Content must not only be kept current and relevant but connected to cultural and normative issues.

The selection of teaching methods and materials is perhaps as important to the learning process as content is. Inappropriate teaching methods or materials will prevent students from understanding content.

7

INSTRUCTIONAL MANAGEMENT

Key Terms

Academic learning time
Actual instructional time
Allocated instructional time
Attack strategies training
Cognitive behavior management
Engaged time
Environmental management
History
Immediacy
Learning climate
Family Educational Rights and
   Privacy Act (FERPA)
Multidimensionality

Organizational time
Publicness
Self-graphing
Self-instructional training
Self-recording
Self-reinforcement
Simultaneity
Time leaks
Time management
Transition time
Unpredictability

Objectives

After completing this chapter, the reader will be able to:

1. Identify environmental management factors that must be considered when organizing instruction.
2. Identify several strategies for establishing a positive learning climate.
3. Structure the physical environment to support specific activity areas.
4. Discuss the effective use of seating arrangements and display space.
5. Develop strategies to manage classroom time and avoid timewasters.
6. Devise techniques to maximize academic learning time.

7. Organize class time into a daily schedule that reflects educational priorities.

8. Create a practical recordkeeping system for student work.

9. Outline strategies for teaching learners to monitor their own learning.

PROFILES OF MANAGEMENT

Judy West

After teaching nine- to eleven-year-olds for three years, Judy West had grown comfortable with the barrage of interactions that filled the classroom every day. She observed so many different shapes, sizes, and minds yet was restrained by limited space and time. But hers was fast becoming a solid classroom environment, in part because Judy felt much more confidence with her ability to manage the multitude of events taking place at any given time. She believed in the benefits of success and had developed several techniques that guaranteed success for every student present.

Judy used a variety of teaching methods. Some topics lent themselves to group inquiry; others were better suited to whole class presentations or individual studies. As a result, students readily demonstrated their preferred learning styles, and Judy used this information to plan future lessons. She was an active member of three professional organizations that represented her teaching and research interests and read from all of their journals on a regular basis. She had also benefited from carefully planned teacher in-service programs, particularly the two-year-long studies on cooperative learning and academic learning time. Every month the group came together in a seminar to explore a new feature of cooperative learning and discuss their teaching in light of what they had learned.

Judy found that she naturally enjoyed her work, and this summer she was planning a totally new classroom layout. Her design was more responsive to students' learning needs. She worked for weeks setting up the room, and when it was done she felt proud. Children would definitely want to come into this room! Judy was more relaxed about the many decisions she faced daily. She had created three professional goals for the coming year, and one of them was to give herself time for her own 3Rs: rest, reading, and recreation. Another was to think more about her teaching. She planned to keep a journal, like some of the journals she had written as a student at San Angelo State. This decision blended in well with Judy's third goal, which was to embrace a fully inclusive class as part of a team of educators. Thirty nine- to eleven-year-olds would be in the group, and the adults included Judy, the speech/language therapist Pat Scott, and resource teacher Joe Monroe. With the support of the principal, the three teachers constructed an agreeable schedule. They knew their collaboration depended on their willingness to communicate and work together, and all three were excited about the coming year.

Over three years, Judy had acquired an in-depth knowledge of the curriculum and an equally thorough appreciation for teaching students, not just teaching curriculum. She had carefully organized files on the students, the curriculum, and lesson ideas. She found that she could also teach students a variety of strategies to organize themselves as well. As a result, they took more responsibility for their learning and were more motivated, too.

Tom Shushman

What was all the fuss about discipline problems? Sure, Tom Shushman remembered his first year of teaching sixth grade and how hard he had worked to gain control of his class. But since then he had really not had any major problems with students. If one of them did not belong in Tom's class, he or she was just shipped off to special ed. Special ed had small classes, and they could handle the real problem kids. In Tom's room, when he talked, the class listened and that was that. When the class door closed, so did students' mouths.

As far as he was concerned, the problems that students may have at home were to be left outside the school door; school curriculum was the order of business between 9 and 3 o'clock. Students arrived and immediately began the seatwork listed on the board. Tom corrected it at his desk and dutifully recorded the grades. He seated students in rows so they had a harder time cheating. Anyone caught talking during a test would be given a zero.

Tom had experimented with groups but found them too noisy. Those in-service days were usually a waste of his time. With all the craziness going on in the community, Tom preferred to not list his home phone number and liked living thirty miles from work. At school, he joked with the other teachers, mostly the guys. But he taught largely by himself. He liked his privacy. His classroom was very quiet, and very competitive.

Mary Faddington

What a workshop! All those neat ideas for teaching long and short vowel sounds— Mary Faddington couldn't wait to try them out in her class. Her kids loved to play the games she bought *and* the games she made herself. It was funny because kids sometimes told her it was too noisy. But they were usually the smarter ones, so they could learn something from it. Besides, she had read somewhere that kids needed to learn to block out noise.

Everyone always told Mary that she was the "kindergarten teacher" type. She just loved little kids and wanted them to feel comfortable in her room. The classroom was full of color and sound, with eye-catching displays all over the walls and twenty-five four- and five-year-olds running around and talking (some actually yelling) amid a storm of decisions about where to "play." Unfortunately, it seemed that every time Mary got a really fun activity going, the class had to go to physical education, or art, or some dumb assembly. The principal, after six years, was visiting Mary's room more than she thought he needed to. When he had commented for five years that her lesson plans were fragmented, Mary just argued that her activities were very beneficial to the young learners. It wasn't that she didn't want anyone watching her teach; she just preferred to do it her way.

Record keeping was nothing but a hassle for Mary, so she did as little as possible. She had a good eye for children's progress and could tell when a child was ready for any activities she planned. They had a fun time, that's for sure. Anyone walking by her room would think it was pretty wild, but Mary knew the children needed to exercise their bodies as well as their minds. Oh, a few parents usually got angry whenever a child got hurt in the classroom. It had never amounted to anything as far as Mary knew. Now, which of the fun ideas she heard about today would she do at school tomorrow?

ENVIRONMENTAL MANAGEMENT

Most teachers would agree that teaching is a demanding task. All students must be provided with instruction in reading, writing, language arts, mathematics, health, history, geography, science, music, art, physical education, and on and on. Schedules must be devised that will allow many students to come and go to receive special instruction (art, music, physical education) or related services. Time must also be allocated for collaborative lesson planning, preparing materials and assignments, assessing and evaluating students' work, filing reports, meeting with parents and colleagues, and, above all else, projecting a positive countenance throughout the day. The goal of instructional management is to create an environment that clearly supports meaningful learning experiences among all students in an efficient manner. This environment must reflect the importance of the home and family and must also be able to change to meet the needs of students.

To gain a fuller understanding of the way that the environment affects instructional management, educators need to consider various components of the environment that remain constant no matter who the students or the teachers may be. Doyle (1980) describes six factors that must be taken into account in effective **environmental management:** multidimensionality, simultaneity, immediacy, unpredictability, publicness, and history.

Multidimensionality

When we stop to count all of the decisions educators must make to effectively balance students and curriculum, it's not unusual to feel overwhelmed. The sheer number of events, or the **multidimensionality** of the typical classroom, is characterized by the number of different students in the room, the different goals and abilities of those students, the demand for planning different outcomes using different types of materials, and the different situations that arise constantly during the school day. Educators must juggle individual rates of learning with schedules, limited resources, assessment techniques and records, and moment-to-moment exchanges of information. One seemingly minor occurrence can have a surprisingly dramatic effect on the entire learning atmosphere. Teachers, therefore, must make many careful and sound instructional decisions for each lesson.

Simultaneity

Classrooms are amazingly dynamic, with many events taking place simultaneously throughout the day. **Simultaneity,** or the occurrence of many events at the same time, is an inevitable feature of any classroom environment. During a whole class presentation, the teacher has to present new learning in an organized manner, use age-appropriate language, visually monitor students around the room, adjust the level of questioning depending on the student, judge the accuracy of student responses, provide meaningful examples of the new learning, consider which students to engage, and clarify the learning when necessary with alternative strategies. If all of these decisions are required of the teacher in a whole class presentation, there are many more similar challenges when the teacher works with a small group within the larger classroom. Kounin (1970) uses the term *overlapping* to describe the educator's ability to manage several classroom events that occur simultaneously.

Immediacy

In addition to the many events occurring in a classroom and the simultaneous nature of these events, they happen at a pace that would surely baffle the keen observer. The **immediacy** of the classroom environment suggests that events take place quickly and constantly over time, demanding that the teacher think on his or her feet in a rapid, at times instantaneous fashion. Because immediacy leaves little room for reflection in the midst of a flurry of events, teachers in many cases should organize their day to allow reflection outside the classroom environment.

Unpredictability

A fourth component of the typical classroom environment is **unpredictability.** Interruptions, unexpected turns of events, and departures from the teacher's intended instructional procedure are everyday features of the contemporary classroom. Even without these common occurrences, the nature of the teaching/learning process (always involving two or more individuals) is so complex that it is usually impossible to predict exactly how any activity, no matter how well planned, will turn out.

Publicness

The fifth component of every classroom setting is its **publicness.** Every event that takes place in a classroom is usually witnessed by other students, sometimes by a large number of students. If a teacher does not see a student writing and passing a note, then other students quickly learn that they can pass notes without being seen by the teacher. If and when the teacher does confront a disruptive student, the other students quickly judge whether the teacher or the student deserves their support, and the result can be, on occasion, even more disruptive.

History

The last component of all classrooms is their **history,** or the accumulation of events over weeks and months that creates a common knowledge among students about the expected procedure for the entire year. This history is almost always a factor in the daily planning of learning activities, and students benefit from having these historically based routines acknowledged or confirmed by the teacher.

Reflect for a Moment

Are you overwhelmed by the classroom demands outlined? Though teaching is truly a challenging experience, you undoubtedly have instances in your own private life that present each of these environmental factors. For example, what do you do each day that is guaranteed to be unpredictable? When do you consciously do more than one task at a time?

REFLECTIONS ON RESEARCH

Bossert (1979) found, in studying fourth grade classrooms, that teachers used more desists and reprimands during recitation activities than during seatwork or small group activities. Seatwork activities, in general, were characterized by teachers helping individual students, but also by lower student involvement rates and more reprimands (Gump, 1967).

Doyle (1986) has concluded that these interactive events reflect a relationship between the teacher's management skills and the multiple variables of the environment. Studies of classrooms in which several activities take place simultaneously have shown that this type of environment produced fewer teacher reprimands, more individual directions, and more peer discussion focusing on higher-complexity tasks, but only when teachers could establish and maintain a sense of order in the classroom (Bossert, 1979; Wilson, Rosenholtz, & Rosenholtz, 1983; Soar & Soar, 1983). Arlin and Webster (1983) reported that mastery learning activities, in which individuals or small groups require more teacher help to achieve a given mastery level, were more difficult to manage instructionally because of an inherent disruption in time flow.

There is widespread recognition that instructional management is influenced by the interaction between environment and student (Evans, Evans, Gable, & Schmid, 1991). The best laid instructional plans, for example, are worthless if a student is suffering from a lack of food or rest. Likewise, the student who has constantly experienced failure and public humiliation during music class will not respond to even the most engaging activity in that environment. In another class, the noise level, although not openly distracting to most students, may totally obstruct a certain student's ability to concentrate on reading a book. Environmental variables and student behavior interact to create physiological, psychosocial, and physical obstacles to learning.

Many researchers have examined interactive events in classrooms. Gump (1967), in observing third grade classrooms, found that about half of teachers' actions were instructional and that almost one-quarter related to organization for learning. The remaining quarter was fairly evenly divided between managing inappropriate behavior and taking care of individual noninstructional needs.

Students in Gump's study (1967) were most involved during teacher-led small groups and least involved during peer presentations. Other studies concluded that students were more involved during recitations and teacher presentations and less involved during seatwork (Atwood, 1983; Kounin, 1970; Rosenshine, 1981; Silverstein, 1979). During seatwork, students tended to become active only toward the end of the designated seatwork time and did indeed finish at different times (deVoss, 1979; Stebbins, 1974).

Implications for Instructional Management

It appears, then, that many aspects of teacher and student behavior do interact with characteristics of the environment to create different outcomes for instructional management. Regardless of how the teacher spends school time, there are ten ways, according to Sabatino (1987), to help build a positive **learning climate:** (1) Be sure students know what is expected of them, academically and socially. (2) Be consistent; otherwise, in many cases, students will be confused, and learning adversely effected. (3) By all means, provide meaningful instruction. Students are more interested and more successful when learning is responsive to their real lives and needs. (4) Threats must be avoided. They serve no other purpose than to create conflict between people. (5) Treat students fairly. This is not the same as treating all students the same way; it means that individual needs should be considered in dealing with disruptive behavior. (6) Model self-confidence for students. The surest way to build self-esteem in each and every student is to relate to them all on a personal level and in a positive, supportive manner exuding self-confidence. (7) Make the effort necessary to provide sincere positive feedback to every student on a regular basis, whether it is for picking up a piece of scrap paper left on the floor, for getting an A on a test, or for being honest about an incident on the playground. Accentuate the positive! (8) Provide this positive feedback immediately, and constantly be on the lookout for acceptable conduct that reaffirms a positive school atmosphere. (9) Display those behaviors and attitudes that contribute to a positive school climate. Enthusiastic, courteous, and constructive teachers provide excellent models of learning for all students and have an effect on student behaviors. (10) Structure the environment so that students are challenged but not frustrated, encouraged to take responsibility for their learning and conduct, and expected to make steady progress. The probability of success will be higher if educators consider Sabatino's ten suggestions every time they design lessons and if their content is good. Simply following a checklist, however, does not always guarantee success.

Reflect for a Moment

Look over Sabatino's ten suggestions. Recall one of your best teachers ever, and check her or his effectiveness against the ten suggestions. Even if she or he does measure up fairly well on all ten, can you also recall less than successful experiences in that class?

ENVIRONMENTAL FACTORS

Louisell and Descamps (1992) emphasize four features of the environment that contribute appreciably to positive learning experiences for students. One feature is the amount of weight the teacher places on openness with feelings. Some teachers keep their feelings to themselves, and consciously or subconsciously expect students to do the same. Other teachers express their feelings openly and readily accept students' feelings as well. A second dimension is the way success and mistakes are regarded. Some teachers punish students who make mistakes. Failure occurs regularly for many in the class. Other teachers plan for high rates of student success. Help is readily available, and students do not hesitate to seek it from adults or peers in the classroom. Mistakes are anticipated and viewed as building blocks of the learning process rather than as reason for shame. A third basic dimension is the amount of enjoyment experienced by participants, both teachers and learners. Some classrooms are characterized by boredom, fear, and lack of laughter. Other classrooms are happy, productive, energetic places where students laugh and learn with enthusiasm. The fourth and very critical feature is how well the teacher tolerates open-ended experimentation and discovery learning along with the increased confusion and student talk that accompany it. Some teachers structure environments so that exploration and questioning is expected, whereas other teachers (and students) follow strict, predetermined procedures, with little time or room for student-initiated learning.

Reflect for a Moment

Can you recall a class where you felt free to express your feelings or a teacher who viewed mistakes as truly worthwhile learning experiences?

Many environmental factors that affect student learning are beyond the control of the teacher. Broader societal issues, including poverty, violence, family structures, and the media, all exert influence on students' readiness for learning. Other environmental variables, such as student empowerment, relevant learning experiences, and self-confident teacher behaviors, have a tremendous effect on student behavior and can be directed by the teacher. Among the many environmental variables within the teacher's control is the physical design of the classroom.

Classroom Design

Each year, before students arrive, reflective educators design the physical space in their classrooms. The physical layout of a classroom contributes to student learning (Meese, 1994; O'Connor, 1988; Stainback, Stainback, & Froyen, 1987), but only when educators first clarify what they want to achieve with that classroom design. The physical environment can contribute to a sense of community in a classroom. Rigid rows of desks, for example, do not support cooperation and communication among students as much as clusters of desks or circular arrangements do.

Prescott, Jones, and Kritchevsky (1967), in a study of the total amount of classroom space available, found some interesting outcomes. Smaller classroom size correlated with less sensitive, less friendly teachers; less interested, less interactive students; and more negative student interactions. Further, Silverstein (1979) found that students in more crowded classrooms were more distracted by other students. Needless to say, there should be plenty of physical space for people to move about in the classroom.

Specific Activity Areas

More specifically, space should be clearly defined for different learning areas in the room, and these areas should be arranged to complement each other. The design of the classroom should support a variety of learning settings. Louisell and Descamps (1992) emphasize, for example, the importance of having flexible arrangements in which tables, chairs, and desks can be moved around to accommodate various learning situations. This feature permits easier transitions from whole class presentations to small group activities. It is important for students to learn, at the beginning of the school year, how to transform the room from a whole class set-up to a small group arrangement.

Further, teachers should be able to visually scan the room and account for the learning that students are engaged in at any given time (Stainback, Stainback, & Froyen, 1987). On the other hand, all students should be able to clearly see the chalkboard, screen, or any other materials used to present instruction (Kauchak & Eggen, 1993). Teachers should also be able to move among students and instructional aids freely, with quick access to learners and teaching aids. Any individual student learning materials (paper, scissors, books) should be quickly accessible and returned to their proper storage place after use. Traffic patterns throughout the room should allow students to move about without distracting others (Bellon, Bellon, & Blank, 1992). Teachers can plan for traffic patterns by actually drafting a typical schedule, identifying what students will be doing, and walk through student behaviors. This way they can get a sense of the traffic patterns likely to emerge. Classroom partitions are often used by teachers who want to break up classroom space and minimize distraction among students. Paine, Radicchi, Rosellini, Deutchman, and Darch (1983) also suggest the use of self-correction stations where students can go to check a particular work exercise without relying on the teacher.

Evans, Evans, Gable, and Schmid (1991) describe eight types of specific activity areas that can be identified in most classrooms: large group, small group, individual student, teacher, paraprofessional work, recreation, audiovisual, and miscellaneous areas. The *large group area* can be used for whole class instruction and also for some discussions, guest speakers, and special events. *Small group areas* are usually located at tables or on a carpet in a designated spot where three to five students can work together with or without the teacher. *Individual student areas* are important because they provide each learner with a private space for her or his belongings. Some students benefit from the use of personal study carrels, where they can work with a minimum of distraction. The *teacher area*, usually around a desk, should be free of clutter, arranged neatly, and visible to all learners. Some teachers use their area for individual student conferencing.

Many classrooms include a *paraprofessional work area,* where staff members and volunteers can prepare materials or work with small groups of students. This area should be across the room from the teacher area to provide adequate monitoring of classroom activity. The *recreation area* is an important place for students to go and relax with a book, game, or cassette tape player when their classwork is completed. The *audiovisual area* can accommodate computers, tape recorders, self-instructional devices, and other equipment used by students for independent learning activities. Finally, numerous *miscellaneous areas* are possible for specific purposes, including cubbies, a variety of learning centers, self-correction stations, cabinet top display areas, and shelf or cabinet space.

Reflect for a Moment

Do you think all of these activity areas should be planned into high school classrooms, or only into elementary classrooms? Why or why not?

Extraneous Stimuli

Outside interferences, or *extraneous stimuli,* can distract students from classroom activities. Knowing the distractibility of individual students will help an educator determine who should be seated away from windows, doorways, or high traffic areas. Some students, when seated near each other, will socialize during instructional time and benefit from carefully designated seating. The physical layout of the room must also minimize the chance that students will be distracted by other students, even when they are actively engaged in meaningful but different activities. These distractions can be avoided by setting up quiet activity areas, like the library corner, away from active areas, such as the block area.

Seating Arrangements

Seating arrangements tend to vary depending on the instructional strategy being implemented. Educators can create a variety of teaching/learning situations in their minds and arrange desks or tables to best suit the instructional approaches they have selected. Group or cooperative learning, for example, will require a very different layout than individual, self-paced learning. Good and Brophy (1986) observed a fourth grade classroom where students were seated at individual desks but clustered in groups. A creative writing lesson was taught that required discussion followed by individual writing. Students found being in groups helpful for the discussion phase, but more difficult when they tried to concentrate on their individual writing assignment because of the proximity of classmates. Educators must constantly assess the relationship between the physical setting of the classroom and the intended instructional activities. If this relationship is not complementary, students' learning will be compromised.

Another factor influencing seating arrangements is the nature of the students involved. Most students who are off task are located farther from the teacher than other students; students who interact most with the teacher are those seated front and center (Adams, 1969; Adams & Biddle, 1970). Therefore it is wise to spread evenly around the room those students who model good behavior. Doyle (1986) suggests that nontraditional arrangements (circles, clusters) encourage more student-to-student interaction and independent learning than traditional rows. Separate activity areas and work spaces are important to consider if teachers want to support personalized student learning experiences, various collaborative structures, and inclusive education.

Display Space

Display space can be planned to support any and all student learning. It is important for students to build displays throughout the classroom to reflect and reinforce their learning. Some displays can be primarily informative; others can be examples of successful student work. Displays can also be used to provide information about schedules, rules, assignments, and general school policies. The overall visual appearance of the room can communicate a great deal to students and visitors. A room that is vibrant, colorful, filled with objects, live plants and animals, and students' successful projects sends a very exciting and positive message to anyone who enters. Educators should be cautioned, however, against overdoing classroom displays, thereby creating a sense of congestion among students. The classroom should project an aesthetically pleasing feeling of warmth and support to all learners. Artwork, plants, and music can all contribute to the aesthetic features of the classroom and encourage more positive student attitudes and behaviors.

Actually drawing a plan, with details of square footage, furniture, storage, teaching/learning materials, displays, lighting, temperature, and color, is a valuable

TABLE 7.1   Questions Related to Classroom Design

1. When someone stands at the entrance to the classroom, does its visual appearance make them want to come in and investigate further?
2. Can all learners easily see the chalkboard or area where large group presentations originate?
3. Can the teacher move freely among learners, with immediate access to any learner at a given time?
4. Are frequently used learning materials (for teachers and students) readily accessible?
5. Are high traffic areas (pencil sharpener, sink, doorway, etc.) located away from where all learners are seated?
6. Do the displays throughout the room reflect the work of students or provide necessary school/class information?
7. Are the displays carefully arranged to avoid a congested look?
8. Can students engage in independent activities without distracting other students? Are there places for students to go when they want to be alone with their thoughts?
9. Does the seating arrangement support the type of learning setting desired (cooperative, individualistic, competitive)?
10. Do the lighting and temperature in the room facilitate student concentration and learning?
11. Is there enough storage space so that materials not being used can be kept out of the way of current learning activities?
12. Is the classroom arranged in a way that allows furniture to be moved around without major difficulty?
13. Is the atmosphere comfortable, inviting, and reflective of you as an individual?

activity for any educator who intends to consciously reflect on her or his classroom design in an effective manner. Another strategy is to visit a variety of other classrooms and discuss the advantages and disadvantages of different designs with colleagues. The questions in Table 7.1 can assist educators in assessing the physical design of a classroom. Ultimately, there are dozens of classroom designs to consider, and each educator will come up with his or her own unique arrangement, keeping in mind the importance of providing a place where students feel comfortable, important, and ready to do their best.

Reflect for a Moment

Do you ever recall standing at the entrance to a classroom, looking in, and getting excited about being there? How did the room look? How was the furniture arranged?

MANAGEMENT OF TIME

"Problems concerning time management contribute to teacher stress and burnout and possibly, to attrition from the field. Since time is not replaceable or expandable, it must be allocated judiciously to provide the most service to the greatest number of people" (Dettmer, Thurston, & Dyck, 1993, p. 196). Unfortunately, educators have a tendency to compensate for loss of time by trying to work faster and do more things. Maker (1985) states that the purpose of developing effective time management practices is not to complete everything, but rather to accomplish professional and personal goals. Being productive is very different than being busy. Not unlike reading, time management is a skill that needs to be learned and will improve with practice. Dettmer, Thurston, and Dyck (1993) point out that personality differences and cultural diversity affect the way in which an individual values and uses time and therefore must be considered when developing management practices.

Reflect for a Moment

Do you get more done when you systematically plan your time? Do you have days when you are busy all day, and other days when you have more free time? How well do you manage your time on such days?

Dettmer, Thurston, and Dyck (1993) suggest a four-step plan for developing productive **time management** practices that let educators achieve personal and job satisfaction, enjoy feelings of self-worth, and make progress toward long-term goals.

Establishing clear goals and developing plans carefully prevents educators from wasting their time, energy, and resources. By reflecting on what they wish to accomplish and how they might achieve it, they activate the planning process. Goals, once developed, become the means by which the use of time is planned. When educators know where they wish to go, they can map out a plan of action for arriving there.

The second step is *identifying and eliminating timewasters.* Lakein (1973) identifies four basic types of time: payoff, investment, organization, and waste. The first three are productive, and the last serves no useful purpose. Wasted time may result from ineffective communication, indecision, lack of proper planning, confusion about responsibilities, and the inability to say no. By identifying and making an effort to eliminate time-wasting habits, educators are taking the first step toward *establishing positive time management strategies.*

As stated earlier, the value and use of time is a personal matter. Although there are no universal strategies, Davis (1983) provides fourteen suggestions for the positive management of time in Table 7.2.

Taking care of oneself is an extremely effective time management strategy. To develop a feeling of personal and professional satisfaction, educators must develop skills for taking care of themselves. The educator who is overburdened and exhausted is of little use to his or her students. Learning to say "no," using a "Do Not Disturb" sign, getting adequate rest, and rewarding themselves for personal successes are just a few of the ways educators can take care of themselves.

Along with the personal benefits educators reap from positive time management practices comes the modeling effect created for learners. Learners not only profit academically from having an organized and productive teacher, they also begin to adopt their own personal time management skills.

TABLE 7.2   Applications for Using Time Wisely

1. Make a "To Do" list.
2. Learn to say no.
3. Rearrange your personal schedule.
4. Plan for bits of time. Keep "Can Do" lists for periods of 5, 15, and 30 minutes.
5. Delegate.
6. Break mountains of work into molehills.
7. Set deadlines and time limits.
8. Organize your desk and office area.
9. Handle the C (lesser priority) tasks.
10. Overcome procrastination.
11. Take less time to do routine things.
12. Get a "Do Not Disturb" sign and use it adamantly, without guilt.
13. Plan time for yourself.
14. Plan treats to reinforce your own efficiency and measurable progress toward goals.

Source: Davis, W.E. (1983), in Dettmer, P., Thurston, L.P., & Dyck, N. (1993). *Consultation, collaboration, and teamwork for students with special needs.* Boston: Allyn & Bacon.

Classroom Time

"Time is the coin of teaching. That is what we have to spend to obtain learning. We can spend that time wisely on quality learning, or we can fritter it away, when students waste time waiting or doing busywork" (Hunter, 1994, p. 155). Effective time management is a critical feature in the development of a classroom environment that is conducive to learning. The carefully structured curriculum becomes meaningless if time management has not been undertaken. The manner in which educators and students manage time has an enormous impact on their success in the classroom.

A strong relationship exists between the use of school time and students' learning (Corno, 1979; Emmer, Evertson, & Anderson, 1979; Kounin, 1977; Paine, Radicchi, Rosellini, Deutchman, & Darch, 1983). To give a learner every possible chance to be successful, an educator must make the most appropriate use of time. Although they are the primary time managers within the classroom environment, educators should not take sole responsibility. Aides, volunteers, parents, and students can play critical collaborative roles in the effective management of time. Aides and volunteers can assist with instructional and organizational activities that will reduce empty time. Parents can maximize their children's learning time by making sure they eat a nutritious breakfast, arrive at school promptly, and attend daily. Last, learners cannot be viewed as bystanders in their own educational process. They should also be accountable for their instructional time by using it to the fullest.

Two major elements are involved in the management of instructional time: allocated time (or activity scheduling) and actual time (or maintaining schedule). Paine, Radicchi, Rosellini, Deutchman, and Darch (1983) describe three levels of allocated time: (1) school time, (2) class time and, (3) instructional time. In any schedule educators must consider the length of time learners are in school, the time they and students are in the classroom, and the time that should be set aside for each instructional activity. Discussion of the first two levels is limited because they are not within educators' control. The amount of time learners are in school and in the classroom is largely dependent on policy set by school boards that determine length of school day, recess time, and lunch period.

Within the two major elements of allocated versus actual, there are four basic categories that classroom instructional time can fall into: (1) allocated instructional, (2) actual instructional, (3) engaged, and (4) academic learning time (Gartland & Rosenberg, 1987). The amount of time the school or educator sets aside to teach a given content area or lesson is **allocated instructional time.** Critics of the educational system often advocate increasing allocated instructional time as a means of correcting what they view as the less than adequate learning going on in schools. Lengthening the school year or day will increase allocated instructional time, but does it increase learning? Karweit (1984) found a positive but weak correlation between increased length of allocated instructional time and learning. Simply put, even if allocated time for any given subject were to be doubled, students would learn only slightly more than they did with originally allocated time.

Actual instructional time, on the other hand, is the amount of time when instruction is actually taking place and can be viewed as a subset of allocated instructional time. Unlike allocated instructional time, when actual instructional time is increased there is a direct effect on learning. Effective educators understand that well-planned and well-used actual instructional time is valuable not just for learning but to help manage behavior within the classroom. Fewer management problems occur in classrooms where educators structure high rates of instructional time that in turn result in increased engaged time for the learner (Emmer, Evertson, Sanford, Clements, & Worsham, 1994).

Reflect for a Moment

When is allocated instructional time not actual instructional time? In what way is allocated instructional time used that keeps it from being actual instructional time?

Engaged time refers directly to the amount of time the learner spends attending to a lesson or task. According to researchers (Berliner, 1987; Karweit, 1984; Rosenshine, 1983), classrooms vary widely in rates of engaged time, ranging from as low as 50 percent to as high as 90 percent. Rosenshine (1983) found an engagement rate of about 74 percent in his study of second and fifth grade classrooms. There appear to be significant differences between more and less effective educators in the amount of engaged time exhibited by their students. At the fifth grade level, effective educators' students had engagement rates over 80 percent; with less effective teachers, their rate dropped to almost 60 percent (Rosenshine, 1980). Engagement time is important as a gauge of an educator's impact on his or her students; if learners are not attending, the most carefully organized and well-presented lesson will be lost

Additionally, there is a difference in engaged time rates and student achievement levels. Low-achieving students frequently have engagement rates below 50 percent, whereas high achievers are generally engaged for 75 percent of the time or more (Evertson, 1980; Frederick, 1977). Kauchak and Eggen (1993) point out that these lapses of engaged time (almost 50% for low achievers and 25% for high achievers) present educators with a challenge.

The link between engaged time and achievement is a complex one involving more than amount of time attending. The educator must also be aware of behavior patterns of learners as they relate to engaged and nonengaged time rates. "High-ability students finished their academic tasks and *then* went off-task; low-ability students went off-task *while* they were working on academic tasks" (Kauchak & Eggen, 1993, p. 106). Anderson, Brubaker, Alleman-Brooks, and Duffy (1985) found that low-ability first graders were frequently given tasks beyond their ability level. These tasks were too difficult for the learners to complete, which created frustration and interfered with engaged time. This behavioral pattern of lost engaged time should be of particular concern to educators pointing out the necessity of academic learning time.

The most important of these categories is **academic learning time.** This category incorporates active engaged time and the appropriateness of instruction. Instruction during this time is at an appropriate level of difficulty, learners are *actively* attending, and a high rate of success exists. "During academic learning time, the students assessed strengths and weaknesses are accurately matched to the assignments or to the instruction" (Meese, 1994, p. 81).

The key feature of academic learning time is success. The desired rate of success is governed not only by the situation but also by the learner's ability level and the content. Diggory (1966) suggests that following successful experiences learners raise expectations and aspire to higher goals. Success rates should be 90 percent or higher when the potential for confusion and frustration is greater (as with homework) (Berliner, 1984). "Younger students, low achievers, and students from lower socioeconomic backgrounds need higher rates of success than do their older, higher achieving, or more advantaged counterparts" (Kauchak & Eggen, 1993, p. 107). Learners such as those indicated have a history of failure in the classroom and are inclined to become frustrated by low success rates. Higher rates of success should be required when the material presented is sequential—that is, built on previous knowledge and skills—than when lessons are based on less structured content. Educators can increase learner success rates by: (1) Breaking instruction into smaller segments, allowing learners to master concepts or content before moving on to next segment. (2) Being explicit about content, modeling skills. (3) Using questions to maintain attention and assess learners' comprehension. (4) Providing guided practice before learners work independently. (5) Providing opportunity for learners to over-learn concept or content. (6) Using formative assessment and reteaching if necessary. (Rosenshine & Stevens, 1986)

As stated earlier, the amount of time spent in a particular school or classroom is often limited by policy. The National Commission on Excellence in Education (1983) suggests that educators must learn to maximize school, classroom, and instructional time. Although educators may not be able to lengthen allocated instructional time, they can successfully increase it by using a variety of well-researched techniques (Gartland & Rosenberg, 1987). All methods have as an essential component, the concept that preactive and proactive planning (see Chapter 6) are fundamental.

A variety of effective teaching behaviors relate directly to engaged time, resulting in increased student attention to task and therefore impacting on academic learning time. Gartland and Rosenberg (1987) state that at least 50 percent of class time should be devoted to interactive activities and 35 percent of instructional time be spent monitoring controlled and independent practice (see Chapter 8 for examples of each).

Educators must also minimize interruptions from persons outside the class during their presentation of materials, instruction, or directions. Cohen and Hart-Hester (1987) suggest arranging the room so the educator is not facing the door during instruction. This will reduce the possibility that a passerby might be encouraged by eye contact to interrupt.

Additionally, educators need to begin and end classes on time. The movement from one activity to another is known as **transition time** and needs to be completed both smoothly and quickly. Transition involves not only the educator but the learner as well. Paine, Radicchi, Rosellini, Deutchman, and Darch (1983) provide three reasons for planning and actively teaching lessons on transitioning to learners. First, it will minimize the amount of nonacademic time learners spend in school. Second, it will also provide educators with more academically engaged

TABLE 7.3   Transition Checklist

1. Are all materials ready for each lesson or activity?
2. Are materials organized and easily accessible?
3. Has a daily schedule been posted?
4. Have transition time rules been established and reviewed?
5. Has a warning been given that an activity or lesson is going to end?
6. Do students have their materials ready for each lesson or activity?

Source: From "Managing life in the classroom: Dealing with the nitty gritty," by J. Olson, 1989, *Academic Therapy*, 24(5), pp. 545–553. Copyright 1989 by PRO-ED, Inc. Reprinted by permission.

time. Third, it will decrease behavior problems that often result when learners are given too much unstructured or down time.

The development and use of verbal and nonverbal signals may help to eliminate confusion and extraneous movement during transition times. Posting the day's schedule and announcing transitions in advance also helps students prepare themselves for change. Table 7.3 offers educators a checklist of transition reminders.

Additionally, it is extremely important for educators to have prepared all the materials for each lesson before the beginning of the instructional day. Educators will have more time for instruction when their materials are available and organized, and they may enlist the assistance of aides, volunteers, and/or learners in this organizational task.

Reflect for a Moment

What are some examples of transition times in your elementary school experience? Your secondary school experience? What do you recall doing during these "down" times as a student?

Timewasters

According to Hunter (1994), **time leaks** may occur during three phases of the teaching/learning process: (1) transition time; (2) instructional time; and (3) postinstruction, independent practice time. During these three periods, "potential time leaks can be plugged when students are *taught* to maximize use of that time for generating meaning, thinking, and learning. Notice that the verb is 'taught,' not 'told' or 'admonished'" (Hunter, 1994, p. 156). Time leaks are common during the transition that occurs at the beginning of a school day. Children may arrive at varying times and there are often unexpected visitors and problems. Poor directions, learning tasks that are either too difficult or too easy, and use of nonrelevant materials all create time leaks that are related to instructional time. Time leaks during postinstruction include students working independently on materials that produce little academic gain or students not lining up quickly.

Educators often do not realize how much time is spent on noninstructional activities until they do a detailed time analysis. Organizational and transition times account for the largest block of noninstructional time. Noninstructional or organizational activities are negatively correlated with academic achievement. Stallings (1980) found significant increases in student achievement, when noninstructional or **organizational times** or activities were decreased. Unfortunately, as much as one-third (Berliner, 1979; Leinhardt, Zigmond, & Cooley, 1981) of actual instructional time is lost as a result of noninstructional or organizational activities. Of that one-third, 20 percent or more of actual instructional time is lost as a result of activities outside the educator's control, such as assemblies, standardized tests, and fire drills (Berliner, 1987). Essentially, the more time an educator spends on these type of activities (discipline, announcements, transitions, etc.), the less time there is for academic instruction. Gartland and Rosenberg (1987) suggest that in order to maintain higher levels of academic achievement, less than 15 percent of class time should be spent on organizational or noninstructional tasks.

Schedules

Another important aspect of time management is scheduling. Careful scheduling not only serves to increase instructional time but also decreases time spent on discipline. Scheduling involves arranging the time for each day. A carefully planned daily schedule ensures not only that enough activities have been developed but also that there is sufficient time to complete and evaluate them. Daily schedules should reflect maximum time for instruction in each of the content areas; activities should be selected to offer the greatest potential for teaching and learning. A well-developed schedule alternates more enjoyable activities or lessons with those less appealing to learners (Polloway, Patton, Payne, & Payne, 1985).

Unfortunately, there is little empirical advice to guide educators in developing their classroom schedules. Orelove (1982), discussing the implication of the time-achievement relationship, emphasizes that if educators expect students regardless of instructional needs to achieve the goals established for them, daily schedules must be designed to reflect those priorities, and they must be adhered to. Thus, it is imperative for a classroom to work efficiently so that the educator or collaborative team can maintain a daily schedule. Posted daily schedules help to provide structure for students and eliminate the "What's next?" or "When do we have . . . ?" type of questions that draw away from academic content. That is not to say that changes to the schedule cannot occur. However, these changes should be announced in advance to decrease the confusion they create.

The daily schedule provides the foundation for all classroom learning. Educators need to develop their scheduling practices early in the school year and use them consistently. Gallagher (1979) provides specific suggestions for planning effective schedules for both large classroom groups and individual students. Each student should have a clear understanding of the daily schedule (see Table 7.4) and be given work that can be completed by the end of that day. Educators should build extra time into the daily schedule, remind students of time limits, and avoid assigning more of the same type of work to students who finish early. Activity choices are a far more appropriate alternative. Educators should continually preplan according to learners' needs, alternate less appealing and more appealing

TABLE 7.4   Daily Schedule

8:30	Students arrive
8:45	Planning and set up
9:00	Opening exercises/organizational tasks
9:15	Math instruction
10:00	Language arts instruction
10:30	Recess
10:45	Reading instruction
11:30	Journal writing
11:45	Story reading (by educator, parent, or aide)
12:00	Lunch
12:20	Recess
12:50	Return from recess/ bathroom and drinks
1:00	Social studies instruction
1:40	Science instruction
2:15	Art/music/physical education
2:45	Closing exercises
2:55	Dismissal
3:00	Collaboration time

tasks, and try not to spring unexpected activities on students. Daily positive feedback to individual students is strongly suggested.

The initial step in developing a daily schedule involves the analysis of actual classroom time. Exactly how much time do learners spend under educators' direction? In an average day, learners may be in the school for six hours. However, not all of that time is spent in the classroom; between lunch and recess(es), as much as 65 to 70 minutes a day may be lost. Time should be allocated for activities based on their importance and time slots should be determined in a manner that maximizes students' learning potential. The basic format for a daily schedule is presented in Table 7.4. It should be noted that the content areas and their order are presented merely as an example (see Chapter 8 for scheduling as a thematic unit). Collaborative teams must work together to select actual content areas according to a diverse set of criteria , such as learners' cultural backgrounds, achievement levels, related services, and available resources.

Polloway et al. (1989) suggest that a schedule such as the one presented in Table 7.4 serves a variety of purposes: to meet prescribed learning goals and objectives, to facilitate the planning process, to assure varied activities, and to provide for structured instructional time. "A well-designed schedule is valuable because it assists the teacher in planning a series of different activities and events that make coming to school interesting and stimulating enough for children and structured enough for efficient teaching" (Polloway et al., 1989, p. 79).

In an inclusive classroom, children may be operating on schedules that differ somewhat from one another. Here individual schedules (see Table 7.5) will be subsets of the larger group schedule. For example, within the time allocated for language arts, Mr. Domenici, the speech pathologist, works with a small group of

TABLE 7.5 Individual Daily Schedule

8:30	Students arrive
8:45	Math sponge
9:00	Opening exercises; turn in homework & lunch money
9:15	Math
9:15	Instruction with teacher
9:30	Independent work
9:45	Computer activity related to math
10:00	Language arts instruction
10:00	Instruction with teacher
10:15	Small group with speech therapist
10:30	Recess
10:45	Reading instruction
10:45	Instruction with collaborative teacher
11:00	Small group reading activity
11:15	Book conference with teacher
11:20	Computer activity related to reading
11:30	Journal writing
11:45	Story reading (by educator, parent, or aide)
12:00	Lunch
12:20	Recess
12:50	Return from recess/bathroom and drinks
1:00	Social studies instruction
1:00	Instruction with postmaster
1:20	Social studies project
1:40	Science instruction
1:40	Instruction with Native American guide
1:20	Small group identification project
2:15	Music
2:45	Closing exercises; turn in completed work; copy homework assignments in notebook
2:55	Dismissal

fourth graders on the expressive language skills objectives included on Mary Lou's IEP. Thanks to advance scheduling, this activity is coordinated with the language art activity; it is designed to allow students to receive their initial instruction from the fourth grade teacher and complete the activity with Mr. Domenici's assistance. Collaborative teaching is a critical feature of all effectively managed inclusive classrooms. Only when adequate professional resource support is present can educators take on truly collaborative roles and accomplish their goal of providing appropriate instruction to all learners.

Time limits are implicit in any classroom schedule and should be used to assist students in structuring their learning. When learners are given a predetermined amount of time to work on a task, they can budget their energies accordingly. Time should not be used competitively among students, but rather as a tool. The fact that some may finish more quickly should not be used to belittle students who take longer.

Collaboration Time

The inclusive classroom requires that educators collaborate. Lack of time is the major deterrent to successful collaboration (Dettmer, Thurston, & Dyck, 1993; Idol-Maestas & Ritter, 1985; Johnson, Pugach, & Hammittee, 1988; McGlothlin & Kelly, 1982; Speece & Mandell, 1980). According to Stainback and Stainback (1985), many general and special educators report that their school day is not designed to accommodate collaboration. Additionally, even when a meeting can be arranged and schedules coordinated, the amount of time is not sufficient for productive collaboration to occur.

Time to meet and collaborate is essential for school staff, classroom teachers, and support personnel if inclusive schools are to be successful. Administrators must assume the primary responsibility for scheduling the time needed for teams to collaborate. By lending both support and authority to the process, administrators can establish an environment in which school staff will be more willing to brainstorm methods for teaming and collaborating. During their discussions with school-based collaborative teams, West and Idol (1990) noted a variety of creative solutions to the time management factor (see Table 7.6). Every inclusive system is

TABLE 7.6   Possible Time Management Solutions

1. Regularly bring large groups of learners together for special types of school experiences (e.g., guest speakers, films, plays) with fewer staff supervising.
2. Have the principal or other support staff/supervisor teach a period a day on a regularly scheduled basis.
3. When learners are working on the same independent assignment or study activity, arrange for them to be clustered together in large groups (e.g., in the multipurpose room or library).
4. Hire a permanent rotating substitute or two part-time substitutes for same half-day (this may be done at no cost to the school district by business community school adopters).
5. Utilize aides or volunteers to guide or supervise groups/classes of learners at class-changing time, lunch, recess, or music or physical education classes.
6. Utilize volunteers(e.g., parents, grandparents, community business leaders, retired teachers).
7. The principal could assign specific times each week for staff collaboration only (documentation required).
8. Alter the school day to provide staff collaboration time without learners (e.g., last Friday afternoon each month).
9. Utilize student teachers.
10. The principal could set aside one day per grading period as "collaboration day" (no other activities can be substituted on this day).
11. The faculty could vote to extend the instructional day 2 days per week for 20 minutes to provide a collaborative period for staff (days can be staggered as well as time periods each day of the week to free staff on different days/times).

Source: From "Collaborative consultation in the education of mildly handicapped and at-risk students." by J.F. West and L. Idol, 1990, *Remedial and Special Education, 11* (1), pp. 29–31. Copyright 1990 by PRO-ED, Inc. Reprinted by permission.

unique, and West and Idol note that there is no universal strategy that will work for all school systems. Each school has to devise the time management system that works best under its unique set of circumstances. However, Schenkat (1988) believes that if schools restructured working conditions to permit greater flexibility in scheduling, educators could find time to collaborate and more creative solutions would be developed to deal with the diversity of learning and behavior problems present in any classroom.

Reflect for a Moment

If collaboration is necessary to provide inclusive programs, when would you, as an educator, be able to find time to meet with colleagues?

MANAGEMENT OF RECORDS

Before any discussion on managing records, it is imperative to understand the legal aspects of this subject. The **Family Educational Rights and Privacy Act** (FERPA) (1974), most commonly known as the **Buckley Amendment,** was designed to provide protections in two major areas—access and accuracy. Although often cited in discussions of the information maintained on children with disabilities, this act covers any type of student record a school keeps (e.g., attendance, cumulative files, test scores). The Buckley Amendment requires public schools to permit parents and students over age eighteen to have, under certain circumstances, access to their records. The purpose behind this provision is to allow a parent or student the opportunity to ascertain whether the information in the records is complete and accurate. If it is deemed inaccurate, there are special provisions for making appropriate changes and corrections. A second provision is designed to protect the individual student's school records from unauthorized inspection, allowing access only to persons with privileged reason.

Froyen (1993) identifies accountability as a motivating factor in establishing and maintaining records throughout the school. Recording and maintaining accurate information about their teaching and learning allows both teachers and students to reflect on their efforts more productively. Information related to student characteristics, curriculum, instruction, student performance, materials and supplies, and professional development is vital to a successful teaching/learning environment. Gathering, storing, and accessing this information requires the teacher to establish and implement an efficient system for maintaining it.

The school can support this effort by maintaining current and accurate information on each student, including attendance, personal information, achievement data, and health status. In most schools this cumulative file is regarded as the official record for a student and is updated annually. It is a valuable source of information when students move from one district to another. The cumulative file also serves to help teacher and parent understand the student's academic and social behavior.

The same benefits come from maintaining accurate records on the organization of the curriculum. Before the beginning of any school year, well-organized teachers spend time creating a flow of curriculum and map out the units of instruction for the year. They do not start at Chapter 1 in all the textbooks and follow them to their conclusion; instead, teachers familiarize themselves with the state curriculum guidelines and develop a plan for active learning toward those curriculum outcomes. The plan becomes activated by short-term objectives that are recorded under each long-term goal and tentative activities that are recorded for each short-term objective. The organization continues on a weekly and daily basis as materials are prepared and adjustments made to meet individual student needs.

In organizing the curriculum for instruction, teachers must often use a recognized hierarchy or sequence of learning both across and within grade levels. Again, the school or district can actively support teachers' efforts to organize the curriculum with a clear framework of content and expectations at a broader level. Under no circumstances, however, should the academic progress of any student be compromised by the use of organized curriculum. For example, the skilled, avid, and fluent reader should not be subjected to a lockstep reading program.

Teachers often group students for instruction in a variety of ways depending on the nature of the lesson. Whether it is ability grouping, cooperative learning, multi-age grouping or interest grouping, teachers will find that keeping records of different grouping configurations helps them make future grouping decisions. Billy, normally a rather passive, nonverbal student, participates actively with older students and may benefit from being grouped with older students more often. Another group of students may share an avid interest in a local sports team and may benefit from working together on a research project. The teacher can help this process by making sure that the group has an adequate plan for completing their work, including a timetable for completing any number of subtasks. In both of these situations, well-organized records facilitate the learning process.

One of the most successful elements of effective teaching is using students' prior learning to plan subsequent lessons. Assessment of student learning is a critical aspect of recordkeeping and will be addressed throughout Part III. All teachers, however, should have individual student files (portfolios) with a collection of data, including projects, cassette tapes, drawings, written work, anecdotal notes and observational data, conference information, student self- and peer evaluations, and parent communication. One valuable strategy is to keep comprehensive records in either a pre- and posttest fashion or in a dated sequence, to emphasize students' progress over time instead of just how they compare with other students or some remote norming population. Maintaining student files such as those just discussed has an added advantage of beginning the process of portfolio assessment (see Part III).

Hunter (1994) points out the value of gathering student information during a lesson to reduce the need for hours of correcting student papers. In fact, many teachers keep logs of information on index cards, charts, graphs, or just note paper throughout their lessons. Others use audio- or videotaping as a means of recording student behavior. Cullen and Pratt (1992) present an information sheet which can be used to maintain valuable student data (see Figure 7.1).

Areas to Consider	What Do I Already Know About This Child?	What More Do I Need to Know?	How Do I Find Out?
Physical			
Behavior Social-emotional			
Speech & Language • Oral • Written			
Cognitive			
Academic • Reading • Writing • Math • Other			

FIGURE 7.1   Information-Gathering Guidelines

Source: Cullen, B. & Pratt, T. (1992). Measuring and reporting student progress. In S. Stainback W. Stainback, *Curriculum considerations in inclusive classrooms Facilitiating learning for all students.* (p. 185). Baltimore: Brookes, P.O. Box 10624, Baltimore, MD 21285-0624.

Assignment sheets are yet another means of recording and managing data, and can be kept by teachers and students. Most will be in chart form (see Figure 7.2). These records of teaching and learning need to be filed and stored in the classroom, where they can be accessed quickly.

Student _____   Subject _____

Date	Assignment	Results	Implications

FIGURE 7.2   Basic Assignment Sheet

Reflect for a Moment

Have you ever looked at a teacher's gradebook? How often do you think teachers should enter assessment results in a gradebook for each student?

Ultimately, if records of curriculum organization and student performance are maintained, the teacher is equipped with sufficient student data to answer three fundamental questions.

1. What does this student know, and what can this student do as a consequence of instruction?
2. How much progress has this student made toward attaining the ultimate goals of the curriculum?
3. How does this student's performance compare with that of other students pursuing a similar program of studies? (Froyen, 1993, p. 91)

Answering these questions can keep accountability fanatics at bay (although they need far more than test scores), and at the same time assist educators in providing an appropriate program for every student in an inclusive setting.

Organizational Skills

Organization is a process of using categories, orders, and frameworks for arranging information, resources, and materials (Freiberg & Driscoll, 1992). Whether it is scientific data, student work samples, or class time, organizing for teaching and learning is essential. Good teachers are well organized. They have materials fully prepared ahead of time. They spend very little time in transitions. Routines are carried out expeditiously. They have carefully considered how time and space influence each and every lesson. Their instructional objectives, procedures, and assessments are planned out ahead of time to maximize student learning.

Well-organized teachers often establish and maintain accurate records of equipment, books, furniture, and other instructional materials. By having clear and current records of materials, teachers can plan more creatively and meet more individual student needs.

Organizational skills must be evidenced by carefully maintained records that reflect individual student characteristics, curriculum information, instructional planning, assessment of student performance, materials and supplies, and teacher professional development. These records should be organized so that they can be easily accessed and updated.

Student Self-Management and Record Keeping

Teaching involves more than providing learners with a series of facts or a set of skills. Educators must also be concerned with assisting students in developing responsibility. Many students in the educational system have become overly dependent on educators for most of their direction, thus developing into passive learners. Students who wait for learning to happen to them rather than seeking it out often fail to accept responsibility for their academic achievement. This effect, coupled with the diversity of learners in an inclusive classroom, makes it impossible for the educator to monitor every learning behavior and reinforce all resulting actions. Therefore, learners must be shown how to take responsibility for and monitor their own learning behavior.

Educators may help students develop responsibility both indirectly and directly. Indirectly, educators help learners by organizing new information in a manner that makes clear the importance of observation, analysis, and reflection. In introducing new information, educators should incorporate expected learner outcomes as advanced organizers to help focus students' observations. Additionally, educators should cue learners to listen carefully to the introduction of new information, concepts, and materials. Educators should draw clear connections that provide learners with an explanation of the relationship between what they previously learned and the new content being introduced.

Students should also be assisted by educators to develop graphic organizers. This can be accomplished by providing guided notes or outlines and using graphs, timelines, and charts. Additionally, educators can help students generate cognitive organizers or develop semantic maps.

Meichenbaum (1986) suggests that **cognitive behavior management** (CBM) offers students a means of taking charge of their learning. Cognitive behavior management provides learners with the strategies needed to monitor and improve their academic performance in the classroom. Additionally, since procedures associated with cognitive behavior management are not content specific, they can be adapted to fit a variety of classroom activities performed by learners. CBM involves five general procedures: self-recording, graphing, reinforcement, instructional training, and instruction training through attack strategies (Williams & Rooney, 1986).

Self-recording is a tool for learners to use to keep track of their own behaviors. Students are instructed to record the occurrence of one of their learning behaviors. The simple act of recording and counting this and other learning behaviors makes the student more acutely aware of these behaviors. An extremely versatile technique, **self-graphing,** is used in conjunction with self-recording. By graphing their own learning behaviors, learners are able to visualize change; they can easily see improvement in accuracy or frequency of academic response. The technique of **self-reinforcement** is aimed at promoting learners' independence from external reinforcers. Through self-reinforcement, learners are able to provide themselves with both verbal and nonverbal praise, thus helping to develop an internal locus of control.

Self-instructional training, finally, provides students with an effective method for learning a variety of academic and social skills. Williams and Rooney (1986) recommend using the following five-step procedure when teaching learners how to use self-instructional training:

1. First the educator provides a cognitive model while completing a task (talks through task while performing it). The model should:

   a. define problem—"What is it I have to do?"
   b. focus attention—"Think clearly."
   c. guide response—"I need to do this and then I can do this."
   d. self-reinforce—"I'm really doing an excellent job!"
   e. direct coping strategies—"If I make a mistake, I can fix it by . . ."

2. Learner performs task while educator provides overt external guidance.
3. Learner performs task using overt self-guidance (actually verbalizes self-instruction).
4. Learner fades overt self-guidance by whispering self-instruction instead of speaking aloud.
5. Learner performs task using covert self-guidance (via private speech).

Although it is essential to provide learners with all these steps, some learners may not need to follow every one in sequence. Some learners may be able to skip step 4 and move directly to step 5, or may prefer to skip step 3 and go directly to step 4. It is, however, important to encourage them to reflect on what is useful and to develop their own verbalizations. Meichenbaum (1981) suggests the following guidelines for developing a self-instructional training program:

1. Task analyze academic behavior, including all necessary requirements for successful performance.
2. Listen to learners and seek out ineffective strategies that they may currently be using.
3. Select learning tasks that approximate academic behavior you've targeted.
4. Be certain that the learner has developed all the necessary prerequisite skills for using self-instruction.
5. Explain to the learner the utility of self-instruction.
6. Have the learner assist you in devising self-instruction.
7. Promote generalization of self-instructional training by doing it with a variety of academic tasks and in various settings.
8. Attend to the management of failure by incorporating specific coping skills into the self-instructional training.

Self-instruction training through **attack strategies training** has been used effectively to teach a wide variety of academic skills. This technique differs from self-instructional training because it expands on self-talk, incorporates specific strategies for problem solving, and is much more teacher directed. This technique examines the uniqueness of each activity for the development of very specific strategies. While the overall techniques may be applied to a wide variety of academic situations, the specific strategies tend to be less generalizable. Meese (1994) provides the following eight steps for developing a strategies training approach:

1. Define a group of related problems that a student needs to be able to solve (e.g., addition with regrouping).
2. Devise a strategy for attacking and solving the problems.
3. Specify the skills required in each step of the strategy.
4. Assess student performance on each of the component skills and teach separately those prerequisite skills not yet mastered by the student.
5. Model the strategy for the student while "talking aloud".
6. Guide the student through the strategy, verbalizing each step.
7. Provide practice and give corrective feedback.
8. Reinforce (praise) the student for correct use of the strategy (p. 192).

Hunter (1994) points out the importance of learners being able to "file" information so that, when needed, it may be retrieved quickly. Educators should demonstrate for learners how to establish an individual filing system. Because it is very difficult for learners to find and retrieve separate pieces of information, a "folder system" is a useful tool. When relationships are established among ideas, information is more easily learned and retained. Through the process and practice of organizing information, learning can become more focused.

Reflect for a Moment

Have you ever actually been taught a technique for self-monitoring or record keeping? If so, what was it? If not, what techniques do you presently use to write notes, keep records of your learning, or in some other way take charge of your learning?

SUMMARY

Several management factors must be considered when organizing a learning environment. Educators should be clear about expectations and student responsibilities, provide meaningful instruction, be positive role models, and offer appropriate feedback. Positive learning experiences occur when educators draw clear limits on personal expression, plan for student success, and view mistakes as learning opportunities.

Features of the physical environment which contribute to effective learning are adequate overall space, complementary work areas, and clear visibility throughout the room. Several different activity areas are described. Student seating arrangements should minimize distractions, but be flexible with different teaching strategies. Display space should showcase students' accomplishments and provide information about schedules, school policies, and class rules.

Productive time management requires that personal and professional goals be established, and that the physical and mental health of the educator be among these. Instructional time can be broken down into allocated, instructional, engaged, and academic learning, and transition time. Good managers of time maximize academic learning time, and teach transition procedures to minimize the time lost in this area.

Carefully constructed schedules allow adequate time for a variety of learning activities, and intersperse less appealing activities with more enjoyable ones. Schedules are established at the beginning of the school year, but only after class time has been analyzed. Time for collaboration must also be scheduled, and supported by district administrators.

Accurate recordkeeping allows educators and students to reflect upon learning experiences, assess academic progress, and plan future activities. Recordkeeping systems should be simple. Several strategies are described for teaching students to monitor their own learning.

8

UNIT AND LESSON PLANNING

Key Terms

Advance organizer
Anticipatory set
Attitude objective
Balance
Bibliography
Bridge
Broad field units
Checking for understanding
Closure
Continuity
Cooperative teaching
Coordinated teaching
Discipline-oriented unit
Evaluation
Group choral response
Guided practice
Immediate objective
Intermediate-level objective

Independent practice
Individual private response
Instructional input
Key questions
Long-range objective
Modeling
Overplanning
Preintegration
Resource unit
Teaching unit
Thematic unit
Sampling
Scope
Sequence
Signaled response
Statement of objective
Unit

Objectives

After completing this chapter, the reader will be able to:

1. Distinguish among the types of units.
2. Discuss learning theory as it relates to units.
3. Identify the benefits of using themes in teaching and learning.
4. Design a thematic unit.
5. Describe the important components of a lesson plan.
6. Create a comprehensive lesson plan.
7. Determine appropriate adaptations in unit and lesson plans.

PROFILES OF A UNIT

Mike McCarty's Unit on Clouds

As usual, he was already falling behind. It was January, and Mike McCarty was only on the fifth chapter in the textbook. It looked like the chapter on clouds would have to get done in just a week if he was going to stay on schedule to complete the text by June. He always seemed to fall behind, usually because the students kept taking so long to write answers to the end of the chapter questions. They always wanted to get him off the topic, asking questions about weather reports, poems about clouds, or some ancient ritual one of them read about that involved clouds. This was science class, not English or social studies. It was all he could do to get them to read the text, so he made them read it aloud in class.

Ms. Dawson, the other third grade teacher, kept coming to him in the teachers' lounge wanting to organize field trips or team teach a lab on the water cycle. Mr. Jenkins, the special education teacher who taught four students from his class every day (and who knew what he taught them), was constantly trying to get Mike to let him come into the general classroom during science. But the chapter was basically clear, and Mike saw no reason why he needed to get into all kinds of extraneous arrangements. He figured that the material covered in the text was what the curriculum required and any other ideas for clouds would take too long to teach. One week was all he needed to get them through the chapter and give them the test at the end. He would skip the essays and just use the multiple choice questions to be sure students remembered the important facts.

Judy Cavanaugh's Collaborative Unit on Clouds

It was July, and Judy Cavanaugh had just returned from a meeting at Mr. Ianowski's house. Four teachers from school were planning thematic units for the upcoming year, and they were meeting throughout the summer to carefully integrate important learnings from the entire curriculum.

The group had actually begun to meet before school got out in June, deciding on a schedule of summer meetings and deadlines. The team had determined early on that each theme would fully integrate all the major subject areas, including music and art. At this point they had used input from a student survey and selected four themes for the year. Long-term goals for each theme had been written, and they were now developing short-term objectives for the second theme, clouds. The team was careful to design activities appropriate for all students that collectively represented the entire range of learning domains and levels. They studied the local community, including typical family environments, and outlined activities that had real meaning in the everyday lives of students and their families.

The schedule was starting to look like a dream come true. Mr. Ianowski (special educator), Judy Cavanaugh and Mr. Tavares (third grade teachers), and Ms. Carr (physical therapist) were promised a half day of planning time each week. They would teach art and music through the themes and could therefore determine how the entire school day would be organized. After several meetings, the team decided to devote approximately 80 percent of students' time to the themes. This left plenty of time to teach any essentials that students might not encounter in the themes. Judy smiled as she greeted her family in the kitchen. Collaborative thematic teaching was challenging, exhilarating, and effective.

TYPES OF UNITS

As the profiles suggest, units can vary in scope, length, and organizational structure. What follows is a rationale and model for thematic learning that has as its foundation the unit concept. **Units** are plans that structure ideas, concepts, knowledge, and learning into meaningful teaching events (Lemlech, 1994). Content is of primary importance to the unit because it facilitates the communication of knowledge. Additionally, units provide learners a means of developing more generalizable understanding, values, and skills through integrative experiences. Lemlech (1994) describes four basic types of units: discipline oriented, broad field, resource, and teaching.

Discipline-oriented units are intended for a single subject area only. Mike McCarty's approach to teaching units appears to be discipline oriented; content is structured around a single discipline. **Broad field units** are designed to cover content from a wider perspective, such as social studies, global studies, or life sciences. Both discipline-oriented and broad field units are relatively narrow in scope because they relate to only one content area, such as science, history, health, music, art, physical education, or mathematics.

Resource units are generally developed by a committee of educators from specific disciplines at the district level. A resource unit is not planned with any specific set of learners in mind because its purpose is to provide large amounts of information on a variety of means for teaching specific topics. Generally, resource units include a broad range of objectives and questions, learning activities, resource materials, and methods of evaluation. Cognitive objectives should include all levels of thinking, from basic knowledge to critical evaluative reasoning. Additionally, activities should be aimed at developing learners' attitudes and psychomotor skills (Esler & Sciortino, 1988).

Teaching units are focused on and designed for a particular group of learners. Such units represent long-term planning by the collaborative team for curriculum teaching. Judy Cavanaugh's collaborative thematic unit represents a teaching unit. Teaching units provide purpose for the day-to-day lesson plans and ensure that a broad range of processes and experiences (e.g., problem solving, research skills activities, language development, physical activities, and dramatic activities) are incorporated. In an inclusive learning environment, it is imperative that the teaching unit be thematic in nature.

RATIONALE FOR A THEMATIC APPROACH

The overwhelming majority of schools in Western society are organized around subject areas (mathematics, English, science, social studies, writing, art, etc.). Even the casual observer can quickly identify, on entering a classroom, the subject being taught. Many elementary school teachers post a daily schedule that states the time allotted to each subject: reading class ends, and science begins. Science ends, and math begins. This phenomenon exists throughout the public school world, and it has not changed in years. As discussed in Chapter 7, the distributing or posting of a daily schedule is an efficient time management concept that assists in transitioning from activity to activity.

In light of the domination of subject area curriculum, what would be the reasons for using **thematic units**? Why would anyone want to suggest an approach in which many traditional subject areas are blended together around a single topic or theme? Ellis and Fouts (1993) offer two primary reasons. First, there is just too much information to be learned. An interdisciplinary approach can help manage information more efficiently. Second, an interdisciplinary approach acknowledges the natural relationships between traditionally segregated subject areas. When students are presented with a thematic unit of instruction, they experience firsthand the valuable and meaningful connections that have always existed among different subject areas.

A third justification is based on classroom teachers' common complaint that their schedules are so fragmented that they never have time to really teach any substance (Jacobs, 1989). Some state curriculum requirements are even listed in terms of how many minutes per week are to be allocated to various subject areas, a practice that exacerbates teachers' concerns. Students are sensitive to this fragmentation and seem to spend as much time moving from one subject to another as they do studying academic content.

Learning Theory

Thematic learning has been around for ages, and more recently was a major component of the progressive education movement led by John Dewey in the early twentieth century. Several interdisciplinary products of that era, such as language arts and social studies, should not, however, be interpreted as evidence of thematic curriculum. They do share a common rationale—namely, that all learning is connected in some way and that learner rather than subject matter must be the focus of instruction. This rationale, to a large extent, derives from the learning process that people of all ages, abilities, and backgrounds undertake in a natural manner on a daily basis, a process that is not driven by subject specific facts, or textbooks. In this manner, a thematic approach utilizes group interaction, student projects, and detailed discussions, not simply textbooks, worksheets, and multiple choice tests. The content that arises from thematic units is usually highly relevant and important to the learners instead of being presented through a state curriculum committee or commercial publishing company in New York City.

Furthermore, the planning of a thematic unit is frequently the joint undertaking of teachers and students and can be represented by webs or semantic maps that lend both a visual framework and a cognitive coherence to the content (see Figure 8.1). Critics of the thematic approach contend that invariably there are critical essentials of school learning, particularly in the area of mathematics, that are neglected in the pursuit of thematic units. The choice ultimately comes down to either teaching any essential curriculum within the context of the theme or clinging to the more traditional segmented subject matter approach and hoping for meaningful context on a random basis.

Reflect for a Moment

Can you remember any of your teachers ever using thematic units in elementary, middle, or high school? Did you find learning easier when it was connected?

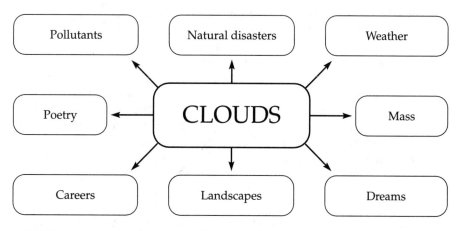

FIGURE 8.1   Semantic Map of Clouds

The thinking of contemporary scholars such as Jean Piaget, Lillian Katz, George Forman, and Catherine Fosnot has contributed to a resurgence of interest in the relationship between personal experiences and meaningful learning. More recently, a rationale for thematic curriculum has emerged in the notion of *constructivism*. Fosnot (1989) describes four major aspects of constructivism. First, knowledge is never objective because it is made up of constructions (people's own unique cognitive frameworks, used to understand their environment) that evolve through individual transformations, organizational schemes, and perceptions. Second, constructions develop through assimilation and accommodation as individual learners modify old learning to incorporate new information. A preschool child, for example, may at one point decide that he or she likes all soft, cuddly stuffed animals, and later may determine that large teddy bears are more likable than small bunny rabbits. Third, learning is not an accumulation of information but a complex series of predictions, manipulations, questions, wonderment, and creations as new constructions are pieced together. This feature of constructivism raises the importance of learner-centered theme-based curriculum and redefines the roles of teacher and learner. Fourth, in the process of learning, reflection and conflict resolution are vital in order to build deeper, more complete understanding in the learner.

Collectively, these four aspects of constructivism clearly indicate that a curriculum that truly utilizes student experiences is more likely to stimulate continuous learning and that this curriculum does not neatly sort itself into separate disciplines of language, mathematics, social science, art, and so forth. A more logical approach to curriculum uses a meaningful concept as a focal point (such as endangered species or clouds) and generates investigations in a variety of directions depending on the experiences of the learners. When Judy Cavanaugh's collaborative planning group studied the community in which the students lived, they made a commitment to learning activities that reflected students' experiences. Although many literature-based units have been described as thematic, they are actually discipline oriented, encompassing the language arts (reading, speaking, listening, and writing). A thematic unit includes a variety of subject areas. In fact, if the constructivist principles just presented are carefully applied, there would be a very natural balance of content from all traditional disciplines because of the emphasis placed on the experiences of the learner.

An additional feature of thematic units is the increased opportunity for collaboration among educators who may have different areas of content knowledge to contribute. Many middle school educators have found that their work as a team has given rise to more thematic curriculum planning and that students have not only become more aware of the connections between the traditional subjects during thematic instruction, but also have benefited from both deeper expertise and more personalized assistance from the educators on the team.

Research

Several experiments have been conducted to explore the effects of a thematic curriculum. The first was the Dewey School, founded at the University of Chicago in 1898. Its goals were to develop a cooperative community to meet students' social needs and to develop the students' intellect through activities (Martinello & Cook, 1994). Subject matter was chosen in relation to students' experiences and interests and therefore took on a naturally integrated form. Then in 1921, the Lincoln School of Teachers College emerged from the writing of Alexander Flexner, using New York City as a laboratory for student learning. Interdisciplinary units arose from the emphasis on "real-life situations," but just as frequently there were concurrent, related units (a Social Studies unit on Eskimos and a Geography unit on Alaska) evident and even unrelated units (a Social Studies unit on Eskimos and a Geography unit on the desert regions). Whenever a unit did not include enough mathematics or reading, it was taught separately, and some classes opted to have daily reading skill lessons.

During the late 1920s and early 1930s, the Houston City Schools researched and implemented an integrated districtwide curriculum. Unlike the earlier projects, this experiment included a study to determine the effects of the integrated curriculum on the fourth and fifth grades. Using an activity approach, teachers planned units that met grade level curriculum requirements and included all traditional subject areas. "Big themes" centered in the social studies and included interdependence, control over nature, adaptation, and cooperation. Results of the study indicated success in a number of areas, including skills, creativity, problem solving, academic achievement, student attitudes, organizational skills, study habits, and even teaching effectiveness (Oberholzer, 1937).

A fourth experiment took place in New York City when the Bank Street College of Education worked with several large urban elementary schools to design a curriculum "suited to children in modern-day United States" (Mitchell, 1950, p. 81). Again, social studies served as the focal point, and different themes emerged at different grade levels. There was, however, never a concerted effort to integrate all subject areas. Amid this less formal curriculum reconstruction, teachers found new levels of self-confidence and new knowledge of both subject matter and curriculum construction.

A more recent interdisciplinary venture is taking place in Elizabeth, Colorado, where for many years a team of first grade teachers has spent some 80 percent of their instructional time with thematic units (Gilbert, 1989). Two of the earliest themes were dinosaurs and space; over time the space unit has become a schoolwide pursuit. Other themes have included Stone Soup, the circus, rodeos, and the five senses. Teachers find that one of the most appealing aspects of the team approach is that each unit is optional. Exit standards are established for students, and among the results are enhanced conceptual understandings, increased interest in hobbies, and higher rates of student participation overall. Teachers are sharing more, and there is greater enthusiasm evident among all involved. Support and active involvement from the community has increased as well. Other outcomes include improved attendance, better homework completion rates, fewer visits to the school nurse by students, and more creative, collegial teachers who use time more effectively and take more pride in their work.

Collectively, these projects in thematic or integrated curriculum reveal a variety of benefits to both teachers and students. A thematic unit may in some cases integrate all of the traditional subject areas, but in other cases it may not. Relevance and meaningfulness to the learner is paramount, and when certain curricular areas are not suitable to full integration, educators should plan supplemental instruction. How much supplemental instruction is needed will depend on the theme and the needs of the students.

Reflect for a Moment

Now that you have read a bit more detail on how thematic units can be carried out schoolwide, can you recall a schoolwide theme from your elementary, middle, or high school days? What types of activities took place? What were some examples of collaboration that took place?

Essentially, thematic curriculum reflects a decidedly different focus for all those involved. It represents significant change in curriculum planning and implementation and as such requires time to become an established and accepted approach to teaching and learning. It requires educators to reconsider the basic purposes of schools on a broad scale. Experimentation by both educators and students is the norm, with risk taking, questioning, and problem solving very routine behaviors.

Thematic curriculum places considerable decision-making responsibility on teams of educators who in turn carry out their work at all levels of the school, from head administrator to youngest kindergarten child. It is this last aspect of the thematic unit approach that holds the greatest promise for strengthening the relationship between the educational community and the larger surrounding community. The development of a thinking individual who is able to contribute to the betterment of the human condition is a common thread in each of the thematic projects described here. Curriculum derived from learners' experiences in the larger community, and based on inquiry, logical and critical thinking, and meaningful problem solving, will contribute to a world of the future in clearly positive ways.

Benefits of Themes

How can educators use a thematic approach to teaching and still be accountable to curricular goals and objectives? One exciting aspect of thematic units is that amid concern over meeting curriculum requirements, which are in fact minimum standards, the thematic curriculum can provide students with experiences that far exceed minimum standards.

If the commitment is complete, then supplemental instruction in separate subject areas will be minimal, and the creative process of thematic planning will be the norm. It must be remembered, though, that educators are required by law in most states to follow curriculum guidelines designed to ensure a complete educational offering for all students. Unfortunately, state-mandated curricula are generally written by experts in and for single content areas such as science, mathematics, or social studies. Additionally, when textbooks are the primary source of student information, the curriculum becomes increasingly segmented and students do not easily grasp the fluency that exists among the traditional disciplines. As students prepare for life in the twenty-first century, they must understand not only the facts, but the way in which information is interrelated. Thematic units can fulfill this need, inviting the learner to create and solve problems through an interdisciplinary study format that draws on a variety of teaching and learning strategies. Learners are the builders of meaningful new experiences using existing knowledge.

There will, of course, be limitations on how many of the grade level curriculum requirements can be meaningfully addressed through a particular theme. A sensible procedure would include the examination of grade level curriculum requirements, followed by the application of the requirements to the study of clouds. Martinello and Cook (1994) suggest identifying a major generalization or statement of concepts that activates the theme. One such statement about clouds might be, "Clouds play an important role in the changing environment." This central idea can then be the main idea of the clouds theme, and teachers can bring their texts, materials, and resources together to plan a long-term sequence of learning. Different grade levels will determine their own generalizations, depending on their curriculum requirements and, just as important, the nature of the learners in their classrooms.

Going back to the theme of clouds, the major academic area is science. Yet when learning activities are chosen with a commitment to providing meaningful and relevant experiences, then knowledge, skills, and attitudes traditionally part of other academic areas often become necessary prerequisites. For example, one of the important applications of knowledge about clouds is being able to track their movement. To do that, students will need to calculate how long it will take a cloud moving at a certain speed to travel a certain distance. They will need to calculate the speed of clouds by using a timer and a locator, and the distance traveled using another type of instrument; there are clearly several mathematics skills required to understand cloud movement. Another way cloud movement can be investigated is through music. Learners can be asked to view various cloud movements and select musical passages that reflect a sense of the movement. In addition, one of the most effective ways for students to develop such understandings is to visit a weather station and learn about the career of a meteorologist. Learning about possible careers is a requirement found in most social studies curriculum guidelines.

The final thematic unit for any group of participants, then, will be fully integrated, with teachers and students asking and attempting to answer questions about clouds. Individual and group studies will be the most frequent approaches to learning observed, and decisions about future areas of study are often influenced by input from students. This inquiry-based curriculum stimulates more abstract and complex levels of thinking because it emerges from students' own interests and experiences. A common respect is fostered between and among teachers and students because of their shared interest in learning.

Reflect for a Moment

Do you think thematic planning requires more or less organization and collaboration than conventional subject area planning? Why is this the case? Which type of unit do you feel is more beneficial for learners?

UNIT DESIGN

Martinello and Cook (1994) provide a set of questions to be addressed early in the design of a thematic unit. Educators collaborating to design a unit should decide:

- whether the unit will embrace all subject areas or concentrate on one or two subject areas
- how long the unit will last
- what types of instructional organizations will be used (independent study, whole class instruction, small group learning)
- whether the unit will have a predetermined beginning, middle and end or will grow according to student-directed exploration

Four organizational factors must be considered in designing a unit: scope, sequence, continuity, and balance. Each of these four factors affects the unit's function, content, and length. Whether the unit will provide an in-depth understanding or broad coverage is determined by the unit's **scope**. The scope dictates the breadth and depth of the content to be covered. Essentially, the greater the scope, the wider the breadth and the shallower the depth. Linear organization and logical flow of content result from a clearly developed **sequence**. A variety of sequential patterns may be used based on the content selected and the learning styles of the students. Unit sequencing may be simple to complex, chronological, or whole to part/part to whole.

Any time content is introduced, it should tap into and expand on learners' existing knowledge base. This focus provides students with a sense of **continuity** during the new learning event. Because of their very nature, thematic units have continuity as a primary function. Using a theme to tie various subject areas together produces continuity in the learning process from one cognitive, affective, or psychomotor level to the next. Content or themes reoccur frequently through a student's formal learning career. Dewey stressed that each time a learner is reintroduced to content, the level of conceptual understanding must be increased for it to continue to have educational value. Each time the concept of clouds is reintroduced in the thematic unit through a new subject area, understanding is extended and expanded.

Common threads can be interwoven when educators organize units for **balance**. As previously stated, though clouds may appear to be most closely related to science, an equitable balance can and must be maintained among all the subject areas. A collaborative effort by educators from each field to contribute ideas and activities will help to assure that this balance has been gained.

Once these four organizational factors have been taken into account, the actual process of developing a thematic unit can begin. This planning process starts not only with educators' relevant knowledge of all the learners involved but also an awareness of their own level of understanding of subject matter and instructional processes.

Theme Selection and Development

The first step in unit design is selecting a theme. Here several related suggestions are important to note. Human experiences that cross age and grade levels, such as the environment, communication, and measurement, usually serve well as themes (Hartoonian & Laughlin, 1989). Jacobs and Borland (1986) caution, however, that themes should be somewhat limited in scope because broad topics such as "life" can present problems. Additionally, they suggest that the theme be conceptual in nature and that, whenever possible, learners be allowed to help select themes, thus enhancing their interest.

Not all topics are suitable for thematic units. Martinello and Cook (1994) offer criteria for theme selection:

> Is the big idea true over space and time?
> Does it broaden students' understanding of the world or what it means
>   to be human?
> Is the big idea interdisciplinary?
> Does it relate to students' genuine interests?
> Does it lead to student inquiry? (p. 63)

Some teachers will take a highly directive role in the development of the theme, whereas others will elicit varying amounts of student input during the development phase. In some cases, the different roles are a factor of the educator's experience with thematic units or familiarity with the required curriculum. Judy Cavanaugh's collaborative team was in their first full year of thematic planning. They utilized data from the student survey in their planning but had not yet determined how much input students would have during the actual implementation of the unit. Though student input is critical, many beginning teachers may find a directive role more stable and turn to student input at a later time. This is not only understandable but wise in light of the need for a thorough framework for meaningful learning experiences.

Subtopics can be identified once a theme has been generated (see Figure 8.1). These subtopics are still at the "big idea" stage and must be focused further into narrower subtopics (see Figure 8.2) and learner outcomes. Developing a topic into a theme requires in-depth elaboration that can be facilitated in several ways. One possibility is to devise a comprehensive list of **key questions**. According to Lemlech (1994), these key questions enable educators to develop the unit's continuity, scope, and sequence. Additionally, the key questions assist educators in the development of objectives and learning experiences necessary to aid students in successfully developing their knowledge, skills, and attitudes. Students can contribute appreciably to such a list, and educators can analyze the list for curricular breadth. For example, if the clouds theme is being developed, a list of questions could be examined to see how mathematics, literature and music are integrated (see Table 8.1).

Another way for educators to develop a theme is to test its level of interest. The

TABLE 8.1   Key Questions

How much do clouds weigh?
How large are they?
How fast do clouds move?
How are clouds depicted in fairy tales?
What have writers used clouds to symbolize?
How have clouds influenced songwriters?
Which musical instruments or rhythms seem to conjure up images of clouds?

topic must be worthwhile for students. They must have convincing responses to the question, "What makes clouds interesting?" In the case of clouds, several possibilities exist.

Clouds are always different.

Some clouds look like other objects or creatures.

Other clouds are dark and ominous.

Clouds sometimes move very fast.

Clouds are full of make believe stories.

Each of these statements contains concepts that can be developed through interdisciplinary learning activities. The statement "Clouds are always different" could lead to artistic explorations of shape, texture, and dimension as well as scientific investigations of how the shapes are created and what the significance of different shapes might be for weather conditions. The statement "Clouds sometimes move very fast" begs a study of the mathematical relationship between wind velocity and different types of clouds. Of course, concepts and statements vary depending on students' prior understandings and experiences, but numerous ideas can emerge from an inquiry into the importance of a particular topic.

Reflect for a Moment

Using the theme of "Seashore," think of three convincing responses to the question "What makes the seashore interesting?"

One fairly common approach to developing a theme is to examine the literature available on a potential topic. Although children's literature should be a major source of information in any thematic unit, it is helpful to identify how different books can support concept learning in specific ways in considering a topic for unit planning. When literature is used as a focus for developing themes, children develop skills in, and enthusiasm for, reading. They also have immediate access to opportunities for higher-order thinking and vast resources for finding information beyond the textbook. On the other hand, literature must be chosen carefully, with particular attention to thematic value, literary elements, interest to learners, readability, and evidence of stereotyping.

Often a combination of approaches is used in selecting and developing a theme. Questions are used to organize the unit, student input is used to heighten interest in the unit, and literature is used to enhance language learning and deepen content understanding in the unit. When a student arrives at school with an earthworm, the potential for a thematic unit presents itself to the educator and the potential for meaningful learning across the curriculum arises for students.

Collaboration

Once key questions have been developed, the collaborative team should now brainstorm. Brainstorming involves writing down all related activities, skills, knowledge, materials, and resources that can in any way be related to the topic. According to Osborne (1963), a brainstorming session produces a large quantity of ideas from which the best quality of ideas can be selected. Osborne suggests that collaborative teams consider the following basic principles for brainstorming:

1. During the brainstorming session, criticism is not permitted.
2. Since spontaneous and unusual responses promote creativity, "freewheeling" should be encouraged.
3. Since the desire is to elicit a quantity of ideas, evaluation should follow the session.
4. Collaborators can improve proposed ideas by attempting to combine two or more of them. (1963, p. 156)

Additionally, Osborne recommends that each collaborator spend 2 minutes doing personal brainstorming before the group begins. This initiates the flow of creativity and increases group productivity. From the list generated by the collaborative teams, items can be added or deleted to help create balance and continuity. With the finalized list in hand, the development of a written thematic unit can continue.

Flexible brainstorming is critical if educators across grade levels are going to collaborate in the development of a thematic unit. Using the theme of clouds, educators can generate ideas at every grade level that relate to the knowledge, skills and attitudes found in respective curriculum requirements or state guidelines. They can then organize these ideas into a web using subheadings (see Figure 8.2). Students can develop webs of ideas as well and contribute to the content of the study. Webs clarify prior knowledge and map out desired learning.

Following the brainstorming phase, participants critically examine the ideas. In some cases, ideas are combined to form new ideas. In most cases, ideas are transformed into questions, a process presented earlier in the chapter. One approach to formulating these questions is to think of questions people from different professions or careers might ask. For example, using the clouds theme, a ship captain might ask how clouds can be used to predict sea conditions, whereas a car salesman might want to devise a strategy or slogan for advertising that capitalized on large fluffy clouds. An orchestra leader would select music that conjured up images of clouds; a historian might ask about how different ancient civilizations used clouds in their rituals and customs. The more diverse the viewpoints, the more

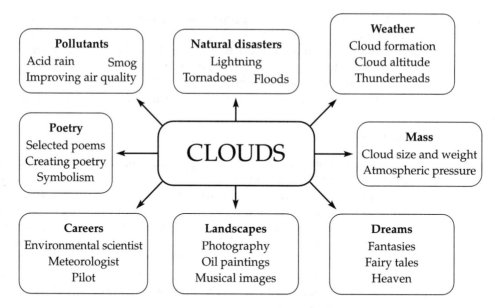

FIGURE 8.2 Possible Web for Third Grade Study of Clouds

interdisciplinary the theme can become (Martinello & Cook, 1994). Then, in turn, as a viewpoint is pursued in detail, the interdisciplinary inquiry becomes a reflection of both lower and higher levels of thinking, and specific questions that continuously emerge represent the full range of Bloom's *Taxonomy of Educational Objectives* (1956). Again, students can provide relevant input during the questioning process.

Before long, there will be enough questions to bring the planning to a phase where curriculum guidelines help organize the questions into groups for student inquiry. At this point, participants use specific disciplines to confirm the curricular accountability of the thematic unit. What began as a highly creative process evolves into a critical thinking experience as participants organize, combine, analyze, and evaluate the developing theme.

Time Management

The importance of having adequate time to plan together cannot be overstated, for it is critical to the success of any thematic unit. In developing long- and short-term goals and objectives for a thematic unit, the effective educator must take into consideration the relationship between time and mental process. Bernabei and Leles (1970) have developed a model for designing objectives that incorporates the principle of cognitive complexity with days or weeks of instructional time. Three levels are provided: immediate, intermediate, and long range. **Immediate objectives** take from one to four days to accomplish and have a knowledge or comprehension level of cognitive complexity (See attitude objective in Table 8.5). The second or **intermediate-level objectives** incorporate the comprehension, application, and analysis tasks and may take from five days to six weeks to complete (see the concept objective in Table 8.5). **Long-range objectives** may last from six to twelve weeks up to a full year, and involve analysis, synthesis, and evaluation levels of cognitive processing (e.g., the students will plan and construct a working weather station).

It is important to understand that these three levels are somewhat progressive and interdependent. For example, learners must acquire the ability to think about clouds at the knowledge level before the comprehension level, the comprehension level before the application level, and so on. Although all levels are not strictly progressive (synthesis need not always precede evaluation), it typically takes longer to work up to thinking about clouds at the more complex levels because of the need to understand them at lower levels. If a student has already shown the ability to compare and contrast clouds, it will only take a few days in most cases before that student will be able to explain how to classify clouds.

Long- and Short-Term Planning

Although the process of long-range planning appears simple, it is an extremely complex task that fortunately improves over time and with experience. Long-range planning requires judgments about reasonable time allocations for each of the proposed learning activities. This is the point in the planning process when educators must develop the appropriate sequence of learning activities and estimate the amount of time needed to reach the intended goals.

Overplanning, the developing of more learning activities for a given time frame than can be accomplished, is a common situation for many educators. Often educators using a thematic approach are faced with decisions not only on the rate of instruction, but also on deleting or adding certain activities. Esler and Sciortino (1988) point out that educators face the dilemma of determining proper topic coverage nearly every school day, and the concept of "the best laid plans of mice and men" applies to the development of any long-range plans. Inclement weather, fire drills, and unscheduled assembly activities are but a few of the interruptions that may impact long-range plans. Even given the range of uncontrollable interruptions, it is imperative that educators create and follow through with their long-range plans, keeping in mind that the keys to creating and executing instructional plans are flexibility and sound judgment (Esler & Sciortino, 1988).

Reflect for a Moment

How flexible are you? What is your response when you find out that an appointment you made has been canceled? What is your response when you do not finish a task when you wanted to because you have to do something else instead?

Short-Term Planning

Short-term planning takes place at four levels on a weekly and a daily basis: reexamining short-term objectives, detailing the procedures needed, preparing the materials, and allocating the time for carrying out a given activity. Objectives may need to be modified when students are progressing at different rates and by different means. When objectives are modified on a short-term basis, students spend more time participating in appropriate learning activities. Detailing procedures will consistently contribute to the smooth implementation of an activity because the teacher will examine each step ahead of time. When procedures are carefully thought out, students are more informed and able to approach activities with confidence.

Time must be set aside for educators to gather materials, on a daily basis in most cases. Classrooms full of paint, lab equipment, computers, yarn, cooking utensils, or unifix cubes are far more stimulating learning environments than classrooms with desks in straight rows, one or two maps on the wall, and a few dictionaries and encyclopedias on the shelf.

Finally, educators must allocate the time needed to successfully implement the activity in a realistic manner. When they plan time for a thematic unit, collaborators like Cavanaugh may find that they have more flexibility than if they were to allocate instructional time for all of the subject areas separately. On the other hand, overplanning often occurs because students take more time to acquire new learning than the educators who planned that same learning. A lesson that looks on paper like it would take 15 minutes ends up taking at least 30 minutes. The experienced learner usually underestimates the time needed for less experienced to acquire new knowledge, skills, or attitudes.

Short-term planning includes decision making in all four areas on both a weekly and a daily basis. In collaborative teaching settings, clear communication is critical whenever changes in short-term plans occur. Time for reflective thought, discussion, and writing all contribute to smooth short-term planning.

Scheduling

Long- and short-term planning should really precede scheduling, and as such both types of planning have a direct effect on actually setting up time for instruction. In many elementary schools, time must be scheduled for separately taught art, music, and physical education. In many secondary schools, time is scheduled for separately taught subjects all day, every day.

Collaborative Thematic Planning

Erb and Doda (1989) describe scheduling implications at four levels of collaborative thematic planning: preintegration, coordinated or overlap teaching, cooperative teaching, and interdisciplinary thematic unit. At the first level, **preintegration**, collaborators alter their respective schedules to utilize field trips, guest speakers, laboratories, and other special opportunities. The process of scheduling learning activities according to how long they would naturally take instead of trying to block out 30 minutes for math and 45 minutes for reading every day is in itself evidence of collaboration.

Coordinated or **overlap teaching**, the practice of teaching related topics simultaneously, can be done alone or as a member of a collaborative team. Educators at this level who are secure with their content knowledge will sometimes adjust their own schedules to coordinate their teaching with a colleague.

The third level, **cooperative teaching,** occurs when educators change the way they teach something to facilitate a mutually beneficial learning environment. Members of a teaching team can each identify learning outcomes in their respective subject areas, selecting an outcome every week: one week it may be a math application, the next week a persuasive speech. Each team member then plans and schedules an activity to reinforce the outcome for that week.

The fourth and final level, **interdisciplinary thematic unit,** includes both long-term and short-term collaborative planning. These units can last as long or short a time as the planning team judges necessary. At this level educators can, as collaborators, design an entire curriculum of learning experiences appropriate for all students and create their own team schedules. Collaborative thematic units can be scheduled only when building administrators support educators involved in the process. In most situations this includes the allocation of time for teams to meet to plan and schedule instruction. Educators themselves must be flexible and willing to give up traditional scheduling practices.

The four levels described can offer professionals a variety of strategies for changing their schedules, and provide a progression toward truly collaborative thematic planning for inclusive classrooms. Table 8.2 provides a basic schedule format that can be followed when designing a written unit plan. Following Table 8.2 is a partially completed unit plan to help clarify some of the subheadings in the format that have not be previously discussed.

TABLE 8.2   Unit Format

A. Title

B. Introduction
   Target group
   Length of unit
   Time per day
   Curriculum areas covered (should be able to include all)

C. Rationale
   Why is this topic important?

D. Motivation/Initiation
   How will you get students interested?

E. Diagram of content areas

F. Behavioral objectives
   By content area
   1. Science
   2. Social studies
   3. Mathematics
   4. Language arts
   5. Music
   6. Art
   7. Practical arts
      a. Home economics
      b. Industrial arts
   8. Health
   9. Motor, recreational, and leisure skills
   10. Drama
   11. Other

TABLE 8.2   (continued)

G. Materials and resources (What will you use? What will students use?)
   1. Films
   2. Filmstrips and slides
   3. Prints
   4. Music
   5. Computer programs
   6. Other technology
   7. Teacher-made materials
   8. Community resource persons
   9. Other

H. Bibliography
   Teacher's
      1. Books
      2. Places to write
      3. Magazines
   Student's
      1. Books
      2. Special materials

I. Daily schedule
   Matrices (objectives)

J. Lesson plans (daily plans)
   1. Day 1
   2. Day 2
   3. Day 3 (etc.)

K. Adaptations
   General
   Specific

Adapted from: deGrandpre, B. (n.d.). *EDS 382: Curricular Practices in Special Education Packet.* Unpublished ms.

Partial Unit Plan

A. Title: Clouds

B. Introduction

This unit is designed to be completed in three weeks for an inclusive class of middle elementary students (third, fourth, and fifth grade). Three hours or 180 minutes a day will be focused on various concepts related to the study of clouds. Math, social studies, language arts, science, art, drama, motor skills, practical arts, health, and music are the curriculum areas included in this unit.

C. Rationale

Why is this topic important?

The movement, shape, and placement of clouds in the sky is a natural phenomenon that has excited children for ages. Clouds are elusive forms that seem to shift and change constantly. Clouds play an important part in our changing environment. By developing an understanding of clouds, students will be able to see how they effect their lives in a number of different ways. Understanding the relationship between clouds and the weather will help students plan their daily activities.

D. Motivation/Initiation

How will you get students interested?

Students will be taken outside and asked to lie on their backs in the grass. The teacher will pose a series of questions about those clouds visible. Some questions will involve the use of imagination and others will be factual.

What do you think of when you look up at the clouds?

What are clouds made of?

What keeps the clouds from falling out of the sky?

What do clouds feel like?

E. Diagram of content areas

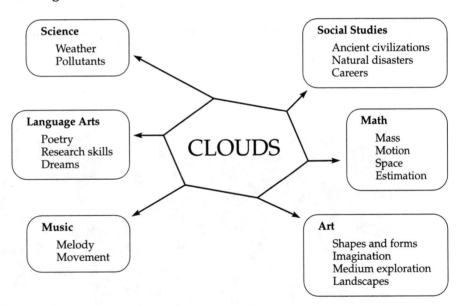

F. Goals (see Table 8.5 for an example of a goal statement), behavioral objectives, and activities:

Science

1.1. The students will investigate the effects of pollutants on cloud formation.

1.2. The students will classify clouds by genera and species.

1.3. The students will develop a variety of methods to demonstrate the water cycle (e.g., plastic bags, terrarium).

Social Studies

2.1. The students will explore careers that require the study of clouds (meteorologist, environmental scientist, rainmaker).

2.2. The students will describe the relationship between clouds and different cultural customs/beliefs.

Math

3.1. The students will monitor, record, and chart the various types of cloud formations.

3.2. The students will determine cloud movement through the atmosphere.

Language Arts

4.1. The students will develop a pamphlet that provides tips on different kinds of weather hazards.

4.2. The students will create poetry about clouds.

Music

5.1. The students will interpret clouds through music.

5.2. The students will compose instrumental melodies symbolic of clouds.

Art

    6.1. The students will sculpt clouds, exploring the various media available for this creative activity.

    6.2. The students will create a collage using items representing clouds (words cut from magazine, cotton balls, etc.).

G. Materials and resources

1. Films

2. Filmstrips and slides

3. Prints

    Weather maps

    The Cloud Charts

4. Music

    Both sides now—J. Collins

5. Computer programs

    The Children's Writing and Publishing Center (Grades 2–12)

    Cause and Effect: What Makes It Happen (Grades 4–8)

    Teddy Takes a Rainwalk (Grades PreK–3)

    Measure Works (Grade 2–6)

    Echo Speech Synthesizer (all grades)

    Crossword Magic (Grade 3–12)

6. Other technology

7. Teacher-made materials

8. Community resource persons

    Jay Manx, meteorologist from PSUC Channel 6

9. Other

    Clay

    Cotton balls

    Magazines

    Newsprint

    Newspapers

H. Bibliography

Teacher

Bureau of Curriculum Development. (1989). *Mathematics K–6: A recommended program for elementary schools.* Albany, NY: The State Education Department.

Bureau of Curriculum Development. (1988). *Social studies program: Grade 3.* Albany, NY: State Education Department.

Bureau of Curriculum Development. (1988). *English language arts syllabus K–12: A publication for curriculum developers.* Albany, NY: The State Education Department.

Bureau of Curriculum Development. (1972). *Music K–6: Experimental edition.* Albany, NY: The State Education Department.

Freedman, R. L. H. (1990). *Connections: Science by writing.* National Science Teachers Association.

Graf, M. (1994). *The weather report.* Palo Alto, CA: Seymour.

Koenig, H. G., DeMarco-Keating, M. L., & Lansing, J. A. B. (1989). *RCT science review*. Middletown, NY: N & N.

Koenig, H. G., DeMarco-Keating, M. L., & Lansing, J. A. B. (1988). *Earth science: A concise competency review* (Teacher annotated ed.). Middletown, NY: N & N.

Malehorn, H. (1975). *Encyclopedia of activities for teaching grades K–3.* West Nyack, NY: Parker.

Miller, A., Thompson, J. C., Peterson, R. E., & Haragan, D. R. (1983). *Elements of meteorology.* Columbus, OH: Merrill.

Seed, D. (1994). *Water science.* Palo Alto, CA: Seymour.

Shymansky, J. A., Romance, N. & Yore, L. D. (1988). *Journeys in science* (teacher's ed.). New York: Macmillan.

Strongin, H. (1994). *Science on a shoestring.* Palo Alto, CA: Seymour.

Tolley, K. (1994). *The art and science connection.* Palo Alto, CA: Seymour.

Wright, R. (1994). *Event-based science: Hurricane.* (teacher's ed.). Palo Alto, CA: Seymour.

Student

Barrett, J. (1978). *Cloudy with a chance of meatballs.* New York: Scholastic Book Services.

Koenig, H. G., DeMarco-Keating, M. L., & Lansing, J. B. (1988). *Earth science: A concise competency review.* Middletown, NY: N & N.

Shymansky, J. A., Romance, N. & Yore, L. D. (1988). *Journeys in science.* New York: Macmillan.

The Black River Depressed Republican. (local newspaper)

Wright, R. (1994). *Event-based science: Hurricane* (student's ed.). Palo Alto, CA: Seymour.

I. Daily schedule

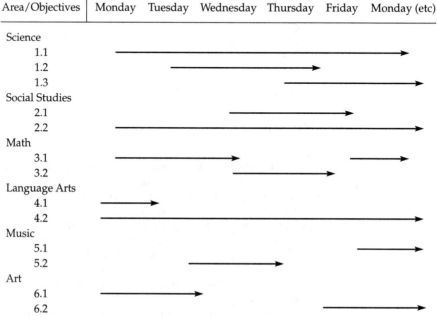

Area/Objectives	Monday	Tuesday	Wednesday	Thursday	Friday	Monday (etc)

Science
1.1
1.2
1.3
Social Studies
2.1
2.2
Math
3.1
3.2
Language Arts
4.1
4.2
Music
5.1
5.2
Art
6.1
6.2

The introduction of an objective is indicated by the beginning of the arrow. The arrowhead indicates projected date of completion.

J. Lesson plans (see Table 8.3 and Table 8.5)
Please note that lesson plans must be reviewed and altered as the unit progresses so that they continue to meet the unique needs of all students.

K. Adaptations

General
Three types of general adaptations can be made to the overall unit or individual lessons: teacher modifications, student instructional modifications, and environmental modifications. *Teacher modifications* are changes educators make in the manner in which they address students. Examples of general adaptations of this type may include adjusting language structures and speed, modeling organization through advance organizers, giving prompt feedback often, utilizing resource personnel and peer tutors, and assisting students to reflect on their learning.

Student instructional modifications are changes that can be made to alter the method of instruction or testing. Providing untimed tests; extending assignment completion times; and providing study guides, concept previews, aids (calculators, word processors) and guided notes are a few of the adaptations that can be made to assist students in the learning process. Additionally, rephrasing instructions, varying response mode, and adjusting length of activity may also be helpful.

Environmental modifications are changes that can be made to the classroom structure and organization, which may include the deletion or addition of resource materials. Examples of general adaptations of this type include changing the learner's location in room, marking clearly all centers, and providing visual displays and distraction-free work areas.

Reflect for a Moment

All of these modifications may appear daunting at first, but pause and reflect on the ways you modify your plans and behaviors routinely on a given day. You modify your conversation, your posture, your writing, your actions, and your expectations in response to the people and events around you, right?

Specific Modifications

In addition to the general types of adaptations mentioned previously, an effective educator will also develop more student-specific adaptations. The following are some specific examples of adaptations that can be made during the thematic unit.

Teacher
- The educator will develop a subtle signal for students who become anxious about being called on so they will know when a question will be directed to them. One such signal could be the movement of the educator toward the student just before asking the question. (This is also an appropriate strategy to use with students who experience processing problems.)

- When the educator asks a question such as, "What are the species classifications for clouds?" sufficient wait time will be given and then the learner with a processing problem will be asked, "Jenny, can you give me one?"

Student Instructional

- When lecturing about species and genera, the educator supplies guided notes for all learners, assisting those who may have difficulty filtering out extraneous information without calling attention to them.
- The educator supplies several students in class with paper that will produce multiple copies of their notes. The duplicates can then be made available to those learners who have difficulty taking notes or copying information from the board.

Environmental

- Within the classroom library, a variety of research and reading materials related to clouds will be made available at various reading levels.
- A large three-dimensional poster of the various cloud types clearly labeled in both print and braille, hung at an appropriate level to ensure that all children will have easy access.

Practice

1. Under part F in the unit, goals, objectives, and activities are listed. Based on your understanding of these 3 terms, label each statement as G, O, or A. Take any statements you feel are not objectives, and rewrite them so they are objectives.

2. Under part F in the unit, objectives have been omitted for drama, practical arts, motor skills, and health. Write two for each area.

3. You have in your classroom a visually impaired student. What specific adaptations could be made for 3.1 under part F in the unit plan?

LEVELS OF LEARNING

The levels of learning are a rough draft of what we learn (see Chapters 2, 3, and 6). The cognitive, psychomotor, and affective domains each have their own type of learning. The integrated nature of thematic units allows more diversity of learning activities and more balanced learning in all three domains. The clouds unit should offer a strong combination of different levels of learning, and all students must have access to all learning activities. Adaptations are made whenever necessary to ensure this access.

Cognitive

Students will name five different types of clouds. (*Knowledge*)

Students will describe how tornadoes are created. (*Comprehension*)

Students will report cloud conditions across the country or region. (*Application*)

Students will determine the influence of pollutants from clouds on the region. (*Analysis*)

Students will compose melodies that represent certain cloud conditions. (*Synthesis*)

Students will establish precautionary measures for high-risk riverfront communities. (*Evaluation*)

Affective

Students will be aware of cloud movement. (*Receiving*)

Students will offer to record cloudiness daily. (*Responding*)

Students will choose among careers related to clouds. (*Valuing*)

Students will take a position on the control of acid rain. (*Organization*)

Students will change their out-of-school plans because of cloud conditions. (*Characterization*)

Psychomotor

Students will draw different types of clouds. (*Imitation*)

Students will construct a graph of cloud movement. (*Manipulation*)

Students will measure the speed of a cloud moving across the sky. (*Precision*)

Students will paint a landscape with their choice of cloud formations. (*Articulation*)

Students will write in response to music with a clouds theme. (*Naturalization*)

LESSON PLAN DESIGNS

Effective learning experiences need to be organized in a systematic way. Each new lesson builds on or reinforces what went before and complements those to follow. A thematic unit lesson should be organized so that complexity increases and learners' visions are broadened by the integration of information across subject areas (Lemlech, 1994).

Although as preservice teacher you may believe that once student teaching has been completed you will never write another lesson, in reality the most effective educators continue to develop and use lesson plans. As an educator becomes more experienced, the details of a lesson plan may diminish, but the importance of thoroughly organizing the learning experience does not.

Prior to planning any lesson, the educator must make four important decisions:

1. What *specific content* will be taught—division long or short, with or without remainders?
2. What are the learner's *present abilities* in this specific content area—basic multiplication and division facts, multiple digit multiplication?
3. What is the *expected learner behavior*—complete a worksheet, do problems on the board, take a test?
4. What *teacher behaviors* will be exhibited—model problem solving, verbal rehearsal, lecture? (Batesky, 1987)

Armed with the answers to these questions, the educator can now select from several lesson design formats and begin the process of formally planning for instruction.

One of the most widely recognized models for lesson design is the Hunter seven-step model (see Table 8.3 for a sample plan). Hunter (1994) emphasizes that

TABLE 8.3   Cloud Lesson Plan Using the Hunter Model

Title:	Clouds as weather predictors
Statement of objective:	Today, students, you will learn to predict weather based on information regarding cloud formation. This is important because it will enable you to make plans that are not in conflict with weather conditions.
Anticipatory Set:	Show class slides of destruction related to weather and have them brainstorm ways in which these weather disasters could have been predicted and perhaps lessened. Write ideas on board.
Input:	Show slides of each of the types of cloud formations. Students should devise list of characteristics that distinguish different cloud types. Teacher should add to each list the types of weather indicated by clouds if students fail to recognize from picture. Responses should be recorded by different students on the flipchart.
Modeling:	Teacher should show a picture of a particular cloud type and discuss characteristics present and type of weather associated with.
Check for Understanding:	The teacher should facilitate discussion and periodically check for understanding of cloud characteristics with questions regarding size, length, color, amount of sky showing, and so on.
Guided Practice:	Show pictures of cloud formation and have students write type on slate or response card. Erase. Now have students write typical weather associated with that type of cloud.
Independent Practice:	After selecting a picture or story about a weather disaster from a magazine or newspaper, students will write a paragraph describing the type of clouds that would have been present.

for every learning event, the educator needs to carefully consider each of seven elements separately to determine those relevant for the specific content, learners, and selection of instructional strategies. The seven elements are anticipatory set, objective, input, modeling, check for learner understanding, guided practice, and independent practice. Elements can be either excluded or combined with one another to form the instructional plan. The seven elements are hierarchical, each derived from and having a relationship to the previous element. Therefore the educator, when designing lessons, needs to consider each of the elements in a particular order.

The **anticipatory set** is designed to direct learners' focused attention on the instructional content to follow and develop a mental "set" (readiness) for it. The "set" should be brief, continuing only long enough to get learners ready and set to go to accomplish the current learning objective. If it will help the learner achieve the current objective, the "set" may include a review of previously learned information. However, routine review of prior learning is not a necessary component of the anticipatory set. Educators may also use the set to obtain diagnostic information that may be needed for the current objective. Hunter (1994) points out that if learners are already alert and ready, the anticipatory set can be excluded. Developing a strong anticipatory set will increase motivation and retention as well as make the use of class time more efficient.

Reflect for a Moment

Have you ever been in a class where the instructor started the session by simply launching, without warning, into a barrage of new information, never indicating where it was leading? How did you feel?

After gaining learners' attention, an educator should provide a succinct statement relating the purpose of the lesson. This is generally accomplished by a **statement of the objective** and reason(s) that it is of importance for the learner. Some educators prefer to write the objective on the blackboard so that they may refer to it frequently during the lesson. Additionally, some educators may have students record the objective in their journals or notebooks, so that at the end of the day they can more easily reflect on their learning. This also becomes the first step in learners' development of notetaking, self-recording, and self-evaluation skills. This process enables students to organize their thoughts in advance, thus accelerating their learning. This overview is often called an **advance organizer** in the research literature on lesson planning. When educators fail to develop a clear lesson plan objective, neither they nor the learners have no sense of direction. For a lesson to be effective, for there to be quality attached to both teaching and learning, a well-developed objective must be present (for writing objectives, see Chapter 6). Furthermore, the objective must discuss the skill or knowledge to be learned and not be an abbreviation of the activity to take place (see Table 8.4 for examples).

TABLE 8.4   Objectives versus Activities

Well written	Poorly written
Students will follow three-step directions, increase their fine motor skills, and work cooperatively for 15 minutes.	Given magazines and scissors, the students will make a collage that represents clouds.
Students will predict weather based on information about cloud formations.	Following a lecture, the students will complete a worksheet on weather prediction.
Students will discuss the importance of recognizing various cloud formations.	After presenting several scenarios, the teacher will lead a discussion of the importance of recognizing various cloud formations.
Students will integrate information from various resources on weather hazards.	The students will develop a colorful pamphlet that provides tips on different kinds of weather hazards.

The next element, **instructional input**, is the nuts and bolts of the lesson plan. The instructional input portion provides the means by which the educator intends to get the learner to achieve the objective. Educators should develop concise, well-organized, step-by-step explanations for learners in a language that they will understand. For some learners, a brief demonstration that is focused, explicit, and repetitive may be most effective (Ysseldyke, Christenson, & Thurlow, 1987). The input section of a lesson plan is generally directed by the teaching strategies selected by the educator: discovery, expository, inquiry, or discussion (see Chapters 9 through 12). How much of the input is student directed or teacher directed depends on the strategy selected. The educator identifies the essential components or skills needed to accomplish the objective by use of task analysis. *Task analysis* is the process by which an educator breaks down complex learning into simpler sequential learnings for efficient and effective student achievement (Hunter, 1994).

Many educators include **modeling** as part of input. Modeling provides the student with both a visual and verbal example of an acceptable learning outcome. For learners to focus on the essentials rather than transitory or nonrelevant factors in the process or product, the visual aspect of modeling must be accompanied by verbal input that labels critical elements of what is occurring (Hunter, 1994).

Checking for learner understanding is an essential feature of any lesson. The educator does this to determine at what point learners grasp the information and/or skill necessary to achieve the objective. Checking for understanding can be accomplished in a variety of ways such as sampling, signaled response, group choral response, or individual private response. When an educator poses a question to the total group, provides wait time, and then calls upon a single student for a response, she or he is **sampling**. Central to this technique is the strategy of calling on students in such a way as to provide a representative sampling of ability levels from within strata of the group. Sampling focuses the entire class (group) on generating an answer and creates a readiness within the student to respond. As a check for understanding, sampling is limited by time and number of questions asked.

Group choral responses require the total group to listen, think, and answer questions presented by the educator. The strength of the response gives a slightly better indication of group understanding but still tends to not be effective for determining individuals who may be having difficulties. Many educators prefer methods that provide them with immediate feedback for all students rather than just a few. **Signaled responses** such as thumbs up or down, showing number of fingers to indicate selection of an answer from multiple choices, or other types of hand gestures give the educator an opportunity to quickly survey the entire group. Learners experiencing difficulty can then be provided additional instruction.

Possibly one of the most effective measures of understanding is the **individual private response**. This can be accomplished easily with response cards or slates. The educator asks a question, provides wait time, and then signals the group to hold up their cards or slates. A quick scan will reveal who understands and who needs further instruction.

Reflect for a Moment

Did they say "slates"? Yes, indeed. Chalkboard slates have become very popular among educators who want to know frequently and precisely how well students understand the new learning. Slates are probably one of the best classroom materials available today, just as they were over one hundred years ago!

Once an educator has a clear picture of learners' understanding, he or she can move on to closely supervised practice trials. **Guided practice** provides monitored practices which allow the educator to correct learners' errors quickly, preventing students from learning incorrect responses (for an example, see Table 8.3). Guided practice also gives learners opportunities to practice and receive immediate feedback and reinforcement.

After learners have successfully completed several practices, they can move on to **independent practice**. During independent practice the educator does not directly monitor completion of the task. This is the learners' opportunity to practice their newly developed skill. Homework, a written exam, a student demonstration, or out-of-school activities are examples of independent practice. Educators should not assign independent practice unless they are sure that learners will be able to successfully complete the tasks. Learners who experience difficulty with independent practice are more likely to give up on the task. Additionally, if learners have not grasped the concept or skill, they may be practicing errors. It is much more difficult to correct a practiced (learned) error.

Some educators, when writing lesson plans, seem to have a great deal of difficulty separating input, guided practice, and independent practice, often confusing the three. Input is the teaching/learning portion of the lesson. Guided practice is the teacher-monitored performance of the skill or concept. Independent practice is done without teacher input. Of the three, independent practice should never be given until the student has a clear understanding of the new material.

Hunter (1994) points out that her model for lesson design relies on teacher decision making and should not be viewed "as a rigid system of steps that must be included in every learning situation" (p. 3). In a recent study, Sousa and Donnavon (1990) found statistically significant gains in student achievement for four of six content areas when educators used the Hunter model. However, the Hunter model is not without its critics. Berg and Clough (1991) contend that "Hunter's design is not consistent with many goals of a science education, it is not appropriate for every lesson in science, and it contradicts important principles of science teaching" (p. 73). (For an in-depth analysis of this debate, consult *Educational Leadership*, December 1990/January 1991.)

As previously stated, there are many types of lesson plan formats. However, most have not experienced the commercial success of the Hunter model. Esler and Sciortino (1991) provide the following format for writing a complete lesson plan (see Table 8.5 for a sample):

1. Topic
2. Goal statement(s)
3. Objective statement(s)
   a. Concept objective(s) when appropriate
   b. Skill/attitude objective(s) when appropriate
4. Materials required
5. Procedure
   a. set
   b. lecture outline or questions if the expository method is used
   c. examples (and non-examples) of concepts
   d. review/closure/bridge to the next lesson
   e. evaluation procedures.

While there is overlap between Esler and Sciortino's lesson design and the Hunter model, the former has incorporated three elements that are critical: materials, review/closure/bridge, and evaluation. Including these elements helps to strengthen the educator's planning effectiveness.

A written lesson plan should have a section that proceeds instructional input and provides the educator with a concise list of all necessary materials. The inclusion of a materials section helps the educator to preplan the instructional day by readying in advance all needed materials. As noted in Chapter 6, this type of planning helps to increase instructional time while decreasing time leaks.

Following the assigning of independent practice (if appropriate), the educator needs to assist the learning and transition process by bringing the lesson to **closure**. Closure is generally accomplished through review or summary of the main concepts learned. To the greatest degree possible, closure should be a student-directed task or event. An educator may ask learners to summarize in their own words, dis-

TABLE 8.5   Cloud Lesson Plan Using the Esler and Sciortino Format

Topic: Clouds

Goal Statement: Students will understand the connection between various cloud formations and weather fronts.

Objective statements:

Concept objective: Students will predict weather based on information about cloud formation.

Attitude objective: Students will discuss the importance of recognizing various cloud formations. Two recent examples of how this information could have prevented tragedy should be given.

Materials: Photos or slides of cirrus, cumulus, stratus, and nimbus clouds and their combinations; filmstrip *Clouds and Weather Prediction*; film clips and slides of recent weather-related disasters; slide projector; flipchart with newsprint; markers; filmstrip projector.

Procedure:

Set: Show class slides of weather-related destruction and have them brainstorm ways in which these weather disasters could have been predicted and perhaps lessened. Write ideas on board.

Outline: Show slides of each of the types of cloud formations. Students should devise a list of characteristics that distinguish different cloud types. Teacher should add to each list the types of weather indicated by clouds if students fail to recognize them from picture. Responses should be recorded by different students on the flipchart. If students have difficulty coming up with characteristics, the teacher can facilitate discussion with questions regarding size, length, color, amount of sky showing, and so on.

Examples: Teacher should show pictures of various weather conditions and discuss types of clouds present.

Review/closure/bridge: Have students restate names of and types of weather they are associated with. Do a semantic web of other cloud associations (see Figure 8.2).

Evaluation: Was the objective met? Was the student response method appropriate? Was wait time effective and appropriate? How could the lesson be expanded? If I were to reteach, what would I keep, what would I change?

Source: Esler, W.K., & Sciortino, P. (1991). *Methods for teaching: An overview of current practices,* 2nd ed. Raleigh, NC: Contemporary Publishing Company, p. 43–44.

play their work, verbally share their conclusions, or brainstorm about the followup lesson (**bridge**).

Evaluation is perhaps the most critical feature of a lesson plan in terms of future planning. To be useful in future planning, evaluation must be two pronged, examining not just student success but teacher effectiveness as well. Not only do educators need to develop a systematic set of procedures for determining whether learners have accomplished the instructional objective, they must also examine how effectively they facilitated the learning process. A lesson plan evaluation needs to involve more than simply stating, "The students enjoyed the lesson and the objective was met." What portions of the lesson drew student attention? Was the modeling effective and clear? Was there a good match between the lesson objective and guided or independent practice? Was the pace appropriate? Was appropriate wait time provided? How successful were attempts at reteaching? These are but a few of the questions that an educator should ask in evaluating a lesson. Answers can then be used in a formative manner to strengthen future lessons.

Lesson plans are developed to implement unit plan goals and objectives. As such, they need to focus on the details of organization and implementation that create a successful learning environment for all students. When formulating a lesson, the educator is strongly advised to develop alternative procedures or explanations (*contingent planning*). There is nothing more frustrating for educators to realize that the learners are lost and an alternate explanation or presentation is not available. Learners become frustrated and behavior problems may occur when an educator is forced to offer the same explanation over and over because of lack of contingency planning.

Reflect for a Moment

As a learner, what do you do when you do not understand what is being taught in a class? Do some instructors just plow ahead, oblivious? Do others encourage learners to raise questions when they do not understand? Do they then restate, or even reteach the learning?

Practice

Given the objectives you developed in the unit plan, select one and develop a lesson plan.

SUMMARY

Units vary in scope, length, and structure, but fall into one of four basic types: discipline oriented, broad field, resource, and teaching. Thematic units help educators and students in inclusive classrooms connect subject areas and manage large amounts of information. Consistent with constructivist thinking, these units also bring relevance to student learning.

Four organizational factors (scope, sequence, continuity, and balance) influence the development of any unit. Unit planning begins with selecting a theme. The educators then brainstorm with students and/or colleagues to generate subtopics, develop key questions, and create a list of activities and available literature. The planning team then can combine ideas and develop goals and objectives. Objectives can be immediate, intermediate, or long range.

Long range planning requires flexibility and sound judgment, as it can easily become overplanning. When planning for the short term, attention must be paid to objectives, procedures, materials, and time allocation on a daily and weekly basis. Adaptations for the educator, the students, and the setting must also be considered during planning a unit. It is important, when planning, that thematic units lend themselves to a diversity of learning activities across the three domains of learning. The final stage of planning units is the scheduling of instructional time for activities, and must be done collaboratively with other team members.

Content, learner readiness, and expected behavior for both educators and learners must then be examined prior to lesson planning. Most lesson plans include a statement of objective, set, instructional input, modeling, checking for understanding, guided and independent practice, and closure. Several strategies are offered for each of these stages. Educators must also evaluate learners and the lesson itself to enhance future planning.

PART III

THE TEACHING/LEARNING EXPERIENCE

INTRODUCTION

The following four chapters examine four major teaching strategies: expository, discovery, discussion, and inquiry. Each chapter provides examples of cooperative learning, peer tutoring, and mastery learning as applied to the teaching strategy under consideration. Let us look first at each of these three teaching innovations.

COOPERATIVE LEARNING

In an attempt to create and maintain a learning environment that is less competitive and more cooperative, teachers have devised lessons that focus on interaction among students and emphasize helping each other achieve common goals. **Cooperative learning** has helped students from different cultures and with varying abilities understand and help each other during the learning process (Slavin, 1990).* It has been used to teach skills at all levels of learning as well as to promote cooperative behavior among an increasingly diverse group of students.

Well-developed cooperative methods have been successful for four major reasons: Cooperative groups stimulate higher-order thinking (reasoning skills), create constructive controversy that results in the use of problem-solving techniques and understanding of others' perspectives, enhance the use of essential cognitive processes, and increase active involvement in learning (Bossert 1988–89; Johnson & Johnson, 1985). Further, Good, Mulryan, & McCaslin (1992) note that cooperative learning enhances children's achievement and social relations by increasing subject

---

*References cited here are included with those from Chapter 9.

matter knowledge, allowing students to regulate their own resources, teaching them to coordinate various information sources, modeling appropriate behaviors by group for group members, and expanding understanding of self and others.

Slavin (1990) has established three basic features of cooperative learning: the presence of group goals, individual accountability, and equal opportunity for success. The **group goal** is a single outcome that all students in a group work toward during the lesson. Group goals motivate students to seek assistance from peers and give them assistance as well. Success depends largely on a group's ability to interact cooperatively. **Individual accountability** requires that the success of the team be dependent on the learning of its individual members. This aspect of cooperative learning prevents situations where highly capable students do all the work and other students do nothing. When all students in a group can contribute meaningfully to the successful outcome of an activity, then there is **equal opportunity for success**. This final component often requires instructional **adaptations**, which will be addressed separately in each of the four chapters.

Among the many cooperative learning variations, the best-known and most widely researched are learning together, group investigation, student team achievement divisions (STAD), teams-game-tournament (TGT), team-assisted instruction (TAI), and jigsaw I and II (Aronson, Blaney, Stephan, Sikes, & Snapp, 1978; Good & Brophy, 1994). The **learning together** model (Johnson & Johnson, 1975; Johnson, Johnson, Holubec, & Roy, 1984) has evolved since it was first introduced and features four elements: positive interdependence (with goals, task, role, and reward), student face-to-face interaction, individual accountability, and student instruction in interpersonal and small-group skills. **Group investigation**, a model developed in Israel, requires learners to select and develop their own two- to six-person group. Each cooperative group selects a subtopic from a total class study unit, breaks that into individual tasks and completes all necessary activities to prepare a final report.

Student team achievement divisions (STAD) is a model that involves mixed-ability groups of four or five students who, following teacher-directed presentations, work together until each group member achieves a perfect score on a quiz. Recognition is a major feature of STAD, and groups change every five or six weeks to allow maximum opportunity for interactive learning. The **teams-game-tournament (TGT)** approach (DeVries & Slavin, 1978; DeVries, Slavin, Fennessey, Edwards, & Lombardo, 1980) requires learners to work in four- to five-member heterogeneously grouped teams mastering content materials and preparing for team competition. **Team-assisted instruction (TAI)** is similar to TGT, but students take more responsibility for monitoring and managing the progress of group members. Individual students must have the approval of their group to take a final test on a given topic.

The **jigsaw I** classroom, finally, is more suited to the secondary classroom. Students work on more elaborate projects largely independent of the teacher, sharing materials, checking each other's work, and meeting both in and out of class. Teachers set deadlines, and groups may present their work to others. Students form groups on the basis of interest but also mix ability, gender, and ethnicity as much as possible. In **jigsaw II**, an adaptation of jigsaw, learners begin with a common reading rather than individual materials.

Clearly, cooperative learning is a major component of collaboration and inclusion in schools. Students are placed in situations where they must develop collaborative skills in order for their group to succeed. The social skills of all students are enhanced during cooperative learning activities, and students with disabilities can participate in a wide range of roles within a cooperative learning group. Traditional classroom activities, such as whole class lectures and daily worksheets, are not conducive to either inclusive settings or cooperative learning situations. Last, educators who plan cooperative learning activities are very likely to seek out other adults in the school and surrounding community as resource persons, supervisors, or collaborators in the planning of such experiences.

For a more in-depth explanation of cooperative learning, see Johnson and Johnson (1987), Bohlmeyer and Burke (1987); DeVries and Slavin (1978); DeVries, Slavin, Fennessey, Edwards, and Lombardo (1980); *Educational Leadership* (December 1989/January 1990); Slavin (1983, 1990a,b), or Slavin, Sharan, Kagan, Hertz-Lazarowitz, Webb, and Schmuck (1985).

MASTERY LEARNING

Because students learn in different ways and at different rates, the mastery learning strategy is important for educators to understand and be able to integrate into their repertoire of teaching techniques. In the strictest sense, **mastery learning** is characterized by frequent tests or quizzes that determine whether a student moves onto the next level/skill or needs to gain a better understanding of the materials at hand before moving on (Jacobsen, Eggen & Kauchak, 1993). Major summative tests constitute a means of evaluating student mastery at the end of a unit or semester.

Mastery learning has become more widespread recently largely because of its usefulness in helping manage a variety of learning rates and styles. Another important reason for the popularity of mastery learning is the steady flow of research supporting its success in helping students achieve academically (Okey, 1977; Hyman & Cohen, 1979; Whiting & Render, 1987) and attitudinally (Gusky & Pigott, 1988; Kulik & Kulik, 1990).

Jacobsen and colleagues (1993) identify seven basic components of mastery learning: (1) The teacher must first present to the learner a *clearly stated goal*, so both parties are fully aware of the desired outcome. (2) Using a *preassessment*, the learner's prior knowledge is accessed. This allows the educator to plan for individual needs. (3) *Primary instruction* is usually carried out with a group of students in a teacher-directed setting. (4) Frequent practice activities or quizzes serve as *formative assessment* tools and are not normally graded; their purpose is to clarify whether or not a student has achieved mastery of the material. (5) In some cases, *additional instruction* comes next. Any student who does not demonstrate the desired level of mastery on a formative assessment is provided with further instruction, modified teaching, or just more practice. (6) Those students who demonstrate mastery on a formative assessment may in some cases move on to the next task or level of learning and in other cases participate in additional *enrichment activities* designed to deepen their understanding of the material they have mastered. This may take the form of applications or more elaborate perspectives but in all cases goes beyond the behavior and criteria originally established for mastery. (7) The final component, *summative assessment*, usually represents a final test of mastery over a larger amount of information and occurs at the end of a unit of instruction.

Collectively, these features of mastery learning make this technique highly compatible with more traditional teacher-directed approaches to instruction (see Chapter 9), although the addition of preassessment and additional instruction typically improves traditional teaching. In addition, although mastery learning can be implemented quite logically in teaching facts or basic concepts, it can also be used when teaching higher levels of thinking, such as application or analysis.

Another important benefit of the mastery learning strategy, beyond its usefulness in accommodating diverse learners, is the opportunity for reflective teaching. The process of preassessment, primary instruction, formative assessment, and alternative/enrichment instruction demands that educators constantly look closely at the effectiveness of their instructional strategies and make adjustments continually to help students experience academic success and subsequently increase their self-confidence and motivation to continue learning. This reflective behavior, together with the suitability of mastery learning to diverse groups of learners, lays a foundation for professional collaboration and facilitates inclusive schooling.

PEER TUTORING

Many enrichment activities suitable for implementation in a mastery learning strategy involve **peer tutoring**. Perhaps the most popular type of peer tutoring is the case in which a student who has mastered certain learning objectives actually enriches her or his learning by teaching another student (Slavin, 1991). This can be an effective strategy because students are often more willing to ask questions with peers than when the teacher conducts a large-group lesson. Other factors also suggest that this type of peer tutoring can be effective (Ornstein, 1990). It is less threatening to be criticized by a peer than by the teacher. The language a peer uses can often be clearer and more understandable than the language of the adult and lead to a better grasp of a new concept or collection of new information. Furthermore, the peer tutor, having recently learned the material, may actually have an easier time diagnosing another student's specific area of difficulty and therefore may provide more precise intervention.

In other settings, students in pairs can take turns being teacher and both give and receive valuable instructional feedback during drill-and-practice sessions. Yet another peer tutoring scheme, cross-age tutoring, is the practice of having older students work with younger students in a wide range of situations. Among the benefits of this arrangement are the incentives for prosocial behavior among both groups of learners (Borich, 1992).

Regardless of the form peer tutoring takes, there is, in most cases, feedback, reinforcement, and support coming from another student. If the full potential of peer tutoring is to be realized, however, all students being tutored should also serve as tutors under different circumstances. The educator can model and help create an environment in which helping others is a common vehicle for learning. Various forms of peer tutoring can become integral parts of the daily schedule so that students know when, how, and with whom it can be utilized. Students should work closely with different peers during the year. In addition, peer tutoring is an opportunity for parents and other members of the community to play an active role in the school—as facilitators, resource assistants, or managers of multifaceted peer tutoring arrangements. This approach supports a strong commitment to building community awareness among and between learners and contributes to the development of collaborative skills as well. Friendships can also emerge as a result of peer tutoring, sometimes between learners who might not otherwise have reason to spend time together. The development and support of a natural support network is fundamental to inclusive classrooms. It represents a significant feature of schooling that serves as a building block for inclusive education.

When it is well planned, peer tutoring has the obvious advantage of allowing the teacher to work with different students and not neglect any of them. On either end of the peer tutoring arrangement, however, the primary beneficiary is the student. Pierce, Stahlbrand, and Armstrong (1989) found academic gains, positive social skills, and increased self-esteem among students being tutored. Enhanced communication skills, increased self-esteem, and higher-level thinking and curriculum knowledge are among the benefits for the tutor (Pierce, Stahlbrand, & Armstrong, 1989; Gartner, Kohler, & Riessman, 1971; Johnson et al., 1984). Educators must, however, be cautioned not to keep tutors who may happen to be high academic achievers from opportunities to work at their own challenging tasks.

9

THE EXPOSITORY APPROACH

Key Terms

Adaptation
Advance organizer
Authentic assessment
Checks for understanding
Comparative organizer
Comprehension question
Conclusion
Convergent question
Divergent question
Expository teaching
Expository organizers
Extending question
Good question
Guessing questions
Individualization
Input

Mastery learning
Mnemonics
Negative example
Overview
Peer tutoring
Performance assessment
Positive example
Preassessment
Probe
Product evaluation
Prompting
Recall question
Redirection
Tugging
Yes-no question

Objectives

After completing this chapter, the reader will be able to:

1. Understand and explain expository teaching.
2. Identify when to use the expository approach.
3. Examine the connections between effective teaching research and the expository approach.

4. Develop expository teaching lessons.
5. Incorporate appropriate adaptations into an expository lesson plan.
6. Develop appropriate questioning strategies.
7. Formulate appropriate student assessment strategies.
8. Incorporate personal reflection into expository teaching.

PROFILES OF EXPOSITORY TEACHING

Ethel's Expository Excellence

During her college program, Ethel Watson became acutely aware of the importance of providing concrete, active learning experiences for students. She also found, however, that she could use other, more teacher-led teaching strategies in certain situations and still teach successfully. In her field experiences, Ethel saw plenty of teachers relying heavily on textbooks and workbooks, especially in the upper elementary grades. Many of these teachers were not really teaching at all. Instead, they were just having students take turns reading the material aloud and then assigning them the questions at the end of each section for seatwork or homework. But other teachers were actually using the text very skillfully, and students were motivated and confident respondents to highly organized teacher presentations. Ethel knew then that, with adequate planning, she could use the expository approach effectively.

Now, as a third year teacher, Ethel was seeing the results of her efforts. She determined early on that she was going to use the expository method only under certain conditions. Contrary to what she had observed in some classrooms, her expository lessons would be very carefully crafted, with each step detailed to illuminate the advantages of direct instruction. The objectives of her expository lessons would be at the knowledge or comprehension levels of the cognitive domain, primarily concerned with the learning of basic facts like geographic features or safety tips. Some of the advanced students who already knew certain facts would be spared these lessons, but other students who showed a need for precise, step-by-step presentations would benefit from such an approach.

In planning her expository lessons, Ethel always began with a performance objective that she could write on the board and have students read or write in their notebooks. Students had to know where they were headed and when they arrived. After the objective had been recorded and understood by students, the procedure would unfold, step by step, beginning with a clear review of prior learning. This review sometimes included an assessment of what each student already knew because Ethel found that there was quite a range of prior knowledge and that some students could actually facilitate learning for other students more easily than she could. Once Ethel had determined where to begin with the majority of the students, she always used visual aids to present the new information, using vocabulary they were able to understand.

Definitions, when presented, were written down by students. She kept in mind the adaptations for individual students and monitored their effect on learning outcomes. Ethel met with other professionals (special educators, speech therapists, counselors) on at least a weekly basis to discuss individual students and build more effective learning opportunities for them. Examples, both positive and negative, were introduced early in the lesson. Students were constantly questioned, and all were expected to respond in some manner. Ethel had developed an impressive array of techniques for checking for individual understanding. She always elicited responses from every student during each lesson and provided every student with supportive feedback after her/his response. Each lesson included ample time for guided practice (closely monitored), and independent practice often emerged in the form of a homework assignment. Students were quizzed, frequently without warning. They learned of the benefits of preparing for class. Ethel constructed each quiz, based on the information she had recently presented. She had mastered the ability to reinforce student responses without changing the momentum of the lesson.

Students, parents, and others often remarked about Ethel's engaging personal style both in and out of the classroom. She certainly loved to teach.

Douglas Ontivares

"Where are my notes?" hollered Mr. Ontivares. The sixth grade veteran of twenty-six years could not find the notes he used for his Battle of Gettysburg lecture. If he had a dollar for every time he had to rewrite lost notes! Well, he could always just go ahead and give them the Industrialization lecture. He had just spotted that one on top of a stack of papers in his classroom.

"Okay, class, settle down. During the late nineteenth century, the invention of a number of machines contributed to the period known as Industrialization." Douglas usually got started right away. Any students who had been absent or who were not ready would have to get the information from someone else after school. He could not slow down or review the previous day's material because he had to finish the unit by the end of the week. Every time he thought of an example of something in the lecture, it made him think of a story from his past, which he then shared with the students. They just looked at him. Other times students would actually start telling remotely related stories to each other, and the class time just flew by.

It would have been a lot easier if they had not adopted new textbooks last year. He hated having to read a whole new text and decided to keep using his own notes. After all, they had worked fine for the past seven years. Students often asked how the lectures he gave fit in with their reading assignments, but he knew they were just looking for excuses.

After a lot of persuasion from his building principal, Douglas agreed to go to a workshop on cooperative learning. Just another fad, he decided. To appease the principal, Douglas even had his students do the questions at the end of the chapter in groups one week. Some of the questions required some complex thinking, which they had said was a valuable feature of cooperative learning. But even after assigning the reading and working in groups, many students did not have much success with the tougher, higher-level questions. Instead of getting "+" on their answers, many got "−", and Douglas just decided to stop the cooperative business. The two test grades would have to be good enough for the nine-week marking period. Besides, with the multiple choice tests he used from the instructor's manual, all he had to do was to just mark the answers that were wrong and use the tables to figure out the percentage grade for each student.

Douglas never quite understood why his students did so poorly on the tests. The questions were right out of the book, and he himself had read them to students just the other day. Before that, he told them everything that was on the tests. Some wrote this information down, but only a few. Douglas decided that the best solution for this problem was to begin reading the textbook aloud to the class. That way he knew they were hearing the material. But again, many failed the tests, even though he actually read the text to them, told them what would be on the tests, and then took the questions right out of the text. Students occasionally asked him for examples, but they could look those up in the book later if they were lost. Just to be sure students were paying attention, he would, on a regular basis, jolt a student out of his dream with "Jim, what did I just say?" Any students who learned anything were making connections on their own.

Douglas Ontivares saw no good reason to change a system that was simple and convenient. His system was: lecture, ask a few factual questions or repeat what he said just to keep them on their toes, and assign end-of-chapter questions. Any students with learning disabilities or anything else would either have to get help from a friend after school or rely on the resource teacher because he was not going to make exceptions for every student who had any kind of problem.

EXPOSITORY TEACHING

Both Ethel and Douglas might be surprised to learn that the expository approach they used was alive and well over two thousand years ago, evident in the writings of such Greek philosophers as Socrates, Plato, and Aristotle. Two reasons for the continued popularity of this teaching technique, in spite of criticism during the twentieth century, are its familiarity and efficiency. In fact, effective teaching research has continually identified **expository teaching** as a valuable approach at both the elementary and secondary levels (Freiberg & Driscoll, 1992; Lloyd, 1988; Englert, 1984)). Jacobsen, Eggen, & Kauchak (1993) also indicate that expository teaching is a popular strategy because of its time efficiency and control features. Teachers can often cover more material when they use convergent questions within an expository approach, and inexperienced teachers find that they feel more secure delivering the content directly. On the other hand, lectures can become dull, and students will stop paying close attention when they are uninterested. Ultimately, clear, well-organized, enthusiastic, and audience-appropriate presentations can be dynamic learning experiences for a wide range of students.

Expository teaching has been labeled in many different ways in professional literature: as *direct instruction, demonstration teaching, competency-based instruction, presentation, explicit instruction, deductive* or *didactic teaching,* and *teacher-directed instruction.* Regardless of the name given, expository teaching is a multifaceted presentation that involves not only large amounts of verbal lecture but also teacher-student interactions involving questions and answers, review and practice, and the correction of student errors. (Borich, 1988, p. 143)

Expository teaching, a teacher-centered approach, is characterized by four major features: clearly articulated instructional goals, teacher-led instruction, accurate record keeping of student learning, and ongoing evidence of effective organizational and management skills (Jones & Jones, 1990).

How Expository Teaching Is Used

The focus of the expository approach is on the teacher, and the success of the approach depends on the educator's ability to communicate information to students. The form that expository teaching usually takes is some version of a lecture with questions and responses, with an emphasis on acquiring knowledge or understanding new concepts or generalizations. The classroom environment is characterized by full class instruction (not small groups), little if any interaction among students, a fairly high level of structure, and teacher-student interaction via questions and answers.

Lessons are organized around key questions, concepts, or generalizations, with ample opportunity for practice. New learning is presented in a carefully designed sequence, and some level of mastery is ideally attained before students move on to new material.

Rosenshine (1983) identified several functions of one type of expository teaching, direct instruction, that can contribute to improved student achievement (Anderson, Evertson, & Brophy, 1982). He determined that direct instruction could be effectively used to review previous learning, organize and present new material, and provide adequate time for both monitored or guided student practice (which includes constructive feedback and reteaching) and additional independent practice.

Reflect for a Moment

You probably have no difficulty recalling teachers who taught in a somewhat expository manner, but can you recall a teacher who actually applied the specific techniques mentioned here, and made expository teaching work effectively?

When Expository Teaching Can Be Used

Perhaps the most appropriate time to use the expository approach is when the educator wishes to provide learners with information not sufficiently presented in class texts or other developmentally appropriate printed materials (Borich, 1992). The task of organizing the information into manageable pieces is the educator's, as it should be under any circumstances.

Another suitable use of the expository approach occurs whenever the educator feels the need to add vitality and personalized interpretations of what might be otherwise seen as a dry, uninteresting text reading experience. Talented educators will provide both a humane version of, and a practical rationale for, text materials that students view as irrelevant or useless.

Rosenshine's (1983) functions of direct instruction mentioned above are central to structuring expository lessons for **mastery learning** by students. Whenever the educator wishes to determine students' level of mastery, these functions can offer specific procedures for assessment. Because expository teaching is best used in teaching facts, rules, and sequential information, observable student behaviors for assessment in the cognitive domain might include describing, recalling, listing, demonstrating, using, and summarizing. In the psychomotor domain, expository teaching can provide opportunities for students to repeat, follow, or perform, and in the affective domain students can be assessed on their ability to attend, obey, display, or comply.

Borich (1992) suggests inappropriate uses of expository teaching (which Douglas Ontivares often employed!). The first is teaching at more complex levels of thinking. Peterson and Janicki (1979) found that students who had been given direct rather than more open instruction did not perform well on tasks requiring creativity and problem-solving behavior. The second is teaching large amounts of new material over a long period of time. In this case students must be exposed to more than one approach to learning, especially whenever there is a large amount of information to be learned. The third inappropriate use of expository teaching is an outcome of learner type. It is generally not an approach to use in working with intellectually advanced students who are familiar with the information being presented. Lemlech (1994) concluded from research that higher-ability students may sometimes have more difficulty with direct instruction because of their strong task orientation and inclination toward higher, more complex levels of thinking. Wright and DuCette (1976) furthermore found that students with a more developed internal locus of control, who believe that they control their successes and failures, are actually often frustrated by the heavily teacher-directed expository approach.

Reflect for a Moment

Can you recall a teacher you had who was a highly organized, well-controlled, enthusiastic role model of expository teaching? What specifically did this teacher model? To what extent have you acquired these behaviors?

EFFECTIVE TEACHING

The expository approach is a strategy that lends itself well to the teaching of facts, rules, sequential information, and procedures. Research (Stevens & Rosenshine, 1981; Stallings & Kaskowitz, 1974; Soar, 1973) related to the expository model delineated four basic characteristics of effective skills instruction. Expository teaching, according to Stevens and Rosenshine (1981),

1. Is group instruction
2. Is educator directed
3. Has a clearly focused outcome
4. Is oriented to individual learners in the group (individualization). (p. 3)

In these learning events the educator is the major provider of information. Expository teaching allows the educator to closely monitor the progress of the group, encouraging active engagement and higher levels of learning. Taking on the role of conveyor of information (facts, rules, and procedures), educators pass their knowledge on to the students. This passing on of knowledge is done in the most direct manner possible, usually a lecture format that Rosenshine (1976) terms the demonstration–guided practice–feedback paradigm. Given this paradigm, the expository method needs to be recognized as a multifaceted presentation technique, one that involves not simply large amounts of lecture but educator-student interactions through the use of questions (teacher's) and answers (students'), practice and the correction of learners' errors. As can be seen, the **individualization** of the expository lesson relies on the educator's belief that each student can learn and his or her ability to assist individual learners through direction, checks for understanding, and feedback.

Rosenshine and Stevens (1986) equate the expository method with an effective demonstration. During this "verbal demonstration," an educator must (1) clearly explain goals, objectives, and primary points; (2) sequentially present content; (3) be specific and concrete; and (4) systematically check for learner understanding.

Effective expository instruction is a direct result of the educator's knowledge of content, understanding of the instructional process, and ability to present materials. Bellon, Bellon, and Blank (1992) point out that different types of content will require variation in instructional processes as well as presentation skills. The teaching of facts, details, and dates requires the educator to present in a clear manner and provide learners with examples that are meaningful to their lives. On the other hand, when content knowledge consists largely of structure and organization (e.g., the composition of the Confederate army in a study of the Civil War), an educator needs to reflect enthusiasm and incorporate multiple examples, analogies, or stories into his or her presentation. Key concepts are best taught using a clear sequential approach and call for the educator to enunciate, pronounce, and present herself or himself clearly.

Additional features related to the effectiveness of the expository method are the weekly and monthly reviews. Borich (1992) points out that these periodic reviews serve to ensure that all material or information related to successful learning in future lessons has been taught. Additionally, periodic reviews help educators identify the facts, rules, and sequences that may need to be retaught. Without periodic review, educators have no idea of whether facts, rules, or sequences taught through the expository approach have been retained. Periodic review is not unique to the expository approach, but it does have increased significance because of the brisk pace at which teaching occurs using this method. Posner (1987) notes the necessity of planned, regular, weekly reviews that gradually increase in breadth and depth of content, culminating in a comprehensive monthly session. This gradual increase of material explored prevents students from being overwhelmed by the cumulative effect of a single review session per month.

PLANNING PROCEDURES

As with any lesson, planning is imperative. Ethel and Douglas present two contrasting styles of planning (although Douglas may not actually have a style of planning). Rosenshine (1987) formulated ten general principles to be considered when planning an expository lesson (see Table 9.1):

- Begin a lesson with a short statement of goals.
- Begin a lesson with a short review of previous, prerequisite learning.
- Present new material in small steps, with student practice after each step.
- Give clear and detailed instructions and explanations.
- Provide a high level of practice for all students.
- Ask many questions, check for student understanding, and obtain responses from all students.
- Guide students during initial practice.
- Provide systematic feedback and corrections.

- Provide explicit instruction and practice for seatwork exercises and, when necessary, monitor students during seatwork.
- Continue practice until students are independent and confident. (p. 76)

TABLE 9.1   Expository Cloud Lesson Plan

Topic: Clouds

Title: Clouds as weather predictors

Goal Statement: Students will understand the connection between various cloud formations and weather fronts.

Statement of objective (overview): When shown slides of weather conditions, the students will identify the cloud formation involved in 8 out of 10 scenarios.

Materials: Photos or slides of Cirrus, Cumulus, Stratus, Nimbus clouds and their combinations; slides of various weather conditions; slide projector; response cards; filmstrip projector

Anticipatory Set: Teacher led review of the types of clouds, teacher describes what each looks like and asks students to name clouds.

> *Teacher states:* "Now that you know the names and features of different clouds, you will learn to identify the types of cloud formations associated with particular weather conditions. This is important because it will enable you to make plans that are not in conflict with weather conditions" (comparative advance organizer).

Teacher Input:
Teacher shows a picture of a particular weather condition and describes the cloud formation.

Show slides of each of the types of cloud formations. Teacher asks students a series of questions related to the characteristics of the clouds that distinguish the formations.

If students fail to recognize the cloud from the slides, the teacher should return to the pictures of clouds used in review. Hold up both a positive and negative example, have students identify each and match positive example to slide.

This process is continued until all cloud formations have been identified in the weather conditions presented.

Check for Understanding: The teacher checks for understanding of cloud characteristics throughout the lesson with questions regarding size, length, color, amount of sky showing, etc. Group response can be given with use of slates or response cards.

Guided Practice: Show pictures of cloud formations. Have students write name of formation on slate or response card. On a checklist teacher records student performance. Erase. Now have student write typical weather associated with that type of cloud.

Review/closure/bridge: Have students restate names of and types of weather they are associated with. Do a curricular semantic web of other cloud associations (See Chapter 8, page 255—"Diagram of content areas").

Independent Practice: After selecting a picture or story about a weather condition from a magazine or newspaper, students will write a paragraph describing type of clouds that would have been present.

Evaluation: Was objective met? Was student response method appropriate? Was wait time effective and appropriate? How could lesson be expanded? If I were to reteach what would I keep, what would I change?

The planning process can be broken down into a series of steps that, when followed, will ultimately result in the implementation of an effective expository lesson. To begin the planning process, an educator must first deal with the philosophical factors or questions (such as educators' function, meeting of learners' needs, and school role) that are associated with the expository method. Once these factors are dealt with the educator needs to develop the overview, input, and conclusion for each learning event.

Overview

As stated in previous chapters, topics for instruction are often dictated by the state curriculum guides, textbooks, and/or competency exams. Once the topic has been selected, the **overview** of the expository learning experience can be developed. This involves determining specific content to be learned, identifying the rationale for learning the content selected, establishing criteria for student success, and planning advance organizers. In developing this overview, the educator must formulate a goal and specify an objective. Structuring the goals and objectives will help the educator to formulate a clear and concise rationale for the learning experience, and confidently identify successful student behaviors.

The expository lesson begins with the use of advance organizers (see Chapter 8). **Advance organizers** facilitate the explanation of goals, objectives, and primary points of the learning event. Ausubel (1968) proposed the use of one of two advance organizers: expository or comparative. The **expository organizer** is most appropriate when the information is new to the learners because it provides an overview of the subject or content to be learned (e.g., "Clouds are formations created by water vapor. There are four major types, each having specific characteristics. Today you are going to learn about two such formations."). In contrast, the **comparative organizer** is most useful when the material is familiar to the learners because it provides them with a link between existing knowledge and what they will be learning. It is important during this introductory phase that the educator use the advance organizer to help clarify the goal(s) and objective(s) of the lesson (see Table 9.1 for an example). Each important feature should be focused on, one at a time, to help avoid digressions and ambiguity.

Reflect for a Moment

Can you find an example of an expository organizer in this chapter? How about a comparative organizer? They are both there!

Input

Content needs to be developed in such a way as to guarantee that information will be presented in a fast-paced, well-sequenced, and highly focused manner. Content needs to be presented in a sequential manner, allowing learners to master one point before moving on to the next. This process of teacher **input** necessitates that the educator present materials in small steps, give explicit directions (step by step), and, if the information is complex, present learners with an outline. Additionally, the expository presentation requires the material to be taught in a specific and concrete manner. When appropriate, the educator needs to model the skill or process, providing learners with a variety of real examples. Explanations that are detailed and redundant are important when the point to be made is difficult. Therefore, repetition of key elements must be built into the content (teacher input) portion of the expository lesson. The ability to develop and implement creative redundancy is extremely important for the success of an expository lesson.

Imperative to the success are the **checks for understanding** that must occur throughout the expository lesson. Checks for understanding should be made before the educator moves on to a new point or skill within the lesson and can be accomplished in a variety of ways. Learners may be asked to answer a series of questions designed to demonstrate their understanding of the material that has been presented or to summarize, in their own words, the main points. Additionally, checks can take the form of **peer tutoring**, allowing the learners who understood the information to present difficult portions to a fellow student who did not. However, educators must remember that when necessary reteaching (sometimes from peers) may also need to occur when further explanation is required.

Perhaps the most critical element for a successful expository lesson is the planning of salient **positive** and **negative examples**. Jacobsen, Eggen, and Kauchak (1993) point out that although the selection of examples appears simple conceptually, in practice it is difficult to accomplish. Listing the characteristics necessary for teaching a concept or the relationship needed for a principle is relatively easy, they feel. Difficulty arises, however, in actually finding or developing examples. Additionally, the more abstract the content, the more difficult it becomes to find or develop clear examples. Often what results are several poor or fuzzy definitions rather than clear examples.

Tennyson and Cocchiarella (1986) point out the necessity for both positive and negative examples when the content being taught can be easily confused with other closely related content. Positive examples help learners to clearly visualize the content, whereas negative examples demonstrate what the content is not. An educator who wants learners to understand the concept of mammals, for example, would include insects as a negative example.

In selecting positive examples, the educator should develop essential characteristics into a checklist and compare them to the example. By making such comparisons, the educator assures that the example adequately conveys the content. Additionally, each area should be examined in terms of coordinate and subordinate factors. Coordinates fall into groups within a larger concept. For example, *table* and *chair* are coordinates because they are types of furniture, and *robin* and *sparrow* are coordinates because they are types of birds. Subordinates are subsets of a concept: Using the sample concepts, *table* is a subordinate of *furniture*, and *robin* is a subordinate of *bird*. Positive examples can be generated from subordinate concepts, negative examples from coordinate concepts. Using these techniques tends to produce more salient examples, ones that have clear relevance to the concept.

The development of examples to enhance generalizations is a complex process. The educator must convey clearly how the concepts interact in the generalization. The use of division and multiplication often becomes clouded when dollars and cents are attached. Therefore, examples should include both whole numbers and decimals.

Examples can also be used as a method of reinforcing content or checking for understanding. Learners can be provided with examples that they must then classify and explain, or learners could also be asked to supply additional examples of their own. Either one of these strategies will provide the educator with insight into learners' levels of understanding.

Thus far, input in the expository approach has been teacher centered. There are other means of providing or developing information that require less overt educator involvement. Programmed instruction, peer or cross-age tutoring, technology-assisted instruction (computers, audiolingual devices, or CD-ROMs), and single-concept videos are just a few of the methods for input delivery in an expository lesson.

Conclusion

The final component in lesson planning is the organization of the learning events' **conclusion** (for an example, see Table 9.1). Educators need to carefully plan how key points will be summarized, what type of postorganizers will be used, and how postlesson assessment will be conducted.

Review at the end of the lesson can be used as a method of summarizing or abstracting key points from the information delivered. When educators point out the most salient information as a postorganizer, students are able to organize their thoughts and learning is improved (Sparks & Sparks, 1984). Additionally, summary and review provides the learner with a sense of finality to the content or procedure being taught and signals transition.

Postinstructional assessment is embedded in the lesson closure. This assessment may take different forms, such as responding to oral questions, taking a quiz, or completing independent practice. "Independent practice provides the opportunity, in a carefully controlled and organized environment, to make a meaningful whole out of the bits and pieces" (Borich, 1992, p. 199). The educator should be able to determine through independent practice whether individual learners have been able to complete unitization and automaticity of the material presented. Unitization occurs when the learner is able to successfully consider all the units of a problem simultaneously. Once this has occurred, the learner is able to connect these units into a harmonious sequence of action, thus demonstrating automaticity. To maximize recall and understanding, independent practice should follow the instructional portion of the lesson as soon as possible (Borich, 1992).

Although the expository method is frequently used to teach facts, rules, or procedures, it may also be appropriate when working with concepts or principles. According to Jacobsen, Eggen, and Kauchak (1993), the expository event will differ slightly depending on whether the lesson involves teaching a concept or principles. Both begin with advance organizers, the first expository, the later comparative. Positive and negative examples are also presented during both types of expository lessons. Additionally, both engage the learners in a similar fashion by having them clarify teacher examples as either positive or negative and provide additional positive examples. The main difference occurs within the material context; during the teaching of a concept educators define the concept and clarify terms, then provide links to superordinate concepts. In teaching principles, however, educators state the principle and clarify concepts within the principle.

Reflect for a Moment

If you were teaching the concept erosion, what would be a good positive example for students where you live? What would be a good negative example?

AN EXAMPLE OF EXPOSITORY TEACHING

Consider the following example of a direct instruction lesson in which the college educator is teaching the characteristics of Dreikurs' model of discipline. This example is offered because of its obvious relevance to readers of this text. The educator begins with an example of attention-getting misbehavior and then informs learners of the lesson's objective:

EDUCATOR: As you know, we have been examining models of discipline. Today you will learn about Dreikurs' model for discipline (write "Dreikurs" on the board). At the end of class, you will complete an informational form on Dreikurs' model. Dreikurs believes, as does Glasser, that children have a strong desire to do what, Lora?

LORA: To belong.

EDUCATOR: Yes, Dreikurs feels that all behavior results from children's desire to belong. Misbehavior is then a result of misguided or mistaken goals that children adopt, believing they will help them belong. There are four mistaken goals that children follow: attention getting, power seeking, revenge, and displaying inadequacies (writes heading "mistaken goals" on board, then lists the four goals). Dreikurs describes the child who has the mistaken goal of attention getting as one who tries through misbehavior to gain the educator's and classmates' attention. Can you describe an attention-getting behavior, Seth?

SETH: Would that be like Redl and Wattenberg's class clown?

EDUCATOR: Good comparison. How do you as an educator think that an attention-seeking child might make you feel, Jennifer?

JENNIFER: Angry, I guess.

EDUCATOR: Angry perhaps, and most definitely annoyed. Can anyone give me an example of a behavior that would be power seeking—Carolyn?

CAROLYN: Would that be someone like Redl and Wattenberg's instigator?

EDUCATOR: Exactly! The instigator, as described by Redl and Wattenberg, may be seeking power but is covert in that action. The child involved in power seeking, on the other hand, is outwardly confrontational. This child will make you feel threatened by becoming involved in a power struggle with you. How do you think a child who is unsuccessful at power struggles and moves on to revenge would make you feel, Tina?

TINA: I would have thought you might feel threatened, but I guess a child seeking revenge would be trying to make me feel bad.

EDUCATOR: Yes. The child who is involved with revenge shows this by attempting to hurt you. I do not mean that they are going to necessarily physically harm you. More often than not it is an emotional attack, such as saying "I hate you!"

The lesson would progress in this manner until the educator has delivered all the relevant information. As can be seen, the educator is the primary speaker. Learners are asked simple questions but not asked to truly explore the material.

Practice

Using the example,

1. Develop a lesson plan, including an objective, procedures, and evaluation, defining the subject matter and the grade level.

2. Describe the type of advanced organizer used.

ADAPTATIONS

The classroom teacher in an inclusive setting is a member of a collaborative team of professional educators responsible for planning instruction. Ethel Watson knew the benefits of actively participating in the collaborative team process. She realized that to ensure that all learners have access to curricular material, it is always necessary to plan **adaptations**—alternate objectives, materials, and methods—for any given lesson. Adaptations are almost always beneficial for students who have *not* been identified as having any type of disability. For example, providing a study guide is beneficial to many students, not just those with auditory perception difficulties. Teaching students to use self-instructional strategies (see Chapter 7) as they attempt to understand a new concept is going to enhance learning for many students, not just those with cognitive processing problems.

Many types of instructional adaptations can be considered in conjunction with the expository approach. Most of these are specific to using textbooks and other printed materials, presenting information, giving assignments, and conducting assessments.

Textbooks and Other Printed Materials

Textbooks are often not well matched to the reading level of the students who use them. Selecting readable texts that also include aids such as introductory and summary paragraphs, margin notes, supportive pictures, charts and tables, and bold-faced content vocabulary will increase student text comprehension. High-interest, low-vocabulary printed materials are available for all grade levels from a variety of publishers, but they may serve to stigmatize students with disabilities or just not provide enough breadth or depth of content. An alternative to these materials is tape recordings of the regular text. Although this can be a time-consuming task, it is yet another opportunity for members of the larger school community to contribute to improving the services schools aim to deliver. Adults who help develop recordings should include questions periodically to keep listening students engaged. Another technique of adapting the textbook relates to the procedure the educator uses in beginning a new unit or chapter. Giving students time to look through the chapter and examine pictures, charts, graphs, headings and subheadings can help generate a better focus or mindset and promote higher interest in the

chapter topic, especially when the educator elicits interpretations from learners. Study guides and graphic organizers (see below) can also contribute to better student learning via the textbook.

Instructional Procedures

Although the expository approach is more commonly aligned with secondary schools than elementary schools, many lessons at the elementary level follow an expository procedure more than any other major teaching strategy. Any time the educator presents new information, whether through lecture, demonstration, or carefully sequenced presentation replete with examples, the expository approach is being implemented. During the preparation of these lessons, the educator should remember to plan for a wide range of learning rates and styles, selecting from among several instructional adaptations.

The first place an adaptation may occur is within the advance organizer, the preinstructional strategy that lends structure and clarity to the lesson about to begin. The educator will have to decide whether to use an expository or comparative organizer (see earlier section of this chapter), but there are many possibilities, including outlining on a handout or the chalkboard, having students copy down the lesson objective from the board, preteaching new content vocabulary, changing voice tone, and pausing to ask and answer questions. Other organizational aids might be verbal cues like "This is important," "Write this down," or terms such as "first," "next," and "finally" during the presentation. Regardless of the type selected, educators need to teach students to recognize and utilize these advance organizers before their benefits can be realized.

Reflect for a Moment

When using an advance organizer, what other changes could you make to meet the needs of diverse students?

Another type of organizational aid is the *graphic organizer*, sometimes found in the form of a semantic map or web (Meese, 1994). The advantage of these aids over other advance organizers is that they provide a clear visual display of the new concept and how it relates to other, more familiar information. As a result, the graphic organizer provides learners with more access to understanding the relationships among familiar and unfamiliar concepts and content vocabulary than just printed information. Examples of graphic organizers would be a chart depicting stages of plant growth for a primary grades class or a web of contributors to the U.S. national debt for an older social studies class. Like most adaptations for expository teaching, the graphic organizer relies on a text reading experience. Also consistent with good expository teaching is the frequent use of positive and negative examples to help learners understand the chart or web.

A totally different type of adaptation from any type of organizer is the use of **mnemonics** to facilitate the storage and retrieval of information. As with any other adaptation, mnemonic aids must be actively taught to learners, although in some cases these aids are utilized by some students without prompting or direct instruction. *First letter acronyms*, such as Huron, Ontario, Michigan, Erie, and Superior, are one fairly successful and popular mnemonic device. The *keyword method* invites learners to construct an unusual drawing or mental picture linking new information to known material. Many find that this approach helps them associate and be able to recall the new information. The concept of emancipation might be better understood if a learner created an image of a black family breaking free of the bonds around their wrists and ankles and use the *man* in the family as a keyword. A third well-known mnemonic device is the *pegword* method, in which students learn a number-object rhyming poem (*one-sun, two-shoe, three-blind mice, four-seasons . . . 12-dozen eggs*). Then they create a picture of the new information, using its major features along with the pegword object for the number related to the new information. If the lesson focuses on knowing the (one) President has power over the (two) houses in the legislative branch of the United States government, learners can draw a sun and a pair of shoes. Each drawing can be labeled and a poem developed to enhance the connection. All of the mnemonic aids described here need to be explicitly taught, but only when a student clearly needs assistance with recall of information.

One final approach to adapting instruction in expository lessons is the use of technology (Meese, 1994). The recent explosion in educational technology has opened up a huge new arena of possibilities in presenting information to students. Laser videodiscs, computer telecommunications, and traditional in-class experiments and demonstrations all offer elaborate multisensory immersions in new information. As such, they can be the key for students who have limited auditory processing ability.

Assignments and Assessments

Independent assignments or homework should only be given as practice for a *learned* skill, not as a means of teaching a new skill. Independent assignments or homework that present unlearned information create two major problems for students. First, students end up practicing errors, and this type of learned misinformation is difficult to unlearn. Second, faced with an assignment that they cannot do, students become frustrated with learning and have possible motivation problems. Additionally, it is important for the educator to correct and return the assignment within a day; feedback is useless if it is given after moving on to a new topic.

In giving assignments, a consistent routine in which students copy down assignments in a specific way from the same chalkboard every day, is helpful. Alternate forms of student work (tapes, photographs, drawings) are sometimes arranged. Adding to or subtracting from the number of items to be completed also demonstrates flexibility in giving assignments. Flexibility with the time allowed, use of cooperative groups, checking for understanding of procedures for an assignment, and even breaking long assignments down into several smaller tasks can all help educators adapt assignments for different learner needs.

Reflect for a Moment

Remember when you worked for hours on an assignment, turned it in and never saw it again. How did that make you feel?

Several general strategies can alleviate the wide variety of problems affiliated with tests. Frequent, weekly assessments can check for student retention of smaller, more manageable amounts of new information much better than monthly exams. Multiple choice questions can have three choices instead of four or more. The time permitted can be more relaxed. Well-planned review classes can be highly effective in helping learners prepare for any more formal assessment. Students can tape-record their responses instead of writing them down. Likewise, tests can be tape-recorded so that students can respond to items regardless of their reading ability. A number of **authentic assessment** techniques are discussed in Chapters 10 through 12, and a few that also serve as evaluative adaptations can be implemented during and after expository lessons. Using actual student work samples, original writings and drawings, and daily evidence of student learning can always provide a more accurate description of student progress than weekly tests, and each of these techniques can be integrated into expository instruction. There are also many ways that educators can adapt their tests for individual students.

Assignments should always provide either effective practice with recent learning material or carefully organized and monitored long-term, out-of-school learning experiences. In either situation, the adaptations an educator makes can improve students' self-esteem, interest in learning, social skills, and academic performance.

Practice

Using the example lesson provided earlier, develop adaptations that might be made for a student experiencing auditory processing problems.

QUESTIONING STRATEGIES

A variety of studies have been undertaken to determine the relationship between types and levels of educators' questions and learner achievement. Although a commonly held belief is that **divergent** (thought) **questions** are better than **convergent** (fact) questions, most researchers have concluded that type or level of questions does not consistently correlate with gains in learning (Dunkin & Biddle, 1974; Rosenshine & Furst, 1973; Winne, 1979). In fact, studies by Dillon (1981), Soar (1973), and Stallings (1975) found that factual convergent questions are preferable to more complex divergent questions in working with economically disadvantaged learners in the early elementary grades (more detailed explanation of divergent and convergent questions to follow).

The relationship of learning gains to frequency of questioning has also been studied and seems to yield much more consistent findings (Brophy & Evertson,

1976; Soar, 1973; Stallings, 1975). High rates of good questions correlate with achievement gains. This may be, however, more the result of the nature of the educator than the questions themselves. Findings have demonstrated that educators who use a high rate of academic questions usually had well-organized and managed classrooms, permitting them to spend most of their energies and time in the active pursuit of teaching. Additionally, educators who questioned frequently tended to supplement the learning event with a variety of examples and experience when students had difficulty responding.

Questions are used by the educator for a variety of reasons. Among these are:

1. Checking for learner understanding
2. Evaluating lesson effectiveness
3. Increasing cognitive level
4. Encouraging learner involvement

Additionally, educators may employ questions to control learner behavior, manage lesson pace and direction, and bridge activities. The utility of different types or forms of questions is more appropriately determined when examined on the basis of the instructional goal. Appropriateness of questions depends more on the learning event and student characteristics. A good question, developed to encourage learner involvement, may not be a valuable question for evaluating the lesson effectiveness.

Good Questions

The complete definition of a **good question**, therefore depends on the context. However, certain basic guidelines can be applied to most questions. Five factors should be considered in developing good questions (Groisser, 1964): (1) clarity, (2) purposefulness, (3) brevity, (4) naturalness and adaptability to individual learners, and (5) provocativeness.

Good questions are not vague. They possess *clarity*—that is, they describe precisely the nature in which learners are to respond. Clarity is necessary to avoid ambiguity, which may confuse students and interrupt the learning process. Questions with clarity typically direct the type of response (Should known felons be allowed to buy handguns?) rather than leaving responses (What about handguns?) totally open ended. Loss of clarity can also occur when questions are asked as part of an uninterrupted series. What about handguns? Should certain persons not be allowed to buy handguns? Should known felons be allowed to buy handguns? Each of these successive questions was an attempt to clarify the first, causing the learner more confusion and wasting valuable educational time. "Questions should clearly cue students to respond along specific lines" (Good & Brophy, 1984, p. 348).

Reflect for a Moment

You can surely recall an instructor or teacher asking a question or questions you simply did not understand. Was it because you were not listening? Because you were not prepared for class? Or because the question itself was unclear? If it was happening in high school and college, imagine how often it can happen in elementary school!

Good questions are those that demonstrate *purposefulness*. Questions that are not planned in advance often fail to match the intent of the lesson. Good and Brophy (1984) point out that educators "who ask most of their questions 'off the cuff' will ask many irrelevant and confusing questions that work against achievement of their own goals" (p. 348). *Brevity* is another crucial aspect of a good question. The longer a question becomes, the more unclear and difficult to understand it also becomes.

The phrasing of a question should be in simple language. Questions should convey a *naturalness* of language that does not require learners to spend more time processing the question than they do the answer. Simple language does not mean that an educator cannot use big words, but rather that the language to be used should match learners' vocabulary level. Questions should not be used to introduce new vocabulary unless the educator is trying to have the class brainstorm possible meanings. Besides having naturalness of language, the question also needs to be *adaptable* to the cognitive level of the learner being asked to respond. When learners do not understand the question, they will be unable to provide the educator with the information needed.

Good questions are *provocative*. This feature is extremely important when the questions are designed to enhance discussion. Provocative questions should entice learners to integrate and apply the facts they possess in new ways. Questions that are provocative also enable learners to engage in higher-level cognitive skills such as analysis and synthesis.

Effective Questioning

There are procedures or techniques that educators should employ to assure maximum learner participation in the questioning process. Educators must examine how they question to prevent the learning process from being overtaken by a few students.

The most obvious technique is to address questions to the entire class. This is easily accomplished by stating the question, pausing for a few moments to allow learners to formulate a response, and then calling on a nonvolunteer. This method of questioning creates a need for all learners to develop an answer in their own minds. Additionally, by calling on nonvolunteers, it eliminates the monopolization of responses that occur when a small number of students are the only ones to consistently raise hands.

Groisser (1964) does point out that there are situations, however, when it is necessary to call on a learner before asking a question: (1) When the question asked is a followup to one previously asked and the educator may need to direct it at a specific learner; (2) when the question being asked is done to draw an inattentive student back into the learning event; and (3) when the learner the question is targeted for is extremely shy and may be flustered by an unannounced inquiry.

Another essential feature in effective questioning is wait time. Research shows that providing learners with a 3- to 5-second lag between the question and the call for a response increases average length of response, frequency of appropriate unsolicited response, incidence of speculative responses, student-to-student comparisons, drawing of inferences from evidence, frequency of student-initiated questions, and variety of student verbal contribution. Additionally, this provision of wait time resulted in a decrease in nonresponsive behavior (Rowe, 1974a).

Interestingly, Rowe (1974b) found that educators, after calling on learners, also failed to wait long enough for them to respond. Additionally, educators tended to wait longer for responses from students they perceived as more capable. This tendency thus created a situation in which students viewed as less capable were given a shorter amount of time to respond.

Educators are encouraged to reflect not only on the types of questions they ask but also the strategies they employ. There are three questioning strategies that not only support but enhance the learning event: (1) redirection, (2) probing, and (3) prompting.

Redirection is a strategy that helps the educator establish positive questioning patterns and high levels of learner interaction in the classroom. This technique involves developing a question in such a way as to have many plausible responses, assuring that a wide variety of learners are called on to respond. Redirection is designed to eliminate the phenomenon of directing questions only at those learners perceived to be high achievers. The following are examples of how an educator might accomplish this task for both a convergent and divergent question.

Convergent

EDUCATOR: What were the major causes of the Civil War? [pause] Harold?

HAROLD: Controversy over slavery.

EDUCATOR: Juanita?

JUANITA: The issue of states' rights.

EDUCATOR: Geoffrey?

GEOFFREY: The struggle between agricultural and industrial societies.

Divergent

EDUCATOR: Having completed our study of the Civil War, who do you think were some of the most critical players? [pause] Mary?

MARY: Abraham Lincoln.

EDUCATOR: Oscar?

OSCAR: U. S. Grant.

EDUCATOR: Mike, who would you choose?

MIKE: John Brown.

The educator does not respond to the replies. She or he simply redirects the original question to another student. This method eliminates the possibility of a few learners dominating the discussion and serves to increase question frequency.

EDUCATOR: Some of you have told us who you believed were key players in the Civil War. Why do you think they were important? Andrew?

ANDREW: I think Lincoln was because he freed the slaves.

EDUCATOR: How about you, Horace?

HORACE: John Brown was important because his raid triggered the war.

Learners with processing difficulties or limited recall should be given, after sufficient wait time, the opportunity to respond first. Additionally, in the followup question here, the educator may want to limit responses to a single key player ("Why do you think John Brown was so important?"). This will reduce confusion for learners who may not be able to follow the transitions from one person to another and back again.

Bellon, Bellon, and Blank (1992) suggest that redirection appears to have greater utility with higher- or middle-ability learners. Learners with lower abilities may experience greater gains if the educator employs a probing strategy.

Probing strategies should be used when the learner's reply is correct but lacks depth. Probing should also occur when the original question does not clearly indicate to the learner the need for an expanded response.

EDUCATOR: Do you think oxygen is important to us? [pause] Hector?

HECTOR: Yes.

EDUCATOR: Why, Hector?

Clearly the learner failed to recognize that the educator expected more than a yes/no response and the question similarly lacked that clarity.

Reflect for a Moment

You ask a group of fourth graders, "Why was slavery so common in the South?" and Jeremy says, "Because they were farmers." How would you probe Jeremy?

Another useful questioning strategy is **prompting**. Prompting deals primarily with the learner who either fails to respond or responds incorrectly. Rather than simply moving on to another learner, the educator may rephrase the question or break it into smaller segments. Regardless of the manner in which the question is altered, the educator always adds hints, clues, or elaborations. These hints, clues, or elaborations are incorporated into the question to provide the learner with prompts to the answer.

Ineffective Questioning

Some question types are either unproductive or counterproductive and should therefore be avoided by the educator. These are: (1) yes-no or simple choice questions, (2) tugging, (3) guessing, and (4) rhetorical or leading questions (Groisser, 1964).

Because of their high guess factor, **yes-no** or **simple choice questions** (Was Washington or Lincoln first president of the United States?) have low diagnostic value and waste educational time. When a learner has a 50 percent chance of simply guessing the correct answer, the question fails to provide a basis for deciding whether or not the material has been mastered. Moreover, since these types of questions are often used during the beginning stages of a lesson as warmups, they have a tendency to misdirect the focus, thus wasting valuable instructional time. When the goal of a lesson is to discuss why the sky appears to be blue in color, asking a question like "Is the sky blue?" draws away from the original purpose of the lesson.

Tugging questions are those intended to elicit a response when a learner is unable to provide an answer. Educators are under the mistaken belief that rephrasing or reasking the question will bring about the correct response, when in fact the student simply does not know the answer. Brophy and Evertson (1976) suggest that it is counterproductive to nag learners in this manner because they would have already responded if they knew the answer. It is therefore better for the educator to give the correct response and not pressure the student for a response.

Questions that force learners to respond when they do not have the information needed to answer are **guessing questions**. Guessing questions that are used to spark interest or encourage discussion are valuable. However, when they are overused or inappropriately used, they tend to promote thoughtless or random responses. The key to the productivity of guessing questions rests in the reason they are used. "Guessing questions are useful if they are tied to teaching strategies that help students think rationally and systematically and if they are designed to arrive at a thoughtful response" (Good & Brophy, 1984, p. 351).

EXPOSITORY QUESTIONING STRATEGIES

Questioning in the expository method is used extensively to check for understanding, evaluate lesson effectiveness, encourage learner involvement, and manage lesson pace and direction. Asking questions that pertain to each point being mastered is essential in the expository method. Furthermore, research findings demonstrate that these questions are most advantageous to the learning process when they are used during the instructional period rather than following it (Anderson & Biddle, 1975). Good and Brophy (1991) feel that the effectiveness of an educator's questions can be determined by examining four factors:

1. Type of question
2. Phrasing of the question

3. Order or sequence of questions
4. Selection of respondent

Types

Convergent or divergent questions, already discussed, can be developed or organized on the basis of the thought process a learner must use to respond. Convergent questions often focus on learning that requires students to acquire facts, rules, and sequences. Generally, convergent questions necessitate learners' having either a single best response or a small number of clearly definable answers. The cognitive focus of convergent questions tends to remain at the lower levels of Bloom's taxonomy: knowledge, comprehension, and, to a lesser degree, application. Types of questions employed in an expository lesson that come under the global heading of convergent are recall and comprehension questions. **Recall questions** require the learner to recite specific facts, principles, or generalizations. Questions of the recall type are usually characterized by such key words as who, what, when, or where. Questions that require the learner to demonstrate an understanding or manipulation of the information through interpreting, summarizing, providing examples, or defining are **comprehension questions**. Comprehension questions tend to be characterized by terms such as how or why.

Divergent questions encourage a diversity of responses. Although generally having no single correct answer, divergent questions do have incorrect responses. Using divergent questions requires the learner to expand on the basic facts through analysis and synthesis. Although mentioned here, divergent questions are rarely used with the expository method and will be discussed in greater detail in following chapters.

Phrasing

Questions developed for use with the expository method need to be direct. The *phrasing* of the question should be clear and focused on the ability level of the person for whom it is targeted. The only time an educator should incorporate new vocabulary in a question is when the response requires learners to define the new word. Here is an example of this problem:

EDUCATOR: On whom or what do we place the *onus* for the Civil War?

There is no response from the class, not because they lack the factual information to respond but because they have failed to understand a key word (*onus*) in the question. The educator must reflect on his or her phrasing in formulating questions.

Reflect for a Moment

How could you rephrase the preceding question so that learners can respond? Is there one answer to this question?

Sequence

Questioning in the expository method most often follows the sequence identified by Brown and Edmondson (1984) as extending. **Extending questions** tend to be a series or string of the same type (recall or comprehension) and on the same topic. Additionally, questions should be sequenced in such a way as to follow any and all major points to be learned. This form of sequencing allows for frequent checks for understanding as well as flagging information for learners that the educator deems important.

Selection of Respondents

Educators who use the expository method need to be mindful of their audience at all times. Questions are used not merely as checks for understanding, but also to draw learners' attention back to the information being taught. The educator needs to recognize body language that indicates confusion, boredom, or frustration, and direct questions accordingly.

Handling of Correct and Incorrect Responses

An important facet of the expository process involves the educator's handling of correct and incorrect responses. Rosenshine (1983) identified four categories of learner response: correct, quick, and firm; correct but hesitant; incorrect but careless; and incorrect because of lack of knowledge.

Obviously, *correct, quick,* and *firm* responses are those most desired by the educator. It should be noted that these types of responses tend to occur toward the end of a lesson. Borich (1992) points out that active engagement of learners requires a moderate to high percentage of correct, quick, and firm responses. This is not to say that every learner response must be correct. However, for learning that involves knowledge acquisition, the steps between successive portions of the lesson sequences should be small enough to produce approximately 60–80 percent correct answers during checks for understanding, practice, and feedback sessions (Borich, 1992). Additional research by Bennett, Desforges, Cockburn, and Wilkinson (1981) and Brophy and Evertson (1976) found that asking the same learner another question appeared to be the best way to respond to correct, quick, and firm responses. The brisk pace of the expository lesson, coupled with a brisk pace of correct responses, helps to ensure increased learner attention and engagement. This pace tends to keep at a minimum irrelevant learner responses and classroom distractions.

Responses that occur at the beginning or middle of an expository lesson tend to be **correct but hesitant**. The educator should respond to this type of answer with a positive reinforcing acknowledgment because it provides an environment in which the hesitant but correct response is more likely to be retained. Additionally, this positive feedback increases the likelihood that the learner's next response will be correct, quick, and firm. Although positive feedback to this type of reply is imperative, it is also important to address the hesitancy by briefly restating the facts, rules, or steps. The restatement provides two direct benefits. The first, as stated before, is the decrease in hesitancy of learners' responses. The second is a reduction in the number of subsequent wrong responses from other learners who have heard the restatement.

Depending on time of day, level of fatigue, inattentiveness, or comfort, as much as 20 percent of learners' responses can fall into the third category, *incorrect but careless.* Effective educators deal with such responses by acknowledging answers as incorrect and quickly redirecting the question to another student. To stop and admonish a learner for his or her carelessness breaks the pace or momentum of the lesson, rarely producing positive results.

The final category of responses, *incorrect because of lack of knowledge,* most frequently occurs during the initial stages of the expository lesson. Since eliciting correct responses is more desirable than giving learners correct answers, the effective educator provides hints or probes, or alters the question. These techniques are designed to assist the learners in developing a process for finding the correct response. It is far more productive to channel a learner's thoughts in the direction of a correct response than simply to provide one. Borich (1992) states that the most common strategies employed in responding to an incorrect answer are:

1. Reviewing key facts or rules needed for a correct solution
2. Explaining the steps used to reach a correct solution
3. Prompting with clues or hints representing a partially correct answer
4. Taking a different but similar problem and guiding the student to the correct solution. (p. 104)

Bennett, Desforges, Cockburn, and Wilkinson (1981) suggest that the strategies of reviewing, reexplaining, and prompting should be employed only until approximately 80 percent of the learners are responding correctly. Once that percentage has been obtained, it is far more effective to deal with responses that are incorrect because of lack of knowledge by making correctives brief and directing respondents to remedial exercises.

In using the expository method, it is essential that an incorrect response never be left as that. Each and every incorrect response must be dealt with by using the strategies noted earlier. Learners who may have shared the same incorrect response may be led to believe it was an appropriate answer, thus learning inaccurate information.

Practice

Using the example lesson provided earlier,

1. Describe the types of questions used.

2. Discuss the educator's strategy, focusing on features of expository teaching.
3. Discuss how responses were handled.

STUDENT ASSESSMENT AND EVALUATION

Historically, one of the most significant outcomes of educational assessment has been the systematic exclusion and segregation of certain groups of learners. There is clearly then a need, in developing inclusive settings, for an evaluation process that is effective yet still humane. Cullen and Pratt (1992) suggest that evaluation should be

1. Continuous, and diagnostic/remedial in nature
2. Presented in a developmentally appropriate forum
3. Student friendly
4. Presented through a variety of techniques
5. Affective, not just cognitive and psychomotor
6. Facilitated by communication among all parties
7. Supportive of student self-evaluation

In addition, Cullen and Pratt (1992) encourage a collaborative decision-making process for effective evaluation that draws on data gathered from observations, student-teacher interviews, teacher-made tests, group projects, student contracts, and peer and self-evaluation.

Student assessment in the expository method must begin before the lesson is actually developed. **Preassessment** of requisite skills, facts, or rules is a necessity in this method. An effective expository lesson is one that builds on the learner's current level of performance through the expansion of the informational or knowledge base.

Reflect for a Moment

How could you preassess at the outset of the lesson? Better still, how could you preassess well in advance of a lesson with, say, ninth graders? How about with second graders?

During the lesson, *advance organizers* can be employed to quickly reassess the various levels of understanding students are bringing to the learning event. Effective educators assess at this time to enhance personalization of the lesson and determine appropriateness of predeveloped checks for understanding.

Checks for understanding are the second assessment tool used during the expository lesson. As stated before, frequent checks allow the educator to gauge the level of student understanding of material being taught. Checks provide the educator with the information necessary to decide the next stage of the lesson: Is there need to reteach or can I move on to the next step? Assessment via *direct communication* may take place during the lesson (checks for understanding) or after the lesson. Personal or direct communication are both forms of authentic assessment and are helpful for learners who have difficulty with more traditional forms of assessment.

In selecting the next level of assessment, it is important to align achievement targets and assessment methods. Achievement in an expository lesson is generally targeted at the mastery of knowledge, skills, or rules. *Selected response, objective paper-and-pencil*, or *fill-in-the-blank tests* are frequently employed to measure learners' memorization of facts and information. These types of assessments, however, tend to examine learners' knowledge of elemental facts in isolation.

An educator who selects objective paper-and-pencil assessment must recognize the unique testing needs of each learner. Learners with reading difficulties may need to have the objective test read to them or tape-recorded. Learners who have b, d reversal problems need to have response indicators capitalized (B, D) to decrease confusion. Some learners may need to mark answers directly on the test because transposition of responses to an answer or scantron sheet is extremely difficult for them. Learners with visual impairments may require enlarged print.

In addition to those adaptations previously discussed, a fill-in-the-blank test should not be developed without a word list. Learners who experience retrieval problems or spelling difficulties are unable to communicate their true level of content understanding without such lists.

When the level of facts, skills, or rules is defined not as isolated pieces of knowledge but as larger interrelated structures, the use of short essay questions or application exercises is appropriate. These forms of assessment require the learner to do more than simply memorize facts.

A good method for enhancing the typical format tests take is to provide the learners with the answers and have them develop the questions. This technique allows the educator to analyze learners' responses for misunderstanding or confusion of information presented.

Stiggins (1994) points out that there will be a need for citizens of the twenty-first century to be able to retrieve massive amounts of information on demand. The twenty-first century will present a world in which memorizing the needed facts and information will not be functionally possible. Therefore, Stiggins believes it is important to assess learners' ability to use reference materials as tools for gaining control over facts, skills, and rules. This form of testing can be accomplished through the use of **performance assessment**, observation of learners in the process of accessing reference materials. Through this observation process, the effective educator can assess learners' proficiency in the area of inquiry.

Product evaluation is another method for assessing learners' mastery of content knowledge. This method is particularly useful in the inclusive classroom, where each lesson presented may have a variety of outcomes as a result of learner diversity. Learners are able to apply the skills, facts, and rules they have learned through the expository lesson into the development of a product. Students in an inclusive setting will demonstrate their knowledge of the Civil War, for example, in different ways. One student may write a summary of the Lincoln-Douglas debate, a second student may design a battleground for a reenacted Gettysburg, and a group of three students produces a play about the *Monitor* and the *Merrimack*. Problems may arise in the evaluation of poor-quality products. Educators must devise a means of determining the reason for quality deficiency: lack of informational mastery, difficulty arising from creating the product, or lack of effort (Stiggins, 1994). It is essential to make this determination so that educators know how to best support learner improvement. Product assessment can be accomplished through the more traditional forms of assessment discussed previously.

Practice

Using the profile of Douglas Ontivares, create an evaluation process appropriate for his classroom.

TEACHER REFLECTIONS: EFFECTIVENESS OF THE LESSON

Throughout this text, use of reflective teaching is reinforced. All educators must allocate time and energy to look at their work, and the area of expository teaching is no exception. To modify instruction for greater student learning, educators who use the expository approach can reflect on their teaching by means of a series of questions like those presented in Table 9.2.

TABLE 9.2   Reflective Questions

1. At the outset, were students aware of the intended outcome of the lesson?
2. Was a review conducted (if necessary)?
3. Were there organizers or mneumonic aids used?
4. Did organizers/aids contribute to student learning?
5. Were teacher-initiated positive examples used?
6. Were teacher-initiated negative examples used?
7. Were student-initiated positive examples used?
8. Were student-initiated negative examples used?
9. Did questions meet the "good question" criteria?
10. Did questions serve to check for student understanding?
11. Did questions result in more student involvement?
12. Did questions support a brisk pace?
13. Did questions reinforce the direction of the lesson?
14. Were adaptations used?
15. Did adaptations contribute to student learning?
16. Did all students have practice time during the lesson?
17. Did all students receive specific and relevant feedback during the lesson?
18. Were all students aware of having had learning success during the lesson?

SUMMARY

Expository teaching, a popular instructional method, generally consists of a lecture which includes questions directed at students. It is best used when teaching facts, rules, or basic concepts. Good expository teachers engage their students through checks for understanding, guided practice, and corrective feedback. They also know their content, present material clearly, and review it routinely with students.

A good expository lesson begins with an overview of content, criteria for success, and advance organizers. The presentation is paced, sequenced and focused, and includes frequent checks for understanding. Links to broader, but related, concepts or rules are established. The lesson ends with a summary of key points and an assessment if and when learners are ready for it.

Adaptations to objectives, materials, or methods can be made in any expository lesson. Assessment of learning must go beyond tests and quizzes when using expository teaching. Observation can be a valuable assessment tool in expository lessons, especially in inclusive settings.

Questions can be used for a variety of reasons, and educators who develop and use good questions contribute to student achievement gains. Educators should consider the six factors discussed when formulating questions. Other important issues regarding questioning include what to ask, when to ask, who to ask, wait time, convergent and divergent questions, phrasing, and the handling of correct and incorrect responses.

10

THE DISCOVERY APPROACH

Key Terms

Abstraction	Intrinsic reward
Active engaged time	Learned helplessness
Attribution theory	Metacognition
Authenticity	Nonexample
Cognitive-developmental theory	Objective
Computer-assisted instruction	Peer tutoring
Constructivism	Problem question
Cooperative learning	Problem solving
Discovery teaching	Process question
Divergent questions	Questioning strategies
Essential questions	Rationale
Extrinsic reward	Reciprocal teaching
Formative evaluation	Scaffolding
Guided discovery	Sociohistorical theory
Heuristic question	Socratic question
Instructional variety	Summative evaluation
Intellectual potency	Wait time

Objectives

After completing this chapter, the reader will be able to:

1. Define the discovery approach.
2. Identify when to use the discovery approach.
3. Examine the connections between effective teaching research and the discovery approach.

4. Develop discovery teaching lessons.
5. Incorporate appropriate adaptations into a discovery lesson plan.
6. Develop appropriate questioning strategies.
7. Formulate appropriate student assessment strategies.
8. Incorporate personal reflection into discovery teaching.

PROFILES OF DISCOVERY TEACHING

Marie Torres

It was another day in Ms. Torres's class, and Randy and Lisa were really getting upset. Ever since the first day of fifth grade, they had been sitting at the same table, and although they really did not know what they had learned in math or science, they had become pretty good friends. Maybe it was because they shared the same concern about school. It wasn't that Ms. Torres didn't have any good ideas. In fact, she brought lots of neat things into the class. One day it was a live snake, the next day it was Chinese artifacts that her brother had brought back from Shanghai, and another day she gave each of them a coin from another country and had them tell the others at their table how they were different from American coins.

The trouble was—well, there were several problems. First, students in the class seemed to take Ms. Torres's teaching style as a signal to goof off, and almost every time she started a lesson, the talking in the room got so loud that Randy and Lisa couldn't even hear what Ms. Torres was saying. To make things worse, she did not even seem to mind that students were talking loudly while she was trying to teach. When the period was over, Randy and Lisa usually felt like they had done practically nothing! They were having this kind of experience a lot and worried that they were not learning what they needed to know. Second, Ms. Torres never really seemed to have a clear idea about what they were supposed to get out of these classroom activities or how they were to go about using the materials she had brought into the class. Randy and Lisa had to admit that, on the rare occasions when they could hear it, what Ms. Torres was saying during a lesson was confusing and vague. She did not seem to have planned any specific outcome for the lessons but just wanted them to "figure out" the materials she distributed among them. A third problem related to what Ms. Torres had told them at the beginning of the year. She had gotten them excited about upcoming activities because she said they would be working in cooperative groups, and the groups would include different students at different times. They would be learning to problem solve, work together cooperatively, and teach and learn with each other. Well, it was almost December and the groups were the same all the time. Students in almost all the groups were definitely not cooperating; they were just trying to show each other up. Some students in groups were being left out altogether. A student who had been in special education class until this year was not working out in class, mainly because Ms. Torres had not wanted him there in the first place. Randy and Lisa asked if he could be in their group, and they were really learning a lot about how to work with him, but they got frustrated at times, too.

There were other, perhaps smaller problems that Randy and Lisa were noticing, like the messiness of the room and the lack of assignment grades. They had told Ms. Torres about their concerns, and she just told them that it would work itself out in time. Unconvinced, they were not sure what to do next.

As a third year teacher, Marie Torres was convinced she could mold her classroom into an atmosphere of cooperative discovery if she could just get the students to cooperate. During her first two years at Howard Elementary, she had known a first grade teacher who had transformed his classroom into an exciting student-centered problem-solving setting where young five- and six-year-olds worked in individual small group and whole class settings, developing tremendous critical thinking skills that they applied on a daily basis to real-life problems in literature, science, mathematics, and social studies. Now, at Weber Community School, Marie had been assigned to an inclusive collaborative team with other educators in the upper elementary cluster. She had heard of inclusion and collaboration but really did not have any idea what either concept was like in action or whether she was ready to be an active collaborator in an inclusive setting. But here she was, in a collaborative team, in an inclusive setting, and she felt overwhelmed by all the new demands being placed on her. Her plans to transform her classroom into a true discovery setting were becoming an afterthought as she struggled to maintain classroom control and learn to adapt her plans for Cory, a student with behavioral problems who was in her class all day, every day.

She sensed that some of the students were getting very little out of her attempts at discovery teaching. If only she had more time to learn about discovery teaching, or about inclusion and collaboration!

Aaron Cohen

The students practically jumped out of their seats when Mr. Cohen challenged them to use statistics in explaining the jobs people in their families had at home. First graders, he knew, were very interested in exploring their own families, and now, about halfway through the year, they were proud of how they had learned to use statistics and were eager to use them again and again.

Aaron had never taught this lesson on family roles before, so he had spent hours carefully organizing the content so that there were plenty of abundantly clear examples and nonexamples he could refer to as he introduced the concept of "family role." He had also worked diligently to group the students into heterogeneous cooperative learning groups. He had met with the collaborative team to be sure that his adaptations for different learners in the class were appropriate and that Jo Weeks, the team special educator, could work with him during certain phases of the activity.

Planning lessons such as these had been quite time consuming back at the beginning of last year, when Aaron and the other educators at Lakemont Elementary made the transition to collaborative inclusive instruction. But the more they got used to the planning schedules, the opportunities to integrate the curriculum around themes (Aaron's activity was part of a larger schoolwide theme on families) and their own ability to develop instructional adaptations for all learners (even those with fairly severe disabilities), the less time it took to prepare discovery activities.

From the very first day of the school year, Aaron had actively taught the first graders not only specific collaborative and cooperative skills, but the standard procedures for discovery learning activities as well because he knew that they would use the skills throughout the year on a daily basis. Now, almost halfway through the year, he was seeing the benefits of the time spent during the first few weeks. The students were willing and able to work collaboratively with each other in many different groupings, and they were quite interested in learning just about everything he planned. Aaron felt that this motivation was in part the result of the discovery strategy he used, which put students in a position to bring their own personal experiences to the learning setting and develop a deeper, more meaningful understanding that they always had an opportunity to apply beyond the lesson itself.

Aaron was looking forward to the activity because he knew that several important concepts beyond "family role" would emerge, including the concepts "most" and "few" and the emergence of creative new ways to statistically display the data that students provided during the activity. Now both Jo Weeks and Ms. Earl, one of the volunteers from the neighborhood, had arrived, and it was time to get started. "Students, you need to organize your group and construct a list of the things your parents do at home."

Aaron Cohen's example shows that successful use of discovery teaching demands a great deal of skill from educators. The discovery approach requires educators to be constantly involved in making decisions. They must be able to think on their feet, recognize when to channel divergent learner responses toward the objective, and be aware of when and how to pose questions or prompts so that student responses begin to narrow. At the same time they must also be monitoring learners' responses to reformulate questions, thus ensuring successful learning. Educators must remember that the old adage "Practice makes perfect" applies especially to the development of an effective discovery approach, and that careful planning is a must. Educators cannot be discouraged if a lesson does not produce the results hoped for; they must analyze what went wrong and try again. After all, even Aaron Cohen was not successful the first time he attempted the discovery approach.

DISCOVERY TEACHING

The twentieth-century roots of discovery teaching are embedded in Johann Friedrich Herbart's inductive teaching of the early 1900s and John Dewey's problem-solving strategies of the 1930s (Morine & Morine, 1973). Contemporary educators who embark on discovery teaching, however, are applying what Henry (1994) refers to as a paradigm shift in their thinking about how students learn. The underlying principle of discovery teaching is the belief that children learn best by doing, not by sitting and listening or watching. It is vital, however, to understand that while this strategy is commonly known as **discovery teaching**, from the learners' perspective the process is more appropriately known as **guided discovery**, in which the educator guides learners step by step through the process of discovering new information, concepts, ideas, or understanding.

One way to gain a perspective on discovery teaching is to contrast it with the more familiar strategy of expository teaching. Whereas expository teaching relies heavily on a behaviorist approach to learning, in which the teacher presents information clearly enough for learners to understand, discovery teaching relies much more heavily on the student's ability to learn on her or his own when given a structured series of procedures carefully created by the educator. Jacobsen, Eggen, and Kauchak (1993) have also delineated the similarities and differences between expository and discovery teaching. They suggest that the two strategies are similar in that both (1) can be used to teach the same objective, (2) involve teacher-student interaction, (3) use questioning to build student understanding, and perhaps most important, and (4) are teacher directed. However, their differences are vital to understand if educators are going to be able to use both strategies effectively and when most appropriate. First, in expository teaching the teacher presents the new idea or information, followed by positive and negative examples. Thus, expository teaching is largely deductive in nature. In discovery teaching, the teacher first presents positive and negative examples of the new learning, and then guides the students to identifying the new idea or determining the new information. Guided discovery experiences are thus inductive, not deductive, in nature.

Here is an example of how the two strategies are applied. Using the theme of clouds from an earlier chapter, the expository educator teaching the basic types of clouds would name them and identify their characteristics in a presentation (hopefully with a visual format!). Then she or he would present positive and negative examples of the different cloud types, and students would gradually learn to identify the cloud they were seeing. The educator using a discovery strategy, in contrast, would provide a series of visual examples of clouds and students would organize the examples into two groups, those that were alike and those that were not. Learners would then describe the shared characteristics of the clouds in each group and in the process discover a cloud type. In this approach the educator may provide the names of the cloud types, but learners who have discovered similarities among clouds are motivated to label their findings and are usually very receptive to using correct labels when they are provided.

Second, there are significant differences in the types of questions used in the expository and discovery approaches. Although the majority of questions used by the expository educator are convergent, discovery teaching is characterized by many divergent questions and frequent redirecting, a practice that often results in a greater variety of learners participating openly in the lesson. Third, and related to this difference in questioning techniques, using divergent questions and redirecting often takes more time. This can sometimes be a problem when educators are not working with a thematic multidisciplinary curriculum and feel obligated to cover a certain amount of material on a particular topic in a given time period.

Fourth, and related to the third difference, is the focus of the lesson. In expository teaching, the topic of cloud types is the only focus of the lesson, and the educator, by using convergent questions and clearly directing the procedures throughout, can prevent other topics from being explored during the lesson. In discovery teaching, other curricular material can easily enter into the discovery process. For example, if learners are grouping pictures of clouds into two groups, they may begin to get interested in the capacity of different clouds to hold moisture or where certain cloud types are more likely to be found. They may express a desire to draw the cloud types or chart cloud types over a month's time. While discovery teaching invites these opportunities, expository teaching does not.

These four differences between expository and discovery teaching allow us to draw a few general conclusions about discovery teaching. One is that the strategy must be viewed as an opportunity for the learner to explore, compare, and in general become a skilled observer of her or his environment. In guided discovery lessons, the learner is also required to think consistently in order to proceed from one step to the next in the process. Furthermore, the discovery approach facilitates the acquisition of new information beyond that actually planned for the lesson. As we saw in the example about cloud types, learners actively organize information using their accumulated knowledge and understanding, frequently becoming interested in seeking additional related information as they are guided to discover learning intended. Lastly, discovery teaching requires educators to develop highly acute questioning skills, decision-making abilities, and monitoring techniques. It is simply a more difficult teaching strategy than the expository method, and one that many beginning teachers may have to practice for a time before feeling comfortable with in the classroom.

Reflect for a Moment

Think about a recent shopping trip you took where you actually considered several similar items before deciding on buying one of them. Maybe it was clothes, or a CD, or even groceries. What important features were you looking for in each item? What comparisons did you make? What other related items entered into your thinking as you compared items? How did you feel after you made your decision? How is shopping like discovery learning?

ADVANTAGES

Gilstrap and Martin (1975) point out that **discovery teaching** has two important advantages. First, learners' curiosity is aroused using the discovery method, thus motivating them to continue to work until a satisfying solution is found. Second, the discovery approach provides a model for independent problem solving that in turn gives learners the opportunity to analyze and manipulate information. Given the data of various national school reform groups (e.g. Holmes Group, Carnegie Forum Task Force) on the need to develop learners who have the ability to think clearly, analyze problems, and create solutions, this second advantage is of particular significance.

Bruner (1961) describes four benefits students derive from the opportunity to learn through the process of guided discovery. Through this approach, he believes students learn how to problem solve and develop an understanding of their own learning processes—both features of **metacognition**. This learning approach therefore increases **intellectual potency**. Bruner suggests this benefit occurs as learners engage in the discovery of answers and learn how to reduce sidetracking by recognizing the perimeters associated with any possible solution they explore. A second benefit of guided discovery is that the process of learning becomes rewarding to the student. The need for immediate **extrinsic rewards** (those given by someone else) gives way to the ability to delay gratification. The rewards become **intrinsic** (internalized) when a learner arrives at his or her own solution.

Bruner further feels that guided discovery aids the learner's memory processing. The ability to remember and retrieve information that a learner has "discovered" appears to be greater than that associated with dictated learning. Bruner believes that this outcome in part results from the fact that a student who develops good problem-solving skills also discovers better techniques for remembering information. Finally, the process of guided discovery engages the student in learning how to develop a problem in such a manner that it can be solved. Only by being involved in the guided discovery process and practicing the structuring of hypothesis and solutions can a learner best develop his or her problem-solving skills.

How Discovery Teaching Is Used

Unlike the expository strategy, discovery teaching places a primary emphasis on the learner and his or her behavior even though the success of the strategy still depends, to a great extent, on the educator's ability to structure the environment in a way that supports learner understanding. Although expository teaching usually involves a chalkboard or overhead projector and a lecture, discovery teaching is characterized by students manipulating objects or less concrete learning materials and discussing their observations, usually with a few other students at first and then with the entire class. It is not unusual, however, for the activity to be conducted with an entire class, and the educator is always required to carefully structure the procedures for the lesson. Just as learning concepts, patterns, and generalizations is a more complex process than learning facts and rules, the instruction needed to help learners successfully understand concepts, patterns, and generalizations is more complex than straightforward direct instruction.

The discovery lesson also centers around a simple new concept, key question, or generalization. But whereas students in an expository lesson must listen and watch to take in new learning, students in the discovery activity are actively pursuing that concept, answer, or generalization throughout the lesson, sharing their observations with their peers and being closely monitored and guided by the questions and comments of the educator until they demonstrate mastery or adequate understanding.

The discovery educator typically generates interest among students by presenting exciting or provocative materials or a challenging question, either way creating a need to know or understand in the minds of the learners. Then the educator provides data, usually in the form of concrete objects or printed examples, and challenges learners to find the pattern(s) in the data and then generalize by adding their own additional examples or data. Learners are also expected to examine and explain their thinking (metacognition) and apply their reasoning to additional data or examples. The questioning and monitoring of students serve to promote higher levels of thinking and a deeper understanding of the new concepts, patterns, or generalizations; the educator is constantly adjusting the process to ensure that these outcomes occur.

Reflect for a Moment

When was the last time a teacher really got your attention at the beginning of a lesson? What did she or he do or present?

When Discovery Teaching Can Be Used

Discovery teaching is a form of informal instruction and can be used to teach new concepts, patterns, and generalizations. However, before these concepts, patterns, and generalizations can be fully understood and applied, students typically need to learn many lower-level facts and rules. When the desired learning response is similar to the stimulus given, as in the learning of facts or rules, discovery teaching is not the recommended approach (Borich, 1992). Of course, not all learning takes place at such a simple cognitive level, and educators know that students must be able to do far more than memorize information to succeed in subsequent years, both in and out of school. Because higher-level thinking behaviors are needed to function effectively in the working world, instructional strategies that help students practice higher levels of thinking, such as guided discovery, are important for educators to utilize.

Students in guided discovery lessons often work in pairs or small groups. Therefore cooperative learning activities are appropriate settings for discovery teaching. Lessons in which students share responsibility for organizing materials provided to them can be found throughout any curriculum and offer educators opportunities for planning discovery learning.

Reflect for a Moment

Reflect on a recent situation when you were part of a group of people who were jointly responsible for getting a job done. How was the experience valuable? What cautions can you offer, based on your experience?

Many curricular expectations involve a student's ability to take specific information and discriminate it from other information. Other curriculum outcomes require students to take specific information and generalize from it to other similar information or circumstances. Both learning situations depend on learners' abilities to distinguish critical attributes in objects, concepts, and abstractions. Educators who are sensitive to these learning processes will utilize the discovery strategy more frequently and provide students with many opportunities to practice both thinking behaviors.

As implied earlier, the discovery strategy is also a suitable approach for thematic curriculum in which incidental learning is anticipated on a regular basis. Although the educator always has a highly structured plan for the discovery lesson, opportunities and questions leading to additional student-initiated learning will undoubtedly occur. Educators, particularly collaborative educators in inclusive settings who are committed to an ongoing thematic curriculum, are also prepared and receptive to the so-called "teachable moments" that discovery teaching provides.

As already discussed, discovery teaching is an appropriate approach when educators want to encourage higher levels of thinking among learners. During such activities, student ideas and experiences play an important part in the lesson, and students are encouraged to evaluate their own thinking. Analysis, synthesis, and evaluation levels of cognitive behavior are facilitated by discovery lessons.

Educators who wish to plan experiences in problem solving should also use the discovery strategy because of its exploratory and investigative nature. In other words, educators who are interested in not just the outcome of a student's thinking, but the actual thinking processes the student uses during the lesson, will find the discovery strategy very worthwhile. Beyond the thinking processes so evident in a discovery activity are the opportunities for students to engage in metacognitive behavior. Educators can have learners describe the thinking processes they used in their work or the strategies they use to solve a particular problem.

Guided discovery experiences, while providing problem-solving opportunities, also offer learners practice in collaboration with their peers. Learners must share responsibility for thinking, consider other students' thoughts, and, in some cases, be willing to follow the directions given by a peer. Furthermore, these types of lessons can be structured to meet the needs of a wide range of learners, whether in a whole class setting or in small groups or pairs.

There are clearly a wide range of occasions when discovery teaching can be beneficial for all learners. In thematic curriculum; in teaching concepts, patterns, and generalizations; in eliciting higher levels of cognitive behavior; in cooperative learning; in encouraging sometimes complex thinking skills; and in collaboration among learners—these are only a few of the instructional areas in which guided discovery is frequently implemented.

EFFECTIVE TEACHING

Discovery learning lends itself well to the development of concepts, principles, problem-solving skills, and a deeper understanding of abstractions. The ideas students use to describe, understand, and simplify the world in which they live are **abstractions** (Jacobsen, Eggen, & Kauchak, 1993). Learners gain an understanding of an abstraction when they are guided through the development of patterns or relationships and are assisted in summarizing experiences in an economical manner. As an example of the concept of abstractions as relationships, think back to the unit on clouds. As students learn about thunderclouds over a period of time, they begin to associate cloud formation with rain, lightning, and an increase in wind velocity. Additionally, through continued observation, they begin to develop ideas about the precautions they should take when they see thunderclouds forming. These learners have formed an abstraction. Knowing patterns clarifies the world and provides learners with enormous power because they need not remember specific examples.

Reflect for a Moment

Reflect on the last time you were in a car looking for a place you had never been to before. What landmarks or objects did you use to associate with the place you were headed? What did you do to simplify the task? What mistakes were you most concerned about making?

Bruner (1966) suggests that children learn best through active involvement with concepts, principles, problem-solving skills, or abstractions. "The premise of discovery learning is that information students discover for themselves will be learned easier and remembered longer than information acquired some other way" (Murray, 1989, p. 8). Educators therefore need to construct experiences, problems, or experiments that allow learners to discover principles, concepts, or abstractions.

As a cognitive approach, discovery learning is a well-planned strategy implemented by educators to guide students through the process of learning. Presseisen (1986) classifies cognitive or thinking skills into three categories: (1) essential cognitive processes, involving observation, comparison, inference, generalization, hypothesizing, and reasoning both inductively and deductively; (2) higher-order cognitive processes that include problem solving, decision making, and critical and creative thinking; and (3) metacognitive processes.

The discovery approach meets many of the effective teacher behaviors (see Chapter 4 for a complete list) detailed by Borich (1992). A critical aspect of effective teaching is **instructional variety**. Discovery teaching employs a variety of different materials, questioning procedures, and feedback techniques. Educators who effectively implement discovery learning also use a variety of visual aids, reading materials, audiovisual technology, reference materials, and computer-assisted instruction.

Student involvement in **active engaged time** is a major factor of the effective discovery lesson. Educators who use questions, materials, and learner curiosity effectively are able to draw students into the lesson. Because responses by the educator are designed to be both neutral and encouraging, many learners who normally are not risk takers become actively involved. Besides active engaged time, discovery learning also uses learners' ideas. Educators who use the discovery approach effectively consistently acknowledge, summarize, or apply learners' comments. By doing so, they are able to reap the benefits of higher levels of learner participation while also eliciting higher levels of thinking from students. Students welcome opportunities to restructure learning by examining their own hypotheses. Wyne and Stuck (1982) and Brophy and Evertson (1976) suggest that students who engage in learning with a minimum of errors have higher achievement and a better attitude toward school.

Clearly defined **questioning strategies** are yet another key factor in effective teaching. **Process questions** (see Chapter 4), a vital part of the effective discovery lesson, are used to elicit the deeper, more complex student thinking that is an essential feature of learning through discovery. In effect, this form of questioning empowers students to discover new concepts, principles, and abstractions.

During discovery activities educators provide direction, guiding students to discover the relationships or patterns that will assist them in developing abstractions, concepts, or principles. Like the expository approach, discovery teaching or guided discovery allows educators to closely monitor the progress of the group, encouraging active learner engagement and higher-level thinking skills. Taking the role of guide, educators lead students through the learning event. The development of abstractions is done in a teacher-directed fashion, usually through the use of questioning. Discovery teaching relies on the use of multifaceted presentation techniques that involve sharing a wide variety of examples and nonexamples provided not only by the educator but by students as well. Educator-student interaction is absolutely necessary because it is the teacher's responsibility to assist the learner in reaching the appropriate outcome through questions, examples, and clarification of discoveries.

PLANNING PROCEDURES

Not unlike the expository method (discussed in Chapter 9), discovery teaching requires careful planning to be effective. Effective discovery teaching

1. Is directed by a clearly developed objective.
2. Is a set of structures designed to guide learners through an exploration.
3. Is educator directed.
4. Is relevant, challenging, and interesting to learners.
5. Focuses on individualization of learning.
6. Focuses on higher order thinking skills.

Many educators have the misconception that discovery learning is a student-directed approach that needs little or no planning. Its implementation is not an easy task, however, and not one in which learners are simply turned loose; educator mediation is required (Corno & Snow, 1986). "Left alone, students are not apt to make mathematical discoveries that took the best mathematicians in history thousands of years to discover" (Simon, 1986, p. 41).

Simon (1986) feels that educators must meet five responsibilities for successful implementation of the discovery learning approach. Educators should

1. *Identify and prioritize what needs to be learned.*
2. *Distinguish among facts, procedures, and concepts.*
3. *Organize concepts hierarchically.*
4. *Divide the material to be learned into appropriate increments.*
5. *Create or adapt activities that stimulate the development of the desired concept. (p. 42)*

To be effective, discovery learning requires advanced planning and preparation, but this advanced planning does not need to be done solely by a single educator. In an inclusive setting educators need to combine their skills to ensure that all learners are benefiting from the discovery approach. Collaborative planning from a variety of educators can produce a lesson that provides all students the opportunity to move beyond the memorizing of facts to the development of generalized skills. Burden and Byrd (1994) believe that the discovery approach is most effective when learners work collaboratively with the educator in designing or planning the lesson. Additionally, educators need to combine visual aids, technology, and appropriate reading materials to permit students the opportunity to draw conclusions, make generalizations, and form abstractions through discovery.

The guided discovery or discovery lesson (see Table 10.1 for a sample lesson plan) has six critical components: objective, rationale, content, materials, procedures (discovery episodes), and evaluation (of educator, students, and the lesson plan itself).

TABLE 10.1   Sample Lesson Plan

Objective:	The students will discover the phonetic pattern "*i* before *e* except after *c* and except when they say *a*, as in *neighbor* and *weigh*," so that in writing the words in a story, poem, or friendly letter they will be able to use the pattern to spell at least eight of the words correctly.
Rationale:	Learners need to understand the pattern to spell words having the *ie* or *ei* vowel combinations.
Content:	When a word has the vowels *i* and *e* placed together, *i* usually comes before *e* unless they follow *c* or are pronounced with an *a* sound.
Materials:	List of words, learners' word bank.
Procedure:	Display the following words on the board:

fierce	diet
field	fiery
receive	conceive
lieutenant	ceiling
neighbor	yield
weigh	die
hieroglyphics	heir

Have learners describe the words (brainstorming).
Ask a learner to pronounce the word *neighbor*.
What vowel sound do you hear?
Have another learner pronounce *field*.
What vowel sound do you hear?
Have another learner pronounce *fiery*.
What vowel sound do you hear?
Is the vowel sound the same?
Have the learners pronounce all words to see if that helps to establish any type of pattern.
What do the *ie* words have in common? The *ei* words
Identify generalization (pattern).
Have the learners brainstorm words containing *ie* or *ei*.
Are there exceptions to this generalization?
The educator may have a list ready such as the one below to help learners brainstorm exceptions.

being	height	deify	heist
either	leisure	deice	
neither	feisty	reinforce	geisha
seismic	heifer	seize	weird

Evaluation:	Have learners write a story that requires the use eight of words with *ie* or *ei*.

Objectives and Rationale

The planning process for the discovery approach begins with the careful develop-ment of a behavioral **objective** (learning outcome). In selecting an objective, the ed-ucator must carefully consider the background information each student must possess to be involved in the learning process. Learners must have sufficient back-ground to build on so that they will not become frustrated by their attempts to discover.

A clear understanding of why the learner needs to learn particular patterns, concepts, principles, or abstractions helps the educator to develop a strong ratio-nale. **Rationale** is a critical component of the discovery lesson because discovery learning is related more to the "knowing" than the "knowing-how-to" (Copeland, 1982); discovering patterns is more difficult than reciting correct answers. Knowing-how-to involves the simple plugging in of answers or information to complete a task. Knowing consists of conceptualization and requires an internalization rather than externalization of knowledge. Therefore learners need to feel that the issue, problem, or dilemma is relevant, challenging, solvable, and interesting.

Reflect for a Moment

Think about how motivated you are when you are embarking on a task that you be-lieve will get you somewhere. Then try to think about how motivated you feel when you are doing something that has no real meaning to you aside from the fact that someone has told you it must be done.

Content

Once educators have determined the objective and outlined the rationale, they must develop examples, nonexamples, and questions. These three components help to direct learners through their examination of the content. Educators who use the discovery learning approach must develop a series of problems and/or expe-riences that offer learners the chance to investigate and discover key patterns, concepts, principles, or abstractions. The presentation of examples can be as straightforward as a list of words (as in sample lesson in Table 10.1) or a series of mathematical problems, or more elaborate, such as a scenario involving an under-standing of the concept of gravity. Examples should develop in such a way that they enable learners eventually to develop their own examples. **Nonexamples** are also important because they enable learners to rule out unimportant or insignifi-cant commonalities shared by examples and nonexamples in the development of key patterns, concepts, principles, or abstractions.

Materials

Materials for the discovery lesson must be carefully considered and may vary greatly. It is especially important for the educator to think through in advance what learners may need to assist them in their quest for understanding. Prior organization of materials prevents the loss of active engaged learning time. Motivation and momentum may be lost if learners need to search out the needed materials to assist them in making their discovery.

Discovery teaching requires the educator to gather a sufficient amount of materials related to the concept to be learned so that all learners can have access to them during the learning activity (Eby, 1992). In selecting materials, educators should look particularly for unfamiliar, interesting materials that will stimulate thinking and questioning among learners. During the activity, learners are directed by questions posed by the educator and manipulate the materials to examine their properties. For older students, the process may go beyond studying the physical properties of objects to critical examinations of the more abstract features of poetry, physics, or social theories.

Procedures

Jacobsen, Eggen, and Kauchak (1993) suggest a nine-step procedure for the delivery of an effective discovery lesson. *Step 1* is the educator's presentation of an example. (In the lesson plan on the spelling pattern in Table 10.1, the educator begins with a word list.) Learners often become more interested if the presentation involves a problem scenario or the development of a "mystery" they must solve.

Step 2 is learner directed; students are asked to describe or perhaps brainstorm about the example. This can be done in either a large group or in smaller cooperative groups or pairs (sometimes called discovery teams). However the educator completes this second step, there needs to be a method for the learners to record their descriptions and ideas. The educator can write ideas on the board, an overhead projector, or easel tablet. In small cooperative groups one learner can be assigned the job of recorder.

Step 3 again requires the educator to present further examples. She or he may do this by moving from one discovery team to the next or as a large group. This second example should be designed to clarify and/or expand on the original, further directing learners toward their goal. Learners then move to *step 4*, which involves describing this example and comparing it to the first. During this step, students are able to study the examples to see if a pattern is emerging. The educator presents additional examples and introduces nonexamples during *step 5*. These are given to allow learners to further compare and contrast (*step 6*), refining their discoveries.

In *step 7*, the educator prompts learners to share the characteristics, patterns, or relationships they have uncovered through their exploration of examples and nonexamples. This might be accomplished by having a group spokesperson read their (the group's) discoveries or by having learners post their discoveries on large sheets of paper for the whole class to see. From this sharing process *step 8* emerges, in which learners are asked to state what they believe to be the key concept, principle, or abstraction.

Step 9, finally, calls for the educator to draw from the learners further examples. By requiring learners to provide this last set of examples, the educator is able to assess whether they have understood and internalized the pattern, concept, principle, or abstraction.

Evaluation

As in any lesson, evaluation must take place in discovery teaching. It may take many forms, such as responding orally to questions, taking a quiz, or completing an independent activity. However, the educator needs to not only evaluate learners' understanding but himself or herself as well (see Teacher Reflections later in this chapter).

Unlike the expository method, evaluation of the discovery lesson is not embedded in lesson closure. Learners' understanding must be judged on a formative and summative basis if the discovery approach is to be properly evaluated. One reason Maria Torres was unsuccessful in her use of the discovery approach was because she failed to evaluate learner understanding. Randy and Lisa began the year with excitement but were worried that they were not learning what they needed to know for the next school year. **Formative evaluation** takes place during large group discussion and small group investigation through questions and the monitoring of group activities. Formative evaluation allows educators to alter instruction, provide new examples, reorganize instruction, and redirect learners' investigations.

Summative evaluation occurs at the end of the lesson in a variety of ways. As the following sample lesson will show, Joan Potts has the children write a story, poem, or friendly letter using the words they have discussed. She also uses the words as spelling words to give a more formalized assessment of her students' knowledge.

AN EXAMPLE OF DISCOVERY TEACHING

Joan Potts wants to teach her students a generalization about spelling ("*i* before *e* except after *c* and except when they say *a*, as in *neighbor* and *weigh*") so when they encounter such words they will be able to use the generalization to spell them correctly. To accomplish this, she directs learners' attention to the following list of words she had written on the board earlier:

fierce	diet
field	fiery
receive	conceive
lieutenant	ceiling
neighbor	yield
weigh	die
hieroglyphics	heir

MRS. POTTS: Children, please look at the words on the board and tell me what you see. [Mrs. Potts provides appropriate wait time.] Patrick?

PATRICK: They all have *i*s in them. [Mrs. Potts writes Patrick's idea on the board.]

MRS. POTTS: Excellent, Patrick. Can anyone see anything else? [Mrs. Potts provides appropriate wait time.] Barb?

BARB: Well, they all have *e*s, too.

HARVEY: Actually, it seems that they all have either *ie* or *ei* in them.

MRS. POTTS: Yes, is there anything else about these words? [Mrs. Potts provides appropriate wait time.] Mickie?

MICKIE: I'm not sure.

ANDREA: Is it that they are either nouns or adjectives? [She also adds these ideas to the board.]

EMILE: No, that can't be it, 'cause some are verbs, too. I think that we should put question marks up next to noun, adjective, and verb because I'm not sure that is important.

MRS. POTTS: Children? [The group concurs so Mrs. Potts follows Emile's suggestion.]

MRS. POTTS: Frank, could you please pronounce this word? [Mrs. Potts points to the word *neighbor*.]

FRANK: Neighbor.

MRS. POTTS: Nice job! What vowel sound did you hear?

FRANK: A long *a* vowel sound?

MRS. POTTS: Yes. Now I'd like you to break into your discovery teams and see if you can find some other similarities or differences in these words. You may want to try saying all the words on the board and recording what you hear.

Joan Potts moves from group to group passing out large sheets of paper and a marker. The group recorders will write down everyone's ideas. Joan Potts provides additional examples to the groups when necessary. She also asks questions to help redirect groups who have strayed too far afield of the generalization she wants them to discover.

MRS. POTTS: Children, let's come back together as a large group. Will the spokespersons from each group please hang your sheets up for all to see?

MELANIE: All the words with a *c* have *ei*. [Mrs. Potts writes this on the board, as she does all the ideas.]

HARVEY: The words that have a long *a* sound have *ei*.

FRANK: All the others have *ie*.

MRS. POTTS: Did it matter whether it was a noun or verb or adjective? [Mrs. Potts provides appropriate wait time.] Andrea?

ANDREA: No, doesn't seem to.

MRS. POTTS: Good. You have established some patterns—what will knowing these help you do? [Mrs. Potts provides appropriate wait time.] Patrick?

PATRICK: If I have a spelling word and I know it has an *i* and an *e* in it, I'll be able to spell it.

MRS. POTTS: Yes, can anyone think of a way to remember these patterns? [The group will write a statement reflecting the patterns that they can remember while spelling.]

HARVEY: Mrs. Potts—the word *science* doesn't follow our rule because it's spelled *s-c-i-e-n-c-e*.

MRS. POTTS: Yes, Harvey that's true. As with many patterns, we learn there are always exceptions. [Mrs. Potts writes *follows the generalization* over her examples and *some exceptions* on the board over the word *science*.] Can anyone else think of a word with *ie* or *ei*?

[The group brainstorms additions to both lists.]

being	height	deify	heist
either	leisure	deice	geisha
neither	feisty	reinforce	weird
seismic	heifer	seize	

MRS. POTTS: What I'd like you all to do is to write these words on file cards for your word banks and write the new generalization in your spelling journals. These words will be your spelling words for the week. From these words please select five and use them in a story, poem, or friendly letter that you will complete by Friday. Be sure to share your piece with your writing partners.

Practice

Given the following objective, develop a discovery lesson plan:

The students will discover the patterns of weather associated with various cloud formations so that when they are shown a cloud, they will be able to predict the weather correctly.

ADAPTATIONS

As a member of a collaborative team in an inclusive school, the classroom teacher has a number of fundamental advantages over the educator in a more traditional setting when it comes to planning and implementing instructional adaptations. First, all the members of the inclusive school community have made a commitment to providing appropriate educational opportunities for all learners. It has already been established that adaptations are an ongoing part of the school's services, are considered every time a group of educators collaboratively plan together, and take place on a daily basis in every classroom. Educators expect to adapt instruction regularly. Second, the school has been restructured, in terms of both resources and time. Special educators are accustomed to meeting with classroom educators. Therapists expect to work in general classroom settings most if not all of the time. Classroom teachers know that they have specialized instructional support when it is needed and routinely utilize community members as volunteers. The school schedule has been modified to provide collaborative planning time on a regular basis, either daily or weekly, depending on which arrangement is better for the professionals involved. Classroom teachers also know that they can integrate the curriculum using themes and as a result can use instructional time more flexibly. It is not uncommon to devote an entire school day to a single activity, especially when the collaborative instructional team has identified curriculum outcomes for all learners in several areas that the activity can directly support.

A third advantage that collaborative educators in inclusive settings have when planning and implementing instructional adaptations is that they have come to understand and value the importance of using learner-centered instructional strategies, including the discovery strategy. Although this shift in thinking about learning usually takes time, it is time worth investing and results in more frequent use of such techniques as cooperative learning, peer tutoring, and active involvement with concrete materials in all classrooms. Educators who have embraced learner-centered strategies utilize the world outside the classroom more fully and find that students are more curious, more motivated, and more capable of thinking creatively and critically than they are when reading textbooks and filling in blanks on worksheets. In many situations, educators find that the learner-centered instructional strategies themselves provide the adaptations needed to facilitate learning for many students.

Reflect for a Moment

Can you think of a recent situation in which you were at a distinct disadvantage because of a lack of skills or experience? What would have helped you feel more capable, or at least more eager to participate?

Textbooks and Other Printed Materials

Instructional adaptations appropriate for implementing guided discovery lessons require a closer examination. First, both expository and discovery lessons may require the use of textbooks and other printed materials, and the adaptations suggested in Chapter 9 in using these materials (appropriate levels of readability, tape recordings, student scanning to develop a mindset) are also appropriate for any discovery lesson. Because the discovery educator must provide extremely clear positive and negative examples of the new learning, it is very important for those examples to be understood by all learners. Regardless of whether they are presented in a book, on the chalkboard or overhead, or distributed to each student or group of students, the examples must be meaningful and clearly understood by all learners. One of the most reliable ways to ensure that all learners do understand the educator's examples is to utilize a variety of grouping techniques.

Computer-Assisted Instruction

Many persons have the misconception that the discovery method and **computer-assisted instruction** are not compatible. In fact, computer-assisted instruction is very useful in the discovery approach. Computers can provide learners with opportunities to investigate databases, approach information inductively, conduct trial-and-error problem solving, and test their hypotheses. Computer-assisted instruction is also a formative means for adapting instruction to meet the needs of individual learners. Databases can be selected that are compatible with the academic levels of a variety of students. Additionally, technologies such as switches and voice synthesizers can be added to the computer to enable physically challenged and nonverbal individuals to participate in class discussions and cooperative groups.

In computer-assisted instruction the educator's role remains the same in presenting the basic problem and monitoring learners' progress. The computer can then be used to enhance the discovery process by presenting learners with greater access to information at their reading level, storing data, and permitting search procedures. Learners are able to make and test hypotheses, a process that assists them in developing principles, rules, or abstractions. Heinick, Molenda, and Russell (1989) suggest that computer-assisted instruction is most useful in the discovery approach when applied to problems in the areas of social science, science, and career exploration.

Instructional Procedures

Educators can use a number of potential adaptations during the discovery activity depending on the needs of the learners. Table 10.2 provides a list of a few of the possibilities.

Grouping Techniques

Discovery lessons can be facilitated by using various groupings of students, depending on the objective of the lesson. Whether using whole class, small groups, pairs, or even individualized arrangements, educators can enhance the discovery process by selecting the arrangement with students' needs in mind.

Whole Class Grouping
Some lessons may call for a whole class grouping, particularly when the educator wishes to demonstrate a procedure, clarify a point, or have the entire class work on the same problem using the same materials. In such an arrangement, the edu-

TABLE 10.2   Adapting Instructional Procedures in a Discovery Lesson

1. Make learners aware of precisely what they are expected to do at each stage of the activity or lesson.
2. Structure the procedures carefully to be sure the examples and nonexamples are first relevant and abundantly clear, then gradually become more and more difficult.
3. Be sure to provide an adequate number of examples and nonexamples, and allow plenty of time for learners to work on mastering the concept, principle, or pattern.
4. Build a pattern of frequent feedback that reduces the possibility of student error, yet still supports the guided discovery process.
5. Be prepared to respond to inappropriate or inaccurate learner responses. Acknowledge them as incorrect when necessary, and then use them to build better understanding.
6. Use relevant, actual objects as much as possible.
7. Always break down the task or the procedure into smaller parts so that all learners can easily see the transition from one phase of the activity or lesson to another phase.
8. Continue to act as a model of positive interdependence and discovery by openly considering a change in presentation style or acknowledging when an example is not well suited.
9. Be prepared to use frequent verbal clues or physical support with learners with more severe disabilities.
10. Whenever necessary, demonstrate the procedure learners will use in their discovery activity.
11. Stay focused on the features of the concept, principle, or pattern being learned, avoiding digressions and verbose explanations.
12. Remember that with the process of discovery, the challenge serves as a motivator and can be presented as such by the educators present.
13. Educational technology can and should be used to facilitate students' understanding and application of new concepts and generalizations.

cator can adapt to individual student needs by directing questions in specific ways to support individual student understanding, plan for different response modes from different learners, monitor students in relation to anticipated needs, work with students on an individual basis, or establish a seating plan that allows certain students to offer or obtain peer assistance when necessary. In situations where alternative objectives and activities are appropriate as determined by a collaborative instructional team, the whole class arrangement can still be utilized. Peer tutoring and carefully prepared instructional materials can ensure that students participating with alternative objectives and activities are able to proceed with the lesson.

Small Groups

Small groups are frequently used to implement discovery lessons. The small group setting facilitates the process of adapting instruction to meet a wider range of learner needs while pursuing higher levels of thinking dictated by the lesson objective. For example, the small group setting, with no more than six students per group, allows every learner to become actively involved in the learning process. Burden and Byrd (1994) organize the small group setting into three categories: the ability group, cooperative learning, and peer tutoring. While the ability group category has been a common practice in elementary reading and mathematics, it has not shown consistently positive results for any group of learners and does not represent a viable approach in inclusive settings.

Cooperative Learning

On the other hand, the **cooperative learning** technique has been discussed frequently in research on inclusion, and can be used with learners of varying abilities in a variety of academic situations (Will, 1986; Slavin, 1990; Johnson & Johnson, 1986; Thousand & Villa, 1991; Putnam, 1993). O'Connor and Jenkins (1993), however, offer a few valuable cautions. When adults intervene *inappropriately* during cooperative learning activities, peer cooperation is disrupted and some learners, particularly those with disabilities, may not benefit academically from the cooperative setting. This is not to say that educators can or should not join in group discussion but that they monitor their own involvement to keep from interfering with the students' cooperative process. Additionally, learners, particularly those unaccustomed to cooperative learning activities, should have ample time to develop and demonstrate a cooperative, helping ethic in their academic and social conduct. Otherwise, some students, again those with disabilities, may not be included in group work. Jakupcak (1993) suggests teaching students cooperative skills, including positive feedback, group unity, recording, leading, and productive interactions.

Teacher behavior and expectations clearly play a significant role in the successful functioning of cooperative learning groups. To maximize the effectiveness of cooperative learning activities, educators can openly and frequently model encouragement and acceptance of all learners in all types of group arrangements and plan carefully to ensure that all learners participate in group work. In a discovery lesson, learners in small groups can usually discuss among themselves the examples and nonexamples presented by the educator using a structured interactive procedure that includes all group members. In some cases, the group of learners themselves can actually decide on an appropriate task for each member, including those with disabilities.

Johnson, Johnson, and Holubec (1987) offer a set of strategies for maximizing the success of cooperative lessons, particularly for inclusive classrooms. (1) Correlate lesson objectives for the entire class with IEP objectives for students with disabilities. (2) Group learners with heterogeneity and diversity in mind. (3) Be sure the classroom is arranged so that group members face each other. (4) Structure the lesson outcomes so they reflect interdependence throughout the activity. (5) Make criteria for success, both academic and social, clear to all learners prior to the activity. (6) Monitor all learners carefully. (7) Intervene to support academic or social skills when necessary. (8) Be sure to have an evaluation procedure for both academic and social performance. These strategies are highly consistent with the goals of a collaborative inclusive instructional setting.

Adapting discovery lessons using cooperative groups also frequently involves collaboration among adults, but in ways that are unobtrusive and do not either disrupt or segregate learners. If a cooperative group of learners is using a discovery process to distinguish different cloud types, for example, it may be beneficial to have a therapist work with an entire group (which includes a learner with cerebral palsy) as they construct a collage of the different cloud types from the various photographs they have collected from different magazines. This example illustrates how discovery teaching can be implemented with cooperative learning groups. It also serves as an example of discovery teaching that is carefully planned by the adults involved yet highly student centered in its actual procedures.

Although there are a number of recognized forms of cooperative learning (group investigation, teams-games-tournament, student teams–achievement divisions, jigsaw I and II, learning together) the learning together strategy has been regarded by some as the most appropriate for inclusive settings or making curricular adaptations (Salend, 1994; Udvari-Solner, 1994). This strategy, devised by Johnson and Johnson, has been characterized as a conceptual rather than a direct approach to learning (Johnson & Johnson, 1991). A conceptual approach does not follow a strict step-by-step procedure like the other popular cooperative learning strategies. Rather, it requires educators to thoroughly understand and apply the important features of cooperative learning and can be applied to a variety of grade levels and curricular areas (Udvari-Solner, 1994). As such, the conceptual approach requires the educators leading the activity to engage in metacognitive behavior.

The *learning together* strategy is highly compatible with discovery teaching, largely because it places the educator in the position of being a facilitator and manager instead of information giver (Udvari-Solner, 1994). It is the educator's responsibility to identify both academic and social objectives; either type can be group or individually focused, depending on learners' needs. The assignment of learners to different groups, group size, the establishment of positive interdependence within each group, the explanation of criteria for academic and social success, the close monitoring of learner performance by the educator, and the consistent use of a closure period in which learners share their work and raise additional questions are all features of the learning together procedure. They are also clearly opportunities for adaptations in planning and implementing discovery activities.

Among the more specific types of curricular adaptations possible during discovery activities implemented with cooperative learning groups are several that can be determined during collaborative planning beforehand. Keeping the individual learner's unique needs in mind, the collaborative team can, for any specific lesson or activity, address whether the cooperative group approach is appropriate, how the lesson objectives might need to be modified, which tasks within the activity would be most appropriate for the specific learner, how the learner's performance will be assessed, how the classroom environment and activity materials might be arranged to support the learner's participation, and what kind of personal support the learner may benefit from during the activity. Using these areas of consideration, the collaborative team can design any adaptations necessary to maximize the success of all learners during a discovery lesson with cooperative groups.

Reflect for a Moment

What social skills can you identify that an educator might observe during a cooperative learning activity? Why are they worth observing?

Peer Tutoring

Peer tutoring consists of students teaching each other, and arranging learners in pairs is one approach to peer tutoring that can be effective in discovery lessons. In some classrooms where learners are not experienced with cooperative learning groups, the pairing technique can provide an opportunity to build collaborative skills with a peer and usually offers a convincing invitation for every learner to actively participate. In discovery lessons, it is not unusual for learners, after acquiring a fragile understanding of a concept from the adult educators present, to gain a deeper and more solid understanding when they are paired together to discuss or work together on the new learning. Another interesting aspect of peer tutoring in discovery lessons is found in the tutoring style of the learners. In many situations, they instinctively avoid simply telling each other answers or examples, opting instead for the questioning techniques that are in fact central to the discovery teaching process, permitting their peers to actually discover the common features of examples or even the underlying generalization or pattern itself.

In planning a peer tutoring arrangement for a discovery lesson, educators should consider the success learners are likely to encounter with the new learning. McNeil (1994) found that learners were successful working in pairs when one student's skill level was judged to be slightly different from the other student's skill level. This case study would suggest that the most advanced learners in a class not be paired with the least advanced learners. One of the most valuable results of many peer tutoring arrangements is the self-confidence learners gain as they see themselves in a helping role with a peer, especially in an area where they have previously experienced frustration. During discovery activities, in which learners in pairs are challenged to solve a problem, they must exercise their collaborative skills and work together, helping each other develop a deeper, more meaningful understanding of the new concept or pattern.

Assignments and Assessments

In considering adaptations to assignments and assessments in discovery learning experiences, it is valuable to consider the suggestions described in Chapter 9. However, the importance of **authenticity** can not be overstated. Authenticity, in terms of assignments, refers to those out-of-school tasks that give learners opportunities to transfer, apply or generalize their new understandings in meaningful ways. Using the cloud collage activity as an example, the educator might have learners take photographs of clouds, draw clouds they observe using features of known cloud types, or watch the weather station on television and note descriptions of different kinds of clouds offered by the meteorologist. All of these assignments can emerge logically from the discovery activity in which groups of learners created collages of different types of clouds. The variety of possible authentic assignments is itself a means to adapting learning for different learner needs.

Authenticity, in terms of assessment, refers to the assessment of student learning by meaningful tasks requiring the students to apply that new learning. Using the cloud activity, the educator must first revisit the rationale of such an activity and clearly determine why the students learned the different cloud types. Then a task can be devised that assesses learners' ability to apply their knowledge of cloud types in a meaningful way. One group of learners could use their knowledge of cloud types to describe the weather in certain regions around the world, whereas another group of learners could develop a recordkeeping system and chart the frequency of different cloud types over the school. Both are meaningful tasks that offer real or authentic evidence of student understanding of cloud types.

Keeping in mind, as Cullen and Pratt (1992) have suggested, that assessment also serves to guide future planning, it is critical for educators using the discovery strategy to use criterion-referenced forms of assessment rather than norm-referenced forms, particularly if they are going to be flexible about adapting assessment techniques. Incidental observations are an important means of assessing a wide range of students during a discovery activity (Wolf, 1984). Student portfolios are yet another valuable assessment tool in a discovery learning environment. In using the cooperative learning approach, educators can use a combination of individual and group assessments, all criterion referenced or authentic in nature.

Practice

Using the following lesson outline, devise adaptations for learners with cognitive, mental, or behavioral disabilities. Create two ways to modify each of the following aspects of the activity:

objectives	instructional procedures
materials	assessment, assignments

Lesson Topic: Classifications of animals

Lesson Goal: Students will learn to organize animals into meaningful groups in order to bet-

ter understand the balance of the wildlife environment.

Lesson Setting: Collaborative, inclusive classroom; small, cooperative groups

Lesson Materials: Large supply of pictures and picture books; other materials (you choose)

Lesson Procedure: Standard discovery format; you decide extent of adult intervention.

QUESTIONING STRATEGIES

The deliberate series of questions developed by an educator to accomplish a specific objective or goal is a questioning strategy (Bellon, Bellon, & Blank, 1992).

> The key to preparing an effective questioning strategy is developing clearly defined learning objectives. The level and sequence of questions to be asked depends entirely on the knowledge that is to be acquired and cognitive processes necessary to respond to the strategy. (Bellon, Bellon, & Blank, 1992, p. 320)

Although good and bad questioning techniques (see Chapter 9) are somewhat universal, questioning strategies for the discovery teaching approach are very different from those used in the expository method.

Since the purpose of this learning approach is to allow students to discover key concepts for themselves, educators must ask heuristic questions. **Heuristic questions** guide learners to discovery by moving them along empirical lines. Questions that are heuristic may also be called *thought questions*. Such questions may be convergent, divergent, or evaluative in nature. Thought questions differ from memory questions because the answers are derived from learners' thinking rather than their rote memory.

DISCOVERY QUESTIONING TECHNIQUES

Wiggins (1987) proposed that learners' thought processes are awakened not by the authoritarian claims of an educator or textbook but by a problem. If this is the case, then knowledge must be envisioned as a product of questioning. Therefore, in order for learners to engage in an intellectual endeavor, they must be provided with questions that assist them in focusing their curiosity and setting them along a path to discover key concepts, principles, patterns, or abstractions. A discovery lesson needs to raise unsettling questions (essential questions) to ensure students will think seriously about what they are learning. Therefore, Wiggins believes that educators organize lessons "not around 'answers' but around essential questions to which 'content' represents answers" (p. 12).

Wiggins (1987) suggests four questions that, answered in the positive, can identify **essential questions**: (1) Do the questions go to the heart of the discipline? (2) Do the questions have no single obviously "correct" answer? (3) Do the questions involve the use of higher order thinking skills (analysis, synthesis, and evaluation)? and (4) Do the questions develop or generate "personalized" interest? Through the use of essential questions Wiggins also believes that educators model the skills a learner needs to develop their own questions. Learners need to develop and refine their questioning skills as part of hypothesis building and testing.

Rakow (1986) states that "open-ended questions, extended wait time, and neutral praise stimulate students to think more divergently, to give more complete answers, and to participate in classroom discussions" (p. 17). Questions in the discovery approach should therefore be designed to encourage reflection, provide subtasks when the original problem is recognized as too difficult, and evaluate learners' understanding regularly. Additionally, questions should be designed to assist students in learning about how they learn or think (metacognition).

Socratic and probing questions are very useful strategies in the discovery process. **Socratic questions** are based on the belief that an educator should never tell a learner what to think but should act as a catalyst for the growth of the student's ideas. Socratic questioning is guided by the belief that the educator must first elicit from the learner a statement of belief or opinion that can then be tested. This may be accomplished by employing a simple expository statement, by asking learners to express their belief or opinion, or by using a springboard technique. Once this has been done, probing questions should be implemented to examine the situation, belief, or opinion.

Probing questions are designed to stimulate learners to think about the problem and to consider the implications of their solutions. Good and Brophy (1984) believe "probing techniques should be gentle ways to focus student's attention and to help them think" (p. 9). These probing questions should attempt to solicit certain answers while challenging learners to examine their own ideas and beliefs. Probing questions need to be brainstormed before the lesson delivery because they need to be asked in a logical sequence; using off-the-cuff questions will confuse the learning process. Well-developed, logically sequenced questions aid learners in developing their own ideas while leading them to the educator's predetermined concept, principle, or abstraction.

Phrasing

Questions developed for use with the discovery approach need to assist learners in discovering key concepts, patterns, principles, or abstractions, Therefore, in phrasing discovery questions, educators should be sure they have developed questions to enable the lesson to proceed as planned, help students learn how to accomplish the task at hand, and allow assessment (of both lesson and students) on a continual basis. As in the expository approach, phrasing should be clear and focused on the ability level of the student to whom it is targeted. The question should create disequilibrium within the learner's thought process without causing confusion or frustration.

Sequence

The use of carefully sequenced questions by the educator during this exploration by learners facilitates the discovery process. Discussions that follow the exploration bring out the new understandings and concepts. Whether it is primary-grade children constructing sets of objects on their way to understanding multiplication or high school students finding out about civil rights in twentieth-century America, guided discovery experiences have tremendous value for all learners if they are structured in a developmentally appropriate sequence.

Taba (1967) maintains that when questions are sequenced appropriately, educators can program cognitive processes. Questions should be sequenced in a manner that stimulates learners' processing information. Taba's questioning strategies are based on the belief that learners need to be able to complete three cognitive tasks to successfully generate principles, patterns, and abstractions.

To facilitate cognitive task 1, *concept formation*, the educator must develop questions that stimulate learners to enumerate and list, group together, and label items using common characteristics. Questions may include: *What did you see? What did you hear? Which things go together? Why did you decide they went together?* (Lemlech, 1994). *Data interpretation*, cognitive task 2, is encouraged by asking learners questions that help them identify points, explain or describe identified information, and develop inferences or generalizations. These are questions such as: *What did you notice? What did you discover? Why did this event happen? What conclusions do you draw from the information? Why?* (Lemlech, 1994). Cognitive task 3, *application of principles, abstractions, and concepts*, can be developed through the following types of questions: *What might happen if . . . ? Why do you think that would occur?* (Lemlech, 1994). Cognitive task 3 questions enable learners to predict consequences, explain unfamiliar phenomena, test their thinking, and support and verify predictions or hypotheses (Bellon, Bellon, & Blank, 1992). Ornstein (1987) points out that using Taba's questioning strategies can take several days to complete but will lead to qualitative changes in learners' thought processes.

Wait Time

Appropriate **wait time** is an essential feature in the sequencing of questions in the discovery approach. Research demonstrates that increased wait time improves the quality of learners' answers (Rowe, 1986). Since the very nature of discovery learning is to increase the quality of the learners' thought processes, it seems only logical that wait time must be taken into consideration in sequencing questions. Bellon, Bellon, and Blank (1992) emphasize that learners "give more complex answers, provide more logical arguments, and are willing to speculate" (p. 319). Additionally, with appropriate wait time, learners reduce their need to compete with their responses and the communication pattern within the class becomes much more student centered.

Practice

Using Joan Potts's lesson about *ie* and *ei*, classify her questions to learners as stimulating cognitive task 1, 2, or 3. Were the questions se-quenced appropriately? If no question was asked for a particular cognitive task, develop one.

Selection of Respondents

The importance of establishing an environment in which learners feel free to respond is magnified in the discovery approach. By its nature, the discovery approach produces a greater level of participation than does the expository approach. In the selection of respondents, the educator needs to be sure to not allow a single student or a small group of learners to monopolize discussion or answers. For the discovery method to work effectively, diversity is needed. Divergent responses create a thinking environment, one in which learners begin to look at others' points of view in an attempt to clarify their own.

Handling Correct and Incorrect Responses

All the question types discussed in this section are divergent in nature. As such, they encourage a diversity of responses and therefore variation in the way in which answers are handled. **Divergent questions** require the learner to expand on what she or he knows already through analysis and synthesis. Incorrect responses to divergent questions need to be viewed not as wrong but as an opportunity for the educator to gently redirect the learner's thinking.

As noted earlier by Rakow, the educator's responses to learners' replies are perhaps more important than the original questions. Educators' responses must encourage learners to explore further or reevaluate their replies. The most typical communication cycle in a learning event involves the educator's question, a learner's response, and some form of reaction by the teacher to the student's answer. Gage and Berliner (1984) point out that what an educator says to or about the learner's response may clarify, expand, synthesize, or evaluate it. Thus educators' responses should never be negative in nature. Learners will not venture speculative ideas when the fear of being judged or evaluated is present (Bellon, Bellon, & Blank, 1992).

STUDENT ASSESSMENT AND EVALUATION

Student assessment and evaluation in a discovery setting reflects current changes that are taking place in the curriculum and methods of instruction. More actual life activities and meaningful outcomes are becoming part of the assessment process, including hands-on performance tests and community-based activities designed for a wider range of student abilities (Wiggins, 1989; Gardner, 1989). Rating scales of critical thinking, demonstrations, simulations, and portfolios are gradually replacing formal pencil-and-paper tests as assessment techniques (Stiggins, 1988; Gardner, 1989; Berk, 1986; Wolf, 1989). In most situations, the transition to these more authentic forms of student assessment involves collaboration among school psychologists, classroom teachers, special educators, therapists, and even assessment specialists (Peterson, LeRoy, Field, & Wood, 1992).

If educators have prepared a comprehensive lesson objective, the evaluation statement will indicate the criteria for student success and guide them in conducting any form of planned assessment. However, one important feature of discovery teaching must be considered in developing assessment techniques. Whereas in an expository lesson educators present the new concept or generalization in clear form to the learners, in a discovery lesson they do not (Jacobsen, Eggen, & Kauchak, 1993). Because of the more intrinsic source of motivation for learning characteristic of discovery activities, it is easier for learners themselves to self-assess and record accurate information about their own learning. For example, if a group of learners are keeping a record of the occurrence of different cloud types over their school, their daily drawings and corresponding labels can serve as self-corrective features of their learning and reinforce their understanding of the cloud types. As a result, the learners may, at various times during the discovery activity, demonstrate their learning at the expected level of mastery. In fact, learning and assessment often occur simultaneously, requiring the educator to observe and evaluate continuously (Sizer, 1986).

This outcome suggests that educators must change their thinking about assessment so that they can observe and note student learning throughout the activity, not just at a designated test time or assessment phase. This formative approach to assessment is a major aspect of discovery teaching and is facilitated when learners are organized into pairs or small groups, mainly because the educator can observe more individual learning here than in a whole class format. This style of assessment, however, does not preclude the implementation of a summative assessment near the end of the instructional period. In fact, it invites educators to customize the summative assessment and challenge certain individual learners to demonstrate more complex levels of understanding. At some point in their work, learners can be challenged to think more complexly by being asked to explain why they think a particular drawing is actually a certain type of cloud or what might happen if there were two different types of clouds in the same sky. Educators can assess thinking beyond the stated objective in situations such as these because they have structured the activity to allow learners to self-assess. They can also extend their assessment to include learners' metacognitive behavior by having students detail the steps they used to come up with their response.

Observing learners as a means of assessment is a skill that requires a committed effort from educators. Cullen and Pratt (1992) offer several suggestions to educators who wish to become better users of observation as an assessment tool. First, it is important to revisit the literature on child development and become reacquainted with the developmental characteristics (cognitive, affective, and psychomotor) of the learners under observation. Second, observations must be carefully planned. The desired behavior(s), means of recording information, and time/location for observations must be predetermined to make the observations useful. Third, during the observations, only those behaviors directly related to the desired behavior should be objectively recorded, avoiding any interpretation of what the child is doing. The learner ideally should be observed working both independent of teachers and during a teaching activity for a later comparison. Details of how the learner is actually performing a certain task may be helpful as long as these details do not include interpretations. Fourth, group projects may be used as settings for observing not only academic performance, but interpersonal skills as well. The two areas of learning are interdependent and should both be assessed carefully. Fifth, cooperative learning and peer tutoring settings should be used as opportunities to implement peer evaluation, particularly with learners above third grade. If all learners are helped to understand the procedures for observation, they can provide each other with valuable observational data.

Reflect for a Moment

Having one learner evaluate another learner in some way is a strategy that some of your peers might not accept. What do you think?

Stiggins (1994) presents four assessment options, three of which are appropriate for the many complex responses from learners that often characterize a discovery activity. The four options are selected response, essay, performance, and personal communication. Selected responses include the traditional multiple choice, true-false, matching, and fill-in items. Essays and performances are self-explanatory. Personal communication includes conversations, questioning, interviews, conferences, and other exchanges between teachers and learners or even between learners. Although all four may be useful in discovery lessons, the selected response option falls short in assessing reasoning and application of skills. The performance and personal communication options, however, are both highly effective and accurate options for assessing the wide range of cognitive learning that typically occurs during discovery lessons. In assessing affective outcomes, often critical in cooperative learning groups and peer tutoring, Stiggins (1994) recommends that even though all four options may be used, caution should be exercised in considering the performance option. If performance is poor, affect may or may not be a contributing factor.

One increasingly popular strategy for gathering and evaluating information about student learning is the development of a portfolio. Although there are endless ways to use portfolios, Arter and Spandel (1992) provide four basic guidelines for the successful implementation of a portfolio assessment strategy. First, there need to be clear guidelines for deciding what materials will go into the portfolio. Otherwise, it can become a disorganized and confusing experience for all concerned. Second, learners must have a major role in the process of material selection and portfolio discussion. Third, there must, of course, be a well-understood set of criteria for evaluating the portfolio materials, both individually and as a total package. If the criteria are comprehensive and cohesive, they can also help educators and learners reflect on the evaluation process itself. Fourth, if the portfolio includes a substantial opportunity for learners to examine their own educational progress, it can help them become more aware of how much they can influence their own learning.

Taking these guidelines into account, the discovery teaching strategy appears to be an excellent candidate for portfolio assessment and evaluation, but by no means the only candidate. Teacher and peer observation is critical to effective assessment and evaluation during discovery activities. Student and teacher reflection after discovery activities is also of great value during the process. In short, although traditional objective pencil-and-paper tests may have some use, there are several informal assessment procedures that should take priority in planning any discovery lesson.

Practice

Use the lesson outline on the classification of animals to design an evaluation procedure for learners. The procedure should include:
- Formative and summative procedures
- Specific criteria for evaluation throughout the procedure
- At least three levels of complexity
- At least two of the options outlined by Stiggins (1994)
- Evidence of learner self-assessment
- Selection of materials for a portfolio used to keep parents informed of learners' progress on a biweekly basis

---

TEACHER REFLECTIONS: EFFECTIVENESS OF THE LESSON

The nature of a discovery lesson lends itself to both teacher and learner reflection. The educator's reflection can take place during and after the activity and should result in more effectively planned future discovery lessons. An educator who evaluates the quality of learners' performance must use the lesson's objective(s), criteria, and standards as a basis for judgments. Educators themselves need to conduct self-evaluations that are both formative and summative.

Formative evaluation occurs during the lesson and helps educators maintain a high rate of success in the learning event. This can be accomplished through the use of self-questioning as the lesson progresses. Questions include: *Am I making myself clear? Are my examples logical? Am I interceding too often or much in the learners' independent investigations? Am I talking too fast? Too slow?*

Summative evaluation provides educators with a systematic method of reflection on their teaching so that future improvements can be made. This form of reflection has a set of predetermined goals. After the lesson is completed, the educator must reflect carefully on the examples and questions she or he used to direct the process of discovery. Were they effective? How might they have been sequenced differently? Were they sufficient to allow the learners to work independently? In addition, the educator needs to examine the pace of the discovery lesson.

It is clearly imperative for educators to develop a systematic series of questions to help guide their reflection. While some of the reflective questions included in Table 9.2 (Chapter 9) are applicable to discovery lessons, Table 10.3 provides a separate set of questions that, taken together, can aid educators in reflecting specifically on discovery lesson effectiveness.

TABLE 10.3   Reflective Questions for Discovery Teaching

1. If necessary, was prior student learning assessed?
2. At the outset, were exciting and provocative materials or a challenging, relevant question presented to learners?
3. Were examples and nonexamples organized carefully (from simple to more complex) ahead of time?
4. Were learners grouped in a manner that provided for active and positive participation for all?
5. Were there student questions or responses that could have redirected the learning for some or all learners? How were these questions or responses integrated into the activity?
6. At what point(s) during the examination of examples and nonexamples did learners encounter difficulty? What adjustments were made, and with what results?
7. Were there materials not present that would have improved learner understanding?
8. Was there adequate time for the discussion following the discovery activity? If not, how will you adjust the next lesson?
9. In examining the assessment and evaluation procedures, were the criteria clearly stated? Were all learners, regardless of their ability, challenged to think?
10. How did learners monitor their own learning? How did they self-assess?
11. If cooperative learning or peer tutoring was used, what affective outcomes were achieved?
12. Was observation used to assess learners? Were the observation procedures specific enough?
13. Were adaptations used? How did they contribute to student learning?
14. How did learners apply their learning to a real world task?

SUMMARY

Discovery teaching relies on the educator's ability to guide students to learn independently, to understand facts, rules and concepts through a logical process they themselves create. Like expository teaching, discovery teaching is teacher directed and relies on questions the teacher develops.

But where expository teaching is deductive, discovery teaching is inductive. Because learners seek information in discovery lessons, they are often more motivated, and have more opportunities to analyze and manipulate information. Educators, however, must structure the lesson carefully to aid learners in the discovery process. They must organize questions and concepts hierarchically, and use appropriate increments of understanding throughout the lesson. They also must utilize the collaborative opportunities inherent during discovery lessons. The discovery classroom is an active learning environment with a variety of instructional materials and techniques. Learners' ideas are the critical component in discovery lessons.

Both formative and summative evaluation are important in discovery teaching. Adaptations can be found in instructional materials and procedures, the use of cooperative learning and peer tutoring, and in techniques of assessment as well. Questioning is vital to discovery teaching because the questions guide learners to their understandings, so planning questions carefully is essential. Wait time is particularly important when questioning during a discovery lesson, and its effective use will increase the number of learners who actively participate during a given lesson.

Because discovery teaching invites more intrinsic motivation in the learner, student self-assessment techniques (portfolios, reflective journals) are encouraged.

11

THE INQUIRY APPROACH

Key Terms

Advanced organizer
Alternative path
Attention-gaining technique
Brainstorming
Conceptual movement
Critical thinking
Decision-making organization
Deductive question
Fluent thinking

Flexible thinking
Inductive question
Instructional variety
Networking organization
Problem-centered organization
Reflective thinking
Self-evaluation
Student-directed

Objectives

After completing this chapter, the reader will be able to:

1. Define the inquiry approach.
2. Identify when to use the inquiry approach.
3. Examine the connections between effective teaching research and the inquiry approach.
4. Develop inquiry teaching lessons.
5. Incorporate appropriate adaptations into an inquiry lesson plan.
6. Develop appropriate questioning strategies.
7. Formulate appropriate student assessment strategies.
8. Incorporate personal reflection into inquiry teaching.

PROFILES OF INQUIRY TEACHING

Mai Lin

If the media hype about poor children and dead-end education was to be believed, most of the children in the fourth and fifth grade cluster at Astronaut Elementary were prime candidates. At least three out of four came from homes with one parent. Well over half were eligible for free breakfast and lunch services. The unemployment rate in the metropolitan Davis County area was over 10 percent. All of the signals for school failure were present, according to the "research."

Yet over the past five years Mai Lin had seen a gradual change in climate in the Astronaut neighborhood. More families were coming to the monthly conferences. Donations from area businesses were higher every year. Teachers were no longer looking for transfers. Reports from the district middle school and high school were coming back to Ms. Evans, the principal at Astronaut, about the positive traits of former Astronaut students. Mai knew it had something to do with the transition to inquiry learning that had taken place at the school. Actually the transition was still taking place, and though most of the teachers knew that not everything would be ideally suitable for inquiry teaching, they had come to appreciate the changes, both academic and behavioral, they had observed in the students. They were excited about the research currently going on in Mai's fourth and fifth grade classroom, and several had asked her to schedule a time so that students could share their studies with other classes.

Mai had begun to integrate popular culture into the curriculum, and her collaborative team had liked her ideas for organizing the class into cooperative groups. Although there were probably seven or eight students in the class whose problems with the curriculum challenged Mai in one way or another, she had requested a meeting with the special educator to discuss adaptations for just two of them. When Jeff Ward, the special educator for the fourth-fifth clusters, met with Mai to plan adaptations for Heather and Adam, he saw that Mai was becoming more and more confident about working with the full range of students. When the inquiry groups had decided on their respective strategies, she had volunteered to meet with the adults in the community whom students wished to visit so they would feel ready when the students came to meet with them.

The community volunteer program at Astronaut, spearheaded by Ms. Evans and supported by the teachers, had been a huge success. Most teachers could count on having an extra pair of skilled, compassionate hands on a daily basis, and whenever a special event arose that warranted more help, the coordinator, Sam Minor, had been able to turn to a pool of community members identified just for that purpose. Mai was so grateful for the volunteers who worked with the students in her classroom; this volunteer program was a critical component of the successful transition to inquiry teaching taking place in each of the classrooms.

One of the most important features of the inquiry program, Mai learned, was careful planning of each activity. She had initially spent several weeks actively teaching, demonstrating, and coaching students through the inquiry process. Their reaction had really surprised her; they loved the idea of making so many decisions on their own. Mai knew, too, that her responsibility was to design the experiences so that all students acquired the necessary knowledge and developed the requisite skills as set forth in the state guidelines and/or students' IEPs. Planning was critical.

Mai knew that the culture around these students, the urban life of Davis County, was their reality. But she also knew that there was a pulse in that urban life, a spirit that she could draw from when she chose the themes for the year. She knew that a theme of health and nutrition would be both relevant and challenging for part of the year. Students almost immediately began raising questions about what they ate at school, about what the school was doing to improve the environment in the neighborhood, about how television viewing influenced their physical and mental health. She and two other adults met to discuss the ways in which the fourth and fifth grade curriculum goals could be served during inquiries into these issues. Jeff met with the three adults to discuss adaptations for certain learners, including alternative objectives and responsibilities, and then the three adults met again to determine the placement of students in each group. They all knew that adjustments would later be likely but felt confident about moving ahead with the theme. Then the adults met with each group of students to discuss the potential for an inquiry into their concerns. Each group was charged with the responsibility for devising a question, a set of hypotheses, and a procedure for gathering data. Mai and her colleagues established a tentative timeline and shared it with students.

The climate was a serious one, but there was a ripple of excitement as students gathered with each other to begin mapping out their investigations. If this inquiry was anything like past efforts, Mai knew that there would be fantastic strides in cognitive and social learning for all students.

Sally Ossian

How on earth had she gotten so far behind? Here it was April, the Iowas were a month away, the CRTs coming up, too, and Sally hadn't gotten even halfway through the math book! Parents had been sending notes with their children, asking to see some of their worksheets. Tom Clark, the principal, had suggested that Sally seek help from Ann Haviland and Megan McConnell, the two other second grade teachers. But Sally knew that she could not live with herself if she had to rule over the students the way those two did. They were actually mean at times, and the students looked like they were miserable. These teachers certainly didn't believe that there was anything needed to teaching reading beyond the basal, and they loaded the students up with worksheets and dittos every day. Sally had been taught not to rely on dittos, but she was beginning to panic.

The opening had come up suddenly, in late August, and Sally had been in the right place at the right time. In the two weeks before school started, she had hurriedly gathered together a collection of materials she thought would help students investigate the change of seasons. She had managed to identify some math and language arts objectives that could be reached during a study of the changing seasons, and felt that the topic was perfect for the early fall in northern Minnesota. Now, as she looked back to that first month, Sally began to wonder if she had made the wrong decisions.

Well, maybe she didn't know the students very well at the outset, but after all, she was new and had only been in the community for two weeks before school started. It had taken her two months to find out who among the students in her class had been classified because the special education director was so far behind with the placements. Sally wondered if those special education programs were really worth all the trouble. The two other second grade teachers were polite but really standoffish, and Sally had been warned by the art teacher not to make waves with either of them. Mr. Clark had patted her on the back and told her not to worry about that; she would do just fine. He even showed her the maps and construction paper that had been left behind in the room she now occupied. He seemed nice enough, but when Sally raised the possibility of starting a community volunteer program to help support her plans for inquiry activities, he suggested she just wait a while and see what happened. Then Sally had asked him point blank if she could plan a few inquiry activities. He had said, "Sure! Who knows, maybe something will come of it!"

So Sally had struck out on her own and patched together her curriculum for the inquiry into the changing seasons. The students had struggled with the process, but Sally figured this was only beginning-of-the-year sluggishness and launched into a second inquiry, this time focusing on poetry. She was really excited about the way she had integrated social studies, science, and even music into the inquiry. By late November, the students were asking when they would start in their spelling books, complaining that they were tired of poetry. So Sally switched to another inquiry, just in time for the holiday season. Students were excited, but she was not sure if it was about the upcoming holiday or the inquiry into international festivals. Around mid-January parents began sending notes, asking to see the work their children had done in school. Sally proudly wrote back to each one, describing the inquiry approach to them and assuring them that their children were doing more important and worthwhile things than worksheets and dittos.

When Sally and the class stumbled to the end of another inquiry, she wondered if she should change the groupings. She also wondered if she shouldn't expect at least something from Leroy and Angie, the two students who had been classified but stayed in her class most of the day. They weren't disruptive, but they didn't do much, either. By February, Sally wasn't sure if any students were really getting much out of the attempts at inquiry. Even those who had started out the year energetic and bright eyed looked confused and frustrated whenever Sally asked them how they could find an answer. They were also very upset because, in a bold move, they had tried to get information from a local family who had recently arrived from El Salvador and couldn't understand anything the family said to them.

Now several students were complaining about the absence of worksheets. Others were bickering about who would do what, none of them wanting to do anything. Sally was on the verge of tears.

Reflect for a Moment

Look back over the two profiles. What are some of the reasons that Mai Lin's classroom is so vibrant and energized? In turn, what are some of the reasons that Sally's classroom is deteriorating?

INQUIRY TEACHING

Sally Ossian was struggling with the implementation of the inquiry approach, but it was clearly not the only struggle she faced professionally. Mai Lin, on the other hand, was seeing the benefits of years of work in the inquiry activities taking place at Astronaut Elementary. Although inquiry learning has many important characteristics, we must mainly remember that in the real world new information is found only through inquiry. This seemingly simple declaration presents the strongest rationale for using the inquiry approach as educators and learners. No highly sophisticated minority of scientists holds the patent on inquiry, either. Every day, people the world over conduct inquiries: the handyman trying to find a leak in the water system, the two-year-old searching for her blanket, the fifth grade teacher experimenting with ways to introduce a new lesson. Because humans instinctively seek new knowledge in an effort to improve their lives, the eternal inquirer resides in us all.

Reflect for a Moment

Consider a problem you have encountered during the past week. If the problem was important enough, you pursued it. What outcome did you expect (hypothesis)? How did you proceed to resolve the issue? Did you succeed?

Yet in spite of the universal need to seek new information, one of the major concerns among educational leaders is the lack of self-direction among young learners. The various curriculum areas all have their buzzwords—"critical thinking," "creative expression," "logical reasoning"—but "self-directed seeking of new knowledge" is too often missing from the list. Even advanced graduate students often feel more concern to fulfill requirements than hunger to search for new directions and answers. The inquiring learner is in seriously short supply. Learners need to raise more questions and search out more answers if they are to acquire and maintain intellectual strategies that can sustain them through countless challenging problems, both personal and professional, over a lifetime. They need frequent opportunities, from an early age, to actively use their innate inquiring behaviors in a wide variety of contexts, both in and out of the formal school setting. Developing this intellectual curiosity, resulting in specific inquiry skills, is the overall goal of inquiry teaching.

Although inquiry learning has obviously been around for as long as humankind has, the application of inquiring behavior to a teaching methodology has only been a recent development. Dewey (1910) proposed a teaching model that has remained the most accepted to date. Dewey's version of inquiry teaching includes problem identification, hypothesizing, gathering data, analyzing data to test hypotheses, and forming conclusions. Suchman (1962) is generally given credit for designing a teaching model, called the Suchman Inquiry method, that capitalizes on the inquiry skills and language that are characteristic of more naturalistic inquiries in everyday life. Suchman, after studying the techniques used by creative researchers, based his model on the scientific method. He applied such procedures as identification of the problem, stating hypotheses, gathering and analyzing data, and offering conclusions and recommendations to a classroom instructional sequence and encouraged its use with lessons that focused on creative thinking and problem solving. Since its introduction to the educational community, **inquiry teaching** has been effective with both elementary and secondary students with and without disabilities (Voss, 1982; Elefant, 1980).

Of all four approaches to instruction, the reflective educator is perhaps most visible in the inquiry approach. Discovery and inquiry teaching alike assume that the learner is actively seeking new information, not passively accepting it from the educator. Both approaches are firmly focused on the process of problem solving. A major difference between discovery and inquiry teaching, however, is who determines the problem to be solved (Kellough & Roberts, 1994). In guided discovery lessons, the educator often presents the problem and the means to solve it to learners. They usually reach the solution in part because the educator has already determined it and is intent on guiding learners through a series of questions and steps to that end. This character of discovery teaching makes it particularly useful in teaching new rules, principles, and concepts.

True **inquiry learning**, on the other hand, occurs when learners become creators of the problem and architects of the process they will use in trying to find a solution. In this manner, the stimulus or event that initiates the inquiry already has a puzzling and meaningful nature, acting as a lure in the minds of the learners (Joyce, Weil, & Showers, 1992).

Reflect for a Moment

Have you ever had a class or experience where you had to come up with the problem yourself? Was it a little disconcerting, at least at first? Many learners are so accustomed to being given information that they find it difficult to design their own learning.

In developing his model, Suchman used initial events with outcomes that made it difficult for learners not to pursue explanations and answers. In such situations, learners genuinely feel they must find out why something is the way it is. Science demonstrations are ideal for the inquiry approach, but all traditional subject areas have similar, mentally disruptive episodes. During these inquiry activities, learners also begin to understand that many problems have only tentative solutions that are open to change. These problems themselves are closer to real-life situations that learners read about and often experience themselves.

Many inquiry activities of this nature take the form of individual and group projects and are often conducted more independently of the educator than any of the other teaching/learning approaches described in this text. Learners usually brainstorm possible solutions and construct ways to test out each one. Critical thinking skills practiced during the inquiry process include recognizing the problem, organizing and analyzing data, controlling variables, being alert for discrepancies, suspending judgment, synthesizing data into a model, and drawing tentative conclusions. This type of decision-making experience can help all learners cope with the often vague realities of true-life problems (Kellough & Roberts, 1994).

There are, then, a number of characteristics that belong to inquiry teaching. The first is emphasis on process. Although the eventual outcome of an inquiry activity certainly has value as an important solution or conclusion, the process of learning that takes place during an inquiry activity has far greater value to the learner. This is because of the variety of thinking behaviors that are called on during the activity and the unlimited demand for these behaviors in real-life situations that the learner will continually face throughout her or his life. Second is the link to higher-order thinking. Perhaps more than any other approach, the inquiry process focuses on problem solving and thus relies consistently on complex cognitive behaviors. In all inquiry lessons, a problem is defined, hypotheses are generated, data are gathered and analyzed, and conclusions are formed. All of these basic steps in inquiry learning require thinking behaviors beyond the knowledge and comprehension levels of Bloom's cognitive taxonomy.

A third significant feature of inquiry learning is the extent of student-centered activity. As mentioned earlier, a true inquiry begins with a problem generated by learners. Even when the educator has input in defining the problem, learners are the leaders in the learning process throughout the inquiry experience. The fourth and perhaps most important characteristic of inquiry learning is its interdisciplinary nature (Martinello & Cook, 1994). By its very nature, genuine inquiry always draws from more than one area of knowledge. Martinello & Cook (1994) use the ripple image to symbolize the expanding opportunities for learning that the many questions in an inquiry activity present. They also point out the value of creativity in developing and maintaining enthusiasm and divergent thought during inquiry experiences. Clearly, then, a fifth major characteristic of the inquiry approach to teaching and learning is creative thinking.

Reflect for a Moment

What are some problems our major political leaders face today? Select one and identify how the different characteristics of inquiry learning are present in determining a solution.

Inquiry teaching offers learners other opportunities as well. Because of the tentative nature of any knowledge gained, they will gain a greater understanding and tolerance of ambiguity. They will extend their own thinking to include the points of view of others because problems are explored in small groups. Further, they will begin to realize that they have the ability to plan a method themselves in order to answer their own questions or to solve problems. The inquiry process in action offers these and other benefits to both educators and learners.

How Inquiry Teaching Is Used

If an observer were to visit a classroom where the inquiry approach was being used, chances are the room would be empty. In some instances, inquiry teaching requires educators and learners to be outside the classroom, seeking the information they need to understand the problem or question that has gained their attention. Although most educators are bound to certain curriculum guidelines, the inquiry process can elevate the cognitive climate used to pursue those curriculum mandates. For example, during a unit of study on the settling of the western United States, the question of what happened to all of the Native American peoples and their homes can be the impetus to an inquiry activity. As they learn about the settlers and their struggles, learners can also investigate the plight of indigenous peoples and use outside sources to gather information. To pursue such an inquiry, learners will have to visit museums and college libraries, and track down historians or historical societies that can offer accurate historical information related to the problem.

Of course, in most cases learners will be in the classroom, but even though problem identification, data analysis, and reporting of conclusions usually occurs there, the data gathering that is necessary in most cases will require learners to go elsewhere. In most elementary classrooms, learners work in pairs or small groups during the inquiry process because there is usually a need to share both the responsibilities of the investigation and their findings before concluding the study. In some cases, the entire class can engage in researching one basic question or problem; in other cases, it is more feasible for small groups to investigate different problems or aspects of a larger problem. For instance, if a second grade class of some twenty-five students generated several questions about recycling efforts in their school, it might be valuable for one group to generate hypotheses and gather data related to materials being recycled while a second group generates hypotheses and gathers data related to what happens to these materials, a third group works on how much of each material is recycled per day, and a fourth group investigates the actual benefits of the school's recycling efforts over a month's time.

Reflect for a Moment

Surely you went out of the classroom to conduct an inquiry when you were in elementary school. What was the problem or question? How did you organize yourselves to go out and study it?

Such inquiries are characterized both by an initial series of questions and problems and, after generating hypotheses, by another stream of problems and questions during the gathering of information. The logistics of organizing the data collection phase are often quite demanding of learners, and they have to make myriad decisions for the data collection to be successful. Such responsibilities also require the educators involved to have carefully prepared lesson procedures in place so that they can advise learners whenever necessary.

The role of the educator in the inquiry approach is that of facilitator. However, as in the discussion approach (Chapter 12), the educator must also be prepared to actively teach learners the skills and language helpful to a successful inquiry process. When educators are teaching learners to use inquiry skills and language, it is helpful to use a simple inquiry problem so that learners can concentrate on acquiring the necessary skills and language. On the other hand, Joyce, Weil, and Showers (1992) warn educators not to use a problem for inquiry unless it is a genuinely puzzling event for learners. If educators use any interesting question as an inquiry exercise, they can end up with little more than a series of questions leading to an answer.

Another important responsibility of the educator in the inquiry approach is to monitor the gathering of data. Learners who lack experience in the inquiry approach are often inclined to dismiss certain hypotheses or variables in the data before they have sufficient evidence to do so. Educators must check students' analyses while they are being conducted and watch for unsupported or premature decision making of this nature. Yet another role for the educator in an inquiry session is help learners see as much as possible in the information they gather. For example, learners who are examining different cloud types on the playground should be encouraged not only to identify the cloud type, but to observe how the cloud moves over time, how the appearance of the cloud changes over time, and what relationship the cloud has to the environment around it. Many additional bits of information can and should be gathered to help learners more fully understand the specific information they are primarily gathering.

Finally, when it is time for learners to form their conclusions based on their thorough examinations of the data, educators may need to be ready to ask probing questions that will encourage learners to think more deeply about their conclusions and even about their data. A successful inquiry depends on the abilities of group members to articulate the often complex explanations they have found for the problem or problems they originally investigated.

Because inquiry learning almost always involves an integration of traditional subject matter, any educator conducting such a lesson is wise to identify the curricular relevance of the inquiry along several lines of subject area content or goals. This multidisciplinary feature of inquiry teaching also lends a wonderful flexibility to the scheduling problems so common to many educators.

When Inquiry Teaching Can Be Used

Inquiry activities can be scheduled flexibly as long as educators can construct experiences that clearly draw from several subject areas. Thematic curriculum, described in an earlier chapter, is a highly compatible context for inquiry learning, not only because of the flexible scheduling it allows but also because of its inherent multidisciplinary character, which constantly raises questions and problems for inquiry. For instance, when Mai Lin and her colleagues at Astronaut Elementary School planned a thematic unit on seacoasts, they found themselves frequently stumbling across genuine inquiry questions that required learners to work on several curriculum goals as they searched for their answers. (Is there more sand now than there was five hundred years ago? Why or why not? What job opportunities have emerged as a result of people's use of the seacoasts?)

The reader has by now deduced that inquiry learning is not a particularly appropriate vehicle for teaching basic facts, rules, and other lower-level cognitive

information. However, when educators are seeking to increase the demands on learners' higher-level thinking behaviors, including analytical thinking, critical thinking, creative thinking, and problem solving, an inquiry experience is highly appropriate. The caution described earlier in this chapter against unchallenging questions and problems is still important to keep in mind. Inquiry learning will not take place if the question presented for study can be answered without true investigation from learners. For example, a fifth grade teacher working on a unit on the solar system believed that the students were asking some questions that warranted an inquiry activity. One student asked if humans could live on Venus, and another wondered how long it would take to get to Jupiter in a spaceship. Although both are valuable questions, neither needs an inquiry process primarily because the answers are readily available. What the educator expected to be a valuable research study ended in 5 minutes when students read about Venus and Jupiter in the encyclopedia.

One indication of whether a problem or question warrants an inquiry is whether educators themselves know the answer. Although some inquiry processes are posed by educators, they themselves may not fully understand the precise solution or answer. In other situations, educators may know the answer, but the problem and/or the process may be intriguing enough to learners and well enough understood by educators to warrant an inquiry activity.

The inquiry approach presents a very appropriate model of instruction whenever educators are seeking an opportunity for learners to collaborate. As mentioned earlier, practically every inquiry activity requires more than one learner to participate in hypothesizing, gathering data, analyzing information, and generating logical conclusions and recommendations. Many experienced learners are able to readily initiate inquiry sessions and organize themselves as a group prepared to proceed with a study. In this manner, with experienced learners inquiry activities may occur unexpectedly at any time in the classroom. The confident and well-organized educator, having a fairly thorough understanding of and appreciation for the advantages of the inquiry experience, can usually respond constructively to these impromptu requests.

What type of student can successfully participate in an inquiry activity? With adequate inquiry skill acquisition, all learners can initiate and engage in inquiry learning regardless of their age or ability. If the curriculum is developmentally appropriate for the learners present, then inquiry opportunities will arise rather naturally in the course of instruction. Cooperative learning groups are a frequent occurrence when inquiry activities take place; when shared responsibility and problem solving are primary goals, inquiry lessons are an appropriate instructional approach. Furthermore, if educators are interested in goals and objectives that focus on the process of learning rather than a specific outcome, then inquiry experiences can serve the purpose well.

Reflect for a Moment

Reflect back to an investigation you participated in as a younger student. Do you remember the other students involved? Who did what? Did certain students dom-

inate? Were any particularly good at cooperating? Do students in general need more opportunities to build these collaborative skills?

Finally, the inquiry approach can be highly effective in inclusive settings for several reasons. Students with disabilities can always gain tremendous collaborative experience through the inquiry process, whether in pairs, small groups, or as part of a large group inquiry. In addition, the special talents and skills of all learners can be utilized during group inquiry. One learner may contribute more in the area of hypothetical reasoning, and another may provide access to sources needed for data collection; in the inquiry process all group members can contribute in meaningful ways to the success of the effort. Finally, when the inquiry process takes place in an inclusive setting, cognitive challenges occur for all learners that might not otherwise have been possible. Talented educators never underestimate the abilities of learners, and inclusive classrooms provide imminent cognitive benefits for every student.

EFFECTIVE TEACHING

The inquiry approach meets many of the effective teacher behaviors (see Chapter 4 for the complete list) detailed by Borich (1992). Not unlike the discussion or discovery approaches, the inquiry approach relies on the educator's use of **attention-gaining techniques** to get learners interested in finding out more about some event, topic, or phenomenon. Once the lesson is started the educator needs to demonstrate *enthusiasm* in students' discoveries to assure that they remain engaged in inquiry.

Effective teachers plan carefully. Although this approach is student directed, it requires educators to be *creative* and *well prepared* if the lesson is to be successful. In addition to careful planning, effective teachers are also flexible in their management of the classroom. Burden and Byrd (1994) point out that a critical variable in the effective implementation of inquiry learning is the ability of the educator to be flexible in his or her management of the classroom.

Strategies used in the inquiry approach are not very effective in the teaching of specific content because they are *student directed* and more time consuming. There are, however, a variety of situations when the objective cannot be adequately met by either the expository, discovery, or discussion approach. Therefore, goals that involve skills such as applying learned information, developing problem-solving strategies, constructing a concrete foundation for abstract thinking, gaining new experiences, making new discoveries, understanding cause and effect relationships, taking on responsibility for one's own learning, and the ability to analyze, synthesize, and evaluate are well served by the inquiry approach.

The inquiry approach requires an interchange of ideas among learners in small groups that they then share with the educator and the larger class. Inquiry lessons may be conducted in small cooperative groups or between two learners, thus allowing educators the opportunity to move about the room and monitor students' progress. For an inquiry to be effective, there must be a climate of investigation that allows for reflective hypothesizing, respect for the speaker's ideas, and a sharing of both concrete and abstract concepts. When this occurs, inquiry lessons are characterized by:

1. The identification of a problem through recognition of a contradiction
2. Student development of a research objective
3. Interaction among all participants in the collection of data or information
4. Shifting or altering of ideas as data are interpreted and hypotheses are tested
5. The drawing of conclusions or generalizations based on reevaluation of hypotheses

Reflect for a Moment

When do you think a whole class inquiry would be more appropriate than a small group or individual inquiry? When would an inquiry done in pairs be better?

A critical aspect of effective teaching is *instructional variety*. Inquiry teaching employs a variety of different materials, exploration techniques, and evaluation strategies. Educators who effectively implement the inquiry approach must supply learners with a variety of visual aids, reading materials, audiovisual technology, and reference materials from which they can gather information and data.

Student involvement in *active engaged time* is an essential factor of the effective inquiry lesson. Educators must create contradictions in students' knowledge base in order to pique their curiosity, thereby effectively drawing them into the inquiry event. Input from the educator is to be kept at a minimum, used primarily as a means of encouraging learners who normally are not risk takers to become actively involved and thus enhancing student-to-student interactions.

Inquiry learning also uses *learners' ideas*. Educators who use the inquiry approach effectively allow students the opportunity to explore a variety of solutions for resolving a problem. By doing so, they are able to reap the benefits of higher levels of learner participation while also eliciting both critical and creative thinking from students.

The inquiry approach provides learners with the opportunity for *reflective thinking* (see Chapter 4 for more on this topic). Learners are encouraged to develop their own *clarity* by formulating research objectives before initiating an inquiry. Educators give directives to help learners formulate a plan of action to resolve the problem. Review and summary are also provided as needed during the inquiry, most often by the students.

An effective classroom inquiry allows *high rates of successful participation* by all learners. The pace varies as learners develop their ideas or database, consider others' information or data, and rethink their hypotheses. Additionally, students welcome the opportunities that the inquiry approach provides to learn in a **student-directed** manner. As a result of the inquiry approach, students begin to develop and refine their metacognitive skills, through the **self-evaluation** necessary in the testing and reformulation of hypotheses.

PLANNING PROCEDURES

The inquiry or Suchman Inquiry method is based on the assumption that each content area or discipline has vast mysteries awaiting the inquisitive mind. This model then builds on the strategies employed by scientists for solving problems. There are primarily six steps the educator must follow in the development and implementation of an inquiry lesson: (1) the educator selects and researches a problem, (2) the educator presents the problem to the class and reviews, if necessary, the process of inquiry, (3) learners ask questions for the purpose of clarifying their research objective, (4) learners are encouraged to test various hypotheses and formulate a theory, (5) rules or effects related to the theory and how the theory might be verified are discussed, and (6) the process is revisited and the class as a large group discusses the steps they used to solve their research objective (Gunter, Estes, & Schwab, 1990).

Developing a Problem and Reference Materials

The first step an educator must take in formulating an inquiry lesson is to identify a problem for learners to solve. This step requires the educator to carefully examine the content area to determine whether the use of a problem-solving inquiry-based approach is appropriate. Jacobsen, Eggen, and Kauchak (1993) found that problem situations often arise during other lessons that educators must identify to capitalize on this learning opportunity. These problem situations can then be applied at a later date to deepen the conceptual base of a previous lesson.

The next step in the planning stage is to make arrangements for the data-gathering process. The educator must be sure that all needed materials will be available for students' investigation. If the inquiry approach is to yield successful results for learners, they must be able to access all necessary data and equipment. Once these two steps have been completed, the educator is ready to develop the details of the lesson, which begins by creating advance organizers.

Advance Organizers

Although it is a student-centered approach, inquiry requires a great deal of teacher planning. For the most part, teaching behaviors at a higher level of complexity does take more planning. By its nature, the range of content in an inquiry lesson is expansive and complex, so the introduction of the lesson must have well developed structures, such as advance organizers, that organize content into meaningful parts. **Advance organizers** help to ensure that learners have a conceptual preview by providing them with a framework by which they can organize content for later use (Ausubel, 1968; Luiten, Ames, & Aerson, 1980; Borich, 1992). Though their overall purpose remains the same, advance organizers in the inquiry lesson differ dramatically from those discussed in other approaches. Because inquiry learning demands higher levels of thinking, advance organizers for this approach are much more complex and lengthy. Presented orally or in the form of charts and diagrams, they are concepts that must be carefully knitted into the fabric of the lesson to provide an overview of both the immediate problem or contradiction at hand and subsequent related topics to follow (Borich, 1992)—for example, when the educator shows several clips of commercials and/or media events before having the students explore the impact media has on their lives. Advance organizers for inquiry lessons should identify the highest level of behavior resulting from the investigative process.

Reflect for a Moment

What might serve as a good advance organizer if you were going to investigate the cost effectiveness of recycling at your school?

Content

The purpose of inquiry is to stimulate scientific thinking, develop problem-solving skills, enhance learners' metacognitive strategies, and provide an opportunity for students to formulate and ask good questions. Therefore, the content selected must lend itself to critical thinking activities. Content involved in this approach must be something that learners can generate hypotheses about and then work to prove or disprove through the collection and analysis of information or data. An exciting by-product of this strategy is the fact that students learn not only the content directly related to the problem, but also procedures for solving future problems.

Procedure

As the educator moves into the procedural portion of an inquiry lesson, there are several avenues or organizational approaches that can be used. Problem-centered, decision-making, and networking approaches are the three most frequently used (see Table 11.1 and 11.2 for lesson plan examples of each). It is important to note that any one of these three types of organization can be used for the same problem. Educators can select the one that best fits the needs of students in a given situation.

Problem-centered organization identifies in advance the steps needed to solve a particular problem. Learners begin this inquiry by first looking at the problem presented and establishing all possible inconsistencies or incongruities. The educator may trigger this process by asking such questions as, "Why does this happen?" "What causes us to react in this manner?" Such questions help to set the problem. The educator may assist learners by establishing a problem-solving sequence while leaving precise methodology up to them. There are five components to the problem-centered approach: identifying the problem, stating research objectives, collecting data, interpreting results, and drawing conclusions. Learners first

TABLE 11.1   Lesson Plan Format

Unit:
Objective:
Rationale:
Materials:
Advanced organizer:
Content:
Procedure:

> *If a problem-centered approach is used, students will:*
> *Identify problem:* seeing, observing a contradiction
> *State research objectives:* establish a plan of action
> *Collect data:* gather appropriate information
> *Interpret results:* develop patterns in the data
> *Draw conclusions:* reevaluate hypotheses and make generalizations from data.

If a decision-making approach is used:
A question is asked:
If the answer is yes, stop.
If no, move on to next question until a yes response is reached.

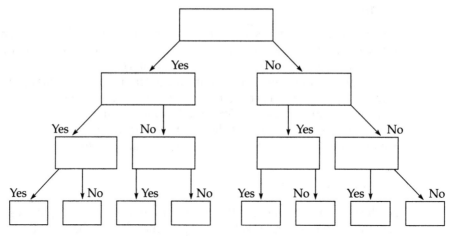

If a networking approach is used:

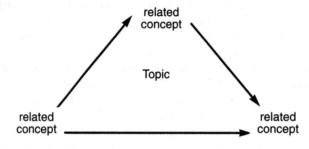

Closure/Conclusions:
Evaluation:

TABLE 11.2　Sample Lesson Plan

Unit:	Plant Life
Objective:	Third and fourth graders will understand the effects of light, water, and oxygen on the growth and development of various plants, so when given a plant type they will be able to identify the relationship between the three elements previously mentioned and growth.
	Students will understand the inquiry process, so when given a problem they will be able to formulate a hypothesis, conduct research, collect and interpret data, and reach a conclusion or solution.
Rationale:	Understanding the impact of water, oxygen, and light on a variety of plant life.
	Understanding the inquiry process will help learners make decisions based on research rather than emotion or unfounded hunches.
Materials:	Textbooks, CD-ROMS, potting soil, pots, seeds, paper, various potted plants, graph paper, encyclopedias, access to library and computer, Farmer's Almanac, planter's guide, other reference materials
Advance organizer:	We have discussed plants for several weeks and you have listed here some things you believe all plants need to survive. However, it appears from some people's observation that not all plants need oxygen, light, and water to survive.
Content:	Some forms of plant life appear not to need the essential elements of light, oxygen, and water. Are these really plants, or is it a misperception that these essentials are not needed?
Procedure:	

If a problem-centered approach is used, the students will:
    Identify problem
    State research objectives
    Collect data
    Interpret results
    Draw conclusions

If a decision-making approach is used:

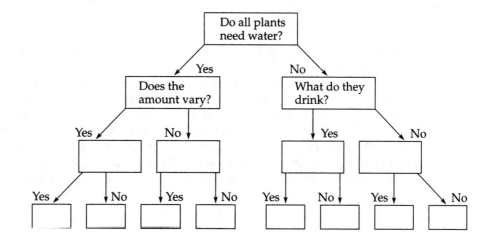

TABLE 11.2 (*continued*)

Learners will generate questions like these until they have systematically explored all their options. The same diagram will be used for oxygen and light.

If a networking approach is used:

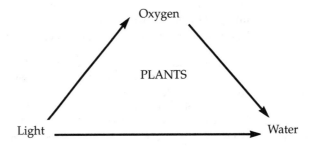

Closure/ Conclusions:	The students will present their findings and discuss their conclusions.
Evaluation:	Using Beyer's eight actions, students will ask themselves the following questions:

1. What method(s) did I use to distinguish between verifiable facts and value claims?
2. How did I distinguish relevant from irrelevant information, claims, or reasons?
3. Were my methods for determining the factual accuracy of a statement efficient?
4. How did I determine the credibility of a source?
5. Have I identified ambiguous claims or arguments?
6. Have I identified unstated assumptions?
7. Is there bias in my solution or methods?
8. How have I determined the strength of my argument or a claim?

identify the problem by looking for or observing contradictions or incongruities in the advance organizer. Once these have been established, each learner must *state his or her research objective(s)*, thus establishing a plan of action for the actual inquiry. The next step in the action plan must always involve the *collection of data*, for only through the gathering of appropriate information can learners move forward to the *interpretation of results*. Through this interpretation learners seek to develop patterns in the data that will assist them through the final stage in the problem-centered approach, *drawing conclusions*. During this final stage students are required to reflect on their original hypotheses and make generalizations from the data (Borich, 1992).

The same problem or dilemma can be organized using **decision-making organization**. In this approach learners organize their inquiry by using internal branching, or steps, that must be completed in a heirarchial fashion in order to reach a final conclusion. The decision-making approach differs from the problem-centered approach in that it focuses on **alternative paths** rather than a straight linear path. During their inquiry students set up a series of questions that, depending on the answers, cause them to go off in different directions. This approach can be used in a large or small group with each student contributing a branch to investigate.

The third type of organization, **networking**, provides both educator and learners with a way of structuring and organizing the lesson in advance. By building a pictorial representation of the relationships among all the components needed to develop a solution, learners are able to visualize the connections. The triangular network (Table 11.1 or 11.2) highlights the importance of lesson goals by indicating the relationship between a variety of events that may provide learners with the best solution to the problem.

Reflect for a Moment

Which of the three organizational approaches to inquiry are you most able to relate to your own intuitive problem-solving strategies? What is an example of a problem you recently addressed using an approximation of that approach?

Closure/Conclusion

Lesson closure should be student directed. Although the educator may initiate the actual closure process by drawing the small groups back together, learners actually provide the conclusions. During closure learners can detail their hypothesis, discuss their findings, and if necessary reevaluate their information. The educator may ask an occasional clarifying question but should otherwise remain in the background.

Evaluation

As in any lesson, evaluation must take place. However, the educator needs to evaluate not only learners' understanding of the problem but also their ability to collect and analyze information or data. Therefore, evaluation in the inquiry lesson must occur in a variety of forms. Not unlike the expository method, the inquiry lesson can embed evaluation in the lesson closure. Because learners during closure share what they have learned in their small groups with the class as a whole, this sharing time presents the educator with a perfect opportunity to make a *summative evaluation.*

Learner understanding must also be given a *formative evaluation* if the inquiry approach is to be useful. Formative evaluation, which takes place during the small group investigation through educator questions and monitoring of group activities, allows educators to provide examples (hints) and gently redirect learners' investigations.

Learners need to develop *self-evaluation* skills using the process of *critical thinking*. Critical thinking is a process that enables learners to determine the value of their ideas, solutions, or information. Beyer (1988) provides a list of eight actions used by learners during an inquiry that determine the worth of their solution:

1. Distinguishing between verifiable facts and value claims
2. Distinguishing relevant from irrelevant information, claims, or reasons
3. Determining the factual accuracy of a statement
4. Determining the credibility of a source
5. Identifying ambiguous claims or arguments
6. Identifying unstated assumptions
7. Detecting bias
8. Determining the strength of an argument or a claim. (p. 27)

Educators can assist learners in this process by helping them formulate questions related to Beyer's eight actions.

AN EXAMPLE OF INQUIRY TEACHING

Dan Tufts and Gloria Fairchild, a collaborative multiage teaching team, were working on a unit on plants. During the course of the unit, their class was discussing what conditions were needed to sustain plant life. As the discussion continued, a difference of opinion developed about whether or not oxygen, water, and light were essential. It was obvious from this discussion that the students had differing perceptions of essential conditions. The recognition of a contradiction, or dissonance, among them, was confirmed, and Dan Tufts and Gloria Fairchild decided to let their students gather information and conduct experimentation about this topic. Dan Tufts begins the inquiry lesson.

MR. TUFTS: We've talked a great deal about plants. What are some of the things you've found out?

AUDREY: Plants are living things.

MALCOLM: Because they are living, they need oxygen, water, and light.

ABBY: I'm not sure all plants need those things. Don't some plants grow in the dark like mushrooms?

CHARLEY: No—mushrooms are fungus, not plants.

KEN: Fungus is a plant. Besides, mushrooms grow in the middle of my yard and there is lots of light there.

MS. FAIRCHILD: Sounds as if we are having some problems here. What is our dilemma? [Waits for several hands to go up.] Abby?

ABBY: Deciding what is essential for plants to survive. [*Problem identification*]

MR. TUFTS: Are there any other problems? [Waits for several hands to go up.] Matthew?

MATTHEW: Is a mushroom a fungus, and if so is it a plant?

MS. FAIRCHILD: What are some questions you could ask in order to find a solution to this problem?
Students brainstorm a variety of questions. [*Students begin to develop research objectives.*]

MR. TUFTS: Ms. Fairchild and I would like you to get into your science groups, formulate your research hypotheses and objectives, and begin to gather materials. You'll need to decide what procedures you will use to investigate and solve your problem. We have a variety of materials available for you and there are passes to the library if needed. You will work on this for two weeks, so don't feel as if you must have a conclusion today.

The students break into their cooperative learning groups to begin *data gathering*. Ms. Fairchild and Mr. Tufts move from group to group, asking questions only if necessary. Students may opt to use the technology center, where they can develop a simulation program that will demonstrate their solution. Others may select materials to set up a hypothetical garden, eliminating an essential item from each plant, then recording data. Still others can head off to the library to begin in-depth research to find a solution.

During the second week the two teachers meet with each group to discuss methods of *data analysis* that might match particular types of data being gathered. For some, it may be photographs of plant growth over time; for others, it may be verifying the credibility of research studies found in the library. When each group *reports conclusions* after two weeks, oral reports, photo displays, and charts and graphs dominate the presentations.

Practice

Select a problem or contradiction that has been puzzling you. Using the problem-centered, decision-making, and networking approaches, outline how you would go about finding a solution.

ADAPTATIONS

In previous chapters, the existence of an inclusive school atmosphere has been recognized as a critical factor in planning instructional adaptations. Several characteristics of that type of school environment have been described along with the ways these features facilitate the process of adapting instruction. Although those advantages need not be repeated here, the inclusive school is also the preferred setting for adapting inquiry experiences.

Another attribute of the inclusive school community becomes particularly vital when inquiry teaching and learning is adapted—namely, the families and members of the community around the school. Because inquiry often involves interaction between learners and families or between learners and members of the larger community surrounding the school, these other adults become much more aware of what students are doing in school, and simultaneously more sensitive and responsive to the special needs of individual learners. For instance, in Mai Lin's class there are two students with disabilities. Heather has moderately involved distractibility, and Adam is severely mentally disabled and wheelchair bound. When the class undertook an inquiry activity in small groups, Heather's group chose to pursue the question, "Where do all the fresh fruits and vegetables we buy come from?" Adam's group chose to investigate the problem of how schools might provide a healthier lunch program without raising the cost. Heather's group of four went to the produce manager at the nearest supermarket. The special educator on Heather's team spoke with the manager before the visit and suggested that she give each student a good-sized piece of fruit to munch on during the meeting. It was also suggested that the manager take students through the different fruit displays as she talked. When the special educator called the manager afterwards to thank her, the manager commented on the effectiveness of the suggestions given and expressed interest in hosting more groups of students in the future. In this way the collaboration for inclusive education extended beyond the school walls and the process of adapting instruction became a communitywide effort.

Adam's group, meanwhile, decided they needed to determine the cost per pupil of the current lunch program and its nutritional value as well. They gathered the information and, after sketching it out, displayed it on large posterboards. One critical factor in deciding which foods were acceptable and which were not was their flavor and taste. Adam was an excellent judge of whether a current food or a food being suggested for the new program was actually tasty enough. He also helped the group by having a cart attached to his motorized wheelchair so the group could take their posterboard, scissors, tape recorders, food samples and other equipment along. The members of the cafeteria staff, especially the food manager, were most eager to work with Adam and the members of his group. They were familiar with each of the students and provided assistance to Adam whenever he needed it. A group of about a dozen parents, including Adam's mom, had worked out a rotating volunteer schedule so he had direct volunteer assistance three hours each day in addition to the therapist who worked with him for an hour in the morning and an hour in the afternoon. For both Adam and Heather the inquiry process was successful, not only because they themselves were enthusiastic about the inquiries, but also because the inclusive community had taken responsibility for participating in the educational process in a positive, supportive role.

It is important to understand that all learners can successfully participate in inquiry learning, regardless of their ability. Inquiry teaching is not typically conducted without extensive planning on the part of the educator. This planning, done collaboratively with other educators in an inclusive school, will consistently take into account the interests and abilities of every student. The range of questions and problems available for student inquiry need to be consistent with the range of interests and abilities among learners. Educators can organize group inquiry to increase the value of the experience for each individual.

Reflect for a Moment

In what other ways could the investigation into the school lunch program be adapted to support Adam's involvement? Remember, he is a member of the school community at Astronaut Elementary.

Textbooks and Other Printed Materials

As with any instructional approach, textbooks and other printed materials are often critical to the overall content of an inquiry lesson. Therefore, adaptations may take a variety of forms, most of which have been described in earlier chapters. For some learners, low-vocabulary, high-interest materials are helpful. Because such materials can sometimes contribute to stigmatizing effects, other more popular materials like newspapers, magazines, and videotapes are especially valuable for inquiry activities. If texts are used, tape recordings can be prepared and learners can use illustrations in the text to acquire a sense of sequence and context as they listen. Here community volunteers can be very instrumental in building a library of book tapes for an entire school, and the result can be a much more motivated and involved school community of learners, educators, and neighbors. Study guides and advance organizers are helpful for inquiry activities. Charts, graphs, and maps are all valuable visual formats for information, which can in turn be the focus for data analysis during the inquiry process.

Instructional Procedures

The unique features of the inquiry process are important to consider in making adaptations to instructional procedures. The inquiry process typically places students in a more independent learning role than any of the other approaches. Therefore it is very important for both educators and learners to have confidence in learners' ability to apply inquiry skills and language to a chosen question or problem. It is equally important that learners have the necessary skills to cooperate with peers in an independent research process. The collaborative skills and discussion skills described in earlier chapters are both critical to students' success in inquiry experiences.

Because of the complex nature of the inquiry process and its emphasis on higher-order thinking, technology can enhance the experience for all learners and prove highly effective as an adaptive tool for students with disabilities. The multisensory nature of many recent technological developments—including simulations, laserdiscs, interactive communications networks, sensory stimulation devices, and electronic aids for self-reinforcement, self-monitoring, and self-assessment—brings much more information and cognitive challenge to learners who might otherwise not be engaged. Educators in inclusive schools are committed to identifying those technological devices that can best serve all their students and making sure that students are able to use these devices as members of learning communities on a daily basis. Other suggestions for adapting the instructional procedures in an inquiry lesson are found in Table 11.3.

TABLE 11.3 Adapting Instructional Procedures in an Inquiry Lesson

1. Teach and check to be sure that all learners have acquired the skills and language of inquiry.
2. Be prepared with a variety of inquiry questions or problems so that all learners can be part of a group pursuing a question or problem that is meaningful and manageable for them.
3. Check to be sure that the prerequisite knowledge base has been established with all learners.
4. When inquiry activities are conducted in small groups, be sure that learners are grouped in a manner that supports each individual's interests and abilities.
5. Plan to have other adults involved with inquiry groups so that research efforts are efficient and individuals within each group are actively involved.
6. Whenever possible and wherever necessary, have specific materials and strategies to help get groups to initial stages of data collection.
7. Consider a whole class inquiry demonstration so learners can participate in a simple but successful inquiry experience.
8. Keep in mind that the most authentic inquiry experiences are those that you the educator do not actually have a precise answer for and that learners have a role in determining.
9. Communicate with families and outside resource persons well in advance to ensure successful modifications for specific learners during the process.
10. Because the data analysis phase of inquiry is often cognitively challenging, consider using advance organizers (outlines, charts, etc.) for data during early inquiry activities.
11. Advance organizers may also be helpful with the actual method(s) for testing hypotheses with data collected.
12. Actively support learners' efforts to draw conclusions by asking leading questions that will take their thinking further if necessary.

Assignments and Assessments

Another interesting feature of the inquiry teaching approach is the close relationship between student success and teacher effectiveness. Even though considerable time is spent on independent learning, the success of that learning is highly related to how well the educator has prepared students for the inquiry experience. Educators need to take whatever steps are necessary to be sure that all learners have acquired the skills and language inherent in the inquiry process before making any assignments. One possibility involves checking carefully to be sure learners can actually describe the process itself. Another might be to practice the process with a mini-inquiry at a relatively simple level.

Reflect for a Moment

Do you know what it is like to be told to do something when you do not know how to do it? Even the most confident among us have some insecurities about such a situation. At the same time, with some positive encouragement, can't learners benefit from their mistakes? There is a fine balance here, isn't there?

Although learners may know all the steps in the inquiry process, they may still have difficulty putting that knowledge into action. The ways that assignments and assessments are adapted for individual learners can therefore greatly affect the development of those cognitive goals fundamental to inquiry learning. As with any instructional approach, flexibility with time, cooperative groupings, and individual responsibilities are important considerations in making assignments. In many cases, the nature of the inquiry process is itself quite time consuming, more so than other instructional approaches. However, providing additional time is just as important with the inquiry approach as it is with any other method of instruction. Individuals or groups may demonstrate a need for additional time to successfully complete an inquiry activity. Cooperative groups, a major format for inquiry activities, are not always going to function smoothly. Learners will have a more positive experience with assignments when educators are willing to change group members when the occasion calls for change. Peer collaboration is a valuable and significant aspect of independent group inquiry because learners are making so many decisions on their own. Some learners clearly benefit from peer assistance in working through certain assignments, and educators can adjust groupings to meet these needs, even if groups have already been formed.

With a wide range of interests and abilities within any one group, educators must realize that assignments are intended to strengthen each learner's understanding of the content and that learners are functioning at different levels of understanding for any given inquiry experience. It is therefore important to be prepared to challenge learners at different levels when responsibilities are assigned for an inquiry activity. Group members who are part of an inclusive school community will acquire, over time, an understanding of and appreciation for the ways that every individual can contribute to the overall quality of the group effort. Each student is entitled to take responsibilities commensurate with her or his developmental abilities, and the educator can make certain that those responsibilities are directed to the collective group process.

Fortunately, if the problem or question being studied in an inquiry activity is of genuine concern to learners, the authenticity of the assessment procedure is reasonably assured. When educators are aware of and planning for different learning objectives for some learners, the authenticity of the assessment process increases further. However, adaptations to the assessment phase of inquiry learning can still increase the confidence and motivation of certain students who may have difficulty with some aspect of inquiry. It is, of course, important to use a variety of assessment tools (observation, interviewing, student self-evaluation) so that the process is the focus of study, not just the end result. Each of these tools, used repeatedly over the course of an inquiry activity, will reveal much more accurate and valuable information about student learning than a single summative essay question or singular group demonstration or sharing episode. These informal tools are also, by their own nature, adaptable to the individual differences among all learners, and therefore highly appropriate for inquiry activities in several ways. When summative assessments are administered, educators should be able to provide alternative modes of performance (oral reports, tape recordings, drawings, or models) for those students who can better demonstrate their learning in some other manner.

The adaptability of the student portfolio makes it an appropriate means of assessment when educators wish to maintain personalized, individually monitored assessment procedures. Inquiry activities provide excellent student materials that can be included in their portfolios (charts, tapes, statistics, maps, self-determined inquiry strategies). These materials can also serve as a means to communicate with peers, parents, and others in the school community about the types of investigations taking place in the inclusive classroom and can increase general understanding of the inquiry approach to teaching and learning.

As long as collaborative professionals use assessment information to plan future learning activities or to modify ongoing activities, they will continue to focus on each learner's progress toward specific goals instead of on how a particular student compares with others in the class or grade. The adaptability of certain assessment procedures (observations, alternative modes of performance, interviews, and student portfolios) makes them invaluable as educators work together to measure student learning.

Practice

Tonya is a seven-year-old who has been having difficulty with many aspects of school. She shows her displeasure by verbally degrading the people around her and the activities in the classroom, intensely and continuously. You are the special educator for the second grade cluster and a member of that collaborative team in the inclusive Massey Park Elementary School. Although meetings with Tonya's mother have resulted in some insight (Tonya's parents are separating), Tonya's behavior has gotten worse almost daily and the team needs to improve the situation. As someone who highly values the inquiry approach to teaching and learning the second grade teachers are using, what adaptations would you suggest that could be applied to a range of inquiry situations?

QUESTIONING STRATEGIES

As earlier chapters have emphasized, a key to being able to develop an effective questioning strategy is clearly defining learning objectives or outcomes. The level and sequence of questions that an educator will ask depends entirely on what cognitive processes are needed and the type of knowledge the learner is expected to acquire.

Good and bad questioning techniques, of course, (see Chapter 9) are universal. However, questioning strategies for the inquiry approach, though similar to those used in the discovery approach, are vastly different from those used in the expository method. Questions in the inquiry approach should be designed to encourage students to engage in reflective thinking, expand on hypotheses that are too narrowly focused, and move forward in the investigative process.

In generating hypotheses, learners must engage in *brainstorming* all possible solutions, then eliminate all but those that are truly plausible. Brainstorming involves **fluent thinking** and **flexible thinking** traits that are important to productive inquiry. Thinking fluently allows learners to generate a large number of ideas, even if some appear to be similar. When learners generate ideas that fall into different classes they are thinking flexibly. During the hypotheses generation stage, educators should use questions that cause learners to think creatively. These types of questions are always divergent, demanding more of the learner's thought processes. Divergent questions also draw from the learners their opinions and conjectures about the problem at hand.

Since the purpose of this learning approach is to allow students to develop hypotheses and test their own thinking, educators must ask deductive questions. **Deductive questions** guide learners by moving them through the scientific process. Questions that are deductive should be designed to encourage the clarification of a concept, known as **conceptual movement**. Such questions may be convergent, divergent, or evaluative in nature. Deductive questions differ from **inductive questions** because the answers are derived from the learners' development of a hypothesis, collection and interpretation of data, and drawing of conclusion rather than developing generalizations from discrete sets of data presented by the educator.

Reflect for a Moment

What types of questions do educators typically ask students? Can you think of some deductive questions an educator might use with a group of students planning to investigate the life of a famous writer like Shel Silverstein?

Handling Correct and Incorrect Responses

The majority if not all of the questions asked in the inquiry approach call for interpretation or evaluation. As such, they encourage a diversity of responses and therefore variation in the way in which answers are handled. Divergent or deductive questions require learners to expand on what they know already through analysis and synthesis. With the use of divergent or deductive questions, invalid or partially correct responses need to be viewed not as wrong but as needing more research or exploration.

As noted in Chapters 9 and 10, the educator's responses to learners' replies are perhaps more important than the original questions. Thus educators' responses should never be negative in nature but rather should encourage learners to continue sharing their opinions and beliefs. Remember that typically the communication cycle in a learning event involves the educator's question, a learner's response, and some form of reaction by the former to the latter's answer. Since communication in the inquiry approach is student directed, the educator must also instruct learners about how they should respond to one another's hypotheses, solutions, and information.

Reflect for a Moment

In your experience as a student, what have teachers actually done that made you feel you could solve a problem in class? Have you ever been in a classroom situation when you felt the teacher stifled your creative thinking by the manner in which she or he dealt with your response?

Inhibiting Inquiry Through Questions

Questions are a valuable means of enhancing the inquiry approach, but overuse of questioning by an educator can be an inhibitor to implementing this strategy effectively. When brainstorming becomes teacher dominated, the educator needs to pull away from the role of gatekeeper. Educators must be aware that what may be an attempt to keep the learners focused through questioning actually results in drawing learners away from their investigation.

STUDENT ASSESSMENT AND EVALUATION

As with all plans for assessment and evaluation, it is wise to match the type of achievement expected with methods of measurement and evaluation (Stiggins, 1994). When the educator is most interested in how many mathematics facts students can correctly answer in one minute, the method of assessment is a timed test. When the educator is most interested in whether students can compare and contrast types of clouds, the method of assessment may be a short essay using pictures of clouds. In inquiry lessons, the educator must first decide what the target behavior is because the method of assessment will logically follow.

Because most learning that takes place during inquiry activities involves higher-order thinking, such summative assessment methods as multiple choice, true-false, matching and fill-in items fall short of measuring the actual learning that occurs. The essay, in which the learner is required to express ideas in an organized manner based on conceptual understanding, is a much more appropriate method of summative assessment for inquiry activities.

Another method, performance assessment, may be useful with inquiry activities in either a summative or formative manner. Learners can demonstrate the ultimate outcome of their inquiry as part of a summative assessment, but they can also provide data for a formative assessment by demonstrating the inquiry skills and language they have acquired during the inquiry process. In the case of the summative outcome, the individual learner or group will have a tangible product or products that can be judged for quality with predetermined criteria. One classic example of such a product is the science fair exhibit. In the case of the formative assessment, learners are observed carrying out a set of procedures and are judged on the basis of how effectively they perform those procedures. An example of such a process, obviously, is an individual or group who performs each step of the inquiry process in investigating the cost effectiveness of recycling.

Another type of assessment that can be applied to inquiry activities is personal communication (Stiggins, 1994). Although not viewed as a traditional assessment method, personal communication, or just talking with learners, in its various forms can be an invaluable way to gather accurate information about student learning, particularly in an inquiry lesson. There are many forms of personal communication, but the most common are conferences and interviews, question and answer sessions, oral examinations, and conducting or listening to conversations with or among learners or other adults. Such assessment methods can be either formative or summative, but in either case the educator must establish criteria to use in judging the success of the learners involved. These criteria may be simply a matter of correctness or based on a more subjective determination of a quality indicator.

Reflect for a Moment

Did you have teachers who used any form of personal communication as a means of assessment and evaluation? Was it overly subjective, or did the teacher have a clear system? How clear was it that she or he was using the time for assessment or evaluation?

Because several methods can be used to assess student learning in inquiry activities, educators can use portfolios to organize student work samples. The complexity of student responses during inquiry lessons results in a wide variety of materials for the portfolio. Educators and students must prepare a system for organizing and evaluating the different materials and be able to devote significant amounts of time to the evaluation process. Finally, the importance of accurate and systematic recordkeeping cannot be overstated. Portfolios are one recordkeeping strategy, but only to the extent that they are structured to serve their purpose effectively. Whether or not portfolios are used, the educator must establish a well-organized system of recordkeeping to maintain an accurate and reliable profile of each student.

Martinello and Cook (1994) have thoroughly examined evaluation in the context of interdisciplinary inquiry and place a solid emphasis on the need for flexibility in terms of the variety of tasks performed, the unique characteristics of individual learners, and the nature of interdisciplinary inquiry itself. They also specify three critical features of any evaluation procedure: the use of portfolios to maintain evidence of individual student progress; the establishment of a clear set of criteria for every task to be assessed; and a workable recordkeeping system that learners, educators, and other significant adults can understand and use to keep track of student learning.

The purposes of portfolios within the interdisciplinary inquiry program include showing evidence of student progress over time, stimulating student self-evaluation, helping those involved set goals, lending credibility to the learning processes at work, linking the process of learning to the final outcome or product, promoting student autonomy in the learning process, focusing more intently on building thinking skills, determining academic needs, and strengthening communication lines (Martinello & Cook, 1994).

As with most of the approaches to instruction included in this book, the basis for establishing criteria with any one task is not norm referenced. It is, of course, criterion referenced. Although one set of criteria may be created that can be applied to a wide array of tasks, there is also good reason to design other sets of criteria for specific tasks in which more detailed or task-dependent criteria is warranted. For example, if a group of learners has completed an inquiry into the cost effectiveness of recycling in their school, it may not be enough to apply a broad set of criteria that focuses on the extent to which the group proceeded successfully through the inquiry process. Instead, the criteria may need to relate to tasks specific to the recycling inquiry, such as short-term and long-term costs or cost benefits of one recyclable material compared with other materials.

Whether the issue is portfolios, sets of criteria, or recordkeeping systems, learners need to participate in the development of the assessment and evaluation procedures as much as possible. They will have a higher level of motivation and a clearer understanding of where they are headed in their inquiries if they are part of the planning process for assessment and evaluation. At the very least, learners must be fully cognizant of the procedures by which their work is being evaluated at all times and must have opportunities for self-evaluation with every inquiry task.

The importance of student involvement in the assessment and evaluation process also represents evidence of the educator's commitment to collaborative decision making. Of course, collaborative decision making typically involves other professionals on a collaborative team and is concerned with the unique strengths and needs of each student. Any system of assessment and evaluation must be sensitive to the range of learner characteristics present and flexible enough to provide accurate and meaningful information on every student's learning progress.

Reflect for a Moment

Think of a class or course where you had a say in the assessment or evaluation process. Were you assessing or evaluating yourself, peers, the teacher? What was the effect of this assessment on you and other students? Might it have been modified and improved in some way?

Practice

Select a sample of student work from the sample lesson plan to include in a portfolio. Then establish a set of criteria, along with a set of points or credits for each level of success, that might be used to assess the sample of student work.

TEACHER REFLECTIONS: EFFECTIVENESS OF THE LESSON

The complexity of the inquiry lesson invites teacher reflection not only after the lesson has ended, but throughout the inquiry process as well. It is important, therefore, for educators to consider the questions in Table 11.4 before, during, and after the inquiry activity. Equally important is the written information the educator accumulates by responding to these questions, and the decisions he or she makes as a result of his or her reflections.

TABLE 11.4   Reflective Questions for Inquiry Teaching

1. Was the original question or problem a valid basis for inquiry? Was it so in the minds of the learners?
2. Did all learners have sufficient inquiry skills and language to pursue the problem or question?
3. Would it have been beneficial to conduct a review of the process?
4. How effectively did the different groups work? Would changes in group makeup improve the dynamics of any group?
5. What resources were particularly helpful? What resources were not? What resources would have been helpful but were not available?
6. To what extent did individual learners participate in forming hypotheses?
7. Was there adequate time to conduct the inquiry? Did it take longer than anticipated? Why?
8. Were there suitable data collection techniques in place? How could the process of collecting data have been enhanced?
9. Did any learners encounter difficulty cognitively during data analysis? Did you intervene, and if so, for what reason?
10. Which of the three organizational approaches (problem centered, decision making, networking) did you use? Was it an appropriate choice?
11. Were there questions planned which you found particularly helpful? Others you did not find useful?
12. What was the role of advanced organizers in the lesson? Was it effective?
13. Did you plan adaptations for individual learners, particularly those with disabilities? What was the effect of the adaptations?
14. How did you gather information about student learning during the inquiry? How did you assess the outcomes of student work?
15. Were you able to monitor student learning satisfactorily throughout the lesson?
16. How did students reflect on their learning?

SUMMARY

All people instinctively inquire whenever they seek new knowledge. A more formal approach to inquiry includes the steps of problem identification, hypothesizing, data gathering, data analysis, and forming conclusions. The inquiry approach lends itself to all grade and ability levels. Inquiry emphasizes process and higher order thinking, is student centered and interdisciplinary in nature, and almost always results in creative thinking. It often takes place outside the traditional classroom.

The educator must plan carefully and be well organized to facilitate inquiry lessons. Thematic units often culminate in inquiry lessons. Collaboration is also expected—due to the interdisciplinary nature of most inquiries. Cooperative inquiry is a popular feature of inclusive classrooms, where students model skills for other students. Aspects of effective teaching found in inquiry lessons include student directedness, reflective thinking, incorporating learners' ideas, and active engaged time.

When planning inquiry lessons the educator must select and research the problem, present the problem to the class, elicit learner questions, encourage hypothesizing, offer rules for judging hypotheses, and support post-inquiry discussion. Having materials available is very important in inquiry lessons. Likewise, advance organizers must ensure a conceptual framework with learners. Content must invite new ideas. Educators must choose from three procedures: problem centered, decision making, and networking.

Formative and summative evaluation are equally important with inquiry lessons. Self-monitoring and hypothesis testing are also essential aspects. Adaptations to reading materials and assignments are feasible. Questioning should elevate the cognitive levels of all learners, in brainstorming, data analysis, and hypothesis testing. Educators should also encourage learners through their responses to learner ideas. Personal communication and performance assessment are both valuable evaluative tools.

12

THE DISCUSSION APPROACH

Key Terms

Active engaged time
Attention-gaining techniques
Basic questions
British-style debate
Caption statement
Clarity
Critical thinking
Debate
Discussion teaching
Divergent question
Divergent thinking
Error analysis
Establishing a focus
Evaluative question
Factual question
Follow-up question

Forum
Instructional variety
Interpretative questions
Observation
Panel
Partner learning system
Questioning strategies
Refocus
Round table
Self-evaluative questionnaire
Student journal
Successful participation
Summary sheet
Symposium
Think aloud technique
Using learners' ideas

Objectives

After completing this chapter, the reader will be able to:

1. Define discussion approach.
2. Identify when to use the discussion approach.
3. Examine the connections between effective teaching research and the discussion approach.
4. Develop discussion teaching lessons.

5. Incorporate appropriate adaptations into a discussion lesson plan.
6. Develop appropriate questioning strategies.
7. Formulate appropriate student assessment strategies.
8. Incorporate personal reflection into discussion teaching.

PROFILES OF DISCUSSION TEACHING

Sandra Weidlich

Nestled in the rolling hills of western Massachusetts, Reston Elementary School stood proudly among the brilliant colors of autumn, a testimony to the days of three-story brick school buildings. In spite of a changing economy and an influx of minority families, the students in Sandra's fourth grade class were predominantly from white middle class homes where parents still dutifully checked their children's homework before letting them turn on the TV. She knew that many of her old college classmates were teaching in much more difficult surroundings, and she was grateful for her own good fortune.

Sandra had, over her eight years of teaching, gravitated toward a fairly traditional style of pedagogy, using textbooks, written assignments, and an occasional play or group project in her classroom. Most students had been successful, although Sandra knew that their family backgrounds had played a major role in that school success. Students at Weston had always had the highest test scores in the region, and Sandra was not so foolish to believe that the scores were simply the result of superior teaching. She had decided that students in her fourth grade were ready for more mature class activities and decided to try some group discussions in the coming year. She knew that social studies would be a good candidate for discussion lessons, and because she always started off the year with a unit on how the Pilgrims settled eastern Massachusetts, she decided to have small group discussions about the Pilgrims.

Sandra assigned the class the first ten pages of the book for homework and told them to prepare for a discussion about the assignment tomorrow. The next day, she told them to divide up into groups of four for the discussion. What happened next took Sandra by surprise. It took the students ten minutes to just get into groups! The bickering and squabbling was unbelievable, and Sandra finally shouted "Quiet down!" When they were finally calmed down, Sandra told them that in groups they were to tell what the Pilgrims did during their first year in the New World. When she informed them that they could begin, the students looked at each other as if she had spoken to them in a foreign language. Some raised their hands, and began telling her their answers. "No, no," Sandra said, "Work with the people in your group!"

After about a half hour of grumbling and half-hearted scribbling on paper, a few students brought their answers up to Ina's desk, where she had been grading their spelling work from that morning. Most of the students were either talking to their friends about what they were planning to watch on TV that night or shouting across the room at other students who were yelling at them for one reason or another. Sandra got up and once again shouted "Quiet down! Now if you can't have a discussion like mature fourth graders, I guess we'll have to go back to doing book assignments like last year's class. I thought that maybe you were different, that you could handle a little responsibility. I guess I was wrong."

After they settled down a second time, Sandra told them again that they had to work together on the assignment. Some students mumbled something about its being a boring lesson. A few waved their papers around in the air, oohhing and aahhing about how much they had written, and others just sat, dazed by it all, staring into space. Sandra collected the papers and told the students to line up for physical education. They rambled down the hall rather noisily and out the door to the playground. Sandra slumped in her chair. If this was a fair example of discussion lessons, she wanted no part of them.

Like a veteran boxing champion, however, Sandra was determined to keep fighting. She decided to try a discussion lesson next in reading and thought that the first story in the second unit would be perfect. It was a good story about a family in the wilderness and how they survived a terrible winter together. The students would enjoy the adventure theme, she thought; they'd really get into a good discussion. Sandra told them to read the story on Tuesday, and on Wednesday she started class by asking the group to tell her if they liked it. She remembered hearing somewhere that questions that asked for students' opinions were good for discussion lessons. They all said that they did like it, and several even gave examples of what they liked best. Sandra then asked them what hardships the family faced, and they excitedly responded. It was going great, thought Sandra. The students were enthusiastic and the discussion was lively. Then Sandra told them to discuss the ending among themselves and write about it. Each student promptly got out a piece of paper and began writing. The only exception was Janine, a student with cerebral palsy who just looked at Sandra as if to say, "What about me?" The discussion and all the energy that accompanied it came to a screeching halt. Sandra felt lost. The lesson had started well, but . . .

Kirk Tucker

Students came into Kirk Tucker's classroom buzzing about the news. They had finally reached the end of the unit on movement and knew that now they would get to critique each other's futuristic wellness systems. Kirk had carefully planned out a symposium setting for the hour-long class time and, with the help of Renee Waters, the special educator in the primary wing, had adapted the scenario so that all learners could contribute to the event. They had worked collaboratively for several hours during the days leading up to the symposium, trying to anticipate anything that could possibly happen and how they would be prepared.

The inclusive classroom Kirk taught in was great for seven-, eight-, and nine-year-olds, and Kirk had been able to use a flexible schedule to accommodate some of the exciting learning activities in the multidisciplinary movement unit. Learners had used biographies of well-known athletes to gain an understanding of successful movement fitness, nutrition, and wellness. They had created their own biographies—fictional, of course—of kids their own age who had improved their physical and mental health through movement and wellness activities. They had taken a field trip to the university an hour away, where they had toured the sports science department and videotaped the different programs going on there. With the help of professional movement specialists from the local YMCA, they had even begun their own wellness movement programs. They calculated daily their own body fat content; heart rates before, during and after movement activities; and cholesterol counts. Most insisted that they would continue their programs after the unit had ended!

But now the symposium was near, and learners were anxiously making last-minute checks of the organization of their respective wellness systems. They had studied wellness among people in the immediate community, interviewing dozens of citizens in their neighborhoods. From this information they had worked in groups to design a wellness program, revolving around movement and nutrition, that would attract all kinds of people in the area and improve the health of all involved. They had also calculated the savings in health costs that different people could expect and had even developed a publicity campaign as part of their overall system.

All this information had to be prepared so that each group could share their ideas in 10 minutes, so there were lots of carefully designed visual aids that offered plenty of information in a relatively efficient manner. Every student in every group had several responsibilities, usually depending on how his or her individual talents could best be utilized. In one group, Tara, who had a specific learning disability in the area of mathematics, took the sketches for the visuals and transferred them onto large pieces of posterboard using bright, clear colors and symbols. Gus, another member of the same group, helped the others with daily calculations of heart rates, cholesterol, and body fat and the construction of bar graphs that displayed the changes over time. Jesse worked out a procedure for interviewing members of the community that the others, after some editing, adopted for their fieldwork. The groups had met on a daily basis, discussing their accomplishments and plans for the next day. The unit had taken up a large chunk of the school day, but Kirk knew that he had the support of the building principal, Judy Sharlin, and had shared his plans with parents in a memo well in advance of the unit. In fact, several parents had accepted his invitation to join them for lunch and the afternoon symposium, and they now settled into the extra chairs that had been brought into the room.

Kirk intended to welcome everyone—he had heard a rumor that the superintendent might be there!—give a brief summary of the unit, and turn the discussion over to the first group. After each group had used their time to share their ideas, then Kirk would lead a discussion with the entire class to formulate a plan that would include ideas from each group. Parents and visitors would be encouraged to make suggestions as well. The local newspaper was there, planning a photo story on community wellness. Kirk and the students were avid, critical thinkers, and today's discussion lesson was the culmination of their work together.

DISCUSSION TEACHING

In a democratic society, people as a collective group participate actively in the process of governing themselves. Through elected officials at the local, state, and national level, citizens have a say in the decisions that affect their daily lives. They serve on decision-making boards and committees, appeal decisions that are made, stand up for their beliefs as part of a majority or a minority, persuade others to support their views, vote on important proposed changes to their lives, and constantly discuss the various strengths and weaknesses of specific positions taken on numerous issues. If there is any teaching strategy that helps prepare young learners to be citizens in a democratic society, it is discussion teaching. When students engage in discussion lessons, they think critically. They listen to what others say and weigh the merits of what they hear. They reflect constantly on their own thinking and are able to change that thinking if the evidence warrants. They continually analyze and evaluate information as they attempt to solve problems. In short, the discussion approach is a classroom version of the democratic process (Hollingsworth & Hoover, 1991). Kirk Tucker's symposium was very clearly democracy in action.

Reflect for a Moment

When was the last time you participated in a real decision-making process? Was it as a member of a club at school? Was it a decision that was made with others on the job? How many of the behaviors just described can you recall as part of your thinking at the time?

Discussions take place constantly, usually revolving around issues that hold some element of controversy. The controversy may not always be of great magnitude, but it is enough to provoke two or more individuals into a discussion about the issue. If they are to effectively discuss the issue, discussants need to be open minded, flexible, objective, and reflective (Hollingsworth & Hoover, 1991). If they are open minded, they are able to consider new information along with the information they already have, take into account their own personal biases, and realize that very few situations call for all-or-nothing answers. If they are flexible, they can see a situation from another person's point of view and, after considering others' ideas, either reject the other position or, when necessary, abandon their previously held position. If they are objective, they avoid, as much as possible, emotional features of the discussion such as voice changes and unrelated appeals, judging the situation instead on the merit of the information and ideas presented. Finally, a reflective discussant can use the ideas of others and the questions put forth by the teacher or discussion leader to analyze and evaluate the situation thoughtfully.

Although the term **discussion teaching** sounds almost like a contradiction in terms, a solid base of support exists for the use of class discussions as a teaching strategy. There are, however, substantive differences between the discussion approach and the teaching approaches presented in the previous three chapters. Expository teaching is teacher centered, teacher directed, and most effective when the learning outcomes are facts or concepts. Discovery teaching is student centered, teacher directed, and most effective when the learning outcomes are concepts or generalizations.

Discussion teaching, on the other hand, is student centered, often student directed, and most effective when the learning outcomes are complex and often abstract in nature. In most discussion lessons, learners are expected first to analyze and interpret what they hear, and then to change their thinking in some way. Examples of possible outcomes of discussion lessons are:

- Learning to take another person's point of view
- Reaching a group consensus on a current events issue
- Improving self-confidence
- Creating solutions to a problem
- Learning to response effectively to conflict
- Summarizing an activity or event
- Developing an evaluation procedure for field trips
- Improving listening skills

The educator's role in discussion lessons is also different than it is in either expository or discovery lessons. Although the educator is still very much the planner, carefully preparing objectives, materials, procedures, questions, and evaluation techniques, the lesson itself may take a different shape because of student contributions. Consequently, the direction of the lesson may change, and the time planned for the lesson can easily increase. The educator is, however, still responsible for making sure outcomes are attainable and must occasionally intervene to promote the student interaction and discussion content needed to achieve those outcomes.

A successful classroom discussion features participation by everyone rather than domination by a few. Class members who simply sit and listen are not contributing their ideas and opinions and therefore not participating in the discussion. There is also usually a core of background information that may be a recently completed unit of study, a current event in the news, or an ongoing topic of importance that students have been keeping abreast of on a regular basis. In addition, discussion questions, those prepared in advance and those that come up spontaneously, are critical to the success of the discussion. The questions that the educator and learners use during the discussion are almost always higher-level questions, requiring more than just remembering or comprehending information. Questioning techniques for discussion lessons will be explored in depth later in this chapter.

Reflect for a Moment

Recall a class—in middle school, high school, or college—that was, in your mind, a real discussion class. Which of the preceding features did it have? Which did it not have? Which of the listed learning outcomes did it help you achieve?

In short, several aspects of the discussion approach are unique to this strategy and vital to a deep understanding of when and how to use it in teaching. First, even though the goals of a discussion lesson are more abstract and complex than those of an expository or discovery lesson, they are nonetheless essential if learners are to develop critical thinking skills, listening skills, and many other complex behaviors central to becoming an effective citizen in a democratic society. Second, because students take part in discussions as a natural part of their daily lives, they are developing the skills (open-mindedness, flexibility, objectivity, and reflection) necessary to participate actively in a class discussion. Third, the educator in a discussion lesson must plan carefully and monitor the discussion to be sure that background information has been provided, that all class members participate actively, and that questions are used skillfully to promote the learning intended.

How Discussion Teaching Is Used

What would an observer see taking place during a discussion lesson? Lemlech (1994) describes a number of characteristics of effective discussion lessons. In general, even a casual observer can see that the discussion must have a clear focus. A purpose is set forth that holds meaning for learners. An entire discussion usually displays fairly discernible steps, including (1) a time for organizing and checking for understanding of the topic, (2) a time for focusing specifically on the problem, (3) a time for the group(s) to gather their information together, and (4) a time for a summary or conclusion phase involving the entire class.

If a whole class discussion is the intent, the classroom seating arrangement should allow students to see one another at all times. A large circle or two semicircles will satisfy this need. This way all students can see the face of the speaker and are thus more likely to stay attentive (assuming the topic is relevant and meaningful to them). The teacher who is able to create an open, encouraging atmosphere in a whole class discussion will facilitate a smooth flow of student-student interaction involving all learners. If the format is small discussion groups with four to six members, it is easier to situate learners so they can face others in their group. In this setting the teacher moves freely from group to group, monitoring and redirecting when necessary.

In other discussion environments, there may be a leader besides the teacher. Small group discussions usually need student group leaders, with all students eventually taking on this role at some point during the year. An effective small group discussion features (1) an accepting, nonjudgmental attitude, particularly from the group leader, (2) an avoidance of personal comments or evaluations of anyone's response, (3) a series of questions, usually when a point needs further clarification or input from a quiet group member is desired, and (4) a conclusive statement that the entire group agrees on (Lemlech, 1994). The discussion leader, teacher or student, will be that individual who demonstrates each of these behaviors most clearly.

Others in the discussion group will also demonstrate aspects of these behaviors. In addition, their conduct will be characterized by a generally sensitive demeanor, a decidedly inquisitive yet patient manner of listening and questioning, and a sense of responsibility for contributing to the overall group effort. Most small groups also have recorders who have learned, with the help of other group members, both how to keep a written account of the discussion and how to report it to other groups. An account of the general flow of the discussion is required, and the recorder can occasionally summarize parts of the written record aloud to be sure the account is being accurately kept or to get the group back on track.

Although discussion lessons rarely proceed exactly in the sequence just described, effective discussion is basically characterized by a smooth flow of meaningful chatter that moves among everyone in the class or group. There is an air of positive feeling as individual responses are sought out (but not judged) from all learners. The educator rarely breaks into the natural give-and-take of the peer conversation because she or he knows that such interventions almost always inhibit the expression of ideas and sense of group cohesiveness (Lemlech, 1994). Students are listening to each other, taking turns talking, avoiding the temptation to whisper to the person next to them, and thinking carefully about what they will say next.

One way to help learners build their discussion skills is to plan frequent discussion lessons for pairs and small groups before trying a whole class discussion (Pasch, Sparks-Langer, Gardner, Starko, & Moody, 1991). In these preliminary discussion lessons, the topic can be highly enjoyable, designed primarily to build discussion skills, and the structure can be carefully monitored.

Some discussions will look different from others. The sharing time in a primary grades classroom is less structured and designed for language expression, both planned and spontaneous. Educators at this level also use discussion to find out what students already know before beginning a new unit of study. A slightly more structured discussion might be found in a classroom where small groups of learners, after working with various types of rocks, report during a whole class discussion on the ways that they grouped the rocks. Yet a more structured discussion can be observed in a class of sixth graders where a series of questions, sequenced from factual to evaluative, provide the guidelines for small groups of learners who are expected to decide on the best way to raise money for a stated purpose and why they feel it is the best way. Discussions can meet the cognitive and social needs of a wide range of learners through an equally wide range of formats.

Exactly what is the educator doing during all of this discussion activity? The educator is constantly aware that the discussion lesson has two desired outcomes. One is clearly related to the subject matter that is the focus of the discussion, and the other is the process of the discussion itself. One way to make sure that groups stay focused is to provide them with a list of questions at the outset and set a time limit for the discussion. Even so, the educator may find a group off the topic and have to redirect them. During the same discussion activity, the educator may find that some groups finish the discussion assignment before others. When this happens, the educator must be able to suggest an extension to the discussion so that learners can develop their thinking more deeply.

Reflect for a Moment

When you were involved in discussion classes, were you aware that social skills were being developed, not just academic outcomes? Did you actually learn how to listen better? How to take another's point of view more readily? Did you engage in discussion activities in elementary school that contributed to these social skills?

To make an ongoing assessment of the discussion process, the educator will change the makeup of the groups so that learners work with a range of peers; members of each group will also be different from each other to enrich the exchange of ideas. In addition, the educator will move among the groups, reinforcing the rules and roles of the discussion process whenever necessary. At times this may require reteaching such discussion behaviors as recognizing when another student is about to speak or when a student has finished speaking. The teacher may also need to reinforce the role of the leader or the recorder during the discussion activity. At times, a student may need clarification from a peer but may not request it. The educator must prompt further explanation, reminding students of the need to ask for elaboration if something is not clearly stated.

An educator who wants learners to develop the positive, accepting attitude toward others that is so important to successful discussion lessons will consciously model that attitude. This might be done by responding to learner comments so objectively that they cannot tell whether there is approval or not (Lemlech, 1994). This also means that educators may also model ways of requesting clarification whenever necessary, especially when the student's comment is clearly questionable or irrelevant. During the final phase of the discussion activity, when groups report back to the whole class, the teacher will usually encourage learners to reflect on (1) any aspect of the question they may have forgotten, (2) what they have actually achieved during the lesson, and (3) the effectiveness of various roles and rules for their discussion group.

When Discussion Teaching Can Be Used

It is important to understand that the mundane teacher-directed question-and-answer period is not in any way a discussion lesson. Furthermore, if an educator wishes to teach facts, concepts, generalizations, rules, and the like, the discussion strategy is not recommended. Discussion teaching is a carefully organized instructional strategy that is used when the desired learning outcome(s) reflect higher expectations for cognitive behavior from learners. Reflective teachers who themselves spend considerable time pondering alternatives and debating ideas with others will undoubtedly value discussion teaching and plan for it often in their curriculum. Teachers who want to develop students' problem-solving and decision-making skills will find themselves making frequent use of discussion teaching. However, they must have a thorough understanding of the problem-solving or decision-making process so that they can structure the discussion to give learners opportunities to practice these skills (Eby, 1992).

Discussion teaching is used when brainstorming activities are an integral part of the lesson. The educator provides the question or dilemma, with prompts if necessary, and students generate numerous responses. The number of responses is narrowed by using student input to determine the most important responses. An example might begin with the question, "Who might make a good president?" The teacher could prompt learners by asking, "What makes a good president?" "What skills should a president have?" and "How could the current president do a better job?" Answers to these questions could help narrow the list of student responses. Throughout such a discussion, learners are thinking analytically, considering several alternatives, and debating the merits of various criteria to be used in judging the alternatives.

Discussion teaching is also used when educators wish to promote **critical thinking** (Eby, 1992). Critical thinking is "skillful, responsible thinking that facilitates good judgment because it (1) relies upon criteria, (2) is self-correcting, and (3) is sensitive to context" (Lipman, 1988, p. 39). Although it is similar to brainstorming to solve a problem, critical thinking includes such additional affective goals as independence, avoiding egocentric behavior, and suspending judgment (Paul, 1988). In fact, Raths, Wasserman, Jonas, and Rothstein (1986) suggest that educators who are planning and implementing discussion lessons should focus on a single thinking skill, such as summarizing, and make learners fully aware of the focus.

Educators can also implement discussion lessons when they want to develop students' creative thinking abilities. **Divergent thinking**, a major feature of creative thinking, is characterized by the ability to generate numerous ideas, change one's thinking, come up with new and relevant ideas, and contribute additional details to an idea (Eby, 1992). Discussion lessons can strengthen divergent thinking because learners are frequently given open-ended situations to complete or resolve and will consequently create numerous possibilities. They will also, in most discussion lessons, listen to the ideas of others in their group and, in some cases, change their thinking on a particular topic. Part of a successful discussion is the process of checking each other's input for relevance, and one of the most reliable ways to confirm relevance is to provide details about an idea to others in a group discussion. Whether it is a problem to be solved or an exploratory venture into a truly hypothetical scenario, learners in discussion activities are building creative thinking in several ways.

Reflect for a Moment

Do you really think these lessons that focus on critical thinking, creative thinking, and problem solving are better than rote memory drills? Why or why not? Will learners ever get the "basics" if we are forever concerned with divergent thinking and reasoning skills?

Cooperative learning is frequently used as a grouping technique for discussion lessons. As we have seen, cooperative learning is characterized by positive interdependence, individual accountability, face-to-face interaction, and various social and cooperative skills (Putnam, 1993). Discussion lessons offer highly compatible procedures and levels of learning for cooperative learning groups and should be strongly considered if the instructional goals are higher-level thinking and cooperative skill building.

Clearly, the discussion approach provides many obvious opportunities for both collaboration and inclusion. Collaboration among educators is, of course, a prerequisite for any successful activity in an inclusive setting, and discussion lessons are no exception. Many successful discussion lessons in inclusive settings are the result, in part, of strategic groupings; specific questioning sequences; and the overall positive, accepting atmosphere of a cooperative small group or whole class discussion. Collaboration among learners in discussion lessons is essential for group success regardless of the task or problem facing the group members. Because the features of an effective discussion are entirely complementary with the features of a successful inclusive classroom, discussion activities are wholly compatible with efforts to collaborate among adults and students in inclusive settings.

EFFECTIVE TEACHING

The discussion approach relies upon the educator's use of **attention-gaining techniques** to get the discussion started. Once started, the educator needs to demonstrate *enthusiasm* to keep the learners engaged in discussion.

Discussion strategies are very different from expository and discovery strategies. They are less effective for teaching specific content because they are less educator directed and more time consuming. As stated previously, there are a variety of situations in which the objective cannot be adequately met by either the expository or discovery approach. Therefore, goals that involve the development of skills such as leadership, summarizing others' opinions, active listening, and the ability to analyze, synthesize, and evaluate are best served through the discussion approach.

The discussion approach requires an interchange of ideas between the educator and learners or among learners (Freiberg & Driscoll, 1992). Discussion lessons may be conducted in a whole group setting, within small cooperative groups, or between two learners. For a discussion to be effective, there must be "a climate of reflective listening, respect for the speaker's ideas, and noninterference from the teacher" (Freiberg & Driscoll, 1992, p. 226). When this atmosphere is present, discussion lessons are characterized by:

> (1) the probing exploration of ideas, concepts, and issues; (2) building upon student responses in a developmental flow; (3) interaction among all participants; (4) shifting leadership among participants; (5) questioning, sharing, differing, conjecturing on the part of all; (6) student participation in decision making; (7) hypothesizing and problem solving. (Callahan & Clark, 1988, p. 211)

Reflect for a Moment

In working with younger children, have you ever found yourself developing and using a series of questions intended to help them understand or solve a problem instead of always just telling them what to do, or what's wrong or right? Perhaps you have simply asked a young child a question that openly perplexed him or her? Caused him or her to think more deeply, as if in a discussion activity (see above)?

The discussion approach meets many of the effective teacher behaviors (see Chapter 4 for a complete list) detailed by Borich (1992). A critical aspect of effective teaching is **instructional variety**. Discussion teaching employs a variety of different materials, questioning procedures, and feedback techniques. Educators who effectively implement the discussion approach may use a variety of visual aids, reading materials, audiovisual technology, and reference materials.

In addition to variation in material, an educator can also implement any number of interaction techniques. Several presentation-type techniques such as panels, symposia, debates, forums, and round-table discussions can enhance interaction. All of these techniques allow learners to share ideas, opinions, information, and differing points of view.

Student involvement in **active engaged time** is an essential factor of the effective discussion lesson. Educators use provocative questions and materials to pique learners' curiosity, thereby effectively drawing students into the discussion. Responses by the educator are designed to be kept at a minimum to encourage learners who normally are not risk takers to become actively involved and to enhance student-to-student interactions.

Discussion learning also features **using learners' ideas**. Educators who use the discussion approach effectively acknowledge, summarize, or apply learners' comments (when appropriate) without judging. By doing so, they are able to reap the benefits of higher levels of learner participation while also eliciting higher levels of thinking from students.

Clearly defined **questioning strategies** are yet another key factor in effective discussion teaching. During discussion activities the educator provides direction to students only as needed, thus making them responsible for their own learning. Like the expository and discovery approaches, discussion allows the educator to closely monitor the progress of the group, and encourage active learner engagement and higher-level thinking skills. Taking the role of facilitator, educators lead students through the learning event. Discussion is teacher directed, usually through the use of questioning. Discussion teaching relies on the sharing of a wide variety of opinions not only from the educator but from students as well. Educator-student interaction is necessary only when the teacher needs to assist the learners through questions, examples, or reclarification of the issue. **Interpretative** and **evaluative questions** are a vital part of the effective discussion lesson. Both interpretative and evaluative questions are used to elicit deeper, more complex student thinking which is an essential feature of learning through discussion. In effect this form of questioning empowers students to investigate through discussion new issues and old or new beliefs.

The discussion approach provides **clarity**. Learners are informed of the objective before the discussion begins. Directives are given to help learners participate. Review and summary are also provided as needed during the discussion, sometimes by the educator but often by students.

An effective classroom discussion allows **high rates of successful participation** by all learners. The pace varies as the learners present their ideas, consider others' opinions, and rethink their own. Students welcome opportunities to restructure learning by examining their own hypotheses. Wyne and Stuck (1982) and Brophy and Evertson (1976) suggest that students who engage in learning with a minimum of errors have higher achievement and a better attitude toward school.

TABLE 12.1   Discussion Lesson Plan

Unit:	Constitution: Civil rights and constitutional rights.
Objective:	Students will understand the relationship among fact, interpretation, and opinion so that when given an issue they will take a position and defend it with evidence. Students will demonstrate the appropriate discussion manners.
Rationale:	The ability to distinguish among fact, opinion, experience, and interpretation is important in the development of higher-level thinking skills. Participating and communicating effectively during a discussion is an important skill both in the workforce and everyday life.
Materials:	Articles supplying students with information on both sides of the issue. Video newsclips on cases where children seem to be denied their civil rights and cases of children legally divorcing their parents.
Content:	The issue of civil rights is not a new one. However, there appears to be a difference in your rights depending on how old you are. There has been a lot in the news lately about children exercising their due process rights by suing their parents for divorce. Should children be allowed to do this? Should civil rights be different for children than for adults?

Procedure:	Show video clips. Have class identify possible positions, the black and white areas as well as the gray. Divide the class into smaller groups and give each group a set of articles that discuss different aspects of the issue. Have the groups meet to do the following:
	   Take a position on the issue and document it.
	   Summarize the information from your article to report to the rest of the class.
	   Come to a group consensus. If not possible, prepare a minority statement.

Discussion Questions:

> *Basic Question:* Should children have the same civil and constitutional rights as adults? Be treated as equals under the law?

> *Follow-up Questions* [a]
> How do you think the law differs?
> What rights do you see as being for adults only?
> What rights do you see as being for children only?
> Are there some laws that protect adults more? Which ones?
> Are there some laws that protect children more? Which ones?
> Parents can divorce themselves from their children (give them up for adoption or over to the state). Should children have the right to divorce their parents? Under what circumstances? Money? Abuse?
> People who divorce sometimes remarry—should children be allowed to undivorce their parents?

Summary of Students'

Observations:	Learners should be asked to orally list points and draw conclusions.
Review of Process:	Have students discuss the discussion. Were there any problems? How could things be done differently?
Evaluation:	Have students write a brief paper that includes a position, supporting evidence, and a summary.

[a] Sometimes follow-up questions may not be delivered by the educator as they are hopefully spontaneously generated by the group during discussion.

PLANNING PROCEDURES

In planning and implementing an effective discussion lesson (see Table 12.1 for sample plan) there are eight general guidelines that should be considered (Borich, 1992; Freiberg & Driscoll, 1992; Jacobsen, Eggen, & Kauchak, 1993; Passe, 1984). First, educators must carefully consider the objective of the discussion and structure the discussion lesson accordingly. If the objective focuses on cognitive skills such as analysis, synthesis, and evaluation, then questions that draw on those skills are appropriate. When the objective is directed toward affective development, then questions related to valuing, organization, and characterization are more appropriate.

Second, educators need to consider learners' ability, experience, and developmental level. Young, inexperienced learners or learners with disabilities may need more direction from the educator during discussion. Directions and questions need to be developed that will help all learners participate in the discussion process. Additionally, ability, experience, and the developmental level of the learners involved will impact on the amount of time a discussion can continue effectively. As learners gain confidence and are exposed to the discussion approach, directions and questions will become less explicit and more student directed. This process can be enhanced by developing the discussion around a unit or a series of related lessons. This framing helps to ensure that the learner has a sufficient information base to allow him or her to discuss the issue or idea comfortably.

Reflect for a Moment

Speaking of experience, if you are not enamored with complex mathematics, how long do you stay interested in a discussion of differential equations? Speaking of ability, how much would you want to contribute to a discussion of vowels? Have you witnessed young children in church? Or in the living room with a group of adults who are discussing politics?

Third, an effective educator must study the issue and/or materials to be considered during the discussion. Often educators have the misconception that discussion lessons can be thrown together with little or no preparation on their part. Reading a single article or examining a single point of view does not prepare an educator to conduct or facilitate a profitable discussion lesson (cognitively, affectively, or academically). A thorough understanding of the issues involved will help the educator keep the discussion from drifting to issues that are only tangentially related to the original topic.

Fourth, learners need to understand the goals or objectives of the discussion. Having a clear understanding provides the students with a guide for the learning event and also alleviates their concerns about "What are we supposed to be doing?"

Fifth, the educator needs to provide a supportive environment by actively listening while learners are talking. Learners must feel they are able to contribute to the discussion without fear of mockery or embarrassment. A moderate environment should be sought, one that is neither too permissive or too rigid. An effective educator will develop such an environment.

Sixth, the effective educator will refrain from commenting or elaborating after each learner's statement. By doing this, the educator encourages more learner-to-learner dialogue that does not rely on the teacher as a conduit. Practicing such restraint will increase both the available time and number of learners participating. However, Taba (1967) cautions that an educator who abandons the discussion totally to learners will have an extremely limited and chaotic lesson.

Seventh, even though the educator should show restraint in commenting, it is necessary to occasionally review, summarize, or meld opinions and facts into a meaningful relationship. Educators need to recognize when it is appropriate to restate the major concepts to help provide meaning and structure to the lesson. The restatement can be done by the educator or a learner, depending on how the discussion has progressed.

Eighth, because discussions can sometimes touch on sensitive topics that produce stress, educators need to be able to use humor. By using humor appropriately, an educator is able to reduce tension in a classroom discussion and redirect or defuse remarks made unintentionally that may be seen by some as offensive.

Once these guidelines have been carefully considered, the educator is ready to carefully organize the discussion lesson. Jacobsen, Eggen, and Kauchak (1993) point out that "it is absolutely critical that the activity be carefully organized, or the activity will result in nonlearning at best or disintegrate into chaos at worst" (p. 207).

There are five steps that an educator needs to complete to conduct a successful discussion lesson:

Step 1. Read materials and develop questions.

Step 2. Plan and group questions.

Step 3. Introduce the model to learners.

Step 4. Conduct the discussion.

Step 5. Review the process and summarize learners' observations. (Gunter, Estes, & Schwab, 1990)

As these five steps indicate, a great deal of the actual structuring of the discussion lesson relies on the use of appropriate questioning strategies. For that reason, this chapter will deviate slightly from the other methodology chapters by discussing questioning in the planning section.

The quality of any discussion is directly related to the level and caliber of the questions being asked. To develop such questions, the first thing an educator must do is read and understand the materials under discussion. Then, in preparing questions, the educator must be able to distinguish between factual, interpretive, and evaluative questions. "Understanding the distinctions between these three types of questions makes it much easier to generate provocative questions" (Gunter, Estes, & Schwab, 1990, p. 150).

TABLE 12.2   Factual, Interpretative, and Evaluative Questions

Factual:	Who was swallowed by a whale? What was Gepetto's wish? How many organs are there in the human body? What are the five basic senses? From what type of cloud formation can we expect thunderstorms?
Interpretive:	Why was Jonah swallowed by the whale? Why wasn't Gepetto's wish granted right away? Why do human beings have organs that they do not need (that are not essential for life)? Is any one sense more important than another?
Evaluative:	If you could gain his insight, would you switch places with Jonah and why? In what other ways could Pinocchio been "cured" of lying? If asked to give up one of your organs, such as a lung or kidney, to help someone else, would you do it and why? Which of your senses would you least like to give up and why?

QUESTION TYPES

When a question can be answered by direct repeating of words from a text, lecture, or other materials, that question is considered **factual**. Factual questions call on the learner to respond with answers already provided by the assigned material, even if these assertions are counter to the student's conception of reality. For example, the existence of winged monkeys that fly is a "fact" in *The Wizard of Oz,* although the reality is that they do not exist. Personal experiences of students are not a source of facts and should not be used to answer factual questions. In dealing with factual questions (examples can be found in Table 12.2), the educator must help learners perceive reality from the perspective of the material being presented. The Great Books Foundation (1965) recommends that a good rule of thumb to follow when trying to decide if a question is factual is to determine whether it could be answered satisfactorily by the learner's covering his or her mouth and pointing to a passage in a book, line on a chart, or some other part of the materials used.

Reflect for a Moment

What limitations can you see to the recommendation of the Great Books Foundation? How would you refine this "rule of thumb" for determining whether or not a question is factual?

Questions that are developed to allow the learner to explore not only what the material states directly but also what the material means are **interpretive questions** (examples can be found in Table 12.2). Materials are not always as clear to others as they are to their creator. As with all things in life, written and visual materials are limited by the developer or author's perspective, personal experiences, meaning placed on certain words, and ability to translate thought and feelings into concrete form. It is therefore the function of interpretative questions to assist the learner in exploring these areas of ambiguity to obtain a better sense of what the developer is trying to communicate. "The ultimate justification for interpretation is the text itself; the ultimate burden of interpretation is on readers" (Gunter, Estes, & Schwab, 1990, p. 151). However, the "burden of interpretation" for the learners can be lightened if the educator has prepared a set of well-designed interpretative questions.

When a question is designed to have learners probe the relevance of the material for themselves it is **evaluative**. However, before a learner can respond to an evaluative question (examples can be found in Table 12.2), she or he must have a well-developed understanding of the issue presented. Hence evaluative questions should be used only when the educator is positive that students have developed this understanding. Evaluative questions should provide learners with an opportunity to bring into a discussion their own personal experiences and standards of value.

Discussion lessons represent the perfect time for collaborative teaching. Talking about the materials prior to the lesson gives the collaborators an opportunity to compare ideas, reactions, and questions—step 2 of the discussion lesson presentation process. Because deeper insights can be generated by two persons, collaboration creates better questions.

Step 3 of the process requires the educator to introduce the class to the discussion model. As we have already seen, students learn better when they are made aware of what they are going to do and why. Discussions must have a purpose; that is what distinguishes them from conversations.

It is also at this step of planning when the educator selects the presentation technique to be employed: large group, round-table, panel, forum, symposium, debate, and/or British-style debate. When the issue is best discussed in a less formal manner with five or fewer participants, a **round-table technique** may be best. A **panel** allows for several small groups of four to six students, with a chairperson to discuss a topic among themselves then expand to a larger give-and-take session with the entire class. The **forum** technique incorporates the panel format, but discussion occurs between the panel and the entire class rather than among panel members.

The next three techniques are much more formal than the previous three (note that formality does not presuppose more or less planning). Discussions can be developed in a **symposium**, with a single student or small group of students introducing differing positions on a topic and then opening up the discussion to include all members of the class. **Debate**, an extremely formal technique, can be used to break the class into smaller opposing teams with arguments and rebuttals by each participant. A final technique that can be used by the educator is the **British-style debate**, a modification of the standard debate format in which the class is divided into parties whose members may ask questions, make comments, or share opinions.

The success of the discussion approach also depends on introducing learners at this time to discussion manners and skills. Lemlech (1994) points out that only when the flow of conversation moves around the students and encourages individuals to respond does the discussion approach work. Although most discussion manners are common sense, the educator should not take for granted that learners know them.

During step 3 students should also be asked to refamiliarize themselves with the material to be discussed, perhaps through a second reading. At this time learners may also develop questions they wish to have the class discuss based on the materials. This is an opportunity for learners to analyze the material and is an excellent source of questions.

Step 4 involves the actual conduct of the discussion. Prior to beginning, learners should be made aware that the educator(s) will begin with questions that create conflict or doubt. Learners will be encouraged to ask their own questions and share concerns or opinions. The fact that there is no single right or correct answer should be stressed so that learners will not waste energy in search of one. Students should be reminded that they are to respond to each other's ideas and should not talk over others or between themselves when someone else has the floor.

The discussion can be enhanced by having learners share equal space with the educator(s). This can be accomplished by having everyone, including teachers, put their chairs or desks in a circle or sit on the floor in a circle. When teachers join the circle, students' perception of them changes from that of an authority figure to a participant.

Discussions can also be enhanced by dividing the class into smaller groups. However it is important to be sure that learners understand what they are to discuss before breaking into groups. This involves **establishing a focus** so that the natural tendency to digress is curbed. A focus can be developed by providing each group with a series of questions or having the entire class brainstorm a series of questions that they wish to discuss.

An educator who circulates from group to group often finds the discussion has veered away from the problem focus. When this has occurred, the educator needs to help the group **refocus** by asking a question or making a statement. Refocusing may also be used if a group is not discussing the topic in enough depth.

During the discussion the educator needs to be constantly aware of ways to extend and deepen students' level of thought. To do this, Lemlech (1994) recommends the following:

1. Ask the students to review the major points already discussed, or summarize what has been said yourself.
2. After the summary, ask "What do we still need to consider?"
3. If there has been conflict over definitions or values expressed, ask the class if Billy and Susie meant the same things when they discussed *communication*.
4. Remind students that they have already discussed several means of communication. Then ask, "Are there some things we have forgotten?" Or, "How else might we think about . . .?" (p. 129)

Unlike other lessons, there is no true or absolute closure to a discussion lesson. Because discussion represents a process rather than a product approach to learning, step 5 involves reviewing the process and summarizing students' observations (Gunter, Estes, & Schwab, 1990). Although the educator may conduct this activity, it is far more beneficial to have the learners perform the review and summary. This is not to say that there can be no product. Often this product will be oral rather than written; a list, summary, series of conclusions, or something similar may serve the purpose. Regardless of the form of the conclusion format, one sure sign of a successful discussion lesson is when learners continue their conversations during lunch or recess.

Reflect for a Moment

When, recently, did you leave a class and continue to discuss the topic of the class with one or more classmates? What was the topic? What type of teaching strategy was used with the topic that day?

DEVELOPING GOOD DISCUSSION QUESTIONS

As stated in previous chapters, an important facet of any question is wording. Therefore, the educator must make the intent of any question perfectly clear, regardless of question type. When a question is worded ambiguously, the learner is left to decide whether the educator is asking for a factual, interpretative, or evaluative response. Learners will be less confident about responding and the discussion may end up becoming a teacher monologue.

Questions should be developed that help learners to reason aloud. This provides the educator with an excellent opportunity to examine students' thought processes. Additionally, learners are able to assess their own cognitive strategies as they verbally work through their responses.

Sequencing of Questions

Once questions have been brainstormed, they should be clustered, determining which are basic questions and then placing under each the appropriate follow-up questions. Questions that are brainstormed should be clustered with one basic question followed by ten to twelve follow-up questions. Three to four such clusters generally provide sufficient questions for a well-rounded discussion.

Although both basic questions and follow-up questions are interpretative, their scope and expected results vary. Gunter, Estes, and Schwab (1990) refer to **basic questions** as "umbrella" questions because they are designed to raise an issue and are, therefore, broad in scope. Because basic questions are designed to inspire discussion, they must be provocative. Note that learners should be able to answer the basic question in several ways. If only a single answer is required, the question is neither basic or interpretative.

Questions that help to develop the issue are **follow-up questions**. Follow-up questions move learners away from their initial reaction by creating an opportunity to look at the issue in a broader context. Follow-up questions and successive clusters need to be logically sequenced, just as in the discovery approach. Successful discussions to a large extent depend on the logical flow of questions.

Selection of Respondents

The importance of the educator's ability to establish an environment where learners feel free to respond is magnified by the discussion approach. By its nature, the discussion approach produces a greater level of participation than does the expository approach. In the selection of respondents, the educator needs to be sure to not allow a single student or a small group of learners to monopolize the discussion. For the discussion method to work effectively, a diversity of participants are needed. Divergent responses create a thinking environment, one in which learners begin to look at others' points of view in an attempt to clarify their own.

Handling Correct and Incorrect Responses

Generally, questions that call for interpretation or evaluation are *divergent* in nature. As such, they encourage a diversity of responses and therefore variation in the way in which answers are handled. Divergent questions require learners to expand on what they already know through analysis and synthesis. With the use of divergent questions, invalid or partially correct responses need to be viewed not as wrong but as requiring validation. When a comment or response is invalid, learners should be asked to support their point of view.

As noted in Chapter 10, the educator's responses to learners' replies are perhaps more important than the original questions. Thus, educators' responses should never be negative in nature but rather should encourage the learners to continue sharing their opinions and beliefs. Typically, the communication cycle in a learning event involves the educator's question, a learner's response, and some form of reaction by the teacher to the student's answer. Since the discussion approach relies more on student-to-student communication, the educator must also instruct learners in how they should respond to one another.

Once an initial question has been asked, sufficient wait time must be allowed before the educator(s) calls for a response. Educators should wait until several hands are up. By not always calling on the learners whose hands went up first, the educator makes it clear that she or he wants the students to think before responding.

Several responses should be solicited before moving on to another question. "It is the richness of varying perspectives that makes the insights so penetrating" (Gunter, Estes, & Schwab, 1990, p. 159). The educator needs to be aware of the content of the responses so that when they become redundant the discussion can be moved ahead.

Reflect for a Moment

In your experience as a student, what have teachers actually done that made you feel you could answer questions in class? What teacher responses to incorrect responses made you feel less inhibited about answering? What did teachers say that made you afraid to respond in class?

Inhibiting Discussion Through Questions

Although questions are an important part of the discussion approach, Dillon (1988) cautions that educator questioning can be a primary inhibitor to implementing this strategy effectively. The discussion can become teacher dominated if the educator is unable to pull away from the role of gatekeeper. Educators must be aware that what may be an attempt to keep learners focused through questioning actually results in drawing learners away from the discussion. This change of roles is made even more challenging by the fact that many educators have had little or no opportunity to see effective discussion modeled during their own schooling.

Practice

Select a topic for discussion. Develop an umbrella question and six follow-up questions that you might use to enhance the discussion.

AN EXAMPLE OF DISCUSSION TEACHING

Rose Augusta and Alan Jacobs have been working with their inclusive sixth grade classroom on a unit about the U.S. Constitution.

MR. JACOBS: You've been learning about the U.S. Constitution and Bill of Rights, the documents that form the foundation of our legal and civil system.

MRS. AUGUSTA: Many of you have commented that you believe they are documents written by adults for only adults. Is that a fair representation of what Mr. Jacobs and myself have been hearing? [A loud "yes" comes from the group, with only a few "no's".]

AARON: Children aren't specifically mentioned in the Constitution or the Bill of Rights.

MINDY: But neither are women, so does that mean that women are not covered by those documents?

OSCAR: No "man" was a generic term used to cover all people, not just adults and not just men!

MR. JACOBS: Before we continue with our discussion, we are going to show you some newsclips, and while watching please keep the following question in mind: How do you think the law differs for different people? [Show video. Lights come on. Hands go up.]

MRS. AUGUSTA: Wow, everyone is excited to talk! But put your hands down for just a minute. Now that you have watched these newscasts, we have several articles for you to consider while forming your arguments and opinions. Please get into your small discussion groups. All groups are getting the same set of articles. Each person in the group will get a different article. Read and then summarize findings for your group. Then Mr. Jacobs and I would like you to discuss the following questions.

MR. JACOBS: How do you think the law differs for different people? What rights do you see as being for adults only? What rights do you see as being for children only? Are there some laws that protect adults more? Are there some laws that protect children more? Parents can divorce themselves from their children (give them up for adoption or over to the state). Should children have the right to divorce their parents? Why? Under what circumstances? Money? Abuse? People who divorce sometimes remarry—should children be allowed to undivorce their parents? Why? When?

MRS. AUGUSTA: Remember, you only have 30 minutes before we come back together for our large discussion group. [Mr. Jacobs and Mrs. Augusta circulate from group to group, listening and only asking questions to help focus and redirect discussion.]

Practice

Put yourself in the place of Mr. Jacobs or Mrs. Augusta. You are listening to one of the groups.   Write a scenario that reflects this discussion.

ADAPTATIONS

Given the nature of discussion teaching, there are several reasons to suggest that instructional adaptations for inclusive classrooms are immediately apparent, if not embedded in the approach itself. Among the characteristics of discussion teaching that inherently lend themselves to adaptable instruction are active participation, cooperative learning groups and pairs, emphasis on interactive skills, relevance of content, and student collaboration. Each of these characteristics can be examined as part of the goals and objectives, textbooks and other printed materials, grouping techniques, instructional procedures, or assessments and assignments sections that follow.

Recall the basic advantages that an inclusive environment brings to the process of adapting instruction mentioned in Chapter 10. These advantages apply equally well to making adaptations in using the discussion approach and can be the foundation for making successful adaptations for individual learners. As a result of the three advantages described in Chapter 10, educators are working together, collaborating on appropriate adaptations, using a flexible thematic approach to planning curriculum, and implementing lessons that reflect a student-centered attitude about learning. Such an atmosphere accommodates instructional adaptations more easily than a traditional teacher-centered, subject area curriculum where educators work largely on their own.

Goals and Objectives

Out of an atmosphere such as that just described comes the growing recognition that instructional goals and objectives cannot be strictly academic or rigidly applied to all learners in a classroom. Effective inclusive settings place a priority on learners' being accepted, having friends among both peers and adults, and developing a positive sense of self based on success both academically and socially (Stainback, Stainback, & Moravec, 1992). Although academic challenges should begin on the first day of school, these affective goals are prerequisites to academic learning for all students and are the first priority in the minds of successful inclusive educators. This approach to curriculum goals reflects a new awareness that traditional academic goals need to be reconsidered and, in some cases, replaced by wholly different emphases—including learning how to learn, learning by using individual background experiences, learning relevant and meaningful material, and giving the learner more control over the learning process (Smith, 1986). If these emphases are honored, learners will spend their school time interacting much more with each other as they pursue tasks with relevance to their lives.

Nevin (1993) suggests that instructional goals and objectives can be adapted for cooperative learning groups. The response mode can be changed according to the learner's sensory abilities, and the amount of work or the amount of time given to complete the work can be adapted. All these adaptations, when applied to a discussion activity, do not need to single out a particular student or be obtrusive. The objective is usually the most critical element of the planning process and needs to be clearly and succinctly stated prior to implementing the discussion. In addition, a cooperative learning discussion activity has both academic goals and social goals, and adaptations may need to be considered in one or both areas. For example, a social goal for a learner with multiple sensory disabilities may be to willingly accept guidance from a peer, whereas a social goal for the peer who is without disabilities may be to use positive statements.

Reflect for a Moment

Have you ever, as a student, been aware of a lesson where some students had different learning objectives than others? Why was this? Did it affect you in any way?

Textbooks and Other Printed Materials

Several strategies already mentioned in Chapters 10 and 11 also apply to adapting textbooks and other printed materials for discussion lessons. In many discussion activities, learners are expected to have read and understood a printed passage or chapter in a text. If they are not able to participate actively in the discussion, it is often because they were not able to manage the reading assignment. Readings with clearly marked subheadings, margin notes, charts and graphs, and summaries can help, as can efforts to provide nonreaders with tape recordings of reading passages. As stated in Chapter 9, those in the school community who tape-record reading passages can help learners prepare for discussion lessons by interjecting comprehension questions and answers during the tape recording. Study guides and teacher-directed structured overviews are also helpful in preparing for a group or class discussion.

Grouping Techniques

Because the discussion approach relies heavily on careful grouping of learners, adaptations in grouping techniques are likely to have a major impact on the success of all learners, particularly those with different disabilities. A number of adaptations are possible, depending on whether the educator is planning a whole class discussion, discussions in pairs, or small group cooperative learning discussions.

Whole Class Discussions

When a whole class discussion is planned, the educator must be fully aware of individual learners and how they are likely to respond to a whole class discussion on a particular topic. Whole class discussions are more likely to succeed when the topic is of particularly high interest to all learners. For example, a whole class discussion in a fifth grade class on student council elections or yesterday's lightning storm will more easily capture the attention of the entire class than a discussion on Iroquois farming techniques or the growing season in the Middle Atlantic states.

In addition, educators should provide opportunities for specific learners to respond to specific questions, offer more than one response mode to learners, and move about the classroom to prompt specific respondents or simply to maintain the attentiveness of certain learners. In some whole class discussions, other members of the collaborative planning team may be able to monitor the attentiveness of certain learners and even accompany the educator as she or he queries them on various aspects of a topic. Peer assistance arrangements can also improve the responsiveness of certain learners during whole class discussions. If brainstorming is a phase of the whole class discussion, the educator can more easily pursue active participation with all learners because responses are elicited from every student. Wait time, rephrased questions, and a variety of prompts can all increase response among learners with disabilities.

As mentioned earlier in this chapter, the atmosphere in the classroom will certainly contribute to the responsiveness of learners. Setting the right tone, so that all

learners feel that their efforts to participate will be welcomed, is critical to any whole class discussion and will require sensitivity of any educator. Finally, it is imperative that all learners possess the prerequisite knowledge for active participation in the whole class discussion, and it is the educator's responsibility to be sure that this is in fact the case. If a learner with a reading disability has not been provided with appropriate access to the assigned information, that learner will not be able to contribute confidently to the class discussion.

Small Groups

In adapting discussion lessons involving small groups, educators are constantly looking for the most effective combinations of learners. These combinations may vary depending on the topic, the tasks, or the various interests and abilities of the learners, but in each situation the makeup of the small group can greatly improve the effectiveness of a small group in a discussion. In some cases, the educator may choose to group learners by interest, while in others she or he may choose to place high-, middle- and low-ability students in each group. In any small group discussion activity, learners must not only have clear instructions, but must also confirm their understanding of the instructions before beginning the activity. Closely monitoring the time for the activity and making sure that learners are focusing on the topic are also important general adaptations for small group discussions.

One cooperative learning format that can be used to adapt discussion activities for individual learners is the Number Heads Together system (Maheady, Mallette, Harper, & Sacca, 1991). This approach increases participation among low-achieving learners and maintains participation levels among high-achieving learners. Small groups include high-, average-, and low-achieving students, and each member of a group is assigned a number from 1 to 4. Each teacher-directed question is addressed to learners with a certain number, but only after groups are given a short period of time to discuss the answer(s) to each question and make sure that all members have the needed response(s). In this manner, all learners, including low achievers, are usually prepared with sufficient information to respond successfully.

Pairs

There is an increasing awareness that pairing students together for a variety of lessons, including discussion activities, is an effective strategy (Good & Brophy, 1987; Harper, Maheady, & Mallette, 1994; Greenwood, Delquadri, & Hall, 1989). These pairings, often referred to as partner learning, peer-mediated, or peer learning programs, can occur across a wide range of settings and among an equally wide range of learners. When applied to a discussion activity, the **partner learning system** can help all learners and specifically those learners who have not experienced many positive relationships with others (LaPlant & Zane, 1994). Given an opportunity to teach others, students more often than not will find a new, positive sense of self-worth that they take with them to other school tasks. In discussions, partner learning arrangements can help learners who would become easily frustrated if left alone. The level of active involvement is obviously high when learners are paired together for discussion activities. The exchange of ideas, evaluation of each other's thinking, and ultimate consensus of judgment is facilitated when learners work in pairs. As an adaptive strategy, partner learning is very well suited to discussion lessons.

Reflect for a Moment

Which of the grouping arrangements mentioned has been your most successful format as a learner? Did your preference depend on the topic? Did your preference change from elementary to high school?

Instructional Procedures

In planning and implementing a discussion activity, regardless of the grouping arrangement or the topic, a wide range of adaptations are possible. The procedures of the discussion activity can be altered to meet the individual needs of

TABLE 12.3   Adapting Instructional Procedures in a Discussion Lesson

1. Check thoroughly for student understanding of prerequisite knowledge before launching into the discussion activity. Time to review the needed information is often very helpful. All learners must begin the discussion activity secure in knowing the information needed to contribute to the discussion, regardless of the grouping arrangement.
2. Be sure that all learners know that there is not necessarily a right or wrong answer to the questions that will frame the discussion activity and that talking to each other is not only permissible but quite important if they are going to learn from the activity.
3. Alert students to the importance of using their social skills (listening, accepting others' input, being open to suggestions, etc.), and that their ability to participate in the discussion is just as important an outcome as the content of the discussion.
4. Be careful to plan each step of the discussion lesson with specific time limits and objectives. Some learners will become easily distracted or frustrated with any sign of vagueness or ambiguity during the discussion activity.
5. Meet with other members of the collaborative team in advance to be sure their roles are clear as facilitators during discussion lessons.
6. In using discussion groups, consider individual student needs when identifying certain roles within a group (leader, recorder, reporter, etc.).
7. Sometimes it is helpful to provide learners with study guides or advance organizers so they can more confidently participate in a discussion.
8. Consider arranging specific question and answer exchanges with certain learners ahead of time to ensure positive and successful participation, especially during whole class discussions.
9. Move about the room, and monitor the discussion or discussion groups closely enough to be sure that learners are focused on the task at hand and that every learner is actively participating.
10. When it comes time for a group or class to produce a specific outcome from a discussion, be prepared to offer certain learners alternative response modes.
11. In planning a learning outcome for an individual within a cooperative group, be sure that it is meaningful and contributes to the group's expected learning outcome and not simply a task related to the topic.
12. Be sure to utilize any and all educational technology that can enhance the discussion experience for certain learners.
13. Collaborate with other educators on the team to structure behavior management plans for certain learners. Place an emphasis on strategies that utilize aspects of self-monitoring and self-reinforcement.

learners, and Table 12.3 presents a partial list of adaptations to instructional procedures.

Assignments and Assessments

In addition to those suggestions already made in Chapters 10 and 11, several specific ideas are appropriate in considering adaptations to assignments. Educators can give extra time for assignments; break down one long, complex assignment into several shorter, clearer assignments; make the original assignment shorter;

use the same procedures and formats for assignments over and over again; match the skills of the learner to the demands of the assignment; organize any written materials so that learners can easily follow the sequence of items; make directions as clear as possible and check for understanding; assign fewer items; and include familiar questions that learners already know among the questions that reflect new learning.

Many of these suggestions do run the risk of stigmatizing the learner with a disability, separating her or him from peers in terms of assignments. The stigmatizing effect can be lessened by nurturing a more collaborative atmosphere in the school and the classroom. As learners see educators needing each other's help or approaching the same task in two very different ways, they begin to realize that different people have different abilities and needs, that it is not a matter of one person's being better or worse than another person. One of the most powerful aspects of the discussion approach is its potential for building this collaborative ethic (see Chapter 5) among learners. When educators actively teach discussion skills to students, they also are imparting many collaborative skills that help students work together and learn to appreciate the unique contributions each can make to a cooperative group effort. This understanding in turn minimizes the stigma that might otherwise be attached to adaptations made to assignments and assessments.

Because of the highly interactive nature of the discussion approach, many assignments and assessments are group oriented, requiring learners to demonstrate collaboratively their understanding of a particular issue or topic. Many of these postdiscussion tasks are natural consequences of the discussions themselves and can be cooperative efforts in the classroom. For example, following a small group discussion in which learners had to develop a public relations campaign to help stop acid rain, the assessment could consist of actually presenting their campaigns to the whole class. Each member of the group would present the section that he or she had contributed and field questions from the class as well.

The authenticity in both assignments and assessments, initially described in Chapter 10, applies to the adaptation of discussion lessons as well. Because goals and objectives in discussion lessons are typically beyond the knowledge and comprehension levels of the cognitive domain and frequently include affective goals and objectives as well, assessment of learning must go far beyond the traditional low-level, pencil-and-paper tests so characteristic of many memorization tasks. Educators must adapt assessments to meet the authentic outcomes of the discussion activities themselves. Portfolios, debates, speeches, group presentations, community-based projects, student constructions (both individual and group), and written compositions are among the many vehicles available as educators adapt both assignments and assessments to meet the needs of all learners. These more authentic, descriptive approaches to assessment are of particular importance to educators who are pursuing collaborative, inclusive programs as they work to meet the needs of a wide range of learners.

Practice

You are planning a discussion activity for fourth grade students designed to build their critical thinking skills. As one of the concluding activities for their unit on poetry, they will, in small groups, select three poets they liked the best. Your task is to develop appropriate objec-tives, including criteria, for the four individuals in the group and the group as a whole. Keep in mind that one of the group members is nonver-bal and another has a moderate mental dis-ability.

STUDENT ASSESSMENT AND EVALUATION

Now you are ready to plan a unit on democracy with your third grade class. You have, with the help of the collaborative team and the students, identified a set of goals, have gathered materials from parents, community resources, and other peo-ple, and are including a real-life election in the school as part of the unit. You have laid out a tentative schedule of activities, investigations, and small group discus-sions to help students think carefully about what they are learning. But as you re-examine the goals and begin to build lesson objectives, you realize that several of the discussion lessons are more difficult to assess. How will you know what stu-dents have learned, and how will you evaluate it?

Here the reflective process is well under way in your planning and will lead you to a variety of useful and appropriate assessment and evaluation procedures. The key is to utilize not just one technique but several as you implement the unit, because one assessment or evaluation technique will not work effectively across a variety of tasks and instructional methods. What informal procedures will be help-ful? How will you assess those important affective outcomes from the discussion lessons? Are there essays the third grade students can work on to demonstrate their learning? Since there will be cooperative learning discussion groups, how about oral reports? Are there tests you can create to assess the higher levels of learning you anticipate? How about interviews and checklists? You have portfolios already in place, so what will their role be during this unit? Just how will you as-sess the cooperative groups themselves? And finally, how will you assign grades to these assessments?

Informal Techniques

One of the most valuable informal assessment techniques is **observation**. Obser-vation is, in the case of most teachers, a routine, ongoing process used every day. In discussion lessons, naturalistic observations can be used in a number of ways to gather data about student learning. Whether they use index cards or checklists or individual student folders with anecdotal entries, educators can gain valuable in-formation as they observe any discussion activity. They can observe how individual students relate to one another in whole class, small group, and partner learning settings. They can observe potentially disruptive grouping combinations. Simply watching the facial expressions of learners can often tell an educator whether they are interested, bored, frustrated, or nervous, resulting in an on-the-spot instructional adaptation. During a discussion group, the skilled observer can detect when an individual within a group is having difficulty participating or grasping the topic or the flow of the discussion. Educators can determine through observation when an individual or a group is ready to move on to the next phase of a discussion lesson, and when another group may need more time.

Another valuable informal assessment strategy for discussion activities is the use of **student journals** or *logs*. While offering the educator important information about the individual learner's progress, journals also support self-evaluation and metacognitive behavior among students. They can serve as either a formative or a summative assessment tool and address both academic and affective learning. They can be diagnostic and serve to alert educators of difficulties learners are having, or they can help both students and teachers understand what learning processes are successful for different individuals. They can accommodate a variety of the more complex learning behaviors inherent in discussion activities more fluently and honestly than can most paper-and-pencil tests.

A variation on the student journal is the **self-evaluative questionnaire** or *interview*, which invites learners to report orally to the educator about their learning experiences. The interview or questionnaire can tap information about individual student learning in much the same naturalistic manner as the journal, except that the educator is there in person asking the questions. If the arrangement appears to influence or inhibit a student's responses, it can be adapted so the learner can fill in answers privately and turn in the completed questionnaire. In either case, the learning that takes place during and after a discussion activity can be assessed using either the questionnaire or interview approach.

Another informal assessment practice, the **think-aloud** technique, can be used to confirm how well learners understand each other's points of view. Although often used in assessing basic reading comprehension, the think-aloud technique offers students an opportunity to demonstrate their ability to interpret each other's input during a discussion by restating what the other person said in their own words. When the think-aloud technique is used, the problem of misinterpretation and miscommunication can be greatly reduced, opening the door to clearer, more effective discussion activities. Still another informal technique, **error analysis**, can allow educators to break down the learner's responses so that the specific point of misunderstanding can be identified and remedied. During a discussion, there is always the risk that a learner may not have accurately understood or interpreted a question. Error analysis can zero in on which aspect of the issue or challenge has been misunderstood, permitting both learner and educator to correct the miscommunication and proceed with the discussion. Much like the other informal strategies already mentioned, error analysis can improve not only the learner's cognitive behavior, but also discussion skills and/or affective learning.

Much if not all of the evidence gathered using these techniques can be included in a portfolio so that the learner, the learner's parents, and the educator can all maintain an accurate awareness of the learner's progress during discussion lessons. In fact, discussion activities are ideally suited for assessment by means of a portfolio because the learning that takes place is often of a more abstract and complex nature, more accurately described in narrative, descriptive, or collective form than as a quantitative measure. It should be remembered that caption statements and summary sheets are important components of the portfolio (Salend, 1994). The **caption statement** is a brief written explanation attached to each item that includes some background information about the item and the rationale for its inclusion in the portfolio. The **summary sheet** is an organizer for the entire contents of the portfolio that draws all of the enclosed materials together in a cohesive manner to facilitate future instructional planning. Students are encouraged to contribute their own written or tape-recorded reflections of any and all materials included in the portfolio. These aspects of the portfolio make it a valuable tool for conferencing with students, parents, collaborative team members, and future teachers.

Reflect for a Moment

Think about the class you are taking now. What materials from the entire course would you include in a portfolio to reflect a composite of your work for the semester or quarter? On what basis would you make your selections?

Formal Techniques

One of the most common techniques used in the formal assessment of discussion activities is the **essay**. Essays are an effective way for educators to assess learners' understanding, ability to apply new information, and capacity for analyzing and evaluating new learning (Eby, 1992). As a result, they are appropriate assessment tools for discussion activities. If learners are going to write successful essays, it is necessary to provide them with certain guidelines. Millman and Pauk (1969) offer a three-step process. First, learners should read the questions carefully and jot down any relevant points to be made next to each question to avoid forgetting the critical information they want to include. Second, learners should reread the easiest questions first, adding or deleting information to what they have already jotted down. They should also build an outline from the information, using both main points and supporting statements. Third, they should compose each essay from the outlines, using the question in statement form at the outset, maintaining a logical flow of information, using specific details and examples when necessary, and summarizing at the end. As a summative assessment of a discussion activity, the essay can be adapted in a number of areas, including length, response mode, time allowed, and number of questions to be answered.

Some essays can actually take on an objective dimension. For example, an educator who wants to assess the extent of learner understanding of the different cloud types could, following a small group discussion period, have learners write an essay explaining each of the types in some detail. This type of essay is usually more structured in terms of length, time allowed, and specific content expected. Other essays are designed to tap learners' ability to analyze information, create new possibilities, or justify their view on a topic. During the unit on clouds, they may ask learners to describe a method for predicting the type of clouds that will arrive on a given day and why their method will work. Still other essays can be used to assess affective outcomes. Using the unit on clouds, learners can write poetry about clouds, selecting a particular type with aesthetic appeal to them. Even with such open-ended essays, educators can structure the assessment in terms of time allowed and other specifications. Regardless of the form used, educators can use essays to help learners develop the complex thinking skills that are the basic academic and affective goals of most discussion activities.

Reflect for a Moment

Think about some of the essay test items you have encountered in the past year or two. In your opinion, what are some characteristics of a good essay question?

Oral reports are another type of formal assessment educators can use with discussion lessons, largely because of their capacity for capturing the complex thinking behaviors of individual students who have been participating in group discussions. As with essays, oral reports can be objective, focusing on basic comprehension of discussion topics, or they can be more open ended, allowing learners to demonstrate their deeper thinking abilities. Debates can also be used as formal oral assessments of discussion learning. Educators who use debates as assessments are usually looking for learners' basic understanding of an issue and their ability to provide supporting evidence for whatever position they may take.

Educators have several techniques for gathering data from oral reports and debates. They can use videotaping and meet with learners individually or in small groups to view the tapes and provide time for student self-evaluation. Self-evaluation, always a valuable and accessible procedure for discussion lessons, may be implemented through a conference or a written format. Educators can also take written notes during the reports or debates and use specific criteria (shared with learners ahead of time) to award credit to individuals or groups. Each type of formal assessment needs to have a set of criteria established ahead of time and shared with learners.

Many of the techniques described here are applicable to cooperative learning groups, but a more detailed description of just how those groups can be assessed is needed here. Both individual and group assessment is valuable for academic and affective outcomes. Criteria for both can be established prior to the cooperative group discussion activity, but it will vary from lesson to lesson depending on the goals and objectives identified. In some cases, individuals or groups can earn points with certain levels of cooperative behavior. With academic outcomes, educators are encouraged to consider not only the final level of individual performance, but the amount of progress from a previously established starting point for individuals. During a cooperative discussion focusing on pollution in clouds, one learner may have accumulated a great deal of knowledge from reading on the subject and excel by writing about the effectiveness of different methods of combatting acid rain. Another learner in the same cooperative discussion group, who happens to be moderately mentally disabled, may excel by drawing a picture of acid rain and its effect on mountain foliage. Both outcomes can be easily assessed by collaborative educators. The group's academic outcome can be a collaborative mural depicting cloud pollution as interpreted by each group member and assessed on the basis of content accuracy and how well each member's work contributes to one cohesive mural.

Because of the nature of learning that takes place during discussion activities, the assessment and evaluation process is often more subjective and as such demands that educators structure it carefully to avoid errors in either the data-gathering phase or the evaluation of student work. On the other hand, discussion activities give educators and learners alike excellent opportunities to strengthen those critical and creative thinking abilities that are essential to problem-solving and decision-making skills. The affective and cognitive outcomes of discussion lessons can be assessed, and the results can help both educators and learners become more open minded and reflective thinkers.

Practice

You are rapidly becoming convinced of the merits of small group discussion activities. As an elementary educator, build a list of discussion skills that you would strive to assess on a regular basis in your classroom. Then take the sample discussion lesson from earlier in the chapter and set up specific criteria for assessing individual learning, both formatively and summatively.

TEACHER REFLECTIONS: EFFECTIVENESS OF THE LESSON

Teacher reflections before, during, and after discussion activities are a prerequisite to the continued effectiveness of such activities in the future. Although the reflective questions provided in Tables 9.1 and 10.3 are helpful, several areas of reflection are specific to the discussion approach to instruction. Educators who plan to become truly effective with discussion activities, regardless of grade level, subject area, or characteristics of learners, will want to consider the questions in Table 12.4.

TABLE 12.4   Reflective Questions for Discussion Teaching

1. Was the topic chosen for the discussion lesson important to the learners and divergent enough to stimulate critical thinking among individuals in the class?
2. Did all learners have adequate prior knowledge to engage confidently in the discussion?
3. Among the various discussion formats, was the format used a good choice? Why or why not?
4. If not, which other format would have worked more successfully? Why?
5. How clear were learners on the intended learning objective(s) for the discussion?
6. Were the questions used to stimulate, maintain, and evaluate the topic clear to learners?
7. How much did you need to intervene in the discussion? Did you feel that it was too much? Not enough?
8. How could the activity have been restructured to improve the intervention factor?
9. To what extent did certain learners dominate the discussion? Were there any learners who may not have participated enough?
10. Because time is often a problem in discussion activities, how well was it managed? Was there adequate time for review and reflection from learners?
11. Were the adaptations made for individual learners successful? If not, how will they be changed for future discussion activities?
12. Were there adequate resources/materials available for learners to use during the discussion? Were the resources/materials appropriate for the topic and learners involved?
13. Were the questions prepared for the activity sequenced well, and needed?
14. How were learners assessed? What formative and summative techniques were used? Informal techniques? Were the techniques sufficiently structured?

SUMMARY

Discussion teaching is a student centered, student directed approach with complex learning outcomes. It still requires educators to plan carefully and evaluate skillfully. A good discussion involves many participants, and involves critical thinking and listening skills. Discussion lessons must allow time for participants to organize and understand the topic, focus the problem, gather information, and summarize or draw conclusions.

Seating for discussions depends on the size of the group, but eye contact is crucial. Leadership may come from students as well as the teacher. Recorders keep a written account to facilitate the summary session. An even flow of dialogue, with many different participants, is ideal. Discussion skills, however, may need to be taught. The educator monitors the process to ensure the desired outcomes. Good discussions can enrich brainstorming, problem solving, and decision making skills. Cooperative learning groups can be used in discussion lessons.

Effective teaching features in a discussion lesson include reflective listening, active engagement, use of learners' ideas, questioning strategies, and clarity. When planning, educators should determine the lesson objective, consider learner readiness, study the issue, alert learners to goals and objectives, model active listening, resist commenting after each statement made, resist getting involved in general, and use a sense of humor. Questions should be developed and grouped in the appropriate context, and encourage learners to reason aloud.

Among the formats for discussions are round tables, symposia, large group, panels, and debates. Discussions should not be dominated by a single student or a small group. All student responses should warrant validation, but educators should be careful not to draw learners away from the discussion. Grouping techniques can provide learners with differing abilities opportunities for participation in a discussion. Checklists, journals, and observation are frequently used assessment techniques.

PART IV

BACK TO THE FUTURE

We can, whenever and wherever we choose, successfully
teach all children whose schooling is of interest to us. We
already know more than we need in order to do this.
Whether we do it must finally depend on how we feel about
the fact that we haven't done it so far.
                                    —*RONALD EDMONDS (1979, p. 24)*

INTRODUCTION

Chapter 13's title delivers a very clear message. Schools in the twenty-first century must break from the tradition of segregation, whether it results from tracking, special education, or the methods by which schools are funded. Even if the learning environment that results does not demonstrate the academic gains traditionally seen as desirable, inclusion is the only morally appropriate setting for learning.

Realizing the kinds of schools needed for the twenty-first century means beginning with the reality that the school must be the focal point for the community. Communities must take the necessary steps to ensure that all students have adequate health and safety so that they are ready to learn. This means they must be well fed, warm, and safe from harmful influences such as weapons, drugs, and violence at home, in school, and in the community. To successfully meet this challenge, all citizens must take active roles in the effort. Although this chapter will provide profiles of students, teachers, and schools for the future, the nature of the community is the one factor that will most influence those students, teachers, and schools.

What is needed, according to Clark and Astuto (1994), are more imaginative ideas from educational leaders. Instead of developing outcome-based assessment programs that fit neatly with existing standardized tests, educators need to engage in planning youth centers in schools where round-the-clock health care, social and psychological services, and nutritious meals are available. Instead of lengthening the school day by one hour in hopes of improving students' test scores, educators need to engage collaboratively in the sort of curriculum creation in which no subject matter is sacred and schedules are constructed according to students' developmental levels and existing knowledge as well as flexible allotments of time appropriate for different topics of study. Educational reform needs to become authentic change, major reconstruction at a fundamental level, rather than so many fix-it proposals dependent on other existing and tragically flawed school practices.

Schools in crisis or education in crisis have been buzz phrases of the twentieth century. Ayers (1994) notes that

> school crisis is not a natural phenomenon. In this time of catastrophic earthquakes, devastating hurricanes, and biblical floods, it is well to remember that the schools we have are neither acts of God nor freaks of nature, neither accidental crack-ups nor natural disasters. We have got the schools we built, and we are reaping the crisis we ourselves have sown. (p. 61)

13

TOMORROW'S SCHOOLS: MODELS FOR INCLUSIVE COMMUNITIES OF THE TWENTY-FIRST CENTURY

EVOLUTION OF GRADUATES

If the twenty-first century is to be a time for improving the human condition and preserving the earth as a place of residence, it will be essential for all citizen to contribute their unique skills and understanding in a productive, harmonious manner. Unfortunately, many communities underutilize their most valuable resource, people. This problem can be the result, in part, of the mismatch between what students are learning and what employers are looking for in knowledge, skills, and attitudes. If communities are going to be strengthened by contributions from all citizens, it will be necessary to understand the uniqueness of individual community members, including the children.

Reflect for a Moment

Create a mental image of the people in your neighborhood. To the best of your knowledge, how does each person contribute to community life? What roles does each neighbor fill in the community?

The school-age population is steadily changing. The number of children living in poverty is increasing at an alarming rate. In today's turbulent economic times, it is important to note that whereas one of five preschool children lived in poverty in 1975, by the year 2000 one of four preschool children will live in poverty (Children's Defense Fund, 1989). More and more children arrive at school sick, hungry, and abused. Many lack the language skills, social skills, or cognitive behavior seen as necessary for school success. Children from poor families are a challenge to educators. They usually live by a set of values very different from those of school professionals. For example, aggressive behavior may be part of the value system of

certain low-income families, and children may hurt others in an early childhood classroom because they have had to fight for everything they could get. Professionals working with these children need to provide genuine, direct guidelines in a supportive, compassionate manner by utilizing the individual child's strengths.

The increasing diversity of learners will challenge educators in many ways. Twenty-three of the twenty-five largest American cities have school enrollments made up primarily of students from minority backgrounds (Villegas, 1991). During the 1980s, as the number of European-American children in U.S. public schools increased 8 percent, the number of African-American children went up 16 percent, Hispanic-American children 44 percent, and Asian-American children 65 percent (Hodgkinson, 1991). The vast majority of elementary school teachers in America are European-American women. Although King (1993) found no significant relationship between student outcomes and teachers' ethnic background, more teachers with minority backgrounds are needed so that cultural ties can serve to facilitate student success. In any event, it seems quite certain that all educators will need to take responsibility for teaching all students.

Because of the rapid increase in school-age children from different cultural backgrounds, it is important to know what values, behaviors, and learning patterns are typically found among minority groups. Guild (1994) reports that Mexican-American students value personal relationships with the teacher and prefer learning broad concepts over specific factual information. African-American students prefer learning experiences that involve discussions, physical activity, and working with peers. Native American students prefer visual skills, global patterns, and opportunities for reflection. These learning preferences stand in stark contrast to those of mainstream white Americans, who value independent, analytic, and objective learning situations that feature competition, literal information, and the testing and grading procedures characteristic of schools in the United States.

The economic, cultural, and physical differences among school-age children will continue to create confusion and misunderstanding unless learners are given ample opportunities to work with each other on cooperative tasks. Mead (1934) asserted that cognitive development occurs when one person actually integrates another person's judgment or perspective into her or his own thinking. This process is facilitated by peer collaboration in elementary classrooms. When more diversity exists in a group of learners, there is greater opportunity for different perspectives to emerge and better cognitive development. These groups of learners develop broader perspectives by grappling with complex problems that require critical thinking and reasoning behaviors and draw from a multidisciplinary curriculum theme.

The number of students with disabilities being served in the general classroom is steadily increasing. Because a segregated special education delivery system has not significantly improved learning among children with disabilities, more and more local districts are providing full services in the general classroom for all students. Although in a very small number of cases students with intensively involved medical or behavioral conditions may require outside services, the general classroom will continue to include more and more students who previously were segregated from their age mates.

Significant environmental factors that continue to exert influence on students were described briefly in Chapter 1. Family influences, such as divorce, are not going to change dramatically in the next twenty-five years, so many students will continue to be from single-parent households in schools. The majority of these single-parent families are headed by women who struggle to provide for their children's basic needs. Because of the parent's work schedule, these children often come home to empty houses. Ironically, even the child who comes from a two-parent home often leaves school to arrive at an empty house or apartment. They may not have an adult checking to see that they have done their homework or had a nutritious snack. Although the availability of time does not guarantee a more adequate parent-child relationship, it does offer an opportunity for developing a more communicative relationship. Unfortunately, most single parents do not have as much time to spend with their children as couples do.

Reflect for a Moment

Remember when you were in fifth or sixth grade? Who was present when you arrived home after school each day? What, if any, adult supervision was there? What was the effect of that supervision on your activities? If there was an after-school routine, describe it in some detail.

Technology has already had a significant influence on today's students. Many educators confess to knowing less about computers than some of the students in their classes. An eight-year study of the impact of computers on classrooms revealed, among other trends, that children actually cooperated more naturally with computers than without them, that children's interest in technology increased with use, and that the keyboard was not an obstacle to learning to use technology, even to the youngest learners (Dwyer, 1994). Across the world, elementary school-age learners are linking up with each other to study a wide variety of topics, from the monarch butterfly to political campaigning in different nations to basic correspondence as pen pals.

In many schools, learners are increasingly involved in internships or apprenticeships. Although primarily focused on the secondary school population, these real-life experiences can offer even younger children successful, reality-based learning opportunities. Programs where children spend time at their parents' workplaces and community-based, career-oriented field trips can provide hands-on work experiences for elementary school students.

Evaluation practices in schools will become more diverse as the learners who attend the schools become more diverse (Cullen & Pratt, 1992). Students will be evaluated by more authentic procedures, reflecting their individual learning characteristics and the processes they use on a daily basis. As a result, learners of the twenty-first century will concentrate more on using strategies for learning and less on memorization of unrelated bits of information. Students will see the grading system as a way to inform themselves and others of their progress during a particular theme of study, not as a competitive, relatively noninformative labeling arrangement designed to separate them from their peers. Students will understand why they are studying a particular topic or performing a certain task and what the criteria for success or mastery is in advance. They will consequently take risks with their learning behavior, understand the value of mistakes, and learn to practice often before they realize success.

Rogers and Freiberg (1994) asked students what they wanted out of their school experience and got some very interesting responses (see Table 13.1). Educators who carefully consider such data will undoubtedly rethink their classroom atmosphere.

To address the problem of mismatch between learned skills and skills needed in the day-to-day world, some fundamental assertions must be made. First of all, all children can learn. They do learn differently, in different areas of content, through different learning processes, and at different rates. These differences do

TABLE 13.1   What Students Want From School

To be trusted and respected	to make decisions about learning to do their best work to talk with educators, not be talked down to
To be part of a family	to feel at home to see school as an extended family
Teachers as helpers	to each individual student to a wide range of students
To take on responsibilities	to speak and vote at school meetings to participate in student governance
Freedom, not license	to know structure without rigidity to have freedom of expression
People who care	to have warm, supportive settings to work collaboratively to be directed to study
Teachers who help them succeed, not fail	to be led away from failure to be able to confide in teachers to never be let off the hook
To have choices	to have a say over what they learn to do community service

Source: C. Rogers & H. J. Freiberg. (1994). *Freedom to learn* (3rd ed.), © 1994, pp. 5–7. Adapted by permission of Prentice Hall, Upper Saddle River, New Jersey.

not, however, warrant labeling children as "slow" or "disabled," lumping them together and separating them from other children in their age range. Instead, these children need more than ever to participate in a general classroom with committed adults who are willing and able to facilitate their success in pursuit of common learning goals (Barth & Mitchell, 1992). Secondly, children come to learning events with a rich and varied background of experience and, regardless of the intentions of the educator involved, interpret these events in their own unique ways. The construction of meaningful units of information is the work that young learners are constantly engaged in regardless of age, ethnic background, or intellect. The development of language and a variety of motor skills from birth is clear evidence of this conscious constructing by children throughout the world.

Third, children possess a natural curiosity about their world and will become excited about learning a wide variety of new material. They all want to learn to read, add and subtract, closely examine a butterfly, or visit the hospital and see the work that goes on there. They all want to sculpt with clay, or play the recorder. In the schools of the twenty-first century, learners will undoubtedly still need to explore, ask questions, and gather new experiences and knowledge.

Children are, by nature, active thinkers, not passive listeners. They will develop skills for problem solving, making inferences, conflict resolution, and collaboration if educators empower them to think for themselves (Fosnot, 1989).

VISIONS OF TOMORROW'S GRADUATES

Just who is the learner of the twenty-first century? A profile, although overly general in nature, would depict a child who is more likely from a minority background, and living in a household headed by a single female at some point during her or his childhood. The learner will attend the school closest to his or her home, and regardless of ability, be assigned to a class with others in the same age range.

Students in the twenty-first century will be ongoing and active members of instructional teams, for both themselves and their peers (Villa & Thousand, 1992). They will team teach with peers and educators. They will help plan instructional programs for their peers and themselves. They will tutor and be tutored by their peers and other students, too. They will form a variety of cooperative learning groups, depending on the topic, the tasks, and the other students involved. They will serve as peer advocates on individualized education program teams and will form peer support networks and buddy systems as well as circles of friends (Snow & Forest, 1987). They will serve on school boards and schoolwide committees. In these settings, students with disabilities will play an active, integral role in their own success as well as the success of the group. For example, Villa and Thousand (1992) describe a cooperative group activity in which John, an eight-year-old with multiple disabilities, participated by turning the tape recorder on and off, with hand-over-hand assistance, for a group of students who were listening to a "talking book."

With few, if any exceptions, learners with disabilities will be educated in the general classroom. All recommended services will be provided in the general classroom, and learners will participate in all aspects of the school day with their peers. Learners who have severe disabilities will also receive professional support services in the general classroom. They will learn functional skills, such as dressing and grooming, in the general education setting with the help of peers, the efficient use of noninstructional school time, and opportunities for parallel instruction in which the disabled learner works on related functional skills while peers work on academic skills (Hamre-Nietupski, McDonald, & Nietupski, 1992). All students will be frequent participants in community-based activities. Learners will go out to the community for some lessons, and the community will be brought into the classroom for other lessons. Specific learning outcomes will be established for the severely disabled student which may differ from those of his or her nondisabled peers.

All students will be given frequent opportunities to take on supportive roles with each other, regardless of the presence or absence of a disability. These opportunities will represent a shift in what students are expected to learn that reflects a significantly greater emphasis on developing a positive sense of self and demonstrating concern and respect for others (Ford, Davern, & Schnorr, 1992).

Reflect for a Moment

What could you learn from a severely mentally disabled person your age? What do you think that person could learn from you?

Students with severe maladaptive behaviors will continue to present a challenge to educators. They will, however, be helped by an open communication process that capitalizes heavily upon input from their peers (Forest & Pearpoint, 1990). With an understanding of the importance of confidentiality, peers may be asked for their perceptions of a particular situation involving a specific student. After offering their perceptions on the situation, peers are guided through an exercise, called the *circle process*, in which they use concentric circles to list the people in their lives who they love or spend quality time with in some activity. Then they are asked how they would feel and what they would do if those persons were not in their circles. In this manner, peers are more able to relate to a particular student's difficulties and are able to suggest ways to help that student that usually include more social integration with them. Through activities similar to the circle process, friendships develop that include students with severe disabilities, and the general classroom becomes the setting for open communication and honesty.

If there is one word that most describes learners in the twenty-first century, it is *inquisitive*. As a result of dramatic changes in the way schools are structured and educators plan, learners of the future will spend considerable time systematically exploring, questioning, experimenting, observing, and constructing meaningful knowledge about their environment. Katz and Chard (1993) detail the project approach, in which learners, alone or in small groups, explore a topic in depth, after a period of advanced planning, for a period of several days or weeks. They use an example of several small groups of young children working on different projects, all related to the school bus. In such situations, learners are intellectually engaged in a study that interests them and are also gaining a better understanding of their world. In this manner the learners of the twenty-first century see school as an extension of life and not as a separate, illogically contrived arrangement of their time. The key ingredient of the project approach is the way the learners interact with people, objects, and their environment to construct personal meaning. Learners in an urban setting might actively analyze traffic patterns, while learners in rural settings might focus on crops raised in the community. Each learner will work frequently with other learners during these inquiries and develop a variety of cooperative and collaborative skills as a result.

Practice

Given the previous discussion of school serving as an extension of life how might you use the cloud unit discussed in Chapter 7?

Given the knowledge explosion taking place in contemporary learning, students of the twenty-first century must develop not just knowledge but wisdom. This wisdom, according to Wiggins (1989), will be evidenced by the ability to suspend belief, receive new information efficiently, ask probing questions to clarify values, be open to new and different ideas, and question any confusing language.

Students will work together constantly and learn to seek out diversity, become lifelong learners, and demonstrate social competence and effective communication skills (Benjamin, 1989). As they work in cooperative groups, all students, including those with varying levels of disabilities, will find increases in academic achievement, self-esteem, applicable learning, social skill development, and friendships (Putnam, 1993). In addition, students from minority groups will find cooperative learning to be more consistent with their cultural values than competitive learning.

Students will receive feedback, not only on their academic performance and motor skills, but on their affective behavior, too. They will become accustomed to reflecting on their efforts specifically, constructively, and frequently, allowing them to make subsequent modifications to their work. This evaluative process will focus on the learner and his or her peers and will consistently emphasize the importance of self-evaluation and reflective thinking. Learners will regularly participate in interviews and conferences with educators and other learners as an integral part of the evaluative process. These meetings may focus on any of a number of issues, including interests, self-esteem, strengths and weaknesses, and learning strategies. Students will, as part of the process, also have input into any possible changes needed in the curriculum or the methods of instruction.

Because of an increase in cooperative group work, learners in the twenty-first century will find themselves in situations where the group they belong to is the focus of evaluation instead of the individual student. In these situations, they will also reflect themselves on how effectively their group functioned. Learners in a group can even designate one of their members to observe the group's dynamics and then complete a written evaluation (Putnam, 1993).

As active, engaged participants in the evaluation process, learners in the twenty-first century will develop and maintain their own performance portfolios. These collections of student work, which represent the breadth and depth of learning that has occurred, will be constantly revised and updated by the students themselves. The portfolios will contain stories, reports, artwork, cards, notes, tapes, and any other material that is evidence of student learning; they may take the form of a folder, a box, a crate, or even a place on a shelf. Portfolios constitute an authentic assessment strategy because they are concrete evidence of real-life tasks undertaken by learners (Farr & Tone, 1994).

EVOLUTION OF EDUCATORS

Berns (1993) believes that the most powerful influence on the school remains the educators, because they are the persons who translate program goals into actions. Educators create the environment for learning through their understanding of children's needs, interests, capabilities, and diversity. "The teacher has the ability to encourage children to explore, satisfy their natural curiosity, and to love learning—to love it so much that it becomes part of their lives forever" (Berns, 1993, p. 250). The educator who works closely with each learner and understands group dynamics will be more apt to provide a successful and rewarding learning environment. The effective educator of the twenty-first century must know how to collaborate, not simply with colleagues but with children, parents, and community members.

For collaborative teaching and inclusive schools to develop concurrently, there must be a paradigm shift or change in thinking among educators, who at present are constantly concerned with performance on standardized tests and how their students compare with other students in the same grade. If real sharing among educators is to become a reality, then policymakers must give more responsibility to those practitioners who are so anxiously waiting to steer their own course in schools and classrooms across the country and throughout the world (Gough, 1994). Educators themselves also have to become more willing to be reflective, self-evaluate their work, and take constructive criticism.

Educators engage in multiple interactions per day with their students. Little time, however, is spent with colleagues discussing important educational issues. Goodlad (1984) and Lortie (1975) have cited this lack of substantial communication as one of the greatest problems facing educators. The complexity of an inclusive school demands that educators be able to take the time to step out of challenging situations and reflect on their practices.

Educators too often fail to provide learners with opportunities to apply knowledge in new and different situations. Gardner (1991) speaks directly to the problems learners have in developing this process and suggests that teachers must make dramatic changes in their assessment techniques before learners can acquire any semblance of what he terms "deep understanding."

Reflect for a Moment

Applying what we have learned is clearly a worthwhile pursuit. Revisit your own education, particularly in the elementary grades. Do you remember class projects, group activities, or field trips in which you actually applied what you had learned in mathematics, science, social studies, or language? Describe a few of these experiences.

Related to Gardner's concern is the knowledge explosion of the late twentieth century. Given the exponential increase of new information in the modern world, it makes little sense to try to teach bits and facts of knowledge such as famous names, dates, and exact measures if learners are going to make valuable contributions to the complex society of the twenty-first century. As the twentieth century comes to an end, it is clearly more important for educators to help learners develop strategies for learning than to try to simply teach them hundreds and hundreds of bits of information. Among the steps necessary for helping students develop their own strategies for learning are giving them respect, building on what learners specifically already know, giving them more control over their learning, providing clear connections among traditional subject areas, and building cooperative learning skills (Lipsky & Gartner, 1992).

If educators are indeed the major influence on what students learn in schools, then their decisions are of utmost importance in the areas of curriculum and instruction. Ellis and Fouts (1993) have developed a set of principles that collectively can guide educators to an energizing new level of global learning for all students. First, as society enters the information age, traditional curriculum simply may not have sufficient meaning or value to warrant its continued use. Second, if modern society is based on democratic values, then those values (freedom, justice, a sense of duty) must be extended to all members of the school community on a daily basis. Third, the traditional teacher-based curriculum arrangement, segregated by subject areas, grade levels, and even self-contained classrooms, must be replaced by a structure that is flexible and responsive, first and foremost, to individual learners in a school as they pursue intellectual, moral, and physical goals of learning. Fourth, the structure of the curriculum must present students with a myriad of possible connections among disciplines and opportunities for reflection instead of presenting the disciplines separately and expecting students to establish the connections totally on their own, outside the academic schedule. Finally—and perhaps the most critical starting point for educators in the twenty-first century—is the task of really finding out what kinds of knowledge are important for success in the future. Knowledge with lasting value for the global citizens of the twenty-first century must be the focus of educators' curriculum and instruction efforts and students' valuable learning time.

Clearly, educators must engage in a dramatic overhauling of the traditional subject-centered curriculum. The work of the Alpha Team at Oakland University, which has produced curriculum themes such as change and adaptability, global interdependence, and technology, is characteristic of the evolution in curriculum that must be led by educators themselves (Alpha Team, 1991). Such efforts will unquestionably require intensive collaboration, reflection, and community involvement if they are to result in the curriculum necessary for the inclusive school community of the twenty-first century.

Linked closely to this evolving curriculum in the hands of educators is the importance of developing those instructional approaches that have, over time, been highly successful in certain areas of learning. At the same time, other approaches will typically be altered or replaced, often after years and years of use.

For children to learn to read, for example, it is important for the debate between whole language and phonics advocates to subside so that the two components can coexist within the context of a language-rich learning environment made up in part of the experiences children themselves bring to school. Barth and Mitchell (1992) urge the use of children's own personal stories in helping them learn to read, an approach that allows mastery of skills and understanding of content to complement each other. When children learn to write, for example, the expression of ideas should drive the process, with accurate spelling, punctuation, and grammar brought in to polish the work after the ideas are captured. This sequencing again allows the mastery of skills and the deeper understanding of written expression to complement each other.

The traditional social studies curriculum, commonly referred to as *expanding environments*, purports to teach children about family, school, and neighborhood right through grade three. Unfortunately, this approach is flawed because all children have been learning about these aspects of their lives quite fluently for years before even entering school. Instead, they should be offered more substance in the form of historical heroines and heroes, exotic mountain villages, and tropical islands through real literature and other readily available community resources. Stories again can be the foundation for substantive learning in history and geography for primary grades learners. Educators who are willing to utilize curriculum approaches such as these will collaborate closely with resource personnel in the community, librarians, and others to support development among all students, both academically and morally.

Approaches to learning mathematics have traditionally followed a process of board demonstration and worksheet practice followed by the same procedure with the next skill, with no opportunity to use the skill in a different situation to help develop deeper understanding. Educators in the twenty-first century will work with other members of the community to provide opportunities for learners to apply their mathematics skills in useful ways on a regular basis.

Although many states issue curriculum guides and mandate standardized tests, daily decisions about what to teach and how to teach it are largely made by educators in communities across the nation. Those educators who fully grasp these opportunities are in a position to develop learning experiences that are highly appropriate for all students in the inclusive schools of the twenty-first century.

VISIONS OF TOMORROW'S EDUCATORS

Tomorrow's educators will be leaders who act as agents of systems change. Educators even more than administrators must be responsible for developing networks within the community that will ensure the inclusion of all students in a variety of settings both in and out of school. Educators will develop collaborative working relationships among parents, other educators, school personnel, and community members.

Educators will have a clear understanding of how their behaviors affect the persons around them. They will, through their actions, model social and political adaptability and change. Educators will be politically aware and socially responsible, emphasizing to learners that having strong beliefs is not enough by itself. Beliefs and ideals must be acted on to have meaning. For example, all educators will be actively involved in the community. Although educators may not necessarily live in the community where they teach, they will attend community and school functions and help to raise funds for special community projects. Educators will not dictate what children are to believe, but they will stress the importance of the old adage, "Actions speak louder than words."

Reflect for a Moment

Can you recall a teacher from your past or present who demonstrated his or her convictions with more than simply words? What do you feel strongly about? How would you demonstrate your conviction to students? Should educators be held to a higher moral standard than other professionals?

Educators will establish classrooms that are controlled and purposeful, viewing learning as a cooperative venture rather than a competitive event. The atmosphere will not necessarily be quiet, but rather a model of active learning. Educators will be found either moving among small groups or team teaching the whole class. They will give up ownership of the classroom to the children, who will take responsibility for class decor.

The sense of ownership of a small group of learners by a single classroom teacher will be replaced by a sense of responsibility, among all members of the school community, for all children who attend the school. The climate this commitment produces will be one of caring adults in which a child can feel comfortable going to any teacher for assistance. Educators will have learned how to collaborate to ensure the academic success of all children.

Work schedules for educators will be similar to those of other professionals. Educators will have twelve-month contracts, teaching three quarters and studying an academic discipline or conducting field-based research during the fourth quarter (Barth & Mitchell, 1992). This flexible scheduling will allow teaching teams to take workshops, develop programs, and plan instruction during the fourth quarter as well. In addition to the fourth quarter, one afternoon per week will be devoted to schoolwide reflection, collaboration, in-service, or personnel meetings. During this time learners will be in the library, technology center, or at the senior center involved in enrichment activities developed by community volunteers or volunteering in the community.

School days for educators will begin at 7:30 and end at 4:30. Both individual and collaborative preparation times are structured into the day. Table 13.2 pro-

TABLE 13.2   Typical Learner's Daily Schedule

Monday	Tuesday	Wednesday	Thursday	Friday
7:30–8:00 Before-school care—child care center				
8:00–12:00 Instructional time				
12:00–12:30 Lunch with teachers		Enrichment activities	Lunch with teachers	
1:00–3:00 Instructional time			Instructional time	
3:00–4:30 Afterschool care program		Volunteer at various locations	Afterschool care program	
4:30–7:30 Afterschool care program				

TABLE 13.3   Typical Educator's Daily Schedule

Monday	Tuesday	Wednesday	Thursday	Friday
7:30–8:00 Personal prep time—readying daily materials				
8:00–12:00 Instructional time				
12:00–12:30 Lunch with students	Teacher luncheon		Lunch with students	
1:00–3:00 Instructional time	Collaboration		Instructional time	
3:00–4:30 Personal reflection	In-Service		Personal reflection	
4:30–7:30 Collaboration with teams				

vides an idea of what a typical day might be like for an educator in the twenty-first century.

During the development of a positive learning environment, educators will understand that much of any one learner's disruptive and dangerous behavior is a function of faulty communicative systems. Therefore, in developing interventions or behavior change plans, they will focus on enabling students to learn how to communicate in more effective ways. Educators will accomplish much of this by creating for students a safe environment and a feeling of trust, and delivering instruction that is interesting, fun, and worthy of children's participation.

A variety of teaching strategies will be used to address the unique needs of each child. The cornerstone for selecting methodology is the recognition that learning for all students involves determining what learning means and how it fits into the child's understanding and experience (Ferguson & Jeanchild, 1992). Since this understanding and experience changes over time, educators of the twenty-first century must be able to perform authentic assessments. Teaching strategies will be selected to ensure maximization of variation across learner characteristics, positive interdependence, and individual accomplishments (Ferguson & Jeanchild, 1992).

Understanding that mere physical proximity is not sufficient to learn about diversity, educators will develop groups that can take advantage of differences. Careful consideration will be paid to assure that each group represents a range of characteristics, including ability levels (social, academic, motor, and language), gender, and ethnicity (Ferguson & Jeanchild, 1992).

Reflect for a Moment

As a student, can you recall being placed in a learning group that was effective? ineffective? What made each group the way it was?

Educators will organize each group's learning experiences in such a way that learners will develop interdependence. Through their own teaming educators will model the ways in which reciprocal relationships and shared experiences are developed, an appreciation of each member's uniqueness, and skills needed for collaboration and cooperation. Learners will be able to see firsthand the benefits of accomplishing a shared goal.

Although it is important for educators to facilitate social interactions and the development of friendship, learners must still master instructional content. Educators will plan activities and learning events that are applicable to students' daily lives. Practices will be designed that help learners become active community members.

Another focus for educators of the twenty-first century will be to facilitate creative thinking. Therefore, teachers must reexamine their role as information givers. Educators will engage students in learning not merely the "correct" response, but in understanding why and how some responses are more appropriate than others. Educators will foster a sense of "deep understanding" not by teaching bits of information but by engaging students in developing learning strategies. Through the use of modeling, discussion, and meaningful practices, educators will help students organize their learning, become successful researchers, and communicate their learning clearly and precisely. Strategies such as these will provide students with a lifetime passion for learning. This type of teaching will further require educators of the twenty-first century to be technologically literate, because techniques of seeking knowledge and using reference materials will be more important skills than rote memorization of facts.

Educators will need to develop different methods of assessing learning for themselves and their students. Because process will take on greater importance than content, assessment must go beyond whether or not an answer is correct. Assessment will need to investigate the thought processes used in reaching an answer, and so educators must use formative assessment techniques that will enable them to build on or redirect learning. Multiple choice and true-false forms of assessment will be obsolete because they fail to provide educators with any cogent information. Educators will monitor learner progress through anecdotal reports (observations) and mutually developed portfolios.

Personal reflection will be fundamental in evaluating teacher effectiveness. Promotion, tenure, and salary increases will in part be based on portfolios that educators develop. Educators will need to demonstrate effectiveness in three areas: teaching, community service, and scholarship. Therefore, portfolios will include lesson and unit plans, writings, and self-reflections. Indications of ongoing learning will also be included. Performance assessments will be completed by peers, students, administrators, parents, and educators themselves. As with any portfolio, all materials will be discussed by the person submitting them as well as evaluators. Based on discussion, mutually agreed-on individual goals and objectives will be developed to further educators' professional growth.

Reflection will also take place on a daily basis as each educator assesses her or his role in learning events as well as those of team members. Opportunities will be provided for teams to discuss both personal and group perceptions during part of their collaborative planning time.

EVOLUTION OF SCHOOLS

Kozol (1992) states that "every teacher knows schools are never neutral. Consciously or not they shape the soul and style of the future adult population" (cited in Noll, 1993, p. 172). Inclusive schools will reshape the attitudes of all present and future adults on the acceptance of diversity and learning as a neverending process.

The change to inclusion brings with it many challenges and many consequences. Whether these consequences are positive or negative depends on whether individuals will work collaboratively to meet the changes and challenges that accompany them. One of the challenges of inclusion is the development of a true sense of community. "Community is not only a place to be, it is a feeling of belonging among other human beings" (Taylor, Biklen, & Knoll, 1987, xvii). Far more than a geographic location, a community involves a network of interactions between and among people.

The first step in developing an inclusive community is to establish the size and domain of the school. Economics became the primary reason for the disappearance of small community-based schools in favor of more "cost-effective" large regional schools. Economics has also spurred entrepreneurs such as Christopher Whittle to enter the field of education. Whittle's Edison Project proposes the opening of a nationwide franchise of 1,000 profit-making private schools by the year 2006. The Edison schools will service 2 million children with student/teacher ratios of 10,000 to 1 or 100,000 to 1, which will be accomplished by the use of "electronic" lectures. Morris (1992) quotes Whittle as saying "We want to provide a better education at a lower cost. Currently public school spending per student averages about $5,000. We want to come in at $4,995" (cited by Morris, 1992, p. 51).

Reflect for a Moment

Thinking back to your years in school, what were the sizes of your classes? How would you feel about attending classes where you would be one student out of 10,000 or one out of 100,000? Did you feel like teachers knew you at your elementary school? Or did you often feel like just a number, lost in the shuffle in a large school?

Educational benefits that were derived from community-based schools have been and may continue to be given up in favor of economic cost benefits. However, Ravitch (1983) believes that

> unlike some present schools, which are as vast and impersonal as factories, the school of the future should be modeled on a family; here, caring, knowledgeable adults would guide and instruct young people—and each person would be special. (p. 320)

McDaniel (1974), Suppes (1975), Cornish (1986), and Benjamin (1989) have predicted that schools will have to become smaller, not larger as Whittle believes, if we are to combat the alienation and violence plaguing schools today. Rates of absenteeism and classroom disorder are higher in larger schools. Grant (1994) found that the dropout rates in high schools of more than 2,000 students were twice that of schools with fewer than 667 students. Additional evidence to support smaller schools is growing rapidly. In both urban and rural settings, small schools are having very positive effects on students. Goodlad (1993) describes healthy schools as having a stronger human connection, with a large proportion of parents, teachers, and students taking care of routine school matters, a larger percentage of students taking part in extracurricular activities, and in general more personal teacher-student relationships. He also observed a clear pattern of small schools that met the criteria for the healthy category and large schools that fit the unhealthy category. A recent study found that schools with less than 350 students had more success in creating a systemic method for school improvement (Consortium on Chicago School Research, 1993). During a two-year period in Chicago, over fifty small schools effectively used a grassroots approach to school improvement, each designing its own focus for reform.

Many observers suggest that smaller schools cost more to operate, but a number of recent studies have found that smaller schools are actually more cost effective than big schools (Public Education Association, 1992). Klonsky and Ford (1994) offer valuable ideas for small school efforts. First, elementary schools must actually *be* small, enrolling between 200 and 400 students. Second, active participation must be the driving force among teachers, parents, and administrators who share a clear vision. Third, teachers and students must choose to participate and not be forced into joining the effort. Fourth, students must reflect the full range of diversity in the community in which the school is located, and fifth, the schools must have a high level of autonomy, with teachers as the primary decision-making body. Grant (1994) suggests, as part of a set of five themes for schools, that smaller schools have more success making students feel a part of the community. He found students in smaller schools were more likely to spend time both with peers and with older or younger students, in and out of class, than students in larger schools.

Stainback, Stainback, and Jackson (1992) recommend that schools serve only those students who live within the natural geographic boundaries for that school. By doing this, schools can more realistically avoid the dilemma of serving disproportionate numbers of students with severe disabilities. Furthermore, students who would have formerly been excluded from attending their home school because of a severe disability could be assigned to a classroom with other children in their neighborhood.

The second step in developing an inclusive community is to foster interaction between home and school. Educators can no longer overlook the importance of the social context in which learners live and operate. To attempt to bandage familial problems simply with free breakfasts and lunches is to overlook a very vital connection required for educational success. Recognition of home and social context is particularly important because the active involvement of family members in the education of children is a recent phenomenon in the United States. In the seventeenth and eighteenth centuries, school-family roles were clearly defined: moral development was taught at home, and the teaching of reading, writing, and arithmetic was the school's responsibility. As the nation moved into the nineteenth and twentieth centuries, parent-teacher associations grew rapidly (O'Brien, 1990). By the end of the twentieth century, however, a significant change in the family structure had taken place. Elkind (1986) reports that the "traditional" two-parent family, with one parent at home, makes up only about 7 percent of family units today. By the year 2000, more than half the children in this country will reside in single parent households (Jellinek & Klavan, 1988).

The educational model for family involvement has ignored this enormous change in the reality of family structures and still operates as if the two-parent, economically stable, nuclear family with a working father and a stay-at-home mother is the norm (David, 1989). The educational system, rather than adjusting to support or nurture the changes in family structure, has simply assumed more and more family responsibilities. This shouldering of responsibility did not arise from open communication between home and school, but a paternal or maternal attitude adopted by educators. Rather than attempting to understand, support, encourage, and assist single or working parents in their homes, schools moved to place blame and assume the role of parents. "Instead of assuming that absence means noncaring, educators must understand the barriers that hinder some parents from participating in their child's education" (Finders & Lewis, 1994, p. 50).

Edmonds once asked, "How many effective schools would you have to see to be persuaded of the educability of poor children?" (Ayers, 1994, p. 61). To which he then responded:

> If your answer is more than one, then I submit that you have reasons of your own for preferring to believe that basic pupil performance derives from family background instead of school response to family background. . . . Whether or not we will ever effectively teach the children of the poor is probably far more a matter of politics than of social science, and that is as it should be. (Ayers, 1994, p. 61)

The third step in developing an inclusive community is to provide all members with a sense of belonging that does not force them to negate their own diversity or that of others. Sapon-Shevin (1992) points out that:

> Students cannot become a community or be comfortable if they believe that they must ignore their own differences and those of their classmates in order to belong. The goal cannot and should not be to become oblivious to differences, to not notice the diversity in society. (p. 19)

Children are given a clear message by the many adults they encounter that differences should not be discussed. This teaching becomes apparent to anyone who has seen an embarrassed parent drag an inquisitive child away from a person who uses a wheelchair for mobility. This child acquires the idea that being different is unacceptable and that being curious about differences is not permitted. Conversely, the parent cannot be blamed for reacting in a manner that was modeled for them as a child. Therefore, according to Sapon-Shevin (1992), the pursuit must be a straightforward explanation of differences, the chance for children and adults to experience and understand diversity within a safe and supportive community. Diversity must be valued because it strengthens the community, school, or classroom by offering all members a greater opportunity to learn. Barth (1990) makes clear his belief in the value of diversity in his personal vision of a good school.

> I would prefer my children be in a school in which differences are looked for, attended to, and celebrated as good news, as opportunities for learning. The question with which so many school people are preoccupied is, "What are the limits of diversity beyond which behavior is unacceptable?" . . . But the question I would like to see asked more often is, "How can we make conscious, deliberate use of differences in social class, gender, age, ability, race, and interest as resources for learning?" . . . Differences hold great opportunities for learning. Differences offer a free, abundant, and renewable resource. I would like to see our compulsion for eliminating differences replaced by an equally compelling focus on making use of these differences to improve schools. What is important about people—and about schools—is what is different, not what is the same. (pp. 514–515)

Reflect for a Moment

Think back to your childhood. Do you remember how your parents viewed people who were different than they were? Just how did they regard people with disabilities? What messages did they send to you about these people?

Unfortunately, diversity is often seen as adversity and children as obstacles and impediments to the learning process (Ayers, 1994).

VISIONS OF TOMORROW'S SCHOOLS

Schools of the twenty-first century will be caring communities. Care will be taken to develop communication, feelings of interaction and mutual dependence, common and shared experiences, attachment and bonding, an internalized set of moral standards, and an ethic of concern for all members (Williams, 1993). Schools will organize themselves using the nine-step process for developing caring environments outlined by Sapon-Shevin (1990). The philosophy of schools in the twenty-first century will be based on inclusion and the celebration of diversity.

Schools of the twenty-first century will be inclusive by definition, because all learners will be educated in the general education environment. There will be no labels. Students will be viewed as individuals with unique talents and educational needs. Labels will similarly be removed from educators so that they will be identified by their expertise instead of by a largely arbitrary title. In-service will be for all persons who work within the school building. Periodically, staff meetings will be held to highlight personnel and their work with learners, parents, and community members.

All learners, educators, and staff will celebrate birthdays, assemblies, and other school functions together. Each class will publish a bimonthly newsletter that will be sent home. Personal items such as birth announcements of siblings will be included as well as public thank-yous for volunteers. Current and future topics of study will also be discussed, with calls for assistance in the new areas of investigation. Individual class newsletters will be collated into a larger school newspaper so that accomplishments can be recognized schoolwide. Lunchrooms will be organized in a familylike manner. Educators and staff will serve as discussion moderators, and children will be able to sit at tables based on their interest in the topic being discussed.

Diversity will be both honored and celebrated. Bulletin boards and displays will reflect the richness of the community's various ethnic origins. Community volunteers will be invited to share stories, traditions, and experiences from around the world. Multicultural education will be the vehicle by which diverse groups will be included and the nation's schools will be transformed (Banks, 1994). Curriculum will be designed to eliminate single group studies. For example, the impact of African Americans, Asian Americans, and Native Americans on the settlement of the West, not just that of European Americans, will be discussed. Although celebrating diversity is an essential first step, twenty-first century schools will also assist learners in understanding social inequalities. Schools will be unconditionally antiracist and antisexist, thus empowering learners, school personnel, and community members to actively work toward societal change.

Multiage grouping and multilevel curriculum, in which students of various ages and abilities can work together studying a given topic, will be the norm. Schoolwide themes will allow all learners to investigate the same broad topic in ways that best suit their learning styles.

A tenth step might be activity afternoons, held twice a month. Students could sign up for activities that interest them and change activities every two months. These activities could be led by educators, administrators, parents, other school employees, or community volunteers. Activities could run the gamut from basic sign language lessons to gourmet cooking, from community recycling projects to babysitting tips, from chess to becoming an entrepreneur. Other offerings could include reacting to behavioral outbursts, seizures, and other behavioral emergencies (Meyer & Henry, 1993).

Reflect for a Moment

Now that you have had a look at ten steps that can help build an inclusive school community, which of them were present in your elementary school? Which are most ambitious, in your view? Why?

Competition must give way to cooperation, modeled by the staff of the school and various agencies located within the building. Cooperation is also expected of learners as they are encouraged to develop a sense of responsibility for each other. Task forces that work on school problems will enlist the support of a diverse group of persons. Parents, support personnel, educators, students, and administrators will come together to develop solutions collaboratively for difficult problems.

Schools of the twenty-first century will be small as well as inclusive. Elementary schools will have student populations between 200 and 400, while middle schools and high schools will have no more than 600 and 800, respectively. Some larger schools are already restructuring by breaking up into two or more totally separate smaller school units within the same walls. Funding for smaller community schools will not rely on property taxes, but rather on a graduated income tax that is equitably dispersed to all schools. Additional funds will come in the form of grants offered by major industries such as Microsoft or McDonalds as well as community-based corporations.

Inclusive schools of the twenty-first century will have strong ongoing family (home)-school interactions. From the birth of their first child to the graduation of their last and beyond, parents will be involved with decision and policy making in the community-based school. Starting at children's birth, parents and their infants will be welcomed into the school family in a variety of ways. A welcome letter will be sent to explain services located within the school that may be of particular importance for the family of a newborn. The building of communication with parents thus begins on a positive note, allaying the fear that letters from school are generally bad news.

Services to parents of newborns, infants, and toddlers will include monthly home visits by a certified parent educator; periodic screenings for vision, hearing, language, motor and social development; and support group meetings. Additionally, the school will house a community resource center that is open year round, offering parents an age-appropriate playroom and a lending library of books and videos. Support groups will be formed to ensure that new parents do not develop a feeling of isolation.

Reflect for a Moment

If you could brainstorm ways to strengthen the home-school relationship, what ideas would you have? What are some ways that community and school can support each other?

Schools providing these services will be open year round. The curriculum will be structured for a nine-month calendar, but students may use the entire year if necessary to achieve academic milestones or to explore certain topics in more depth. Students will be encouraged to take time off when their respective families are on a vacation from their jobs. The stigma of summer school will be eliminated as community services and school curriculum become more and more blended.

Careful attention will be paid to ensure that the school and its personnel recognize the diverse school experiences, economic and time constraints, linguistic and cultural backgrounds that each family brings to the system. Parents will be encouraged to be assertive, speaking up for their family's needs. They will be called on for their expertise, helping to contribute to the development of relevant units of study. Skills ranging from housekeeping to building design will be called into play. Parents will be asked to allow students to job shadow (when possible) to help them explore careers.

Volunteerism, modeled by adults and peers, will be an integral part of the school philosophy and required of all members of the school community. Younger students will volunteer within the smaller school community, whereas older students may volunteer in the larger neighborhood community. Additionally, community volunteers will be a necessary part of the school. Community volunteers will use their expertise to enhance concepts discussed in the classroom. For example, in discussing either the Armenian, Jewish, or Croatian holocausts, survivors will be asked to come and speak about their experiences. A local builder will come in to present the importance of mathematics in house construction. Practical uses of chemistry will be demonstrated by both a farmer and a janitor. The neighborhood grocer can provide learners with hands-on experience in marketing, unit pricing, and supply and demand. Volunteers will also join school personnel in the lunchroom, on the playground, and on field trips.

Reflect for a Moment

Look back at your own school activities. What types of volunteer work did you do in the community? What did some of your classmates do as volunteer work in the community? Was it seen as an integral part of your school experience or as a separate effort you undertook on you own?

Schools of the twenty-first century will serve as the focal point for communities. Schools will provide space to programs such as Head Start, child care, community health, visiting nurses, senior citizen groups, and selected municipal or social service agencies. The funds normally paid out in rent by such organizations will be directed to the educational budget.

Services will be intertwined within this community setting. Senior citizens will be able to volunteer in the classrooms or child care center and children will spend time in the senior center. When a child requires social service assistance, social workers and educators will be able to pool their collective information effectively to help develop sound programs. These collaborative efforts will be enhanced by the fact that both the senior center and social service agency are located within the school. Parents and other community members will also be drawn into the school through their use of the community health, child care, or social services available. As more people are drawn into the building, schools can readily showcase the talents of their students and school personnel through displays and demonstrations.

The community-based school building will be open every working day of the year (Monday through Saturday from early in the morning until early in the evening). Nutritious breakfasts, lunches, and snacks will be available for children. School-age children will leave to attend classes and return at the end of the school day if necessary. High school students and teachers may volunteer their time to the afterschool care program by reading, supervising games, organizing community-based field trips, or tutoring. Tutoring may be in the more traditional subject areas, but it may also be in the visual or performing arts.

Child care services will be available to all parents in the community. Teen parents will especially benefit by being provided a safe environment for their children while they continue their high school education. Teens will be expected to provide some type of community service as reimbursement for child care, such as volunteering in the school-based child care program during study halls and after classes. Additionally, the presence of social services on the premises allows parenting classes to be offered frequently and at times convenient for all teens and others who are interested.

Technological devices will be as commonplace in schools of the twenty-first century as paper, pencils, and encyclopedias. Students will develop analytical skills by evaluating various types of hardware and software supplied free of charge to the school. Companies will gain valuable marketing information and learners will have access to the most innovative technology. Mutually beneficial cost-effective arrangements such as these will be evident in most if not all schools.

AGENTS OF SOCIAL CHANGE

Students are the centerpiece for the schools of the future. Each child is unique, with special talents and needs. When the school and the surrounding community work together, the results can be quite exciting for both learners and educators.

Melissa Gomez

Melissa Gomez is a happy, outgoing eight-year-old who attends Cook's Grove Elementary in El Paso, Texas. Her parents never married, and she does not know her father. A talented musician, Melissa, often plays the piano for school programs, and her mother has learned the importance of Melissa's private lessons. Melissa can recognize people from their voices but sees only shadows and shapes.

Academic subjects were never difficult for Melissa. Her third grade teacher described her as a "popular" third grader who excelled, especially in the areas of math and science. She did not have brothers or sisters, so her mother, a legal clerk, was her primary role model. They spent a lot of time together reading, writing, and playing games. They also spent a lot of time together grocery shopping, swimming, and cooking. They enjoyed each other, and their relationship helped Melissa develop a quiet self-confidence that clearly helped her in school.

Most of the Cook's Grove school community had heard Melissa play the piano during a concert or school program. Most of them also knew Melissa before she was old enough to enter kindergarten. Through support from a variety of community resources, adaptive materials (including large-print literature and videotapes), and student-centered instructional approaches such as peer tutoring and cooperative learning were written into the educational plan for Melissa.

Last week, Melissa had celebrated the coming of spring vacation with her classmates. But Melissa went a step further and proposed that a committee of students beautify the school by planting flowers in flower boxes to be secured on the window ledges of every school window. One committee member, Taylor, drew up a list of tools and materials. Another, Eugene, figured out how many flowers, how much dirt, and how many boards were needed at the lumber yard. Melissa was working out a time schedule for students who had volunteered to work on the boxes. Mr. Hester and Ms. Nagowski, the two educators Melissa worked with, each helped, one by discussing Melissa's plan on a daily basis with Melissa and the committee, and the other by doing whatever was necessary to facilitate student-community collaboration. After three days, Melissa and the committee decided that they needed to plan more specifically, extend the schedule for completing the job, and organize a tighter, larger network of workers. Parents and grandparents, firefighters and insurance agents were all invited to join the work team. The changes in planning had an immediate effect. Within two weeks, the boxes were made by one subcommittee, headed by Jasmine, and the flowers were planted by another group. A schedule for flower care had been filled in with volunteers, and they were all provided with a brief orientation to the job by Mr. Claussen, a local gardener.

Melissa had made progress in a number of curricular areas. Academically, she strengthened both her organizational skills and her estimating skills in the process of developing the volunteer work schedule. Her abilities to sequence tasks and solve problems were enhanced as the leader of the project. Melissa also increased her ability to communicate persuasively during the initial proposal of the project, and she demonstrated her flexibility and willingness to accommodate the needs of others in coordinating the network of school community volunteers. She willingly accepted help from her peers and adults when she needed to revise the project implementation. Melissa also noticed, as a member of the planting subcommittee, that she became more and more adept at the task of digging the right size hole, holding the plant in place, and gently filling in around it without assistance. Her strength and balance were both tested as she carried a flat of plants up the school steps.

One of the most valuable roles Melissa took on was as a member of the student committee that developed a supportive role for Ray, a nine-year-old who had severe behavior difficulties. Based on their understanding of Ray's strengths and interests, the group decided that he could be a big help in the construction of the boxes and the loading and unloading of building and planting materials. They recommended to the respective subcommittee heads that Ray be invited to help them, and he was more than happy to join both groups. During the self-evaluation of her affective learning outcomes, Melissa focused extensively on her increased understanding of the needs of others and specifically identified her role in including Ray in the project. She really valued her school community and looked forward to returning to school after spring vacation.

Ho Ling

Although his undergraduate degree was in physics, Ho Ling found that he was fascinated by the way that young children interacted with their environment. During his senior year, he had helped develop a series of physics demonstrations for a younger audience, and when he and his classmates actually took their presentation to the schools around Houston, Ho Ling found himself wanting to work with the younger learners more and more. After graduation, he entered the graduate teaching program at Southeast Texas State College, and two years later he was certified in inclusive education. During his graduate program, Ho Ling took coursework in adaptive instructional technology and became involved with using technology to facilitate learning for students with disabilities.

Ho Ling was highly impressed with the comprehensive community involvement in the Cook's Grove Elementary interviewing process, and he was thrilled when Mr. Richardson called to offer him a position in the K–2 cluster. The younger learners, he was convinced, were the more curious, more enthusiastic learners. He soon met his K–2 team colleagues Nellie Bordeau, Cindy Robinson, and Betsy Hibbert, and immediately they began helping him adjust to the Cook's Grove community. In addition, when he moved into his apartment, he found welcome cards and letters from the children at the school and a huge packet of community information from the Chamber of Commerce. Everyone was so helpful.

As soon as he had a chance to settle in, Ho Ling visited the school and volunteered to work on the technology committee, which was currently exploring new adaptive devices for several students. They were more than happy to respond to his inquiries and hear his comments. Ho Ling was grateful because he had an opportunity to meet not only his colleagues but parents and others from the Cook's Grove community. One priority the entire committee agreed on was the need to provide full access to learning for all students, and to make all technology-assisted learning applicable to real world, on-the-job technology utilization.

Some of Ho Ling's expertise would definitely facilitate program planning for Arnie and Sally, two students on the K–2 team he was part of during the upcoming year. Arnie, orthopedically disabled, was a very active young student who would benefit from a touch sensor screen. Sally, a big seven-year-old who always wore a smile, had severe brain damage as a result of an automobile accident and would be more successful with self-management skills if she could monitor her own needs using a microphone that transmitted to earplugs that her teachers wore. Ho Ling or Cindy Robinson, the colleague who provided a broad range of instructional adaptations, could both hear Sally's almost inaudible call for assistance and be ready to help her almost instantly.

Although he had now been at Cook's Grove for ten years, Ho Ling had found that every year he was able to learn so much more about the strength of community involvement and collaboration. Every other semester he supervised a student teacher from nearby El Paso State and really found that collaboration with college students and college faculty opened up new areas of learning for him. A few years back he had formally completed the structure for implementing portfolio assessment with every student in the K–2 cluster, due in large part to his collaboration with the college. Just last year he had worked with the school psychologist, studying the effects of a play-based curriculum that stressed the child's interactions with the physical environment. This year he had helped a group of students during the ecology unit who had wanted to design and build a can and bottle crusher.

Ho Ling was convinced now more than ever that young children were capable of highly complex learning under the right conditions. He was also happy to be in a school community where those conditions were possible.

A MODEL OF COMMUNITY

The Martels

David and Linda Martel have been married for fifteen years and for the last eight have resided in Cook's Grove. They have two adopted children, six-year-old Adam, and two-week-old Jessica Sue. They chose Cook's Grove because of the community feeling and the excellent reputation of the school district. So far they have not been disappointed.

When Jessica Sue arrived, the Cook's Grove Elementary school sent her a welcome-to-the-community letter signed by all the school personnel and a welcome

banner signed by all 300 of the students. Adam had quickly pointed out his signature to David and Linda. He was exceptionally proud of the fact that he and Arnie had colored the second *s* in Jessica's name. They had hung the banner across their front porch for everyone to see. This, along with the community baby shower, was a big part of what made Cook's Grove a real home.

David is a contractor and has been volunteering with the local meteorologist on Wednesday afternoons. Together with a group of Cook's Grove Elementary students, they are building a weather station. Billy Jones, a member of the flower box committee, had called last week to ask if David could help with the flower box project. David checked his schedule and spoke with his customers. They did not seem to mind his starting earlier and leaving at about 3:00 to assist the students. Actually, several offered to donate any usable scrap wood from their building projects.

Linda is a visiting nurse, working primarily with senior citizens and persons who have difficulty leaving their homes. Her office is located in Cook's Grove Middle School, which shares the same block as the elementary school. Although the Middle School is somewhat larger, Linda feels it has the same warmth and community involvement as the elementary school. This location is extremely convenient for Linda because many of the persons she sees go to the senior center at the elementary school. She also gets daily updates through the computer communication project on the persons who have difficulty leaving their homes. Since the project began, Linda has noticed real positive changes in many of the persons she works with.

She is also able to bring Jessica Sue to school with her and feels comfortable about leaving Jessica Sue in the child care center when she is out visiting in the homes. Linda has also volunteered time to Cook's Grove Elementary, helping Connie and Yvonne develop a student-centered first aid training program.

Both David and Linda have earned credits to attend El Paso State as a result of their school volunteering. They took a course together from Dr. Maze on developing collaborative relationships and they have also donated some of their tuition waivers to the scholarship program.

At first Linda and David were concerned about the inclusion of a child with severe disabilities in Adam's child care group. Like many other parents, they were afraid Arnie's disabilities would demand too much of the caregivers' time. The child care staff at Cook's Grove held an open forum to discuss those concerns. Arnie's parents, Mike and Juanita Brown, also attended to introduce themselves and answer questions. Linda and David found the Browns to be frank open people who, like themselves, only wanted the best for their child. From their first encounter, Adam and Arnie became the best of friends. Linda and David quickly realized that Arnie was not a disabled person to Adam, but rather his buddy, the kid who rode a wheelchair instead of a bicycle.

The Browns' and Martels' friendship has grown. Mike coaches teeball and Linda, David, and Juanita are the cheerleaders. Arnie helps Adam with his swing, and Adam helps Arnie get his catcher's gear on. As Linda and David watch the two boys, they wonder why they ever had concerns about inclusion.

Karen Maze

Karen Maze is a faculty member at El Paso State University in the Center for Educational Studies and Services. She has lived in the Cook's Grove community for seven years, having come from a previous position in upstate New York. Dr. Maze has been very happy with her decision to settle here. When she bought her home, she received welcome-to-our-community letters from the Cook's Grove Elementary School and Chamber of Commerce. The welcome letter from Cook's Grove Elementary extended to her an invitation to one of their Wednesday afternoon faculty meetings. The inclusive program was what drew her here, so Dr. Maze was anxious to meet with the school staff. The letter from the Chamber of Commerce set out the community services available, many of which she was surprised to see shared the same address as the school. A list of upcoming community events was also included. Again, most of these were held at the elementary school. She was pleased to be in a community that appeared to value education, where school seemed to be at the heart of the action.

Dr. Maze was also excited about the faculty-teacher exchange that took place between all the El Paso schools and the university. She was part of a team that included a curriculum specialist and professors from the biology, mathematics, English, and history departments.

Although she had no children, Dr. Maze received the school's monthly newspaper and had become a frequent visitor to the school. She noted that school board meetings were always well attended, and she rarely heard complaints when she was in the audience. In fact, the Cook's Grove school board meetings were some of the most productive she had ever seen. Parents, business leaders, community members, and school personnel worked together to make difficult decisions. Student representatives from each of the teams in the school were also included. Funding problems were generally dealt with by everyone during a brainstorming session. Several ideas were then selected for the finance committee to examine and choose from for implementation. People were actually willing to become involved in a variety of different subcommittees.

Several of the local businesses, in conjunction with El Paso State, offered tuition waivers for students and community members who were active volunteers. Students were able to accumulate their waivers until after graduation, and adults could use theirs to take courses or special workshops. College faculty like Dr. Maze were able to pool theirs and offer several full-tuition scholarships each year.

The subcommittee on grant writing, which included a variety of persons from the community and the school, worked on funding school and community projects. The latest project funded was a joint community-school venture that provided a group of citizens who had difficulty getting out of their homes with laptop computers and modems that were voice, key or switch activated. Students wrote to these citizens every day, via E-mail, keeping abreast of their health and happiness. A variety of friendships resulted, and students learned far more than written communication skills. Many of the citizens were elderly and able to share El Paso's rich cultural history. Others were victims of their own mistakes and able to talk with students about the dangers of drug or alcohol abuse. Some were able to come out of their homes for the first time in years because of a new friendship.

The school flower box project organized by Melissa Gomez was another wonderful collaborative community-school effort. The K–2 cluster turned in recyclable bottles and cans to help fund materials for the flower boxes. Businesses in town sold materials at cost and donated expertise in various areas: planning, construction, and planting. Dr. Maze was impressed by Melissa's abilities to organize and lead a group of such varying ages and abilities. She was equally impressed by the adults involved, who were able to give up control of the decision-making process, thereby allowing the children to learn even more.

Unlike other places where Dr. Maze had lived, this community really seemed like home. She felt warm and welcome!

THE HEART OF THE COMMUNITY

Cook's Grove Elementary is an inclusive school of 300 children from families that make up one of the subcommunities of El Paso. The school has multiage classrooms that are split by grade groups of K–2 and 3–5, with three teams at each level. This division was adopted after much discussion among teachers, parents, and administrators. No class has more than seventeen students, including one or two with disabilities; instead of labeling students, educators at Cook's Grove follow a more developmental model of education. There are twenty-six certified teachers and six aides. The K–2 teams have educators with expertise in early childhood and elementary curriculum as well as special education. The grades 3–5 teams have elementary curriculum and special education expertise. Each team has an aide, and everyone benefits from the expertise of the speech therapist, occupational therapist, music, art, technology, and adaptive physical education teachers.

The doors at Cook's Grove School open at 6:30 to permit the child care center to begin its day. This child care center is one of the best in El Paso, having recently received accreditation from the National Association for the Education of Young Children. Many of the parents in Cook's Grove take advantage of the early child care hours to begin their work day at 7:00. Several of the companies in this area have, after consulting with their employees and the school, adopted a more flexible work schedule. Parents are permitted to begin their eight-hour day earlier so that they may have more late afternoon and evening time with their children. The child care center provides before- and afterschool care as well as full-day care. Several high school students, whose parent(s) leave for work early, volunteer at the child care center before school begins, while others volunteer their time after school. Each group is expected to organize and carry out activities or tutoring while there. This arrangement has proven helpful for all concerned. Parents know their teenagers are helping in the school community before or after school, high school students' academic work benefits from this opportunity to develop their organizational skills, and the children in the center benefit from the lower adult-child ratio.

Teachers and staff start to arrive about 7:00, and at 7:30 their official work day begins with a half hour of personal prep time or, if needed, an early meeting with parents. Mrs. Nagowski, Mr. Hester, Ms. Carter, and Mrs. Holmes (one of the grades 3–5 teams) each arrives carrying an armful of newspapers that the third, fourth, and fifth grade students typeset at the local newspaper office the day before. This is the final project in a month-long thematic unit on newspapers. The children developed cooperative learning groups based on interest. Some became journalists, cartoonists, editors, or photographers, while others wrote and sold advertisements, developed crossword puzzles, or reviewed movies and books. Each student had contributed to the paper, and the teachers knew how anxious students would all be to see everyone's name on a byline, cartoon, or advertisement.

Mr. Richardson, the school's principal, arrives at 7:15, walks with his mother to the senior center, then continues down the hall to his office. Several of the K–2 children have "adopted" Mrs. Richardson as their foster grandmother, and she visits their classroom frequently to read or create story books with them. She is an exceptionally vivacious lady of ninety who says the children help her stay young.

At 7:50, Mrs. Englebright and Ms. Markum, the classroom aides, are seen headed toward the child care center to gather up the students who go to before-school care. Mr. Whitman and Ms. Hemmingford have been out on the playground, so they gather children from there. Today is Wednesday, so the children are talking about their special projects for this afternoon. Several are discussing the weather station they are building with the Channel 5 meteorologist and a local subcontractor. Some are talking about their peer-to-peer counseling meeting, while others are trying to guess what they might be cooking in the community kitchen with their "foster grandparents" in the senior center. John and Archie are grumbling because they have appointments for vaccinations at the community health center. June has a meeting with her case worker. The senior and community health centers as well as the social service agency are all located within Cook's Grove Elementary, providing easy access to these services for both the children and school personnel.

Because Cook's Grove Elementary houses these various services, many community residents visit the school. Someone is always stopping by Mr. Richardson's office to comment on a display or bulletin board. Although he does have an office, Mr. Richardson prefers to spend his working days in the classrooms and hallways of Cook's Grove Elementary. Mr. Richardson is looking forward to talking with both teams this afternoon at their meeting about his plans for teaching next week. He feels that teaching keeps him in touch with the needs of both students and staff.

The diaper coupon box is overflowing as Ms. Reynolds, the school secretary, gathers a handful to be included in the Martels' welcome packet. Besides the coupons, the packet contains a welcome letter signed by all of the school personnel and a congratulations banner colored and signed by the students. The Martels have just adopted their second child, a baby girl, and the school community celebrates this exciting event. Several new mothers stop on their way to the infant playroom to pick up some diaper coupons, commenting to Ms. Reynolds about how much money they are saving.

As the academic day begins, the K–2 groups are continuing with their ecology unit by estimating the total number of trash bags collected by the sanitation workers in their neighborhood per week. Mr. Henry, from the sanitation department, will be there shortly to talk with students about their estimates and what happens to the bags. After Mr. Henry leaves, the students break into small learning groups to develop proposals, providing detailed descriptions for cooperative projects related to garbage. One group has decided to write a mystery story, "The Case of the Missing Garbage," that will incorporate fact as well as fiction. Another group is designing an art project for all members of the grades 3–5 cluster group that will involve the creative use of garbage. A third group is investigating the development of a schoolwide recycling project. Some of the recycled items will be sold to buy materials for the school flower boxes.

Janet and George are going from class to class delivering a copy of the grades 3–5 newspaper to each staff member. George carries the papers on the tray of his wheelchair and Janet distributes them to the staff. They start laughing because a pile of papers slides off his tray onto the floor as they round the corner. They decide, after picking up the papers, that maybe George should hold on to the pile while Janet pushes the chair.

At about 11:45, the Wednesday afternoon enrichment volunteers arrive. Because the companies in this area feel volunteerism increases productivity, they provide their employees with release time. The volunteers begin by eating lunch with their group, since groups are formed based on interest. Students of all ages are involved in a single activity. Because the weather is so nice, several groups have opted for a picnic lunch today.

The staff has decided to have a progressive potluck luncheon today. They begin at the senior center with salad and a brainstorming session with the seniors, trying to find some new ways to bring school students and senior citizens together. After salad, they move on to the K–2 team's rooms for various casseroles and to discuss their upcoming switch month. Each team has a favorite unit they have adapted for all the learners in the school. One month of the year, they switch groups to teach those units. The grades 3–5 team comments on the wonderful ecology displays and skims the portfolios of those students moving into their team next year.

Dessert comes last in the classrooms of the grades 3–5 team. Today the middle school teams have been invited in to share coffee and dessert. The group will discuss transition day and the joint elementary and middle school science fair.

The transition day discussion takes only a few minutes for last-minute ironing out of details. The fifth graders will go over to the middle school on the same day the eighth graders go to the high school. This year each fifth grader will shadow a sixth grader. The grades 5–6 pairs were set up in September and have been getting acquainted as pen pals through the electronic mail network.

The grades 3–5 team is particularly eager to share Raymond's progress with the middle school team. Raymond, an elective mute with behavior problems, has discovered through the E-mail experience that he had a passion for writing and communicating via computer. As a result, he has organized several members of his class, taught them a rebus system for writing letters, and begun a pen pal system with the preschoolers in the child care center. With encouragement from the computer communication group, Raymond has begun to verbalize.

Because this is the first time they attempted the joint science fair, the teams have some problems and concerns. When will the groups work together? How will educators divide responsibilities? How can they get multi-age groups of K–8 grades? How will older students involve the younger students? All are pleased and surprised to find that the students have already resolved many of those concerns among themselves. Several of the collaborative groups have actually selected the younger students as team leaders. Responsibilities are divided among all the elementary and middle school science teachers, with each taking on several teams according to their own expertise.

At 3 o'clock, the middle school teachers head off to a collaborative meeting at the high school and the elementary teachers go to the library to meet with library staff about their book requests. Mr. Gibson, the adaptive physical education teacher, has discovered several wonderful children's books written by athletes with disabilities. Ms. Nagowski has had the student newspaper laminated so that it can be displayed in the library. Mr. Hemp, the school librarian, is excitedly sharing a combined economics and mathematics life skills lesson he has designed. It seems that he discovered some grocery ads from the 1960s while rummaging through his grandmother's trunk. He proposes using them to do a comparison of prices from then to now, with students drawing hypotheses about the reasons for price changes and analyzing changes in people's eating habits.

Mr. Richardson will be team teaching a lesson on ecology that combines reading, research, art, and math with two of the K–2 teams. In the grades 3–5 team he will be taking over storytelling to introduce them to their next unit—undersea life. Mr. Richardson, an experienced diver, will present his own slide show on underwater subjects.

As 4:30 approaches, many of the school personnel are met by family members. Hispanic-American community members are hosting a Cinco de Mayo celebration in the school cafeteria. A local storyteller will be relating the history of the festival, authentic food will be served, and everyone will learn several Hispanic dances. Some of the money collected from tonight's celebration will go toward the acquisition of Hispanic sculptures for the school's art museum. The museum began four years ago with the donation of several pieces from the school's artist-in-residence. A local philanthropist donated several pieces from her African and Asian collections.

Mr. Richardson's wife and mother meet him at his office. They greet the Martels, who have arrived for the celebration and are showing off Jessica Sue. The musicians are warming up and the spicy smell of Hispanic cuisine drifts over from the cafeteria. Mr. Richardson smiles. He considers himself lucky to be the principal of the best elementary school in the world.

PARTING COMMENTS

With the exception of those persons named in the Chapter 3 profiles, all subjects of our profiling are fictitious and overdramatized to make a point. The profiles in this final chapter represent our hope for schools and communities of the twenty-first century. Some features are drawn from the more progressive schools we have been fortunate enough to visit. Others are simply our vision for the future. Idealistic, unrealistic? Perhaps. But so, at one point in history, was the dream of traveling to the moon. Anything can be achieved if we put our children and their education above all else.

How can these dreams be realized? The first place to start is to utilize what you have in place already and network with others who have already experienced success (and failure). In short, use all resources available to you. If there is an inclusive program near you, ask for their help. That school has in place materials, methods, and approaches that have already been effective.

Second, keep in mind that the development and implementation of an inclusive environment is not something that occurs randomly or overnight. Before starting up an inclusive program, substantial time must be spent on staff development. Staff must be prepared to work collaboratively with one another for the betterment of all children. Educators must learn to drop their defenses and open their classroom doors to one another.

Third, faculties undertaking the development of inclusive programs must avoid getting weighed down by overly elaborate schemes. Problem-solving techniques should be developed and implemented regularly. However, trying to anticipate and solve every problem before beginning is ludicrous. Some problems are better resolved along the way, providing those involved with a means to expand their affective and cognitive skills.

Fourth, the purpose for developing an inclusive environment cannot be solely to reduce a school's budget. Careful planning must be undertaken to ensure that general educators are not being overburdened. Appropriate support services must be available to both students and faculty. Technical clerical assistance must also be available to expedite printed materials and electronic communications. Access to information must be quick and efficient.

Fifth, keep in mind that today's learners are tomorrow's leaders. The standards by which collaborative, inclusive communities are constructed must be the very highest possible. Shortcuts and decisions driven by convenience are not in the best interest of children. They must have the most compassionate, most talented educators. Nothing less will do.

Finally—get started today.

REFERENCES

Chapter 1

American Council on Education and the Education Commissioner of the States. (1988). *One third of a nation: A report of the Commission on Minority Participation in Education and American Life*. Washington, DC: American Council on Education.

Anastasiow, N. (1983). Adolescent pregnancy and special education. *Exceptional Children, 49* (5), 396–401.

Armstrong, D. G., Henson, K. T., & Savage, T. V. (1983). *Education: An introduction*. New York: Macmillan.

Banks, J. A., (1993). Multicultural education: Characteristics and goals. In J. A. Banks, & C. A . McGee-Banks (Eds.), *Multicultural education: Issues and perspectives* (pp. 3–28). Boston: Allyn & Bacon.

Brown v. Board of Education of Topeka, 347 U.S. 483, 74 S. Ct. 686, 98 L. Ed. 873 (1954).

Cannell, J. J. (1987). *National norm-referenced elementary achievement testing in America's public schools: How all fifty states are above the national average*. Charleston, WVA: Friends of Education.

Carlile, C. (1991). Children of divorce: How teachers can help ease the pain. *Childhood Education, 67* (4), 232–234.

Dettmer, P., Thurston, L. P., & Dyck, N. (1993). *Consultation, collaboration, and teamwork*. Boston: Allyn & Bacon.

Dodson, F. (1987). *How to single parent*. New York: Harper & Row.

Doll, R. C. (1992). *Curriculum improvement: Decision making process* (8th ed.). Boston: Allyn & Bacon.

Doyle, D. P. (1991). America 2000. *Phi Delta Kappan, 73* (3), 184–191.

Dye, T. R. (1985). *Politics in states and communities,* (5th ed.). Englewood Cliffs, NJ: Prentice Hall.

Elam, S. M., Rose, L. C., & Gallup, A. M. (1991). The 23rd annual Gallup Poll of the public's attitudes toward the public schools. *Phi Delta Kappan, 73* (1), 41–56.

Elkind, D. (1986). Helping parents make healthy educational choices for their children. *Educational Leadership, 44* (3), 36–38.

Gayle, M. (1990). Toward the 21st century. *Adult Learning, 1* (4), 10–14.

Geiger, K. (1993). Beyond 'A Nation at Risk.' *Education Week, 12* (3), 15.

Gray, K. (1993). Why we will lose: Taylorism in America's high schools. *Phi Delta Kappan, 74* (5), 370–374.

Grunwald, P. (1990). The new generation of information systems. *Phi Delta Kappan, 72* (2), 113–114.

Hatch, J. A., & Freeman, E. B. (1988). Who's pushing whom? Stress and kindergarten. *Phi Delta Kappan, 70* (2), 145–147.

Hirsch, E. D., Jr. (1993). The core knowledge curriculum—What's behind its success? *Educational Leadership, 50* (8), 23–30.

Hochschild, J. (1985). *Thirty years after Brown.* Washington, DC: Joint Center for Policy Studies.

Holmes Group (1986). *Tomorrow's teachers: A report to the Holmes Group.* East Lansing, MI: Author.

Holt, M. (1993). The educational consequences of W. Edward Deming. *Phi Delta Kappan, 74* (5), 382–388.

Huelskamp, R. M. (1993). Perspectives on education in America. *Phi Delta Kappan, 74* (9), 718–721.

James, T., & Tyack, D. (1983). Learning from past efforts to reform the high school. *Phi Delta Kappan, 64* (6), 400–406.

Jellinek, M., & Klavan, E. (1988, September). The single parent. *Good Housekeeping,* p. 126.

Kelly, H. (1990). Technology and the transformation of American education. *T.H.E. Journal (Technological Horizons in Education), 18* (1), 60–63.

Kozol, J. (1967). *Death at an early age.* Boston: Plume.

Kozol, J. (1985). *Illiterate America.* Garden City, NY: Anchor Press/Doubleday.

Kozol, J. (1992). *Savage inequalities.* Boston: Plume.

Kuhn, T. K. (Ed.) (1962). *The structure of scientific revolutions.* New York: Basic Books.

Legislative update. (1993). *Education Week, 12* (3), 15.

Lieberman, A. (1991). Accountability as a reform strategy. *Phi Delta Kappan, 73* (3), 219–220.

Linn. R. L., Graue, M. E., & Sanders, N. M. (1990, Fall). Comparing state and district test results to national norms: The validity of claims that 'everyone is above average.' *Educational Measurement: Issues and Practices,* pp. 5–14.

Lipsky, D. K., & Gartner, A. (1992). Achieving full inclusion: Placing the student at the center of educational reform. In Stainback, W. & Stainback, S. (Eds.). *Controversial issues confronting special education: Divergent perspectives* (pp. 3–12). Boston: Allyn & Bacon.

Mecklenburger, J. A. (1990). Educational technology is not enough. *Phi Delta Kappan, 72* (2), 104–108.

Mills v. Board of Education, 348 F. Supp. (D.D.C. 1972).

Morrison, G. S. (1993). *Contemporary curriculum K–8.* Boston: Allyn & Bacon.

Morrison, G. S. (1997). *Teaching America.* Boston: Allyn & Bacon.

National Assessment of Educational Progress. (1985). *The Reading Report Card: Progress toward excellence in our schools* Princeton, NJ: Educational Testing Service.

National Association of Elementary School Principals & Charles F. Kettering Foundation (1980). One parent families and their children: The school's most significant minority. *Principal, 60,* 31–37.

National Center for Educational Statistics (1984). *The condition of education* (1984 ed.). Washington, DC: U.S. Department of Education.

National Center for Educational Statistics (1990). *Proceedings of the second annual federal forecasters conference.* (NCES-90-862). Washington, DC: U.S. Department of Education, Office of Educational Research and Improvement.

New Jersey v. T.L.O., 469 U.S. 325 (1985).

Newman, D. (1992). Technology as support for school structure and school restructuring. *Phi Delta Kappan, 74* (4), 308–316.

O'Looney, J. (1993). Redesigning the work of education. *Phi Delta Kappan, 74* (5), 375–381.

Orlich, D. C. (1989). Education reforms: Mistakes, misconceptions, miscues. *Phi Delta Kappan, 70* (7), 512–517.

Ornstein, A. C. (1989, February). Emerging curriculum trends: An agenda for the future. *NASSP Bulletin, 73* (514), 37–38, 40–44, 46–48.

Pallas, A. M., Natriello, G., & McDill, E. L. (1989). The changing nature of the disadvantaged population: Current dimensions and future trends. *Educational Researcher, 18,* 16–22.

Pennsylvania Association for Retarded Children (PARC) v. Pennsylvania, 344 F. Supp. 1257 (E. D. Pa. 1971).

Reed, A. J. S., & Bergemann, V. E. (1995). *In the classroom: An introduction* (2nd ed.). Guilford, CT: Dushkin.

Resnick, L. B., & Resnick, D. P. (1992). Assessing the thinking curriculum: New tools for education reform. In B. R. Gifford & M. C. O'Connor (Eds.), *Future assessments: Changing views of aptitude, achievement, and instruction.* Boston: Kluwer Academic.

Rossow, L. F. & Hiniger, J. A. (1991). *Students and the law.* Bloomington, IN: Phi Delta Kappa Educational Foundation.

Schmoker, R., & Wilson, R. B. (1993). Transforming schools through total quality education. *Phi Delta Kappan, 74* (5), 389–395.

Shane, H. (1989). Educated foresight for the 1990s. *Educational Leadership, 47,* 4.

Shane, H. (1990). Improving education for the twenty-first century. *Educational Horizons, 69* (1), 11–15.

Shepard, L. A. (1991). Will national tests improve student learning? *Phi Delta Kappan, 73* (3), 232–238.

Smith, M. L. (1989). *The role of external testing in elementary schools.* Los Angeles: Center for Research and Evaluation, Standards, and Student Testing.

Snyder, T. D. (1988). *Digest of education statistics 1988.* Washington, DC: Center for Educational Statistics.

Stainback, S., Stainback, W., & Jackson, J. H. (1992). Toward inclusive classrooms. In S. Stainback and W. Stainback (Eds.), *Curriculum considerations in inclusive classrooms: Facilitating learning for all students* (pp. 3–18). Baltimore: Brookes.

Stevens-Long, J., & Cobb, N. J. (1983). *Adolescence and early adulthood.* Palo Alto, CA: Mayfield.

Tinker v. Des Moines Independent Community School District, 393 U.S. 503, 89 S. Ct. 733, 21 L. Ed. 2nd 731 (1969).

United States Constitution. Washington, DC: Office of Government Publications.

Usiskin, Z. (1993). Lessons from the Chicago mathematics project. *Educational Leadership, 50* (8), 14–18.

Wattleton, F. (1989, July). Teenage pregnancy: The case for national action. *The Nation,* 138–141.

Weitzman, L. J. (1985). *The divorce revolution.* New York: Free Press.

Wishnietsky, D. H. (1991). *Using electronic mail in an educational setting.* Bloomington, IN: Phi Delta Kappa.

Chapter 2

Aikin, W. M. (1942). *The story of the Eight-Year Study.* New York: Harper & Row.

Alpha Team (1991). *A vision of a preferred curriculum for the 21st century.* Rochester, MI: Oakland University School of Education and Human Services. (ERIC Document Reproduction Service No. ED 344 275.)

Anyon, J. (1980). Social class and the hidden curriculum of work. *Journal of Education, 162* (1), 67–92.

Apple, M. W. (1982). *Education and power.* Boston: Routledge & Kegan Paul.

Aronwitz, S., & Giroux, H. A. (1985). *Education under siege.* Boston: Bergin & Garvey.

Bagley, W. C. (1941). The case for Essentialism in education. *Today's Education: Journal of the National Education Association, 30* (7), 201–202.

Banks, J. A. (1991). *Teaching strategies for ethnic studies* (5th ed.). Boston: Allyn & Bacon.

Bloom, B. S. (Ed.) (1956). *Taxonomy of educational objectives: The classification of educational goals, Handbook I: Cognitive domain.* White Plains, NY: Longman.

Combs, A., & Snygg, D. (1959). *Individual behavior* (2nd ed.). New York: Harper & Row.

Conant, J. B. (1959). *The American high school today.* New York: McGraw-Hill.

Dewey, J. (1902). *The child and the curriculum.* Chicago: University of Chicago Press.

Doll, R. C. (1992). *Curriculum improvement: Decision making and process* (8th ed.). Boston: Allyn & Bacon.

Educational Policies Commission and the American Council on Education. (1951). *Education and National Security* (pp. 17–34). Washington, DC: National Education Association.

Ernst, G. (1993). A multicultural curriculum for the 21st century. In G. Hass & F. W. Parkay (Eds.), *Curriculum planning: A new approach* (6th ed., pp. 84–90). Boston: Allyn & Bacon.

Flavell, J. (1992). Cognitive development: Past, present, future. *Developmental Psychology, 28,* 998–1005.

Ford, A., Davern, L., & Schnorr, R. (1992). Inclusive education: "Making sense" of the curriculum. In S. Stainback & W. Stainback (Eds.), *Curriculum considerations in inclusive classrooms: Facilitating learning for all students* (pp. 37–64). Baltimore: Paul H. Brookes.

Forman, E. A., Minick, N., & Stone, C. A. (Eds.). (1992). *Contexts for learning: Sociocultural dynamics in children's development.* New York: Oxford University Press.

Fosnot, C. T. (1989). *Enquiring teachers, enquiring learners: A Constructivist approach for teaching.* New York: Teachers College Press.

Gagne, R. M. (1977). *The conditions of learning* (3rd ed.). New York: Holt, Rinehart and Winston.

Harrow, A. J. (1972). *A taxonomy of the psychomotor domain: A guide for developing behavior objectives.* New York: Longman.

Hass, G., & Parkay, F. W. (1993). *Curriculum planning: A new approach* (6th ed.). Boston: Allyn & Bacon.

Hilgard, E. R. (1956). *Theories of learning* (2nd ed.). Englewood Cliffs, NJ: Prentice Hall.

Hutchins, R. M. (1938). The organization and subject-matter of general education. An address to the annual convention of the National Association of Secondary School Principals, Atlantic City, NJ, February 26.

Jersild, A. T. (1952). *In search of self.* New York: Teachers College Press.

Jersild, A. T. (1955). *When teachers face themselves.* New York: Teachers College Press.

Kilpatrick, W. H. (1941). The case for Progressivism in education. *Today's Education: Journal of the National Education Association, 30* (8), 231–232.

Krathwohl, D. R., Bloom, B. S., & Masia, B. (1964). *Taxonomy of educational objectives: The classification of educational goals, Handbook II: Affective domain.* New York: David McKay.

Maccoby, E., & Jacklin, L. (1974). *The psychology of sex differences.* Stanford, CA: Stanford University Press.

MacKenzie, G. N. (1964). Curriculum change: Participants, power, and processes. In M. B. Miles (Ed.), *Innovations in education.* New York: Teachers College Press.

Maslow, A. H. (1962). *Toward a psychology of being.* New York: Van Nostrand Reinhold.

Matyas, M. & Kahle, J. (1986). Equitable precollege science and mathematics: A discrepancy model. Paper presented at the Workshop on Underrepresentation and Career Differentials of Women in Science and Engineering. Washington, DC: National Academy of Sciences.

McNeil, J. D. (1995). *Curriculum: The teacher's initiative*. Englewood Cliffs, NJ: Prentice-Hall.

Morrison, G. S. (1997). *Teaching America*. Boston: Allyn & Bacon.

Morrison, G. S. (1993). *Contemporary curriculum K–8*. Boston: Allyn & Bacon.

National Center for Education Statistics, U.S. Department of Education (1990). *The condition of education. Vol. 1. Elementary and secondary education*. (NCES 90-681). Washington, DC: U.S. Government Printing Office.

National Commission on Excellence in Education. (1983). *A Nation at risk: The imperative for educational reform*. Washington, DC: U.S. Government Printing Office.

National Education Goals Panel. (1991). Goals report. Washington, DC: U.S. Government Printing Office.

Oliva, P. F. (1992). *Developing the curriculum* (3rd ed.). New York: HarperCollins.

O'Neil, J. (1990, September). New curriculum agenda emerges for '90s. *Curriculum Update*, 1, 8.

Penna, A. N., Giroux, H. A., & Pinar, W. F. (Eds.) (1981). *Curriculum and instruction: Alternatives in education*. Berkeley, CA: McCutchan.

Piaget, J. (1965). *The moral judgment of the child*. New York: Free Press.

Poplin, M. S. (1988). Holistic/constructivist principles of the teaching/learning process: Implications for the field of learning disabilities. *Journal of Learning Disabilities*, 21, 401–416.

Reid, D. K., Kurkjian, C., & Carruthers, S. S. (1994). Special education teachers interpret Constructivist teaching. *Remedial and Special Education*, 15 (5), 267–280.

Simpson, E. J. (1972). The classification of educational objectives in the psychomotor domain. *The psychomotor domain*, Vol. 3. Washington, DC: Gryphon House.

Sizer, T. (1984). *Horace's compromise: The dilemma of the American high school*. Boston: Houghton Mifflin.

Stainback, W., Stainback, S., & Moravec, J. (1992). Using curriculum to build inclusive classrooms. In S. Stainback and W. Stainback (Eds.), *Curriculum considerations in inclusive classrooms: Facilitating learning for all students* (pp. 65–84). Baltimore: Brookes.

Taba, H. (1962). *Curriculum development: Theory and practice*. New York: Harcourt Brace Jovanovich.

Tanner, D., & Tanner, L. (1995). *Curriculum development: Theory into practice* (3rd ed.). Englewood Cliffs, NJ: Prentice Hall.

Tyler, R. W. (1949). *Basic principles of curriculum and instruction*. Chicago: University of Chicago Press.

Watson, G. (1960). What psychology can we feel sure about? *Teachers College Record*, 61(5) 253–257.

Weiner, B. (1980). *Human motivation*. New York: Holt, Rinehart and Winston.

Wiles, J., & Bondi, J. (1993). *Curriculum development: A guide to practice* (4th ed.). New York: Merrill.

Zais, R. S. (1976). *Curriculum: Principles and foundations*. New York: Crowell.

Chapter 3

Adelman, H. S., & Taylor, L. (1983). Enhancing motivation for overcoming learning and behavior problems. *Journal of Learning Disabilities*, 16, 384–392.

Alabiso, F. (1972). Inhibitory functions of attention in reducing hyperactive behavior. *American Journal of Mental Deficiency*, 77, 259–282.

Ames, R., & Ames, C. (1984). *Research on motivation in education. Vol. 1. Student motivation.* New York: Harcourt Brace Jovanovich.

Andrews, G. R., & Debus, R. L. (1978). Persistence and causal perception of failure: Modifying cognitive attributions. *Journal of Educational Psychology, 70,* 154–166.

Armstrong, T. (1994). *Multiple intelligences in the classroom.* Alexandria, VA: Association for Supervision and Curriculum Development.

Ausubel, D. P. (1959). Viewpoints from related disciplines: Human growth and development. *Teachers College Record, 60* (5), 245–254.

Banbury, M. M. (1987). Testing and grading mainstreamed students in regular education subjects. In A. Rotatori, M. M. Banbury, and R. A. Fox (Eds.), *Issues in special education* (pp. 177–186). Mountain View, CA: Mayfield.

Bandura, A. (1986). *Social foundations of thought and action: A social-cognitive theory.* Englewood Cliffs: Prentice Hall.

Banks, J. A. (1988). Ethnicity, class, cognitive, and motivational styles: Research and teaching implications. *Journal of Negro Education, 57* (4), 452–466.

Banks, J. A. (1991). *Teaching strategies for ethnic studies* (5th ed.). Boston: Allyn & Bacon.

Banks, J. A. (1993). Multicultural education: Characteristics and goals. In J. A. Banks & C. A. McGee-Banks (Eds.)., *Multicultural education: Issues and perspectives* (pp. 3–28). Boston: Allyn & Bacon.

Banks, J. A., & McGee-Banks, C. A. (Eds.). (1993). *Multicultural education: Issues and perspectives.* Boston: Allyn & Bacon.

Berliner, D. (1987). Simple views of effective teaching and a simple theory of classroom instruction. In D. Berliner & B. Rosenshine (Eds.), *Talks to teachers* (pp. 93–110). New York: Random House.

Blackman, S., & Goldstein, K. M. (1982). Cognitive styles and learning disabilities. *Journal of Learning Disabilities, 15,* 106–115.

Borich, G. (1992). *Effective teaching methods* (2nd ed.). New York: Merrill.

Bruner, J. (1969). *Toward a theory of instruction.* New York: Norton.

Carnine, D. (1990). New research on the brain: Implications for instruction. *Phi Delta Kappan, 71,* 372–377.

Deshler, D. D., Schumaker, J. B., & Lenz, B. K. (1984). Academic and cognitive interventions for L.D. adolescents: Part I. *Journal of Learning Disabilities, 7,* 108–117.

Eggen, P. D., & Kauchak, D. (1988). *Strategies for teachers: Teaching content and thinking skills.* Englewood Cliffs, NJ: Prentice Hall.

Eisner, E. W. (1985). *The educational imagination: On the design and evaluation of school programs* (2nd ed.). New York: Macmillan.

Ellis, E. S., Lenz, B. K., & Sabornie, E. J. (1987). Generalization and adaptation of learning strategies to natural environments: Part I: Critical agents. *Remedial and Special Education, 8* (1), 6–20.

Ennis, R. (1987). A taxonomy of critical thinking dispositions and abilities. In J. Baron and R. Sternberg (Eds.), *Teaching thinking skills* (pp. 9–26). New York: Freeman.

Epstein, H. (1977). A neuroscience framework for restructuring middle school curricula. *Transescence: The Journal of Emerging Adolescent Education, 5,* 6–11.

Epstein, H. (1981, May). Learning how to learn: Matching instructional levels. *The Principal,* 25–30.

Epstein, H., & Toepher, C. F., Jr. (1978). A neuroscience basis for the reorganizing of middle grades education. *Educational Leadership, 35,* 656–660.

Farr, C., & Moon, C. (1988). *New perspectives on intelligence: Examining field dependence/independence in light of Steinker's triarchic theory of intelligence.* Paper presented at the annual meeting of the American Educational Research Association, New Orleans.

Farr, M. (1986). Language, culture, and writing: Sociolinguistic foundations of research on writing. In E. Z. Rothkopf (Ed.), *Review of research in education* (Vol. 13, pp. 195–223). Washington, DC: American Educational Research Association.

Fennema, E., & Peterson, P. L. (1987). Effective teaching for girls and boys: The same or different. In D. C. Berliner and B. V. Rosenshine (Eds.), *Talks to teachers* (pp. 111–125). New York: Random House.

Flavell, J. H. (1979). Metacognition and cognitive monitoring: A new area of cognitive-developmental inquiry. *American Psychologist, 34,* 906–911.

Flavell, J. H., Beach, D. R., & Chinsky, J. M. (1966). Spontaneous verbal rehearsal in memory tasks as a function of age. *Child Development, 37,* 283–299.

Gagné, R. M. (1985). *The conditions of learning* (4th ed.). New York: Holt, Rinehart and Winston.

Gardner, H. (1983). *Frames of mind: The theory of multiple intelligences.* New York: Basic Books.

Gardner, H. (1993). *Multiple Intelligences: The theory in practice.* New York: Basic Books.

Glasser, W. (1986). *Control theory in the classroom.* New York: Harper & Row.

Gredler, M. E. (1992). *Learning and instruction: Theory into practice* (2nd ed.). New York: Macmillan.

Hallahan, D. P., Kauffman, J., & Lloyd, J. (1985). *Introduction to learning disabilities* (2nd ed.). Englewood Cliffs, NJ: Prentice Hall.

Haring, N. G., Liberty, K. A., & White, O. R. (1980). Rules for data-based strategy decisions in instructional programs: Current research and instructional implications. In W. Sailor, B. Wilcox, & L. Brown (Eds.), *Methods of instruction for severely handicapped students* (pp. 171–172). Baltimore: Brookes.

Hass, G., & Parkay, F. W. (1993). *Curriculum planning: A new approach* (6th ed.). Boston: Allyn & Bacon.

Heath, S. B. (1983). *Ways with words.* Cambridge: Cambridge University.

Herndon, J. (1971). *How to survive in your native land.* New York: Simon & Schuster.

Hilgersom-Volk, K. (1987). Celebrating students' diversity through learning styles. *OSSC Bulletin, 30* (9), 1–26.

Hulse, S. H., Egeth, H., & Deece, J. (1980). *The psychology of learning* (5th ed.). New York: McGraw-Hill.

Huston, B. (1985). Brain growth spurts—What's left by the middle school years? *The Middle School Journal, 16* (2), 8–11.

Jacobsen, D., Eggen, P., & Kauchak, D. (1993). *Methods for teaching: A skills approach* (4th ed.). New York: Merrill.

Kagan, J., Pearson, L., & Welch, L. (1970). Conceptual impulsivity and inductive reasoning. *Child Development, 37,* 123–130.

Katims, D. S. (1990). Theory-based instructional practices in the classroom. *Preventing School Failure, 34* (2), 45–47.

Kauchak, D. P., & Eggen, P. D. (1993). *Learning and teaching: Research based methods* (2nd ed.). Boston: Allyn & Bacon.

Keefe, J. (1982). Assessing student learning styles: An overview. In National Association of Secondary School Principals (Ed.), *Student learning styles and brain behavior* (pp. 18–21). Reston, VA: Author.

Keller, H. (1903). *The story of my life.*

Kolb, D. A. (1984). *Experiential learning: Experience as the source of learning and development.* Englewood Cliffs, NJ: Prentice Hall.

Le Mehieu, B. (1981). Learning to choose. *Theory into Practice, 20,* 273–277.

Lerner, J. W., & Egan, R. W. (1989). *Learning disabilities: Theories, diagnosis, and teaching strategies* (5th ed.), *Study guide.* Dallas: Houghton Mifflin.

Maccoby, E., & Jacklin, L. (1974). *The psychology of sex differences.* Stanford, CA: Stanford University Press.

Madison, J. P. (1995). Personal communication.

McCarthy, B., & Lieberman, M. (1988). Learning styles dialogue. In *Report of the New York State Board of Regents' Panel on Learning Styles* (ED 348 407).

McKim, R. (1980). *Experiences in visual thinking.* Boston: PWS Engineering.

Meichenbaum, D. (1977). *Cognitive-behavior modification.* New York: Plenum.

Mercer, C. D., & Mercer, A. R. (1989). *Teaching students with learning problems* (3rd ed.). Columbus: Merrill.

Mercer, C. D., & Snell, M. E. (1977). *Learning theory in mental retardation: Implications for teaching.* Columbus: Merrill.

More, A. J. (1990). Learning styles of Native Americans and Asians. Paper presented at the 98th annual meeting of the American Psychological Association, Boston, MA.

Morrison, G. S. (1993). *Contemporary curriculum K–8.* Boston: Allyn & Bacon.

Moses, M. (1985). Thinking and excellence in education: Pieces of the same puzzle? *Journal of Creative Behavior, 19,* 113–119.

National Association of State Boards of Education. (1988). *Right from the start: A report on the NASBE task force on early childhood education.* Washington, DC: Author.

National Commission for Excellence in Education. (1983). *A nation at risk: The imperative for educational reform.* Washington, DC: U.S. Government Printing Office.

Nicholls, J. G. (1978). The development of the concepts of effort and ability, perception of academic attainment, and the understanding that difficult tasks require more ability. *Developmental Psychology, 49,* 800–814.

Nickerson, R. (1988). On improving thinking through instruction. In E. Rothkropf (Ed.), *Review of research in education* (pp. 10–33). Washington, DC: American Educational Research Association.

Orr, E. W. (1987). *Twice as less.* New York: Norton.

Overton, T. (1992). *Assessment in special education: An applied approach.* Columbus, OH: Merrill.

Piaget, J. (1970). Piaget 's theory. In P. H. Mussen (Ed.), *Carmichael's manual of psychology* (pp. 703–732). New York: Wiley.

Piaget, J., & Inhelder, B. (1975). *The origin of the idea of chance in children.* New York: Norton.

Polloway, E. A., Patton, J. R., Payne, J. S., & Payne, R. A. (1989). *Strategies for teaching learners with special needs* (4th ed.). Columbus: Merrill.

Presseisen, B. (1986). *Thinking skills: Research and practice.* Washington, DC: National Education Association.

Pressley, M., Woloshyn, V., Lysynchuk, L., Martin, V., Wood, E., & Willoughby, T. (1990). A primer of research on cognitive strategy instruction: The important issues and how to address them. *Educational Psychology Review, 2,* 1–58.

Ramirez, M., & Castaneda, A. (1974). *Cultural democracy, bicognitive development, and education.* New York: Academic Press.

Reid, D. K. (1988). *Teaching the learning disabled: A cognitive developmental approach.* Boston: Allyn & Bacon.

Reid, D. K. & Hresko, W. P. (1981). *A cognitive approach to learning disabilities.* New York: McGraw-Hill.

Resnick, L. (1987). *Education and learning to think.* Washington, DC: Academic Press.

Ritter, D. E. (1988). *Curriculum content today and tomorrow: Will students be motivated to learn?* Report to U.S. Department of Education Office of Educational Research and Improvement (ERIC Document Reproduction Service No. ED 303 443).

Romberg, T. A., & Carpenter, T. P. (1986). Research on teaching and learning mathematics: Two disciplines of scientific inquiry. In M. C. Wittrock (Ed.), *Handbook of research on teaching* (3rd ed.; pp. 850–873). New York: Macmillan.

Rothman, R. (1993). Testing smarts: Boston schools pilot urban assessments. *Education Week, 12* (38), 1,13.

Sadker, M. P., & Sadker, D. M. (1980). *Teachers make the difference: An introduction to education.* New York: Harper & Row.

Sax, G. (1989). *Principles of educational and psychological measurement and evaluation* (3rd ed.). Belmont, CA: Wadsworth.

Schmeck, R. (Ed.). (1988). *Learning strategies and learning styles.* New York: Plenum.

Shade, B. J. (Ed.). (1989). *Culture, style and the educative process.* Springfield, IL: Charles C Thomas.

Skinner, B. F. (1968). *The technology of teaching.* New York: Appleton-Century-Crofts.

Smith, D. D. (1981). *Teaching the learning disabled.* Englewood Cliffs, NJ: Prentice Hall.

Stigler, J. W., & Baranes, R. (1988). Culture and mathematics learning. In E. Z. Rothkopf (Ed.), *Review of research in education* (Vol. 15, pp. 253 306). Washington, DC: American Educational Research Association.

Stipek, D. J. (1988). *Motivation to learn: From theory to practice.* Englewood Cliffs, NJ: Prentice Hall.

Suppes, P. (1974). The place of theory in educational research. *Educational Researcher, 3* (6), 3–10.

Swartz, R. (1987). Critical thinking, the curriculum, and the problem of transfer. In D. Perkins. J. Lochhead, and J. Bishop (Eds.), *Thinking: Progress in research and teaching.* Hillsdale, NJ: Erlbaum.

Thorndike, E. L. (1931). *Human learning.* New York: Century.

Toepher, C. F., Jr. (1986). *Improving instruction in middle level schools: Implications of neurological data for curriculum development.* Paper presented to New England School Development Council Middle School Workshop, Massachusetts (ERIC Document Reproduction Service No. ED 270 883).

Torrence, E. (1982). Hemisphericity and creative functioning. *Journal of Research and Development in Education 15* (3), 29–37.

U.S. Department of Education. (1986). *First lessons: A report on elementary education in America.* Washington, DC: U.S. Government Printing Office.

Wallace, G., & McLoughlin, J. A. (1988). *Learning disabilities: Concepts and characteristics* (3rd ed.). Columbus, OH: Merrill.

Wang, M. C., & Stiles, B. (1976). An investigation of children's concept of self-responsibility for their school learning. *American Educational Journal, 13,* 159–179.

Weiner, B. (1979). A theory of motivation for some classroom experiences. *Journal of Educational Psychology, 71,* 3–25.

Wiles, J., & Bondi, J. (1993). *Curriculum development: A guide to practice* (4th ed.). New York: Merrill.

Witkin, H., Moore, C., Goodenough, D., & Cox, D. (1972). Field dependent and field independent cognitive styles and their educational implications. *Review of Educational Research, 47,* 1–64.

Wittrock, M. C. (1986). Students' thought processes. In M. C. Wittrock (Ed.), *Handbook of research on teaching* (3rd Ed.; pp. 297–314). New York: Macmillan.

Zeaman, D., & House, B. J. (1963). The role of attention in retarded discrimination learning. In N. R. Ellis (Ed.), *Handbook of mental deficiency.* New York: McGraw-Hill.

Chapter 4

Anyon, J. (1981). Social class and school knowledge. *Curriculum Inquiry, 11* (1), 3–42.

Bellon, J. J., Bellon, E. C., & Blank, M. A. (1992). *Teaching from a research knowledge base: A development and renewal process.* New York: Merrill.

Bennett, W. J. (1986). *First lessons: A report on elementary education in America.* Washington, DC: U.S. Government Printing Office.

Berliner, D. (1984). Research and teacher effectiveness. In *Making our school more effective: Proceedings of three state conferences.* San Francisco: Far West Laboratory.

Berliner, D. (1987). Simple views of effective teaching and a simple theory of classroom instruction. In D. Berliner & B. Rosenshine (Eds.), *Talks to teachers* (pp. 93–110). New York: Random House.

Borich, G. D. (1992). *Effective teaching methods* (2nd ed.). New York: Merrill.

Bossert, S. (1981). Understanding sex differences in children's classroom experiences. *Elementary School Journal, 83,* 255–268.

Brophy, J. E. (1983). Classroom organization and management. In D. Smith (Ed.), *Essential knowledge for beginning educators* (pp. 42–59). Washington, DC: American Association of Colleges for Teacher Education.

Brophy, J. E. (Ed.). (1989). *Advances in research on teaching* (Vol. 1). Greenwich, CT: JAI Press.

Brophy J. E., Evertson, C., Anderson, L., Baum, M., & Crawford, J. (1981). *Student characteristics and teaching.* New York: Longman.

Brophy, J. E., & Evertson, C. (1976). *Learning from teaching: A developmental perspective.* Boston: Allyn & Bacon.

Brophy, J. E., & Evertson, C. (1981). *Student characteristics and teaching.* New York: Longman.

Brophy, J. E., & Good, T. (1974). *Teacher-student relationships: Causes and consequences.* New York: Holt, Rinehart and Winston.

Brophy, J. E., & Good, T. (1986). Teacher behavior and student achievement. In M. C. Wittrock (Ed.), *Handbook of research on teaching* (3rd ed.; pp. 328–375). New York: Macmillan.

Bruner, J. (1960). *The process of education.* New York: Vintage.

Bullough, R. (1989). Teacher education and teacher reflectivity. *Journal of Teacher Education, 40* (2), 15–21.

Cazden, C. B., & Mehan, H. (1989). Principles from sociology and anthropology: Context, code, classroom, and culture. In M. C. Reynolds (Ed.), *Knowledge base for the beginning teacher* (pp. 47–57). Oxford, UK: Pergamon Press.

Clark, C., & Peterson, P. (1986). Teachers' thought processes. In M. C. Wittrock (Ed.), *Handbook of research on teaching* (3rd ed.; pp. 255–296). New York: MacMillan.

Collins, J. (1986). Differential instruction in reading groups. In J. Cook-Gumperz (Ed.), *The social construction of literacy* (pp. 117–137). Cambridge, UK: Cambridge University Press.

Comer, J. P. (1987). New Haven's school-community connection. *Educational Leadership, 44* (6), 13–18.

Cooper, H. (1979). Pygmalion grows up: A model for teacher expectation communication and performance influence. *Review of Educational Research, 49,* 389–410.

Cooper, H., & Good, T. (1983). *Pygmalion grows up: Studies in the expectation communication process.* New York: Longman.

Dewey, J. (1933). *How we think: A restatement of the relation of reflective thinking to the educative process* (Rev. ed.). Lexington, MA: D. C. Heath.

Doyle, W. (1977). Paradigms for research on teacher effectiveness. *Review of Research in Education, 5*, 163–198.

Doyle, W. (1986). Classroom organization and management. In M. C. Wittrock (Ed.), *Handbook of research on teaching* (3rd ed.; pp. 392–431). New York: MacMillan.

Duffy, G., Roehler, L., & Herrmann, B. (1988). Modeling mental processes helps poor readers become strategic readers. *The Reading Teacher, 41* (8), 762–767.

Dunkin, M. J., & Biddle, B. J. (1974). *The study of teaching.* New York: Holt, Rinehart and Winston.

Eby, J. W. (1992). *Reflective planning, teaching, and evaluation for the elementary school.* New York: Merrill.

Evertson, C., Anderson, C., Anderson, L., & Brophy, J. (1980). The Texas junior high school study: Relationship between classroom behavior and student outcomes in junior high math and English classes. *American Educational Research Journal, 17* (1), 43–60.

Feistritzer, C. E. (1983). *The making of a teacher: A report on teacher education and certification.* Washington, DC: National Center for Educational Information.

Flynn, G. (1989). *Toward community.* Paper presented at the 16th Annual TASH Conference, San Francisco, CA.

Ford, A., Davern, L., & Schnorr, R. (1992). Inclusive education: "Making sense" of the curriculum. In S. Stainback & W. Stainback (Eds.), *Curriculum considerations in inclusive classrooms: Facilitating learning for all students* (pp. 37–64). Baltimore: Brookes.

Futrell, M. H. (1989). *An open letter to America on schools, students, and tomorrow.* Washington, DC: National Education Association.

Good, T. L. (1970). Which pupils do teachers call on? *Elementary School Journal, 70*, 190–198.

Good T. L., & Brophy J. E. (1986). School effects. In M. C. Wittrock (Ed.), *Handbook of research on teaching* (3rd ed.; pp. 570–602). New York: MacMillan.

Good, T. L., & Brophy, J. E. (1994). *Looking in classrooms*, 6th ed. New York: HarperCollins.

Good, T. L., & Brophy, J. E. (1987). *Looking in classrooms*, 4th ed. New York: Harper & Row.

Good, T. L., & Findley, M. (1985). Sex role expectations in achievement. In J. Dusek (Ed.), *Teacher Expectations.* Hillsdale, NJ: Erlbaum.

Grant, L. (1985). Race-gender status, classroom interaction, and children's socialization in elementary school. In L. Wilkinson & C. Marrett (Eds.), *Gender influences in classroom interaction.* New York: Academic Press.

Hall, A. G. (1981). Points picked up: One hundred hints on how to manage a school. In E. W. Johnson (Ed.), *Teaching school: Points picked up* (pp. 209–216). New York: Walker.

Heath, S. (1983). *Ways with words.* New York: Cambridge University Press.

Hilliard, A. (1989). Teachers and cultural styles in a pluralistic society. *NEA Today, 7* (6), 65–69.

Holmes Group (1986). *Tomorrow's teachers: A report to the Holmes Group.* East Lansing, MI: Author.

Idol, L., Nevin, A., & Paolucci-Whitcomb, P. (1994) *Collaborative consultation*, (2nd ed.). Austin: Pro-Ed.

Irvine, J. J. (1990). *Black students and school failure.* New York: Greenwood Press.

Jackson, P. (1968). *Life in classrooms.* New York: Holt, Rinehart and Winston.

Kauchak, D., & Eggen, P. D. (1989). *Learning and teaching: Research based methods.* Boston: Allyn & Bacon.

Kohlberg, L. (1987). *The measurement of moral judgment: Vol. 1. Theoretical foundations and research validation.* London: Cambridge University.

Kounin, J. (1977). *Discipline and group management in classrooms* (Rev. ed.). New York: Holt, Rinehart and Winston. [Original work published 1971.]

Leacock, E. (1969). *Teaching and learning in city schools.* New York: Basic Books.

Lehr, J. B., & Harris, H. W. (1988). *At-risk, low-achieving students in the classroom.* Washington, DC: National Education Association.

Louisell, R. D., & Descamps, J. (1992). *Developing a teaching style: Methods for elementary school teachers.* New York: HarperCollins.

Maccoby, E., & Jacklin, L. (1974). *The psychology of sex differences.* Stanford, CA: Stanford University.

Macrorie, K. (1984). *Twenty teachers.* New York: Oxford University Press.

McDermott, R. P. (1977). Social relations as contexts for learning in school. *Harvard Educational Review, 47* (2), 198–213.

Meese, R. L. (1994). *Teaching learners with mild disabilities: Integrating research and practice.* Belmont, CA: Brooks/Cole.

Morse, L., & Handley, H. (1985). Listening to adolescents: Gender differences in science class interaction. In L. Wilkinson & C. Marrett (Eds.), *Gender influences in classroom interactions* (pp. 37–56). New York: Academic.

Motta, R., & Vane, J. (1977). An investigation of teacher perceptions of sex-typed behaviors. *Journal of Educational Research,* 363–368.

National Commission on Excellence in Education. (1983). *A nation at risk: The imperative for educational reform.* Washington, DC: U.S. Department of Education.

Oakes, J. (1986). Tracking, inequality, and the rhetoric of school reform: Why schools don't change. *Journal of Education, 168* (1), 60–80.

Pugach, M. C. (1992). Unifying the preservice preparation of teachers. In W. Stainback and S. Stainback (Eds.), *Controversial issues confronting special education: Divergent perspectives* (pp. 255–269), Boston: Allyn & Bacon.

Pugach, M. C. & Lilly, M. S. (1984). Reconceptualizing support services for classroom teachers: Implications for teacher education. *Journal of Teacher Education, 35* (5), 48–55.

Ratzi, A. (1988). Creating a school community: One model of how it can be done: An interview with Anne Ratzki. *American Educator, 12* (1), 10–17.

Reed, A. J. S., & Bergemann, V. E. (1995). *In the classroom: An introduction to education* (2nd ed.). Guilford, CN: Dushkin.

Rist, R. C. (1970). Student social class and teacher expectations: The self-fulfilling prophecy in ghetto education. *Harvard Educational Review, 40* (3), 411–451.

Rogers, J. (1993, May). The inclusive revolution. *Phi Delta Kappa Research Bulletin.* Bloomington, IN: Center for Evaluation, Development, and Research.

Rosenshine, B. (1971). *Teaching behaviors and student achievement.* London: National Foundation for Educational Research in England and Wales.

Rosenshine, B. (1983). Teaching functions in instructional programs. *The Elementary School Journal, 83,* 335–351.

Rosenshine, B., & Furst, N. (1971). Research in teacher performance criteria. In B. O. Smith (Ed.), *Research in teacher education* (pp. 37–72). Englewood Cliffs, NJ: Prentice Hall.

Rosenthal, R. (1973). The Pygmalion effect lives. *Psychology Today, 7* (4), 56–60, 62–63.

Rubin, L. J. (1985). *Artistry in teaching.* New York: Random House.

Sapon-Shevin, M. (1991). Cooperative learning in inclusive classrooms: Learning to become a community. *Cooperative Learning, 12* (1), 8–11.

Schon, D. (1987). *Educating the reflective practitioner.* San Francisco: Jossey-Bass.

Simmons, B. (1980). Sex role expectations of classroom teachers. *Education, 100,* 249–253.

Sizer, T. R. (1984). *Horace's compromise: The dilemma of the American high school.* Boston: Houghton Mifflin.

Skopp, D. (1992). *Bright with promise: From the normal and training school to SUNY Plattsburgh, 1889–1989: A pictorial history.* Norfolk, VA: Donning.

Smith, F. (1986). *Insult to intelligence.* New York: Arbor House.

Solorzano, L. (1983, March 14). What's wrong with our teachers. *U.S. News and World Report,* pp. 37–40.

Stainback, S., Stainback, W., & Jackson, H. J. (1992). Toward inclusive classrooms. In S. Stainback & W. Stainback (Eds.), *Curriculum considerations in inclusive classrooms: Facilitating learning for all students* (pp. 3–17). Baltimore: Brookes.

Stainback, W., Stainback, S., & Moravec, J. (1992). Using curriculum to build inclusive classrooms. In S. Stainback & W. Stainback (Eds.), *Curriculum considerations in inclusive classrooms: Facilitating learning for all students* (pp. 65–84). Baltimore: Brookes.

Stallings, J., Cory, R., Fairweather, J., & Needles, M. (1978). *How to change the process of teaching basic reading skills in secondary schools.* Menlo Park, CA: SRI International.

Tom, A. (1984). *Teaching as a moral craft.* New York: Longman.

Villegas, A. M. (1991, December). *Culturally responsive pedagogy for the 1990s and beyond.* ERIC Clearinghouse on Teacher Education. Washington, DC: American Association of Colleges for Teacher Education.

Villegas, A. M., & Watts, S. M. (1991, April). *Life in the classroom: The influence of class placement and student race/ethnicity.* Paper presented at the annual meeting of the American Educational Research Association, Chicago.

Walberg, H. J. (1986). Synthesis of research on teaching. In M. C. Wittrock (Ed.), *Handbook of research on teaching* (3rd ed.; pp. 214–229). New York: Macmillan.

Walberg, H. J., Schiller, D., & Haertel, G. D. (1979). The quiet revolution in educational research. *Phi Delta Kappan, 61* (4), 179–183.

Weinstein, R. (1983). Students perceptions of schooling. *Elementary School Journal, 83,* 287–312.

Whittier, K. S., & Hewit, J. S. (1993). Collaborative teacher education: An elementary education/special education connection. *Intervention in School and Clinic, 29* (2), 84–88.

Wong-Fillmore, L. W. (1990). *Now or later? Issues related to the early education of minority group students.* Unpublished paper, Council of Chief School State Officers, Washington, DC.

Wyne, M., & Stuck, G. (1982). Time and learning: Implications for the classroom teacher. *The Elementary School Journal, 83,* 67–75.

Chapter 5

Biklen, D. (1985). *Achieving the complete school.* New York: Teachers College.

Biklen, D. (1987, October). *Excellence in education: Can we have it without integration?* Keynote address, Annual Conference of the Finger Lakes Association for Persons with Severe Handicaps, Syracuse, NY.

Boyer, E. L. (1983). *High school: A report on American secondary education.* New York: Harper & Row.

Brandt, R. (1988). On students' needs and team learning: A conversation with William Glasser. *Educational Leadership, 45* (6), 38–45.

Briscoe, D. B. (1991). Designing for diversity in school success. Capitalizing on culture. *Preventing School Failure, 36* (1), 13–18.

Brown, L., Long, E., Udarvi-Solner, A., Davis, L., Van Deventer, P., Algren, C., Johnson, F., Gruenewald, L., & Jorgensen, J. (1989). The home school: Why students with severe intellectual disabilities must attend the schools of their brothers, sisters, friends, and neighbors. *Journal of the Association for Persons with Severe Handicaps, 14,* 1–7.

Buswell, B. E., & Schaffner, C. B. (1990). Families supporting inclusive schooling. In W. Stainback and S. Stainback (Eds.), *Support networks for inclusive schooling: Interdependent integrated education* (pp. 219–229). Baltimore: Brookes.

Carnegie Forum on Education and Economy. (1986). *A nation prepared: Teachers for the 21st century.* New York: Carnegie Corporation.

Comer, J. (1989). Children can: An address on school improvement. In R. Webb and F. Parkay (Eds.), *Children can: An address on school improvement by Dr. James Comer with responses from Florida's educational community* (pp. 4–17). Gainesville, Fl: Alachua County Mental Health Association.

Ellis, N. (1990). Collaborative interaction for improvement of teaching. *Teacher and Teacher Education, 6,* 267–277.

Epstein, J. L. (1989). Building parent-teacher partnerships in inner-city schools. *Family Resource Coalition Report, 8,* 7.

Falvey, M. A., Coots, J. J., & Bishop, K. D. (1990). Developing a caring community to support volunteer programs. In W. Stainback and S. Stainback (Eds.), *Support networks for inclusive schooling: Interdependent integrated education* (pp. 231–239). Baltimore: Brookes.

Friend, M. (1988). Putting consultation into context: Historical and contemporary perspectives. *Remedial and Special Education, 9* (6), 7–13.

Friend, M., & Bauwens, J. (1988). Managing resistance: An essential consulting skill for learning disabilities teachers. *Journal of Learning Disabilities, 21* (9), 556–561.

Friend, M., & Cook, L. (1992). *Interactions: Collaboration skills for school professionals.* New York: Longman.

Forest, M. (1986). *Making a difference: What communities can do to prevent mental handicap and promote lives of quality. Vol. 3. Helping children live, learn and grow in their communities.* Downsview, Ontario: National Institute on Mental Retardation.

Forest, M. (Ed.). (1987). *More education integration.* Downsview, Ontario: Roeher Institute.

Fuchs, G. E., & Moore, L. P. (1988). Collaboration for understanding and effectiveness. *Clearing House, 61,* 410–413.

Galant, K., & Hanline, M. F. (1993). Parental attitudes toward mainstreaming young children with disabilities. *Childhood Education, 69* (5), 293–297.

Gartner, A., & Lipsky, D. K. (1990). Students as instructional agents. In W. Stainback and S. Stainback (Eds.), *Support networks for inclusive schooling: Interdependent integrated education* (pp. 81–93). Baltimore: Brookes.

Giangreco, M. F. (1992). Curriculum in inclusion-oriented schools: Trends, issues, challenges, and potential solutions. In S. Stainback and W. Stainback (Eds.), *Curriculum considerations in inclusive classrooms: Facilitating learning for all students* (pp. 239–263). Baltimore: Brookes.

Giangreco, M. F., & Eichinger, J. (1990). Related services and the transdisciplinary approach. In M. Anketell, E. J. Bailey, J. Houghton, A. O'Dea, B. Utley, & D. Wickham (Eds.), *A series of training modules for educating children and youth with dual sensory impairments.* Monmouth, OR: Teaching Research Publications.

Glasser, W. (1986). *Control theory in the classroom.* New York: Harper & Row.

Graden, J. L. (1989). Redefining "prereferral" intervention as intervention assistance: Collaboration between general and special education. *Exceptional Children, 56,* 227–231.

Graden, J. L. & Bauer, A. M. (1992). Using collaborative approach to support students and teachers in inclusive classrooms. In S. Stainback and W. Stainback (Eds.), *Curriculum considerations in inclusive classrooms: Facilitating learning for all students* (pp. 85–100). Baltimore: Brookes.

Graden, J. L., Casey, A., & Bronstrom, O. (1985). Implementing a prereferral intervention system. Part I: The model. *Exceptional Children, 51,* 377–384.

Green, A. L., & Stoneman, Z. (1989). Attitudes of mothers and fathers of nonhandicapped children toward preschool mainstreaming. *Journal of Early Intervention, 13,* 292–304.

Guralnick, M. (1980). Social interactions among preschool children. *Exceptional Children, 46,* 248–253.

Gutkin, T. B., & Curtis, M. J. (1990). School-based consultation: Theory, techniques, and research. In T. B. Gutkin and C. R. Reynolds (Eds.), *The handbook of school psychology* (2nd ed.; pp. 577–611). New York: Wiley.

Hamre-Nietupski, S., McDonald, J., & Nietupski, J. (1992, Spring). Integrating elementary students with multiple disabilities into supported regular classes: Challenges and solutions. *Teaching Exceptional Children,* 6–9.

Hansen, J. C., Himes, B. S., & Meier, S. (1990). *Consultation: Concepts and practices.* Englewood Cliffs, NJ: Prentice Hall.

Hayek, R. A. (1987). The teacher assistance team: A pre-referral support system. *Focus on Exceptional Children, 26* (1), 1–8.

Hinde, R. (1979). *Toward understanding relationships.* New York: Academic Press.

Henderson, A. T. (1987). *The evidence continues to grow: Parent involvement improves student achievement.* Silver Springs, MD: National Citizens Committee in Education.

Holmes Group. (1986). *Tomorrow's teachers: A report to the Holmes Group.* East Lansing, MI: Author.

Idol, L., Paolucci-Whitcomb, P., & Nevin, A. (1986). *Collaborative consultation.* Rockville, MD: Aspen.

Johnson, D. W. & Johnson, F. P. (1987). *Joining together: Group theory and group skills* (3rd ed.). Englewood Cliffs, NJ: Prentice Hall.

Johnson, D. W., Johnson, R. T., Holubec, E., & Roy, P. (1984). *Circles of learning.* Alexandria, VA: Association for Curriculum Development and Supervision.

Johnson, L. J., & Pugach, M. C. (1992). Continuing the dialogue: Embracing a more expansive understanding of collaborative relationships. In W. Stainback and S. Stainback (Eds.), *Controversial issues confronting special education: Divergent perspectives* (pp. 215–222). Boston: Allyn & Bacon.

Kent, K. M. (1987). Conditions for collaboration among colleagues: Is your district ready? *Teacher Education Quarterly, 14* (3), 50–58.

Knight, M., Meyers, H., Paolucci-Whitcomb, P., Hasazi, S., & Nevin, A. (1981). A four year evaluation of consulting teacher services. *Behavior Disorders, 6,* 92–100.

Kroth, R. L., & Scholl, G. T. (1978). *Getting schools involved with parents.* Arlington, VA: Council for Exceptional Children.

Lavoie, R. (1985). Frustration, anxiety, and tension: FAT City workshop.

Lytle, S. L., & Fecho, R. (1991). Strangers in familiar places: Teacher collaboration by cross-visitation. *English Education, 23* (1), 5–28.

Macchiarola, F. J. (1989). Foreword. In D. K. Lipsky & A. Gartner (Eds.), *Beyond separate education: Quality education for all* (pp. xi–xix). Baltimore: Brookes.

McDonnell, J. (1987). The integration of students severe handicaps into regular public schools: As analysis of parents' perceptions of potential outcomes. *Education and Training in Mental Retardation, 22* (2), 98–111.

Meyer, L. H. & Biklen, D. (1992). *Preparing teachers for inclusive schooling: The Syracuse University inclusive elementary and special education teacher preparation program.* Unpublished ms.

Mittler, P., Mittler, H., & McConachie, H. (1987). Family supports in England. In D. K. Lipsky (Ed.), *Family supports for families with a disabled member* (pp. 15–36). New York: World Rehabilitation Fund.

Murphy, A. T. (1981). *Special children, special parents: Personal issues with handicapped children.* Englewood Cliffs, NJ: Prentice Hall.

National Joint Committee on Learning Disabilities. (1987). Learning disabilities: Issues in the preparation of professional personnel. *Journal of Learning Disabilities, 20,* 229–231.

Nevin, A., Thousand, J., Paolucci-Whitcomb, P., & Villa, R. (1990). Collaborative consultation: Empowering public school personnel to provide heterogeneous schooling for all—or, who rang that bell? *Journal of Educational and Psychological Consultation, 1* (1), 41–67.

Phillips, V., & McCullough, L. (1990). Consultation-based programming: Instituting the collaborative ethic in schools. *Exceptional Children, 56,* 291–304.

Pugach, M. C. (1992). Unifying the preservice preparation of teachers. In W. Stainback and S. Stainback (Eds.), *Controversial issues confronting special education: Divergent perspectives* (pp. 255–269). Boston: Allyn & Bacon.

Pugach, M. C. & Johnson, L. J. (1988, Spring). Peer collaboration. *Teaching Exceptional Children, 75–77.*

Rich, D. (1987). School and families: Issues and actions. Washington, DC: National Education Association.

Schenkat, R. (1988, November). The promise of restructuring for special education. *Education Week, 8,* 36.

Schmuck, P., & Schmuck, R. (1990). Democratic participation in small town schools. *Educational Researcher, 19* (8), 14–19.

Sileo, T. W., Rude, H. A., & Luckner, J. L. (1988). Collaborative consultation: A model for transition planning for handicapped youth. *Education and Training in Mental Retardation, 23,* 333–339.

Simpson, R. L., & Smith-Myles, B. (1990). The general education collaboration model: A model for successful mainstreaming. *Focus on Exceptional Children, 23* (4), 1–10.

Skrtic, T. (1987). An organizational analysis of special education reform. *Counterpoint, 8* (2), 15–19.

Skritc, T. (1989, May). School organization and service delivery: Are schools capable of change? Paper presented at Vermont Association of Special Education Administrators Conference, Stowe, VT.

Stainback, S., & Stainback, W. (1984). A rationale for the merger of special and regular education. *Exceptional Children, 51,* 102–111.

Stainback, S., & Stainback, W. (1990). Inclusive schooling. In W. Stainback and S. Stainback (Eds.), *Support networks for inclusive schooling: Interdependent integrated education* (pp. 3–23). Baltimore: Brookes.

Stainback, S., & Stainback, W. (Eds.). (1992). *Curriculum considerations in inclusive classrooms: Facilitating learning for all students.* Baltimore: Brookes.

Stainback, S., Stainback, W., & Jackson, J.H. (1992). Toward inclusive classrooms. In S. Stainback and W. Stainback (Eds.), *Curriculum considerations in inclusive classrooms: Facilitating learning for all students* (pp. 3–18). Baltimore: Brookes.

Stainback, G. H., Stainback, W. C., & Stainback, S. B. (1988, June). Superintendents' attitudes toward integration. *Education and Training in Mental Retardation, 92–96.*

Stainback, W., Stainback, S., & Wilkinson, A. (1992, Winter). Encouraging peer supports and friendships. *Teaching Exceptional Children, 6–11.*

Strully, J. & Strully, C. (1989). Friendships as an educational goal. In S. Stainback, W. Stainback, and M. Forest (Eds.), *Educating all children in the mainstream of regular education* (pp. 59–68). Baltimore: Brookes.

Thousand, P., & Villa, R. (1990). Sharing expertise and responsibility through teaching teams. In W. Stainback and S. Stainback (Eds.), *Supportive networks for inclusive schooling* (pp. 151–166). Baltimore: Brookes.

Thousand, P., & Villa, R. (1991). Interpersonal skills for effective collaboration. *Impact, 4* (3), 12–13.

Thousand, P., Villa, R., Paolucci-Whitcomb, J., & Nevin, A. (1992). A rationale for collaborative consultation. In S. Stainback and W. Stainback (Eds.), *Curriculum considerations in inclusive classrooms: Facilitating learning for all students* (pp. 223–232). Baltimore: Brookes.

U.S. Department of Education. (1986). Eighth annual report to Congress on the implementation of the Education of the Handicapped Act. Washington, DC: U.S. Government Printing Office.

Vandercook, T., & York, J. (1990). A team approach to program development. In W. Stainback and S. Stainback (Eds.), *Support networks for inclusive schooling: Interdependent integrated education* (pp. 95–122). Baltimore: Brookes.

Viadero, D. (1992, November 4). NASBE endorses "full inclusion" of disabled students. *Education Week*, pp. 1, 30.

Villa, R. A., & Thousand, J. S. (1990). Administrative supports to promote inclusive schooling. In W. Stainback and S. Stainback (Eds.), *Support networks for inclusive schooling: Interdependent integrated education* (pp. 201–218). Baltimore: Brookes.

Villa, R. A., Thousand, J. S., Stainback, W., & Stainback, S. (Eds.). (1992). *Restructuring for caring and effective education: An administrative guide to creating heterogeneous schools.* Baltimore: Brookes.

Webster's new twentieth century dictionary. (1990). New York: Harper & Row.

Wiedmeyer, D., & Lehman, J. (1991, Spring). The "house plan": Approach to collaborative teaching and consultation. *Teaching Exceptional Children*, 6–10.

Whittier, K. W., & Hewit, J. S. (1993). Collaborative teacher education: The elementary education/special education connection. *Intervention in School and Clinic, 29* (2), 84–88.

Will, M. (1986). Educating students with learning problems: A shared responsibility. Washington, DC: Office of Special Education and Rehabilitative Services, U.S. Department of Education.

York, J., & Vandercook, T. (1988). What's in an IEP? Writing objectives for an integration education. *Impact, 1,* 16, 19.

York, J., Giangreco, M. F., Vandercook, T., & Macdonald, C. (1992). Integrating support personnel in the inclusive classroom. In S. Stainback and W. Stainback (Eds.), *Curriculum considerations in inclusive classrooms: Facilitating learning for all students* (pp. 101–116). Baltimore: Brookes.

Zins, J. E., Curtis, M. J., Graden, J. L, & Ponti, C. R. (1988). *Helping students succeed in the regular classroom.* San Francisco: Jossey-Bass.

Chapter 6

American Association of University Women. (1992). *How schools shortchange girls.* Washington, DC: American Association of University Women Educational Foundation.

Banks, J. A., & McGee-Banks, C. A . (1992). *Multicultural education: Issues and perspectives.* Boston: Allyn & Bacon.

Beez, W. (1968). Influence of biased psychological reports on teacher and pupil performance. *Proceedings of the 76th annual convention of the American Psychological Association* (pp. 605–606).

Berliner, D. (1987). Simple views of effective teaching and a simple theory of classroom instruction. In D. Berliner and B. Rosenshine (Eds.), *Talks to teachers* (pp. 93–110). New York: Random House.

Birkel, L. F. (1973, July). The lecture method: Villain or victim? *Peabody Journal of Education,* 298–301.

Blakeslee, T. R. (1982). Brain behavior research. In *Student Learning Styles and Brain Behavior.* Reston, VA: NASSP.

Bloom, B., Englehart, M., Hill, E., & Krathwohl, D. (1956). *Taxonomy of educational objectives. The classification of educational goals. Handbook I: Cognitive domain.* New York: Longman Green.

Borich, G. (1992). *Effective teaching methods* (2nd ed.). New York: Merrill.

Callahan, J. F., & Clark, L. H. (1988). *Teaching in the middle and secondary schools* (3rd ed.). New York: Macmillan.

Carnegie Forum on Education and Economy. (1986). *A nation prepared: Teachers for the 21st century.* New York: Carnegie Corporation.

Chess, S., & Thomas, A. (1985). Temperamental differences: A critical concept in child health care. *Pediatric Nursing, 11,* 167–171.

Clark, C., & Peterson, P. (1986). Teachers' thought processes. In M. C. Wittrock (Ed.), *Handbook of research on teaching* (3rd ed.) (pp. 255–296). New York: Macmillan.

Corno, L., & Snow, R. E. (1986). Adapting teaching to individual differences among learners. In M. C. Wittrock (Ed.), *Handbook of research on teaching* (3rd ed.) (pp. 605–629). New York: Macmillan.

Deshler, D. D., Schumaker, J. B., & Lenz, B. K. (1984). Academic and cognitive interventions for LD adolescents: Part I. *Journal of Learning Disabilities, 17,* 108–117.

Doyle, W., Hancock, G., & Kiefer, E. (1972). Teachers' perceptions: Do they make a difference? *Journal of the Association for the Study of Perceptions, 7,* 21–30.

Duffy, G., Roehler, L., & Herrmann, B. (1988). Modeling mental processes helps poor readers become strategic readers. *The Reading Teacher, 41,* 762–767.

Ellis, E. S., Lenz, B. K., & Sabornie, E. J. (1987). Generalization and adaptation of learning strategies to natural environments: Part I: Critical agents. *Remedial and Special Education, 8* (1), 6–20.

Evertson, C., Emmer, E., & Brophy, J. (1980). Predictors of effective teaching in junior high mathematics classrooms. *Journal of Research in Mathematics Education, 11,* 167–178.

Flavell, J. (1979). Metacognition and cognitive memory. *American Psychologist, 34,* 906–911.

Freiberg, H. J., & Driscoll, A. (1992). *Universal teaching strategies.* Boston: Allyn & Bacon.

Gall, M. (1981). *Handbook for evaluating and selecting curriculum materials.* Boston: Allyn & Bacon.

Good, T. L., & Brophy, J. E. (1994). *Looking in classrooms* (6th ed.). New York: HarperCollins.

Good, T. L., & Brophy, J. E. (1991). *Looking in classrooms* (5th ed.). Cambridge, MA: Harper & Row.

Good, T. L., & Grouws, D. (1977). Teaching effects: A process-product study in fourth-grade mathematics classrooms. *Journal of Teacher Education, 28,* 49–54.

Goodlad, J. (1984). *A place called school.* New York: McGraw-Hill.

Gronlund, N. E. (1991). *How to write and use instructional objectives* (4th ed.) New York: Macmillan.

Hallahan, D. P. (Ed.) (1980). Teaching exceptional children to use cognitive strategies. *Exceptional Education Quarterly, 1* 1–102.

Hansford, B., & Hattie, J. (1982). The relationship between self and achievement/performance measures. *Review of Educational Research, 52,* 123–142.

Haring, N., Lovitt, T., Eaton, M., & Hansen, C. (1978). *The fourth R: Research in the classroom.* Columbus, OH: Charles E. Merrill.

Harrow, A. (1972). *Taxonomy of psychomotor domain: A guide for developing behavioral objectives.* New York: David McKay.

Henson, K. T. (1980). What's the use of lecturing? *The High School Journal, 64,* 115–119.

Hillocks, G., Jr. (1981). The response of college freshmen to three modes of instruction. *American Journal of Education, 89,* 373–395.

Holmes Group (1986). *Tomorrow's teachers: A report to the Holmes Group*. East Lansing, MI: Author.

Idol, L. (1989). The resource/consultant teacher: An integrated model of service delivery. *Remedial and Special Education, 10* (6) , 41.

Idol-Maestas, L. (1983). *Special educator's consultation handbook*. Rockville, MD: Aspen.

Jacobsen, D., Eggen, P., & Kauchak, D. (1993). *Methods for teaching: A skills approach* (4th ed.). New York: Merrill.

Johnson, D., & Johnson, R. (1991). *Learning together and alone* (3rd ed.). Englewood Cliffs, NJ: Prentice Hall.

Johnson, D., Maruyama, G., Johnson, R., Nelson, D., & Skon, L. (1981). Effects of cooperative, competitive, and individualistic goal structures on achievement. A meta-analysis. *Psychological Bulletin, 89*, 47–62.

Johnson, D., Skon, L., & Johnson, R. (1980). Effects of cooperative, competitive, and individualistic conditions on children's problem-solving performance. *American Educational Research Journal, 17*, 83–93.

Kash, M., & Borich, G. (1978). *Teacher behavior and pupil self-concept*. Reading, MA: Addison-Wesley.

Kauchak, D. P., & Eggen, P. D. (1993). *Learning and teaching: Research-based methods* (2nd ed.). Boston: Allyn & Bacon.

Kibler, R. J., Barker, L. L., & Miles, D. T. (1970). *Behavioral objectives and instruction*. Boston: Allyn & Bacon.

Kozol, J. (1967). *Death at an early age*. Boston: Plume.

Kozol, J. (1992). *Savage inequalities: Children in America's schools*. New York: Crown/Harper Perennial.

Krathwohl, D., Bloom, B., & Masia, B. (1964). *Taxonomy of educational objectives. The classification of educational goals. Handbook II Affective domain*. New York: David McKay.

Leinhardt, G., Seewald, A., & Engel. M. (1979). Learning what's taught: Sex differences in instruction. *Journal of Educational Psychology, 71*, 432–439.

Lerner, J. (1993). *Children with learning disabilities* (6th ed.). Boston: Houghton Mifflin.

Mager, R. F. (1984). *Preparing instructional objectives* (Rev. 2nd ed.). Belmont, CA: David S. Lake.

Maslow, A. (1954). *Motivation and personality*. New York: Harper & Row.

Mercer, C. D., & Mercer, A. R. (1989). *Teaching students with learning problems* (3rd ed.). Columbus, OH: Merrill.

Michaels, J. W. (1977). Classroom reward structure and academic performance. *Review of Educational Research, 47*, 95.

Morine-Dershimer, G., & Pfeifer, J. (1986). Instructional planning. In J. M. Cooper (Ed.), *Classroom teaching skills* (3rd ed.; pp. 19–66). Lexington, MA: Heath.

Morse, L., & Handley, H. (1985). Listening to adolescents: Gender differences in science classroom interaction. In L. Wilkinson & C. Marrett (Eds.), *Gender influences in classroom interaction*. (pp. 37–56). New York: Academic Press.

National Commission on Excellence in Education (1983). *A nation at risk*. Washington, DC: U.S. Department of Education.

Newson, J., & Newson, E. (1976). *Seven year olds in the home environment*. London: Allen & Unwin.

Palardy, J. (1969). What teachers believe—What children achieve. *Elementary School Journal, 69*, 370–374.

Polloway, E. A., Patton, J. R., Payne, J. S., & Payne, R. A. (1989). *Strategies for teaching learners with special needs* (4th ed.). Columbus: Merrill.

Pressley, M., & Levin, J. R. (Eds.). (1983). *Cognitive strategy research: Educational applications.* New York: Springer-Verlag.

Reid, D. K. (1988). *Teaching the learning disabled: A cognitive developmental approach.* Boston: Allyn & Bacon.

Richek, M., List, L., & Lerner, J. (1989). *Reading problems: Assessment and teaching strategies.* Englewood Cliffs, NJ: Prentice Hall.

Roberts, J. (1971). Intellectual development of children by demographic and socioeconmic factors. (DHEW Publication No. HSM 72-1012). Washington, DC: U.S. Government Printing Office.

Rosenshine, B. & Stevens, R. (1986). Teaching functions. In M. C. Wittrock (Ed.), *Handbook of research on teaching* (3rd ed.; pp. 376–391). New York: Macmillan.

Sadker, M., Sadker, D., & Klein, S. (1991). The issues of gender in elementary and secondary education. In G. Grant (Ed.), *Review of research in education* (Vol. 17, pp. 269–334). Washington, DC: American Educational Research Association.

Schrank, W. (1968). The labeling effect of ability grouping. *Journal of Educational Research, 62,* 51–52.

Sharan, S. (1980). Cooperative learning in small groups: Recent methods and effects on achievement, attitude, and ethnic relations. *Review of Educational Research, 50,* 241–271.

Simpson, E. J. (1972). The classification of educational objectives in the psychomotor domain. The psychomotor domain. Vol. 3. Washington, DC: Gryphon House.

Slavin, R. (1980). Cooperative learning. *Review of Educational Research, 50,* 315–342.

Sleeter, C., & Grant, C. (1986). Success of all students. *Phi Delta Kappan, 68,* 298.

Smith, C. R. (1983). *Learning disabilities: The interaction of learner, task and setting.* Boston: Little Brown.

Smith, D. D. (1981). *Teaching the learning disabled.* Englewood Cliffs, NJ: Prentice-Hall.

Smith, I. K. (1978). Teaching with discussion: A review. *Educational Technology, 28* (1), 40–45.

Stanovich, K. E. (1986). Cognitive processes and the reading problems of learning disabled children: Evaluating the assumption of specificity. In J. K. Torgeson & B. Y. L. Wong (Eds.), *Psychological and educational perspectives on learning disabilities* (pp. 87–131). Orlando, FL: Academic Press.

Stokes, T. F., & Baer, D. M. (1977). An implicit technology of generalization. *Journal of Applied Behavior Analysis, 10,* 349–367.

Strike, K. A. (1975). The logic of learning by discovery. *Review of Educational Research, 45,* 461–483.

Weiner, B. (1972). *Theories of motivation: From mechanism to cognition.* Chicago: Markham.

Worden, P. E. (1983). Memory strategy instruction with the learning disabled. In M. Pressley & J. R. Levin (Eds.), *Cognitive strategy research: Educational applications* (pp. 129–153). New York: Springer-Verlag.

Chapter 7

Adams, R. S. (1969). Location as a feature of instructional interaction. *Merrill Palmer Quarterly, 15* (4), 309–321.

Adams, R. S., & Biddle, B. (1970). *Realities of teaching: Exploration with videotape.* New York: Holt, Rinehart and Winston.

Anderson, L., Brubaker, N., Alleman-Brooks, J., & Duffy, G. (1985). A qualitative study of seatwork in first-grade classrooms. *The Elementary School Journal, 86,* 123–140.

Arlin, M., & Webster, J. (1983). Time costs of mastery learning. *Journal of Educational Psychology, 75,* 187–196.

Atwood, R. (1983, April). The interacting effects of task form and activity structure on students' task involvement and teacher evaluations. Paper presented at the annual meeting of the American Educational Research Association, Montreal.

Bellon, J. J., Bellon, E. C., & Blank, M. A. (1992). *Teaching from a research knowledge base: A development and renewal process.* New York: Merrill.

Berliner, D. (1979). Tempus educare. In P. Peterson and H. Walberg (Eds.), *Research on teaching* (pp. 120–135). Berkeley: McCutchan.

Berliner, D. (1984). Research and teacher effectiveness. In *Making our schools more effective: Proceedings of three state conferences.* San Francisco: Far West Laboratory.

Berliner, D. (1987). Simple views of effective teaching and a simple theory of classroom instruction. In D. Berliner and B. Rosenshine (Eds.), *Talks to teachers* (pp. 93–110). New York: Random House.

Bossert, S. (1979). *Tasks and social relationships in classrooms.* New York: Cambridge University Press.

Cohen, S. B., & Hart-Hester, S. (1987). Time management strategies. *Teaching Exceptional Children, 20* (1), 56–57.

Corno, L. (1979). Classroom instruction and the matter of time. In D. Duke (Ed.), *Classroom management: Seventy-eighth yearbook of the National Society for the Study of Education.* Chicago: University of Chicago.

Cullen, B., & Pratt, T. (1992). Measuring and reporting student progress. In S. Stainback and W. Stainback (Eds.), *Curriculum considerations in inclusive classrooms* (pp. 175–198). Baltimore: Brookes.

Davis, W. E. (1983). *The special educator: Strategies for succeeding in today's world.* Austin: PRO-ED.

Dettmer, P., Thurston, L.P., & Dyck, N. (1993). *Consultation, collaboration, and teamwork for students with special needs.* Boston: Allyn & Bacon.

deVoss, G. G. (1979). The structure of major lessons and collective student activity. *Elementary School Journal, 80,* 8–18.

Diggory, J. (1966). *Self-evaluation: Concepts and studies.* New York: John Wiley.

Doyle, W. (1980). *Classroom management.* West Lafayette, IN: Kappa Delta Pi.

Doyle, W. (1986). Classroom organization and management. In M. C. Wittrock (Ed.), *Handbook of research on teaching* (3rd ed.; pp. 392–431). New York: Macmillan.

Emmer, E. T., Evertson, C. M., & Anderson, L. (1979). *Effective classroom management at the beginning of the school year.* Austin: Research and Development Center for Teacher Education, University of Texas.

Emmer, E. T., Evertson, C. M., Sanford, J. P., Clements, B. S., & Worsham, M. E. (1994). *Classroom management for secondary teachers* (3rd ed.; Englewood Cliffs, NJ: Prentice Hall.

Evans, W. H., Evans, S. S., Gable, R. A., & Schmid, R. E. (1991). *Instructional management for detecting and correcting special problems.* Boston: Allyn & Bacon.

Evertson, C. M. (1980, April). *Differences in instructional activities in high and low achieving junior high classes.* Boston: AERA.

Frederick, W. (1977). The use of classroom time in high schools above and below the median reading score. *Urban Education, 11,* 459–464.

Freiberg, H. J., & Driscoll, A. (1992). *Universal teaching strategies.* Boston: Allyn & Bacon.

Froyen, L. A. (1993). *Classroom management: The reflective teacher-leader* (2nd ed.). New York: Merrill.

Gallagher, P. A. (1979). *Teaching students with behavior disorders: Techniques for classroom instruction.* Denver: Love.

Gartland, D., & Rosenberg, M. S. (1987). Managing time in the LD classroom. *LD Forum, 12* (2), 8–10.

Good, T., & Brophy, J. E. (1986). *Educational psychology* (3rd ed.). New York: Longman.

Gump, P. V. (1967). The classroom behavior setting: Its nature and relation to student behavior (Final Report). Washington, DC: U.S. Office of Education, Bureau of Research (ED 015 515).

Hunter, M. (1994). *Enhancing teaching.* New York: Macmillan.

Idol-Maestas, L., & Ritter, S. (1985). A follow-up study of resource/consulting teachers: Factors that facilitate and inhibit teacher consultation. *Teacher Education and Special Education, 8,* 121–131.

Johnson, L. J., Pugach, M. C., & Hammittee, D. J. (1988). Barriers to efficient special education consultation. *Remedial and Special Education, 9* (6), 41–47.

Karweit, N. (1984, May). Time on task reconsidered: Synthesis of research on time and learning. *Educational Leadership,* 32–35.

Kauchak, D. P., & Eggen, P. D. (1993). *Learning and teaching: Research-based methods.* Boston: Allyn & Bacon.

Kounin, J. S. (1970). *Discipline and group management in classrooms.* New York: Holt, Rinehart and Winston.

Kounin, J. S. (1977). *Discipline and group management in classrooms.* Huntington, NY: Krieger.

Lakein, A. (1973). *How to get control of your time and your life.* New York: McKay.

Leinhardt, G., Zigmond, N., & Cooley, W. (1981). Reading instruction and its effects. *American Education Research Journal, 81,* 343–361.

Louisell, R. D., & Descamps, J. (1992). *Developing a teaching style: Methods for elementary school teachers.* New York: Harper/Collins.

Maker, C. A. (Ed.). (1985). *Professional management: Techniques for special service providers.* Baltimore: Brookes.

McGlothlin, J. & Kelly, D. (1982). Issues facing the resource teacher. *Learning Disabilities Quarterly, 5,* 58–64.

Meese, R. L. (1994). *Teaching learners with mild disabilities: Integrating research and practice.* Belmont, CA: Brooks/Cole.

Meichenbaum, D. (1986). *Metacognitive methods of instruction: Current status and future prospects.* New York: Hawthorne Press.

Meichenbaum, D. (1981). Cognitive behavior modification with exceptional children: A promise yet unfulfilled. *Exceptional Education Quarterly, 1,* 83–88.

Minner, S., & Prater, G. (1989). Arranging the physical environment of special education classrooms. *Academic Therapy, 25* (1), 91–96.

Morrison, G. S. (1988). *Education and development of infants, toddlers and preschoolers.* New York: HarperCollins.

National Commission on Excellence in Education. (1983). *A nation at risk: The imperative for educational reform.* Washington, DC: U.S. Government Printing Office.

O'Connor, S. (1988). Affective climate. In R. McNerney (Ed.), *Guide to classroom teaching* (pp. 247–261). Boston: Allyn & Bacon.

Olson, J. (1989). Managing life in the classroom: Dealing with the nitty gritty. *Academic Therapy, 24* (5), 545–553.

Orelove, F. (1982). Developing daily schedules for classrooms of severely handicapped students. *Educational and Treatment of Children, 5,* 59–68.

Paine, S. C., Radicchi, J., Rosellini, L. C., Deutchman, L., & Darch, C. B. (1983). *Structuring your classroom for academic success.* Champaign, IL: Research Press.

Polloway, E. A., Patton, J. R., Payne, J. S., & Payne, R. A. (1985). *Strategies for teaching learners with special needs* (3rd ed.). Columbus: Merrill.

Polloway, E. A., Patton, J. R., Payne, J. S., & Payne, R. A. (1989). *Strategies for teaching learners with special needs* (4th ed.). Columbus: Merrill.

Prescott, E., Jones, E., & Kritchevsky, S. (1967). Group day care as a child rearing environment: An observational study of day care programs. Pasadena, CA: Pacific Lakes College (ED 024 453).

Rosenshine, B. (1981). How time is spent in elementary classrooms. *Journal of Classroom Interaction, 1?* (1), 16–25.

Rosenshine, B. (1983). Teaching functions in instructional programs. *The Elementary School Journal, 83,* 335–351.

Rosenshine, B., & Stevens, R. (1986). Teaching functions. In M. C. Wittrock (Ed.), *Handbook of research on teaching* (3rd ed.; pp. 376–391). New York: Macmillan.

Sabatino, D. A. (1987). Preventive discipline as a practice in special education. *Teaching exceptional children, 19* (4), 8–11.

Schenkat, R. (1988, November 16). The promise of restructuring for special education. *Education Week,* p. 36.

Silverstein, J. M. (1979). Individual and environmental correlates of pupil problematic and nonproblematic classroom behavior. Unpublished doctoral dissertation, New York University.

Soar, R. S., & Soar, R. M. (1983, February). Context effects in the teaching-learning process. In D. C. Smith (Ed.), *Essential knowledge for beginning educators.* Washington, DC: American Association of Colleges for Teacher Education.

Speece, D. L., & Mandell, C. J. (1980). Resource room support services for regular teachers. *Learning Disabilities Quarterly, 5,* 49–53.

Stainback, S., & Stainback, W. (1985). The merger of special and regular education: Can it be done? A response to Lieberman and Mesinger. *Exceptional Children, 51,* 517–521.

Stainback, W., Stainback, S., & Froyen, L. (1987). Structuring the classroom to prevent disruptive behaviors. *Teaching Exceptional Children, 19* (4), 12–16.

Stallings, J. (1980). Allocated academic learning time revisited or beyond time on task. *Educational Researcher, 9,* 11–16.

Stebbins, R. A. (1974). *The disorderly classroom: Its physical and temporal conditions* (Monographs in Education No. 12). St. John's, Canada: Memorial University of Newfoundland, Faculty of Education, Committee on Publications.

West, J. F., & Idol, L. (1990). Collaborative consultation in the education of mildly handicapped and at-risk students. *Remedial and Special Education, 11* (1), 22–31.

Williams, R. M., & Rooney, K. J. (1986). *A handbook of cognitive behavior modification procedures for teachers.* Charlottesville, VA: University of Virginia Learning Disabilities Research Institute.

Wilson, B. L., Rosenholtz, S. J., & Rosenholtz, S. H. (April, 1983). Effect of task and authority structures on student task engagement. Paper presented at the annual meeting of the American Educational Research Association, Montreal.

Chapter 8

Batesky, J. (1987, September). Increasing teacher effectiveness using Hunter lesson design. *Journal of Physical Education and Recreational Dance,* 89–93.

Berg, C. A., & Clough, M. (1991, October). Forum: Generic lesson design, Does science fit the mold? The case against. *The Science Teacher,* 26–31.

Bernabei, R., & Leles, J. (1970). *Behavioral objectives in curriculum and evaluation.* Dubuque, Iowa: Kendall/Hunt.

Bloom, B. S. (1956). *Taxonomy of educational objectives: Book 1. Cognitive domain.* New York: McKay.

deGrandpre, B. EDS 382: Curricular Practices in Special Education Packet. Unpublished ms.

Ellis, A. K., & Fouts, J. T. (1993). *Research on educational innovations.* Princeton Junction, NJ: Eye on Education.

Erb, T. O., & Doda, N. M. (1989). *Team organization: Promise, practices and possibilities.* Washington, DC: National Education Association.

Esler, W. K., & Sciortino, P. (1991). *Methods for teaching: An overview of current practices.* Raleigh, NC: Contemporary (CPI).

Fosnot, C. T. (1989). *Enquiring teachers, enquiring learners: A constructivist approach for teaching.* New York: Teachers College Press.

Gilbert, J. C. (1989). A two-week K–6 interdisciplinary unit. In H. H. Jacobs (Ed.), *Interdisciplinary curriculum: Design and implementation.* Alexandria, VA: Association for Supervision and Curriculum Development.

Hartoonian, H. M., & Laughlin, M. A. (October, 1989). Designing a social studies scope and sequence for the 21st century. *Social Education 53* (6), 388–398.

Hunter, M. (1994). *Enhancing teaching.* New York: Macmillan.

Jacobs, H. H. (1989). The growing need for interdisciplinary curriculum content. In H. H. Jacobs (Ed.), *Interdisciplinary curriculum: Design and implementation.* Alexandria, VA: Association for Supervision and Curriculum Development.

Jacobs, H. H., & Borland, J. H. (1986). The interdisciplinary concept model: Theory and practice. *Gifted Quarterly, 30* (4), 159–163.

Koenig, H. G., DeMarco-Keating, M. L., & Lansing, J. B. (1989). *RCT science review.* Middletown, NY: N & N.

Koenig, H. G., DeMarco-Keating, M. L., & Lansing, J. B. (1988). *Earth science: A concise competency review* (Teacher annotated ed.). Middletown, NY: N & N.

Koenig, H. G., DeMarco-Keating, M. L., & Lansing, J. B. (1988). *Earth science: A concise competency review.* Middletown, NY: N & N.

Lemlech, J. K. (1994). *Curriculum and instructional methods for the elementary and middle school* (3rd ed.). New York: Macmillan.

Malehorn, H. (1975). *Encyclopedia of activities for teaching grades K–3.* West Nyack, NY: Parker.

Martinello, M. L., & Cook, G. E. (1994). *Interdisciplinary inquiry in teaching and learning.* New York: Merrill.

Miller, A., Thompson, J. C., Peterson, R. E., & Haragan, D. R. (1983). *Elements of meteorology.* Columbus, OH: Merrill.

Mitchell, L. S. (1950). *Our children and our schools.* New York: Simon & Schuster.

Oberholzer, E. (1937). *An integrated curriculum in practice.* New York: Teachers College Press.

Osborne, A. F. (1963). *Applied imagination.* New York: Charles Scribner and Company.

Sousa, D., & Donnavon, J. (1990). Four-year study of Hunter model shows student achievement gains in some areas. *The Developer, 1* (4), 6.

Tolman, M. N., & Morton, J. O. (1986). *Earth science activities for grades 2–8.* West Nyack, NY: Parker.

Ysseldyke, J. E., Christenson, S. L., & Thurlow, M. L. (1987). *Instructional factors that influence student achievement: An integrative review* (Monograph No. 7). Minneapolis: University of Minnesota.

Chapter 9

Anderson, R. C., & Biddle, W. B. (1975). On asking people questions about what they are reading. In G. H. Bower (Ed.), *The psychology of learning and motivation. Vol. 9. Advances in research and theory*. New York: Academic Press.

Anderson, L., Evertson, C., & Brophy, J. (1982). *Principles of small group instruction in elementary reading*. East Lansing: Michigan State University, Institute for Research on Teaching.

Aronson, E., Blaney, N., Stephan, C., Sikes, J., & Snapp, M. (1978). *The jigsaw classroom*. Beverly Hills, CA: Sage.

Ausubel, D. (1968). *Educational psychology: A cognitive view*. New York: Holt, Rinehart and Winston.

Bellon, J. J., Bellon, E. C., & Blank, M. A. (1992). *Teaching from a research knowledge base: A development and renewal process*. New York: Merrill.

Bennett, N., Desforges, C., Cockburn, A., & Wilkinson, B. (1981). *The quality of pupil learning experiences: Interim report*. Lancaster, England: University of Lancaster, Centre for Educational Research and Development.

Bohlmeyer, E., Burke, J. (1987). Selecting cooperative learning techniques: A consultative strategy guide. *School Psychology Review, 16*, 6–49.

Borich, G. D. (1988). *Effective teaching methods*. New York: Merrill.

Borich, G. D. (1992). *Effective teaching methods* (2nd ed.). New York: Merrill.

Bossert, S. (1988–1989). Cooperative learning activities in the classroom. In E. Rothkopf (Ed.), *Review of research in education* (Vol. 15, pp. 225–250). Washington, DC: American Educational Research Association.

Brophy, J. E., & Evertson, C. (1976). *Learning from teaching: A developmental perspective*. Boston: Allyn & Bacon.

Brown, G., & Edmondson, R. (1984). Asking questions. In E. Wragg (Ed.), *Classroom teaching skills* (pp. 97–119). New York: Nichols.

Cullen, B., & Pratt, T. (1992). Measuring and reporting student progress. In S. Stainback & W. Stainback (Eds.), *Curriculum considerations in inclusive classrooms: Facilitating learning for all students* (pp. 175–196). Baltimore: Brookes.

DeVries, D. L., & Slavin, R. E. (1978). Teams-Games-Tournament (TGT): Review of ten classroom experiments. *Journal of Research and Development in Education, 12*, 28–38.

DeVries, D. L., Slavin, R. E., Fennessey, G. M., Edwards, K. J., & Lombardo, M. M. (1980). *Teams-Games-Tournament: The team learning approach*. Englewood Cliffs, NJ: Educational Technology Publications.

Dillon, J. (1981). Duration of response to teacher questions and statements. *Contemporary Educational Psychology, 6*, 1–11.

Dunkin, M., & Biddle, B. (1974). *The study of teaching*. Holt, Rinehart and Winston.

———. *Educational Leadership*. (1989/1990). 47 (4). Entire issue.

Englert, C. S. (1984). Effective direct instruction practices in special education settings. *Remedial and Special Education, 5*(2), 38–47.

Freiberg, H. J., & Driscoll, A. (1992). *Universal teaching strategies*. Boston: Allyn & Bacon.

Gartner, A., Kohler, M., & Riessman, F. (1971). *Children teach children: Learning by teaching*. New York: Harper & Row.

Good, T. L., & Brophy, J. E. (1984). *Looking in classrooms* (3rd ed.). New York: HarperCollins.

Good, T. L., & Brophy, J. E. (1991). *Looking in classrooms* (5th ed.). New York: HarperCollins.

Good, T. L., & Brophy, J. E. (1994). *Looking in classrooms* (6th ed.). New York: HarperCollins.

Good, T. L., Mulryan, C., & McCaslin, M. (1992). Grouping for instruction in mathematics: A call for programmatic research on small-group processes. In D. Grouws (Ed.), *Handbook on research in mathematics teaching and learning* (pp. 165–196). New York: Macmillan.

Groisser, P. (1964). *How to use the fine art of questioning*. New York: Teachers' Practical Press.

Gusky, T., & Pigott, T. (1988). Research on group-based mastery learning programs: A meta-analysis. *Journal of Educational Research, 8* (4), 197–216.

Hyman, J. S., & Cohen, S. A. (1979). Learning for mastery: Ten conclusions after 15 years and 3,000 schools. *Educational Leadership, 37* (2), 104–109.

Jacobsen, D., Eggen, P., & Kauchak, D. (1993). *Methods for teaching: A skills approach*. New York: Merrill.

Johnson, D. W., & Johnson, R. T. (1985a). Classroom conflict: Controversy versus debate in learning groups. *American Educational Research Journal, 22*, 237–256.

Johnson, D. W., & Johnson, R. T. (1985b). Cooperative learning and adaptive education. In M. C. Wang and H. J. Walberg (Eds.), *Adapting instruction to individual differences*. Berkley, CA: McCutchan.

Johnson, D. W., & Johnson, R. T. (1987). *Joining together: Group therapy and group skills* (2nd ed.). Englewood Cliffs, NJ: Prentice Hall.

Johnson, D. W., Johnson, R. T., Holubec, E., & Roy, P. (1984). *Circles of learning*. Arlington, VA: Association for Supervision and Curriculum Development.

Jones, V. F., & Jones, L. S. (1990). *Comprehensive classroom management: Motivating and managing students* (3rd ed.). Boston: Allyn & Bacon.

Kulik, C. C., & Kulik, A. (1990). Effectiveness of mastery learning programs: A meta-analysis. *Review of Educational Research, 60*, 265–299.

Lemlech, J. K. (1994). *Curriculum and instructional methods for the elementary and middle school* (3rd ed.). New York: Macmillan.

Lloyd, J. W. (1988). Direct academic interventions in learning disabilities. In M. C. Wang, M. C. Reynolds, & H. J. Walberg (Eds.), *Handbook of special education: Research and practice: Vol. 2. Mildly handicapped conditions* (pp. 345–366). New York: Pergamon Press.

Meese, R. L. (1994). *Teaching learners with mild disabilities: Integrating research and practice*. Pacific Grove, CA: Brooks/Cole.

Okey, J. R. (1977). Consequences for training teachers to use Mastery Learning strategy. *Journal of Teacher Education, 28* (5), 57–62.

Ornstein, A. C. (1990). *Strategies for effective teaching*. New York: Harper & Row.

Peterson, P. L., & Janicki, T. C. (1979). Individual characteristics and children's learning in large-group and small-group approaches. *Journal of Educational Psychology, 71*, 677–687.

Pierce, M., Stahlbrand, K., & Armstrong, S. (1989). Increasing student productivity through peer tutoring programs. (Monograph No. 9-1). Burlington: University of Vermont, Center for Developmental Disabilities.

Posner, G. (1987). Pacing and sequencing. In M. J. Dunkin (Ed.), *Encyclopedia of teaching and teacher education* (pp. 266–271). New York: Pergamon.

Rosenshine, B. (1976). Classroom instruction. In L. L. Gage (ed.), *The psychology of teaching methods: The seventy-fifth yearbook of the National Society for the Study of Education*. Chicago: University of Chicago.

Rosenshine, B. V. (1987). Explicit teaching. In D. C. Berliner & B. V. Rosenshine (Eds.), *Talks to teachers* (pp. 75–92). New York: Random House.

Rosenshine, B. V. (1983). Teaching functions in instructional programs. *Elementary School Journal, 83*, 335–351.

Rosenshine, B. V., & Furst, N. (1973). The use of direct observation to study teaching. In R. Travers (Ed.), *Second handbook of research on teaching*. Chicago: Rand McNally.

Rosenshine, B. V., & Stevens, R. (1986). Teaching functions. In M. C. Wittrock (Ed.), *Handbook of research on teaching* (3rd ed.); pp. 376–391. New York: Macmillan.

Rowe, M. B. (1974a). Pausing phenomena: Influences on the quality of instruction. *Journal of Psycholinguistic Research, 3,* 203–224.

Rowe, M. B. (1974b). Wait-time and rewards as instructional variables, their influence on language, logic, and fate control: Part 1—Wait time. *Journal of Research in Science Teaching, 11,* 81–94.

Slavin, R. E. (1983). *Cooperative learning.* New York: Longman.

Slavin, R. E. (1990a). Ability grouping and student achievement in secondary schools. *Review of Educational Research, 60,* 417–499.

Slavin, R. E. (1990b). *Cooperative learning: Theory, research, and practice.* Englewood Cliffs, NJ: Prentice Hall.

Slavin, R. E. (1991). *Educational psychology* (3rd ed.). Englewood Cliffs, NJ: Prentice Hall.

Slavin, R. E., Sharan, S., Kagan, S., Hertz-Lazarowitz, R., Webb, C., & Schmuck, R. (Eds.). (1985). *Learning to cooperate, cooperating to learn.* New York: Plenum.

Soar, R. S. (1973). *Final report: Follow through classroom process measurement and pupil growth* (pp. 170–171). Gainesville, FL: Institute for the Development of Human Resources.

Sparks, D., & Sparks, G. M. (1984). *Effective teaching for higher achievement.* Alexandria, VA: Association for Supervision and Curriculum Development.

Stallings, J. A. (1975). Implementation and child effects of teaching practice in Follow Through classrooms. *Monographs of the Society for Research in Child Development, 40* (7-8), Serial No. 163.

Stallings, J. A., & Kaskowitz, D. (1974). *Follow Through observation evaluation.* Menlo Park, CA: Stanford Research Institute.

Stevens, R., & Rosenshine, B. V. (1981). Advances in research on teaching. *Exceptional Education Quarterly, 2,* 1–9.

Stiggins, R. J. (1994). *Student-centered classroom assessment.* New York: Merrill.

Tennyson, R., & Cocchiarella, M. (1986). An empirically based instructional design theory for teaching concepts. *Review of Educational Research, 56,* 40–70.

Whiting, B., & Render, G. F. (1987). Cognitive and affective outcomes of mastery learning. *Clearing House, 60* (6), 276–290.

Winne, P. (1979). Experiments relating teachers' use of higher cognitive questions to student achievement. *Review of Educational Research, 49,* 13–49.

Wright, R. J., & DuCette, J. P. (1976). Locus of control and academic achievement in traditional and non-traditional educational settings. ERIC Document Reproduction Services, ED 123-203.

Chapter 10

Arter, J., & Spandel, V. (1992). Using portfolios of student work in instruction and assessment. *Educational measurement: Issues and Practice, 11* (1), 36–44.

Bellon, J. J., Bellon, E. C., & Blank, M. A. (1992). *Teaching from a research knowledge base: A development and renewal process.* New York: Merrill.

Berk, R. A. (Ed.). (1986). *Performance assessment: Methods and applications.* Baltimore: Johns Hopkins.

Borich, G. D. (1992). *Effective teaching methods* (2nd ed.). New York: Merrill.

Brophy J. E., & Evertson, C. (1976). *Learning from teaching: A developmental perspective.* Boston: Allyn & Bacon.

Bruner, J. S. (1961). Act of discovery. *Harvard Educational Review, 31* (1), 21–32.

Bruner, J. S. (1966). *Toward a theory of instruction.* New York: Newton.

Burden, P. R., & Byrd, M. (1994). Methods for effective teaching. Boston: Allyn & Bacon.

Copeland, R. W. (1982). *Mathematics and the elementary teacher* (4th ed.). New York: Macmillan.

Corno, L., & Snow, R. (1986). Adapting teaching to individual differences among learners. In M. C. Wittrock (Ed.), *Handbook of research on teaching* (3rd ed.; pp. 605–629). New York: Macmillan.

Cullen, B., & Pratt, T. (1992). Measuring and reporting student progress. In S. Stainback & W. Stainback (Eds.), *Curriculum considerations in inclusive classrooms: Facilitating learning for all students* (pp. 175–196). Baltimore: Brookes.

Eby, J. (1992). *Reflective planning, teaching, and evaluation for the elementary school.* New York: Merrill.

Freiberg, H. J., & Driscoll, A. (1992). *Universal teaching strategies.* Boston: Allyn & Bacon.

Gage, N. L., & Berliner, D. C. (1984). *Educational psychology* (3rd ed.). Boston: Houghton Mifflin.

Gardner, J. (1989). Building community. In W. Pink (Ed.), *Restructuring to promote learning in American Schools.* Elmhurst, IL: North Central Regional Educational Laboratory.

Gilstrap, R. L., & Martin, W. R. (1975). *Current strategies for teachers: A resource for personalizing education.* Pacific Palisades, CA: Goodyear.

Good, T. L., & Brophy, J. E. (1984). *Looking in classrooms* (3rd ed.). New York: HarperCollins.

Good, T. L., & Brophy, J. E. (1991). *Looking in classrooms* (5th ed.). New York: HarperCollins.

Heinick, R., Molenda, M., & Russell, J. D. (1989). *Instructional media and the new technologies of instruction* (3rd ed.). New York: Wiley.

Henry, J. (1994). A letter to my students (from a college teacher). *Young Children, 49* (5), 84–85.

Jacobsen, D., Eggen, P., & Kauchak, D. (1993). *Methods for teaching: A skills approach* (4th ed.). New York: Merrill.

Jakupcak, J. (1993). Innovative classroom programs for full inclusion. In J. W. Putnam (Ed.), *Cooperative learning and strategies for inclusion: Celebrating diversity in the classroom* (pp. 163–180). Baltimore: Brookes.

Johnson, D. W., & Johnson, R. T. (1986). *Learning together and alone* (2nd ed.). Englewood Cliffs, NJ: Prentice Hall.

Johnson, D. W., & Johnson, R. T. (1991). *Learning together and alone* (3rd ed.). Englewood Cliffs, NJ: Prentice Hall.

Johnson, D. W., Johnson, R. T., & Holubec, E. (1987). *Structuring cooperative learning: The 1987 lesson plan handbook.* Edina, MN: Interaction Book Company.

Lemlech, J. K. (1994). *Curriculum and instructional methods for the elementary and middle school* (3rd ed.). New York: Macmillan.

McNeil, M. (1994). Creating powerful partnerships through partner learning. In J. S. Thousand, R. A. Villa, & A. I. Nevin (Eds.), *Creativity and collaborative learning: A practical guide to empowering students and teachers* (pp. 243–259). Baltimore: Brookes.

Morine, H., & Morine, G. (1973). *Discovery: A challenge to teachers.* Englewood Cliffs, NJ: Prentice Hall.

Murray, F. B. (1989). Explanations in education. In M. C. Reynolds (Ed.), *Knowledge base for the beginning teacher* (pp. 1–12). New York: Pergamon.

Nevin, A. (1993). Curricular and instructional adaptations for including students with disabilities in cooperative groups. In J. W. Putnam (Ed.), *Cooperative learning and strategies for inclusion: Celebrating diversity in the classroom* (pp. 41–56). Baltimore: Brookes.

O'Connor, R. E., & Jenkins, J. R. (1993). Cooperative learning as an inclusion strategy: The experience of children with disabilities. Paper presented at the annual meeting of the American Educational Research Association, Atlanta, April, 1993.

Ornstein, A. C. (1987). Questioning: The essence of good teaching. *NASSP Bulletin, 71* (499), 71–79.

Peterson, M., Leroy, B., Field, S., & Wood, P. (1992). Community-referenced learning in inclusive schools. In S. Stainback & W. Stainback (Eds.), *Curriculum considerations in inclusive classrooms: Facilitating learning for all students* (pp. 207–228). Baltimore: Brookes.

Presseisen, B. (1986). *Thinking skills: Research and practice*. Washington, DC: National Education Association.

Putnam, J. W. (1993). The movement toward teaching and learning in inclusive classrooms. In J. W. Putnam (Ed.), *Cooperative learning and strategies for inclusion: Celebrating diversity in the classroom* (pp. 1–14). Baltimore: Brookes.

Rakow, S. J. (1986). *Teaching science as inquiry*. Bloomington, IN: Phi Delta Kappa Education Foundation.

Rowe, M. B. (1986). Wait times: Slow down may be a way of speeding up! *Journal of Teacher Education, 37* (1), 43–50.

Salend, S .J. (1994). *Effective mainstreaming: Creating inclusive classrooms* (2nd ed.). New York: Macmillan.

Simon, M. A. (1986). The teacher's role in increasing student understanding of mathematics. *Educational Leadership, 43* (7), 40–43.

Sizer, T. (1986). Changing schools and testing: An uneasy proposal. *The redesign of testing for the 21st century*. Princeton, NJ: 1985 ETS Invitational Conference Proceedings.

Slavin, R. E. (1990). *Cooperative learning: Theory, research and practice*. Englewood Cliffs, NJ: Prentice Hall.

Stiggins, R. J. (January, 1988). Revitalizing classroom assessment. *Phi Delta Kappan, 69,* 5.

Stiggins, R. J. (1994). *Student-centered classroom assessment*. New York: Merrill.

Taba, H. (1967). Implementing thinking as an objective in social science. In J. Fair and F. Shaftel (Eds.), *Effective thinking in the social studies* (pp. 25–50). Washington, DC: National Council for the Social Studies.

Thousand, J. S., & Villa, R. A. (1991). A futuristic view of the REI: A response to Jenkins, Pious, and Jewell. *Exceptional Children, 57* (6), 556–562.

Uldari-Solner, A. (1994). A decision-making model for curricular adaptations in cooperative groups. In J. S. Thousand, R. A. Villa, & A. I. Nevin (Eds.), *Creative and collaborative learning: A practical guide to empowering students and teachers* (pp. 59–77). Baltimore: Brookes.

Wiggins, G. (1989). Teaching to the authentic test. *Educational Leadership, 46* (7), 41–47.

Wiggins, G. (1987, Winter). Creating a thought-provoking curriculum. *American Educator,* pp. 10–17.

Will, M. (1986). Educating students with learning problems: A shared responsibility. Washington, DC: Office of Special Education and Rehabilitation Services, U.S. Department of Education.

Wolf, D. (1989). Portfolio assessment: Sampling student work. *Educational Leadership, 46* (7), 35–39.

Wolf, R. (1984). *Evaluation in education: Foundations for competency assessment and program review* (2nd ed.). New York: Praeger.

Wyne, M., & Stuck, G. (1982). Time and learning: Implications for the classroom teacher. *The Elementary School Journal, 83,* 67–75.

Chapter 11

Ausubel, D. (1968). *Educational psychology: A cognitive view*. New York: Holt, Rinehart and Winston.

Bellon, J. J., Bellon, E. C., & Blank, M. A. (1992). *Teaching from a research knowledge base: A development and renewal process*. New York: Merrill.

Beyer, B. (1988). Developing a scope and sequence for thinking skills instruction. *Educational Leadership, 45* (7), 27.

Borich, G. D. (1992). *Effective teaching methods* (2nd ed.). New York: Merrill.

Burden, P. R., & Byrd, M. (1994). *Methods for effective teaching.* Boston: Allyn & Bacon.

Dewey, J. (1910). *How we think.* Lexington, MA: Heath.

Elefant, E. (1980). Deaf children in an inquiry training program. *The Volta Review, 82,* 271–279.

Freiberg, H. J., & Driscoll, A. (1992). *Universal teaching strategies.* Boston: Allyn & Bacon.

Gunter, M. A., Estes, T. H., & Schwab, J. H. (1990). *Instruction: A models approach.* Boston: Allyn & Bacon.

Jacobsen, D., Eggen, P., & Kauchak, D. (1993). *Methods for teaching: A skills approach* (4th ed.). New York: Merrill.

Joyce, B., Weil, M., & Showers, B. (1992). *Models of teaching* (4th ed.). Boston: Allyn & Bacon.

Kellough, R. D., & Roberts, P. L. (1994). *A resource guide for elementary school teaching: Planning for competence.* New York: Macmillan.

Lemlech, J. K. (1994) *Curriculum and instructional methods for the elementary and middle school* (3rd ed.), New York: Macmillan.

Luiten, J., Ames, W., & Aerson, G. (1980). A meta-analysis of advance organizers on learning and retention. *American Educational Research Journal, 17,* 211–218.

Martinello, M. L., & Cook, G. E. (1994). *Interdisciplinary inquiry in teaching and learning.* New York: Merrill.

Stiggins, R. J. (1994). *Student-centered classroom assessment.* New York: Merrill.

Suchman, R. J. (1962). The elementary school training program in scientific inquiry. Report to the U.S. Office of Education, Project Title VII. Urbana, IL: University of Illinois.

Voss, B. A. (1982). *Summary of research in science education.* Columbus, OH: ERIC Clearinghouse for Science, Mathematics, and Environmental Education

Chapter 12

Bellon, J. J., Bellon, E. C., & Blank, M. A. (1992). *Teaching from a research knowledge base: A development and renewal process.* New York: Merrill.

Borich, G. D. (1992). *Effective teaching methods* (2nd ed.). New York: Merrill.

Brophy J. E., & Evertson, C. (1976). *Learning from teaching: A developmental perspective.* Boston: Allyn & Bacon.

Burden, P. R., & Byrd, M. (1994). *Methods for effective teaching.* Boston: Allyn & Bacon.

Callahan, J. F., & Clark, L. H. (1988). *Teaching in the middle and secondary schools* (3rd ed). New York: Macmillan.

Dillon, J. T. (1988). *Questioning and teaching.* New York: Teachers College.

Eby, J. W. (1992). *Reflective planning, teaching, and evaluation for the elementary school.* New York: Merrill.

Freiberg, H. J., & Driscoll, A. (1992). *Universal teaching strategies.* Boston: Allyn & Bacon.

Great Books Foundation (1965). *A manual for co-leaders* (Nos. 15–16). Chicago: Great Books Foundation.

Greenwood, C. R., Delquadri, J. C., & Hall, R. V. (1989). Longitudinal effects of class wide peer tutoring. *Journal of Educational Psychology, 81,* 371–383.

Gunter, M. A., Estes, T. H., & Schwab, J. H. (1990). *Instruction: A models approach.* Boston: Allyn & Bacon.

Harper, G. F., Maheady, L., & Mallette, B. (1994). The power of peer-mediated instruction: How and why it promotes academic success for all students. In J. S. Thousand, R. A.

Villa, and A. I. Nevin (Eds.), *Creativity and collaborative learning: A practical guide to empowering students and teachers* (pp. 229–241). Baltimore: Brookes.

Hollingsworth, P. M., & Hoover, K. H. (1991). *Elementary teaching methods* (4th ed.). Boston: Allyn & Bacon.

Jacobsen, D., Eggen, P., & Kauchak, D. (1993). *Methods for teaching: A skills approach* (4th ed.). New York: Merrill.

LaPlant, L., & Zane, N. (1994). Partner learning systems. In J. S. Thousand, R. A. Villa, and A. I. Nevin (Eds.), *Creativity and collaborative learning: A practical guide to empowering students and teachers* (pp. 261–273). Baltimore: Brookes.

Lemlech, J. K. (1994). *Curriculum and instructional methods for the elementary school* (3rd ed.). New York: Macmillan.

Lipman, M. (1988). Critical thinking—what can it be? *Educational Leadership, 46* (1), 38–43.

Maheady, L., Mallett, B., Harper, G. F., & Sacca, K. (1991). Heads Together: A peer-mediated option for improving the academic achievement of heterogeneous learning groups. *Remedial and Special Education, 21,* 107–121.

Millman, J., & Pauk, W. (1969). *How to take tests.* New York: McGraw-Hill.

Nevin, A. (1993). Curricular and instructional adaptations for including students with disabilities in cooperative groups. In J. W. Putnam (Ed.), *Cooperative learning and strategies for inclusion: Celebrating diversity in the classroom* (pp. 41–56). Baltimore: Brookes.

Pasch, M., Sparks-Langer, G., Gardner, T. G., Starko, A. J., & Moody, C. D. (1991). *Teaching as decision making: Instructional practices for the successful teacher.* New York: Longman.

Passe, J. (1984). Phil Donahue: An excellent model for leading a discussion. *Journal of Teacher Education, 35* (1), 43–48.

Paul, R. (1988). *31 Principles of critical thinking.* Rohnert Park, CA: Center for Critical Thinking and Moral Critique.

Putnam, J. W. (1993). The process of cooperative learning. In J. W. Putnam (Ed.), *Cooperative learning and strategies for inclusion* (pp. 15–40). Baltimore: Brookes.

Raths, L., Wasserman, S., Jonas, A., & Rothstein, A. (1986). *Teaching for thinking.* New York: Teachers College.

Salend, S. J. (1994). *Effective mainstreaming* (2nd ed.). New York: Macmillan.

Smith, F. (1986). *Insult to intelligence.* New York: Arbor House.

Stainback, W., Stainback, S., & Moravec, J. (1992). Using curriculum to build inclusive classrooms. In S. Stainback and W. Stainback (Eds.), *Curriculum considerations in inclusive classrooms: Facilitating learning for all students* (pp. 65–84). Baltimore: Brookes.

Taba, H. (1967). Implementing thinking as an objective in social science. In J. Fair and F. Shaftel (Eds.), *Effective thinking in the social studies* (pp. 25–50). Washington, DC: National Council for the Social Studies.

Wyne, M., & Stuck, G. (1982). Time and learning: Implications for the classroom teacher. *The Elementary School Journal, 83,* 67–75.

Chapter 13

Alpha Team (1991). *A vision of a preferred curriculum for the 21st century.* Rochester, MI: Oakland University School of Education and Human Services. ERIC Document Reproduction Service ED 344 275.

Ayers, W. (1994). Can city schools be saved? *Educational Leadership, 51* (8), 60–63.

Banks, J. A. (1994). Transforming the mainstream curriculum. *Educational Leadership, 51* (8), 4–8.

Barth, P., & Mitchell, R. (1992). *Smart start: Elementary education for the 21st century*. Golden, CO: North American Press.

Barth, R. C. (1990). A personal vision of a good school. *Phi Delta Kappan, 71*, 512–517.

Benjamin, S. (1989). An ideascape for education: What futurists recommend. *Educational Leadership, 47* (9), 8–14.

Berns, R. M. (1993). *Child, family, community socialization and support* (3rd ed.). New York: Harcourt Brace.

Children's Defense Fund. (1989). *A vision for America's future: An agenda for the 1990s*. Washington, DC: Author.

Clark, D. L., & Astuto, T. A. (1994). Redirecting reform: Challenges to popular assumptions about teachers and students. *Phi Delta Kappan, 75* (7), 512–520.

Consortium on Chicago School Research. (1993). *A View from the Elementary School: The State of Reform in Chicago*. A Report of the Steering Committee.

Cornish, E. (1986). Educating children for the 21st century. *Curriculum Review, 25* (4), 12–17.

Cullen, B., & Pratt, T. (1992). Measuring and reporting student progress. In S. Stainback and W. Stainback (Eds.), *Curriculum considerations in inclusive classrooms: Facilitating learning for all students* (pp. 175–196). Baltimore: Brookes.

David, M. E. (1989). Schooling and the family. In H. Giroux and P. McLaren (Eds.), *Critical pedagogy, the State and cultural struggle*. Albany, NY: State University of New York Press.

Dwyer, D. (1994). Apple classrooms of tomorrow: What we've learned. *Educational Leadership, 51* (7), 4–10.

Edmonds, R. (1979). Effective schools for the urban poor. *Educational Leadership, 37* (1), 15–18, 20–24.

Elkind, D. (1986). Helping parents make healthy educational choices for their children. *Educational Leadership, 44* (3), 36–38.

Ellis, A. K., & Fouts, J. T. (1993). *Research on educational innovations*. Princeton Junction, NJ: Eye on Education.

Farr, R., & Tone, B. (1994). *Portfolio performance assessment: Helping students evaluate their progress as readers and writers*. Fort Worth, TX: Harcourt Brace.

Ferguson, D. L., & Jeanchild, L. A. (1992). It's not a matter of method: Thinking about how to implement curricular decisions. In S. Stainback and W. Stainback (Eds.), *Curriculum considerations in inclusive classrooms: Facilitating learning for all students* (pp. 159–174). Baltimore: Brookes.

Finders, M., & Lewis, C. (1994). Why some parents don't come to school. *Educational Leadership, 51* (8), 50–54.

Ford, A., Davern, L., & Schnorr, R. (1992). Inclusive education: "Making sense" of the curriculum. In S. Stainback and W. Stainback (Eds.), *Curriculum considerations in inclusive classrooms: Facilitating learning for all students* (pp. 37–61). Baltimore: Brookes.

Forest, M., & Pearpoint, J. (1990). Supports for addressing severe maladaptive behaviors. In W. Stainback and S. Stainback (Eds.), *Supportive networks for inclusive schooling* (pp. 187–197). Baltimore: Brookes.

Fosnot, C. T. (1989). *Enquiring teachers, enquiring learners: A constructivist approach for teaching*. New York: Teachers College.

Gardner, H. (1991). *The unschooled mind: How children think and how schools should teach*. New York: Basic Books.

Goodlad, J. I. (1984). *A place called school*. New York: Mcgraw-Hill.

Goodlad, J. I. (1993). Access to knowledge. In J. I. Goodlad and T. C. Lovitt (Eds.), *Integrating General and Special Education* (pp. 1–22). New York: Merrill.

Gough, P. B. (1994). Flawed 'solutions.' *Phi Delta Kappan, 75* (7), 507.

Grant, G. (1994). Schools where kids are known. *American Educator, 18* (1), 38–43.

Guild, P. (1994). The culture/learning style connection. *Educational Leadership, 51* (8), 16–21.

Hamre-Nietupski, S., McDonald, J., & Nietupski, J. (1992, Spring). Integrating elementary students with multiple disabilities into supported regular classes: Challenges and solutions. *Teaching Exceptional Children,* 6–9.

Hodgkinson, H. (1991). Reform versus reality. *Phi Delta Kappan, 73* (1), 8–16.

Jellinek, M. & Klavan, E. (1988, September). The single parent. *Good Housekeeping,* p. 126.

Katz, L. G., & Chard, S. C. (1993). *Engaging children's minds: The project approach.* Norwood, NJ: Ablex.

Klonsky, M., & Ford, P. (1994). One urban solution: Small schools. *Educational Leadership, 51* (4), 64–66.

King, S. H. (1993). The limited presence of African-American teachers. *Review of Educational Research, 63,* 115–149.

Kozol, J. (1993). Whittle and the privateers. In J. M. Noll (Ed.), *Taking sides* (7th ed.; pp. 169–174). Guilford, CT: Dushkin.

Lipsky, D. K., & Gartner, A. (1992). Achieving full inclusion: Placing the student at the center of educational reform. In W. Stainback & S. Stainback (Eds.), *Controversial issues confronting special education: Divergent perspectives* (pp. 3–12). Boston: Allyn & Bacon.

Lortie, D. (1975). *School teacher: A sociological study.* Chicago: University of Chicago Press.

McDaniel, M. (1974). Tomorrow's curriculum today. In A. Toffler (Ed.), *Learning for tomorrow: The role of the future in education* (pp. 103–131). New York: Random House.

Mead, G. H. (1934). *Mind, self, and society.* Chicago: University of Chicago Press.

Meyer, L. H., & Henry, L. A. (1993). Cooperative classroom management: Student needs and fairness in the regular classroom. In J. W. Putnam (Ed.), *Cooperative learning and strategies for inclusion: Celebrating diversity in the classroom* (pp. 93–121). Baltimore: Brookes.

Morris, G. (1993). Whittling at the wall. *National Review, LXIV (18),* 50–51.

Noll, J. W. ed. (1993). *Taking sides: Clashing views on controversial educational issues,* 7th ed. Guilford, CT: Dushkin.

O'Brien, S. (1990). Parents and schools together. *Childhood Education, 67* (2), 106–109.

Putnam, J. W. The process of cooperative learning. In J. W. Putnam (Ed.), *Cooperative learning and strategies for inclusion: Celebrating diversity in the classroom* (pp. 15–40). Baltimore: Brookes.

Ravitch, D. (1983). On thinking about the future. *Phi Delta Kappan, 64* (5), 317–320.

Rogers, C., & Freiberg, H. J. (1990). *Freedom to learn* (3rd ed.). New York: Merrill.

Sapon-Shevin, M. (1990). Initial steps for developing a caring school. In W. Stainback and S. Stainback (Eds.), *Supportive networks for inclusive schooling: Interdependent integrated education* (pp. 241–248). Baltimore: Brookes.

Sapon-Shevin, M. (1992). Celebrating diversity, creating community: Curriculum that honors and builds on differences. In S. Stainback and W. Stainback (Eds.), *Curriculum considerations in inclusive classrooms: Facilitating learning for all students* (pp. 19–36). Baltimore: Brookes.

Small Schools' Operating Costs: Reversing Assumptions About Economics of Scale. (1992). New York: Public Education Association.

Snow, J., & Forest, M. (1987). Circles. In M. Forest (Ed.), *More education integration* (pp. 169–176). Downsview, ON: G. Allan Roeher Institute.

Stainback, S., Stainback, W., & Jackson, H. J. (1992). Toward inclusive classrooms. In S. Stainback & W. Stainback (Eds.), *Curriculum considerations in inclusive classroom: Facilitating learning for all students* (pp. 3 18). Baltimore: Brookes.

Suppes, P. (1975). The school of the future: Technological possibilities. In L. Rubin (Ed.), *The future of education: Perspectives on tomorrow's schooling* (pp. 145–157). Boston: Allyn & Bacon.

Taylor, S., Biklen, D., & Knoll, J. (1987). *Community integration for people with severe disabilities.* New York: Teachers College Press.

Villa, R. A., & Thousand, J. S. (1992). Student collaboration: An essential for curriculum delivery in the 21st century. In S. Stainback and W. Stainback (Eds.), *Curriculum considerations in inclusive classrooms: Facilitating learning for all students* (pp. 117–142). Baltimore: Brookes.

Villegas, A. M. (1991). *Culturally responsive pedagogy for the 1990s and beyond.* Washington, DC: ERIC Clearinghouse on Teacher Education, American Association of Colleges for Teacher Education (ED 339 698).

Wiggins, G. (1989). The futility of trying to teach everything of importance. *Educational Leadership, 1* (3), 44–59.

Williams, D. R. (1993). Cooperative learning and cultural diversity: Building caring communities in cooperative classrooms. In J. W. Putnam (Ed.), *Cooperative learning and strategies for inclusion: Celebrating diversity in the classroom* (pp. 145–162). Baltimore: Brookes.

AUTHOR INDEX

SUBJECT INDEX